ELEANOR OF AQUITAINE

ELEANOR OF AQUITAINE

QUEEN OF FRANCE
QUEEN OF ENGLAND

RALPH V. TURNER

YALE UNIVERSITY PRESS
NEW HAVEN AND LONDON

For information about this and other Yale University Press publications, please contact:
U.S. Office: sales.press@yale.edu   www.yalebooks.com
Europe Office: sales@yaleup.co.uk   www.yaleup.co.uk

Set in Minion by IDSUK (DataConnection) Ltd.
Printed in Great Britain by T J International, Padstow, Cornwall

Library of Congress Control Number: 2009922522

ISBN 978-0-300-11911-4

A catalogue record for this book is available from the British Library.

10 9 8 7 6 5 4 3 2 1

CONTENTS

ILLUSTRATIONS

1. Church of Notre-Dame-la-Grande, Poitiers. Photo by Photothèque Zodiaque, La Pierre-qui-Vire, 89630 Saint Léger Vauban, France.
2. Seal of Eleanor's grandfather Duke William IX, housed at the Archives Nationales, Paris, Sceaux/E/1. Photo by the Photographic Studio of the Archives Nationales.
3. The Eleanor Vase, Musée du Louvre, Paris. Photo courtesy of Professor George Beech, Western Michigan University, Kalamazoo.
4. Louis VII at Saint-Denis receiving the crusader's banner, painting by Jean Baptiste Mauzaisse (d. 1844), Châteaux de Versailles et de Trianon, Versailles, France. © Réunion des Musées Nationaux/Art Resource, NY.
5. Byzantine walls of Antioch, print from T.A. Archer and Charles L. Kingsford, *The Crusades* (New York: G.P. Putnam's Sons, 1894). Photo by Florida State University Photographic Laboratory.
6. Eleanor's tomb sculpture at Fontevraud Abbey. © Erich Lessing/Art Resource, NY.
7. Henry II's tomb sculpture at Fontevraud Abbey. © Erich Lessing/Art Resource, NY.
8. Cathedral of Saint-Pierre, Poitiers, east (rear) wall. Photo from Photothèque, Centre des études supérieures de civilisation médiévale, Université de Poitiers, France.
9. Cathedral of Saint-Pierre, Poitiers, stained-glass Crucifixion window. Photo from Photothèque, Centre des études supérieures de civilisation médiévale, Université de Poitiers, France.
10. Henry II with his lover Rosamund Clifford, painting by Margaret Dovaston (d. 1954), Walter Hutchinson, ed., *Story of the British Nation: A Connected Pictorial and Authoritative History of the British Peoples,*

Maps

ACKNOWLEDGMENTS

MANY years ago when I arrived in Poitiers as a Fulbright Scholar, it never occurred to me that one day I would write a biography of the town's most famous resident, Eleanor of Aquitaine. My year in Poitiers opened up a different world to me, and it led me to a scholarly career devoted to the Angevin or early Plantagenet kings of England, and to Eleanor, Henry II's queen. Scholars of Eleanor of Aquitaine can now turn to her charters not readily available to earlier writers, thanks to Sir James Holt, founder of the Plantagenet *Acta* Project at Cambridge University that is collecting and editing her charters, along with those of Henry II and Richard I. Without access to Eleanor's collected charters generously shared with me by the Project's staff, it would not have been possible for me to complete this book. I depended also on the work of Marie Hivergneaux, whose post-graduate studies in France have centered on Eleanor's charters. I am indebted to Martin Aurell, professor at the Centre des études supérieures de la civilisation médiévale, University of Poitiers, for organizing a series of conferences on the Plantagenets and their world that bring together both Francophone and Anglophone scholars, as well as for his friendship and encouragement of this project. Two conferences organized by medieval historians at the University of East Anglia on King John and Henry II also provided an occasion for sharing ideas with fellow writers on those two monarchs' reigns.

Any biographer of Eleanor, subject of innumerable studies, must also acknowledge the aid afforded by earlier scholarship. I owe a deep debt to the work of Dr. Jane Martindale, doubtless the premier scholar of eleventh- and twelfth-century Aquitaine writing in English today. The insights in her many papers and articles were invaluable to me in understanding Eleanor and her

Poitevin background. Also helpful were Jean Flori's learned biographies of Eleanor and of her son Richard recently published in France. Emily Amt was kind enough to read and offer suggestions on my chapters treating Eleanor's role as English queen. Other colleagues and friends have shared their work with me, offering advice and sending me copies of their conference papers and articles. They include Martin Aurell, George Beech, Maïté Billoré, John Gillingham, Marie Hivergneaux, Lois Huneycutt, Sara Lutan, Georges Pon, Daniel Power, Ursula Vones-Liebenstein, and John W. Baldwin, my longtime mentor and friend. Constantly giving me encouragement and boosting my confidence during the writing of this book was Heather McCallum of Yale University Press UK.

Over the years, the Department of History at Florida State University provided me with released time and travel funds for research that deepened my knowledge of the early Plantagenets. Also the Strozier Library at Florida State continues to provide resources for my research. Peter Krafft, cartographer with Florida State, prepared the maps, and the University Photo Laboratory provided photographs. For my studies of the Angevins, I have done research at other libraries both in the United States and in the United Kingdom, most recently at the Institute of Historical Research, University of London, and also in France at the Centre des études supérieures de la civilisation médiévale, University of Poitiers.

I am grateful to the following publishers for permission to quote passages: p. 89 reprinted by permission of Oxford University Press from Marjorie Chibnall, ed., *Historia Pontificalis of John of Salisbury*, Oxford Medieval Studies (1986), pp. 52–53; p. 207 reprinted by permission of Taylor and Francis Books, Ltd. from David Douglas and George W. Greenaway, eds, *English Historical Documents*, vol. 2, *1042–1189* (London: Eyre & Spottiswoode, 1968), pp. 387–88; p. 232 reprinted by permission of Boydell & Brewer Ltd. from Catherine Léglu and Marcus Bull, eds, *The World of Eleanor of Aquitaine: Literature and Society in Southern France between the Eleventh and Thirteenth Centuries* (Woodbridge: Boydell Press, 2005), pp. 22–23.

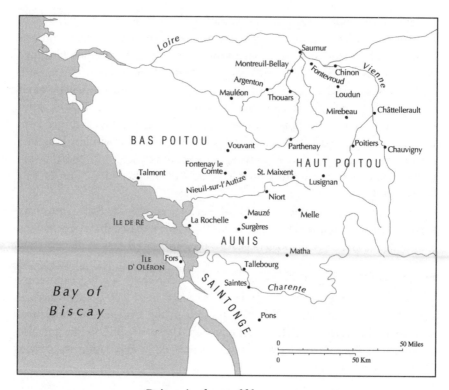

Poitou in the twelfth century

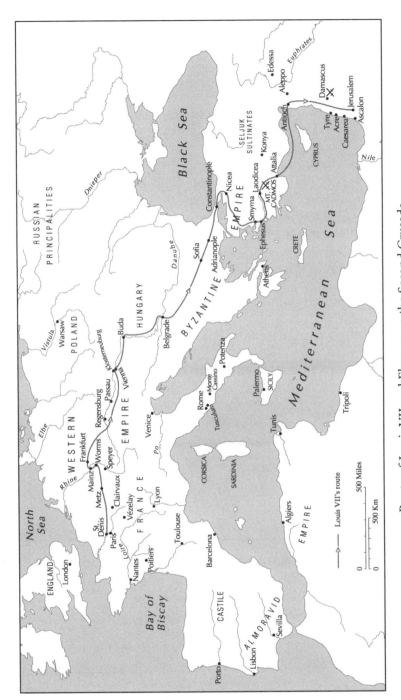

Route of Louis VII and Eleanor on the Second Crusade

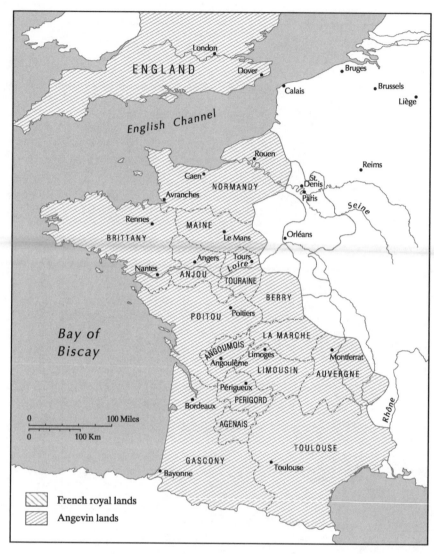

Henry II's possessions at their height, *c.* 1174

England during Eleanor's years as queen

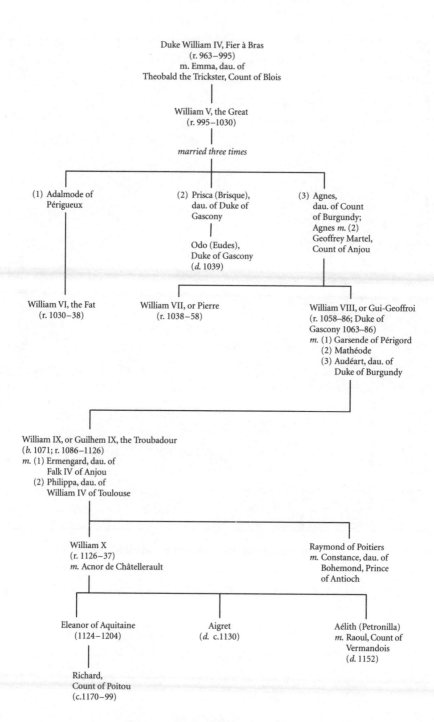

Duke William IV, Fier à Bras
(r. 963–995)
m. Emma, dau. of
Theobald the Trickster, Count of Blois

William V, the Great
(r. 995–1030)

married three times

(1) Adalmode of
Périgueux

(2) Prisca (Brisque),
dau. of Duke of
Gascony

Odo (Eudes),
Duke of Gascony
(*d.* 1039)

(3) Agnes,
dau. of Count
of Burgundy;
Agnes *m.* (2)
Geoffrey Martel,
Count of Anjou

William VI, the Fat
(r. 1030–38)

William VII, or Pierre
(r. 1038–58)

William VIII, or Gui-Geoffroi
(r. 1058–86; Duke of
Gascony 1063–86)
m. (1) Garsende of Périgord
(2) Mathéode
(3) Audéart, dau. of
Duke of Burgundy

William IX, or Guilhem IX, the Troubadour
(*b.* 1071; r. 1086–1126)
m. (1) Ermengard, dau. of
Falk IV of Anjou
(2) Philippa, dau. of
William IV of Toulouse

William X
(r. 1126–37)
m. Acnor de Châtellerault

Raymond of Poitiers
m. Constance, dau. of
Bohemond, Prince
of Antioch

Eleanor of Aquitaine
(1124–1204)

Aigret
(*d.* c.1130)

Aélith (Petronilla)
m. Raoul, Count of
Vermandois
(*d.* 1152)

Richard,
Count of Poitou
(c.1170–99)

The counts of Poitou, dukes of Aquitaine

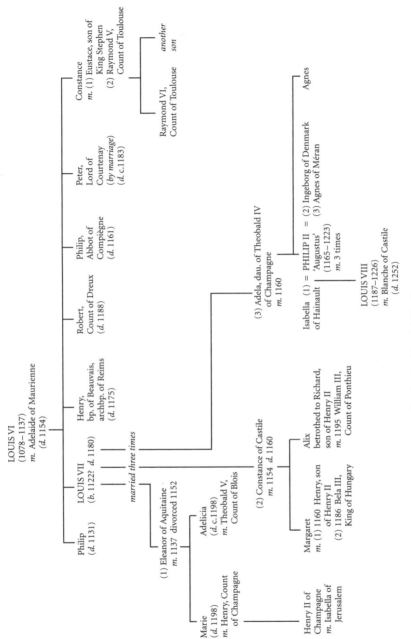

The family of Louis VII of France

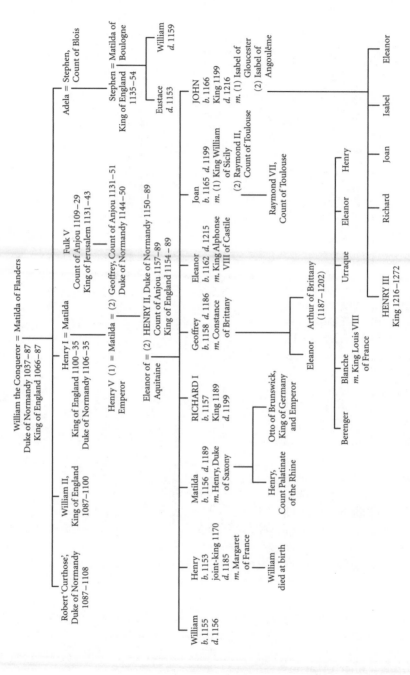

The Norman and Angevin kings of England

INTRODUCTION

SEARCHING FOR A "TRUTHFUL IMAGE" OF
ELEANOR OF AQUITAINE

ELEANOR of Aquitaine (1124–1204) is the most famous queen in all the Middle Ages and one of the most infamous women in history. A renowned beauty, with a headstrong, spirited personality, she has been compared to Cleopatra, the celebrated Egyptian queen, Elizabeth I of England and many others. Eleanor was the proud daughter of a distinguished lineage, the dukes of Aquitaine, successors to Carolingian kings of Aquitaine and rulers of France's largest duchy. Her grandfather was William IX, the "troubadour duke," whose verses reinforced the northern French cliché of the Aquitanians as light-hearted and lusty pleasure seekers. As she grew up, she absorbed her dynasty's sense of its dignity as successors to Carolingian royalty, and she never forgot that her dynasty was France's most distinguished after the royal family, far surpassing the Plantagenets in prestige.

Wife of the king of France, married to the future king of England, mother of three English kings, Eleanor is a larger-than-life figure, embodying the two extremes of hatred and love, escaping from an unsatisfying marriage to Louis VII of France after going on the Second Crusade, and then choosing as her second husband Henry Plantagenet. The young count of Anjou and duke of Normandy was a contender for the English Crown, which became his within three years of their marriage. This marriage would make Eleanor a key figure in Henry's amassing of an assemblage of family lands known as the Angevin "empire." Again disappointed in a marriage that proved to be troubled and tumultuous, she incited her sons to rebel against their own father, enduring a fifteen-year loss of her freedom as a consequence. Then Eleanor emerged from captivity to play an important political role in the reigns of her two surviving sons, Richard Lionheart and John Lackland, some of her most burdensome and eventful, yet rewarding years. Her long life as Henry II's wife and mother of his quarrelsome sons could be taken "directly from the imagination of a romance writer of the time."[1] No other medieval queen's history comes close to matching Eleanor's extraordinary story, and she has attracted attention both from her contemporaries and twentieth-century writers, as well as from rumor-mongers and myth-makers throughout the centuries since her death in 1204.

While Eleanor of Aquitaine represents the problems faced by an ambitious and able woman living in medieval society, her life has still greater significance. Her lifespan of eighty years encapsulates many great moments of medieval history to which she had to adapt herself as her circumstances rapidly changed. The part that Eleanor was called to play mutated almost every decade. Heiress to a vast duchy and bride of Louis VII of France at age thirteen, she soon took the role of her young husband's chief councilor and accompanied him on the Second Crusade. After enduring a harrowing journey, she found herself at the center of scandal in the Holy Land due to rumored sexual misconduct. Malicious gossip followed her to France, resulting in the dissolution of her fifteen-year marriage to the French king. Her quick remarriage to the young Henry of Anjou only added to the scandal. For two decades, Eleanor occupied a central place at the brilliant royal court of twelfth-century Europe's most powerful monarch, her second husband, Henry II. Always aware of her special position as heir to the duchy of Aquitaine, she assumed that in her two marriages, first to Louis VII and then to Henry Plantagenet, she would retain authority as queen-duchess, enjoying a partnership in power. This strong-minded heir to Aquitaine felt entitled to govern her own duchy, and she was resolutely opposed to seeing it lose its separate identity, absorbed into the domains of either of her two husbands.

Feeling entitled to wield power, the queen-duchess came very close to achieving her goal during her marriage to Henry II. At the same time that Eleanor was bearing nine children, she acted as regent in England during Henry's long absences abroad in the crucial early years of his reign, then she returned to Poitiers for several years to take charge of Aquitaine until she joined her sons in rebelling against their father, a move that added to her infamy. Torn by the conflict between her marriage vows, wounded pride, fears for her duchy's future, and ambition for her sons, she went further than any other unhappy high-born wife in literally going to war against her own husband. Following Eleanor's rebellion against Henry, she returned to England a captive and endured fifteen years of confinement. Fortunately, her husband could not risk putting her to death, since his complicity in Thomas Becket's murder was already costing him heavily. After the English king's death in 1189, Eleanor emerged to embark on an active and eventful life during her two surviving sons' reigns, achieving the political influence that she always had craved. She safeguarded Richard Lionheart's lands while he went on the Third Crusade and was a prisoner in Germany, traveling across Europe on his behalf in her seventies when most widows would have retreated to their country estates or to a nunnery. Following Richard's death, she fought to secure her last surviving son's succession. Only a few years before her death in 1204 at the age of eighty, she threw herself into political activity one last time to shore up her Poitevin subjects' support for the beleaguered King John.

Eleanor of Aquitaine's dedication as a widow to preserving intact the block of lands amassed by her hated husband on her sons' behalf refutes historians' charges that she was "an essentially frivolous woman" whose life consisted of a series of scandals.[2] Her role in power politics throughout her life demands a major place in her biography, yet modern writers follow their medieval predecessors in attributing Eleanor's actions to personal, not political motives. Eleanor was a woman who fought for the freedom to make her own choices in life, expecting to find partnership in her two marriages; when that proved impossible, she dared to challenge them and go her own way. Twelfth-century society dismissed women as unfit for wielding power, and Eleanor's claim to liberty could not be tolerated. Fear, revulsion, and hatred stimulated by her desire for independence inspired ugly gossip about supposed sexual indiscretions during her two tumultuous marriages that still sullies her reputation, despite lack of proof. She dared much, and the price she paid for defying custom and religious teaching would be a "black legend" that has stalked her ever since it was elaborated during the Second Crusade.[3] By the thirteenth century, Eleanor's reputation had sunk to such a point that common opinion pointed to her adultery on crusade, perhaps with a Muslim prince, as the cause for Louis VII's divorce. Over the centuries, she came to be regarded as another Messalina, the sluttish and scheming Roman empress, or even worse.

Eleanor ranks among English queens as a favorite subject for modern writers despite the dearth of sources for a comprehensive biography. However, lack of evidence has not deterred authors from producing book-length studies of Eleanor, and a dozen or so have been published in Britain and North America, as well as several in other countries, in the last half-century. She entered popular culture when she appeared on the screen, played by Katherine Hepburn, in the film *A Lion in Winter*.[4] The 1968 film, however inaccurate and anachronistic in many aspects, vividly showed audiences that Eleanor and Henry II's family was not a happy one. By the later twentieth century, writings about this twelfth-century personality had attained the proportions of a "romanticizing 'Eleanor industry.'"[5] Popular biographies in pursuit of a good story have spun a new legend of Eleanor, portraying her as the "queen of the troubadours," a patron of poets pronouncing judgments in courts of love at Poitiers despite scant evidence for her advocacy of the art of courtly love.[6]

Although the subject of numbers of books, Eleanor has not been well served by her biographers.

So much myth and legend have grown up about Eleanor of Aquitaine that another search for the "real" Eleanor presents seemingly insurmountable obstacles. To retrieve a "truthful image," it is essential to grasp not only the facts of her life, but also the image of her held by her contemporaries and passed down to later generations. Public perceptions of Eleanor are crucial. Her subjects had expectations of her in fulfilling a queen's proper role, and they inevitably made comparisons with her predecessors' roles as French and English queens.[7] We must avoid the preconceptions of our own era, resisting temptations to subject Eleanor to Freudian psychoanalysis or to reinvent her as a proto-feminist.[8]

The safest path to reviving figures of the Middle Ages as rounded personalities lies through surviving documents, even if twelfth-century written materials now exist in minuscule numbers and reveal little more than bare outlines of even major monarchs' lives. No contemporary writer left anything approaching a biography of Eleanor of Aquitaine, for the only women likely to find biographers in the Middle Ages were saints or candidates for sainthood. With the exception of saints' lives, biography was not a common genre of literature in the Middle Ages; when penning lives of secular persons, medieval authors showed little taste for expressions of individual personality. They were unlikely to probe in a search for their subjects' inner lives, motivations, or a sense of the individual personality, for today's perception of individuals trying to express a unique self was alien to them. Bound by the Church's accepted models of conduct, medieval authors looked for the individual's place within the Christian community.[9] They thought more about their subjects' conformity to accepted models or types, their usefulness as examples of conduct for Christians, or as warnings of the dangers of not conforming to the Church's models. The handful of surviving biographies of queens written before Eleanor's time linked their subjects with conventional female virtues, chiefly marital and parental duties, and they "passed lightly over their heroines' threatening and unladylike political wheeling and dealing."[10] When twelfth-century writers of histories turned to Eleanor, they hardly knew what to make of her unwillingness to conform to conventional standards of conduct expected of great ladies.

In the absence of writings about Eleanor of Aquitaine dating from her own era, her biographers today must turn to other historical works by her contemporaries, the Latin chronicles, for reconstructing her life. Chronicles grew out of earlier annals kept by monasteries that were little more than lists of key events of each year, continuing this rigid chronological structure. Although medieval writers of chronicles attempted to tell a story, their rambling narratives leave an impression that for them history was "just one thing after another," often literally year after year.[11] Gleaning evidence from twelfth-century chronicles is not easy, for their authors were clerics, chiefly monks, with all the biases of churchmen. The fortunes of popes and prelates, kings and princes, preoccupied them, and they caught sight of Eleanor "only out of the corner of their eyes as they tracked down their bigger game."[12] Indeed, French chroniclers writing under royal patronage after Eleanor's divorce say surprisingly little about her years as Louis VII's queen. Her reputation was so tattered that they tried to write her out of their histories.[13] Chronicles surviving from Eleanor's own duchy of Aquitaine are scarce, and most extant ones are little more than annals with their year by year accounts. Those surviving from her lifetime were chiefly concerned with events surrounding great monasteries such as the abbey of Saint-Martial at Limoges, where a monastic tradition of chronicle writing was strong. Saint-Martial housed two authors whose works are the fullest narrative sources for twelfth-century Aquitaine: the monks Geoffrey de Vigeois (d.1185) and Bernard Itier (d.1225). A third significant writer from the region is Richard le Poitevin, whose chronicle survives in different versions, possibly not all by the same author.

The chronicles that students of Eleanor most often consult are the works of a group of English writers who were well informed about the Plantagenet court, writing during her last years as Henry's queen and as queen-mother. Their works dating from the last quarter of the twelfth century to the first decade of the thirteenth century constitute a medieval "golden age" of historical writing.[14] Chroniclers writing in later medieval England mined this group of chronicles, exaggerating their veiled allusions to Eleanor's behavior into tall tales. These "golden age" chroniclers have continued to influence modern writers on Eleanor, although they were rarely eye-witnesses to events in their queen's life, often writing decades after they had taken place. They supply the paints for a portrait of Eleanor, but mixed in their colors are gossip and rumor as well as their own preconceptions, droplets of a black legend that still shadow her portrait with evil.

All these chroniclers were in clerical orders. Five were secular clerks with ties to the royal court: Roger of Howden (d. *c.*1203), Ralph Diceto (d.1201), Walter Map (d. *c.*1210), Gerald of Wales (d. *c.*1223), and Ralph Niger (d. *c.*1199). Four others wrote in monasteries: Gervase of Canterbury (d. *c.*1210), Ralph of Coggeshall (d.1218), Richard of Devizes (d. *c.*1200), and William of Newburgh (d. *c.*1198).[15] Beginning their careers in the Church in the second half of Henry II's reign, all reflect in their writings the aftershocks of Archbishop Thomas Becket's martyrdom at the end of 1170 that had shattered the king's reputation among churchmen. Becket's death darkened their view of the royal family, whose immoral lives they condemned, especially that of Eleanor, a woman in public life who aroused their suspicion. One of the monastic writers, Richard of Devizes, is noticeably more positive in his treatment of Eleanor than his fellows, however. Writing during her old age, he admires her for her tenacity in fighting for Richard, her favorite son, during his long absence on the Third Crusade.

The secular clerks all had some ties to the royal household, and Howden and Diceto rank as semi-official historians with their access to courtiers and official documents, but they were by no means royalist propagandists. Their treatment of Eleanor comes close to neutrality, though they could not pass over in silence unsavory episodes in her long life. Two others, Walter Map and Gerald of Wales, were not chroniclers in a strict sense but courtiers writing satirical works in which rhetoric often overwhelms facts. Their malicious wit makes it impossible for modern-day writers to resist quoting them. Map's book *On the Follies of Courtiers*, written between 1181 and 1192, is a collection of anecdotes exposing the English royal court's corruption and courtiers' foolishness. His fellow courtier, the thwarted patronage seeker Gerald of Wales, writing over a decade later, proved most malevolent in his denunciations of Henry II and his entire family. Expanding on allegations borrowed from Map's work, Gerald filled his book *On the Instruction of Princes* with spiteful anti-Plantagenet propaganda, slandering Eleanor along with Henry and their sons. Ralph Niger, like Gerald, had joined the English royal court after studies in Paris, but was even less successful in winning favor. His support for Thomas Becket's cause brought his banishment from England, but he returned after Henry II's death. In Ralph's two chronicles dating from Richard's reign, his hostility toward Henry does not extend to Eleanor, whom he may have encountered at the schools of Poitiers in the 1160s and again in England in the 1190s.

As churchmen, these chroniclers were prone to interpret events and evaluate personages in accord with Christian teaching. Not surprisingly, they were influenced by traditions in history writing established by early Church Fathers, chiefly the conviction that history records human progress toward salvation. Twelfth-century chroniclers expected their histories to impress readers with God's power at work in the world. Their powerful belief in a divine purpose behind all that happened on earth led them to see history as a series of examples for their readers' moral edification, recording God's rewards for the righteous and punishment of evil doers. While they took their work as historians seriously, they aimed both to inform and to amuse, and they were not above embroidering the facts to tell a better story. To entertain, they accepted oral tradition, blending rumors and gossip into their accounts, shirking responsibility for any inaccuracy by such asides as "so it is said," providing themselves with cover for evading responsibility for incautious remarks about Eleanor's misconduct. Through an accumulation of elaborations, historical facts were transformed into legends.

It should be no surprise that nearly all chroniclers display the misogyny common among medieval churchmen. An intensified effort at enforcing clerical celibacy during the eleventh-century religious reform movement had encouraged anti-feminist tirades by moralists and theologians. They amplified the pervasive mistrust of women embedded in early Church Fathers' writings portraying Eve as Adam's tempter, the original sinner, and all women as Eve's daughters inheriting her nature as sources of wickedness. In discussions of marriage, theologians stressed the wife's need to submit to her husband's authority. They were following not only Scripture but also classical scientific teaching that women were incomplete or imperfect males, less rational, less capable than men of overcoming the passions.[16]

Not only religious teaching prejudiced males against females in medieval society. In a warlike environment in which rivalries between men often resulted in violent confrontations, the fighting class feared women because they resembled clerics in their skill with non-violent weaponry, using words and sexual wiles to engage in plots and intrigues.[17] Medieval poets and authors of romances, reflecting their noble patrons' outlook, depicted women as incapable of taking on the masculine role of exercising power, unable to act on their own initiative, men's passive victims. Such notions predisposed twelfth-century writers against any woman challenging a masculine monopoly on power; any exercise of power in the public sphere was condemned as "unwomanly," somehow unnatural and wrong.[18] Eleanor's participation in her sons' great rebellion against their father Henry II in 1173–74 would confirm the chroniclers' suspicions of her. It is little wonder that they present a picture of her shadowed with streaks of evil that spread until it became a long-lasting black legend.

The English chroniclers limited their mentions of Eleanor to a few key crises or scandals in her life, and they barely distinguished between the public roles and private morality of rulers, expecting kings to exhibit heroic virtues of chivalric courage and honor, and queens to be exemplars of personal piety and virtue. It is no surprise then that they fail to help in answering questions that twenty-first-century readers find fascinating. They provide only the slightest hints of Eleanor's character or mentality, simply following conventional thinking in attributing her actions to personal, emotional, or sexual motives. Nor do they supply evidence of her psychological involvement with her children or her personal part in their upbringing. Indeed, they tell little more about her role as mother than the dates and places of her children's births, or names of those accompanying her on crossings of the English Channel. None comments on her "outsider" or "alien" status as a woman steeped in the civilization of southern France who encountered ill will at northern royal courts first at Paris and later in England. Nor do they comment on a topic of great interest to admirers of medieval French literature: her alleged role as a literary patron both in her native Poitou and in England, propagating courtly love through troubadour lyrics and chivalric romances. Since chroniclers frowned on women in power, they cast little light on Eleanor's political role at the courts of her two royal husbands or on her activity in the affairs in her own duchy of Aquitaine, other than to acknowledge her hereditary right to hold it.

A diligent biographer must look beyond these partial and biased writings and turn to other evidence for a more rounded portrait of Eleanor of Aquitaine. There is a second category of written sources that only incidentally yield biographical information, non-narrative record materials, an assortment of surviving documents, most of them by-products of the work of royal governments or the Church. Some were meant to be preserved as permanent legal records, but many others had only temporary usefulness and survive only by chance. Such records, though meager, can be pieced together to reveal Eleanor more clearly in her offices of queen and duchess; and neglecting them slights a substantial portion of her life, the part played by her in governing her own duchy of Aquitaine and her two husbands' kingdoms. Almost 200 documents issued by Eleanor are known, only 20 or so from her marriage to Louis VII and about 160 as wife and widow of Henry II.[19] Most surviving documents issued by Eleanor are charters, the most common surviving medieval documents. They are solemn records of grants of land or privileges, valued as permanent proof of rights in legal proceedings, and carefully preserved by churches and monasteries. Charters are documents frozen at one moment in time, but careful detective work in analyzing them, applying hard-won knowledge of medieval documents, can decipher their significance. Among Eleanor's documents there exist today few pieces of her own correspondence, no more than a half-dozen letters. Yet letters of others frequenting the royal court survive, some addressed to her, to afford glimpses of her life there.

Although more record material survives from England than from France, even English documents from Eleanor's time are scarce. Most impressive are financial records, the pipe rolls, enrollments of sheriffs' annual accounts presented to the exchequer that record royal income and expenditure. The pipe rolls, unique in twelfth-century Europe, yield invaluable details of Eleanor's daily life as England's queen, with expenditure on choice cloth, fine food and wine, payments to her household servants, and rewards to favorites attesting to her wealth. Other surviving English public records are writs, brief royal letters most often addressed to the sheriffs ordering the carrying out of some command, often in response to a petitioner's complaint. The royal chancery or writing-office drafted innumerable writs, but only a tiny minority have endured because they were usually soon discarded once they had served their purpose. No more than a handful of Eleanor's writs are extant, but they are vital for appreciating her authority as English queen, acting as Henry II's regent during his many absences from the kingdom.

The queen-duchess Eleanor of Aquitaine had an adventure-filled life, shifting rapidly from high points of success to defeats and back again. During her long years, she played a major role as Henry II of England's wife and widow in both the creation and collapse of the Angevin "empire." It is little wonder that she has always fascinated history lovers, as have few other women in the Middle Ages. This book shares with most earlier biographers of "that incomparable woman" a quest for "a truthful image," a goal that is possibly never fully attainable.[20] Any new look at Eleanor must draw on the same chronicles read and re-read by earlier biographers. Record materials and recent findings of specialists, however, enable a fresh re-creation of the queen-duchess's life. The result is not simply a narration of events, but clues to Eleanor's motivations as well as her contemporaries' understanding of their queen and what they saw as her proper role in that period.

To understand Eleanor today, we must confront the sharply differing standards of her medieval contemporaries and of authors in subsequent centuries right up to today in depicting a powerful woman's place in medieval society and government. Eleanor deserves to be seen on her own terms, not pressed into conformity with twenty-first-century preconceptions. Her story takes on added meaning once her public role as queen and her unwavering quest to protect the integrity of her duchy of Aquitaine take their proper place as essential components of her life. A major aspect of her nature was a pursuit of power, especially through partnership with her husbands, even though her expectations were often disappointed. Not until she was a widow would she achieve the political power that she had long craved, and then she shared it with her two sons, not with her husband. In an age when women were defined by their powerlessness, Eleanor chose to live her life as she saw fit, even though she paid heavily for her defiance of aristocratic custom and religious teaching.

CHAPTER 1

GROWING UP IN THE DUCAL COURT OF AQUITAINE, 1124–1137

On Good Friday in 1137, William X, count of Poitou and duke of Aquitaine, died while on a pilgrimage to Spain, leaving behind his daughter Eleanor of Aquitaine, aged thirteen, and her younger sister Aélith. Although Eleanor's early life is lost in obscurity, her father's death elevated her to a central place in European politics and diplomacy as the greatest marriage prize of the age, worthy of a great prince. The winner of her hand was Louis the Younger, son of Louis VI of France and heir to the French Crown, and she would bring to her betrothed the largest duchy within the kingdom of France. Her girlhood would end on their wedding day, 25 July 1137 in the cathedral at Bordeaux, and she would occupy center stage in history almost continuously until her death in 1204: first as queen of the French through her marriage to the future Louis VII, then through the scandal of divorce and marriage to Henry Plantagenet, future king of England, and later as mother of three English kings. As queen to two major monarchs, she would become one of the most famous or infamous of all women in all the Middle Ages.

By all accounts, the young Eleanor was a great beauty, but no portrait of her survives, for the Middle Ages was not a time when the art of portraiture flourished. Claims for surviving sculptures or wall paintings as portraits of Eleanor as queen are highly suspect.[1] Not even contemporary descriptions can be trusted, for medieval writers made little attempt at accuracy, but merely followed conventional descriptions of beautiful maidens, often handed down from the classics. In imaginative works, the writer's love object always has "hair [that] is golden, forehead milky, eyes sparkling like stars, visage rosy, lips flaming, teeth ivory, neck white."[2] Yet poets and other writers praised Eleanor's charms, and her attractions were evident even in her mature years.

Eleanor of Aquitaine was born and nurtured in a milieu that contrasts with the background of her two husbands. She was born into a dynasty with a rich history ruling over the largest duchy in France, and it was her hereditary right to Aquitaine that gave her such importance in history. Once a part of the ancient Roman province of Gaul, Aquitaine still preserved in Eleanor's childhood customs surviving from Roman rule that guaranteed women greater freedom than those in northern Europe enjoyed. Young Eleanor grew up hearing tales of earlier duchesses of Aquitaine who had sought and sometimes succeeded in grasping power in the turbulent tenth and eleventh centuries, when disorders had allowed some dynamic women to overcome the limitations of a patriarchal society and religion. Eleanor's ducal ancestors, tracing their origins to the Carolingian rulers, considered themselves the equals of kings; and she would take pride in her ancestry, confident that her lineage was as illustrious as that of her husbands, if not more so.

As Eleanor grew up she would have become aware that her ancestors had been counts of Poitou before they were dukes of Aquitaine and that the count-dukes' power rested on their estates in Poitou, providing the bulk of their resources for enforcing ducal authority. Indeed, Eleanor's premier identity was more Poitevin than Aquitanian. Even at the time of her birth in 1124, Eleanor's ancestral duchy was a confusing collection of a dozen or so counties. "Aquitaine," both in Eleanor's lifetime and in modern usage, is an imprecise term, referring to a vast and ill-defined region of France stretching from its northern frontier just below the River Loire to the Pyrenees and extending eastward from the Atlantic coast into the Massif Central. Yet Eleanor's subjects in her two royal husbands' northern kingdoms made little distinction between the peoples of Poitou or Gascony, Aquitaine, or other inhabitants of the Mediterranean south. They simply assumed that all those living in southern French territories known variously as the Midi or the Languedoc (often called Occitania today) shared similar excitable, emotional, and pleasure-seeking personalities. Even modern authors tend to fall back on a similar stereotype, characterizing Eleanor as a "child of the Midi" or "queen of the troubadours."

ELEANOR'S LEGACY, LINEAGE, AND LAND; THE DUCHY OF AQUITAINE

Eleanor was the descendant of proud dukes who ruled over Aquitaine—the largest territorial principality in France—ranking among the kingdom's most prestigious princes. She could take pride in her ducal ancestors' heritage as successors of Carolingian monarchs, and something of a sacred aura of royalty continued to surround them. As the central authority once wielded by ninth-century Carolingian rulers had weakened, political subdivisions of their

Frankish empire fell into the hands of men who inherited or usurped power as dukes, counts, or viscounts. When Eleanor's ancestors, tenth-century counts of Poitou, extended their rule over Aquitaine, the ineffectual late Carolingian kings to the north had little choice but to acknowledge them as dukes. Once the counts gained their ducal title they applied themselves to extending their authority over all ancient Aquitaine, eventually absorbing the duchy of Gascony lying below Poitou and stretching toward the Pyrenees.

The six eleventh-century count-dukes from William V the Great to William IX the Troubadour, Eleanor's grandfather, each succeeded in passing the duchy undivided to a son or sibling. The dukes assumed royal responsibility for enforcing public authority formerly in the Carolingians' hands. It was said of Duke William the Great (reigned 995–1030) that he "was thought to be a king rather than a duke," and chroniclers applied such words as 'most glorious' and 'most powerful' when describing him.[3] Before the mid-eleventh century, Gascony had constituted a separate duchy, ruled by a different dynasty who viewed their territory as entirely exempt from the French king's dominion. Gascon dukes spoke of their 'kingdom' or 'monarchy' before the union of the two duchies in 1058, claiming a divine source for their ducal authority. Duke Guy-Geoffrey of Aquitaine, who gained control of Gascony by 1058, styled himself in his official documents "duke of all the monarchy of Aquitaine."[4] Yet a sense of belonging in some manner to the larger kingdom of France lingered, even though neither the dukes nor their great men took much notice of the Capetian monarch at Paris. Nonetheless, like other powerful French princes, they admitted that his unique status as the crowned and anointed successor to the Carolingian emperors set him apart from them.

Despite the pretensions of Eleanor's Poitevin ancestors, their ducal title, though prestigious, brought them little added power; it merely outstripped in grandeur their earlier title of counts of Poitou that was the source of their actual power.[5] Aquitaine was becoming an almost stateless territory over which they held widely varying degrees of control, despite their pretensions to near-royal authority.[6] Habits of obedience to institutionalized public authority were withering throughout France, and in the century or so after the year 1000 governmental structures were either ineffective or non-existent. Eleanor's ancestors could only preserve their dominance over the counts and viscounts by exploiting the force of their personalities and the prestige of their illustrious ancestry. In Aquitaine as elsewhere in western Europe, the dukes' power came from personal ties or networks of relationships binding their great men to them through mutual trust and friendship or love.[7] If personal ties of friendship and affection between the duke and his magnates failed to bring stability to a society lacking effective governmental institutions, the only other option was military force to overawe them. Talk of friendship and love disguising a tie of lordship may seem a strange conflation of private sentiments and public power, yet Eleanor's contemporaries did not draw the line between 'private' sentiment and 'public' power that is drawn today.[8]

Although heir to the duchy of Aquitaine, Eleanor was more a product of Poitou than of those regions of Aquitaine lying farther south, although according to tradition she was born in the castle of Belin near Bordeaux. She spent most of her childhood at Poitiers, and although she periodically traveled to Bordeaux with the ducal household, as a girl she never visited those parts of Gascony lying south of the Bordelais. So evident was Poitou's position as the heartland and base for ducal power that Eleanor's predecessors' documents often styled themselves simply "Count of Poitou" without the added designation "Duke of Aquitaine." The power base of the counts of Poitou was always their direct control over extensive estates in Poitou, although not even there were effective administrative structures left standing.

It is impossible to map the land belonging to the ducal domain that Eleanor would inherit, but most significant were the fertile lands with fruitful vineyards lying around Poitiers and stretching westward to the region of the Sèvre Niortaise and the Vendée, and Olonnais and Talmondais along the Atlantic coast, extending southward into Aunis and Saintonge. Although more and more of the Poitevin estates were being converted to vineyards, abundant forests gave the dukes pleasure as hunting grounds and also generated funds through sale of timber and other resources, as well as rents from forest dwellers.[9] Less than a half dozen local agents known as provosts collected revenues from the ducal domain in Poitou, and ducal castles scattered over those lands were defended by their custodians, known as castellans. These posts of provost and castellan, like many formerly public offices in the tenth and eleventh centuries, tended to become hereditary, weakening the dukes' control over them. Although Gascony was described as "rich in white bread and in excellent red wine, . . . covered with woods and meadows, rivers and pure springs," the Poitevin count-dukes never succeeded in exploiting its resources.[10] Ducal lands there were not large, located almost entirely in the Bordelais and the adjacent Bazadais, and their effective control did not extend far beyond Bordeaux. Occasionally the dukes marched deep into Gascony to make a show of force and to demand local lords' allegiance, before hastily heading for Poitiers.

Aquitaine had experienced by the mid-eleventh century a commercial revolution fueled by population growth and bountiful crop yields, and traffic was expanding at a dozen or so Atlantic ports in both coastal and overseas trade.[11] As commercial activity expanded, port towns' revenues plus profits from mints produced considerable funds. In the interior, Poitiers was a center for both trade and manufacturing, known for producing helmets as early as the eleventh century. In the Atlantic ports at La Rochelle and Bordeaux the wine trade was expanding. An early thirteenth-century French poem, "The Battle of the Wines," refers to over seventy wines produced in France bearing names of Eleanor's possessions, including the Aunis and La Rochelle, Poitiers, Saint-Jean d'Angély, Saintes, Angoulême, Bordeaux and Saint-Emilion. Salt, essential for a growing fishing industry, was panned from the marshes on the Poitevin coast lying within the counts' domain, and it was a major product in the region's commerce.[12] Farther south, Bayonne on the Gascon coast was important for both salt production and for commercial fishing.

Eleanor would have absorbed in childhood her family's genealogy and stories of great deeds done by her ancestors. Prominent in her past were not only the dukes, but also their strong-willed duchesses and daughters who had considerable influence in political matters. In Poitou in the century before Eleanor's birth, and more so in provinces nearer the Mediterranean, survivals of Roman law traditions for several centuries after Rome's fall ensured women greater freedom than women in northern Europe enjoyed. great ladies had moved easily into positions of political power, attending assemblies of magnates and intervening in the public sphere. Within patrician families of the Midi, women were important actors in preserving and expanding family interests at a time when noblewomen in the north of France were losing power. At the time of Eleanor's birth, strict primogeniture (passing all property to the eldest son) was beginning to prevail in northern Europe as the pattern for aristocratic inheritance, narrowing women's prospects. Since this custom was not yet so widespread in Aquitaine, Gascony, or elsewhere in the Midi, southern fathers were more willing to share lands with their daughters, giving gifts of land on their betrothal, even allowing them to inherit property along with male siblings. Some women even succeeded to lordship of lands, and occasionally to a county or duchy, though probably not without challenges by male claimants or neighboring princes. Eleanor's own contemporary, Ermengard of Narbonne, succeeded her father as viscountess and ruled over Narbonne from 1143 until 1192/93 without sharing power with her husband, who hardly surfaces in the viscounty's documents.[13] As Ermengard's biographer observes, "almost every great Occitan dynasty . . . could name the matriarchs of their near or distant past, women whose lives were as charged with intrigue, ceremony, and warfare as those of their male contemporaries."[14]

Throughout medieval Europe, aristocratic women could come into control of some property. Fathers assigned their daughters substantial dowries or marriage-portions to take with them to their spouses, consisting of one or several estates before the thirteenth century. In addition, a noble bridegroom was expected to assign estates to his bride as dowerland, part of his land set aside to provide her with resources of her own, both during marriage and later as a widow. Aristocratic widows had control of their dowerlands, sometimes forcing sons to wait years before gaining full possession of their father's estates. Even in the south of France, however, women who wielded political power did so most often through their roles as wives and mothers. In the absence of a direct male heir, they had responsibility for ensuring dynastic continuity, selecting daughters or nephews as heirs. Aristocratic wives' authority over the domestic side of noble households also gave them power, demanding that in their husbands' frequent absences on military campaigns or crusades they look beyond their household and act in the public sphere.

Young Eleanor would have heard stories of earlier duchesses of Aquitaine, among them her grandmother Philippa of Toulouse, or more distant ancestors—Emma, a tenth-century duchess, or the eleventh-century duchess Agnes of Burgundy, third of Duke William (V) the Great's three wives. Such women confronted and abandoned ineffectual or adulterous husbands, governed as deputies for weak or absent spouses or for minor children, and claimed lordships as their own hereditary right.[15] Although Agnes of Burgundy is only one of a number of powerful women whose deeds were remembered, she is the outstanding female figure in Aquitaine's history before Eleanor's time.[16] Agnes had most influence following William V's death in 1030, after her remarriage to the much younger Geoffrey Martel, count of Anjou. During her second marriage she managed to play a powerful role in Aquitaine while two sons by her late husband's previous wives and then her own son held the ducal title one after the other, 1030–58. On her elder son's death in 1058, she worked to secure the succession of her younger son, Guy-Geoffrey, to the ducal title. Agnes had added the name Geoffrey to his baptismal name after her second marriage in the hope that the boy, brought up at his stepfather's court, would be the count's choice as heir to Anjou. Her hope was not fulfilled, and Guy-Geoffrey on succeeding to Aquitaine took the traditional name for heads of the Poitevin dynasty, William (VIII). His mother worked to add the duchy of Gascony to his domains, marrying him to a noble maiden who had a claim to the Gascon inheritance. Agnes also succeeded in marrying a daughter to the German emperor, Henry III, adding to the Poitevin lineage's prestige by linking it to Europe's greatest ruling family. Agnes lost influence over her son William VIII once he came of age, and after dominating Aquitaine's history for thirty years, she retired to a convent that she had founded at Saintes.

The duchy assembled by Eleanor's ancestors had a dual character: Poitou was closer in geography, in society, and language to Capetian-ruled northern France, while the remainder of Aquitaine shared the language and outlook of the Mediterranean south. A result of the long Roman occupation of the south of France was the survival of a commercial economy into the Middle Ages with old Gallo-Roman cities continuing as both centers for trade and seats of power for princes, who often occupied old Roman palaces. Bordeaux was in Eleanor's time still enclosed by third-century Roman walls standing as a reminder of the region's centuries as a province of Rome.[17] In some ways, Bordeaux and other Gascon towns with their strong survivals of Roman traditions resembled more closely medieval Italian towns than northern French ones.

Bordeaux lay in a zone where the speech known as *langue d'oc* or Provençal, now called Occitan, prevailed. Although Eleanor doubtless grew up first hearing Poitevin, a dialect of northern French spoken by the servants caring for her, she soon learned as a second language Occitan, the language of the Mediterranean south. Occitan extended as far northward as the Limousin, about 100 kilometers from Poitiers. Located not far south of the River Loire, Poitiers was not an Occitan city, although Occitan was the language of the poets and courtiers of Limousin or Gascon origin gathered at her grand-father's court.[18] Occitan was not a dialect of northern French, but a distinct language, closer to modern-day Catalan or Italian. It was virtually incom-prehensible to speakers of *langue d'oïl*, the language of Paris and northern France, reinforcing regional antagonism between southerners and the Franks of northern France. In the minds of the subjects of Eleanor's two royal husbands in the north, Poitevins, Gascons, and Aquitanians were all lumped together, identified as inhabitants of the Midi or Provence; and they supposed that Poitevins possessed the hot-blooded temperaments found in territories further south. Yet Eleanor's roots were hardly Mediterranean, and regarding her as incapable of adapting to northern France's solemn atmosphere or to England's gloom slights the complexity of her childhood. Growing up in Poitiers, she had lived on the frontier between two languages and two cultures.

In Eleanor's time, northern Europeans felt a contempt for southerners that perhaps masked their own feelings of inferiority. The more urban and secular culture of lands south of the Garonne river had little similarity to the lands to the north, and visitors from the north, particularly clerics, found the Midi "a troubling and frightening world." A twelfth-century guide for pilgrims trav-eling to the great shrine at Compostella in Spain described the Gascons as "thoughtless in their words, talkative, mockers, drunkards and gluttons." When Duchess Agnes's daughter was sent off from Aquitaine to marry the German emperor, a German abbot complained of the scandalous customs and indecent standards for dress that she introduced to the imperial court.[19] Eleanor's Aquitanian childhood would color northerners' perceptions of her when she married and moved away to the courts of her two husbands. When she arrived in Paris as a young bride in 1137, courtiers there had long found the people of the south lacking in gravity; they judged them to be effete and consumed with the pursuit of pleasure, yet incessantly quarreling. Later Eleanor's English subjects would form an equally unfavorable impression of the duchy of Aquitaine. The cosmopolitan twelfth-century scholar John of Salisbury found the duchy's culture so different from that of England and Normandy that he commented on "the peculiar customs and strange laws of the folk of Aquitaine."[20] Indeed, southerners tended to think of themselves as a separate people or nation sharing a common descent, although still belonging somehow within the larger kingdom of France. For the people of Gascony and the Mediterranean south, "France" was the Île de France, the royal domain of the Capetian kings, a foreign land far to the north. This mutual misunderstanding would prejudice Eleanor's new subjects in the north, both French and English, against her even before her arrival at her two husbands' courts.

ELEANOR's GRANDFATHER WILLIAM IX AND HER FATHER WILLIAM X

Shaping the character of the court at Poitiers where young Eleanor spent her most impressionable years was her grandfather, Duke William IX (1071–1126). Eleanor could not have avoided the influence of such a potent personality, even if indirect, since he had died when she was less than three years old. Known as the troubadour duke, William IX's carefree, secular, even anti-clerical spirit would continue to dominate the ducal court during his son William X's reign. Eleanor's grandfather was a worldly man, an exemplar of a type rare in the Middle Ages, impious and anti-clerical, an ardent pursuer of sexual pleasure who flouted the Church's moral teachings. Yet the serious feelings expressed in five of his songs helped raise the value placed on a man's love for a woman. At the same time, he was a warrior who had engaged in hard-fought battles against his rebellious nobles and on crusading expeditions.[21]

The troubadour duke is renowned today for his ribald verses, but in his own day, it was his promiscuity and open adultery that brought him disrepute, entangling him in conflict with the Church. Duke William IX took two wives, separating from the first after two years apparently because of her failure to give him a child.[22] In an age before the Church had brought marriage under its exclusive jurisdiction, matrimony was not yet a sacrament and the tie between wife and husband was not indissoluble. Aristocrats did not take marriage vows very seriously, and an easy excuse for shedding inconvenient spouses was a charge of consanguinity, since the eleventh- and twelfth-century Church barred unions within seven degrees of kinship. Yet it often failed to prevent marriages of cousins in powerful families, and later, kinship afforded a pretense for dissolving them.

In 1094 in a political marriage, William took as his second wife the formidable lady Philippa, daughter of the count of Toulouse and widow of the king of Aragon.[23] Philippa had sought marriage to William after her first husband's death in search of support for her claim to the county of Toulouse. Philippa was the sole child of Count William IV of Toulouse (d. *c.*1093), but following his death her uncle, Raymond of Saint-Gilles (later Count Raymond IV), had succeeded in wresting her inheritance from her. From 1098 Philippa claimed her right to Toulouse as lawful heir. William took up his wife's cause with enthusiasm and asserted her right with force, launching a series of expeditions over thirty years.[24] She and her husband regained the county and held it intermittently; but when William went off to fight in Spain in 1119, the Toulousains took advantage of his absence to raise a revolt. The long struggle by the duke and duchess of Aquitaine for Toulouse finally ended in failure in 1123, when its urban militia rose up to support Raymond V, grandson of Raymond of Saint-Gilles, as their count. Eleanor would take to heart the injustice done to her grandmother, and the long struggle for Toulouse remained a sore point. Years later, she would succeed in persuading each of her husbands to undertake military campaigns to retake control of the county.

Eleanor's grandmother endured William's multiple infidelities and even a long-lasting adulterous liaison for the sake of her struggle to regain her inheritance, and she remained faithful to him during their twenty years of marriage and the births of seven children. In 1115 in the midst of William's most notorious affair, she bore her last child, a son Raymond, born at Toulouse. Philippa's ultimate fate is unclear. According to some accounts, she took refuge at a priory of the new religious order of Fontevraud that she had founded in her ancestral county of Toulouse and died there; other accounts have her outliving her husband and dying on her dowerlands.[25] Whether or not the young Eleanor ever knew her grandmother, she would have grown up hearing stories of the independent-minded Philippa and other women whose discord with their husbands often ended in separation or remarriage.

William IX's partner in the most notorious of his many affairs was the wife of the viscount of Châtellerault, a lordship lying to the north of Poitiers on the road to Tours. She bore the ominous sobriquet "Dangereuse," but once installed in the Maubergeon Tower of the ducal castle at Poitiers, the townspeople came to call her "La Maubergeonne." The adulterous pair could never marry even if William repudiated his wife because the viscountess had a husband still living. The duke had to content himself with living openly with her as his mistress. Not surprisingly, the duke's unconventional conduct earned him the condemnation of clerical contemporaries, chief among them the bishop of Poitiers who excommunicated him. Hildebert of Lavardin, the urbane and learned bishop of Le Mans, a friend of the prelate, dedicated poems to him denouncing William, accusing him of having contaminated Poitiers by relinquishing his wife for a mistress, for rejecting his bishop's moral counsel and for filling his palace with anti-clerical counselors.[26]

Although Eleanor was not descended from William IX's adulterous union, she nonetheless was descended from La Maubergeonne, who was her maternal grandmother. Her grandfather had arranged the marriage of his son, Duke William X, to his mistress's daughter Aénor, born before she left her lawful husband the viscount of Châtellerault. Doubtless, the duke's mistress, unable to marry her paramour, encouraged Aénor's marriage to his son and heir, delighted that one day her daughter would be duchess, though the title was denied to her. The details of Eleanor's parentage would not prevent later moralists from proclaiming that Eleanor was cursed with the inherited licentiousness of her Poitevin lineage, and more than one writer would find in the viscountess's leaving one husband for another man a foreshadowing of her granddaughter Eleanor's scandalous divorce and remarriage.

A monk of the Limousin connected William IX's defeat in his first crusading campaign to his irreligion and his amorous activity, commenting on his failure in the Holy Land, "In truth he bore nothing of the name Christian; he was, as everyone knows, an ardent lover of women, and therefore unstable in all his actions."[27] Although today William, the troubadour duke, is remembered more for his love lyrics than for his political role, he likely enjoyed more success as a ruler than is recognized. However, his military adventures elsewhere—first on crusade in the Holy Land, later in 1119–20 fighting against the Moors and in Spain, and finally struggling to subdue Toulouse—distracted him from the work of subjecting the lords of his own lands to his authority. His first crusading venture proved disastrous when almost his entire army was massacred in a Turkish ambush in Anatolia; yet his second crusading campaign in Spain was a great success, offsetting his earlier humiliation. One souvenir of her grandfather treasured by Eleanor was an elegant pear-shaped rock crystal vase now in the Louvre, probably of Persian origin, brought back by him from Spain, apparently a gift from one of his fighting companions, a Muslim ruler allied with the Christians. The vase passed into Eleanor's hands, possibly as a christening gift from her grandfather not long before his death in 1126.[28]

William IX's reputation for a devil-may-care outlook, hedonism and singular views on sexuality soon reached far beyond Poitou. Far to the north in England, where his granddaughter would one day reign as queen, stories spread of his licentious life, and writers there felt free to repeat and to inflate them. In the view of scandalized northern Europeans, the troubadour duke's wanton ways typified the mores of southern France, and Eleanor's subjects in the French and English kingdoms would assume that she had inherited his unsavory character. It was the writings of two early twelfth-century Anglo-Norman monks that supply most detail on the personality of Eleanor's grandfather. One describes William IX as "a bold and upright man and so gay

that he could outdo even the wittiest minstrels with his many jests." He gives
an account of the disaster that befell William on crusade in 1101, when a
Turkish attack almost annihilated his force. Barely escaping, the duke was left
to wander back to Christian territory alone, living off the land. The duke is
hardly presented as a typical crusader; neither a warrior seeking glory nor a
penitent pilgrim. He writes that after William's return from the East, "Being a
gay and light-hearted man, he often recited the trials of his captivity in the
company of kings and throngs of Christians, using rhythmic verses with
skillful modulations." Another Anglo-Norman chronicler also remarked on
William IX's character. According to him, the duke's sudden fall from wealth
and power after his disastrous crusade made a deep impression, and once back
in Aquitaine he surrendered himself to a life of sin and self-indulgence,
"wallow[ing] in every kind of vice." He depicts William as a wit, eager to
arouse his listeners to laughter with such preposterous proposals as plans to
establish a convent at Niort filled with prostitutes instead of nuns.[29] Such
stories were repeated and embellished in England after Eleanor's arrival there
as a means of discrediting her, and her descent from such a notorious
character would dog her days as the English queen.

Today the reputation of Eleanor's grandfather rests on his poems on
women, love, and lust composed in the language of southern France, *langue
d'oc*, or Occitan, and he is counted as the first of the troubadours. A collection
of troubadour songs dating from the late thirteenth century is accompanied
by a biographical sketch of their composer, an unnamed count of Poitiers
whom few today doubt is Duke William IX. It describes him as "one of the
greatest courtiers of the world and one of the greatest deceivers of women . . .
And he knew well how to compose and sing." About half of his eleven
surviving poems are ribald verses ridiculing the Church's teachings on sexual
morality with occasionally obscene humor, but others adopt a serious tone,
praising the uplifting quality of love between a man and a woman. It is the
themes and vocabulary of these serious pieces that have won William fame as
creator of the poetry of "courtly love," even if the sentimental picture of an
adoring, longing knightly lover pining for a lady of superior rank, later a
staple of chivalric romances, barely emerges in his poems. These first examples of medieval vernacular poetry on secular subjects reveal William's
acquaintance with classical rules of rhetoric and Latin love poetry. A level of
learning in Latin letters exceeding that attained by most eleventh-century
nobles should not be surprising, since William IX's forebears were known for
their interest in letters, and he would see that Eleanor's father acquired an
education in letters at the cathedral school at Poitiers.[30]

On William IX's death in 1126, Eleanor's father succeeded to the ducal title
as William X. Though sharing his father's enormous appetites and impressive

in his physical appearance, he was not the larger-than-life character that the troubadour duke had been. Nor was he a composer of vernacular poetry, but troubadour songs did not cease to be heard in the palace at Poitiers. During Eleanor's childhood troubadours continued to number among the entertainers of all sorts flocking to his court seeking his patronage. Although a monk at the great monastery of Saint-Maixent wrote that William X "was courageous in combating his enemies and placed under his yoke all those whom he found to be rebels in his land," he in fact was not notably successful as count-duke, and he proved less than effective in bringing the Poitevin nobles under his control. His main achievement was regaining possession of the Aunis coast, traditionally claimed by the counts of Poitou. This gave him the town of La Rochelle that would rapidly rise as a major seaport when Eleanor was duchess, important for producing revenues for her and her two husbands.[31]

Duke William X, like his grandfather, quarreled with his bishops, expelling them for their opposition to an anti-pope whom he supported after a disputed papal election in 1130. The price of backing the anti-pope, son of a Jewish convert to Christianity, was his excommunication and an interdict declared on his lands, banning public religious services, although these steps failed to move him. William X's obstinacy impelled Bernard of Clairvaux (d. 1153), primary opponent of the anti-pope, to travel to Poitiers twice to denounce him. In 1135, after experiencing the determined Cistercian monk's holy anger in an emotional confrontation, the duke meekly submitted.[32] Years later Eleanor and her sister at the French royal court would also encounter the still energetic Bernard and earn his wrath. William vowed to do penance for his opposition to ecclesiastical authority by making a pilgrimage to the shrine of Santiago de Compostella in northwestern Spain, a popular destination for Poitevin pilgrims since the discovery of Saint James the Apostle's relics there in the ninth century. When the duke set out for Compostella, he took his two daughters with him as far as Bordeaux, where he installed them in the castle of l'Ombrière to await his return.

THE DUCAL COURT AT POITIERS AND BORDEAUX

Like other princely courts, the model for the court at Poitiers that Eleanor knew in her girlhood was the household of the Carolingian monarchs that the aristocracy adopted throughout the former Frankish kingdom.[33] Years later, as queen in France and England, Eleanor would find the same pattern at the royal households of her husbands, Louis VII and Henry II. The courts of her grandfather and her father consisted of an elaborate household, including the ducal family and all their retainers of various ranks. Persons at the court at

Poitiers ranged from noble friends and companions, chaplains, and other clerics, officers charged with keeping the household supplied with food, wine, and other necessities, to domestic servants who did the cooking and cleaning. Others joining the ducal household on festive occasions were entertainers, all known as *jongleurs,* or *joglars* in Occitan, whether troubadour singers or clowns, actors, acrobats, and dancers.

The Carolingians' organization of such a herd of people derived from functions of the parts of the royal palace: the chapel, the hall, the chamber, and the stable. Staffing the chapel in any aristocratic household was the chaplain and a half-dozen or so lesser clerics attached to the chapel who drafted documents and letters for the duke. Sometimes the chief of the household clerics had the title of chancellor, although it is not certain that such an office existed at the ducal court before Eleanor's time. In some great households, one of the clerks doubled as a physician. The staff of the hall, where guests were greeted and entertained, consisted of various officials occupied with supplying food and drink for the ducal household, such as the butler, who was charged with keeping the wine cellar stocked. The chamber originally signified the duke's bedroom, but as aristocratic housing became more elaborate, it came to refer to his private quarters where he could retreat with his family or meet for frank talks with intimate counselors. This was the sphere of the chamberlain who originally looked after bed-linens and clothing, but became in effect the household treasurer. The kitchen, pantry, and larder were under the chief cook's supervision. In addition, scores of lesser servants—ushers, door-keepers, messengers, maids, grooms—were needed for the ducal household's smooth functioning.

Another household official was the constable, originally the keeper of the stables, responsible for the care and feeding of the duke's horses. He headed a band of household knights needed for the ducal family's protection and for maintaining order in the palace. Through the constable's responsibility for the knights, he became a significant military figure, leading in battle the duke's men fighting on horseback. This is typical of the way that governing was still an informal, part-time activity in Eleanor's youth, and household officials combined their domestic duties with larger administrative responsibilities. A similar shift was seen in the office of seneschal or steward; charged with general oversight of the secular side of the household, he had responsibility for the ducal household's domestic comfort and security. By Eleanor's early years, however, the seneschal was also acting as the count-duke's deputy in Poitou during his absences on campaigns or other circuits of his lands, and he played a significant part in administering the county. William de Mauzé, seneschal under Eleanor's father, belonged to a family that had served the counts of Poitou in administrative capacities since the tenth century.[34] At other princely courts, the office of seneschal changed over time from a working post to a purely honorific one, a sign of favor for important nobles who took on its functions only on great ceremonial occasions.

William IX's court was not only a domestic household, but a center of public authority, where the great men of the duchy assembled to give the duke counsel, discussing matters of war and peace, and to settle disputes, constituting a court in the judicial sense. The term "court" does not refer to a fixed place, for the duke and his household frequently left Poitiers to circulate about his Poitevin domains. In an age of poor communications and rudimentary administrative mechanisms, Eleanor's father and grandfather had to travel about their territories cultivating their great aristocrats' friendship and impressing their authority on their subjects, and their court moved with them. The court was often on the move, traveling to other cities, strategic castles, prominent religious houses, and favored hunting lodges such as Talmont on the Poitevin coast. This travel acquainted young Eleanor with her ancestral lands in Poitou and Saintonge and she developed a deep feeling for them. Occasionally William X's court ventured south of the Garonne river to Bordeaux, seat of government for Gascony; and traveling between the two cities, the court stopped along the way at Saintes for lengthy halts.[35] Eleanor's father visited Bordeaux no more than once a year, if that often, and he rarely traveled beyond the Bordelais to southern Gascony, where the nobility acknowledged only the vaguest ties of lordship to him as their duke. On ducal visits to Bordeaux, Eleanor and her family resided at the eleventh-century castle of l'Ombrière, with its bulky rectangular tower constructed at the southeastern corner of the old Roman wall dominating the river. Built soon after her ancestors' eleventh-century acquisition of Gascony, it served as the Aquitanian dukes' seat of government for their southern duchy.[36]

Poitiers, Eleanor's primary childhood residence, occupied a site high on a hilltop with the River Clain looping around it that contrasted with the flat riverside location of Bordeaux. At Poitiers, the count-dukes' residence stood at the summit of the hill that was the site of the old Gallo-Roman town, surrounded by surviving Roman walls. The palace at Poitiers, dating from Merovingian times, took on the appearance of a medieval castle as a result of renovations over the centuries, such as the eleventh-century addition of the Tower Maubergeon and an encircling moat. Poitou, like the rest of western Europe in the eleventh and twelfth centuries, was "cladding itself in a white mantle of churches"; and carvings decorating even village churches attest to the skill of sculptors working in the new Romanesque style.[37] In Poitiers, young Eleanor was surrounded by impressive churches built in the eleventh century. Standing on the market square near the palace was Notre-Dame-la-Grande with its magnificent sculpted façade. Completed during her early years, it marks the peak of Romanesque architecture.

The schools of Poitiers had kept alive classical letters since the declining days of the Roman Empire, and the early dukes of Aquitaine had a reputation for learning. Eleanor's father and grandfather shared the early dukes' interest in letters, welcoming men learned in the classics to Poitiers. In the eleventh century, the school attached to the church of Saint-Hilaire was the most important cultural center in France south of the Loire, and by the mid-twelfth century both it and a school attached to the cathedral were drawing students from as far away as the Anglo-Norman realm. Illustrating the Latin learning taught at Poitiers is William of Poitiers, author of a book recording the deeds of William the Conqueror completed around 1077. Actually of Norman origin, William acquired his name as a result of his studies at Poitiers from about 1045 to 1050, and he returned to Normandy to serve as the duke's chaplain and biographer. In William's biography of the Conqueror, he reveals himself as "exceptionally well-read in the Classics, and determined to show off his learning." The excellence of his Latin, his knowledge of both the Roman historians and poets, as well as the early Christian histories, all attest to the quality of his education at Poitiers.[38]

The count-dukes' court at Poitiers in Eleanor's childhood was significant not only as a center of power, but also as a cultural center with a reputation for its highly civilized atmosphere. Shining as a center of fashion and culture, the court attracted visits from the Aquitanian aristocracy. William ix and Èbles, viscount of Ventadorn, another troubadour noble, visited one another's courts, and each tried to outdo the other in their display and magnificence. Eleanor's outlook would be shaped by the sophisticated environment of the court of her grandfather and father, renowned for its "ostentatious prodigality," outshining other aristocratic courts further south.[39] Gathered together at their ducal court were persons of many levels of society, from high-ranking ecclesiastics and lay lords and their ladies to "new men" of undistinguished ancestry who had risen to take local offices, as well as household knights of even lower birth, some of them the duke's former fighting companions.

At the ducal court at Poitiers, as in other princely courts in the twelfth century, courtliness, the ethos of courtiers, was infiltrating chivalry, the traditional values of a warrior aristocracy, marking a new sophistication. As with other medieval princely courts, one of its important functions was educational—the training of youths, not only in the use of arms, but also in elegant manners, and perhaps in Latin letters as well. The court of Eleanor's father and grandfather included a corps of military retainers, young knights of varying social ranks, some the younger sons of noble families sent away for instruction and others from modest backgrounds seeking their fortunes as fighting men. Often the sons of poor knightly families or of even lower ranking parentage, they barely had the money for the training, horse, and equipment needed to become mounted warriors, and they expected loyalty to their prince to win them generous rewards. With young single men greatly outnumbering the women, the court in Eleanor's impressionable years was filled with sexual tension; the songs of William IX and Marcabru, a troubadour at his son's court, suggest that cuckoldry of noblemen was common.[40] Eleanor's grandfather, William IX, stamped his character on the ducal court of her childhood. Not only a creator of the medieval vernacular love lyric, but also learned in Latin letters, he welcomed fellow poets and entertainers of all sorts to his court. Two famous Gascon composers and singers of songs, Cercamon and Marcabru, can be identified in the household of Eleanor's father William X, fashioning poems and possibly performing clerical services for him as well. Marcabru's poetry was filled with classical and scriptural references revealing his learning, and both writers show a precocious awareness of the "matter of Britain," Celtic legends that would inspire authors of Arthurian romances later in the twelfth century. Another early troubadour, Jaufre Rudel, lord of Blaye in the Gironde, may have spent his youth at the court at Poitiers.[41]

Courtly love is commonly cited as marking the nascence of the modern era's notion of romantic love. Although Eleanor undoubtedly heard the troubadours' songs as a child, the extent to which their new ideas on love and marriage shaped her own views cannot be known. Too little evidence from Eleanor's early life survives to resolve much debated claims for her role in fostering the doctrines of courtly love disseminated by troubadours or claims that she influenced later notions of romantic love. Troubadour poetry was in its infancy in the years before she left for Paris, and its theme of a young knight's adoration of his superior-ranking lady would not become a literary norm until the later twelfth century.[42] Nonetheless, because the adult Eleanor is so often associated with courtly love and outrageous claims have been made for her as its sponsor and propagator, the unfolding of this phenomenon during her formative years must be understood.

Today it is hard to know what to make of courtly love that seemingly celebrated adulterous relationships between a married noble lady and her knightly admirer; nor can it be known what those living in a Christian society that classed adultery and fornication as serious crimes were to make of it. The troubadours' love was full of contradictions: sensual yet spiritual, both ethically edifying and sinful, open and at the same time secret.[43] The elevation of women in their songs conflicted with teachings of eleventh- and twelfth-century Church reformers who portrayed all women as descendants of Eve, the temptress and source of sin, spreading wickedness and disorder in the world. Because troubadour love contradicted Church teachings on love, marriage, and sex, it was suspected of contamination by the heretical Cathars or even of Spanish Muslim influences. Eleanor's ducal ancestors knew something of Arabic culture, for they had often joined other warriors from southern France in the Christian Spanish kings' struggle to push back Muslim invaders a generation before the First Crusade. Among those campaigning beside the Christians in Spain was Eleanor's grandfather, and Arabic influences may have been at work in his poetry. Whatever courtly love's sources, it is an elusive concept, and its impact on people's behavior at princely courts is impossible to estimate.

Also responsible for blending clerics' courtliness, knights' prowess, and "courtly love" into a new standard for knightly behavior were authors of late twelfth-century vernacular romances. More numerous in northern France and the Anglo-Norman realm than in the south, the romance writers adapted the love portrayed in troubadour songs, making adoration of a noble lady a key characteristic of the perfect knight. Romance writers borrowed from troubadour lyrics language that applied a knight's service to his lord to the language of devotion to his lady. Illustrating this are lines by Bernart de Ventadorn, a poet who would follow Eleanor from Poitiers to the court of her new husband, Henry Plantagenet, and whose songs celebrating his devotion to an anonymous aristocratic lady, sometimes identified as Eleanor, created the model for later troubadour poets: "Good lady [*domna*], I ask nothing from you/but that you take me as your servant [*servidor*]/who will serve you as his good lord [*senhor*]."[44]

Unlike the knights of the romances written in the north, Occitan knights would continue to identify chivalry with purely warlike traits, rather than with exalted love for a lady, and the sponsors of singers of troubadour songs were more likely the husbands of noble ladies than the ladies themselves. Songs of the Périgord knight Bertrand de Born, writing for Eleanor's sons, say nothing of knightly love for ladies, but extoll warfare and taunt those nobles who refrained from fighting. In the few poems that Bertrand authored with amorous topics, his treatment of love is decidedly unromantic.[45]

Courtly love's language of knightly devotion to a lady cannot be regarded as an accurate portrayal of the position of women in the aristocratic society of Eleanor's youth. While power for women of the Midi was possible, and some ruled lands in their own right or on behalf of absent spouses or minor offspring, many others found their fates entirely in the hands of fathers, husbands, or other kin. Indeed, property rights enjoyed by southern women in the eleventh century were weakening in the early and mid-twelfth century.[46] While encouraging courteous conduct toward the ladies at princely courts, it is unlikely that the troubadour love lyrics brought significant betterment of their lives. Perhaps such songs were little more than moves in a complex game of flirtation. Once troubadour poetry reached the French and

English royal courts, listeners there would find the depiction of adulterous love alarming, and such songs may have inclined Eleanor's subjects to believe the worst of her.

At the same time that poetry at the court of Eleanor's grandfather was defining "courtly love", it was also contributing to a new understanding of "chivalry" at Poitiers and at other princely courts. In Eleanor's early childhood, the Old French and Occitan terms that would evolve into the modern "cavalry" and "chivalry" still applied primarily to skill with horses and weapons, the qualities of knights, military professionals fighting on horseback, men in those days often of non-noble rank. In the violence and chaos of the tenth and eleventh centuries, polite manners or moral behavior were little valued, although knights felt a strong sense of honor and shame, making them quick to avenge any affront that dishonored them. Desirable characteristics for knights described in the late eleventh-century epic poems, the *chansons de gestes*, center on prowess, including physical strength, mastery of fighting skills, and courage. Less attractive traits also characterized the epic heroes: pride, arrogance, disdain for lesser persons, and willingness to humiliate others. This individualistic ethos clashed with the Christian contemplative ideal, exemplified by the monastic life, and by the late eleventh century, churchmen were seeking to harness the warrior elite's ferocity for spiritual ends. They tried to channel their fervor toward Christian goals, enforcing the Peace of God to defend the poor and weak and crusades to liberate the Holy Places.

During Eleanor's early years, first as a child at Poitiers and later as an adolescent bride at Paris, courtliness, or courtesy, was beginning to dilute the warrior ethos of chivalry. Courtliness stood for a new standard for the nobility of polite and principled conduct gaining ground in the late eleventh century, inspired by ancient Roman ideals. Cultured ecclesiastics had kept alive classical ideals of conduct advocating upright character, eloquent speech, good taste, and polished manners aimed at preparing Roman youths for the life of statesmen. Under the influence of churchmen at princely courts, this classical ideal began to take on new form among both clerical and lay courtiers.[47] Soon the two concepts of knightly prowess and clerical courtliness were giving rise to a new standard of chivalric conduct that combined fighting skills with learning and courteous conduct. Over the twelfth century, a new definition of nobility was taking root as knights, originally rough soldiers, were exposed to courtly conduct in their lords' households. As models for conduct followed by both landless knights and nobility of ancient lineage meshed together, they coalesced as a single class in people's thinking. The terms "knight" and "noble" were becoming synonymous, and individuals of either status were expected to exemplify chivalry and courtesy as members of a single superior caste standing above the common people.[48] This change in social structure would not be completed until Eleanor's mature years at the end of the twelfth century and the beginning of the thirteenth century.

Eleanor, growing up in William IX's sophisticated court, a model for courts throughout southern France, saw at first-hand the elegant behavior characteristic of a courtly culture. There she would have witnessed women enjoying a more respected position than later at the French or English royal courts, where religious teachings demanding women's deference toward males bore greater weight. Southern women freely joining the men in witty and flir- tatious conversations would have shocked visitors from northern France or England, who feared the skill of ladies with words, their ability to apply verbal weaponry and sexual wiles for plotting and intriguing.[49] Yet court life had less appealing aspects that young Eleanor could have observed. A competitive atmosphere permeated the princely courts, for courtiers flocked there to win the prince's approval and patronage; and in their competition for favors, they resorted to scheming, slander, and flattery. As a girl, she would have heard scurrilous rumors at the ducal court spread by ambitious courtiers about their rivals of the sort that would circulate later at her two husbands' courts about her own alleged sexual misconduct.

A Princess's Upbringing

Eleanor's life as a child growing up in the ducal household is almost completely undocumented. Her name first surfaces in the records in July 1129, when her presence with her brother and her parents was noted at the monastery of Montierneuf at Poitiers, the burial place of her great-grandfather, who also founded the house.[50] Not even the exact date of Eleanor's birth can be known, for few early twelfth-century noble families bothered to record their children's birthdays; and if chroniclers occasionally noted births of sons to princely fami- lies, they were less likely to mention those of daughters. Furthermore, uncer- tainties remain even when dates are recorded, for medieval scribes used diverse dates for beginning the new year, sometimes Christmas, sometimes as late as Easter, but rarely 1 January. Tradition has it that Eleanor was born on one of her parents' visits to Bordeaux, perhaps at the nearby castle of Belin, and her birth year is variously given as 1122 or 1124, although the latter date is now generally accepted.

Earliest evidence for Eleanor's birth year is a late thirteenth-century genealogy of her family listing her as thirteen years old in the spring of 1137, the time of her father's death. We can assume that the genealogy's compiler strived for accuracy, since her marriage later that year would have been invalid under Church law if she were under twelve years old. This fixes her birth in 1124, making her two years younger than the previously favored date of

1122.[51] Since the date of Eleanor's death is known to be 1204, her lifespan measured eighty years, an extraordinary age for anyone to have attained in her era. Because so many deaths came in infancy or early childhood, the average life expectancy in the Middle Ages was only around thirty years, although another decade might be awarded to aristocratic ladies who had the advantage of comfortable lives and abundant food, and who were not required to risk their lives in battle. Eleanor's survival points to good health in her early years; indeed, her longevity suggests that she was unusually healthy throughout her life, capable of surviving a dozen pregnancies and childbirths. Otherwise, illnesses would have brought doctors to the bedside of a lady in her high position, and their ministrations were as likely to kill as to cure.

Eleanor did not grow up surrounded by a large extended family, as did many aristocratic children in the Middle Ages. When Eleanor's grandfather William IX died in 1126, he left only two sons, his elder son and heir, Eleanor's father William X, and his youngest child Raymond, only nine years older than his niece. Raymond left Poitou by 1130, landless after his father's death. He journeyed to England to seek his fortune at the court of Henry I, a king known for his hospitality to young knights. Raymond, who had inherited his father's charm, found good fortune there; but after the king's death he left for the Holy Land, having received an offer from Fulk, king of Jerusalem and former count of Anjou, to wed an heiress there. By early 1136, Raymond had arrived in the crusader kingdom, lured by a marriage that would confer on him the principality of Antioch; and he would remain in the East until his death in 1149, enjoying a reunion with his niece Eleanor when she accompanied her first husband Louis VII of France there on the Second Crusade.[52]

Although Eleanor's father and uncle had five sisters, little or nothing is known of them or of their participation in young Eleanor's upbringing. The best known of the sisters, sometimes called Agnes and other times Mahaut, was married first to the viscount of Thouars, an important lordship lying along Poitou's northern and western frontiers. Several years after her husband's death in 1127 she left Poitou, called to a new life in Spain as the wife of Ramiro, younger brother of the recently deceased king of Aragon. The magnates of Aragon had removed Ramiro, a monk, from his monastery to take the Aragonese Crown in order to prevent it from falling into the hands of the king of Castile. In 1134, they crowned the former monk King Ramiro II and married him off to Eleanor's aunt, known to the Aragonese as Agnes of Aquitaine, in order to perpetuate the royal line. Another of Eleanor's aunts, Agnes of Poitiers, entered the convent of Notre-Dame at Saintes and became abbess there.[53]

Eleanor's mother, Aénor, did not belong to one of the highest ranking princely families of Aquitaine. As we have seen, in 1121 William IX arranged a marriage for his heir to the daughter of his infamous paramour, La

Maubergeonne and her husband, the viscount of Châtellerault. Little Eleanor was named for her mother; according to tradition, her name Aliénor in French, derives from the Latin, meaning "another Aénor." Eleanor's mother died in 1130 while she and her husband were on a hunting party in the marshes of Lower Poitou, and she was buried near the site of her death at Nieuil-sur-l'Autise, a house of regular canons.[54] She left behind three children: Eleanor, aged approximately six, a younger daughter, Aélith, also known as Petronilla; and a son, Aigret, who died in the same year as his mother. The two girls, left without a mother or other siblings at an early age, took comfort in each other's company, and Eleanor's closest childhood tie was likely with Aélith. Their close relationship would continue after Eleanor's marriage when her sister accompanied her to Paris.

Eleanor as the elder of the two surviving children was the putative heir to her father's duchy of Aquitaine, unless he were to take a new bride after Aénor's death who could give him another son as his heir. William aimed to take as his second wife the young widow of the lord of Cognac, the daughter and heir of the viscount of Limoges, but this did not come to pass. Instead, a hostile neighbor, the count of Angoulême, took the young viscountess and won control of her viscounty of Limoges with its chief city, seat of the great monastery of Saint-Martial.[55]

It was Eleanor's maternal Châtellerault relatives who would play important roles during her adult years. Most prominent of all was one of her mother's brothers, Ralph de Faye. Ralph, a younger son of the viscount of Châtellerault, added "de Faye" to his name after his marriage to the heir to the lordship of Faye-la-Vineuse on the Poitevin–Angevin frontier. Because a purely patri-lineal family model did not yet prevail in that region, strong links with maternal relatives—especially between uncles and aunts and their nephews or nieces, and between sons and their cousins—continued in force in noble families. A female heir such as Eleanor could expect to enjoy her maternal uncle's protective concern, and Ralph de Faye would stand beside her, assisting as one of her chief agents and her trusted counselor in governing Aquitaine until 1173. Eventually Ralph's plotting with his niece to encourage her sons' revolt against their father, Henry II, would bring down on him the English king's wrath.[56]

Little information survives about the upbringing of aristocratic daughters in the Middle Ages—even less than about the education of noble sons. Childhood first became a subject for serious historical study almost a half century ago, and for years afterward, studies questioned the universality of the affectionate nuclear family considered the norm today. It was widely assumed that people living in the Middle Ages did not recognize childhood as a distinct phase of development, and that medieval children were integrated into adult activities by age six or so. The "discovery" of childhood was attributed to sixteenth- and seventeenth-century religious reformers, who ended the happy mingling of children and adults and converted the family into a tyrannical institution for disciplining the young. It was taken for granted that the medieval noble family had little "moral and spiritual function," and that it played no significant part in shaping a child's adult character, but was "simply an institution for the transmission of a name and an estate."[57] Further research has caused a reaction against depictions of pre-Reformation parents as uninvolved, cold, and distant, or even abusive. Searches of medieval sources uncover numerous examples of mothers and fathers who were devoted to their children and who grieved at their deaths, pointing to the continuity of parental affection for offspring among all peoples in all ages. As one writer declares, "Parents delighted [in their children] for as far back as there are records. The medieval family was never dead to sentiment; it is only poor in sources."[58]

Yet the fact remains that before the twentieth century, when Sigmund Freud's teachings gained favor, preoccupation with parental "bonding" with their infants was hardly a universal concept. Unlike middle-class western families during the twentieth century, medieval families did not have the luxury of elevating child-rearing to a cult. Although motherhood was much honored in the twelfth century, the rearing of children was not left to mothers alone as in modern societies dominated by a child-centered model of the nuclear family. Instead, a larger group contributed to medieval children's welfare; the village community for peasant families and an elaborate household for aristocratic families. Noble families with households comprising numbers of servants had little in common with today's nuclear family. Families of royalty or great magnates had even less in common with modern families. Indeed, twelfth-century Latin had no equivalent to the modern word "family", and various Latin words for relatives or kin had looser meanings that included related persons outside the nuclear group. The Latin *familia* is a false cognate, better translated as "household" than as "family".

Noble family life did not revolve around the nurturing and socialization of children, and all sorts of retainers, domestics, and other members of noble households took part in their upbringing. This meant that the first close ties of affection formed by aristocratic or royal children were not only with their parents, but spread among other relatives, knightly attendants, household officials, and lower-ranking servants. This would have been all the more true for young Eleanor, whose mother died when she was only six years old. Perhaps the servants charged with little Eleanor's care pitied her because she had no mother and were over-indulgent, spoiling her more than other aristocratic children. In medieval noble families, dependence on servants was little different from that in modern aristocratic families, or at least those before

World War II. Lives of children of the rich and powerful in the nineteenth and early twentieth centuries were ruled first by their nannies and later by governesses or tutors, and they saw their parents only when servants brought them "dressed in their best once a day at tea-time for perhaps one hour of the twenty-four."[59]

Although hardly anything can be known about Eleanor's education, yet evidence is abundant for tutors' presence in eleventh- and twelfth-century princely households; also some noble families sent their children, girls as well as boys, away to religious houses to be educated. While little Eleanor was never sent off to a convent for schooling, there can be no doubt that she received a sound grounding in letters. She almost certainly learned to read Latin, tutored by chaplains in the ducal household. Perhaps taking responsibility for overseeing her education was the archbishop of Bordeaux, her guardian during her father's absence on pilgrimage and in the days following his death. Geoffrey du Loroux was a learned man who had headed the cathedral school at Angers earlier in his ecclesiastical career.[60]

Many great ladies born a generation or so earlier than Eleanor had received excellent educations; Adela of Blois, daughter of William the Conqueror, won praise from clerical authors for her learning, and she corresponded with churchmen such as Saint Anselm, renowned for their writings. A lady of the lesser nobility in northern France at about the same time, mother of a future monastic author, was capable of teaching her young son his ABC.[61] Twelfth-century vernacular romances also lend support for noble maidens educated in letters, depicting their heroines learning to read, often alongside boys. In Renaut's *Galeran*, the heroine was brought up in a convent, where she learned to read and write Latin, as well as to sew, sing, and play the harp.[62] Although an idealized depiction, it suggests that the early education of both aristocratic girls and boys in twelfth-century Aquitaine included at least elementary learning in Latin letters, and now and then more advanced studies for young nobility of both sexes. An intriguing passage in a thirteenth-century English chronicle seems to show that Eleanor was educated in the company of boys. It gives an account of a ring given to St Albans Abbey, alleging that the giver had received it as a gift from Eleanor, his "fellow student and childhood companion," when the two were youngsters studying together.[63]

The tradition of Occitan poetry fostered at Poitiers by Eleanor's grandfather gave her an early acquaintance with vernacular literature and with the courtly conduct praised in troubadour songs. Troubadour poetry authored by female troubadours, *trobairitz*, shows that aristocratic women's training in courtly manners included learning to read the vernacular language.[64] Their poetry suggests that one of the pleasures of social life at princely courts in the south was bantering and flirtatious conversation between women and men. Two didactic poems composed in Occitan as guides for young ladies also reveal women's lively engagement in the courtly activities of princely households in southern France. Compared with similar didactic poems from northern Europe, they indicate that both married and unmarried women at southern courts had more latitude in social life, emphasizing their competence at conversation in men's company.[65]

If young Eleanor experienced the worldly civilization of the south exemplified by troubadour poetry at the Poitevin court, she also had exposure to the Christian teachings that dominated court life in northern France. Like other children growing up in twelfth-century Europe, she saw all around her ever-present reminders of the power of the Church.[66] The lives of Eleanor and the ducal family were punctuated by the liturgical calendar with its feasts and fasts; and the great festivals of the Christian year—Christmas, Easter, and Pentecost—called to mind the Church's central doctrines. These feast days were occasions for impressive assemblies at the ducal court, combining religious, convivial, and political functions.

Christianity had set down strong roots in Roman Aquitaine some 700 years before Eleanor's birth, and Poitiers was an important religious center throughout the Dark Ages. On the slope descending from the palace toward the river lay evidence for Christianity's early presence in the baptistery of Saint-Jean. Dating from the fourth century, it is the earliest surviving Christian structure in France. Around the ancient baptistery a religious quarter arose dominated by the cathedral of Saint-Pierre, which would be reconstructed early in Eleanor's marriage to Henry II of England. In the same religious quarter below the cathedral and near the river was the church of Sainte-Radegonde, burial place of the Merovingian queen who founded the abbey of Saint-Croix, one of the first women's religious houses in the Frankish kingdom. Her tomb attracted such crowds of pilgrims that the church was rebuilt on a grander scale in the eleventh century. Standing on the other side of the city outside its Roman walls was another church that became a pilgrimage goal, Saint-Hilaire-le-Grand, containing the tomb of a fourth-century bishop who ranks among the early theologians of the western Church. The counts of Poitou had close ties to Saint-Hilaire, acting as lay abbots, taking their seats in the choir among the canons, and appointing the church's officials. Pilgrims traveling southward on their way to Spain to worship at the shrine of Santiago de Compostella made a point of stopping at these two churches in Poitiers to pray at the tombs of Saint Hilary and Saint Radegonde.

Instruction in the tenets of the Christian faith would have formed an important aspect of Eleanor's early education, conforming to the pattern for daughters in other medieval aristocratic families. A thirteenth-century guide to children's upbringing sets down that the first thing to be taught to children is belief in God, and that they should learn by heart the Creed, the Lord's Prayer, the Hail Mary, and the first two of the Ten Commandments.[67] Little Eleanor would have learned to make the sign of the cross and to cross herself each night before going to bed. Mothers were charged with helping their young daughters to memorize these fundamental texts of Christianity, but nothing can be known of the role of Eleanor's mother Aénor, whom she lost so early in childhood. Perhaps the motherless child's godparents saw to her religious instruction. Once she learned her ABC, her basic knowledge of Latin would have enabled her to read devotional handbooks. She likely received a psalter for personal devotions in quiet moments alone, and her constant repetition of the psalms that she knew through public devotions in the palace chapel would also have aided in improving her skill at reading Latin.[68] Eleanor would have learned stories of the saints' lives as part of her childhood religious education. Among them was Saint Radegonde, whose life foreshadowed one aspect of Eleanor's own—a loveless marriage ending in separation. A Thuringian princess taken captive by the Frankish king, Clothair I, Radegonde was forcibly married to him in 531. It was hardly a happy marriage, and the queen found consolation in religious devotions. After her husband's murder of her brother, she separated from him, dedicated her life to Christian devotion and founded the abbey of Saint-Croix; and on her death in 587, she was buried nearby in the church bearing her name.

An important aspect of young Eleanor's religious life was attendance at daily masses in the palace chapel, or in some nearby church, possibly Notre-Dame-la-Grande. She would have occasionally confessed her sins privately to a chaplain in her father's household, a pious practise gaining ground in the twelfth century, but that would not win the formal status of a sacrament until 1215. Surveillance of individuals' morality was also fostered by a society composed of people living crowded together with no privacy either in isolated rural communities or in large noble households; both peasants and their lords prized group solidarity and frowned on any unconventional conduct. At aristocratic courts, those who violated customary norms of behavior inspired ugly gossip and risked social isolation or even banishment. They were expected to feel both guilt at being condemned as sinners and shame at their exposure to censure by their lord or lady and their noble companions. At the court at Poitiers, however, where Duke William IX had set the tone, behavioral norms hardly met the serious moral standard prevailing at the royal court at Paris, Eleanor's future home.

Early on, Eleanor encountered the medieval Christian mentality, largely defined by monks, that was suspicious of human bodily needs, especially sexual activity.[69] Reforming moralists and theologians intent on enforcing priestly celibacy sharpened their attacks on the supposedly sinful nature of women, reinforcing the early Church Fathers' pervasive mistrust of the gender and burdening them with guilt on that account. Christian teaching, however, held up the sinless Virgin Mary as the model for women, at the same time idealizing and anathematizing women, trapping them in double jeopardy. In discussions of Christian married life, moralists and theologians reinforced patriarchal traditions that stressed the wife's duty to accept subordination to her husband and condemned women daring to challenge the masculine monopoly on power. Yet during Eleanor's childhood, the Church had not yet succeeded in codifying the early Fathers' misogyny into its later restrictive definitions of women's roles. By the mid-twelfth century, canon lawyers would redefine women's proper sphere to restrict their public roles more and more; they would dismiss Old Testament depictions of women acting as judges as the old law, no longer binding in the Christian era.[70]

It was not only religious teaching that prejudiced males against females in medieval society, stripping from aristocratic women power in the public sphere that they had held in previous centuries, if only precariously. The classical scientific tradition taught in the schools also encouraged masculine superiority, teaching that males were more rational, more capable than females of overcoming the passions. Ideas about female anatomy at the Salerno medical school reinforced the clergy's notion that women were "raging volcanos of sexual desire," and scientific theories followed Aristotle's finding that women were incomplete or imperfect males.[71] Another factor contributing to the reshaping of medieval notions about women's proper place was a militarization of society as the aristocracy adopted the chivalric values of their fighting men. At princely courts, a bellicose environment often existed where rivalries between courtiers resulted in violent confrontations; and rude knights feared women who resembled clerics in their skill with non-violent verbal weaponry, using words and sexual wiles to engage in plots and intrigues.[72] Yet Eleanor, reared in a household under her sensualist grandfather's influence, would succeed in escaping the feelings of guilt and shame that society expected to restrain women from pursuing their personal fulfillment.

As a girl, Eleanor learned that previous dukes of Aquitaine were founders of some of Poitou's most important religious houses, among them Montierneuf at Poitiers outside the old Roman walls, founded by Duke Guy-Geoffrey as recompense for setting aside his first wife to take a second one. Young Eleanor would have visited other monasteries with her father and his household as they circulated about the county, certainly Saint-Maixent, a house not far from Poitiers closely associated with the ducal family. On festival days, Eleanor would have viewed the precious relics of the saints housed in monastic chapels, and she would have heard accounts of miracles performed by the saints for the faithful who venerated their relics. This taught her and other

Christians that God was active in the material world, not only in the past but in the present, continuing to intervene in people's lives with miracles when they called on him or his saints.

Little Eleanor was taught that eternal salvation was not easily attained, and that a Christian owed definite duties to God. She would have equated these obligations with the loyalty and service owed to one's lord, a conviction held by most early medieval aristocrats. Any failure to carry out the duties owed to one's lord, either an earthly one or the heavenly Lord, would mean taking steps to regain his goodwill. Just as the powerless in judgments before a medieval lord's court needed an influential friend to intercede on their behalf, even more did the dead standing before the heavenly tribunal need a saintly intercessor. For the eleventh- and early twelfth-century nobility, "Salvation was a matter of negotiations with God represented by his ministers on earth."[73] Like other aristocrats, Eleanor knew the importance of purchasing the saints' goodwill with gifts to monastic houses, and throughout her life she recognized the importance of monasteries for offering perpetual prayers for intercession with God and the saints. As a queen, Eleanor would be punctilious in providing funds for religious houses for prayers for the salvation of her living kin and for the souls of deceased ancestors.

Eleanor would have grown up with an awareness of earlier duchesses' special place in the sacred sphere. Some aristocratic ladies found in the devotional life of the Church a means of transcending limitations that society imposed on women, winning control over a corner of their lives. In an age of family solidarity, the wives and mothers of princes played an essential part in securing their families' eternal salvation with their devotional practises, their friendships with holy men and women, and their patronage of monastic houses. Duchesses of Aquitaine had founded some of the region's most prestigious religious houses, and their husbands' own foundations often resulted from their urging. Surpassing all other duchesses in her support of religious houses was Eleanor's ancestor, Duchess Agnes of Burgundy. Although few convents existed in eleventh-century southern France for women wishing to enter the religious life, Agnes founded the abbey of Notre-Dame at Saintes.[74] It became a prestigious house for noble ladies, and its abbess during Eleanor's first marriage was another Agnes, her aunt. Agnes of Burgundy was also a benefactor of Saint-Hilaire at Poitiers, constructing a major part of the abbey's buildings. A monk of Saint-Maixent, mindful of her turbulent career, wrote of her, "If that lady offended the Lord in many things, she did much to please him."[75] Eleanor's grandparents William IX and Philippa of Toulouse were early supporters of Fontevraud Abbey, founded at the beginning of the twelfth century as a double monastery for both men and women and headed by an abbess. Philippa visited Fontevraud, and she founded a Fontevraudist priory in her native Toulouse.[76]

Young Eleanor's pampered childhood came to an end with the loss of her father when she was barely a teenager. William X died in Spain at age thirty-eight on Good Friday, 9 April 1137, short of reaching on Easter Sunday his pilgrimage goal of the shrine of Saint James at Compostella. His companions carried his body to the great cathedral in Galicia, and the archbishop of Compostella agreed to his burial before the high altar.[77] The duke's fellow pilgrims returned to Aquitaine as quickly as possible, taking word of his death to the archbishop of Bordeaux, Geoffrey du Loroux, who had been charged with caring for William's two daughters. Perhaps due to the fecklessness of her father, Eleanor had not yet been affianced to some prince to achieve a political objective. Among the aristocracy in that day, betrothals of girls much younger than Eleanor, who was just entering adolescence, were a normal means of uniting two great families. Noble maidens were often married by the time they reached their twelfth year, the age when the Church deemed them capable of giving their consent to taking a husband. Since Eleanor and Aélith's only brother had died in the same year as their mother, and their paternal uncle Raymond was far away in the Holy Land, the young girls were left as William's heirs. It was not only William X's two daughters but his duchy of Aquitaine that faced an uncertain future following his unexpected death. The troubadour poet Marcabru wrote a lament on the duke's death expressing his grief and also fears for the fate of William's lands: "Antioch, Guyenne, and Poitou / Weep for worthiness and valor. / Lord God, in your washing place / Give peace to the count's soul; / And may the Lord who rose from the tomb / keep safe Poitiers and Niort."[78]

Eleanor of Aquitaine's upbringing at the ducal court at Poitiers impressed her with the history of her lineage, making her aware that her ancestors' status had equalled that of monarchs. She learned of powerful women preceding her, leading her to expectations about the possibilities open to an aristocratic woman in the public sphere that were evaporating as she attained her adult years. Born into a society that allowed married women, especially those in Aquitaine's southern reaches, to control property and enjoy a measure of independence, she would witness a decline in the position of her gender that she proved unwilling to accept.

The circumstances of Eleanor's childhood, a pampered princess at a court stamped by the character of her grandfather, the troubadour duke, left her ill-equipped for her future as queen of two northern European kingdoms. On Eleanor's marriage, her new subjects, first at Paris and later in England, would consider her a southerner, and they would judge her as not meeting their standards for a Christian queen's conduct. They assumed that she had inherited the licentious outlook set forth in the troubadour duke's scandalous songs, and no doubt they were partly correct. She could have hardly avoided absorbing something of the urbane and sensual atmosphere of the court at Poitiers, far different from the pious and restrained atmosphere that she would encounter at Paris. Missteps at her two husbands' royal courts in the north could be predicted.

CHAPTER 2

BRIDE TO A KING, QUEEN OF THE FRENCH, 1137–1145

W ITH the sudden death of William X, Eleanor became the most desirable bride in Europe, heir to the prestigious duchy of Aquitaine and the prosperous county of Poitou. Plans that her father had made before setting out for Compostella were merely precautionary, and his unforeseen death left young Eleanor vulnerable. With no powerful kin to protect his young heir, William X knew that she would become the prey of some ambitious prince in search of additional lands through marriage or in need of a rich bride to provide support for a younger son. In the short time left him, the dying William decided to place young Eleanor in the care of Louis VI, king of France, and to charge him with seeing to her marriage. The French king, approaching death himself, had to act quickly to carry out the duke's request. He resolved that Eleanor should be married to his own son and heir, the already crowned King Louis the Younger. When, less than a month after her marriage, her husband succeeded his father as King Louis VII (1137–1180), Eleanor found herself queen of France. She was the first Capetian queen to bring significant territory with her, bringing to Louis the duchy of Aquitaine, potentially an immense addition to the Crown's resources.

The marriage of Eleanor and Louis VII would prove to be a trial for both, bringing the couple little happiness. Neither Eleanor nor her husband, only a couple of years her senior, was prepared for the duties of marriage, much less the heavy responsibilities placed on them by their royal titles. The decade before the royal couple's departure on crusade in 1147 would reveal the young king's poor judgment and impetuous decisions, spurred on in several instances by his bride. Eleanor soon overcame rivals at the royal court to make herself her husband's chief adviser, and her influence would be felt particularly in matters concerning her duchy of Aquitaine, where Louis's right to wield authority was a result of his marriage.

A Spectacular Royal Marriage at Bordeaux

William x had given the archbishop of Bordeaux, Geoffrey du Loroux (d.1158), "a personage of high virtue and great austerity," custody of his two daughters before departing on his pilgrimage to Spain, and Eleanor remained under his protection in the short interval between her father's death and her marriage to Louis the Younger. Geoffrey du Loroux was a former hermit who had become master of the episcopal school at Angers before moving on to a monastic house in the Saintonge, where he had won Duke William x's friendship. Praised by the influential Cistercian monk Bernard of Clairvaux and other monastic reformers for the holiness of his life, Geoffrey had played an important part in ending the duke's long quarrel with his bishops over his support for an anti-pope at Rome. His part in mending William's relations with the Church had won him election to the archbishopric of Bordeaux. It is possible that the learned archbishop had played a part in young Eleanor's education even before her father's death in 1137 left her an orphan.[1]

William x knew well the dangers that would loom over his duchy should he die without a direct male heir of an age to take control of his heritage. The counts of Toulouse could assert some claim to the duchy of Gascony, the counts of Anjou could seek to regain their former foothold in the Saintonge, and turbulent lords on Poitou's southern frontier were always ready to take advantage of weakened ducal authority. No doubt William had intended to remarry and sire a male heir after his wife's death but his attempt to make a second marriage in 1136 was unsuccessful. Surely he had considered the fate of his two daughters and his lands in case of his failure to return from the dangerous journey across northern Spain? Almost the only evidence for events surrounding William's death is the biography of Louis vi written by his friend Abbot Suger of Saint-Denis; according to his account, the duke had made his plans known "before he had departed on the expedition and again on the journey as he lay dying." An alleged will survives supposedly dictated by William before setting out on his pilgrimage, stating his desire that Louis vii take custody of his daughters and marry Eleanor to his son, Louis the Younger.[2] Its authenticity is dubious, however, and it is impossible to know precisely what succession plans the duke communicated to his fellow pilgrims for conveying to the archbishop of Bordeaux.

The only male relative of the duke with a reasonable right to take control of Aquitaine was his younger brother Raymond, who had left his homeland at an early age to seek his fortune. Even if he had wished to stake a claim to succeed his brother as duke, Raymond was far from Aquitaine at the time of his brother's death. By the time the news reached him in the crusader kingdom, the succession had been settled. With Raymond so far away, William could not have contemplated him as a potential successor to the ducal title; nor could he have considered him a possible guardian of his two young nieces, which would have been his responsibility had he remained in Aquitaine. William had to take other measures to safeguard the girls should he not return from his pilgrimage, for not only was his duchy surrounded by dangerous rivals, but there was a real possibility of some Poitevin noble forcibly laying hands on Eleanor in order to marry her and seize the ducal title. Yet it appears that the duke had left no plans with ducal officials acting as his agents in Aquitaine before his perilous journey across the Pyrenees.

Lacking any alternative as guardian for his daughters and his lands, William X confided to his companions his wish that custody be placed in the hands of King Louis VI. Although the dukes of Aquitaine acknowledged a vague tie of lordship to the French monarch, it seems unlikely that a strong sense of Louis's lordship over Aquitaine mandated William's choice of Louis as guardian for his daughter. Recognition of the Capetian kings as lords by previous dukes of Aquitaine had meant little more than acknowledgment of their royal status, ranking them among France's highest nobles only as "first among equals." Even if William acknowledged Louis's lordship, custom in the early twelfth century had not yet established throughout France a lord's right of custody over his deceased vassal's minor children or his right to arrange their marriages; and in the south, these matters were still deemed a family's responsibility. Yet William dared not confide his daughter and her duchy to his father-in-law, the viscount of Châtellerault, or some other Poitevin noble who would arouse other princes' jealousy. The only alternative was an outsider, and the Capetian kings' image that they were creating for themselves as model Christian kings and as peacemakers assured him that King Louis VI would prove a worthy protector of young Eleanor.

Louis VI (d.1137) is considered the first effective Capetian monarch, an energetic ruler despite his bulk that earned him the epithet "the Fat." As was remarked after his death, Louis VI was "huge in body, but no smaller in act and thought."[3] His Capetian forebears had done little more than succeed in getting themselves crowned and anointed as the Carolingian rulers' successors in the Frankish kingdom and producing sons essential for keeping the French Crown in his family's hands. The early Capetians could not control the nobles of the Île de France, their own lands surrounding Paris and Orléans, much less overpower far stronger counts and dukes outside the royal domain, whose allegiance was little more than theoretical. Louis VI devoted himself to enhancing the power and prestige of the French Crown, and by the time of his death he had largely won effective control over the Île de France, subduing nobles who had not hesitated to defy his predecessors. He began to look beyond the lands under his direct control to assert his authority over neighboring French dukes and counts, and he would not let pass an opportunity to acquire the duchy of Aquitaine for his family through his son's marriage to its heir.[5]

Within Louis's own household, he ended his nobles' hereditary control over great administrative offices, and chose as his chief counselor Suger, the ambitious abbot of Saint-Denis (d.1151), the prestigious abbey just outside Paris that sheltered the Frankish kings' tombs. The king and the abbot together constructed an alliance with his abbey and with its namesake Saint Denis, who would become through the abbot's efforts the patron saint of France. Suger's work in strengthening the connection between the French monarchy and the Church would supply Louis VI and succeeding French kings with ideological weapons for Capetian expansionism, surrounding them with an aura of holiness. Not only did Suger contribute to an ideology of kingship, but his practical work as an administrator for Louis VI and later to Louis VII would advance royal governance beyond informal administration by the royal household and toward more developed structures.[4] In addition, Suger's widely read biography of Louis VI did much to secure his historical reputation as the first truly capable Capetian king.

While it was becoming customary in northern France and in England for lordships to be divided among daughters if no son survived to inherit them as a unit, the duchy of Aquitaine was not to be divided between Eleanor and her sister Aélith. As the elder daughter, Eleanor alone was to become countess of Poitou and duchess of Aquitaine and of Gascony. It would not have been unusual for her to have succeeded to the duchy of Aquitaine and her younger sister to some other component parts of their father's principality, perhaps Gascony, absorbed into Aquitaine only in the time of their great-grandfather. William X was not likely to have regarded his two duchies of Aquitaine and Gascony as indivisible, yet he apparently made no provision for a division of his lands between his two daughters. Whatever the count-duke's reasoning, he declared on his deathbed his wish that Eleanor should succeed as sole heir to his lands without making any provision for his younger daughter. Nor did Louis VI settle any property on Aélith to make her a more attractive bride. Eleanor's succession and her marriage to Louis VI's son and heir would fix firmly the indivisibility of the two territories, Poitou and Gascony; and Louis VII, as if acknowledging their unity, would style himself "duke of Aquitaine," discarding the titles "count of Poitou" and "duke of Gascony."[5]

Since no authentic document setting forth William X's wishes survives, it is not at all certain that in naming Louis VI as Eleanor's guardian he intended her marriage to the French monarch's son and heir. Although the duke's wishes were not set down in writing, Abbot Suger of Saint-Denis wrote in his biography of Louis that the duke "had decided to deliver to the king for the purpose of marriage his daughter . . . and all his land, so that he could hold it for her," but Suger's statement relates only to the right to manage young Eleanor's marriage. Yet other chronicles maintain that the duke had arranged Eleanor's betrothal to Louis's heir before his death, placing Aquitaine under the French king's sway.[6] For Eleanor to have been without either fiancé or husband at age thirteen was unusual among aristocratic families, and perhaps it is a sign of her father's fecklessness that he had never arranged a marriage for her. It is possible, however, that Duke William could find no candidate for Eleanor's hand whom he considered worthy of her and concluded that the only suitable husband for such a great duchess was the heir to the French Crown. Whether he thought far enough ahead to see that the marriage might mean the duchy's annexation to the French Crown is problematic.

Probably playing a key role in the marriage of young Eleanor to the Capetian heir was Archbishop Geoffrey du Loroux, an acquaintance of Suger. It was from the archbishop's messengers who reached Louis VI in the Île de France near the end of May 1137 that Suger learned of the duke's death, and possibly they also brought a proposal that Eleanor should marry the Capetian heir. If Geoffrey du Loroux did not suggest the marriage to the French monarch, he at least supported the proposition.[7] Geoffrey and the Bordeaux clergy very much favored the marriage, knowing the Capetian kings' reputation as advocates for the Church and fearing that rivalries among the magnates of Aquitaine damaging to the Church's interests could result if the young duchess were married to one of them. Apparently the lay magnates of Aquitaine raised no objection to a Capetian spouse for Eleanor, preferring a duke residing far away in Paris to one of their own number. They assumed that a Capetian king-duke would be a largely absentee ruler and that he would appoint some local lesser-ranking noble to act as his agent in his new duchy. They were confident that they could intimidate easily such a royal representative, leaving them unfettered in their cherished freedom. Not all the Aquitanians favored a royal marriage for Eleanor, however. In a song by the troubadour Marcabru composed in autumn 1137, his bitter reference to Louis VII's rule over the Poitevins reveals his sense that the county was being subjected to a "foreign" lord's dominion. With the French monarch ruling over Aquitaine, Marcabru and another poet, Cercamon, moved on in search of patronage elsewhere.[8]

Louis VI, in poor health since 1135, knew that his days were numbered and that he must act quickly to carry out his responsibility of finding a husband for Eleanor. At the same time he saw an opportunity to acquire the duchy of Aquitaine for the French Crown by marrying the girl to Louis the Younger, hoping to see his son secure in his possession of the duchy of Aquitaine before his death. Abbot Suger writes in his biography of Louis VI, "Having taken counsel with his close advisors, he happily accepted the offer with his usual greatness of soul and promised [Eleanor] to his dear son Louis." The king and his counselors were not following established laws of inheritance, for such rules hardly existed, but they were hurrying to settle the succession to Duke William's lands before uncertainty led to confusion and collapse of authority there.[9] Louis Senior would have understood that marrying his heir to a girl bringing with her as her inheritance Aquitaine, the greatest duchy in the kingdom, was a huge opportunity for advancing the monarch's position in France. The marriage by no means assured Aquitaine's permanent absorption into the French royal domain, however. The union of the duchy with the French Crown was purely personal, and should Eleanor bear Louis the Younger no sons, the duchy would probably pass out of royal hands. If she should produce several children, a younger son could be designated heir to the ducal title, removing it from direct royal control.[10] Yet Louis VI recognized the Capetians' strategic advantage in possessing Aquitaine. It would assist his son in corralling the expansionist counts of Anjou, whose Loire valley lands lay between the French royal domain in the Île de France and Eleanor's heritage; and also it could strengthen his hand against the expansionist dukes of Normandy who were also kings of England.

To avoid a power vacuum, Louis the Younger headed south from Paris to meet and marry Eleanor at the earliest possible moment. He was accompanied by a very large body of men—500 knights from "the best men in the kingdom and led by powerful nobles." Such a force, swelled by the nobles' retainers, was more an army capable of dealing with resistance either along the route or in Eleanor's patrimony than merely a "stately escort" for the young bridegroom.[11] Heading the royal party were the count of Blois-Champagne, Theobald II, Ralph, count of Vermandois (one of Louis VI's stalwarts), and Abbot Suger himself. Also in the group was the bishop of Chartres, Geoffrey de Lèves, who was familiar with Aquitaine from his visits there as a papal legate. During earlier service as legate in the ecclesiastical province of Bordeaux wooing Duke William X to make peace with his prelates, the bishop had worked closely with the future archbishop, Geoffrey du Loroux. They had become friends, and they again co-operated to facilitate the transfer of Aquitaine into the hands of the French Crown.[12]

Eleanor could not have expected to play any part in choosing her husband, even had her father returned from Spain in 1137. In an age when arranged marriages were the norm among aristocrats, she would have become aware at an early age that marriage was a matter for families, not individuals. All aristocrats viewed the marriages of their children as opportunities for their family's political or pecuniary advantage, not for the personal happiness of their offspring; and a bride and her future husband had little choice in the matter. Eleanor, who had learned in her earliest years of her distinguished ancestry, took pride in her dynasty's ducal title, and the prospect of marriage to the heir to the French Crown must have flattered her. She is unlikely to have had many illusions about finding romantic love in her marriage to young Louis, a stranger to her, although she may have been led by legend or love lyrics, like some other aristocratic maidens, to unrealistic aspirations for happiness in her arranged marriage, anticipating that she would fall in love with her husband eventually, if not immediately.

Although marriages in noble families were matters for the parents, Church teaching was moving toward a requirement of freely given consent by both parties to a marriage. The Church imposed other restrictions on marriages, including the requirement that the betrothed couple be old enough to give their consent—at least twelve years of age for a girl and fourteen for a boy.[13] Yet aristocratic families frequently disregarded this rule, betrothing their children at ages when they were far too young to give informed consent and often securing without difficulty the clergy's concurrence. Although marriage was not yet a sacrament in the early twelfth century, the Church taught that it created an indissoluble bond. Nobles, however, were accustomed to separating from wives and taking new ones as suited their desires or their ambitions, and they favored easy terms for dissolving a marriage if advantageous for the male partner or his family.

Another of the Church's restrictions barred marriages of those related within prohibited degrees of kinship. Theoretically, canon law barred the marriage of any couple within seven degrees of kinship; that is, those with a common ancestor reaching back seven past generations. Such a sweeping prohibition was "perhaps unique in human experience,"[14] and if enforced rigorously would have barred as consanguineous a large number of aristocratic marriages. By the eleventh century the greatest families could hardly avoid marrying cousins, if they were to take wives of appropriately imposing descent. The bar had the effect of providing nobles dissatisfied with their marriages convenient grounds for annulment, for if the couple were discovered to be related within the seventh degree, there was no true marriage. The Church considered them to be committing incest by living together, and it required an immediate separation.

In one way, the marriage of Eleanor and Louis was unusual, for he was also a teenager (born *c.*1120–23) and little older than his bride.[15] In numerous aristocratic marriages, the bride was much younger than her spouse; it was not uncommon for teenaged noble maidens to be married to men in their thirties or older. The couple's similar ages likely gave Eleanor higher expectations that their marriage had more likelihood of turning into a true love match than other aristocratic marriages with great age disparities. No doubt, their similar ages also led Eleanor to assume that their marriage would be a true partnership; and she would feel more free to express her opinions to her young husband and to persuade him to accept her ideas than if he had been a mature, experienced man. In several ways, however, the bride and groom were mismatched. Louis the Younger, apparently a good-looking youth with shoulder-length hair, was quiet, serious, and exceedingly devout. The second son of Louis VI and Adelaide of Maurienne, his upbringing had aimed at preparing him for an ecclesiastical career with studies at the school attached to Notre-Dame Cathedral on the Île de la Cité in Paris not far from the royal palace.[16] Louis's elder brother Philip, heir to the throne, was killed when he was thrown to the ground and crushed by his falling horse after it "stumbled over a diabolical pig" in the road. This unexpectedly elevated Louis to the position of heir to the French throne. The boy left Notre-Dame's cloisters at about age ten to be crowned king in accordance with the custom established by the second Capetian king of installing the current monarch's heir in his own lifetime to ensure a smooth succession. Twelve days after his brother's death, Louis's consecration as king took place at Reims Cathedral in October 1131 in the presence of a great council of prelates presided over by the pope.[17]

Louis VII apparently returned to his religious studies after his coronation, and his clerical education would make a powerful impression on him throughout his life, imprinting on him simple tastes in dress and manners and an earnest piety. His Capetian predecessors had sought to present themselves as models of Christian kingship, stressing their close relations with the Church as compensation for their modest military power. Louis's reputation for piety and spirituality surpassed that of earlier French monarchs, however. As one contemporary wrote, "He was so pious, so just, so catholic and benign, that if you were to see his simplicity of behaviour and dress, you would think . . . that he was not a king, but a man of religion."[18] Young Louis thought of kingship as a religious vocation, and he felt called to govern according to Christian principles. In his first years as king, his confidence that he was God's agent as French monarch gave him an unrealistic notion of his power, and he tended to over-reach, pursuing excessively ambitious political goals.[19] In his youthful enthusiasm, he often displayed an inclination toward rash decisions taken in anger and without reflection. Yet he sometimes seemed sluggish and unenthusiastic for his task of governing, partly due to a distaste for political intrigue, and partly due to a lack of perseverance, his ardor rapidly cooling and giving way to periods of indecision and inactivity. Although he held a very high view of the monarchical office, he could be timid, and he allowed himself to fall under the influence of members of his entourage. Most prominent among those seeking to influence this impressionable youth was his young wife Eleanor, and he readily allowed her to take part in political decision-making.[20]

Such a mild husband as Louis VII was unlikely to find happiness with a wife such as Eleanor of Aquitaine. His young bride had already seen more of life than his sheltered upbringing had allowed him. A girl brought up at a sophisticated and lively court where no more than conventional piety was observed and whose own grandfather had lived openly for years with his paramour would find the Capetian royal court's piety and repression confining. If Eleanor had been too young to remember life at William the Troubadour's court, she grew up surrounded by people who had tasted its pleasures willing to tell her about it. Looking back on her earliest childhood while in Paris "through the prism of her imagination," she could only compare the austere Capetian royal court unfavorably with an idealized image of her grandfather's court.[21] A widely quoted quip ascribed to Eleanor that she felt that she "had married a monk, not a king," while hardly an authentic quotation, captures the feeling that she surely came to hold for Louis.[22] Although his clerical education had not prepared him for a fulfilling marital relationship, Eleanor's beauty and charm captivated him at once and soon he fell deeply in love with her. Indeed, some observers of the couple's marriage described the king's love for his wife as "almost childish" and passionate beyond reason. The intensity of Louis's love for his bride may have made him an anxious husband, easily roused to jealousy.[23]

Despite evidence of Louis's attraction to his bride, the Church's notoriously misogynist view of women and teachings of the early Fathers had ill-equipped him for the robust sexual relationship that Eleanor expected. Louis, brought up in a clerical environment, was prudish and repressed in a way that the queen could not understand.[24] The high value that the Church assigned to sexual abstinence and its linking of the act of procreation with Adam and Eve's sin operated to curb the young king's passion. He had assimilated fully the Church's teaching that for Christians the model life was the monastic life and that marriage was instituted merely as a divine remedy for sexual desire. The early Church Fathers were suspicious of physical love, more likely to denounce all sexual activity than to endorse lawful marital intimacy. Among their teachings was a warning that a man whose love-making with his wife was over-ardent was guilty of a sin worse than adultery.[25] Later, sophisticated twelfth-century clerics, steeped in Stoic teachings, continued to warn husbands against immoderate marital love, fearful that a too powerful love could cripple superior masculine reasoning faculties.[26] Eleanor, coming from a court dominated by the memory of her lusty grandfather William the Troubadour, had absorbed a more earthy and forthright outlook on sexual matters. Doubtless she and her new husband's different expectations for the physical side of their married life would contribute to their unhappiness and the ultimate failure of their marriage.

The royal bridegroom and his entourage reached Limoges on 1 July 1137, and after stopping there for prayers at the shrine of Saint Martial, Louis and his party arrived at Bordeaux on 11 July. They raised tents and camped on the banks of the Garonne river across from the city, where they waited for boats to cross the wide waters. The entry into Bordeaux of Louis the Younger, crowned king six years earlier, marked the first French monarch's visit there in three centuries. The wedding took place on 25 July in the cathedral of Saint-André, constructed around the end of the eleventh century. Today only its surprisingly plain façade survives from Eleanor's time.[27] In full summer heat, a great throng of nobles of all ranks came from throughout Eleanor's lands to witness the couple's exchange of vows. As part of the ceremony, Louis had his bride "crowned with the diadem of the kingdom."[28]

To commemorate the occasion, young Louis had brought along lavish gifts for his bride that a chronicler asserted would have required the mouth of a Cicero or the memory of a Seneca to expose their richness and variety.[29] Usually aristocratic marriages were preceded by lengthy negotiations between the couple's parents about financial arrangements. It was a Poitevin custom in the century before Eleanor's birth that a bride's family should assign her a dowery or marriage-portion at the time of her betrothal, either land or cash, to present to her spouse on their marriage. Then on her wedding day, her spouse was expected to endow his new wife with a portion of his estates, known as her "dowerland," to provide her an income as a widow should she outlive him; in some cases she gained control of her dowerland at once, although more often her husband kept it in his hands.[30] Since Louis VI had arranged Eleanor's marriage, acting as her guardian, no negotiations concerning financial arrangements were needed. In the case of young Eleanor, she was bringing to her husband a great duchy, and no other wedding gift was expected. No doubt she retained revenues from her ancestral estates in Poitou, and it seemed pointless to designate lands from the limited French royal domain as her dowerland. As the young couple set out on their journey to Paris, she offered her new husband another splendid present, however—a vase carved from rock crystal, one of her few possessions that survives today. The vase was a cherished possession, connecting her to her grandfather William IX, who had brought it back to Poitiers after an expedition to Spain.[31]

Louis VI marked the marriage of his son and heir to Eleanor with grants of important privileges to the ecclesiastical province of Bordeaux, acting quickly to secure the support of the bishops in Aquitaine. Before Louis the Younger set out for Aquitaine, the king renounced any claim to rights of lordship over the dioceses of the province of Bordeaux, allowing them free episcopal elections. This concession ended the traditional ducal privilege of playing a part in the selection of bishops in the six dioceses of the province of Bordeaux.[32] Following Louis Senior in making concessions to the Church, Eleanor's young husband as duke of Aquitaine surrendered ducal rights to the homage and fealty of newly elected bishops, and he abandoned his right to take custody of deceased bishops' possessions during an episcopal vacancy.[33] This was a significant reward for Geoffrey du Loroux, archbishop of Bordeaux, granted for his key role in smoothing the way for the French king's wardship of Eleanor and her marriage to young Louis.[34] Later the archbishop would secure another favor from the Capetian king. Louis VII would sanction Geoffrey's placing the troublesome canons of his cathedral under the rule of the Augustinian canons that he favored, converting the cathedral chapter into a semi-monastic institution.[35]

As soon as the wedding celebrations ended in the evening of 25 July, the newly-weds lost no time in beginning their journey toward Paris. Eleanor and Louis stopped to spend their first night together at Taillebourg, a formidable castle looming over the Charente river, where their host was its lord, Geoffrey de Rancon. The most powerful of lords in the Saintonge, Geoffrey held wide lands stretching from his castle of Taillebourg eastward to La Marche, to Poitou proper in the north, and southward into the Angoumois. He and his heirs would be important players in Poitevin politics throughout Eleanor's lifetime.[36] Whether the young couple consummated their marriage that first night at Taillebourg cannot be known, but royal retainers surely looked for evidence, since both the Church and popular opinion held no marriage to be an indissoluble union until it was consummated.

By the beginning of August, the couple arrived at Poitiers, where a week later Suger organized a formal investiture of young Louis in the cathedral of Saint-Pierre, a religious ceremony signaling the Church's sanction for his ducal title.[37] Young Louis, already crowned and anointed king of the French, did not adopt the titles "count of Poitou" or "duke of Gascony" on his marriage; instead, he had only the additional title "duke of Aquitaine" engraved on his seal. The title that he adopted implied that his bride's duchy, though under Capetian administration, was not to be absorbed into the French Crown lands, but would preserve a separate identity with distinct institutions.[38]

Barely after the ceremony had ended, a messenger arrived from Paris with the sad news that King Louis VI had died on 1 August, aged almost sixty. The intense summer heat demanded his immediate burial at the abbey of Saint-Denis without waiting for the arrival of Louis the Younger and his bride from Poitou.[39] Young Louis, already a crowned and anointed king on his father's death, had to take on royal responsibilities at once, and the newly married Eleanor became a queen. Now King Louis VII, he had to leave his bride in the care of Bishop Geoffrey of Chartres to continue her progress toward Paris, while he led a force to subdue the rebel townspeople of Orléans, who had taken advantage of the old king's death to proclaim their city a commune, taking rights of self-government for themselves.[40]

From the Ducal Court at Poitiers to the Royal Court at Paris

When Queen Eleanor arrived in Paris at the end of summer 1137, she likely compared the city unfavorably with Poitiers or Bordeaux. Paris, consisting of little more than the Île de la Cité at that time, did not yet rank among the great cities of Europe. Construction of the cathedral of Notre-Dame in the grand new gothic style had not begun, and the ancient sixth-century Merovingian cathedral still stood on its site at the eastern end of the island. The royal palace occupied the island's western tip, its location contrasting with the commanding position of the ducal palace at Poitiers, dominating the high hill on which the town stood. The Île de la Cité with its crowded houses and narrow streets surrounded by a crumbling Roman wall was connected to an expanding settlement of tradespeople on the right bank of the River Seine by the Grand Pont, a fortified stone bridge lined with shops. The right-bank commercial center did not yet have proper walls for protection, but was surrounded by a wooden stockade. As Eleanor and her entourage approached Paris on the road from Orléans, she would have seen on the southern outskirts of the city ruins of some Roman structures. Scattered among vineyards on the left bank of the Seine were religious houses, Sainte-Geneviève, Saint Victor, and Saint-Germain des Prés. Small communities surrounding them were growing as increasing numbers of ambitious young men were attracted to the schools of these monasteries. To pass from the south bank of the Seine to the Île de la Cité, the queen and her entourage crossed another stone bridge lined with houses, the Petit Pont.[41]

In the early twelfth century, schools at Paris were eclipsing the old monastic schools dating from earlier centuries, and the cathedral school and newer schools on the left bank were making the city western Europe's pre-eminent center for philosophical and theological studies. Charismatic and controversial teachers such as Peter Abelard were attracting students from all parts of Europe, and they were spilling over from the cathedral school on the Île de la Cité to the schools established by religious houses in the countryside on the Seine's left bank. Students in the settlements around these schools that would become Paris's Latin Quarter found "an abundance of all good things, gay streets, rare food, incomparable wine."[42] It was primarily treatises written in Latin by scholars of the Parisian schools that attracted attention and stimulated discussion in Paris, and not vernacular poetry treating secular themes, as was the case in the south of France. The laity of northern France lacked the self-confidence of southerners who had created a vibrant lay culture for a secular society that communicated in their vernacular language, Occitan. Yet on the fringes of the Parisian schools could be found disreputable students who were inspired by the Latin love poets to write licentious lyrics in Latin.

Their poems expressed attitudes toward the love of men for women outside of marriage that resembled strikingly the southern troubadours' songs.[43] The poem of a wandering German student who likely had caught sight of Eleanor as a mature woman declares, "Were the world all mine / From the sea to the Rhine, / I'd give it all / If so be the Queen of England / Lay in my arms."[44]

Accompanying Eleanor to Paris was her younger sister, Aélith or, as she became known at the French royal court, Petronilla. Most likely also accompanying their mistress was a large entourage of Poitevins ranging in rank from noble lords and ladies to knights and domestic servants, although it is impossible to identify them. Eleanor's new subjects were prepared to expect the worst of Eleanor and her Poitevin companions, for writers had long depicted southerners as soft, vain, and corrupt compared with the more vigorous and virtuous northern French. At the first encounters between Eleanor, her entourage, and the Parisians, all experienced a degree of "culture shock." Her elevated rank as duchess of Aquitaine meant that she was accompanied by a larger retinue from Poitiers than previous queens had brought with them to Paris. Eleanor's personal household, like the entourages of other great aristocrats, would have numbered at least forty or more persons.[45] The young queen and her companions stood out at the Capetian court, dressed in the excessive costumes favored by ladies of southern courts. Communicating among themselves in Occitan, their lack of the reserve and propriety expected of northern courtiers shocked members of her new husband's entourage. They could hardly believe the freedom with which Eleanor and her ladies felt at ease joining in the men's conversations. The size of the new queen's household, its large alien element with its unfamiliar ways, and the priority that her servants gave to the needs and interests of her duchy all presented causes for friction between the newcomers and long-serving officials and courtiers of the royal household.

Eleanor, the darling of the ducal court at Poitiers, was oblivious to the offense that she and her "clan" or coterie of Poitevins caused at Paris with ways that were alien to the French royal court. A teenaged girl comparable to the young Marie-Antoinette some six centuries later, she was hardly aware that courtiers could change suddenly from sycophants to slanderers if her thoughtless words or rash acts appeared to threaten their standing at court.[46] Soon a situation would arise similar to that later in mid-thirteenth century England during Henry III's reign, when his consort surrounded herself with an influential "queen's set at court" composed of a number of "foreigners," her countrymen who had followed her from Savoy.[47] Just as those later left outside the English queen's clique feared its becoming "an all-powerful alien faction," so those outside Eleanor's Poitevin clan feared a loss of influence at the Capetian royal court. Clashes over precedence and patronage as well as serious policy disputes could lead to conflicts between Eleanor's retainers and long-serving royal officials, threatening to split the court into something akin to two rival households.[48]

Eleanor soon saw that a restrained and earnest atmosphere prevailed at her pious husband's court, regardless of whether it remained at the royal palace on the Île de la Cité or was going on circuits around the royal domain. Like all princely households, Louis's was constantly on the move, circulating between royal residences at Compiègne, Orléans, Étampes, and sometimes stopping along the way to visit royal monasteries or bishoprics. Eleanor could not avoid noticing the contrast with the boisterous and merry ducal court of her father and grandfather at Poitiers, crowded with singers, mimes, jugglers, and entertainers of all sorts. The Church equated all professional performers from talented musicians to buffoons with prostitutes, and it admonished respectable people to avoid them. The Capetian kings took this admonition to heart, and entertainers learned that their chances of winning favor at their court were slim.[49]

The young queen quickly observed that cultural life in northern France was far more dominated by the Church than in her homeland. The leading person-alities in the political and intellectual life of Louis VII's lands came from monastic backgrounds. At the royal court, Abbot Suger of Saint-Denis was a dominant figure as both ideologue and politician. The king in his youthful-ness and inexperience leaned heavily on Suger, his father's friend and chief minister, and the abbot stood beside him almost as a father-figure. Two other heads of French religious houses also exercised influence far beyond their monasteries. Peter the Venerable (d.1156), head of the prestigious abbey of Cluny and its far-reaching chain of affiliated houses, was a prolific letter writer, winning influence with his pen. He defended his Cluniac order from attacks by Bernard, the overbearing Cistercian abbot of Clairvaux, who repeatedly left his cloister to intervene in both political and religious controversies throughout France.[50]

Because Eleanor of Aquitaine was the granddaughter of William IX, the trou-badour duke, a common assumption is that she introduced an air of sensuality and pursuit of pleasure to the French royal court. In addition Eleanor has an outsized reputation as a patron of poets, supposedly a pioneer in acquainting the French court with troubadour love lyrics promoting the art of courtly love, and redefining the perfect chivalric knight as an admirer of the ladies. While troubadour songs arrived in northern France during Eleanor's years of presiding over the French court, there is little direct evidence of her playing a major role in encouraging this new trend. Following the death of Duke William X and Aquitaine's subjection to French rule, troubadours in his entourage fled Poitiers to search for patronage elsewhere, but no evidence shows them flocking to Paris, drawn there by expectations of patronage from his daughter. Only a single explicit reference to Eleanor of Aquitaine appears in any troubadour love song, and it dates from the years after her separation from Louis VII. In fact, troubadour-style courtly love lyrics were a brief and alien fashion in northern France, and only a few of the northerners who took up the writing of such poetry were from the Parisian region.[51] It cannot be doubted, however, that Eleanor, like other great ladies of her day, gave some encouragement to courtly literature through hearing it, reading it, and enjoying it.

Nonetheless, the subjects of the new queen associated her with her troubadour grandfather's attitude toward love and marriage that conflicted with Christian teaching. For the more pious among them, a linking of Eleanor with southern courtly love poetry tended to tarnish her in their eyes. They would apply to their queen their long-held prejudices about the character and the customs of natives of the Mediterranean south, even though her native Poitou lay on the borderline between northern France and the Midi or Languedoc. In turn, Eleanor's childhood experiences led her to unrealistic expectations about her role at the French royal court. Possibilities for a place in the public sphere that were not yet closed to aristocratic women in the south were rapidly evaporating in twelfth-century northern France. Changes in inheritance practises throughout northwestern Europe that favored the eldest son meant that aristocratic women there were less likely than their southern counterparts to inherit any of their father's property, and they lacked the degree of independence that Eleanor expected a great lady of her status to enjoy.

When Eleanor arrived in Paris, she was ill-equipped for her role as a queen-consort. Because her mother had died young, and her childhood was spent in a court without a duchess to preside over it, she had no model for conducting herself as French queen. Prominent in Eleanor's past, however, were strong-willed women who had exercised influence in political matters in the chaotic conditions of the tenth and eleventh centuries. The few learned men writing histories in those troubled times had expressed no surprise when ladies exhibited leadership abilities equal to those of men, describing them with imagery that was "by no means entirely pejorative."[52] In Aquitaine and in all the Midi, noblewomen succeeded to the rule of principalities, and public roles for aristocratic ladies were not unusual. Eleanor's perception of her role as French queen was shaped by such great women whose stories she had heard as a child. The young queen's unique position as the first Capetian royal bride to have brought with her a great landed inheritance led her to expect that she would share with her husband authority over her ancestral lands.[53] She expected also that she would play a part in the governance of his kingdom.

At Christmas 1137, Louis VII and his new queen traveled to Bourges for a ceremonial crown-wearing at "a great court . . . attended by nobles and middling men from all over France and Aquitaine and other regions round about."[54] The royal court was a center for ceremonies on the Church's great festivals symbolizing the king's lordship and lawful authority, and the queen appeared at her husband's side on these great occasions, participating in ritual and ceremonial that were essential props upholding the monarchy's prestige. This ritual crown-wearing was equivalent to a second coronation for the young king and a formal installation of Eleanor as queen of the French.[55]

At the French court before Eleanor's marriage, a long tradition had been in place of the French queen as "an ally and partner in governing," her royal husband's companion and helpmate. The Capetian queen's power had reached its peak with Louis's mother, Adelaide of Maurienne; she had been Louis VI's partner in ruling after their marriage in 1115.[56] Adelaide's power had rested on her place in the great hall of the royal place, where she was present at her royal husband's side. A queen's role as her husband's counselor and helpmate would endure only so long as royal government continued to be conducted informally through discussions in the king's hall.[57] Such a situation prevailed down to the early twelfth century because royal government was still centered in the royal household. The royal household was not limited to the domestic sphere, but was a public institution, indistinguishable from the royal court, the seat of dispute settlement and decision-making, and household officials performed public functions. Queen Adelaide had occupied a crucial place, openly taking part in the public policy debates and decisions of great councils, and her assent to royal acts was recorded on royal charters.[58]

Louis the Younger's experience of his mother's active partnership with Louis VI in governing led him to assume that his bride would share his work of ruling over the French kingdom, and Eleanor's background likewise caused her to expect to be her husband's chief counselor, in part because she had quickly calculated that hers was the stronger personality of the marriage, despite her youth. Yet Eleanor would never enjoy the participation in royal government that her mother-in-law had relished. Official documents tell almost nothing about either Eleanor's activities or her influence on Louis VII, rarely associating her name with his. The most likely documents to survive from their reign are charters granting privileges to religious houses, charters that the monks took care to save. During Eleanor's years as Louis's consort, the queen's name was disappearing from royal documents; she is mentioned in little more than half those issued during the fifteen years of her marriage, although Louis VI's charters had recorded regularly Adelaide of Maurienne's assent. Those mentioning Eleanor mostly record her assent to Louis's documents concerning Aquitaine. Of Eleanor's own charters as French queen, only some twenty survive, all but one dating from before the couple's departure on crusade; and only three of these, mere confirmations of her husband's documents, treat matters beyond her own duchy.[59]

Any power that Eleanor was to wield in the policy sphere would be personal and indirect, derived from her intimate conversations with her royal husband. As queen, she had a unique opportunity to influence Louis VII through their "conjugal intimacy," which enabled her to express her views in private and to press him to implement them. A queen's ability to persuade the king, taking advantage of her privileged access, was regarded as a benefit to the community, inspiring him to merciful and pious deeds. These queenly responsibilities were not purely "private" matters, but part of the work of representing kingship to the people as merciful, benevolent, and devout.[60] Yet Eleanor's unique access to the king through her sexuality was alarming to clerics at court, who regarded all women with suspicion. The possibility of a queen taking advantage of her intimate contact with her husband for selfish gain or advancement of a court faction inspired envy and distrust among her rivals for the king's ear.

Unfortunately for Eleanor, religious reforms of the late eleventh and early twelfth centuries were inspiring renewed questioning of the queen's shared authority with the king as moralists and theologians were redefining gender roles. No longer were Eleanor's formidable female ancestors in Aquitaine appropriate models for noble ladies, and aristocratic women were being stripped of power in the public sphere that they had previously held, if only precariously. Males were growing less and less tolerant of powerful women, condemning them for any initiatives in the public sphere as "unwomanly," somehow unnatural and wrong. French queens, in addition to their primary function of producing royal offspring, were expected to occupy themselves with pious activities, overseeing their ladies' sewing of vestments and altar cloths for favored religious houses, distributing alms to the poor, and interceding with their royal husbands on behalf of their subjects for mercy. Eleanor's refusal to be forced into such a constraining mold of wifely submissiveness would cause her grief in both her marriages.

Louis VII, like his bride, was young and inexperienced, ill-prepared for ruling over a kingdom, and in his first decade and a half as king—also the first years of his marriage to Eleanor—he displayed a youthful lack of judgment. Naturally mild and meek, Louis would sporadically rouse himself to action, moving with uncharacteristic impetuosity, alienating his great men and quarreling with religious authorities, despite his evident piety. With a youth wearing the crown, the formation of factions at court intriguing for influence was to be expected. His father's capable confidant, Suger of Saint-Denis, viewed by Eleanor as a competitor for influence over young Louis, stayed on as the new king's chief counselor. In addition to Abbot Suger, she had to contend with her mother-in-law, the queen-mother, Adelaide of Maurienne, and their relations were cool almost from the royal couple's arrival in Paris. Trouble between the new queen and her predecessor was not surprising.

Although widowed queens were expected to retire from court to live quietly
on their dowerlands, Adelaide, having enjoyed power as Louis VI's consort,
expected continued influence at court during her son's reign.[61] In her struggle
to preserve her powerful position, the queen-mother found an ally in the
king's cousin, Count Ralph de Vermandois. The count had been a stalwart of
Louis VI, holding the post of seneschal of France, a title that originally had
designated the steward, a domestic officer who supervised a princely household. By Louis VII's time, however, the office of royal seneschal was largely
honorific; and although flattering to its holder, he performed only occasional
ceremonial duties.[62]

In a bid for power, the queen-mother and Ralph de Vermandois provoked
a confrontation with young Louis over his profligate expenditures. Since Louis
was known for his disdain for magnificent display, for his simple dress and
diet, Eleanor and her entourage were obviously the true objects of this charge
of extravagance. Adelaide reproached her son, complaining that her endowment as the king's widow was endangered by his lavish spending; and when
her rebuke was ignored, she insisted on being given full possession of her
dowerlands. The queen-mother's charges masked a three-way struggle for
influence over the young king as she and the count of Vermandois, as well as
Suger of Saint-Denis, opposed Eleanor. Adelaide demanded permission to
withdraw from Paris to her estates near Compiègne, and Ralph de Vermandois
likewise asked to be allowed to retire to his lands. Both Adelaide of Maurienne
and Ralph de Vermandois retired from court out of "abject cowardice," as
Abbot Suger pointed out, and their departure amounted to an admission that
they had lost their struggle for influence over the king.[63] Eleanor must have
shared Suger's relief at Adelaide's departure from court, happy that her
mother-in-law would no longer be a rival for Louis's affection. With Suger left
as her sole rival, she was confident that she could overcome him in the contest
for influence over her husband. In any case, the revered abbot's victory would
prove to be short-lived.

Following her departure Adelaide of Maurienne promptly remarried,
taking as her husband Matthew, lord of Montmorency, a relatively minor
ranking noble. The marriage of a widowed queen was rare in this period, and
many questioned Adelaide's motives. Few could understand why a great lady
who had borne eight children and whose dower freed her from financial
concerns should desire a husband unless her motivation was a thirst for
regaining power.[64] Apparently Louis's devotion to his mother had not ended
entirely, for not long into her marriage, he named her new husband as his
constable.[65]

Soon after the queen-mother's departure from court, Louis VII began
asserting his independence, and Suger's ascendency also began to wane, in all

probability a consequence of Eleanor's rising influence. The young queen was capable of "taking a determined political stance," as the redoubtable Bernard of Clairvaux discovered when he encountered her at the French royal court.[66] The king made a number of changes in the officials of the royal household, recalling Ralph de Vermandois to resume his post as seneschal in 1138; and he appointed an ambitious newcomer to the royal court, Cadurc, as chancellor to head his writing-office in 1140. Suger, realizing that his role as Louis's chief counselor was no longer secure, was too sensitive to insist on retaining his place at the king's side.[67] Although never entirely ceasing to rank among the royal counselors, the abbot of Saint-Denis spent less and less time at the palace on the Île de la Cité. By 1140 he was turning his attention more and more to his ambitious program of rebuilding his abbey-church, pioneering the Gothic style with tall banks of stained-glass windows flooding the interior with light and color.

During the years of Suger's absence from the royal court, no one with his wisdom and experience in government was left to moderate the young couple's frequent thoughtless reactions to events.[68] It is clear that Eleanor desired to involve herself in the business of governing and to influence Louis, and she soon came to be counted among her husband's chief counselors. Both Abbot Suger and the king's mother had failed in their attempts to exert influence over Louis. Nor did any of his younger brothers play roles as royal advisers, with the exception of the eldest of them, Henry, a cleric who became bishop of Beauvais in 1149 and later archbishop of Reims. The young queen helped compound Louis's many mistakes during his first fifteen years as king when he tried with "disorganized ardor to take action almost everywhere at the same time and by any means, including violence."[69]

Eleanor's Poitevin Homeland During her Marriage to Louis VII

Eleanor was not merely Louis's consort; she was duchess of Aquitaine in her own right, and her primary concern was her landed legacy. As duchess, she had a right to intervene, although she rarely acted without her husband.[70] Her ducal inheritance, a vast and ill-defined swath of southwestern France consisting of a dozen or so counties, might be defined as "rather a loose union of principalities than a single one," with Poitou and Gascony as two distinct political entities ruled separately from Poitiers and Bordeaux. On the southern fringes of Poitou separating the county from Gascony lay lands in the hands of powerful and turbulent lords, whose subjection to the count-dukes was little more than nominal, the most dangerous of whom were the counts of Angoulême. Castles of these frontier nobles presented barriers blocking the roads between the dukes' two capitals, Poitiers and Bordeaux.

It was direct control over extensive estates in the county of Poitou that formed the power base of the dukes of Aquitaine, although increasingly revenues from towns and trade added to their wealth. Since the resources for enforcing ducal authority had come almost entirely from their Poitevin lands, they often styled themselves simply "count of Poitou." Eleanor's estates as countess of Poitou were concentrated in central and western Poitou, in Aunis and Saintonge lying along the Atlantic coast. In Gascony, the Bordelais and the adjacent Bazadais contained estates belonging to her in prosperous grape-growing areas, but beyond these two territories the ducal domain had never been extensive. Elsewhere in Eleanor's duchy, lands under her direct control were insignificant; for example, she held no land in the Limousin outside the city of Limoges.

Constant warfare characterized the lands that Eleanor brought to Louis the Younger. She had grown up in a region where the aristocracy had such a reputation for endless strife with each other and with their duke that many histories have labeled Aquitaine's turbulent conditions "feudal anarchy."[71] Although supposedly subject to the dukes of Aquitaine, the greatest nobles resisted interventions by Eleanor's ancestors within their lands, barely acknowledging ducal lordship and only doing homage as an act of reconciliation after rebellion. Their obligations to the dukes remained ill-defined, vaguely set forth in treaties or less formal agreements. By the beginning of the twelfth century, the counts, viscounts, and some lesser lords of Aquitaine were consolidating their power, bringing under their authority local castellans whose castles dominated the countryside and creating large regional lordships within the duchy. The count-duke had either to coax or charm these lords into acknowledging obligations of loyalty and service that his lordship imposed on them. Controlling the neighboring principalities nominally subject to ducal authority had required Eleanor's ancestors to circulate on campaigns from one end of the duchy to the other.

Establishing effective rule over Eleanor's duchy would prove a daunting task for Louis VII, and all his military expeditions undertaken in the early years of his reign were directed toward his wife's domains. Louis visited Aquitaine several times during the first five years of his marriage to Eleanor. She, however, returned to her homeland only three times during the first decade of their marriage. In the spring of 1138, the couple made a visit to the Auvergne on Aquitaine's ill-defined eastern frontier where they attended a traditional celebration in honor of Our Lady of Le Puy. While there, the king-duke took the homage of the nobility of the region. Eleanor and Louis returned to Aquitaine in 1141, when the king intervened in a quarrel over the succession to the viscounty of Limoges and then marched on Toulouse in a military campaign against the count that aimed at enforcing ducal claims to the county, reviving the prior claim pursued by Eleanor's paternal grandparents. Her third visit to her lands was in autumn 1146 when the royal couple held court at Poitiers after taking the cross at Vézelay. The king and queen made a circuit of Aquitaine to provide for the duchy's administration during their absence on crusade and to recruit the nobility of the region for the expedition.[72]

Since none of the royal couple's visits to Aquitaine was of any great duration, they had to rely on a handful of trustworthy Poitevin nobles to safeguard their interests there. Traveling often to the royal court in the Île de France were Poitevins who assisted the royal couple in governing Aquitaine. Among them was Geoffrey, lord of Rancon, the most powerful lord in Saintonge and a land-holder in Angoulême and La Marche as well; and William de Mauzé, member of a family that had served Eleanor's predecessors in administrative capacities since the tenth century.[73] Mauzé had held under Eleanor's father the title of seneschal; under Eleanor and Louis, his title designated a working official, their chief agent supervising Poitou's day-to-day administration. A major part in ecclesiastical aspects of ducal governance was taken by Geoffrey du Loroux, archbishop of Bordeaux, occasionally requiring his presence at the royal court.[74]

Eleanor expected to play a significant part in the governance of Aquitaine, and Louis in governing her duchy needed to associate her with him, since his authority there derived entirely from his position as husband to the lawful duchess. Louis found it essential to identify himself with the lineage of Eleanor's male ancestors by confirming their acts as a sign that they had become his predecessors in bearing the ducal title as well as her own ancestors. Documents from Aquitaine showing Louis acting alone without his queen's participation make clear the limits of her power, however, for the majority of these concern serious matters—the settlement of disputes or threats of action against unruly nobles. Most of Eleanor's charters for Aquitaine show her governing alongside her husband, revealing her relatively limited sphere of authority over her own duchy.[75]

The majority of Eleanor's own documents show her giving assent to Louis's grants to Poitevin religious houses. Such gifts had more than a purely spiritual purpose, for they fostered "networks of fidelity," binding the beneficiaries in loyalty to their duke and duchess. Only four surviving charters show Eleanor acting alone, and all of them were for major religious houses such as the abbey of Saint-Maixent, greatest of the Poitevin ecclesiastical baronies. One bene-fitted the prestigious women's house of Notre-Dame at Saintes, where the abbess was Agnes, the queen's aunt. Abbess Agnes was "insatiable" in her quest for privileges for her convent, and she sought out Louis and Eleanor when they were returning from the 1141 Toulouse campaign to ask for her abbey's release from all subjection to ducal officials. Eleanor, with the assent of Louis and her sister Aélith, issued a charter granting Agnes's request. Later Eleanor issued a charter guaranteeing the liberties of Notre-Dame, Saintes, and another of her charters confirms her husband's charter of liberties for the abbey. To summarize Eleanor's public role in Poitou during her marriage to Louis, it was "far from negligible though it was more restrained than is often asserted."[76]

As duke of Aquitaine, Louis VII attempted sporadically to make his position meaningful, occasionally intervening in successions to lordships and in episcopal elections. In his early exaggerated view of his power, he rejected traditional ties between the dukes of Aquitaine and their great men based on alliance and consensus among near-equals in favor of assertions of the pre-eminence of ducal power. Some of his interventions were of "an extreme brutality," perhaps undertaken to impress his bride with his manliness. Yet Louis's disjointed assertiveness accomplished little other than winning him the disapproval of great families that were traditional supporters of the ducal line and indifference from lesser Aquitanian nobles.[77] The proclamation of a commune by the townspeople of Poitiers in 1138 gave Louis his first opportunity for a show of force against Eleanor's subjects. He regarded their claim to rights of self-government as an affront, and he felt that fortifying their city and trying to form a sort of federation with neighboring towns must be met with strong action. The crisis worsened as some nobles with strong castles in the Vendée rose up in revolt at the same time.[78]

Louis VII moved quickly against the rebels in Eleanor's native city, marching to Poitiers at the head of a force of 200 knights. The king's presence with an armed force outside the town's walls was enough to overawe the inhabitants, and they promptly surrendered. Louis ordered the commune dissolved, and he took severe measures against the town's leading citizens, demanding that they surrender 100 of their children, both boys and girls, to be sent off to remote regions as hostages. He only relented when Abbot Suger arrived at Poitiers; the abbot was so touched by the pleading of the distraught parents that he interceded with the king, who quickly gave in to his chief counselor's request for leniency. Then Louis turned aside to the Vendée to deal with the nobles' rebellion, crushing it forcefully. Eleanor's role in Louis's severity against the Poitevins is unknown. Perhaps she prodded her husband to action, angered and humiliated by the rejection of ducal authority by her own people; or possibly he took the initiative, hoping to please his wife.[79] The young queen likely shared the contempt for the urban merchant class common among the aristocracy. Vernacular poetry often lumped the bourgeoisie with the peasantry, applying to them the term *vilein* and depicting them as reprehensible on account of their greed and gross manners.[80]

The first of Louis VII's attempts to assert his authority by intervening in ecclesiastical affairs occurred at Poitiers over an election to the see of Poitiers in autumn 1140. Louis was angered when the canons of Poitiers Cathedral elected a new prelate without his consent. Following their bishop's death, they chose as his successor an abbot, Grimoald; and three months later Geoffrey du Loroux, archbishop of Bordeaux, consecrated him bishop without Louis's assent. Although Louis VI had granted the churches of the ecclesiastical province of Bordeaux the right to free elections and Louis the Younger as duke of Aquitaine had approved the concession, he insisted that his formal installation or investiture of new bishops was still required. Viewing as an affront to the royal prerogative Grimoald's failure to present himself for royal confirmation, Louis prohibited the bishop-elect from entering Poitiers, and he hailed the archbishop of Bordeaux before the royal court. Soon Bernard of Clairvaux and Pope Innocent II entered the dispute, both showing "profound contempt" for the king's claim of a right to invest newly elected prelates. Bernard wrote to one of the royal counselors decrying the archbishop of Bordeaux's summons before the king's court, and the pope wrote to the people of Poitiers commanding them to obey their new bishop. By the time the pope had issued his order, however, Grimoald had already died (October 1141), making the entire matter moot.[81] Eleanor's father and grandfather had also engaged in quarrels with their clergy, although without great success, and perhaps she shared their hostility for churchmen; however, her role, if any, in her husband's quarrel over the see of Poitiers remains unknown. The crisis at Poitiers would be followed by others as the king continued intervening in episcopal elections. The most serious of these would be Louis's attempt to secure the archbishopric of Bourges for one of his courtiers, his chancellor Cadurc.

No sooner had Louis VII's contest over the bishopric of Poitiers ended than he launched an ambitious new project, an expedition to Toulouse after Easter 1141 to recover by force the county formerly controlled by the dukes of Aquitaine. Louis's attempted conquest of Toulouse is one of the surest signs of his wife Eleanor's influence on him in the early years of their marriage. Suger, whose peaceful instincts would have inspired him to oppose such an adventure, was no longer influential at court.[82] Eleanor's claim of hereditary right to rule the county derived from her grandmother, Philippa, who had never given up her contention that she was the lawful heir to Toulouse (see pp. 17–18), and her claim passed to her son Duke William X, born at Toulouse in 1099 and sometimes known as "le Toulousain." His claim to the county passed to his heir Eleanor, who strongly believed in her lawful right to rule over Toulouse.[83]

Louis VII and his army appeared before the walls of Toulouse on 21 June 1141, but they could not take the strongly fortified city. Apparently the French king had brought neither sufficient forces nor adequate siege equipment for compelling a powerful vassal such as Raymond V of Toulouse to surrender his chief city. Eleanor was disappointed in her hope of sustaining her claim to control over the county of Toulouse, and she had to be satisfied with the count's offer to do homage to Louis in acknowledgment of ducal lordship. The French king and his army then withdrew to Gascony in a campaign to subdue its turbulent nobles. Eleanor seems to have remained behind in Poitiers during the siege of Toulouse and, before returning to Paris, the couple visited the burial place of Eleanor's mother at Nieuil-sur-l'Autise. At nearby Niort, Louis honored his mother-in-law's memory by conferring on the religious house containing her tomb the rank of a royal abbey. His charter states that it was issued "with the assent and petition of Queen Eleanor at our side."[84] Around the time of the royal couple's visit, the eleventh-century church of the canons was being transformed into a fine example of Poitevin Romanesque architecture. Eleanor would not visit her ancestral home again until 1146, when she and Louis made a circuit of Aquitaine after taking the cross at Vézelay.

THE ROYAL COUPLE CONFRONT CRISES OF THEIR OWN MAKING IN THE 1140S

Louis VII's failed attempt to take Toulouse is only one example of missteps made in the absence of Abbot Suger's steadying hand at court during the early 1140s when Eleanor's influence on her husband was most noticeable. Also revealing the couple's immaturity were several clumsy attempts by Louis to insert himself into ecclesiastical matters, notably several interventions after his first inconclusive contest at Poitiers to impose candidates of his choice on vacant episcopal sees.[85] The king's piety combined with his belief in the sacred character of monarchy to convince him that he could speak for the entire kingdom in ecclesiastical matters. A number of episcopal sees and great abbeys outside the royal domain were considered "royal churches" under the king's special protection. In political terms, royal protection for these churches reinforced royal power and prestige, giving the king excuses for intervening in regions far from Paris to protect religious institutions from local lords.[86] For example, the authority of the archbishop at Bourges, a royal see, extended over bishoprics of the Massif Central and over the diocese of Limoges in Eleanor's domains. Yet the young monarch's efforts to implement his belief in the semi-priestly character of kings by controlling episcopal nominations proved futile, an ideology that could not be revived so long after the eleventh-century reform movement had mobilized sweeping ecclesiastical opposition to such practises by lay princes.

The greatest of Louis's quarrels over episcopal nominations centered on the selection of a new archbishop of Bourges, traditionally filled by the king's nominee. When Louis sought the post in 1141 for his chancellor Cadurc, the cleric heading his writing office, the cathedral chapter objected and rallied around their own candidate, a monk. This ecclesiastical matter soon merged with the king's dispute with Count Theobald II of Blois-Champagne, one of France's great magnates, who gave the chapter's candidate refuge in his lands. The disputed Bourges election provoked a conflict between the monarch and the papacy unlike any seen in France since the reign of Louis's grandfather. Pope Innocent II, a supporter of free elections of prelates, strongly backed the chapter's choice for the archbishopric, and he consecrated their nominee. The pope wrote a condescending letter to Louis, addressing him as if he were a youth in need of completing his education, advising him against entangling himself in serious matters that did not concern him. The stubborn young king, shaking with anger, publicly swore a solemn oath, vowing to prevent the canons' candidate for the archbishopric from ever entering Bourges Cathedral.[87] To bring Louis to heel, the pope took the drastic step of proclaiming an interdict on his lands, prohibiting public religious services.

An unseemly love affair between Eleanor's younger sister, Aélith, or Petronilla as she came to be called, and the count of Vermandois, conducted with the queen's connivance, added new complications to the Bourges succession crisis precipitated by Louis VII. By the time of the royal entourage's return from the 1141 Toulouse expedition, Ralph de Vermandois had become romantically involved with the queen's sister despite having a wife of many years. His wife, Eleanor of Champagne, was the niece of Theobald II, count of Blois-Champagne, creating new complexity for an already awkward situation. The queen's influence on the king is evident as this new crisis came to a head, and Louis, "incapable of resisting the insistence of Eleanor," sanctioned her sister's liaison, giving added grounds for his hostile relations with the count of Champagne.[88] When the lovers' marriage took place, not only did the wedding infuriate the bride's uncle, but it also brought down on Louis the Church's wrath. The saintly abbot, Bernard of Clairvaux, always ready for combat, would thrust himself into this conflict, lending support to his friend Count Theobald; and the affair soon attracted the pope's attention. The two, already shocked by Louis's abandonment of his earlier submissiveness toward the Church to intervene in episcopal elections, pounced on him for his new affront to spiritual authority attacking the sanctity of Christian marriage. Many, most likely correctly, attributed the king's new assertiveness to his bride's influence. Eleanor would have remembered that Bernard had been a fierce and unyielding opponent of her father. When she was a young girl, Duke William X had tangled with the holy man, and after an emotional confrontation between the two, the duke yielded completely in a humiliating defeat. Perhaps Eleanor sought to stiffen her young husband's resolve, encouraging him to stand up to the fearsome Cistercian.

An amorous liaison between Eleanor's sister, hardly more than fifteen, and the count of Vermandois, a rough warrior with an eye missing and old enough to be her grandfather, seems ludicrous, yet Petronilla's desire for him appeared heart-felt. Although medieval noblemen often married much younger women, such unions were rarely the consequence of the couple's passion, but resulted from coldly practical concerns for financial gain or cementing family alliances. In this case, the prospect of becoming the king's brother-in-law must have heightened Ralph's passion for Eleanor's sister. Possibly Louis and his counselors had dynastic reasons for supporting the lovers, for Petronilla would become heir to the duchy of Aquitaine should Eleanor die childless. In such a case, Ralph de Vermandois as Petronilla's husband could have claimed the ducal title through her right to the succession, positioning a prominent member of the royal entourage to take control of the duchy.[89]

Louis VII and Eleanor found three compliant bishops to declare Ralph's marriage to his first wife invalid because of her relationship to him within the degrees prohibited by Church law. Petronilla and Ralph's marriage followed in 1142, with the queen's presence as proof of royal approval. Theobald of Blois-Champagne, uncle of Ralph's cast-off wife, was outraged, and he lodged an appeal with Pope Innocent II. A papal legate was despatched from Rome to preside over a council in the count's lands that declared Ralph's first marriage fully valid. The legate then excommunicated the newly wed couple and suspended from their episcopal functions the three prelates who had sanctioned Ralph's separation and remarriage. Louis, already angered by the count of Champagne's opposition in the crisis over the archbishopric of Bourges and by his refusal to contribute forces to the king's military campaigns, launched an invasion of Champagne in the summer of 1142. The war was fought with such fury that it resulted in a terrible and tragic massacre at the town of Vitry. When Louis's forces broke through its defenses, looting and setting fires that soon engulfed the entire town, the people took shelter in the parish church; and soon it caught fire, burning to death several hundred trapped inside, among them many women and children. The king stood watching, horrified but helpless, from a vantage point outside the town.[90]

The catastrophic incident at Vitry filled Louis VII with guilt, grief, and soul-searching; for several days he took to his bed, refusing to eat or speak. The king, fearing that the death, destruction, and disruption of lives due to the fighting were endangering the state of his soul, returned to Paris. Nonetheless, the war in Champagne continued with Louis's army overrunning the countryside, but with the count's forces still in control of the county's chief towns.[91] Negotiations began in 1143 with Abbot Suger, who was still occasionally called on to counsel Louis, acting on the king's behalf and with Bernard of Clairvaux serving as his friend Theobald's agent. A sticking point was Eleanor's insistence that the excommunication of her sister Petronilla and her brother-in-law Ralph de Vermandois be withdrawn. The count of Champagne had to agree that he would work to secure their restoration to communion with the Church, a hopeless task, for the matter lay entirely in the pope's hands and Innocent II was obdurate. The pontiff refused to act unless Ralph left Petronilla and returned to his first wife and unless Louis allowed the duly elected archbishop of Bourges to take possession of his see. In one of Bernard's letters to the French king, he reprimanded Louis for his readiness "to kick aside frivolously and hastily the good and sound advice that you receive," and for following "I know not what devilish advice." He asked, "From whom but the devil could this advice come under which you are acting, advice which causes burnings upon burnings, slaughter upon slaughter." Actually, Bernard knew that such advice came from Eleanor and her "clan" at court. Yet Louis's own unwillingness to bend on the Bourges issue was equally an obstacle. He was adamant in his refusal to renounce his oath that he would never allow the canon's nominee as archbishop to enter his cathedral, fearing that breaking his vow would bring down on him heavenly wrath.[92]

In the summer of 1143, resolution of the conflict appeared hopeless with Louis VII still refusing to heed the counsels of both Suger and Bernard of Clairvaux. Meanwhile, Count Theobald of Champagne was building up alliances that threatened to involve the entire north of France in the conflict in Champagne. Louis VII found a new grievance against Theobald, charging him with constructing his alliances by contracting consanguineous marriages for his relatives in violation of the Church's rules. Louis's venturing into canon law aroused the abbot of Clairvaux's ire, who asked angrily, "How has [the king] got the effrontery to try so hard to lay down laws for others about consanguinity when it is clear that he himself is living with his cousin within the third degree?"[93] Bernard was exaggerating Eleanor and Louis's degree of kinship, but in merely raising the question, he was declaring openly what many ecclesiastics must have known already about the suspect legitimacy of the royal marriage. Certainly Louis and Eleanor also must have realized that their marriage was questionable from their disingenuous raising of the issue of consanguinity as an excuse for annulling Ralph de Vermandois's first marriage.

The impasse ended in September 1143 with the death of Pope Innocent II. His successor as pontiff had a conciliatory character and would prove more accommodating to the French monarch.[94] As a gesture of goodwill toward Louis VII, he removed the interdict imposed by his predecessor on the churches of the French royal domain, but took no action on the excommunication of Eleanor's sister Petronilla and Ralph de Vermandois. Eventually Louis's ill-considered undertakings caused him to turn once more to Abbot Suger, who was re-emerging as the chief royal counselor. Bernard of Clairvaux organized a series of meetings in the winter of 1143–44 that eventually brought the crisis to a conclusion. One of the meetings broke off almost at once, when Louis withdrew in anger at Bernard's words, earning him a rebuke from the outspoken abbot. Bernard attributed the king's annoyance to "the fraud of wicked men and the idle chatter of silly people who do not know good from evil or evil from good." Doubtless the "silly people" he had in mind included Eleanor and her circle at court. Finally, agreement was reached at a conference hosted by Suger at Saint-Denis on 22 April 1144, when many dignitaries had gathered for one of the abbey's feast-days.[95]

Bernard recognized that the chief obstacle to a settlement was Eleanor's opposition to any agreement that did not confirm the validity of her sister's marriage to Ralph, count of Vermandois. During conversations with the queen at Saint-Denis, the formidable abbot exhorted her to cease her agitation against the count of Champagne and to give better counsel to her husband. Somehow the austere monk, who regarded Eleanor as a snare of Satan, won her confidence, and she then confided to him her sorrow at her infertility and asked his aid in obtaining the gift from God of a child. She was aware of whisperings among the courtiers about her failure to produce a child, preferably a male heir, and she knew that her continued childlessness was threatening her credit with her husband. Eleanor, at age twenty, had experienced only one pregnancy in her seven years of marriage, and it had ended in a miscarriage. The abbot of Clairvaux, confident of the queen's power over Louis, then offered her a bargain. He asked her to do all that she could for the re-establishment of peace, and he promised, "If you do what I require of you, I also by my prayers will obtain from the Lord what you request." In effect, Bernard was telling Eleanor that her barren marriage was divine punishment for the royal couple's sins of attacking the Church and making war on the count of Champagne. The queen had to admit that the situation of her sister and her paramour was hopeless, despite all her labors on their behalf; and humbled, she gave her agreement to Bernard's advice and reported his words to her husband Louis. Peace followed, and a year later the queen gave birth to a child as promised. It was a daughter, named Marie in thanks to the Virgin Mary, not the son that Louis and his subjects so fervently desired.[96]

Eleanor's infertility may not have been her fault, but rather a result of her husband Louis VII's piety. Despite evidence of Louis's love for his bride, the Church's teachings had ill-equipped him for a fulfilling sexual relationship with her. The early Church Fathers' suspicion of physical love meant that the Church's views on the act of procreation were contradictory. Expecting Christ's quick return in glory, they had held up virginity and celibacy as superior to the married state; and almost the only happy marriages depicted in medieval saints' lives are those in which the couple vowed to remain continent.[97] Other teachers came to stress the Old Testament injunction to "be fruitful and multiply" once the hope for Christ's speedy return faded, but they also stressed the sinful character of coitus unless for the purpose of producing progeny. Because the sex act's purpose must be bringing children into the world, any non-reproductive sexual behavior was condemned as sinful, a form of sodomy. Clearly, Christian teaching remained suspicious of any sexual activity, and it imposed restrictions on coitus on certain days of the week, during the seasons of Lent, Advent, Easter, or Pentecost, and also at times when women were considered "unclean," such as menstruation, pregnancy, or lactation. One writer calculates, "If all the calendar and physiological periods were observed by a scrupulous couple, the days available for procreation were reduced to only forty-four to fifty-seven a year." He comments that authors of such rules "were evidently little aware of or concerned with the demographic effects of their theory."[98] However ardent Louis's desire for his wife, his wish to obey the Church's many restrictions on marital sex may have proven more powerful. This can account for Eleanor's infrequent pregnancies during their marriage in contrast to her later fruitfulness with her second husband, Henry Plantagenet.

The 1144 agreement at Saint-Denis included terms calling for Eleanor and Louis to end their support for the marriage of Eleanor's sister to the count of Vermandois, but the two refused to separate, and succeeding popes renewed their excommunication. Eleanor stubbornly continued seeking the couple's restoration to communion, and Louis, who considered Ralph one of his chief counselors, continued to press the couple's case before leaving on crusade in 1147. Finally in 1148, while the French king and queen were far away from their kingdom, Ralph de Vermandois's absolution was arranged with the aid of two cardinals at Rome, "not without suspicion of bribery."[99] The Church officially dissolved Ralph's first marriage as consanguineous, leaving no impediment to his marriage to Petronilla, who would give him three children during their life together.[100] Also at Saint-Denis in 1144, Louis had to admit defeat in his attempt to impose his own choice as archbishop of Bourges, and he accepted the canons' candidate, although his conscience continued to trouble him about breaking his oath. In violating canon law at Bourges and taking on the Church of Rome, he had gone down a dead-end road.

These tumultuous years produced heavy strains on Eleanor and Louis VII's marriage. The horrible incineration at Vitry caused the king much soul-searching, and in a penitent spirit he began to turn away from his wife's counsel and look in the direction of the holy men Bernard of Clairvaux and Suger of Saint-Denis. A hint that Louis was undergoing some disillusionment with the marriage is his action at the dedication of Suger's splendid new church at Saint-Denis on 11 June 1144. In the midst of ceremonies attended by Bernard and other important ecclesiastical dignitaries as well as the royal

entourage, Louis chose to commemorate that grand occasion by giving away
the rock crystal vase that had been Eleanor's wedding present to him, handing
it over to Suger for the new abbey church. Suger, "a sophisticated connoisseur
of art," appreciated acquiring the vase for his collection of precious stones and
art objects; his addition of a bejewelled gold neck and base to the vase shows
that he considered it one of the most precious objects in his abbey's treasury.
He had an inscription engraved on its base, "As a bride, Eleanor gave this vase
to King Louis . . ., the King to me, and Suger to the Saints"; and elsewhere he
wrote that Louis had given it to him "as a tribute of his great love." This
gift can be seen as symbolizing the young king's return as a "prodigal son"
to Suger's guidance and some slippage in Eleanor's place as his chief counselor. Perhaps Louis hoped that a gift to Saint-Denis associated with his
queen's family would cause their childless marriage to become fruitful;
whatever his reason, the surrender of the vase must have caused Eleanor
sorrow.[101] The influence of the abbot of Saint-Denis, once restored to the
center of royal power, gradually expanded; and Suger's renewed influence
would culminate in his title of regent while Louis and Eleanor were away on
crusade, 1147–49.

Eleanor of Aquitaine, aged twenty in 1144, had been queen of France for seven
years. Since arriving in Paris as Louis the Younger's bride in 1137, she had
succeeded in overcoming all rivals to secure her position as her husband's
partner in governing. Her mother-in-law's attempt to discredit her with
complaints of extravagant expenditures had backfired, and she had beaten
back Abbot Suger's effort to preserve his place as the king's chief counselor.
Indicating Eleanor's importance for Louis VII in the early years of his reign is
his belligerent attention to her ancestral lands. Yet Louis's early assertiveness
in Aquitaine made little long-term impact on the region, and the ducal
government had no more mastery over powerful nobles than before, despite
his sporadic interventions.

   With Eleanor at Louis VII's side as his most trusted counselor during the
first years of his reign, he had no one to restrain his impetuosity; and he took
actions with little foresight, setting in motion initiatives in several places at
once. In the decade before the Second Crusade, the young king practiced a
"politics of grandeur and delusion" that earned him little credit.[102] The
formerly docile and devout youth uncharacteristically undertook a campaign
to impose his authority over the French Church, underestimating the strong
reaction that he would arouse from French prelates, the pope, and the influential Cistercian preacher Bernard. Aside from the failed Toulouse campaign,
clearest evidence for Eleanor's influence over Louis is his persistent support
for her sister's marriage to the count of Vermandois, and its chief result was

only to complicate his troubles with the count of Blois-Champagne and with the Church that were already difficult enough. Once these crises ended in 1144, Louis began to return to the piety and sobriety of his youth, directing his thoughts toward a pilgrimage to Jerusalem as expiation for his recent sins, and Eleanor's influence was on the wane.

CHAPTER 3

ADVENTURES AND MISADVENTURES ON THE SECOND CRUSADE, 1145–1149

THE Second Crusade was the greatest adventure of Eleanor's life, taking her across eastern Europe to the storied capital of the Byzantine Empire and a harrowing march across Anatolia (the Turkish peninsula) to Jerusalem and the Holy Land's sacred sites. On her return journey she endured a voyage that included capture at sea in a naval battle, then a long journey from Palermo on the island of Sicily across the Norman kingdom in southern Italy to the papal court, before finally reaching Paris after an absence of over two years. This action-packed phase of Eleanor's life was crucial both for her and for her husband Louis VII. He could claim credit as the initiator of the Second Crusade, the first king to pledge himself to undertaking a crusade, for no western monarch had gone on the First Crusade. Yet Louis's crusade ended in failure, and the failed crusade would have dire consequences for his marriage to Eleanor, leading to an irreparable break between them and irrevocable damage to the queen's reputation. It was Eleanor's alleged misconduct during a visit to Antioch following an agonizing crossing of Anatolia that gave rise to a "black legend" that would fasten onto her a reputation for sexual impropriety that remains even today. The French queen's stay with her uncle, Raymond prince of Antioch, brought into the open long-simmering antipathy between spouses ill-suited to each other, beginning a process of unraveling their marriage that not even the pope's efforts could reverse. The incident at Antioch would sway historians' opinion of Eleanor for all time, staining her with infamy as an unfaithful wife long before her death in 1204.

LOUIS VII'S PROJECTED PILGRIMAGE BECOMES A CRUSADE

In the summer of 1145 the shocking news of the fall of Edessa to Turkish Muslim forces on Christmas Eve 1144 spread to France and throughout western Christendom. Edessa was one of four principalities that constituted the western Christian or "Frankish" states created in the Holy Land after the First Crusade; the others were the principality of Antioch, the county of Tripoli, and the kingdom of Jerusalem. Edessa near the headwaters of the Euphrates river had a large native Christian population, and it had become the first of the crusader states when its ruler adopted a French knight on the First Crusade as his son. Edessa's conqueror in 1144 was Zengi, a descendant of Seljuk Turkish fighters who had established their domination over the Arab caliphs at Bagdad by the mid-eleventh century. Governor of the Iraqi region north of Bagdad around Mosul and prince of Aleppo, Zengi was making himself master of all Muslim Syria. His capture of Edessa threatened the existence of the three other crusader states, leaving nothing separating his forces from Antioch on the Mediterranean coast and opening the way for a Muslim assault on Jerusalem. News of Edessa's conquest and the massacre of its defenders horrified Christians in the West and roused them to defense of the Holy Land.[1] The people of France felt particular concern for the threatened crusader states, for a majority of the settlers were French knights, former participants in the First Crusade.

While the news affected Eleanor's husband Louis VII as deeply as anyone, he had already been contemplating a pilgrimage to Jerusalem. Apparently the idea of a penitential journey had come to him once he ended his long quarrels with the Church and with the count of Champagne in 1144, and he announced his aim at the 1145 Christmas court at Bourges. A month earlier, an embassy sent to the West by leaders in the crusader states had reached Rome to acquaint Pope Eugenius III with the extent of the disaster at Edessa, and on 1 December the pope issued a papal encyclical calling on the French and their king to rush to the rescue of their fellow Christians in the Holy Land. This document probably did not reach Louis in France before the new year 1146, after he and Eleanor had held their Christmas court. News of the fall of Edessa had most likely reached them before the arrival of the papal document, and it would cause the transformation of the king's simple pilgrimage vow into a promise to lead a crusade.[2]

Odo of Deuil, a monk of Saint-Denis, who would accompany Louis VII's crusading army as the king's confessor and as the crusade's official historian, lists in *De profectione Ludovici VII* three reasons for the French king's desire to make a pilgrimage to the Holy Land. Two are connected to his struggles with the canons of Bourges Cathedral and the resulting conflict with the count of Champagne: foremost was his wish to do penance for his part in the tragic massacre of non-combatants at the town of Vitry; second, he wished to do penance for breaking his solemn vow never to allow the canons' candidate for archbishop of Bourges to enter the cathedral. The king's third reason was a promise made at the time of his brother Philip's death to carry out his unfulfilled vow of making a pilgrimage to Jerusalem. An unmentioned fourth factor also influencing Louis was his consciousness of the French monarchy's prestige and his desire to add to the Capetians' glory as one of the most devout royal families in Christendom by leading a new crusade. Throughout the crusade, the pious young king would try to make evident the essentially Christian character of his leadership.[3]

At the Christmas court at Bourges, Louis VII first proposed to his bishops and barons a military expedition to the East, and one of the bishops present preached a fiery sermon seconding his call. Even though Louis was not yet proposing a full-scale crusade, only a rescue of Edessa, the French magnates listening to his proposal were notably unenthusiastic.[4] The influential Abbot Suger was disturbed at the possibility of the king's long absence from the kingdom and the risks of such a perilous journey. The response of Eleanor and her Aquitanian "clan" at court was more enthusiastic, however. They were aware that at Antioch, the principality most directly threatened by the Turks' advance in Syria, the prince was Raymond, a fellow Poitevin and Eleanor's uncle. Because Raymond was the only surviving male in the ducal line of Aquitaine, the queen was alarmed by the threat to his lands in the East, and she and her friends were eager to see that a French crusading army came to his assistance.[5]

Louis, faced with his great men's opposition, postponed a decision on his proposed expedition until the 1146 Easter court at Vézelay. The king recruited Bernard of Clairvaux to preach there, confident that the eloquent abbot would prove capable of arousing the necessary enthusiasm. At first neither Bernard nor Pope Eugenius III, a former monk of Clairvaux, was overly enthusiastic about sponsoring another crusade, for both were preoccupied with a revolt by the people of Rome facing the newly installed pope. Ignoring a ban against monks preaching outside their monasteries, Bernard left Clairvaux to go to Vézelay to preach the crusade on 31 March 1146, on the express command of the pope. Bernard gave an account of his preaching to the pope: "You ordered, I obeyed; and the authority of him who gave the order [i.e. the pope] has made my obedience fruitful. I opened my mouth; I spoke; and at once the Crusaders have multiplied to infinity. Villages and towns are now deserted."[6] In his sermon, he depicted in apocalyptic terms the menace facing the Holy Places and the fearsome fate awaiting the embattled Christians in the East.

The enthusiasm and eloquence of Bernard's preaching emphasizing the personal religious significance of the vow for each crusader inspired a vast number of his hearers at Vézelay to take the cross.[7] Most prominent among those to whom the famous Cistercian handed the crusader's cross was King Louis, joined by many of his nobles. Apparently, distribution of crosses was not limited to fighting men, but to pilgrims as well, including many women; and likely among them was Eleanor. For Eleanor to take the cross was not unusual: women were allowed to join their crusading husbands or other relatives if they secured the Church's permission. The First Crusade had been part pilgrimage, and noble ladies had accompanied their husbands.[8]

Eleanor shared conventional religious beliefs, and like any Christian she would have experienced genuine emotion at the prospect of worshiping at the sites of Christ's passion. She probably hoped for some reward for her pilgrimage—and not only in heaven. Even though the French queen had borne a daughter, she must have worried that her marriage had not produced more children; above all, she was troubled by her failure to give birth to a male heir. She must have hoped that by submitting herself to the pains and perils of a long pilgrimage she might merit the reward of bearing a son. Yet Eleanor may have underestimated the discomfort and danger of such a lengthy journey through enemy territory, anticipating eagerly a radical change in her life, breaking away from the tedium of life in the French royal household to experience the adventure and excitement of travel to distant and exotic lands. Eleanor must also have looked forward to renewing her acquaintance with her uncle Raymond and visiting his court at Antioch, for its reputation for adopting a luxurious oriental lifestyle had reached the West.[9]

The French queen's presence on the crusading expedition is often credited to Louis VII's "over-urgent longing for his young wife," an infatuation so intense that the young king could not bear the long separation from his queen that his absence from France would cause.[10] Yet there were sound political reasons for not leaving Eleanor behind. As queen, she would have held a powerful position, perhaps even assuming the title of regent; and she could have disputed the power of Suger of Saint-Denis, Louis's choice for administering the kingdom during his absence. The Poitevins around Eleanor at court had already demonstrated their hostility for the wise old abbot. Furthermore, Louis may have considered his wife's presence on crusade essential for ensuring the participation of the Poitevin barons in his enterprise, as well as the generous financial assistance of the churches and townspeople of Aquitaine. A number of nobles from Poitou would join their duchess on the Second Crusade, among them Geoffrey de Rancon, Hugh de Lusignan, Guy de Thouars, and Saldebreuil de Sanzay, Eleanor's constable. The troubadour Jaufre Rudel, lord of Blaye in Gascony, was also among her nobles traveling to Palestine, a member of the entourage of the count of Toulouse.[11]

For churchmen, women's presence on the Second Crusade threatened the mission's success, and the mere fact of Eleanor's accompanying her husband merited their condemnation. The late twelfth-century English monastic writer William of Newburgh, for example, saw nothing good coming from the queen's presence in the crusading host, feeling it set a bad precedent that would encourage nobles to bring along their wives or mistresses, who would then enlarge the number of women by bringing their maidservants. Whatever the result, noble ladies did join the crusaders; they included the wives of Thierry of Alsace, count of Flanders, and Count Alphonse-Jourdain of Toulouse.[12] Newburgh, along with most medieval monks, held a deep reverence for chastity. He declared that "in that Christian camp [*castris*] where chastity [*casta*] should have prevailed, a horde of women were milling about . . . bringing scandal upon our army." For Newburgh looking back years after the Second Crusade, the knights' sexual license afforded a sufficient explanation for its failure; he wrote of their misfortunes, "It is not surprising that divine favour did not smile at all on the troops, as they were defiled and unclean." He goes on to explain that the word *castra* [camps] "is derived from *castratio luxuriae* [the castration of wantonness], but our camp was not chaste, for the lusts of many spurted forth . . . with a disastrous licentiousness."[13]

Strangely, condemnations of women going on crusade did not mention their leaving behind their young children. For Eleanor to take the cross meant that she would be separated from her daughter Marie, no more than two years old, for over two years. This separation would not have caused great concern for either Eleanor or Louis, however, given the medieval aristocracy's attitude toward child-rearing. If aristocratic mothers had many responsibilities that competed with caring for their children, a queen had even more demands on her time. Nothing is known of Eleanor's role in her young daughter's rearing before she left on crusade, but it is likely that it was limited. If mothering was not Eleanor's first priority, it is no more fair to accuse her of frivolity in abandoning little Marie to go off on such a great adventure than it would be to condemn Louis for going on a crusade for the sake of the Holy Places instead of staying at home to guard his subjects' safety.

In the autumn after taking the cross at Vézelay, Louis and Eleanor made a circuit of Aquitaine to recruit the region's nobles for the crusade and to provide for the duchy's administration during their absence.[14] Then in mid-February 1147, Louis presided over a great assembly at Étampes of French nobles who had taken the cross. Bernard of Clairvaux was present, having returned from a preaching mission in Germany at the end of 1146, and he reported the good news that he had persuaded the German emperor Conrad III to take the cross.[15] At least one foreign ambassador was in attendance, an envoy of King Roger II of Sicily, and the Byzantine emperor Manuel Komnenos sent a message to Louis offering his good offices. The Étampes council's task was to choose a route to the East for the crusaders to follow. Roger of Sicily's envoy urged a maritime route that would make the French crusaders dependent on the Sicilian fleet. Louis and others at Étampes were wary of Roger because he was not on good terms with other powers essential to the crusade's success— neither the pope nor the German and Byzantine emperors. The Sicilian ruler was engaged in rivalry with the eastern emperor for domination over the eastern Mediterranean, and he wished to win the crusaders to his side. Anti-Greek elements at Étampes that deeply distrusted the Byzantine emperor and his subjects lobbied hard for Roger's all-water route.[16]

Whatever part Eleanor and her fellow Poitevins at court played in the debate is uncertain, but her uncle Raymond's relations with the eastern emperor are likely to have influenced their thinking. Raymond's predecessors as princes of Antioch had had bad relations with the Byzantine Empire, refusing to acknowledge the emperor's claim to Antioch, but Raymond had come to terms with Manuel Komnenos once Edessa's fall exposed his principality to the Muslims' attack. In 1145 Raymond went to Constantinople to conciliate the emperor, doing homage to him and acknowledging Byzantine rights over Antioch. Raymond's peace with the emperor possibly inclined Eleanor and the Poitevin clique at court toward support for an all-land route passing through Constantinople, and its selection can be seen as in some measure a victory for them.[17] The pope's opinion was most likely the decisive factor, however. He had high hopes for restoring communion with the eastern Church, and he feared that Roger's conflict with the Byzantines would inflame hatreds and undermine his goal of reuniting the two Churches.

After the assembly at Étampes agreed on the route and set mid-June as a departure date, Louis sent messages to the king of Hungary and to Emperor Manuel Komnenos, asking for safe passage and provisions for the crusaders who would be crossing their lands. A final issue discussed at Étampes was that of providing for France's governance during Louis's absence. The ever-interfering Bernard of Clairvaux pressed for Suger's appointment as regent, but the matter was deferred until the Easter court. The Étampes council then dispersed, leaving major gaps in its planning. It had failed to hammer out a definition of the crusaders' purpose: a pilgrim's goal of praying at the Holy Sepulcher, a limited military goal of liberating Edessa, or a larger one of freeing the crusader lands from the Muslim threat? Another critical gap in planning was a failure to consult with leaders of the Latin Christian kingdom in the Holy Land on their needs.[18]

Final preparations for the crusading army's departure took place at Louis and Eleanor's Easter court at Saint-Denis on 20 April 1147. Pope Eugenius III was traveling in France with a number of cardinals, and his party arrived in Paris for Easter along with Bernard of Clairvaux.[19] The pope as overseer of the crusade had envisioned a purely French force under Louis VII's leadership without divided command. However, enthusiasm aroused by Bernard's preaching had recruited the German emperor Conrad III, and at the same time that the crusaders were to set out for the east, Roger of Sicily was planning a large-scale naval campaign to challenge the Muslims' hold on the North

African coast. With the new crusade turning into an international movement, the pope worried that rivalries among the three monarchs, Louis, Conrad, and Roger, would complicate matters. On Easter Sunday, after celebrating mass at the abbey of Saint-Denis, Eugenius III appointed two cardinals to accompany the crusaders as his legates; and also two French bishops to act as his eyes and ears. This "plethora of legates" would not enhance papal control over the crusade, for their rivalry would only cause confusion.[20]

The essential task remained of providing for the French kingdom's governance during the king and queen's long absence on crusade. At the Easter court at Saint-Denis, Louis formally handed over custody of his kingdom to the pope, who invested the abbot of Saint-Denis as regent. Suger was to have two associates in administering the kingdom, however, and Louis named as co-regent with the abbot Count Ralph of Vermandois, the seneschal of France. Doubtless Ralph's nomination caused both the pope and Bernard of Clairvaux to wince, for he was still excommunicate on account of having abandoned his wife to take up an adulterous relationship with Queen Eleanor's sister. Later Suger appointed a second associate, the archbishop of Reims.[21] Despite Suger's shared authority, he would succeed in seeing that the French kingdom did not suffer undue damage during Louis VII's long absence and early in 1149 he was able to assure the king in a letter sent to the Holy Land, "Your land and your men, thanks to God, enjoy good peace."[22]

On the Road from Paris to Constantinople

Two months after the Easter court of 1147 another impressive gathering took place at Saint-Denis Abbey on 11 June for religious ceremonies marking the crusaders' departure. The royal party left Paris in the morning for the short ride to Saint-Denis, and Louis stopped along the way, visiting a leper hospital. The monk–historian Odo, always eager to depict the king's crusading venture as an internal pilgrimage toward humility and spiritual perfection, was careful to record his pious act as "a praiseworthy thing, which few, perhaps no one of his lofty rank, could imitate."[23] When Louis reached the abbey church, Pope Eugenius III, Abbot Suger, Eleanor, and the queen-mother awaited him. The king humbly prostrated himself on the ground before the pope and the abbot, and they presented him with relics of Saint Denis for his veneration. Next he was handed the oriflamme, the sacred banner that the Capetians carried into battle, received the pope's blessing, and was handed his pilgrim's pouch and staff. Afterward Louis dined in the monks' refectory with a few members of his retinue. Meanwhile, the queen and queen-mother waited until they could no longer endure the crush of the crowd, the heat, and their own tears, and they retreated inside into the monastery.[24]

Later in the day, Louis's army and auxiliary forces, followed by a horde of pilgrims, began marching toward Metz in imperial territory, the designated point for assembling crusaders from other regions of France. As the French troops marched, some took up a song expressing their confidence in their mission: "He who goes with Louis / Will have no fear of Hell, 'For his soul will go to Paradise' / With the angels of our Lord."[25] Eleanor certainly had no intention of dying while on this long journey, but the French crusaders' faith in their king and in their holy war must have raised her spirits, stimulating feelings both of lofty religious sentiments and anticipation of a great adventure. The armies led by the French king and the German emperor formed the largest force leaving for the Holy Land. An army led by the count of Savoy marched down the Italian peninsula to cross the Adriatic and continue across the Balkans to join Louis's forces at Constantinople, and the count of Toulouse would sail later from the south of France, reaching Palestine in spring 1148. Modern estimates place the total number of crusaders, including non-combatants, at between 25,000 and 50,000. Of these figures, perhaps 5,000 were knights and another 10,000 or 12,000 other fighting men, light cavalry, and infantry.[26] Almost all medieval armies included foot soldiers, some of them with special skills such as crossbowmen or siege engineers. In addition, any large army in the field over a long period required thousands of non-combatants employed to perform support services. These ranged from smiths, armorers, and grooms to cooks and common servants, and each knight brought along one or more of his own servants. All were expected to take up weapons when needed, at least guarding the baggage train during engagements.

As well as considerable numbers of women among the poor pilgrims following the crusaders, there were always some working women following medieval armies, some doing laundry and kitchen work or nursing the wounded and others providing sexual services. When fighting broke out, women contributed by carrying drinking water and comforting the wounded. A number of aristocratic ladies in addition to Eleanor followed their crusader husbands, and they brought along servant girls and ladies in waiting, swelling the total number of women. Eleanor's own personal entourage must have been quite large but the legend that she recruited a band of armed and mounted "Amazons" to ride with her alongside the crusading knights can be set aside. This improbable story apparently originated with a Greek chronicler's description of the crusaders' entry into Constantinople, written at least a generation after the event. The legend was taken up enthusiastically by nineteenth-century writers and is repeated in widely read twentieth-century books on Eleanor.[27]

The vast army made its way to Metz after a four-or five-day march from Paris and then marched on to Worms, where it crossed the Rhine.[28] A traveler on horseback could average thirty-five miles a day, but Louis's host was slowed by many persons on foot, slow-moving packhorses, and cumbersome two- and four-horse baggage carts and wagons clogging the roads. At Regensburg in Germany, baggage was loaded on barges to be sent down the Danube as far as Bulgaria, relieving the army of the carts that had "afforded more hope than usefulness" and raised much complaint from military men for holding up their progress on land. A great deal of the supplies belonged to Eleanor, and her bulky baggage would cause criticism later. Even with her more than ample supplies, she could not have found travel conditions comfortable. A medieval road "hardly existed as a physical object," being little more than a track connecting towns and villages, often containing impassable mudholes in wet weather. If Eleanor chose not to ride a horse, she could have had herself carried between two horses on a litter, as was common for noble ladies. She and other aristocratic ladies may have ridden part of the way in "chariots," uncomfortable but highly decorated carts. Wheeled vehicles were not equipped with springs, and nobles usually disdained carts for their rough ride and also for their demeaning associations with peasants and laborers.[29]

While at Regensburg, envoys from the Byzantine emperor Manuel Komnenos arrived to meet with Louis, giving Eleanor her first sight of representatives of the legendary Eastern Christian Empire, fabled for its riches.[30] The eastern emperor desired aid from the French against the advancing Turks, but distrusted them at the same time, knowing of their ties to the Norman Sicilians and to French settlers in the crusader states along the Syrian coast. Nor did the French trust the Byzantine emperor or his people, and a party hostile to the Greeks had formed at the Étampes assembly well before the crusaders' departure. The envoys at Regensburg did not make a favorable impression, delivering their emperor's message with many flattering circumlocutions. Odo of Deuil wrote that the Greeks "sought with such inept humility to secure our good will that I should say the words, too affectionate because they were not sprung from affection, were such as to disgrace not only an emperor, but even a buffoon."[31] It was not only the form of Manuel's message but its content as well that inflamed anti-Greek feelings among the French crusaders. The emperor sought assurances from Louis and his men that they would do homage to him for any former imperial lands they occupied, acknowledging his lordship over any territories once part of the Byzantine Empire. This was a demand that would be made at every encounter, and relations between the French and the Greeks would worsen at each stage of the route to Jerusalem.

From Regensburg, the French king and queen and their host of soldiers and pilgrims followed the banks of the Danube, passing Passau and Klosterneuburg. Leaving Conrad III's domains behind, they spent fifteen days crossing the kingdom of Hungary to reach the Eastern Empire's frontiers, arriving at the fortress of Belgrade by mid-August and pushing on into Byzantine-controlled Bulgaria. The French crusaders marched along a route taken only a few weeks earlier by the German emperor and his army, who had left ahead of them so that provisions needed by the host of hungry marchers should not over-stretch the available supplies along the way.[32] Yet the French, trailing behind, found the countryside stripped almost bare, pillaged by the Germans. Peasants hid whatever meager food supplies were left to prevent them from being taken by the French, and traders demanded steep prices for whatever produce they had to spare. The numerous pilgrims following in the wake of Louis's crusading army quickly ran out of their own food, presenting major disciplinary and logistical problems on the long march to the Holy Land. A failing of Louis and Conrad III as the crusade's commanders was their inability to separate their armies from the pilgrims who constantly slowed the fighting men's progress and competed for provisions, contributing to strained relations between the French and their German allies. The lack of food and fodder forced Louis to spend more money on supplies and even before his army reached Constantinople he had to write to Suger asking for additional funds.[33] Despite shortages, it is unlikely that Eleanor and the ladies of her entourage experienced hunger at this stage of the journey.

In Bulgaria the Byzantine governor at Sofia, a kinsman of Emperor Manuel Komnenos, did what he could to find provisions for Louis's crusaders and pilgrims. The French arrived at Adrianople (today Edirne in Turkey) to discover that the Germans had added to the already difficult relations between the westerners and the Byzantine emperor's subjects, burning an Eastern Orthodox monastery and killing its monks. The authorities at Adrianople, exasperated by the Germans' behavior, tried to persuade Louis to lead his army directly across to Asia via the Dardanelles, avoiding Constantinople, but they had no success. The march from Adrianople to the walls of Constantinople would take five days.[34]

No doubt Eleanor looked forward to remaining in one spot for several days and relaxing after weeks of sleeping in tents across eastern Europe, but she also looked forward to visiting the cosmopolitan city, famed for its rich history, architectural and artistic treasures, and sophisticated inhabitants. Her husband and others among the French crusaders felt some apprehension as they approached Constantinople because of their mistrust of the Byzantines. They were much annoyed to learn when less than a day's distance from the Byzantine capital that Emperor Manuel Komnenos had made a truce with the Turkish sultan of Konya in Anatolia through whose lands they must pass on their way to crusader Syria. They lacked understanding and sympathy for the emperor's problems in dealing with his hostile and aggressive Muslim neighbors: Manuel Komnenos needed a breathing space from his struggle with the Turks in order to cope with the threat from Roger of Sicily's fleets to his territories along the

Adriatic coast. The French crusaders, however, could only see fraud on the emperor's part, and some urged Louis to ally with the Norman Sicilian king against the Greeks.[35] Furthermore, the French were also annoyed to learn that the emperor had forbidden their German allies to enter his great city and that the Germans had crossed the Bosporus without waiting for them as planned.[36]

CONSTANTINOPLE, "QUEEN OF CITIES"

On 4 October 1147, after a five-month journey, Louis and Eleanor arrived before the walls of Constantinople with the crusading army and its accompanying pilgrims.[37] From the first sight of the massive Theodosian walls protecting the western approach, the great city made a powerful impression on Eleanor and her companions, even though at the time of the Second Crusade it was past its prime, the capital of a shrunken and weakened empire. Its great churches and palaces constructed under Constantine and Justinian were still standing and in daily use, unlike in Rome, where the Roman imperial monuments had fallen into ruin long ago. The "Great" or "Sacred Palace" overlooking the sea had periodically been enlarged and renovated and had grown into a city within a city. Connected to the palace complex were the nearby Hippodrome and the church of Hagia Sophia, illustrating the links between the emperor, his people, and the Church. Since the eleventh century, the imperial family had abandoned the Great Palace, favoring the Blachernae Palace built next to the city wall at the western landward edge of the city near the Golden Horn.[38] It was to Blachernae that Louis was led for his first meeting with the emperor Manuel Komnenos. Odo of Deuil describes the palace: "Its exterior is of almost matchless beauty, but its interior surpasses anything that I can say about it. Throughout it is decorated elaborately with gold and a great variety of colors, and the floor is marble, paved with cunning workmanship; and I do not know whether the exquisite art or the exceedingly valuable stuffs endows it with the more beauty or value."[39]

At the gates of the city, Louis and his queen were met by a delegation from the city's nobles and prominent citizens who welcomed them and invited them to meet their emperor. Odo of Deuil, observing the meeting, left a description: "When we approached the city, lo, all its nobles and wealthy men, clerics as well as lay people, trooped out to meet the king and received him with due honor, humbly asking him to appear before the emperor and to fulfill the emperor's desire to see and talk with him." Louis, "taking pity on the emperor's fear," agreed, and his first encounter with the Eastern emperor at the Blachernae Palace was cordial. Byzantine court etiquette with its obsequious obeisance to the emperor scandalized the French, but a concession was made to Louis, allowing him to sit in the emperor's presence. The chronicler notes, "The two sovereigns were almost identical in age and stature, unlike only in dress and manners." Eleanor is not mentioned in the account, but it is probable that she was anxious to accompany Louis on his first meeting with the Byzantine ruler to see him and his court for herself.[40]

Manuel Komnenos made available to the French king and queen the Philopatium, a hunting lodge outside the city wall near the Blachernae Palace, and the army and the many servants and pilgrims following it camped nearby. The French crusading army spent about three weeks at Constantinople, crossing over to the Asian side of the Bosporus on 26 October. The emperor took Louis on sightseeing tours, showing him the many churches and their collections of holy relics, and after their tours he invited Louis to dine with him. The banquets at the emperor's palace "afforded pleasure to ear, mouth, and eye with pomp as marvelous, viands as delicate, and pastimes as pleasant as the guests were illustrious."[41] Meanwhile Eleanor and the empress were exchanging letters and becoming acquainted. The wife of Manuel Komnenos was German, the sister-in-law of the emperor Conrad, Bertha of Sulzbach. She had received a new name, Irene, after her marriage and conversion to the Eastern Orthodox religion in 1146.[42] In theory, respectable Byzantine ladies were expected to be seldom seen and never heard in public. The empress's quarters in the palace were under her sole control, guarded by eunuchs, and men were never supposed to enter—not even the emperor, unless with her permission. Yet in the twelfth century, Byzantine women, except for unmarried girls, were no longer so secluded as in earlier centuries, and the empress and her ladies attended receptions and banquets.[43] Empress Irene and her guest Eleanor likely joined their husbands in the evening to dine with them in the emperor's quarters.

Louis, "a simple man who made a duty of simplicity," soon found the excessive ceremonial and the extravagant titles of the many Byzantine court officials exasperating.[44] His growing distaste for Constantinople was shared by his men as friction arose with the city's money changers and merchants, whom the French suspected of price-gouging and of disdaining them. Eleanor's impression of the Byzantine capital and the imperial court, however, was not likely to have been as negative as that of her husband and her countrymen. Perhaps Byzantium evoked memories of the sensuality and luxury of life at the Poitevin court, and she savored the contrast between the gorgeous spectacle of the imperial court's ceremonies and the dull and drab Capetian royal court that she had left behind. Constantinople's glories opened Eleanor's eyes to "vast, lofty, undreamed-of possibilities for majesty."[45]

Louis was unwilling to leave Constantinople until the arrival of the count of Savoy's forces that had traveled by way of the Italian peninsula, then by ferry to the Balkans and onward to the Byzantine capital. During the wait for their arrival, Louis conducted negotiations with Manuel Komnenos to win his aid on the march across Anatolia, largely under Turkish control. Eventually the eastern emperor agreed to provide guides for the French army and markets for purchasing provisions along the way. In return, Louis agreed that any territories lost by the Eastern Empire to the Turks should be restored to imperial sovereignty, and he required his barons to do homage to the emperor in advance for any lands that they might occupy. The French nobles, deeply distrustful of the Byzantines, were unhappy at this demand for their homage, but Louis thought it essential to keep the emperor Manuel's support, especially once rumors of a German defeat began to spread about the French camp.[46]

In the half-century since the First Crusade, bitterness between crusaders and Eastern Christians had accumulated, building "a wall of incomprehension."[47] Crusading westerners visiting Constantinople felt inferior to the Byzantines, and they compensated by condemning the Greeks as over-civilized, too soft, effeminate, and degenerate for their tastes. Furthermore, western Christians condemned Eastern Orthodox Christians as heretics, and the chronicler Odo of Deuil reveals the ferocity of their hatred of Orthodox doctrinal errors. He writes, "Because of this they were judged not to be Christians, and the Franks considered killing them a matter of no importance and hence could with the more difficulty be restrained from pillage and plundering."[48] Greeks regarded westerners as coarse and crude barbarians, as shown by Anna Komnena's account of the conduct of those passing through Constantinople on the First Crusade. She wrote, "Now the Frankish counts are naturally shameless and violent, naturally greedy of money too, and immoderate in everything they wish, and possess a flow of language greater than any other human race." The behavior of the armies of the Second Crusade did nothing to change attitudes at the imperial court or among the people. Complaints about merchants and money changers' cheating roused the crusaders to violence: they took with force what they could not buy, and they spoke openly of conquering Constantinople.[49]

THE DANGER-LADEN ADVANCE ACROSS ANATOLIA

Once Louis's long wait for the count of Savoy's army ended, the French crusaders began crossing to Asia on 15 October.[50] After they had crossed the Bosporus and made camp at Nicaea, they heard rumors of a grand German victory. Hearsay of the capture of Konya, chief city of one of the chief Seljuk Turkish princedoms in Anatolia, was circulating, but soon it became known that actually the Germans had suffered a dreadful defeat, and that they were making a disorderly retreat back to Nicaea. After ten days of marching, the German crusaders had experienced a surprise attack; the Turks had swooped down before the German knights and infantry, worn down by privations, had

had time to organize into a line of battle. A contemporary account of the sudden Turkish attack on Conrad III and the German crusaders gives a vivid description of the Muslims' tactics and the western knights' ineffective response:

> This unexpected action threw the legions into utter confusion, for they had not foreseen anything of the kind. The strength of the Turks lay in their swift horses . . . and in their light equipment of bows and arrows. With loud cries, they surrounded the camp and with their usual agility fell furiously upon our soldiers, who were retarded by their heavy armor. The Christians were superior to the foe in strength and practice in arms, yet, weighed down as they were . . . they could not combat the Turks, nor could they pursue them very far from the camp. Their horses also, emaciated by hunger and the long marches, were utterly unable to gallop hither and yon. The Turks, on the contrary, charged en masse; while still at a distance they let fly countless showers of arrows which fell like hail upon the horses and their riders and brought death and wounds from afar. When the Christians tried to pursue, however, the Turks turned and fled upon their swift horses and thus escaped . . . . Our army, hemmed in on all sides, was in mortal danger from the constant showers of darts and arrows. They had no chance to retaliate or to engage the foe at close quarters, nor could they lay hold of the enemy. As often as they tried to make a counter attack, the Turks broke ranks, eluded all their attempts, and galloped off in different directions.[51]

Following the terrible butchery of the Germans, which left their emperor wounded and his force decimated, they had no choice but to turn back to Nicaea. When Louis and Conrad III met there, the French king offered to join his own army with the German emperor's remaining force and the two rulers agreed to march together across Anatolia. They rejected a quicker but more dangerous march through the Turkish-occupied interior in favor of a longer but safer coastal route that would avoid the Turks and afford more access to supplies.[52]

The combined French and German armies set out for Ephesus and, almost at once, a small band under Louis's leadership lost its way in the mountains and had to be led back to the main force by rustic mountain dwellers. Already the great caravan was losing pack horses and tossing aside excess baggage, although it is unlikely that Eleanor suffered any loss of supplies.[53] On reaching the ancient city of Ephesus around 20 December, envoys from the Byzantine emperor met Louis and Conrad III, bringing a warning that Turks of the Sultanate of Konya had gathered a great army to confront the crusaders. They advised the two monarchs to halt their advance and take refuge in Byzantine fortresses, but

Louis paid no attention to their advice. The ambassadors also delivered to the German emperor an invitation from their lord Manuel Komnenos to return with them to Constantinople and to recuperate in the imperial palace. Since Conrad's wounds had not healed enough for him to continue, he accepted the Byzantine emperor's offer; and he would remain in the eastern capital until March 1148, when the Greeks ferried him to Palestine to rejoin the crusaders.[54]

The long march along the Anatolian coast would cause the French great suffering, for the countryside was largely devastated and deserted after years of fighting between Turks and Byzantines. The numerous non-combatants following along severely slowed the fighting men's progress and competed with them for provisions. When supplies were sought in Greek towns along the way, they found them empty, for the inhabitants had all fled into the mountains at their approach. Thanks to mounting difficulties as the journey wore on, discipline almost collapsed.[55] The route from Ephesus to the Mediterranean port of Attalia (modern Antalya) where the crusaders expected to take ships for Antioch in Syria was punishing at any time, crossing barren mountain ranges that ran down to the sea. It was worst in mid-winter weather with no means of resupplying and with Turkish horsemen picking off stragglers. Soon after leaving Ephesus, the crusaders had to endure almost constant harassment by the Turks with their completely unfamiliar tactics—firing arrows while riding on fast light horses and unsportingly shooting the crusaders' horses. The first attack came on Christmas Eve 1147, while Louis's army was camped in a valley outside Ephesus. Odo of Deuil with his anti-Greek prejudice wrote that the Turks, "under Greek leadership, tried for the first time to take us unaware by attacking our horses as they grazed."[56]

From Ephesus, the crusading army turned inland to march eastward to the site of ancient Laodicea, where they headed south toward the port of Attalia. The craggy route was punishing, and it was while traversing Cadmos Mountain (Homaz today) at the beginning of January 1148 that the French experienced the worst Turkish attack of their crossing of Anatolia.[57] The marchers were proceeding in three groups ascending one of the highest mountains in their path. The advance guard consisted of men commanded jointly by the aged count of Maurienne, Louis's maternal uncle, and Geoffrey de Rancon, lord of Taillebourg, one of Eleanor's major vassals and the king's standard bearer. In the center the main body of crusaders moved slowly because it included livestock, baggage trains, and pilgrims on foot. Eleanor and other high-ranking ladies moved in the midst of this group, doubtless with a military escort to guarantee their safety. Bringing up the rear was the French king and a force under his command.

The vanguard had orders to halt and pitch their tents when they reached the summit of the mountain and to wait there for the rest of the army to complete its ascent, but somehow they ran far ahead of the main body of crusaders and pilgrims. When the two commanders reached the peak earlier than expected, they decided to disregard Louis's command and to continue their march down into the valley, looking for a more hospitable campsite than the bare and windswept summit. The Turks took advantage of the wide gap that the vanguard's rapid advance had created in the line of march, and they attacked the center, which was slowed by non-combatants and their baggage, and separated from both the advance and rear guards. The suddenness of the Turkish assault spread chaos among the unarmed pilgrims, many of whom were slaughtered or tumbled down the mountainside in futile attempts to escape the fighting. Soon the Turks turned to attack the king and his rear guard, and Odo of Deuil describes the mêlée:

> The Turks killed the horses . . . and the mail-clad Franks, now on foot, were overwhelmed among the thick-pressing enemy as if they were drowned in the sea; they were separated one from another, spilling the vitals from their defenseless bodies. . . . The king lost his small but renowned royal guard; keeping a stout heart, however, he nimbly and bravely scaled a rock by making use of some tree roots which God had provided for his safety. . . . By the will of God his cuirass protected him from the arrows, and to keep from being captured he defended the crag with his bloody sword, cutting off the heads and hands of many opponents in the process.[58]

At the end of that terrible day, the Turks withdrew, taking with them much loot and leaving many wounded and dead, among them some forty knights fighting alongside the king as his escort. This calamity at Cadmos Mountain damaged the military reputation that the French crusaders had won during the First Crusade, and it threatened Louis VII's standing as a commander, calling into question his judgment as a leader. Opprobrium fell chiefly on Geoffrey de Rancon, however; Odo of Deuil writes, "Here Geoffrey of Rancon . . . earned our everlasting hatred," adding that "the entire people judged that Geoffrey should be hanged because he had not obeyed the king's command about the day's march." Louis dared not discipline his own uncle who had shared command of the vanguard with Geoffrey de Rancon, however, and so one of Eleanor's great men also went unpunished.[59]

Soon the anger against Geoffrey aroused rancor against all the Aquitanians, whom the other French denounced as devil-may-care southerners, undisciplined and incapable of obeying commands. Eventually those looking for blame turned to Eleanor, although her only connection to the vanguard's rash action was that Geoffrey de Rancon was her vassal. A story woven by romantically inclined writers has Eleanor, whom they theorize had been entrusted to

Geoffrey's care, urging him to press forward and search out a more agreeable site in the valley for making camp. It strains common sense to suppose that the French queen should have been riding alongside Geoffrey de Rancon at the head of the army, rather than in the center with other non-combatants where she would have had less exposure to danger.[60]

It is not known how Eleanor managed to escape the massacre that so many non-combatants suffered at the hands of the Seljuk Turks at Cadmos Mountain. The nightmare that she had experienced certainly left her shaken, and it must have led her to question her husband's abilities as a strategist. Earlier events had already caused the queen to suspect that "she was entirely as capable as her rather weak husband in making decisions and seeing that they came to a good conclusion." This episode and other ill-conceived decisions made by Louis during the difficult crossing of Anatolia would strengthen this feeling as they approached Antioch.[61]

The crusading army moved on after a day or so, continuing its grueling route across the mountains in the cold of January. A need for better discipline was apparent, and the highly disciplined Knights Templars among the French force provided needed leadership.[62] Eleanor, who had earlier escaped the privations of the poor pilgrims, now traveled in little comfort and perhaps in hunger, having lost nearly all of her baggage and provisions. The Turks had thoroughly plundered the baggage train, and most of the goods left had to be abandoned because of the loss of pack horses. No new provisions could be found, for the Turks and Greeks had destroyed anything of use that lay in the pilgrims' path. However, the soldiers did not starve, for they could survive by butchering and eating the horses that were dying from exhaustion or hunger along the road.[63]

After ten more days in the mountains, the crusaders began descending from the high plateau toward Attalia on the southern coast of Anatolia. Around the end of January 1148, Louis and his queen arrived at the small port town after their months-long march across the peninsula under constant Turkish harassment. Attalia was no longer a prosperous city, and it had few supplies to share with the crusading party. The crusaders, in wretched condition, could not find adequate food or new clothing to replace their tattered garments; nor could they purchase horses to replace those lost along the mountainous road they had traveled. Louis spent weeks trying to hire ships for transporting his army to the Holy Land, but in the dead of winter not enough could be found. He decided that he and Eleanor should set sail for Antioch with a corps of his best knights, leaving the rest of his army and its followers to make their way by land.[64] Although Louis paid the Greeks to provide his soldiers with supplies and guides for their journey, they failed to keep their promise, and only about half of the French fighting men ever reached Antioch. After the royal party had sailed away, the Attalians expelled from their city the thousands of pilgrims who had followed the crusaders, condemning them to die of hunger and exhaustion, or to be massacred by the Turks. The voyage of Eleanor and Louis from Attalia to Antioch, normally three days in duration, took two weeks because of winter winds on the Mediterranean.[65]

The Incident at Antioch and the Beginning of a "Black Legend"

Eleanor and Louis arrived at Antioch's port ten miles from the city on 19 March 1148, eight months after leaving France—considerably later than they had expected to reach the Holy Land. They were welcomed warmly by the prince of Antioch, Raymond, younger brother of Eleanor's father. He led the royal entourage to Antioch "with great pomp," where the clergy and people were waiting to greet them. On Eleanor's arrival in the city after the ordeal of the harrowing crossing of Anatolia, she anticipated relaxing and recovering from her hardships, swathed in luxury at Raymond's palace. During a ten-day sojourn as her uncle's guest, Eleanor enjoyed the company of a number of other Poitevins who had followed Raymond to Antioch, among them his palace chaplain and some of his knights whose families she knew, as well as the patriarch of Antioch who came from Limoges.[66]

Eleanor took great delight in the company of Prince Raymond, only nine years her senior, and his sophisticated court at Antioch charmed her. The city and its palatial residences with marble columns, intricate mosaics, and rich silks called to mind the magnificence of Constantinople. The "Franks," as western Christians settled in the crusader states were called, had adopted Syrian manners and customs that were suitable for the local climate. They took baths and used soap, wore eastern-style clothing, ate the local dishes, including sweets flavored with sugar, and built their houses on the Syrian model with courtyards and fountains. Louis and his men recoiled from the luxurious and self-indulgent way of life they observed at Antioch, regarding it with the same scorn felt earlier for the Greeks at Constantinople. They were shocked and scandalized by Frankish settlers who "went native," making friends with Muslim notables and occasionally even allying with them. It seemed to Eleanor, however, that her uncle and other Poitevins at his court belonged to a more exotic world, living more splendid lives than the richest rulers in the West. Her arrival at Antioch seemed to mark "the sudden revelation of a world in accord with her heart and her dreams."[67]

Conflict between Louis VII and Raymond soon arose over the prince's attempt to recruit the king and his army for an attack on Aleppo, a step that he viewed as essential for Edessa's recovery. That city was the center of power for the Turk Nur ad-Din, younger son of the recently deceased Zengi, who was making himself the dominant force in Syria. Nur ad-Din represented a serious threat, for he had inherited his father's uncompromising goal of unifying Muslim Syria and driving out the western Christians. Indeed, his success in extending his power from northern Iraq to Egypt would pave the way for Saladin's later achievements. Above all, moved by a powerful and aggressive piety, Nur ad-Din felt a visceral hatred of Christians.[68] Raymond saw his proposed campaign to secure control of Aleppo and other strategic cities as an essential first step for defending Jerusalem. Louis's nobles, suspicious of any Aquitanian, suspected that the proposed expedition was merely part of Raymond's plan to enlarge his own principality of Antioch.

Before Louis's departure from France, Raymond had sent him "noble gifts and treasures of great price" to earn his goodwill, and he expected the king to accept his proposal.[69] Louis's concept of his mission had changed, however, and rescuing Edessa was no longer his primary aim; he had become convinced that his crusading vow required him to go directly to Jerusalem to pray at the Church of the Holy Sepulcher. Louis's desire to depart at once for Jerusalem and to defer a campaign against the Turks was perhaps his way of disguising indecision, for other western princes settled in Syria were pressing him for assistance. The French king, newly arrived in the region, could not know the best use to make of his depleted army. His forces at Antioch were only a tenth of their original number, consisting mostly of knights without light cavalry or foot soldiers and, exhausted from the rigors of their crossing of Anatolia, they were hardly ready for battle.[70]

In his attempt to convince Louis VII to join him in recovering Edessa, Raymond of Antioch "counted greatly on the interest of the queen with the lord king."[71] Raymond probably sensed Eleanor's admiration for him, aware that she saw in him a father-figure, a reminder of her father, Duke William X. He knew how to play on his niece's divided loyalties, appealing to her sense of family solidarity; he was her closest living male relative and a reminder of her pampered childhood at Poitiers. In addition, his entourage included a number of Poitevins, so he could arouse her concern for her kin and countrymen dwelling in this endangered Christian outpost.[72] He would have observed that Eleanor was a strong-minded woman. Certainly her interest in political matters had been evident from the first years of her marriage, and then Louis's hopeless love for his bride had won him over easily to her point of view. Yet now Eleanor felt herself capable of openly disputing her husband's policy decisions on the basis of her own judgment.[73] Impressed by Prince Raymond's knowledge gained from a decade's residence in the crusader principality, she quickly grasped the wisdom of his strategy. Despite Raymond's success in recruiting his niece to his cause, neither she nor he had any luck in shaking Louis's determination to proceed directly to Jerusalem.

Louis VII now expected his queen to be a docile wife, submitting to him and not questioning his initiatives in public policy. Yet his indecisiveness during the difficult crossing of Anatolia already had shaken Eleanor's confidence in his judgment, and no doubt her impatience with his austere way of living had deepened during her exhausting and frightening journey across Anatolia. She could no longer deny her unhappiness with her marriage, and she quite possibly confided this to her uncle. Her refusal to be forced into a constraining mold of wifely submissiveness became clear at Raymond's court, and this was her actual crime at Antioch in the eyes of Louis and his entourage. Eleanor's impassioned and forthright support of Raymond's plan only provoked her husband's jealousy. When neither Raymond's private approaches nor a council attended by both rulers' entourages could win Louis's support for his plan of attack, the prince's attitude changed, and he began plotting against the French king.

Eleanor announced to Louis that he could go on to Jerusalem, but she would stay in Antioch and initiate proceedings for the annulment of their marriage. The earliest source for this shocking episode, the infamous incident at Antioch that colored all succeeding assessments of Eleanor, is John of Salisbury. John possessed first-hand information on Eleanor and Louis's marital difficulties from his time at the papal court when the royal couple were guests of Pope Eugenius III on their return from the Holy Land, and he recorded what he had learned in a memoir of his service with the pope, 1146–54. This measured account by the respected English writer, revealing that the source of Eleanor's friction with her husband was the excessive attention and time that she gave to her uncle Raymond, "breathes truth."[74] Because John's recounting is so significant for Eleanor's later reputation, it must be quoted:

> Whilst the king and queen remained [at Antioch] to console, heal and revive the survivors from the wreck of the army, the attentions paid by the prince to the queen, and his constant, indeed almost continuous, conversation with her, aroused the king's suspicions. These were greatly strengthened when the queen wished to remain behind although the king was preparing to leave, and the prince made every effort to keep her, if the king would give her consent. And when the king made haste to tear her away, she mentioned their kinship, saying that it was not lawful for them to remain together as man and wife, since they were related in the fourth and fifth degrees.[75]

The queen was correct about their kinship within the prohibited degrees, for it was an open secret that she and Louis shared a common ancestor. Yet it was a daring declaration for her to make, and she would not have spoken so boldly without her uncle's support, or perhaps his urging. Raymond, angered by Louis's contrariness, saw his niece as an instrument for revenge. No doubt during their many conversations the prince had assured his niece that as senior male of the Aquitanian ducal line he would take her under his protection should she become single again. He knew that the choice of another spouse for her would fall to him, and her marriage could prove useful in cementing some new alliance.[76]

John of Salisbury continued, telling of the advice given to Louis VII by Thierry Galeran, a eunuch who was a trusted counselor of the king. Thierry warned Louis against allowing Eleanor to remain behind in Antioch because, quoting Ovid, "guilt under the guise of kinship could lie concealed." The quotation can be read as a veiled reference to Eleanor's incestuous relations with Raymond, but may be no more than a rhetorical flourish added by John, a scholar proud of his classical learning. Thierry further warned the king that should the crusade result in the loss of his wife, by her desertion or her theft by another, it would bring lasting shame on the French kingdom.[77] John of Salisbury took care to make no overt accusation of adultery, seeming to suggest no more than the queen's immoderate familial affection. If he intended to hint at Eleanor's unfaithfulness at Antioch, it is significant that he chose Thierry Galeran, as a eunuch an object of derision, whom he described as "a eunuch whom the queen had always hated and mocked." John comments that Thierry expressed his view "either because he hated the queen or because he really believed it, moved perchance by widespread rumour," leaving readers free to reject his testimony as unreliable.

John of Salisbury says little about Raymond's role in this matter, other than that as the king prepared to leave Antioch "the prince made every effort to keep [Eleanor]."[78] It is quite clear, however, that John held Raymond guilty for using the queen to pressure her husband into agreeing to his plan for battling the Turks, and for encouraging his niece's decision to seek a separation from her husband once he had failed to influence Louis through her. According to a chronicler writing in Palestine a generation after the events, Raymond became the manipulator of his niece, exploiting her as a means for wreaking his revenge on Louis. He writes that Raymond "resolved also to deprive him of his wife, either by force or by secret intrigue. The queen readily assented to this design, for she was one of the foolish women. She was . . . an imprudent woman and contrary to the king's dignity, disregarding her marriage vows, having forgotten the conjugal bed." He concludes by noting that Louis, becoming aware of Raymond's scheming, "hastened his departure and secretly left Antioch with his people."[79]

What is important about the Antioch incident is not so much what actually happened between Eleanor and her uncle, but what her contemporaries believed or wished to believe had occurred. For John of Salisbury and his clerical contemporaries, Eleanor's violation of the laws of marriage was not adultery with Raymond, nor her demand for an annulment of her marriage so much as her refusal to adopt the subservient role expected of a wife. She had gone against the submissiveness demanded of wives by a male-dominated Church and secular society. Her lack of discretion and obstinate behavior in pressing for her uncle's plan and disputing her husband's decision-making in military matters constituted infidelity by compromising her husband's royal dignity. It was already clear that Louis VII's queen had achieved a place among his chief counselors and had exercised influence over him before leaving France. Clerical authors of the twelfth century could not condone such behavior in a woman: only men were considered capable of acting rationally, and when they encountered women wielding power, they attributed their actions to irrational, passionate motives, not to practical political considerations. In their view, Eleanor was engaging in a pattern of misconduct, "a form of deliberate provocation . . . a will to manifest her independence" that they interpreted as infidelity, whether or not it amounted to outright adultery. For the queen's clerical critics, her conduct failed to conform with the Church's standard for the proper self-effacing role of a wife or a queen, and she acted as "a man . . . even as a king."[80]

Equally shocking to John was Louis VII's excessive love for Eleanor that drove him to surrender to her wishes and to agree to the separation that she desired. This made manifest the French king's ineffectual control over his strong-minded queen. For most medieval males, Louis's inability to resist his wife seemed to threaten a moral and political order that defined female activity in diplomacy and politics as "unwomanly" and a husband unable to master his wife as "unmanly." John, steeped in the Stoic philosophy revived in the twelfth-century Renaissance, held that a man must use his superior rational faculties to control his passions and attain an ideal life of moderation. He concluded that Louis's love for his wife "almost beyond reason" showed the king's dangerous lack of moderation in marital love, allowing passionate jealousy to overwhelm his masculine reason.[81]

Although John of Salisbury's condemnation of Eleanor does not imply actual adultery, rumors about the royal couple's troubled marriage soon spread in the camps of French soldiers bitter at the crusade's inglorious end. In the retelling of the queen's indiscreet behavior in Raymond's presence, "Gossiping courtiers apparently misconstrued and magnified her lively enjoyment of the visit."[82] Soon rumor magnified her deed from an impudent challenge to her husband's authority, disobeying the Church's teaching on wives' submission to their husbands, to outright adultery with her uncle. The incident at Antioch also figured in troubadour poetry, and verses probably composed in Palestine during the Second Crusade allude to Eleanor's alleged adultery. A song condemns women who lie with more than one man: "Better for her never to have been born than to have committed the fault that will be talked about from here to Poitou." The lyric is attributed to Cercamon, a troubadour who had been active at the court of Eleanor's father.[83]

Once the crusaders returned to France, hostile courtiers at Paris would spread tales of the queen's outrageous conduct at Antioch, displeased at her second marriage and Louis's loss of her duchy of Aquitaine to his Plantagenet vassal. Such stories circulated rapidly throughout western Europe, embroidered at each retelling.[84] English writers, even those writing a generation or more after the affair at Antioch, heard such rumors, but contented themselves with oblique references to their queen's alleged sexual impropriety. Richard of Devizes, an English chronicler favorably inclined toward Eleanor, writing in the 1190s when Eleanor was much respected as queen-mother, still managed to remind readers of her questionable conduct. Alongside a passage in his manuscript praising Eleanor, he placed a marginal note, marked off with wavy lines, which stated conspiratorially, "Many know what I would that none of us knew. This same queen, during the time of her first husband, was at Jerusalem [rightly Antioch]. Let no one say any more about it. I too know it well. Keep silent." Over a decade after the queen's death, Gerald of Wales, a frustrated courtier vitriolic in his loathing for the Plantagenet line, was surprisingly guarded, writing only, "It is enough to note how Eleanor, queen of France, conducted herself at first beyond the sea in the parts of Palestine."[85] Writing more than sixty-five years after the incident at Antioch, he was confident of his readers' ability to fill in the details, evidence of the survival of a powerful oral tradition.

ON TO JERUSALEM AND DAMASCUS

Faced with Eleanor's intractability and suspecting her uncle of complicity, Louis VII decided to put an end to his embarrassment by abandoning Antioch for Jerusalem. He left brusquely in the night without bidding his host farewell. By taking Eleanor away by force, the broken nature of their marriage was made clear to all; in John of Salisbury's words, "Their mutual anger growing greater, the wound remained, hide it as best they might."[86] After her abduction Eleanor must have spent much time pondering her alternatives. She doubtless rejected an attempt at flight back to Antioch and reconciled herself to waiting until her return to Paris with Louis for a resolution to her situation. She reasoned that her husband could not hold her a prisoner indefinitely, denying himself the possibility of remarrying and producing a male heir by a new wife, and ultimately she would succeed in securing an end to her marriage. She knew that some churchmen, among them Bernard of Clairvaux, had already questioned the lawfulness of their union. Meanwhile, Louis was following the counsel given by Suger, who wrote urging him "to conceal whatever rancor is in your heart, if there is any, until you return to your own kingdom . . . and you can attend to this and other matters."[87]

When news arrived in Jerusalem of the French monarch's departure from Antioch, the nobles, although elated, were anxious that Raymond might lure Louis back or that the count of Tripoli might persuade the king to stop with him. The Jerusalem nobility sent the patriarch of Jerusalem to meet Louis and escort him to the holy city. The arrival of the French king and his battered army in Jerusalem was a great occasion, and the people came out to greet them. He was welcomed with "all due honor and ceremony," and the patriarch and the Frankish nobles led him to the Holy Places "to the accompaniment of hymns and chants." Louis and Eleanor put aside their bitterness for a time to play their parts as king and queen on the ceremonial entry into Jerusalem, caught up in the intense spiritual feeling that devout Christians experienced on approaching the site of their Lord's passion. Presumably Eleanor accompanied Louis on foot as a pilgrim to the holy city's shrines. The queen was certainly kept under close, though no doubt discreet, surveillance, for overly harsh treatment would have aroused the resentment of her fellow Aquitanians among the crusading host.[88]

Louis went off to a great council summoned by the young king of Jerusalem, Baldwin III at Acre on 24 June 1148. Also attending was the German emperor, Conrad III, who had arrived from Constantinople, and their barons as well as Frankish nobles. Baldwin's mother Queen Melisende, a dominant figure in Christian Syria for many years, was also present, but it is unlikely that Eleanor accompanied her husband. She would probably have been left in Jerusalem to make penitential visits to the Holy Places in the company of dependably devout ladies or nuns. Notably absent from the assembly were two important princes of the crusader states: Raymond of Antioch and the count of Tripoli. Their refusal to attend meant that an alliance of all western Christian princes in the Holy Land would not be achieved. Eleanor's uncle was still infuriated at Louis for his behavior at Antioch, and he washed his hands of the Second Crusade.[89]

At Acre an agreement was reached to attack Damascus, the chief city of Syria and one of the most prestigious Muslim cities after Bagdad. It was a buffer between the Latin Christian principalities and the Turks, and previously it had maintained a truce with the Franks settled in the Holy Land. The Muslim rulers of Damascus found friendship with the Christian settlers useful for preserving their independence in the face of growing threats from the Turks, first Zengi and then his son Nur ad-Din. The princes debating at Acre doubtless hoped that conquering Damascus would prevent unification of all Muslim Syria under Nur ad-Din's rule, but their decision was unwise.

Louis VII and Conrad III of Germany, lacking understanding of eastern politics, could not see that threatening Damascus would simply cause the Damascenes to throw themselves into Nur ad-Din's arms, bringing about his domination of the city.[90]

The invading force consisted of crusaders and Frankish settlers under the joint command of Louis VII, the German emperor, and Baldwin III. The armies gathered in early July 1148 to cross the Golan Heights and march on Damascus. On 24 July, the crusading army reached the outskirts of Damascus, occupying the lush gardens and orchards surrounding it, and by evening they were at the city's walls. The invading army made camp in this cultivated area well supplied with food and water, but its leaders unwisely changed their camp's site to a much less defensible position. As soon as the crusaders engaged troops sent out from the city, the Damascenes lost no time in sending for assistance from Nur al-Din. Only a few days later, Turkish and Arab cavalry arrived from Aleppo and Mosul, leaving the Christians with no option but to withdraw from Damascus. On 28 July, five days after the crusaders' arrival, they packed up and headed back to Palestine, having suffered "a terrible humiliation."[91] They were harried by Turkish light cavalry all the way back into Frankish territory. When Eleanor learned of the crusaders' ignominious climb-down, the news was unlikely to have surprised her, for Louis's earlier leadership of the crusade had given her little reason to expect success from him. Her husband's shortcomings as a leader further undermined her respect for him and reinforced her desire to separate from him.

News of the disastrous defeat at Damascus reached the West before the end of 1148. Some found a moral explanation for the Second Crusade's failure, blaming it on the crusading warriors' sins, while others turned to conspiracy theories, accusing the Byzantines or Frankish settlers in the Holy Land of betraying the crusaders.[92] More clear-sighted observers such as Eleanor saw the fiasco as resulting from a failure of leadership. Whatever the explanation, the Second Crusade's failure was a blow to Louis VII's prestige. Later, when the French king was considering another crusade, the pope reproved him, reminding him that when "you yourself undertook the journey to Jerusalem without caution, you did not receive the expected result and hoped-for profit." He called on Louis to remember "how great a disaster and cost resulted . . . to the Church of God and to almost the entire Christian people. And the Holy Roman Church, since she had given you advice and support in this matter, was not a little weakened by this."[93]

Soon after the defeat at Damascus, Louis VII's army "melted away, impelled by want, until the king of the Franks remained almost alone." Many crusaders left almost at once, among them the king's own brother Robert of Dreux and also the count of Flanders, while Conrad III, alienated from Louis, delayed his departure until September.[94] Louis decided to remain in the Holy Land for several more months, crisscrossing the country to visit holy sites and to distribute money to religious houses. In addition to the shrines at Jerusalem hallowed by their association with Christ's passion, pilgrims wished to see Bethlehem, the Jordan river, and other places important in his life and preaching. The king was earning the esteem of the Christian settlers in Palestine as a sort of "lay-saint" with his pilgrimages and his alms, partially compensating for his failed reputation as general or diplomat. Louis's round of pilgrimage-going did nothing to improve his relations with his wife. The king was in penitential mode, practicing self-denial; and sexual intimacy, perhaps an expedient for easing a reconciliation between the unhappy pair, would have soiled in his eyes the spiritual exaltation that a pious pilgrim should be seeking.[95]

Months went by without Louis showing any sign of preparing to sail back to his kingdom. Perhaps he feared a double humiliation on his return to France, first for failure to lead the crusaders to victory in the Holy Land, but also for failings as a husband.[96] By the time that 1149 approached, Eleanor was probably growing more and more anxious to return to France and reach some favorable resolution of her marital problem. Suger sent pleading letters to the king, asking, "Why do you persist in enduring so many desperate ills overseas after your barons and nobles have returned?"[97] Louis's brother, Robert of Dreux, having returned to France soon after the Damascus debacle, circulated complaints about Louis's shortcomings as a leader, attributing the crusade's failure to his weakness and his piety. No doubt mixed with the news brought back from the Holy Land was gossip about Eleanor's alleged adultery at Antioch. Robert was showing signs of seeking to supplant his elder brother as monarch, and Suger worried that he posed a threat to the kingdom's security. Finally, after numerous letters from Suger begging him to return to his realm, Louis decided nine months after the Damascus expedition to leave the Holy Land. He lingered, however, long enough to experience the joy of celebrating Easter in Jerusalem at the actual sites of Christ's crucifixion and resurrection.[98] The departure was none too soon for his unhappy wife.

The Perilous Voyage Home

On 3 April 1149 Louis and Eleanor left Jerusalem for Acre to take ship for home. Normally travel by sea between Palestine and the West was safer and faster than the long overland journey, but Eleanor's voyage was to be far from normal. This was her first long sea voyage, and she could not have avoided some trepidation; a topic figuring in almost all travelers' tales was narrow escapes from terrible storms during voyages. The French king and queen were sailing with a Sicilian fleet of galleys designed for speed, not simple sailing ships. Some twelfth-century galleys in operation in the Mediterranean were up to 150 feet long with two tiers of rowing banks and as many as 100 rowers; the rowers were not slaves, but free men capable of taking up weapons if attacked by another vessel. The royal couple set sail in two ships, the king on board one vessel and his queen on another. Perhaps practical reasons dictated the choice of separate ships, or perhaps it was a sign of the couple's discord.[99] Although Louis professed his continued love for Eleanor and a desire to preserve their marriage, he probably saw that their unhappy marital relations would be less visible to others if they kept apart on the voyage. Eleanor was no doubt thoroughly sick of the sight of her husband and anxious to avoid continuous contact with him in a small vessel.

The fleet carrying Louis and his party passed through waters where conflict was raging between the Sicilian and Byzantine fleets, and their ships were caught up in a naval battle off the coast of the Peloponnesus. The king's vessel managed to escape capture, but Eleanor's was less lucky and fell into Greek hands. However, the Sicilians soon regained possession, either retaking it or regaining it from their captors at Emperor Manuel Komnenos's command.[100] Later during the two-month voyage, the royal couple's vessels were separated again, this time by storms, and they reached land at two distant points on the coasts of the Norman kingdom of Sicily. Louis landed on the Italian coast in Calabria at the end of July 1149 while, several days later, Eleanor found herself far from him at Palermo on the western shore of Sicily. The mischances of Eleanor's long voyage had left her exhausted and in ill-health. Agents of Roger II of Sicily escorted her to the royal palace where she could recuperate from her ordeal. Eleanor's condition may not have allowed her to appreciate the exotic charms of the palace complex at Palermo with its bizarre blend of Arabic, Byzantine, and western art and architecture. Louis, distressed over his queen's uncertain fate, did not learn until mid-August that she had landed safely at Palermo. Due to Eleanor's illness, it took some time for her to make her way across the island to the Italian mainland, and three weeks passed before she and her husband were reunited.[101]

Once Eleanor and Louis were together again in Italy, they moved on to Potenza to King Roger's court, where they were received with appropriate honors. It was probably there that Eleanor learned of her uncle Raymond of Antioch's death at the end of June 1149. In the course of repulsing an invasion by Nur ad-Din, the prince had launched an ill-conceived and suicidal attack on the Muslims that cost him his life. A chronicler writes that Raymond "fought valiantly, like the high-spirited and courageous warrior he was, but finally, wearied by the killing and exhausted in spirit, he was slain." Later his mutilated remains were discovered among the corpses on the battlefield with his head and right arm cut off. Tradition has it that his severed head was sent to the caliph at Bagdad.[102] It would have been easy for Eleanor to blame Raymond's death on Louis's refusal to join him in attacking Aleppo, adding another grievance against her husband.

Eleanor's capture by the Greeks, though brief and perhaps accidental, had given Louis new reason for mistrusting them, and in conversations with Roger the two found common ground in their mutual animosity toward the Byzantines. Louis was willing to consider organizing a new expedition with the double goal of aiding the Holy Land and also assisting Roger in expanding in the eastern Mediterranean at the Byzantines' expense.[103]

After a brief stay with the Sicilian monarch, the French king and queen left for a visit with Pope Eugenius III, going slowly because of Eleanor's ill-health. They stopped overnight at the famous abbey of Monte Cassino before joining the pope at Tusculum (today Frascati) just south of Rome on 9 or 10 October 1149. Eugenius rejoiced to see Louis and Eleanor safe after their long ordeal and, having been told of their troubled marriage by Suger, he was determined to reconcile them, taking on a somewhat surprising role as "marriage counselor."[104] The pope listened to each one separately, hearing differing versions of their estrangement and chiding both for their conduct. Passing judgment on the legitimacy of their marriage under Church law, he "forbade any further mention of their consanguinity: confirming their marriage, both orally and in writing, he commanded under pain of anathema that no word should be spoken against it and that it should not be dissolved under any pretext whatever." Louis was relieved by the pope's dispensing with canon law concerning consanguinity in their case. The thought that his marriage was unlawful in God's sight had troubled his over-scrupulous conscience, yet he had no wish to separate from Eleanor, whom he still loved "passionately, in an almost childish way." Eugenius saw to it that the couple slept in the same bed, and he personally directed its decoration "with priceless hangings of his own," hoping to create auspicious surroundings for their reconciliation. On the following days he tried by "friendly converse to restore love between them," and "heaped gifts upon them."[105]

In mid-October the couple took their leave of the pope after receiving his blessings for them and for the kingdom of France. Eleanor and Louis traveled overland up the Italian peninsula and passed over the obstacle of the Alps, taking about a month to reach the Île de France. After an absence of more than two years, they arrived in Paris by mid-November 1149.[106] Apparently Eugenius III's attempt at restoring harmony in their marriage had good effect; some time in the next year, the queen bore a second child, likely conceived during the couple's stopover at the papal court. Although Louis was reassured at new proof of the fertility of their marriage, he was disappointed that the infant was not a male heir to the French throne, but another girl. Their new daughter was named Adelicia, or sometimes put into English as Alice, though she may have been christened in 1150 as Aélith, the name of Eleanor's sister.[107]

Louis VII's crusade ended in failure and during the royal couple's long adventure his shortcomings as a leader in military and diplomatic matters became clear to all, especially Eleanor. The Second Crusade was costly for France. Special taxes imposed before the crusaders' departure could not cover the venture's costs, and several times during the long journey to the Holy Land Louis had to ask Abbot Suger to raise more money. Once in Jerusalem, Louis had to borrow money from the Knights Templars and Hospitallers while waiting for funds to reach him from France. For the French king's subjects, however, simply taking on the task of launching and leading a crusade gained him credit as a leader. Paradoxically, the disasters that befell Louis on crusade increased his subjects' respect for their king. His earnest piety while enduring so many travails somewhat counterbalanced his failure, enhancing his reputation as a Christian king; and thanks to Suger's wisdom, his kingdom had not suffered great damage during his long absence.[108]

Eleanor's knowledge of Louis's shortcomings as a leader further undermined her respect for him and reinforced her desire to separate from him. During the long journey from France to the Holy Land she had questioned Louis's decisions, and at Antioch following the harrowing march from Constantinople to the sea, her respect for her husband had reached a low point. She publicly challenged Louis's judgment and openly declared her dissatisfaction with her marriage. During the remainder of Eleanor's year in the Holy Land, once her uneasy marital situation became common knowledge, her misery only increased, and strains on her marriage stretched to breaking point. Not even the pope's attempted reconciliation and the birth of a second child could move Eleanor to give up hope of escaping from her unhappy marriage.

CHAPTER 4

A HUSBAND LOST, A HUSBAND
GAINED, 1149–1154

ELEANOR'S great adventure, filled with both marvelous sights and dreadful hardships, had changed and strengthened her. She would not give up her goal of ending her marriage, not even after the pope's dispensation of the impediment of the couple's consanguinity. Her unhappiness would not dissipate on her return to Paris.

If Eleanor's esteem for Louis had sunk as a result of the crusade, his subjects' regard for him had risen; the disasters endured on the dangerous journey to the Holy Land earned him added respect for piety and won over churchmen who had earlier deplored his clumsy interference in episcopal elections.[1] Although Louis found his kingdom well ordered on his return, thanks to the good work of Abbot Suger, he had much more than his wife's discontents to occupy him once back in France. Especially pressing was the problem of the count of Anjou's expanding power on the fringes of the French royal domain. Count Geoffrey Plantagenet was descended from minor castellans in the Loire valley who had created a remarkably effective state in the tenth and eleventh centuries. His aggressive Angevin ancestors had proved remarkably successful in adding to their landholdings, both by conquest and by marriage, doubling the territories under their rule and consolidating their lordships in the Loire valley—Anjou, Maine, and Touraine—into a single powerful principality. Geoffrey's own marriage represented another addition to the house of Anjou's power and prestige. His wife was the ambitious and headstrong Matilda, daughter of Henry I of England and widow of the German emperor Henry V. Matilda claimed the duchy of Normandy and the kingdom of England as her hereditary right. The couple would produce an assertive and able son, Henry Plantagenet, named after his paternal grandfather, to pursue his mother's claim to the English Crown.

By early 1152, Eleanor would achieve her goal of breaking off her marriage to the French monarch. Wasting no time before marrying again, she would take as her second husband young Henry Plantagenet, already duke of Normandy and count of Anjou, and their lives would become bound together for almost forty years. By a combination of hard fighting, diplomacy, and incredible good luck, Henry would win the English throne by the end of 1154, and Eleanor would become a queen for a second time in a new kingdom.

BACK IN FRANCE AND ESCAPING A FAILED MARRIAGE

When the unhappy Louis VII and Eleanor settled again in France, the king listened to his respected counselor Suger, who advised him to forgive and forget, and to resume a normal married life. The character of the couple's marriage had changed, however, and the partnership that it had been before the crusade could not be revived. Eleanor no longer had any role in governing the kingdom, and the post-crusade period of her marriage marks a decline in French queens' influence in royal governance that would continue after her departure from Louis's side.[2] With the death of Abbot Suger in January 1151, no one at court could give the king sound advice about his marital situation, and some courtiers worked to turn his mind toward setting aside his wife.[3] Eleanor herself had no desire to remain married to Louis; her wish to separate from her husband had remained fixed ever since he had taken her away forcibly from Antioch. Giving birth to a son would have done much to rehabilitate Eleanor's reputation, causing the French to overlook ugly gossip that had reached them from Antioch, but perhaps Eleanor was not utterly disappointed at the birth of another daughter, realizing that her failure to give birth to a son was likely to push Louis in the direction of a divorce.[4]

The king had matters of state as well as his unhappy marriage to occupy his mind, and he had to give attention to the security of his domains. The expanding power of Geoffrey Plantagenet of Anjou presented a serious threat, upsetting a balance of power that Louis had worked to achieve in northern France. Geoffrey of Anjou's wife, Matilda, the only surviving legitimate child of King Henry I of England, had been left a childless widow in Germany on the death of the emperor in 1125. Her father had summoned her to England to be groomed as his heir, and had browbeaten his barons into acknowledging her as his successor by 1127. The English king then looked for a suitable husband for Matilda, settling on Geoffrey le Bel, count of Anjou. She was Geoffrey's elder by a decade and her strong personality and powerful sense of her lofty status as the German emperor's widow ensured a stormy marriage. Yet she would bear her much younger and unloved second husband three sons, Henry, Geoffrey, and William. In 1139, Matilda had sailed to England, launching a struggle to wrest the kingdom from her cousin Stephen of Blois who had seized the throne on her father's death. Matilda's fight for recognition as Henry I's heir would lead to civil war in England and Geoffrey's invasion of Normandy. The possibility of their success bringing an enormous increase in Angevin power concerned Louis, in theory Geoffrey Plantagenet's lord.

Louis VII faced a confrontation with Geoffrey of Anjou by early 1150, only a few months after his return from the crusade. Although several factors contributed to conflict between the king and the prince, a central issue was Geoffrey's occupation of the duchy of Normandy on his wife's behalf in 1144 that led to disputes over lands lying between ducal territories and French royal lands along the Norman frontier. In 1150 Count Geoffrey decided to hand over Normandy to his eldest son Henry, but the new duke was in no hurry to present himself to the French king and do homage to him as his lord. The seventeen-year-old Henry Plantagenet would soon take up the claim to England's Crown that his mother had been pursuing since 1139 against Stephen of Blois. Should Henry become king of England, his combined power as king, duke of Normandy, and heir to his Angevin patrimony in the Loire valley would present a vastly increased threat to Capetian dominance within the French realm.

Faced with this challenge from Count Geoffrey and his son in Normandy, Louis VII responded by supporting the claim of Eustace, son of Stephen the English king, to the duchy and investing him with the ducal title, resulting in war on his Norman frontier against his Angevin foe. With Abbot Suger's guiding hand removed, the aged Bernard of Clairvaux, still determined to take center-stage in French affairs whenever possible, intervened to negotiate a truce.[5] The count and his eldest son came to the French court for peace talks in the summer of 1151, giving rise to a new complication in the royal marriage with Henry Plantagenet's entrance into Eleanor's life. During the Angevins' visit, Eleanor's first meeting with the young duke of Normandy took place, and she renewed her acquaintance with his father Geoffrey. The count, so handsome that his subjects called him "Geoffroi le Bel," had been among the French nobles on the Second Crusade, where he had proven to be one of the more valorous knights. According to some gossips, the French queen knew Geoffrey all too well.[6]

Tales of Eleanor's alleged adultery with Geoffrey le Bel were reported—or fabricated—many years after their meeting in Paris in writings first by Walter Map and later by Gerald of Wales, two courtiers who authored satirical accounts of Henry II's court. Alone among late twelfth-century English writers, the two accused Count Geoffrey of having "carnally known" Eleanor. If true, this rumor revealed the commission of both a sin and a heinous crime. In the

Church's teaching, a son's sharing a woman with his own father was considered a form of incest, and some churchmen would later label Eleanor and Henry's marriage as "incest of the second type."[7] Furthermore, a society based on ties of lordship saw sleeping with the wife of one's lord as a dreadful deed, tantamount to treason and threatening the legitimacy of the lord's lineage. The sharp-witted Map in his book *On the Frivolities of Courtiers* depicts Eleanor as a willing participant in an affair with the count, writing that "she was secretly reputed to have shared Louis's couch with [Henry's] father Geoffrey."[8]

A decade after Eleanor's death, the gossipy and opinionated Gerald of Wales, who had a copy of Map's work at his side to plagiarize, wrote *On the Instruction of Princes*. Gerald was at work on his book at a time when he was thoroughly disillusioned with Henry, his wife, and their sons, who had rebuffed his attempts to profit from their patronage. In a chapter devoted to tracing both Henry's and Eleanor's depraved ancestry, Gerald recalled her grandfather's "manifest and detestable adultery" with the viscountess of Châtellerault, declaring that Eleanor was cursed with the inherited licentiousness of her Poitevin lineage. Gerald, however, depicts Eleanor not as Geoffrey's willing partner as did Map, but as a victim of rape. He writes that the count of Anjou "several times ... forewarned his son Henry, admonishing and forbidding him to touch [Eleanor] in any manner, both because she was his lord's wife, and because she had been known by his own father." Gerald's purpose in this passage is to accuse Henry of having become the queen's lover during his Paris visit, complaining that Henry's own crime exceeded his father's: "King Henry presumed to pollute with adulterous copulation the so-called queen of France, as disseminated by rumor, and took her away from his own lord and joined with her in matrimony."[9] Of course, no evidence survives to prove or disprove the accusations of either Walter Map or Gerald of Wales, but they were no doubt embroidering on medieval legends and romances in which transgressing the incest taboo figured as a theme.[10]

It seems clear that Henry Plantagenet made a powerful impression on Eleanor and that she found him attractive, his youthful vigor and boldness a seductive contrast to her husband's meekness. The youth had only recently become a knight, dubbed by his great-uncle the Scottish king, and he had already proven himself "an intrepid warrior in the making," taking up his mother's fight for the English kingdom.[11] Eleanor would have found young Henry charming and courteous, for he had received schooling in courtly conduct first at his father's court at Angers, which has an important place in the history of courtliness, and later in England in the household of his uncle Robert, earl of Gloucester. Count Geoffrey, sharing a long tradition of learning among the counts of Anjou, made sure that young Henry studied with the best teachers available. When the boy first went to England in 1142 at age nine, he joined the household of his uncle, Earl Robert, who was known for his intellectual interests. Both father and uncle saw that the boy was "imbued with letters and instructed in good manners, as beseemed a youth of his rank," although they were fully capable of setting an example for him in knightly prowess as well as in courtesy and letters.[12] At age eighteen, young Henry's height was average, but he had a striking, though not handsome appearance, with a ruddy complexion and reddish hair, robust and powerful looking, with powerful limbs and a broad chest that gave evidence of strength and vigor.[13] Perhaps Eleanor had heard the legend of the Angevin line's descent from a demon-wife of an early count who always slipped out of church before the elevation of the host, and when forced to remain during that sacred moment, mysteriously vanished into thin air. If so, that diabolical ancestry simply intensified Henry's fascination for her; he appealed to her as an exciting, even dangerous personality compared to the lackluster Louis VII.[14]

Contemporaries commented on the favorable impression that young Henry made on the French queen, and her fascination with him may have been a bit too obvious to hostile courtiers.[15] Some modern writers go so far as to declare that Eleanor fell in love with the young duke of Normandy on meeting him in the summer of 1151.[16] Yet her decision to take Henry for her second husband would not be governed entirely by her heart, but by political calculation. Since he was already duke of Normandy and heir to the Angevin counts' Loire valley lands, the youth was a near neighbor to Poitou, and Eleanor would have seen advantages in marriage to him. In addition he was a pretender to the Crown of England, for which his mother had been fighting for years. At the time, however, Eleanor may not have given too much thought to the possibility of becoming queen of England through marriage to Henry; she is more likely to have seen him simply as suitable to rule Aquitaine at her side as duke.[17] Although Eleanor undoubtedly felt an attraction for the youthful Henry, she may have calculated that should they marry, she—his elder by nine years—could establish herself as the dominant partner, just as she had dominated Louis VII during the first years of their marriage.[18]

Despite the introduction of a new threat to his marriage to Eleanor, Louis VII's talks with the Angevin princes were successful. Count Geoffrey and his son realized that for victory in their struggle against the English king, Stephen of Blois, it was essential to prevent Louis from aiding Stephen, who was claiming Normandy for his son Eustace. They were willing to make generous concessions to Louis, confirming his rights in the Vexin, a disputed Norman border zone, and even conceding that young Henry should do homage to him before leaving Paris.[19] For earlier dukes, homage to the French monarch had only taken place on the Norman frontier as no more than a sign of an alliance of friends and equals, not the subordination of one to the other. No doubt

Geoffrey and the young duke felt homage at Paris was worthwhile if it bought the French king's acknowledgment of Henry's ducal title, and perhaps such a concession was more easily given because Henry had already made some arrangement with the king's wife.

Shortly after the two Angevin princes' visit to Paris, Louis VII warmed to the idea of the divorce long desired by Eleanor, and a decision to pursue a royal separation was reached apparently by mutual consent. It seems that the king was not unmoved by Henry's gallantry toward his queen or by her receptiveness toward the young duke's attentions during his August visit to the French court. Observers commented that Louis was "inflamed by a spirit of jealousy" in the last months of 1151.[20] It is not impossible that Eleanor had gone so far as to try provoking Louis's jealousy by flirting with Henry. Perhaps she hoped by such means to incite her husband to divorce her. In such private conversations as those that had inspired the king's suspicions at Antioch, it is not improbable that she and Henry gave hints to one another of a future together. In any case, warnings from Louis's courtiers that Eleanor's behavior was bringing on public ridicule, threatening to expose him as the laughing stock of all Europe, would have made an impact on the king's thinking.[21]

The first steps toward separating soon followed the Plantagenet princes' departure, and in the autumn of 1151 the royal couple made a tour of Aquitaine that "took on the appearance of a liquidation of the past."[22] Louis knew that a divorce would result in the Capetian monarchy's loss of Aquitaine, but apparently he was reconciled to losing the duchy, for he ordered fortifications demolished and his troops withdrawn in order to make way for Eleanor's men. The couple held their last Christmas court together at Limoges, then moved on to Saint-Jean-d'Angély early in 1152. After presiding at their last court together, they parted company, with the king heading back to Paris and Eleanor staying behind in her duchy, probably moving on to Poitiers.

A ROYAL MARRIAGE ANNULLED

In March 1152 a council of French prelates and nobles assembled at Beaugency in the county of Blois to declare the marriage of Louis VII and Eleanor invalid on grounds of consanguinity. Although their legal separation is often termed a divorce, in the Middle Ages there was no such thing in the modern sense of the word. When the word divorce was used, it either meant an annulment—a judgment that no true marriage had ever existed—or a concession allowing a couple to separate and live apart, but without the right to remarry. Because canon law decreed marriages unlawful if the couple shared a common ancestor within the past seven generations, claiming consanguinity was a common excuse for dissolving aristocratic marriages when the actual reason was incompatibility or childlessness. By the mid-twelfth century, however, the Church was elevating marriage to the status of a sacrament, and it stressed strongly the indissolubility of all marriages. As a result, it was becoming less accommodating in annulling marriages on grounds of consanguinity. As we have seen, the pope had refused to sanction the royal couple's separation in 1149; however, the consanguineous nature of their marriage was no secret, as Bernard of Clairvaux had angrily declared during one of his quarrels with Louis. The couple were related within four degrees on Louis's side and within five degrees on Eleanor's. They shared a common ancestor in King Robert II of France, Louis's great-great-grandfather and Eleanor's great-great-great-grandfather.[23] Yet in Louis's urgency to produce a son, he would not hesitate to enter into two more consanguineous marriages, both to brides more closely related to him than Eleanor. Within two years, he would wed a second spouse, Constance of Castile, and then in 1160 a third wife, Adele of Champagne, less than six weeks after the death of Constance, who had not given him a son.[24]

Despite the pope's earlier counsel, Louis requested the archbishop of Sens to convene a council to consider the legitimacy of his marriage to Eleanor. In attendance were the archbishops of Reims, Rouen, and Bordeaux as well as a number of bishops and some leading lay nobles. At that time, papal courts staffed by professional canon lawyers had not yet overpowered other ecclesiastical tribunals, and such councils were still a common means of settling powerful persons' disputes in matters of Church law. Both English and French chroniclers relate that Louis's relatives appeared at Beaugency, swearing with "a contrived oath" or "the oath that they had promised," bearing witness to the couple's kinship within the degrees prohibited by the Church.[25]

It is clear that however much Eleanor of Aquitaine may have desired a separation, the deciding factor was Louis VII's conviction that she could not give him a son. He felt strongly the Capetian dynasty's mission to be a most Christian monarchy, and he knew that his lack of a male heir to succeed him could undermine its stability and even threaten the French kingdom's security. Eleanor was the first Capetian queen in a century and a half to have reached the age of thirty, and fifteen years of married life, without having already given birth to a son. The disputed succession and resulting civil war in England after Henry I's death, still unsettled in 1152, was a stark warning to Louis of the necessity of having a son to succeed him. Louis knew that the French realm's security demanded an undoubted legitimate male heir.[26]

Louis had always been easily led, and his own relatives as well as malicious courtiers were eager to separate him from Eleanor. They took advantage of the death of the influential Suger, who had favored preserving the marriage, to sway the king toward divorce. Louis's counselors did not hesitate to point out that Eleanor's conduct arousing periodic scandalous gossip was incompatible with her dignity as queen. A weightier argument for Louis, however, was the fact that the queen had given him no son, and all assumed that the fault lay with her, for both folklore and twelfth-century medical teaching held that a child's mother determined its sex. Additionally, members of Louis's clerical entourage encouraged him to view Eleanor's infertility as a sign of divine disapproval of the marriage. In his youth, the Church Fathers' rhetoric tending toward denunciation of all sexual activity had turned him toward over-scrupulous religiosity.[27] Churchmen may have informed Louis of canon lawyers' finding that sex between spouses who felt no affection for each other must be classed as adultery, convincing him that sexual relations with the unloving Eleanor were sinful.

Furthermore, medieval medical faculties followed ancient Greek science in teaching that women only become pregnant if they experience pleasure during sex. Supposedly prostitutes failed to conceive because they took no pleasure in the sex act. Louis could easily be persuaded that if Eleanor no longer loved him, then he could no longer impregnate her since she derived no delight from the conjugal act.[28] Like Henry VIII of England almost 400 years later, Louis came to see his lack of male offspring as proof that God was frowning on his marriage and denying it divine blessing in spite of a papal dispensation. The birth of their second daughter confirmed this thinking and made invalidation of the marriage inevitable.[29]

At Beaugency, the bishop of Langres raised the question of Eleanor's adultery as a cause for dissolution of the marriage, but it was not considered. The bishop, who had accompanied Eleanor and Louis on their crusade, certainly knew of the Antioch affair, but his close association with Bernard of Clairvaux raises suspicion of his motive. He was Bernard's cousin, one of his early companions at Clairvaux, where he became prior, and he owed his election as bishop of Langres to his famous cousin, who had discredited the former bishop and caused the cancellation of his election. Bernard championed Louis's divorce; he considered Eleanor incorrigible in her immoral conduct, corrupted by her ancestry. He may have preferred that a question of morality be put forward as grounds for the separation, aiming at making Eleanor unsuitable as wife to any other prince.[30] Geoffrey du Loroux, archbishop of Bordeaux, devoted to Eleanor and the Aquitanian ducal line, urged that the council only examine the couple's consanguinity, and their relationship within the prohibited degrees was quickly confirmed. The archbishop proceeded to pronounce the official annulment of the couple's marriage that he had celebrated in his cathedral fifteen years earlier.[31] The council also decreed that since the couple had married in good faith, their two daughters' legitimacy was not in question. Custom concerning property was followed, and Eleanor's right to retain her own family lands that she had brought to the marriage was affirmed. Louis did make some effort to preserve their two daughters' rights as heirs to the duchy of Aquitaine, and it was not until 1154 that he finally gave up all claim and abandoned his title of duke of Aquitaine.[32]

After the council at Beaugency annulled Eleanor's marriage, she wished to return to her own lands in Poitou as soon as possible. She had to leave behind her two daughters, Marie, aged seven, and little Adelicia, who was only eighteen months old. No doubt Eleanor felt deep sorrow at parting from her children, but she knew that losing them was inevitable, since law and custom decreed that children were their father's property. There was no possibility of her having custody of them or visiting them, and after the annulment it is doubtful that she ever saw them again. The girls would have little more contact with their father. Soon Louis would affiance them to the two sons of the count of Blois-Champagne (d.1152) to strengthen political alliances essential for countering the growing Angevin threat.[33] A year or two after their mother's departure, the young girls were sent off to their future husbands whose family would supervise their upbringing. While on crusade, Louis had promised his elder daughter to the heir to the county of Champagne, Henry the Liberal, who had impressed the king in fighting against the Turks in Anatolia. Marie's betrothed sent her to the abbey of Avenay in Champagne, near Épernay, to be raised by the nuns, and she remained there for eleven years until she reached marriageable age. Her younger sister may have been sent to Avenay as well. In 1154 Louis would give Adelicia to Henry's brother Theobald v, heir to their father's county of Blois, and they would be married in the early 1170s.[34]

ESCAPE TO POITOU AND A STUNNING SECOND MARRIAGE

Almost at once, Eleanor set out for Poitiers with some members of her household, and Poitevin nobles who had attended the council formed an escort to accompany their duchess.[35] She was in danger of being abducted and forced into a new marriage by some nobleman eager to acquire her inheritance. The former queen knew that she could not remain single for long and that unless she acted quickly to take a husband of her own choosing, she would soon find herself married against her will to a stranger. She had two narrow escapes during her flight from Beaugency: first from the count of Blois and Chartres, Theobald v, later to become her younger daughter's husband, who tried to take her as she traveled past Blois; then she had to evade another attempted abduction by Geoffrey Plantagenet, Henry's sixteen-year-old younger brother. He planned to capture her at Port-de-Piles on the border of Touraine and Poitou, but "warned by her angels" at Tours she took a different road into her own county. As soon as Eleanor was safely at Poitiers, she wrote to Henry that she was free to marry. Modern writers explain her hasty marriage almost entirely in emotional terms, as due either to her falling in love or to her quest for a younger man more vigorous than her former husband. They ignore her vulnerability once she left her former husband's court: a woman alone and in need of a protector—both of her person and of her duchy. She had little choice but to find a new husband capable of defending her and her lands as quickly as possible.[36]

As heir to the largest of the French duchies and as a former queen, Eleanor had few options in marriage partners, but she had to take the initiative in making a new marriage before being forced into wedding someone not of her own choosing. In an act almost unheard of in her time, Eleanor acted independently without consulting her kin or other counselors. Of all available princes, Henry Plantagenet, although nine years her junior, "came nearest to being a worthy partner for a discarded queen."[37] Everything points toward first plans for their marriage having been laid during his August 1151 visit to the French court. Her true feelings toward the Angevin heir cannot be known, but she must have found his youth and ardor appealing. Something definitely happened between the French queen and Henry during the August visit, and it had a dual effect: it resolved Louis on a separation, and Henry, aware of the political advantage a marriage to Eleanor would bring him, determined to have her as his wife.[38]

When Eleanor's message that she was free to marry reached Henry on 6 April 1152, he was at Lisieux in Normandy preparing to sail off on another expedition, resuming his struggle to take the English throne. The young duke of Normandy was now count of Anjou as well, since his father Geoffrey had drowned in September 1151 while taking a swim during his return journey from Paris. An English chronicler writing a generation later notes that, after the council of Beaugency countenanced Eleanor's separation from her first husband, she "with unlawful license soon sent for her new partner."[39] Another tells of Henry Plantagenet's hastening to Poitiers: "The duke indeed allured by the nobility of that woman and by desire for the great honors belonging to her, impatient at all delay, took with him a few companions, hastened quickly over the long routes, and in little time obtained that marriage which he had long desired."[40] Barely two months after the annulment of Eleanor's first marriage, she had a second husband, the future Henry II of England.

Eleanor and Henry's marriage took place in the cathedral at Poitiers in a hastily organized ceremony on 18 May 1152. Preparations for the wedding had been made in secret for fear of attempts to stop it, and the simple service with only a few intimates present hardly matched the couple's lofty status.[41] No doubt the advantage that the marriage would bring Henry was the dominant consideration in his desire to wed Eleanor. It was more than the prestige of the title of duke of Aquitaine that made Eleanor an appealing bride for the young count-duke. The Angevin counts had a long record of trying to expand their power into Poitou, and in the tenth and eleventh centuries they had occupied portions of northern Poitou and the Saintonge stretching along the Atlantic coast and the Charente river. Indeed, the counts of Anjou still held two castles, Loudun and Mirebeau, that lay within Poitou's borders with the counts of Poitou technically as their lords. It has been pointed out that "The union of Anjou and Aquitaine was not only workable, but the culmination of two centuries of Angevin pressure." Furthermore, Henry saw that Poitou in some other powerful lord's possession would threaten Anjou and all his Loire valley lands. He could see more immediate practical advantages too, for possessing Poitou would enable him to deal more effectively with plots by his younger brother Geoffrey, who was count of Nantes.[42]

The young duke of Normandy should have anticipated trouble with his putative lord over his lands, his new wife's ex-husband, Louis VII; as an English chronicler noted, his marriage to Eleanor "was the cause and origin of great hatred and discord between the French king and the duke." It cannot be known whether or not Louis was surprised at Eleanor's quick remarriage but he was certainly enraged when he heard the news, and he never gave up his conviction that her new marriage was somehow displeasing to God.[43] He had good reason for bitter resentment and remorse at losing his wife and her great duchy to such a powerful enemy as the young duke of Normandy, and he must have pondered the possibility of Henry ruling not only both the county of Anjou and Normandy, but one day making good his mother's claim to the kingdom of England. Even without a royal title, Henry Plantagenet had become the largest landholder in France, surpassing Louis in possessions, and his control over all western France seemed to block any expansion of Capetian domains in that direction. If Louis could have seen into the future, he might have found some consolation in the fact that Aquitaine was too large and amorphous, too far from Henry's center of power for him or his sons ever to assimilate it.[44] The French king put no trust in soothsayers, however.

A pressing problem for Louis, faced with this apparently unexpected situation, was safeguarding his two daughters' rights. He had refused to surrender his ducal title, continuing to use it for his children's sake as Eleanor's heirs and only renounced it formally in August 1154, when he and Henry came to terms.[45] One chronicler stated the issue succinctly: "When King Louis heard of [the marriage], he was greatly incensed against Duke Henry, for he had two daughters by the aforesaid Eleanor, who would be disinherited if she should bear a son by any other husband."[46] Louis seems to have believed that Eleanor had no right to marry without first taking counsel with him and that Henry, her chosen spouse, had no right to take her as his wife without consulting him, his lord. Already in England and Normandy, lords' prerogative of controlling their vassals' marriages was customary, but this was not yet accepted in other regions as one of the privileges of lordship. Yet Louis VII could not avoid taking some action if he intended to enforce what he considered his right as lord, and he convened a great council to garner support for an attack on Normandy. It is unlikely that Louis actually summoned Henry to appear before his royal court and, if he did, it is certain that the young count-duke refused to comply. Louis would have realized that Henry's offense in marrying Eleanor was not fixed firmly enough in feudal custom to justify a formal decree of confiscation of his lands.[47] Yet the French monarch had to make some attempt to forestall Eleanor's new husband from consolidating his power over western France, and he organized a coalition that prevented Henry's returning to England in the summer of 1152. Louis's alliance could accomplish little more than harassing Henry along his Norman frontiers and encouraging his younger brother Geoffrey's short-lived revolt in Anjou. Nonetheless, these hostilities mark the beginning of over a half-century of Capetian–Angevin conflicts as first Louis and then his son, Philip II Augustus, attempted to assert royal supremacy over the lands of Eleanor, Henry, and their sons that theoretically lay under French lordship.

In marrying Eleanor, Henry Plantagenet apparently felt concern neither for his bride's questionable fertility during her first marriage nor for her age; as she was approaching thirty, she seemed to her contemporaries to be bordering on middle age. After undergoing no more than three pregnancies as the French king's wife, Eleanor's second marriage would prove remarkably fruitful in sons, a fact that infuriated Louis, but must have pleased her greatly. She would produce eight or nine children by Henry within thirteen years: five sons—and possibly a sixth who died in early infancy—three of whom lived to be crowned kings of England, and three daughters, all of whom married important foreign princes.[48] Eleanor gave birth to her last two children, Joanne and John, when she was over forty. She was a remarkably healthy woman to have survived numerous childbirths in an age when giving birth was a major cause of women's deaths.

Eleanor could be assured of her new husband's virility, for Henry already had illegitimate offspring by the time of his marriage, as was not uncommon among scions of aristocratic families. He acknowledged a bastard son, Geoffrey Plantagenet, whose mother, according to the gossip Walter Map, was a harlot named Ykenai or Hikenai who had duped the young king into admitting that he was her child's father. Whatever Henry's reason, he was willing to acknowledge young Geoffrey and to welcome him into the royal household soon after winning the English Crown.[49] Henry had another illegitimate child born before wedding Eleanor, a daughter named Matilda, whom he would install in the late 1170s as head of Barking Abbey, a convent in Essex. Matilda's predecessor as abbess of this rich and aristocratic house was Thomas Becket's

sister, appointed in 1173 as part of the king's restitution to the martyred archbishop's family.[50] Henry's bride, brought up in the sophisticated atmosphere
of the Poitevin court, would not have found it shocking that her new husband
had fathered illegitimate sons in his youth. Toleration for the offspring of aristocratic youths sired while "sowing their wild oats" was greater than for children resulting from a married man's adulterous affair. Nor would a bastard's
presence in his household have upset her unduly, for she knew that such illegitimate sons frequently found places in their father's household. Indeed,
young Henry's bastard son sent an encouraging signal to Eleanor that he
might give her sons.

Despite Eleanor's need for a protector after her divorce, her speedy remarriage two months later to Henry Plantagenet added fodder for rumors of
serial adulteries, and talk spread of the former French queen's scandalous
conduct. Born in the camps of French crusaders bitter at their expedition's
inglorious end, it was nurtured by courtiers at Paris displeased at her second
marriage that had resulted in their king's loss of her duchy to his Angevin
vassal. Verses by troubadour poets that "play on or echo rumours and scan-
dalised gossip about topical events" signal the impact made by the affair at
Antioch. Two poets, Cercamon and his pupil Marcabru, formerly at the court
of Eleanor's father, composed lyrics condemning a lady who takes more than
one lover that can be read as "distant echoes" of the queen's alleged misconduct.[51] Gossip would follow Eleanor from Antioch to England, where it
metastasized into more scurrilous tales later set down in rumor-mongering
courtiers' writings.[52] It was not only courtiers who were scandalized by their
new queen: a number of English churchmen deemed Eleanor's marriage to
Henry sinful. Some rejected their new queen's second marriage as bigamous
because they considered the Beaugency council's declaration annulling her
marriage to Louis as unlawful. English clerics also denounced the marriage as
incestuous, just as her first one had been, contravening canon law on marriage
within prohibited degrees of kinship. Scandalmongers condemned Eleanor's
marriage to Henry as doubly incestuous, accepting gossip that she had slept
with Count Geoffrey, Henry's father, while still Louis VII's queen. Still others
labelled the marriage felonious because Henry had entered into it for the
purpose of opposing his lord, King Louis.[53]

Two monastic writers, William of Newburgh and Gervase of Canterbury,
depicted Eleanor as taking the initiative in her marriage to Henry. Both were
surprised by a woman arranging her own marriage alliance, a rare occurrence
in the twelfth century, although their impression was none too favorable. Both
presumed to know Eleanor's mind, although they were writing a generation
after the events. Newburgh, profoundly anti-woman like other clerics and
believing that a woman's libido was stronger than a man's, ascribes Eleanor's

quick remarriage to her wish for a new, more virile partner. He writes that after Louis and Eleanor's return from the East, "the former love between them gradually grew cold," and he reports rumors that Eleanor "even during her marriage to the king of France . . . longed to be wed to the duke of Normandy as one more congenial to her character," and that she "eventually obtained the marriage which she desired."[54] Gervase of Canterbury comments that after the divorce Eleanor returned to Poitou, "disdaining [Louis's] decrepit Gallic embraces." Gervase also portrays Eleanor as the initiator of her marriage so soon after Louis VII's repudiation of her; according to him, "by means of a messenger sent secretly to the duke, she announced that she was free and dissolved [from her marriage] and stimulated the duke's mind to contract matrimony." Yet Gervase also admits that Henry "had long desired" the marriage, "above all driven by the desire to possess all the honors that belonged to her."[55]

These chroniclers, following conventional thinking, attribute personal, emotional, or sexual motives to Eleanor's quick marriage to Henry. As one commentator notes, "It is striking that chroniclers consistently avoid any suggestion that Eleanor could have been driven to divorce Louis and marry Henry by any other motivation than sexual desire. [They] consistently sexualize women's power to depict it as a disorderly, uncontrollable force and to discredit it."[56] They take no note of Eleanor's vulnerability as a woman alone and without a protector in a masculine society where single women were expected to be under a male's guardianship. Romantically inclined biographers see her marriage to Henry as a love match, or at least find strong sexual attraction motivating them. No doubt Eleanor did find Henry, aged nineteen, more attractive than Louis, whom she considered insufficiently virile, more monk than monarch, but physical attraction—or lust, in contemporary churchmen's opinion—was certainly not the chief factor in their marrying. The marriage resembled closely that of Henry's parents: the much younger Geoffrey le Bel taking as his wife the older, previously married Empress Matilda, and no one could suspect their marriage of being a love match. It had been the work of Matilda's father, guided by dynastic concerns.

DUCHESS OF AQUITAINE AND OF NORMANDY, COUNTESS OF ANJOU

During the brief period between Eleanor's return to Poitiers and her departure for England to become Henry II's queen, she wielded full authority as duchess of Aquitaine. Two documents issued by her at Poitiers in May 1152 only a week after her marriage to Henry, confirming grants by "her great-grandfather, grandfather and father" to two important Poitevin religious houses, Montierneuf and Saint-Maixent, reveal her acting independently without her new husband's approval. The two charters show her breaking with the Capetian phase of her life and asserting the same authority over her own duchy that her ducal predecessors had wielded. In one, she refers specifically to her divorce from Louis VII, declaring that she was "separated from the king by the Church's judgment." She states that she had given a forest to Saint-Maixent Abbey following her former husband's wishes, "almost without wishing to," that is, not of her free will. Now, however, she was taking the forest back into her own hand and regranting it to the monks "with good grace." The statement seems designed to accent that she was acting entirely on her own authority, separating her gift to the monks from any connection with Louis's authority over Aquitaine.[57]

Eleanor acted without her new husband witnessing or confirming her acts, and Henry is mentioned in only one of the charters and then only in the dating clause, "in the time of Henry ruler of the Poitevins and Angevins," since he had not yet assumed the title "duke of Aquitaine." Possibly Henry did not wish to provoke further Louis VII who continued to use the ducal title for over two years after his divorce. For whatever reason, Henry hesitated to adopt the ducal title until spring of 1153 while on an expedition to England.[58] Why Henry delayed assuming the title until he was in England is a mystery; possibly he saw it as useful there for impressing the English opposition with his powerful position as duke of France's largest duchy. In August 1153, the birth of a son to Eleanor would make the succession of her daughters by Louis a non-issue.

Added evidence for Eleanor's independence just after her new marriage comes from the witnesses to her charters, for they included solely members of her own entourage and no one from Henry's household. Among those attending her court were her uncles Hugh II, viscount of Châtellerault, and Ralph de Faye, and members of the Chabot, Maingot de Melle, and Mauléon families, longtime officials for the Poitevin rulers, as well as Saldebreuil, constable of the duchess's household. These names would recur again and again on Eleanor's documents, and they would remain her trusted counselors and officials, especially her uncle Ralph de Faye. About this time, Eleanor further cemented ties with her uncle the viscount, granting him lands and hunting rights. Two of the charters declare that they were "given by the hand of Bernard, my chancellor," who had become head of her secretariat on her return to Poitiers, if he had not been in her service earlier in Paris.[59]

A few days after issuing the charters for Poitevin monastic houses, Eleanor visited Fontevraud Abbey, the famed double monastery for men and women that had an abbess as its head. Fontevraud lay in Angevin territory, but fell under the bishop of Poitiers' authority and had longstanding ties to the Poitevin ruling line as well as to the Angevin counts. Like the two other charters, this one conveys the message of Eleanor's lawful authority as duchess, and she grandly describes herself as "countess of the Poitevins by grace of God." The document confirming the grants of "my father and my ancestors . . . and particularly this donation . . . that my lord the king of the Franks, who was then my husband, and I had given," again shows her now making former actions by Louis into her own. She is also expressing the lawfulness of her separation and remarriage, stating that she acted "After separating from my lord Louis, the very illustrious king of the Franks, because we were related, and having been united in marriage to my lord Henry, the very noble consul of the Angevins." Then the charter takes a surprisingly personal tone, declaring that "impelled by divine inspiration, I have wished to visit the assembly of holy virgins in Fontevraud, and what was in my mind I have been able to accomplish with the help of God's grace. Therefore guided by God, I have come to Fontevraud and crossed the threshold of these virgins' chapter house."[60]

Eleanor's statements in this document are "moving, dramatic, and unconventional," and with their emphasis on God's role in motivating her action, they illuminate personal feelings expressed in few other charters. Also unusual is the dating clause, in the reign of Henry "governing the empire [*imperium*] of the Poitevins and the Angevins," perhaps an expression of the couple's ambition.[61] This document is Eleanor's first expression of special feelings for Fontevraud, but few other significant gifts to the abbey followed for years. Her visit may not have resulted entirely from her own inspiration, for her new husband must have wished his bride to meet his aunt Matilda who was abbess there. Eldest daughter of Henry's grandfather, Count Fulk v of Anjou, Matilda had followed her father's wishes in entering Fontevraud in 1122, two years after her young husband, the son and heir of Henry i of England, had drowned in the disastrous sinking of the *White Ship*. Throughout Abbess Matilda's life and beyond, her nephew would prove to be one of Fontevraud's greatest patrons and protectors.[62]

To give Eleanor's authority visual representation, she had a new seal made to affix to these documents bearing only her titles of duchess of Aquitaine and countess of Poitou, omitting any title that had come to her through marriage. For a short time in spring 1152, Eleanor of Aquitaine had more power than she had ever held before, and she would never be so powerful again until she was a widow. Soon she had another seal, however, one that bore the new titles resulting from her marriage to Henry Plantagenet: not only "duchess of the Aquitanians" but also "duchess of the Normans and countess of the Angevins." The added titles, deriving entirely from Eleanor's position as Henry's wife, are indicative of her dependence on him, and soon her brief independent authority over Poitou would begin to erode steadily.[63]

After their wedding, Eleanor and Henry spent less than a month together before he headed to Normandy for an expedition to England to pursue his claim to its Crown. He was at Barfleur preparing to set sail when he learned of an attack on the Norman frontier by a coalition assembled by Louis VII. The French king, incensed by Eleanor's marriage, marched on her new husband's duchy in alliance with Eustace of Boulogne, eldest son of Henry's rival King Stephen. Louis's coalition included his own brother Robert of Dreux, also the count of Champagne and the Plantagenet prince's younger brother Geoffrey, angered at Henry on account of his paltry inheritance. While Geoffrey undertook to raise Anjou in revolt against his elder brother, Louis and his allies breached the Norman border and laid siege to one of Henry's frontier castles. Henry left Barfleur on 16 July and made a forced march toward the allied army, causing Louis and his friends to retreat. By the end of August 1152, Henry was free to march on Anjou to confront his younger brother; he managed to rally to his side young Geoffrey's principal supporters, forcing him to capitulate. By autumn, with the war ended and a truce in place, the count-duke was ready to rejoin his bride in Aquitaine.[64]

Following the return of Eleanor's new husband to her side, they set off on a circuit of her lands to acquaint him with his new duchy, and Henry showed his intention to be a forceful ruler. Among the cities that they visited in autumn 1152 was Limoges, location of the great monastery of Saint-Martial. The monks and the townspeople of Limoges welcomed their duchess and their new duke, marching in solemn procession to Saint-Martial; but conflict soon arose, setting off Henry's volatile temper.[65] The abbot of Saint-Martial proved unwilling to offer Henry the funds traditionally afforded to visiting dukes of Aquitaine in hospitality, giving the excuse that Henry had not actually stayed at the abbey, preferring to lodge in his tent or at the viscount's castle. Outraged by the townspeople's violence against his entourage, Henry severely punished them in reprisal; before leaving, he ordered the city's recently constructed walls leveled and a bridge over the River Vienne broken down. This was not the last time that Limoges inflamed Henry's temper, and he would destroy the city's walls twice more in 1156 and 1183.[66] Eleanor's role in this incident is unknown, but her previous husband's strong-armed actions in Poitou early in their marriage suggest that she would have urged on young Henry. No doubt she made him aware, as she had Louis VII, of her sense that the Poitevins needed a strong hand to keep order.

Henry would soon find that as duke of Aquitaine his authority was more limited than in Anjou or Normandy. During Eleanor's childhood, the dukes' power had come chiefly from the prestige of their office, the force of their personality, and from personal bonds of friendship with the aristocracy of Aquitaine and Gascony. The great men acknowledged only the vaguest ties of ducal lordship, their homage often signifying little more than vague promises of friendship and their obligations either ambiguous or unacknowledged.

Louis VII had sought to enforce ducal supremacy, subjecting the nobility through stronger ties of vassalage, though inconsistently and with little success. The French king's efforts had failed, for he never followed through on his vigorous actions in his first years as king-duke. His desultory assertiveness was insufficient to instill fear in the Poitevin nobles, but was enough to arouse their resentment. Henry as count of Anjou held lordships within the borders of Poitou, and he had a better knowledge of the county than had Eleanor's first husband, despite the county's differences from his ancestral Angevin lands and an even greater contrast with Normandy. In pursuing a goal of mastering Aquitaine's aristocracy, Henry's Poitevin policy resembled Louis's. Like his predecessor, he saw violence as the only means of forcing obedience on the turbulent nobility. The result of his effort to impose direct rule over Eleanor's possessions would be repeated cycles of revolts by the nobles followed by harsh repression.

Within Eleanor's lands, her new husband would encounter difficulty in asserting public powers that he enforced effectively in his duchy of Normandy or to a lesser extent in Anjou. The numbers of castles belonging to Eleanor as duchess illustrate differing degrees of mastery over the ducal domains. While Henry Plantagenet held some thirty castles in Normandy and ten in his domains in Anjou, Maine, and Touraine, Eleanor possessed no more in all her vast duchy of Aquitaine. As countess of Poitou, she held perhaps thirty castles in Poitou proper and in Aunis-Saintonge, including citadels of important towns. In large swathes of territory—the edges of Poitou, the Angoumois, Limousin, Périgord, or Auvergne, and almost the whole of Gascony beyond the Bordelais—Eleanor held neither castles nor estates as duchess.[67] Her predecessors as dukes had found themselves incapable of imposing their authority over many of the Gascon lords, and they often neglected to use their title "duke of Gascony."[68]

Late in 1152 Henry left Poitou again, taking with him the now pregnant Eleanor; they stopped at Angers, then moved on to Rouen in Normandy. Henry prepared to return alone to England for another campaign, and after long delays due to winter storms on the English Channel, he finally set sail around 13 January 1153. He would remain in England throughout the year, not returning to his French lands until March 1154. This was the first of many times when Eleanor and Henry would find themselves separated by the English Channel for long periods. Henry left his bride behind at Rouen with her mother-in-law, the formidable Empress Matilda.[69] In 1148, after struggling for a decade for her English inheritance, the empress had settled in Normandy, turning over to her eldest son the task of continuing the fight to dislodge Stephen of Blois from the kingdom of England.

It would seem that Matilda and her daughter-in-law were too much alike to have gotten along well, for their lives paralleled one another in several aspects.

Both had married prestigious monarchs at a very young age and had made second marriages to younger husbands of less exalted rank that proved to be turbulent. Yet no hint surfaces of conflict between Eleanor and her new mother-in-law, and in fact they were not often enough in one another's presence for serious rivalry to develop. Perhaps Eleanor's earlier experience with Louis VII's mother had made her cautious and hopeful of avoiding conflict. She had resented Adelaide of Maurienne's influence over her first husband, and she could recognize that Henry Plantagenet was also very close to his mother. Empress Matilda would remain a powerful influence on her son until her death in 1167; indeed, he took pride in being called Henry fitz Empress.

Eleanor doubtless saw in Matilda a woman similar to the great ladies among her own ancestors whose exploits she learned of in childhood. Furthermore she could easily have seen a reflection of herself when she contemplated her new mother-in-law's life. Both were independent-minded women aware of their exalted lineage, sharing a self-assurance rare among women of their day, certain of their ability to wield power. Matilda, like Eleanor, was subjected to criticism from misogynist churchmen, though the empress had not earned their disapproval for alleged sexual indiscretions, but for masculine traits reckoned unnatural for a woman. She had dared to undertake an armed struggle to replace her cousin, Stephen of Blois, on the English throne.[70]

After Henry's expedition had left for England, Eleanor's movements cannot be traced; possibly she remained at Rouen with Matilda or perhaps returned to Poitou to deal with affairs in her county. It seems probable, however, that she left Normandy, and she settled with her own household at Angers, safe in the heartland of her husband's paternal inheritance.[71] In August 1153, fifteen months after Eleanor and Henry's marriage, she brought forth a baby boy. In Henry's absence it was left to her to choose the newborn heir's name for his christening. Eleanor selected the name William borne by nearly all of her ducal ancestors, who had adopted it on their succession if it was not their birth-name. Although first-born sons in aristocratic families were often given their paternal grandfather's name, William was a more prestigious name than Geoffrey, the name of Henry's father. The name of Eleanor's first-born son expressed her confidence in the continuity of the Aquitanian dynasty through her offspring by her new husband. No doubt Henry agreed with his wife's choice. A monk with close ties to the Plantagenet court, the abbot of Mont-Saint-Michel in Normandy, was aware that the name honored Eleanor's ancestors; he wrote that the couple's first son "was called William, a name that is almost the distinctive attribute of the counts of Poitou and dukes of Aquitaine."[72] In any case, Henry could take pride in the name's significance for his maternal lineage as a descendant of Duke William of Normandy, conqueror of England.

Although the location of William's birth is unknown, it was most likely Angers. Certainly Eleanor was in the city some time between her son's birth and Henry's return, for while holding a court at Angers she heard a petition of the abbot of La Trinité-de-Vendôme, a major religious house in Henry's lands. She granted his request "for the salvation of the souls of my father and mother and of Duke Henry my dearest husband and for his success [in England?] and for the safe rearing of my son William." Present with her was Henry's youngest brother William and also the chief administrative officials of Anjou and Poitou, the two counties' seneschals. One of her Poitevin local officials, Hervey Panetier, was also present, along with two members of Henry's entourage who had long served the counts of Anjou, a Norman William fitz Hamo and Geoffrey de Clères, an Angevin.[73] These two men had been left behind by Henry to safeguard his wife and also to see to his own interests in his absence.

A New Husband and a New Kingdom

At the time of Henry Plantagenet's marriage to Eleanor of Aquitaine in May 1152, he was already in a powerful position—duke of Normandy by 1150 and, after his father's death in 1151, count of Anjou. An even greater prospect, however, was the possibility of becoming king of England. When he sailed away to England in January 1153, it was to continue the contest begun by his mother, Empress Matilda, some fifteen years earlier to wrest the English Crown from Stephen of Blois. Henry's crossing from Normandy in mid-winter, when his opponents assumed that severe storms would keep him on the other side of the English Channel, established him as a major force in the kingdom and encouraged those favoring his cause.[74]

Henry's claim to the English kingdom came through his mother. A female's succession to a royal Crown was unlikely to be acceptable except in extraordinary circumstances. England would not have a queen-regnant as ruler until Mary Tudor in the sixteenth century. With the law of inheritance in early twelfth-century Europe still uncertain, a challenge to Matilda's succession was inevitable; and during the years after Henry I's nomination of her as his heir, a likely challenger was present at the English royal court, Stephen of Blois, the king's nephew. Henry I showered him with favors, enabling him to amass resources to purchase friendships among the baronage. On Henry I's death in 1135, Stephen had moved fast, rushing to England, securing the barons' homage, and, before Matilda had time to react, his coronation as king.

Empress Matilda did not abandon her claim to the English Crown, and once she and her husband Geoffrey of Anjou had established a foothold in the duchy of Normandy, she moved to confront her cousin Stephen in England. A civil war ensued, threatening the strong royal government that the Norman kings had constructed; but by 1148 the situation seemed to have reached stalemate, and a disheartened Matilda left England.[75] She had settled in Normandy just across the Seine from Rouen, near a priory of the monks of Bec at Quevilly, and until ill-health overtook her around 1165, Matilda would act as her son's regent in Normandy during his absences.[76] Slowly the character of the conflict changed, becoming more Henry's fight for his grandfather's heritage than her own. He had first taken up the struggle in 1146–47 and again in the spring of 1149, when he sought out his great-uncle the Scottish king to knight him. Then in January 1150, Henry rejoined his father in Normandy, who transferred to him the ducal title. After fighting off a threat to the duchy from Louis VII, father and son had proceeded to Paris for peace talks and Henry's fateful meeting with Eleanor in August 1151. When the Angevin prince received the message from Louis's ex-queen that she was free to marry the following spring, he was in Normandy, preparing to sail for England to renew his war against Stephen.

As the two sides fought to a stalemate, the English wearied of the long civil war. Many in England were willing to accept Henry Plantagenet as Stephen's successor, if that would bring an end to the fighting. From King Stephen's point of view, however, provision for his son and heir Eustace of Boulogne was all-important—if not succession to the Crown, then at least a guarantee of his father's English and Norman estates. In summer 1153, the situation drastically changed when Eustace died at almost the time that Eleanor was giving birth to her first son. After his eldest son's death Stephen lost heart for the struggle, and he concluded that it was time to make peace. On 6 November, a compromise was reached, allowing King Stephen to wear the English crown for the remainder of his life. He had to agree that the kingdom was not to pass on to his own heirs, and he adopted Henry as his son and acknowledged him as his heir; in return, his sole surviving son, William, was to receive a generous settlement. At the time, no one could have guessed how long Stephen of Blois would live or whether the peace settlement would hold on his death.

In March 1154 Henry felt secure enough in his situation in England to cross the Channel for a first look at his infant son. He celebrated Easter in Normandy, welcomed by his mother Matilda, his wife Eleanor, and little William. Then Henry set out on a quick trip to Aquitaine, accompanied by Eleanor, and there he dealt with some local revolt, likely involving lords of the Limousin and Périgord.[77] Eleanor accompanied him to Périgueux, and while there they each renewed ducal protection for the abbey of Notre-Dame at Saintes where Agnes, Eleanor's aunt, was still abbess. Those witnessing the solemn grant present a snapshot of Eleanor and Henry's entourage at the time. Accompanying them were two Norman bishops, the bishop of Agen, and

Geoffrey du Loroux, longtime archbishop of Bordeaux, on hand at other important occasions in Eleanor's life. Also present were two members of Eleanor's entourage at Poitiers, Saldebreuil, her constable, and Èbles de Mauléon, who was becoming an important lord of lands along Poitou's Atlantic coast. Through marriage and inheritance, he came to hold one of the strongest lordships in the Aunis, Châtelaillon (today Châtaillon-sur-Sèvre), which made him master of the Île de Ré and one of four lords on the Île d'Oléron.[78]

By May 1154 Eleanor and Henry were heading north to Normandy, stopping at Fontevraud Abbey on the way. Apparently Eleanor was unable to take with her many members of the large household that she had assembled at Poitiers following her flight from Beaugency in 1152. Notable among the small group accompanying the duchess was one of her magnates, Geoffrey de Rancon, a dominant figure in Poitevin political life for many years.[79] The party reached Normandy a few days later and the couple were reunited with Empress Matilda. On 24 June they celebrated the feast of Saint John the Baptist at Rouen. In August, Henry met with Louis VII at Vernon near the Norman frontier with the Île de France, and they made peace concerning disputes over some Norman borderlands. As part of their settlement, Eleanor's ex-husband at last relinquished his claims to the duchy of Aquitaine, recognizing Henry Plantagenet's ducal title.

By early November, news arrived from England of Stephen of Blois's death on 25 October. His death at age sixty within a year of the treaty of Winchester was an unexpected piece of good luck for Henry, and now he, Eleanor, and their entourage had to prepare for the voyage to England for his coronation as King Henry II. England remained at peace for six weeks while the people waited patiently for their new king and queen's arrival in the kingdom because, in the words of one chronicler, they were "in such great awe of him."[80] The English were too weary of war and too desirous of an end to the disorder to resist Henry's succession. The youth and modest ambitions of Stephen's surviving son William meant that he would not lead his father's loyalists in resistance to Henry; instead, he would serve the new king and queen faithfully, dying during an 1159 expedition in support of Eleanor's claim to Toulouse.[81]

The English kingdom had passed to the dukes of Normandy with the victory of Henry Plantagenet's great-grandfather William the Conqueror over the last of the Anglo-Saxon kings in 1066. William and his two sons had combined Anglo-Saxon patterns of strong royal control over the shires or counties with Norman traditions of princely power inherited from the Franks. Then Henry's grandfather, the Conqueror's third son Henry I, had added to this combination of governmental traditions effective new administrative structures that set the Anglo-Norman realm apart from other western European countries before the thirteenth century. England's unity, assured by geography and history long before the Angevin kings' accession, would enable Henry Plantagenet and his sons to rule in an authoritarian, if not absolutist manner even when abroad for long periods. The strong government of the Anglo-Norman realm contrasted with weak ducal government in Eleanor's lands, where the dukes of Aquitaine had never succeeded in devising advanced administrative structures.

All Henry's lands on the Continent lay within the kingdom of France, as did Eleanor's; and the French monarch claimed to be their lawful lord, regardless of his ability to exert actual authority over them. From the time of Henry and Eleanor's coronation as king and queen of the English, conflicts first with Louis VII and later with his son Philip II would absorb the energies of Henry and his sons. Both Louis and his successor were determined to weaken and destroy the Angevin assemblage of lands, so much of which lay in France under their sovereignty. Once Henry had won the English throne, he possessed governmental mechanisms for efficient raising of funds for paying mercenary forces to fight on all fronts against his Capetian rivals. England's role was to be the treasury for Henry and his sons in the constant warfare with the Capetian kings, supplying barrels of cash. Henry and even more so his two sons, Richard and John, would engage in a gigantic shakedown of English and Norman landholders. Not surprisingly, many of the English would feel threatened by their arbitrary acts, and even mighty magnates lived in fear of the king's wrath and indignation.

All three of the Angevin kings would value England chiefly for its wealth readily tapped by a strong royal government. Despite the kingdom's importance as a source of funds, they never viewed themselves as English, although they shared English ancestry through Henry I's queen, Edith-Matilda, descended from Anglo-Saxon royalty. As a result, the English would feel little love for Henry II or his sons, in contrast to the fondness of Louis VII's subjects for their God-fearing and good-hearted monarch. Eleanor, regarded by her new subjects as even more alien than her Angevin husband and suspected of immorality on account of poisonous rumors following her from France, could contribute little to her husband's popularity in England. The English would not give Eleanor their affection until she was an aged widow.

On 7 November 1154, Eleanor and Henry arrived at the Norman port of Barfleur where they were forced to wait a month until unfavorable winds let up and allowed them to put to sea and make for their new kingdom.[82] The turning wheel of fortune bringing down the powerful, rich, and proud was a popular motif among medieval writers. Within two and a half years Eleanor had experienced profound turns in her own fortunes, passing from the unhappily married queen of France, to a newly divorced duchess of Aquitaine in flight to her homeland, to the bride of the young prince Henry Plantagenet, and now, in a sweeping upward turn, finding herself on the voyage to her coronation as England's queen. She had secured her long-sought separation from Louis VII and found a husband more to her liking: a younger, bolder, and more worldly prince with apparently limitless ambitions for more possessions and power. After taking Eleanor as his wife, Henry was the greatest prince in the French kingdom, a far larger landholder than the king, and about to be crowned king of England. Soon after Eleanor's second marriage, she would bring forth a son which had the effect of disinheriting her two daughters from her first marriage, and giving Louis an unpleasant surprise, angering him. Eleanor's former husband was not to disappear from her life, however; for Louis's strained relationship with Henry II of England would be a major theme of the rest of his reign. The fortunes of Henry, Eleanor, and their sons would be inextricably bound up with the Capetian ruler's position as their lord and their adversary.

Eleanor's expectations for her new marriage cannot be deciphered. Clearly Henry Plantagenet was a more lively companion than Louis VII, always active and on the move, riding to the hunt when not fighting against rebels. At the same time, Henry's excellent education ensured that learned thinkers and writers would be welcomed at his court, and Eleanor would find life there more stimulating than at Paris. She would not be disappointed in her new husband's virility, and she and Henry would produce many children in rapid succession, seven of them living to adulthood. No doubt Eleanor expected to be Henry's partner in the political sphere, and for the first years of her marriage at least, her position as regent in England would prove satisfying, but the promised partnership would not last. If she had expected love and devotion from her new husband, she was to be disillusioned and disappointed. Henry would prove to be as cynical and despotic in his personal life as in politics, and Eleanor's fate at his hands would ultimately be rejection, not admiration, respect, or devotion.

CHAPTER 5

ONCE MORE A QUEEN AND MOTHER: ENGLAND, 1154–1168

LESS than three years after Eleanor of Aquitaine had separated from her first husband she found herself sailing to England with her new husband to become queen of a new kingdom. After waiting a month for a favorable wind, the royal party crossed the English Channel, landing on the Hampshire coast on 8 December. The couple stopped at the ancient Saxon capital of Winchester before proceeding to London, and they received a joyful welcome from their new subjects along the way.[1] Eleanor attended the coronation ceremony in Westminster Abbey on Sunday 19 December 1154, pregnant for the second time by Henry Plantagenet and doubtless filled with pride at regaining the rank of queen. Whether the archbishop of Canterbury actually crowned her as queen of the English is uncertain; her earlier coronation as Louis VII's queen already entitled her to wear a crown. In any case, the ceremony would have included some symbolic acknowledgment of her as Henry's queen, for special ceremonies had marked installations of the Anglo-Norman queens.[2]

Despite the English people's welcome of their new queen, her arrival among them soon would be shadowed by her tarnished reputation, and the rumors that had followed her from Antioch to Paris would follow her to her new kingdom. However in December 1154, few of Eleanor's subjects outside court circles knew any more about her than that she was the former French queen and heir to the duchy of Aquitaine. At age thirty, she could look on her new situation with satisfaction, confident that she had successfully cast off one husband and taken another, whose ambition and thirst for power matched her own, and she looked forward to her new life as queen of the English. She could lose herself in the task of making her marriage to Henry an effective partnership, heading the royal court and governing as regent during his many absences from England. The king and queen would work harmoniously together as a team during the first decade and a half of their marriage, until about 1170, with Henry's campaign to enforce her claim to Toulouse in 1159 marking a high point of her influence.

Eleanor of Aquitaine could also take pride in her new fecundity, after the difficulty in conceiving she had experienced as Louis VII's wife. She had already fulfilled her duty by producing a son, William, before her arrival in England; and she was pregnant with a second son, Young Henry, born in her new kingdom on 28 February 1155. In her second marriage she would experience almost fifteen years of regular childbearing, giving birth at a rate of one child a year during the first four years as wife to Henry II.[3] Only meager sources survive to reveal her role in her children's nurturing, and these scattered scraps of evidence invite conflicting interpretations, leaving no consensus about the quality of her mothering. Because of her sons' turbulent relations with their father and with one another, the evidence can be read in wildly divergent ways. Some biographers defend Eleanor's maternal instincts as normal, and others, examining the material through the lens of Freudian psychology, denounce her as an indifferent or domineering mother, using her sons by Henry II for revenge against him.[4]

ELEANOR'S ARRIVAL IN HER NEW KINGDOM

As Eleanor and the royal party crossed southern England on their way to London, she must have been pleased by what she saw. She would not have found her new kingdom's climate any more disagreeable or depressing than that of Paris.[5] England's weather in the twelfth and thirteenth centuries contrasted less with milder conditions across the Channel than in modern times, and Eleanor could see vineyards as she crossed the southern shires. Reaching London, the royal party found the palace complex of the Norman kings at nearby Westminster uninhabitable due to neglect during the long civil war between Stephen of Blois and supporters of Henry's mother. As a result, the king and queen took up residence at the royal manor of Bermondsey, across the River Thames from the Tower of London far to the east of the city.[6]

Dwarfing all other towns in England was London, "the capital, the queen of the whole kingdom of England."[7] With a population of some 20,000 by 1100, London's nearest rival Bristol lagged far behind it in population and wealth, and most English towns held fewer than 1,500 inhabitants. William fitz Stephen, a twelfth-century London citizen, who left a description of his city, labeled it as "among the proud cities of the world that are celebrated by fame, . . . one that spreads its fame wider, sends its wealth and wares further, and lifts its head higher than all others." London was well located to be a center for northern Europe's commerce, attracting traders bringing wines from the Loire and Garonne valleys and spices, silks, and other luxury goods from as far away as Constantinople. The king's chamberlain had first choice of all these imported goods for the royal household. By the mid-twelfth century, the richest of the London merchants were mingling with courtiers and noble visitors to the royal court, investing in land in the country and mixing with the rural gentry. As the political center of the kingdom, London drew all the magnates to it, and according to the Londoner's description, they maintained "lordly habitations" along the banks of the Thames, "wherein they make lavish outlay, when summoned to the City by our Lord the King or by his Metropolitan to councils and great assemblies."[8]

Eleanor would soon discover that London was a 'cultural and linguistic melting pot,' less austere than Paris. A late twelfth-century monk left a description of what he saw as the city's wickedness; "Whatever evil or malicious thing can be found anywhere in the world can also be found in that city. . . . The number of parasites is infinite. Actors, jesters, smooth-skinned lads, Moors, flatterers, pretty boys, effeminates, pederasts, singing and dancing girls, quacks, belly-dancers, sorcerers, extortioners, night-wanderers, magicians, mimes, beggars, buffoons." Yet London had an active spiritual and intellectual life as well. Of scores of churches, three principal ones possessed "famous schools by privilege and in virtue of their ancient dignity"; and Londoners took pride in their schools, although the city was hardly an intellectual center comparable to Paris.[9]

Eleanor as queen of the English would spend surprisingly little time in London or at Westminster, the settlement up the river two miles west of the city that was replacing Winchester, the ancient capital, as the kingdom's administrative center. The Anglo-Saxon "palace" of Westminster consisted of a large and impressive group of domestic buildings adjoining the great abbey. Next to the Anglo-Saxon palace complex stood the great hall built in the second Anglo-Norman king's last years, the largest hall in England and possibly the largest in Europe at the time it was built. Westminster Hall had suffered years of neglect under King Stephen. Renovations were badly needed, and soon work was going forward under Thomas Becket's direction on this "building beyond compare," as the proud William fitz Stephen declared in his description of his noble city. Repairs were also made to other parts of the palace complex, including the queen's chambers.[10]

Henry II and Eleanor's court, like other twelfth-century royal courts, was itinerant, moving about visiting castles and other royal residences to the west of London in the Thames valley and central Wessex, where royal residences had stood since Anglo-Saxon times. The royal court ventured less often into East Anglia and rarely to northern England or even into the Midlands.[11] Eleanor's chief residences in England were Old Sarum, or Old Salisbury, and

Winchester followed by Oxford and Bermondsey, just outside London. Lying within the walls of royal castles at Old Sarum and Winchester were groups of houses, including a hall, chapel, and chambers for the royal family, as well as kitchens, stables, and storehouses. Within the large castle complex at Old Sarum stood the cathedral that would be abandoned at the beginning of the thirteenth century for the new cathedral at Salisbury. In addition to castles, the English monarch had a number of unfortified residences, some considered palaces and others simple hunting lodges. An important factor governing the royal court's movement was hunting, for the first of the Plantagenet kings had a great fondness for the chase, just as had his Anglo-Saxon and Norman predecessors. Hunting was a sport much favored by aristocrats throughout medieval Europe, and many of the castles visited regularly by the royal family had their beginnings as hunting lodges in forests. On these hunting holidays, Eleanor would have remembered childhood visits to the forest of Talmont in the Vendée, favored hunting grounds of the counts of Poitou.

Henry II launched a lavish program of renovating castles and constructing new royal residences all around England, at least in part to convey a message to his subjects of their new king's power and wealth.[12] Two of his favorite English residences, his house at Woodstock just outside Oxford, and Clarendon, a "rural palace" near Old Sarum, had their beginnings as royal hunting lodges. Over the years, Henry converted Clarendon into a true palace with an impressive hall capable of accommodating great councils. At Woodstock works were under way almost every year after Henry's accession, including buildings at nearby Everswell with a room that would come to be known later as "Rosamund's chamber," allegedly the bedchamber of the king's favorite mistress. Such provincial royal residences had the amenities of palaces, and Eleanor would have enjoyed standards of comfort as high as those in any palace in northern Europe. Henry spent large sums on renovating these royal houses: over £1,000 was spent on Winchester alone, including major repairs to Eleanor's living quarters, with more than £22 spent on repairs to her chamber, chimney, and cellar. Here and at other royal residences, wall paintings commissioned by the king decorated the rooms.[13]

ELEANOR AND HER NEW SUBJECTS

England, an island kingdom with a majority population of Anglo-Saxon, Celtic, or Danish origin and a ruling minority of Norman French descent, must have seemed in many ways a strange land to Eleanor. Happily for the queen, England since the 1066 Norman Conquest had had close links with the French and Latin culture prevailing on the European mainland. While the majority of the native population spoke English, the language spoken among the aristocracy at the royal court and by London's commercial classes was Anglo-Norman French. The clergy and many royal officials knew Latin as well and easily moved from one language to the other. A number of Anglo-Norman speakers were trilingual, since they found some knowledge of English, the language spoken by the mass of the population, a practical necessity, but French would remain the language of the royal court long after Eleanor's time. One of Henry II's courtiers wrote glowingly of the king's linguistic skill, noting that he "had some knowledge of every language from the Channel to the river Jordan, but himself employed only Latin and French." Probably Henry could grasp the gist of what was said to him in English, but was far from fluent and unable to make himself understood by English speakers. Such linguistic plurality was familiar to Eleanor, who had moved back and forth in her childhood between the two French tongues, *langue d'oïl* and *langue d'oc.* Yet she never learned English, although she must have had many English-speaking servants.[14]

Surviving accounts from Henry II's early years as king mention his marriage to Eleanor of Aquitaine and little more, but there can be no doubt that shocking rumors about her conduct on the Second Crusade followed her to her new kingdom. Large numbers of ambitious English youths who sought out the learning of the schools of Paris doubtless laughed over drinks in their taverns at exaggerated stories told of their new queen's scandalous conduct as Louis VII's consort. On their return to England in search of employment, many gathered at the royal court, a place filled with clever courtiers, ambitious and greedy men of low birth, who traded on amusing stories to stand out from their fellows in the rivalry for patronage. They readily turned their skill with words toward gossip, flattery, lies, and hypocrisy in order to prevail over competitors. Doubtless, one means of impressing potential patrons with their access to power was to retell tales of the queen's immorality that they had heard while in France. Nothing could be kept secret at court, for the royal family lived their lives in public with courtiers and lesser servants constantly present, and they could not avoid being the subjects of much gossip.

It is impossible to gauge how far down among the common people gossip about the new queen penetrated. The majority of Eleanor's new subjects probably knew little more than that she came from a place far away in the south of France and that she had left her first husband, the French king, to marry Henry Plantagenet. Yet court gossip circulated among Londoners and no doubt spread to their acquaintances in the countryside. Eleanor's largely unflattering portrait painted by English chroniclers writing toward the end of the twelfth century probably reflects popular opinion. It shows that she did not meet a standard for queenship being defined in the course of the century, part of a reformulation of gender roles that would impose harsher judgments of her than those passed on earlier English queens.[15]

Despite a growing animus against powerful women, Eleanor's four Anglo-Norman predecessors as English queen-consorts had enjoyed the approval of contemporary writers. The chronicler Orderic Vitalis, an English-born monk writing in Normandy, supplies few signs of women's worsening conditions early in the twelfth century. His stereotypical references to feminine weaknesses are no more than superficial comments made in passing. He portrays queens as companions and helpmates to their husbands, "helping in government in any time of crisis, ruling during minorities, or helping the foundation of churches." Other chroniclers similarly described Anglo-Norman queens in conventional terms as models of piety and purity, making benefactions to religious institutions and supporting literary and artistic patronage at the royal court. These ladies attracted no scandalous gossip, were conscientious mothers and worthy companions of their royal consorts, even if occasionally involved in politics, serving as regents during their husbands' absences from the kingdom. William I's wife Matilda of Flanders escaped Orderic's condemnation for mixing in worldly matters, since circumstances required her to act as governor of Normandy for long periods while her husband was busy consolidating his rule over his new kingdom of England. Orderic recorded without disapproval "the hard facts of her participation in the work of government" later in England, where she acted as regent and even as royal judge.[16]

Henry I's consort Edith-Matilda had exerted similar influence in the political sphere, acting as regent during her husband's absences from the realm. When exercising power on Henry I's behalf, she applied her own seal to royal documents, and she expected royal officials to obey her as they would the king.[17] Yet her activity as her husband's helpmate did not sully her reputation, for her piety staved off writers' objections. Indeed, Edith-Matilda spoke openly of her influence over her husband; in a letter to Anselm of Canterbury, who had incurred royal wrath, she told him, "With God's help and my suggestions, as far as I am able, [Henry] may become more welcoming and compromising towards you." Eleanor's efforts as Henry II's regent during the first decade of their marriage did not win her similar praise, however. Unlike Henry's grandmother, whose intercession with her husband on behalf of worthy petitioners had led churchmen to compare her to the biblical Queen Esther, Eleanor did not earn contemporaries' gratitude for taking advantage of her intimate access to Henry to intervene for the sake of others.[18]

Edith-Matilda with her saintliness represented a model of what was expected and esteemed in an English royal consort. Yet her death in 1118 marked a change for English queenship, for by then the eleventh-century reform movement's fight for clerical celibacy was bringing about a sharpening of gender definitions to deny women any public role. While Eleanor was queen, English churchmen were condemning great women for assuming such "manly" roles as the exercise of power, and they decried husbands who allowed their wives a role in public life as guilty of "unmanly" behavior. Henry II's own mother, Empress Matilda, had suffered from accusations of an "unwomanly" desire for power. Eleanor sought a place for herself in politics that went beyond what northern Europeans considered suitable for a queen. Even as a young wife and a stranger at the court of Louis VII, she had demonstrated a desire to share power with her royal husband; and she had resented both her mother-in-law's influence over her young husband and Abbot Suger of Saint-Denis's role as his senior counselor. As a French biographer writes, "It is that constant political activity and her role at court . . . that makes Eleanor an exceptional woman to the point of astonishing the historians of our time and of shocking the misogynistic chroniclers of her own."[19]

Religious devotion was an important quality for queens, who were expected to be models of piety, using their prominence to promote religion in the kingdom. While Eleanor's predecessors were known to have given pious gifts to monastic institutions, including new foundations, she is not noted for having founded new religious houses in England. A late tradition has it that Eleanor founded the chapel of Blyth at Tickhill Castle in northern Nottinghamshire. She evidently had some connection with the chapel, for as a widow she urged the current holder of the chapel to share some of its income with her aged chaplain, Peter the Poitevin.[20] The infirm of the Queen's Hospital appear on the pipe rolls receiving regular payment from the Surrey account beginning in 1159 of thirty shillings and five pence, but this was probably the leper house of Saint Giles in the Fields, just outside London, founded by Henry I's queen, not Eleanor's personal charity.[21] On lands belonging to the queen's dower lay a house of secular canons at Waltham, Essex, and in 1159 its residents were described as "the queen's canons," benefitting from that relationship to win remission of a tax on their substantial landholdings.[22] After Henry II's death, one of the Waltham canons was Eleanor's clerk charged with collecting "queen's gold"; apparently this was one of their customary services to her.[23] The beneficiaries of most of Eleanor's grants were monastic foundations in Poitou, and not even there was she noteworthy as a founder of new houses.[24] Poitevin monasteries or convents favored by her ancestors seem never to have benefitted from gifts of English lands from her as additions to their endowments. Unlike Henry II, who provided Fontevraud with revenues from English properties and encouraged the foundation of Fontevraudist priories in England, no evidence survives of Eleanor's gifts to that house from her English revenues.[25]

Eleanor formed a special relationship with Reading Abbey where her first son, William, dead at the age of three, was entombed in 1156, apparently while Henry II was abroad. No doubt her husband sent instructions concerning their son's burial; and his body was placed at the feet of his great-grandfather,

King Henry I of England, Henry's model for ruling England. The choice of
Reading as the child's resting place was a means of linking the Angevin king
and his family to Henry I, founder of the abbey, who had intended it to be a
royal mausoleum.[26] Like parents in any age, Eleanor and Henry mourned the
loss of their first child. In making a grant for the little boy's soul to Hurley
Priory, a dependent house of Westminster Abbey, the king declared that the
gift was made at the queen's request and with her assent.[27] Also indicating
Eleanor's grief at losing her first-born son is a letter to her, dated between 1158
and 1165, from the abbot of Reading Abbey. The letter assured the queen that
she would receive on her death all benefits normally accorded to a deceased
monk of the abbey, including the monastic community's commemoration in
perpetuity of the anniversary of her death. Reading's gift to the queen of
membership to the abbey's confraternity seems to have been "exceptionally
early and exceptionally extensive," for such promises to lay persons were
unusual before the thirteenth century. The abbot's letter presents the favor
shown to Eleanor as simply an answer to her request, but doubtlessly it was
also a response to her generosity to the religious foundation housing the
remains of her first son.[28]

Another rare letter to Eleanor as queen of England survives to cast light on
her spiritual life. It was written to her by the prophet and mystic, Hildegard of
Bingen (d.1179), another remarkable twelfth-century woman, and a letter
addressed by her to Henry II also survives. As Hildegard's fame spread, she
conducted a wide correspondence replying to requests for her advice from
powerful persons throughout Europe, including England.[29] Since the letter
cannot be dated more precisely than sometime before 1170, the event that
impelled Hildegard to write to the English queen remains a mystery. She
addresses Eleanor not so much as a sovereign as a woman who is prey to
troubles; and she offers counsel to calm her, advising her to search for stability.
She wrote "Your mind is similar to a wall plunged into a whirlwind of clouds.
You look all around, but find no rest. Flee that and remain firm and stable,
with God as with men, and God will then help you in all your tribulations.
May he give you his blessing and his aid in all your undertakings."[30] The
German nun's description of Eleanor's state of mind recalls critics' complaints
of her "flightiness."

Most significant in setting Eleanor apart from her four predecessors as
queens of England, all either natives of England or northern European principalities just across the Channel, was her association in her subjects' minds with
the Mediterranean south of France.[31] Once Eleanor's marriage to Henry II
acquainted the English with Aquitaine, they would form an unfavorable
impression of the duchy, convinced that it was an ungovernable land inhabited
by rebels and heretics. When troubadour love lyrics began to circulate among

the Anglo-Norman nobility, their portrayals of southern French noblewomen's adulterous loves would taint Eleanor, a child of that exotic culture. For the queen's contemporaries, Aquitaine's mores were typified by Eleanor's grandfather, William IX, the troubadour duke whose licentious life had scandalized the Anglo-Norman chroniclers.[32] They apparently assumed that as a "child of the Midi," she had inherited his louche character.

ELEANOR'S FIRST YEARS AS ENGLISH QUEEN, DECEMBER 1154–DECEMBER 1158

After the coronation ceremony in December 1154, Eleanor and Henry II both remained in their new kingdom for over a year until, in January 1156, the king left for France to contend with his brother Geoffrey's rebellion in Anjou. Eleanor, often parted from her husband for long periods when he was fighting on England's frontiers or on campaigns in his French lands, may have experienced feelings of isolation in England from time to time. Adding to the queen's loneliness was her inability to have the company of more than a handful of her fellow Poitevins serving in her household. Eleanor, living in the midst of foreigners withholding from her the admiration accorded their earlier queens and whose language she never learned to speak, may have faced her days in England with some foreboding.

Henry's frequent absences from his kingdom would become a cause of concern for his English subjects. In a letter addressed to the king by the archbishop of Canterbury in spring 1160, he was urged to return to England, and reminded of his offspring, "those children from the sight of whom scarce even the hardest-hearted father could any longer withhold his gaze."[33] While in England, Henry had much work to do, taking him away from his queen's side in his task of reversing the diminution of royal rights during the civil war under King Stephen. Not long after his coronation, he headed for the north to reassert royal power there, while Eleanor remained behind at Bermondsey in the last stage of her second pregnancy by the English king.

When Eleanor gave birth to their second son on 28 February 1155, Henry II was in Northampton. This was their first child "born to the purple," and he was named Henry to commemorate his great-grandfather King Henry I of England, linking the boy to the Anglo-Norman royal line. At the end of March, the king returned from his northern expedition in time for the Easter festivities at Merton Abbey, and afterward he held a great council at London, where Eleanor had a prominent part in the festivities as the mother of two young princes. Two weeks later another council took place at Wallingford, where little William and his month-old brother were presented to the assembled magnates. The king, mindful of the uncertainty about the succession that had caused years of civil war, 1139–53, insisted that his barons swear their fealty to William and to his infant brother Henry.[34] By June, Henry had left his wife's side again to go on campaign, this time in the west country, conducting sieges of castles at Bridgnorth, Wigmore, and Cleobury.[35]

Eleanor would be separated from her husband for much of 1156, for Henry II crossed the Channel to Normandy in January on his first visit to his Continental lands as English king. He would be absent from his kingdom for the entire year, not returning to England until April 1157, while Eleanor remained in England acting as regent. Some time during Henry's absence, William died at the age of three, although the date of his death is not known. Henry had left Eleanor pregnant for a third time, and in June 1156 she gave birth to a daughter, christened Matilda. The name linked the child to her Anglo-Norman ancestors, honoring her grandmother, the former German empress, whose own mother, William the Conqueror's wife, had also borne the name Matilda. Eleanor's first two children born in England were both christened by Archbishop Theobald of Canterbury at Holy Trinity, Aldgate, a London house of Augustinian canons founded by Henry's grandmother, Henry I's queen.[36] Eleanor joined her husband at Angers in the summer of 1156, following William's death. On that Continental sojourn, she took with her both Young Henry and the infant Matilda, no more than three months old.

The following autumn the royal couple would make a tour together of Eleanor's duchy of Aquitaine, her first visit to her people in over two years. On this first visit since their coronation as king and queen of England, they revisited Limoges. Henry II intervened again in the Limousin to enforce his lordship, this time in the succession to the territory, enforcing his right as lord to guardianship over the deceased viscount's minor son, even though previous count-dukes had not exercised such a privilege. He claimed custody of young Aymar V, and placed the viscounty in the hands of two Norman officials, despite the boy's paternal uncles' claim that tradition gave them the guardianship by their right as his closest kin. Later Henry would take advantage of his lordship to arrange the young viscount's marriage to a daughter of his uncle, the powerful Earl Reginald of Cornwall.[37] Such "feudal" prerogatives of lordship were not customary in Eleanor's lands, and Henry's attempted introduction of them would not be appreciated by her nobility.

From Limoges, Eleanor and Henry continued south, visiting Bordeaux at the invitation of her former guardian Archbishop Geoffrey du Loroux. The state visit to Eleanor's lands culminated with a Christmas court at Bordeaux, where Henry proclaimed his peace to the nobility and people of Gascony. This ceremony marked the end of Eleanor's autonomy as ruler of her duchy. The five surviving documents issued by her as duchess during her 1156 visit reveal the limits of her authority over her ancestral lands, for three are merely confirmations of Henry's acts. The two documents that Eleanor issued, evidently without Henry's sanction, are routine orders to her Poitevin local agents to observe her father's grants of privileges to religious houses.[38] After this visit, Eleanor's name disappears from Aquitanian charters, and none recording her as grantor, either alone or jointly with her husband, is found until her return over a decade later. During those years, Henry was issuing charters for his wife's subjects in Poitou with no mention of her consent, although many of them were likely confirmations of grants originally made by her.[39]

Following the Christmas court at Bordeaux, the queen returned to England with her children early in 1157, pregnant once more, to resume her duties as regent until Henry's arrival in April. Neither Eleanor nor Henry would visit her duchy again until 1159 at the beginning of the failed Toulouse campaign. Prolonged visits to Eleanor's lands by Henry were rare, and most were no more than a month long. Two years after the 1156 visit, Henry would tangle with the viscount of Thouars, the most important noble in the northern and western parts of Poitou with territory stretching from his ancient fortress at Thouars, guarding the Poitevin frontier below the River Loire south of Saumur to the Atlantic coast near the Île d'Oléron. Henry took the castle of Thouars in 1158 after a three-day siege and then sent the viscount into exile, ruling his territory through Angevin or Norman appointees. Supposedly Henry had moved against the viscount of Thouars because of his support for Henry's rebellious younger brother, Geoffrey count of Nantes; but according to some accounts, he acted out of a desire to please Eleanor, who considered the viscount a quarrelsome vassal. She counseled Henry to forceful action, urging him to raze the castle and its walls just as earlier she had pressed her first husband for strong measures against the Poitevins.[40] Whatever the cause, Henry's brutality toward the viscount only alienated the nobles of Eleanor's duchy.

The Poitevin nobility viewed Henry Plantagenet as tampering with their traditional "liberties" in his attempt to transform vague ties that had bound them to Eleanor's predecessors into defined duties owed to him as lord. As usual, the instigators of resistance were the lords along Poitou's southern frontier in the lower Charente and upper Vienne valleys, most prominent among them the counts of Angoulême. Despite the English king's success in taking custody of the minor viscount of Limoges, the great men of Poitou rejected his "feudal" right to wardship and marriage, and Henry would never succeed in imposing on them the obligations owed by his Norman and English nobles. Nor would they admit that they held their lands of him as count-duke conditionally in return for payments and services; they only acknowledged a long-standing duty as landowners to perform ancient "public" services. Eleanor had urged Louis VII to strong measures against her subjects, but eventually she would come to see Henry's authoritarian actions against the Poitevin aristocracy as contrary to her homeland's traditions and her sympathies would shift toward her own people.

After Eleanor's return from Poitou, she would remain in England throughout the summer and autumn of 1157, and on 8 September she was at Oxford, where another son Richard was born.[41] The source of Richard's name is uncertain; it had been borne by several Norman dukes, but Robert was also a common name in the ducal lineage of Normandy. Henry on rejoining his family in England in April 1157 would remain in his island kingdom for fifteen months, except for a Christmas visit to Normandy with Eleanor for the Christmas court at Cherbourg. In mid-August 1158, the king left again for a long absence of four and a half years, not returning until late January 1163. Eleanor would recross the Channel to join her husband for the 1158 Christmas court at Cherbourg, leaving her infant son Geoffrey behind in England little more than two months after his birth on 23 September 1158. Geoffrey's name, of course, honored Henry's own father, Count Geoffrey of Anjou. The name Fulk that alternated with Geoffrey as a male name in the comital family of Anjou was also available for one of the sons, but never selected. Eleanor's own ancestors afforded no additional choices, since all dukes of Aquitaine took the name William.

THE CAMPAIGN FOR ELEANOR'S RIGHT TO TOULOUSE, 1159

Not long after 1159 dawned, the royal couple again headed southward to her duchy of Aquitaine to prepare for a great campaign against the count of Toulouse, whose county Eleanor claimed as her hereditary right. Early in her first marriage she had persuaded Louis VII to launch a war for the recovery of Toulouse, and her marriage to Henry Plantagenet made him a party to her ducal ancestors' long rivalry with the counts of Toulouse. Eleanor's success in convincing Henry to pursue the same goal in 1159 marks the high point of her influence on her second husband. The attempt to conquer the county was not some "harebrained scheme" that she lured a young and rash husband into launching. The queen-duchess, like her grandmother and her father, regarded Raymond of Saint-Gilles and his descendants at Toulouse, including the current count, Raymond V, as usurpers.[42]

Hereditary right no doubt had justified the dukes of Aquitaine in their attempts to take Toulouse, and Henry would have readily seen that his wife's claim to Toulouse was remarkably similar to his mother's and his own claims to the English Crown. Events of his own childhood and youth had centered on his mother's armed struggle to assert their rights as legitimate heirs to the kingdom of England, and he would have seen nothing wrong with winning Eleanor's rightful inheritance by force of arms. Henry also reached the practical conclusion that without controlling the county his ascendancy over Eleanor's lordship of Aquitaine would be "both incomplete and fatally weakened." Mastery of Toulouse would have given Henry as duke of Aquitaine dominion over a wealthy trading zone stretching from the Atlantic coast and the Garonne valley to the Mediterranean. The city of Toulouse stood at the head of the River Garonne's navigable waters and at the crossing of important trade routes, where Roman roads from La Rochelle, Bordeaux, and Bayonne on the Atlantic coast met those running east from Narbonne on the Mediterranean and Arles on the Rhone river.[43] Eleanor found an ally to aid her in convincing the king to take an aggressive stance against Toulouse in his chief counselor and greatest friend Thomas Becket. The chancellor would personally lead a large force of knights that he had recruited and financed, and John of Salisbury, an opponent of the Toulouse expedition, considered him its architect.[44]

Not surprisingly, Count Raymond v of Toulouse denied Eleanor's right to his county, acknowledging neither her own claim to the title of countess nor her lordship over him as duchess of Aquitaine, and he was able to forge an alliance with Louis vii. The French king, knowing Eleanor as well as he did, surely suspected that she would sooner or later urge Henry ii to make good her claim to Toulouse, just as she had persuaded him in 1141. Louis sought to undermine Henry and Eleanor's project on his 1156 visit to Toulouse by confirming privileges of southern bishops and, more importantly, by marrying his sister, the recently widowed Constance, to Count Raymond. This tie of kinship obligated the French king to sustain his brother-in-law's right, despite having earlier led an expedition in support of Eleanor's claim. As a result, Poitevin–Toulousain rivalry would merge with Angevin–Capetian rivalry.

Earlier Louis vii had hoped for peaceful coexistence with Henry, and after initially resisting his succession to the English throne, the French king had tried to befriend him. At a meeting on the Norman frontier in August 1158, they settled their rivalry over the Norman Vexin, with castles vital for controlling the Seine valley route between Rouen and Paris.[45] To mark their agreement, Henry and Eleanor's eldest son, Young Henry, aged three, was affianced to the even younger Margaret, daughter of Louis by his second wife. The Vexin and its frontier castles were her dowry to be handed over to Young Henry at the time of the two children's marriage, which the Capetian king assumed to be far in the future. Henry's plans for the marriage went beyond gaining the Vexin. His ambition seemed almost limitless, and he may even have dreamed of Young Henry succeeding to the French throne.[46] Louis would not produce a male heir until 1165, when finally his third wife gave him a son, the future Philip ii.

Because two of the future couple's parents, Eleanor and Louis, were related within the Church's prohibited degrees, their children's marriage would also be consanguineous, an inconvenient fact that was initially ignored, but later would afford an excuse for challenging the betrothal.[47] Margaret was turned over to her future father-in-law for her upbringing; Eleanor's ex-husband insisted, however, that the child should not be brought up at the Plantagenet court where she was likely to be placed in his ex-wife's household, and Henry handed her over to the care of his seneschal of Normandy.[48] Eleanor must have appreciated the irony of her young son's betrothal to her former husband's daughter. Certainly she took pleasure in the prestige brought by his engagement to a Capetian princess, and given Louis's record of siring three daughters and no son, she could envision Henry Junior's succession to the French Crown as well as to the English Crown as a possibility, even if remote.

Soon after the beginning of 1159, Eleanor was with Henry II at Blaye, an ancient port town on the River Gironde just north of Bordeaux. There the English king met with Raymond-Berengar IV (d.1162), count of Barcelona and prince of Aragon, to form an alliance in preparation for his planned war on Toulouse. Ramond-Berengar had joined together the two territories of Catalonia and Aragon, making himself one of Spain's most powerful princes, and his ambitions reached across the Pyrenees into Gascony and all along the Mediterranean shores of Occitania. In 1144 he had succeeded in securing the county of Provence for his nephew. As he sought to pull into his orbit southern princes from Barcelona to Provence, he threatened to undermine Aquitaine's lordship over southern Gascony, luring to his lordship such Gascon princes as the viscount of Béarn. Since Count Raymond-Berengar's expansionist aim of extending his power eastward toward the Rhone conflicted with the ambitions of the count of Toulouse, Henry II saw an opportunity to secure him as an ally in his planned campaign to take control of the county.[49] The two agreed to young Richard's betrothal at age two to Raymond-Berengar's daughter. A betrothal, though a serious commitment to marriage, could be broken off if no longer useful; and Richard's betrothal proved short-lived. In 1161 he would be promised to another of Louis VII's daughters, Alix of France (sometimes called Alais or Alice), younger sister of his brother Henry's bride.

A Poitevin chronicler writes that in the middle of Lent "An edict went out from King Henry, that the princes and barons of all his kingdom should prepare for a siege of the city of Toulouse in the near future." The date set for the host to gather at Poitiers was the feast of Saint John the Baptist, 24 June 1159; later contingents from Gascony and across the Pyrenees would gather at Agen.[50] Answering Henry II's call were magnates from England, Normandy, Anjou, and Poitou as well as the king of the Scots, Count Raymond-Berengar of Barcelona, and dissident nobles from territories adjoining the Toulousain. The scale and scope of the expedition, the largest army that Henry ever raised, comparable in size to a crusading host, amazed contemporaries. The royal chancellor Thomas Becket came accompanied by a band of 700 knights. Recruiting and supplying such a force would stretch his English administration's resources, but the administrative structure that Henry and his justiciars had been constructing since 1154 "passed this test with flying colors." To secure funds for mercenary forces, Henry subjected England to special levies amounting to over £9,000, more than the total royal income collected the previous year. In addition, he had revenues from his French possessions; a tax was levied on his Norman vassals of sixty shillings per knight's fee.[51] Henry's heavy taxation to finance this military expedition shows the increasing importance of money for a medieval king's power, and it aroused the first outcries against his harsh methods of raising revenues. Prominent English churchmen would view the Toulouse campaign as marking the end of the good days of Henry's government. They decried his demands for money from English churches and monasteries, judging them "improper and unjust extortion," in violation of "ancient custom" and "their rightful liberty," and their disenchantment with his rule grew.[52]

In the summer of 1159, Henry's army marched through Périgord and Quercy, approaching Toulouse by the first week of July. King Louis VII came to talk with Henry but they could not come to an agreement. Louis's response was to go to the city of Toulouse to stand beside his brother-in-law, Count Raymond v. Henry sought to convince the Capetian king and the count of the futility of resisting him by ordering raids on the Capetian royal domain and by ravaging the countryside surrounding Toulouse. Although Thomas Becket pressed for ignoring the French king and launching an assault, Henry withdrew from the city's walls by the end of September, either from deference to Louis, his sworn lord, or in recognition of the difficulty of taking the strongly fortified town by storm. Henry's abandonment of the siege of Toulouse can only have caused Eleanor deep disappointment, and the question of Toulouse's subjection to the duchy of Aquitaine remained "an unfinished business" that would occupy both Henry and his successor Richard I in the politics of the Midi for years. After Henry headed back toward Normandy, Becket took command of a force to salvage something from the Toulouse campaign; and putting on armor and helmet, he captured castles in Quercy, scourging the countryside and bringing Cahors and the entire county under Plantagenet control. His subjection of Cahors amounted to a new addition for Aquitaine, for the counts of Toulouse had controlled the town and its bishops since the tenth century.[53]

For forty years after the failed Toulouse campaign, conflict continued intermittently. Its failure would leave Eleanor bitterly disappointed, and had she accompanied the army, she doubtless would have joined Thomas Becket in arguing that Louis VII's presence in the city should not preclude taking it by force. The queen's whereabouts during the Toulouse campaign are unknown, but it is unlikely that she accompanied her husband's army marching on the city. Possibly she traveled from Blaye to Poitiers to await the outcome of the campaign, more likely she returned to England to resume her responsibilities as regent.[54] Since 1159 passed without Eleanor becoming pregnant, her return to the English kingdom for much of the year seems plausible. In December 1159 she crossed from England to Normandy to rejoin Henry at Falaise for Christmas, following his return from the failed expedition.

Eleanor in the Years From 1159 Until Her 1168 Return to Poitou

After Eleanor and Henry held their Christmas court at Falaise, the queen would continue her crisscrossing of the Channel, returning to England early in the new year. She would remain in the kingdom except for Christmas courts in Normandy or Maine and visits on other special occasions. In September 1160 she again sailed to Normandy, leaving behind in England her two younger sons, Richard, aged three, and Geoffrey, two years old. Accompanying the queen were their elder siblings Young Henry and Matilda. The purpose of Eleanor's voyage was to escort her eldest boy to Normandy for his homage to Louis VII for the duchy and his marriage to the French monarch's daughter Margaret. To placate Louis, the child bride had been kept in Normandy apart from Eleanor since her betrothal two years earlier.

The English king somehow managed to have Young Henry's future father-in-law Louis VII take his homage without his becoming aware that the planned marriage was about to take place. The wedding was solemnized at Neubourg at the beginning of November 1160, even though the bride and groom, at two and five years old respectively, were far too young to give their consent to the marriage, as canon law insisted. Louis VII felt betrayed when he heard that the marriage was to proceed, placing the Norman Vexin in Plantagenet hands at least a decade earlier than he had anticipated. He was also much annoyed that the new Roman pontiff, Alexander III, who was struggling against a rival claimant to the papal throne, was willing to grant a dispensation for the children's marriage in violation of canon law. Hoping to win Henry's support, the pope readily ordered his legates in France to supply the necessary dispensation for the early marriage. Henry saw an opportunity to proceed with the wedding and take control of the Norman Vexin. Around the same time the French king announced his intention to marry Adela of Blois-Champagne less than a month after his second wife's death following the birth of a second daughter. Since Louis's new bride was also related to him within degrees prohibited by ecclesiastical rules, he was in no position to challenge his daughter Margaret's marriage on grounds of consanguinity. Louis, preparing for his own marriage, was too busy to attend his daughter's wedding, saving both himself and Eleanor the awkwardness of a meeting. Like heads of other princely families, Henry placed political goals ahead of the wishes of the two children, who were no more than "pawns in his diplomatic chess game," and his queen would hardly have expected him to do otherwise.[55]

Eleanor and Henry II remained in France throughout autumn 1160, planning to cross to England to celebrate Christmas, but stormy seas kept them on the Norman side of the Channel until January. Delays of days or even weeks due to unfavorable winds were common in winter weather. The royal couple, unable to reach England, spent the 1160 Christmas season at Le Mans, Henry's favorite city and his father's burial place. Some time in the new year the queen is likely to have returned to England, but she was again in her husband's French lands in September 1161, when she gave birth to a second daughter, her namesake Eleanor, at Domfront in Normandy. Presiding at the infant Eleanor's baptism was a papal legate with the abbot of Mont-Saint-Michel as sponsor.[56] The queen remained in the duchy for Christmas at Bayeux, and in March of the next year she was still with Henry for the solemn reburial in the abbey church of Fécamp of the bodies of two of his ducal ancestors. Fécamp Abbey, possessing the revered relic of the holy blood, was an important pilgrimage site, and the two early dukes' re-entombment there exalted their memory as devout Christians and benefactors of the Norman Church. Henry and his queen's presence at the ceremony had a propaganda purpose, calling attention to his descent from such praiseworthy rulers.[57]

In April 1161 the archbishopric of Canterbury had fallen vacant, and Henry II almost at once began to consider naming his great friend and companion, the royal chancellor Thomas Becket, to Canterbury. As soon as Henry nominated his friend, his thoughts turned to securing the coronation of his eldest son, Young Henry, as king in his own lifetime, and he ordered gold for a crown for the six-year-old boy.[58] Eleanor as the French king's ex-wife was familiar with this Capetian practice. It seems that Henry was thinking of setting up in England a subordinate administration with Young Henry as nominal ruler and actual power in the hands of a council headed by Becket as archbishop-chancellor and the chief justiciar, Earl Robert of Leicester.

Eleanor must have had doubts about Henry's decision to elevate the chancellor to Canterbury. It seemed that in both her marriages she was destined to encounter churchmen whose ascendancy at court threatened her own influence on her husband: Abbot Suger in her first marriage and now Thomas Becket. It is impossible to know what Eleanor thought of this complex clerk, an ambitious courtier who had become Henry's best friend, boon companion, and respected counselor. Very likely, she found unseemly his love of splendor, his elaborate entourage, his lavish dinners, his resplendent robes that seemed to express a desire to outshine the royal court's majesty. Yet she may have found a cleric who took so much pleasure in magnificent display and setting a splendid table a charming character, one who enlivened the court and gave her pleasure with his wit and intellect.[59] She may well have tried to win his friendship, preferring such a worldly clerk as Henry's confidant to one such as the saintly Suger of Saint-Denis, so influential on her former husband. Yet Eleanor knew that if Becket were to be both chancellor and archbishop, her political power would be undercut, rendering her regency no longer necessary. Indeed, Henry may have already been contemplating sending his queen off to her duchy of Aquitaine to exercise nominal authority there.[60] It would not be long, however, until growing hostility between king and archbishop invalidated a plan that threatened to deprive Eleanor of her duties as regent.

No more is known of Thomas Becket's feelings about Eleanor than hers for him. Although adopting a worldly courtier's outlook while chancellor, he may have shared other clerics' low opinion of the queen as a loose woman. Yet nothing indicates the usual clerical fear and distrust of women on Becket's part; indeed, in a letter to a nun written when he was a beleaguered archbishop, he would employ "almost feminist rhetoric." He praised the women among Christ's followers whose faith had outstripped that of his disciples.[61] The chancellor was the consummate courtier, skilled in playing the game of patronage, and he probably set out to win over the new queen. Indeed, his ardent support for the 1159 campaign to take Toulouse was perhaps calculated as a stance that would curry favor with her.

Eleanor may have been in Normandy during much of 1162 while Becket was transforming himself from a worldly courtier to a devout churchman. Her whereabouts are uncertain, although it seems likely that she would have returned to England for a time. In any case, she was in Normandy with Henry II in December, when he was preparing to sail to his island kingdom for his Christmas court. With the queen were their two daughters, Matilda and Eleanor, who was being taken to England little more than a year after her birth in Normandy. Foul winter weather once more prevented them from crossing the Channel; and the royal party was forced to remain at Cherbourg for the Nativity celebrations. They did not land at Southampton until late January 1163, where Young Henry and his custodian, the new archbishop of Canterbury, met them. Henry II had been away from England for almost four and a half years, and his subjects were becoming concerned at his long absence. Once the king arrived in his kingdom, he busied himself instituting reforms to strengthen royal power and dealing with unrest along the borders of Wales. During the year that Henry spent in England, moving as far north as Carlisle and York, Eleanor and her daughters seem to have made their home in the traditional royal residences in the southwest—Salisbury and Winchester.[62]

Henry gave greatest attention to restoring the royal control over the English Church once exercised by Henry I, and this would set in motion a great quarrel with Thomas Becket, now archbishop of Canterbury. In mid-October

1163, a council of the English Church at Westminster opened with Henry present for the solemn translation of the relics of Saint Edward the Confessor to Westminster abbey. Since Edward's queen, the reportedly chaste Edith, was reburied with him, no doubt Eleanor also attended the service.[63] Earlier, Henry had worked to secure his Anglo-Saxon predecessor's canonization, and the Confessor's reburial was an event that served to emphasize the English monarchy's sacred character at a time when ill-will between king and archbishop was bursting open for all to see. Later Henry chose to celebrate Christmas of 1163 at the castle of Berkhamstead, seat of a vast estate that was traditionally part of the English queens' dower. The choice appears to have been aimed at humiliating Becket, for he previously had held Berkhamstead as the king's custodian.[64] Henry would remain in the kingdom for two years until February 1165, dealing with worsening relations with his archbishop. In January 1164 the king's issuance of his Constitutions of Clarendon, defining what he regarded as the proper relationship between the monarchy and the English Church, brought matters to a head. By the following autumn, Henry's former chancellor and fast friend had fled to France to seek the protection of the English king's chief competitor, Louis VII.

In May 1165, Eleanor again sailed to the Continent to join Henry, remaining there for a year to act as her husband's regent in Anjou and Maine, while he was in England for a campaign against the Welsh. In October 1165 after three years without a pregnancy, Eleanor gave birth to another child, a daughter Joanne, born at Angers. Eleanor and Henry's choice of the name Joanne for their third daughter is unclear. It seems unlikely that a saint's feast-day determined Joanne's name, for the only saint named John whose feast falls in October is an obscure eighth-century Anglo-Saxon bishop. Eleanor was resident in Anjou until as late as March 1166, and at times she had all of her children with her except Young Henry, who was left in England. Young Geoffrey apparently left his mother's side to cross the sea to England for a time, but was sent back to her.[65]

Eleanor, while in Anjou and Maine, involved herself in the work of governance; records survive of several lawsuits settled "in the court of our lady the queen."[66] The nobles of Maine and neighboring Brittany proved unwilling to submit to Eleanor's authority, however, and revolt appeared to be a possibility, forcing her to turn to Henry. He returned from England in 1166 to assert his authority in the region, making war on the Bretons to subject them to his rule. His victory enabled him to force Conan, count of Brittany, to agree to affiance his heir, his daughter Constance, to Henry and Eleanor's third son Geoffrey. Young Constance also brought to the seven-year-old Geoffrey her English inheritance, the earldom of Richmond.[67]

At the time of Eleanor's regency in Maine, she renewed close ties with her uncle Ralph de Faye; as her kinsman he was prominent in Poitou's governance throughout the years that she was occupied in England, serving as seneschal of the Saintonge and possibly as seneschal of all Poitou by the end of 1160.[68] Between 1154 and 1172, Ralph enjoyed Henry II's favor, and he was often with the king on his Continental circuits, witnessing royal charters. Ralph had a bad reputation among the Poitevin clergy as an oppressor of religious institutions; a decade earlier he had been excommunicated for violating the rights of Sainte-Radegonde of Poitiers and more recently for despoiling the priory of Oléron. Indeed, after Eleanor took charge of Poitou's government in 1168, she had to act on charges by the monks of Vendôme, who complained of her uncle's imposition of evil new customs on one of their priories.[69]

Churchmen had no doubt that the queen's uncle would support Henry II's stand in the conflict with Archbishop Thomas Becket, and they feared that he would exert influence on Eleanor harmful to the Church's cause. The English-born bishop of Poitiers, John of Canterbury, wrote to Becket in August 1165, warning him that "you can hope for no help or advice from the queen, especially since she relies entirely on Ralph de Faye, who is persecuting us no less than before. Every day many tendencies come to light which make it possible to believe that there is truth in the dishonourable tale we remember mentioning elsewhere." The bitterness of Henry's quarrel with Becket was deepened by the exiled archbishop's excommunication in June 1166 of several of the king's most trusted counselors. Late in that year John of Salisbury wrote to the bishop of Poitiers, asking for news of Henry's Christmas court at Poitiers: "It is conjectured that the spirit of Ralph de Faye was powerful there, and so the prophets and heralds of the palace were intoxicated with his wiles and rash daring."[70]

These letters are among the few documents that give any hint of Eleanor's part in the entire Becket conflict. Whether or not she shared her uncle's hostility toward the Church, the letters suggest that Becket and his friends assumed both that Ralph de Faye could influence her and that her advice to her husband was a factor to be taken into account. Another of John of Salisbury's letters, however, suggests the likelihood that the queen shared the moderating opinion of Henry's mother, the empress Matilda, more than her uncle's antagonism toward churchmen. Matilda made attempts at mediating a compromise settlement of the quarrel, and John's letter from late summer 1165 shows Eleanor, then residing at Angers, joining in her effort. He wrote to the exiled Becket, reporting that the count of Flanders was said to be working for a settlement of the struggle, "at the request of the Empress and the queen," and that he had sent "a distinguished party of men" to the king.[71] Eleanor had little reason for confidence in Henry's success in his confrontation with the Church, for she would have remembered ruefully her father's years of fruitless altercations with his Poitevin prelates. Duke William X's stubbornness in a disputed papal election, opposing a claimant favored by his bishops, brought him no benefit; and in the end, pressured by

Bernard of Clairvaux, he finally abandoned his support for the rival candidate. Eleanor could also have recalled a similar ending to Louis VII's ineffectual efforts early in their marriage to exercise control over episcopal elections. His action had only resulted in triggering both Bernard's and the pope's intervention in French ecclesiastical affairs.

In spring 1166 Henry joined his wife in the Loire valley, and they celebrated Easter at Angers. Some time after Easter, perhaps as late as autumn, the queen returned to England, accompanied by her eldest daughter, Matilda. Eleanor remained in England during the Christmas season, while Henry presided over his court at Poitiers. Eleanor's failure to join her husband for the festivities in her native Poitou, on one of the rare occasions when Henry was holding his Christmas court there, has raised red flags for some biographers seeking signs of trouble in their marriage. A simple explanation is her pregnancy; as the time of her delivery drew near, she realized that she was in no condition to undertake the long journey to her homeland.[72] Some time around Christmas Day 1166, she gave birth to John, her youngest son and her last child. His birthplace is usually given as Oxford, but it is impossible to say with certainty where in England Eleanor gave birth to him.[73] The name John was chosen apparently because his birth occurred about the time of the feast of Saint John the Evangelist, 27 December. A possible sixth son of Eleanor and Henry who did not survive infancy is noted only in one English chronicle, although its author had reliable sources at the royal court. Eleanor must have given birth to this unnamed boy, if he actually existed, some time between the births of Geoffrey in autumn 1158 and young Eleanor in 1161 or else after Eleanor's birth and before Joanne's arrival in October 1165.[74]

During much of 1167, while Henry was busy fighting in Brittany, the queen was in England, spending several weeks at Winchester occupied with preparations for her eldest daughter Matilda's marriage to the duke of Saxony. When the girl's grandmother, the empress Matilda, died in September, the dutiful Henry immediately came to Normandy, where she had lived in semi-monastic retirement. It is not known whether Eleanor crossed the Channel to attend her burial service. In December when John was one year old, Eleanor did sail to Normandy for the Christmas court at Argentan; it is not known whether she brought the infant boy with her. Accompanying the queen as far as the port of Dover was Matilda, where envoys of the girl's future husband, Henry the Lion duke of Saxony, were waiting to escort her to Germany.[75] Perhaps Eleanor felt some misgivings about sending off her daughter, a girl of only eleven, to marry the duke of Saxony, a mature man and a widower, even though such great age differences in marriages were common among aristocratic families.[76]

The betrothal and marriage of Matilda to Henry the Lion, placing her in the greatest family in Germany after the imperial family, must have filled Eleanor with pride, as would the royal marriages of her other daughters. When Henry had first entered into negotiations with the German emperor for finding a husband for one of his daughters, Eleanor may have remembered that one of her ancestors as duchess of Aquitaine had succeeded in marrying off her daughter to Emperor Henry III in 1043.[77] Yet it is unlikely that Eleanor played a major part in finding husbands for any of them. For Henry II, the girls were important weapons for winning diplomatic advantage, and like other princes, he always had in mind some goal to achieve through their unions. While other great men in the twelfth century occasionally took some account of emotional compatibility in choosing their daughter's husbands, a powerful monarch could not afford such indulgence, and political calculation prevailed.[78] Distributing daughters in neighboring rulers' households could create new friendships or strengthen old ones, and marriages between the families of negotiating partners often sealed diplomatic agreements. Princely families hoped that their married daughters would produce sons, for nephews and their maternal uncles traditionally felt a close connection, fostering friendly relations between the daughter's new family and her own.[79] Whether or not Eleanor played any part in selecting her daughter's spouses, she must have been aware that they had made better marriages than her two daughters by Louis VII, who were not wedded to kings but to French counts, vassals of their father.

While Eleanor was in England watching over the kingdom in 1167, Henry II was occupied in the autumn and winter in her duchy of Aquitaine, confronting a revolt by nobles. Early in 1168, after the Christmas court at Argentan in Normandy, she would join her husband in Poitou, where it appeared that Henry had suppressed the rebellion; and he settled his queen in her hereditary lands, hoping that her presence could inspire greater loyalty among a nobility so prone to rebellion. She would remain more or less permanently resident in her ancestral homeland until her sons' great rebellion of 1173–74.[80] Accompanying her as she traveled to Poitou were the two of her children still in infancy, Joanne and John, as well as Richard, aged nine, who would be formally invested as duke of Aquitaine in 1172.

ELEANOR AND THE REARING OF HER CHILDREN

Eleanor experienced almost fifteen years of regular childbearing after marrying Henry Plantagenet.[81] It was during her early years as queen, while she was bearing a child almost annually, that she was busiest acting as Henry's regent in England. She would give Henry II nine children within thirteen years. If Eleanor of Aquitaine was a distant figure as mother to her children, so were other aristocratic mothers responsible for supervising complex households. As queen, she had even less time than most for child-rearing. Contact with her children would have been limited while they were growing up. This was due to circumstances and social custom, not to a lack of maternal feeling, and it is not necessary to conclude that Eleanor was indifferent toward her young children nor that she made little "psychological investment" in them. There is no evidence to show that she and Henry failed to cherish their children, to provide for their care, to place their hopes in their futures, or to experience grief at their deaths.

It seems fruitless from a distance of eight centuries to calculate Eleanor's role in shaping her children's adult psyches, when thinking on the topic is still influenced by nineteenth-century bourgeois models modified by twentieth-century Freudian psychology. Yet one fact that stands out is the devotion to Eleanor demonstrated by her sons in their adult lives, and it testifies that their experience of her love was more powerful than their father's fitful affection. Clearly, the queen had cemented solid ties of affection with them at some point, whether during their infancy or adolescence; and strong maternal feelings would prod her to furious activity after Henry II's death, struggling to assist first Richard and then John in securing their thrones. As one writer observes, "It is difficult to believe that the devotion shown [Eleanor] by her adult sons and daughters did not grow out of childhood experience, experience that simply left no record in the account books and annals of the court."[82] Possibly Henry's difficulties with his sons were caused by their early and prolonged separations from their father. The fact that they were near-strangers to one another, in some years together only on great festive occasions, can explain in part the ease with which they took up arms against their father and against each other.

Along with all medieval mothers, Eleanor was unaware of the significance of earliest childhood for shaping adult personality that modern psychology teaches. The early Fathers of the Church had not shown great interest in questions centering on family life, and twelfth-century churchmen with their ambivalent feelings about women provided mothers with little more direction in carrying out their maternal responsibilities. Although concern for the care of children was growing in the twelfth century, encouraged in great part by Christian teaching, spiritual counselors offered mothers little counsel beyond advocating emulation of the Virgin Mary, the ideal mother. An exception to the dearth of literature on motherhood is a biography of Queen Margaret of Scotland, written in the first years of the twelfth century as a guide for her daughter Edith-Matilda, Henry I's queen. It praises Margaret as a model mother, intimately involved with her children's upbringing; yet the daughter who commissioned it hardly knew her mother, having been sent away at age six to be brought up at an English convent where her aunt was abbess.[83] Like many other great ladies living in the twelfth century, Eleanor had larger duties in politics and government that she regarded as equally important and perhaps greater than her responsibility for her children's upbringing.

In Henry and Eleanor's household were retainers of many ranks, ranging from dependent relatives and high-ranking nobles to simple knights or domestic servants of peasant origin, any of whom could be charged with caring for the royal children. As a result, the royal children's ties of affection would not have been focused uniquely on their parents, but diffused among household members of many ranks. While differing from typical nuclear families today, the medieval English royal household, overflowing with servants and retainers, had much in common with other medieval aristocratic families. Like them and like European aristocrats or American plutocrats even in the twenty-first century who turn their children over to a series of servants, Eleanor and Henry did not think it unnatural to hand their children into the care of others in the royal household, or even to custodians far from court. Sons and daughters were often sent away at early ages, daughters to be reared in the households of their betrothed and sons given over to the care of others until early adolescence, when they were established in households of their own. Yet these practices do not negate royal parents' caring instincts or an awareness of the uniqueness of childhood that is innate in all societies. It is clear that Eleanor and Henry showed great concern for the upbringing of their offspring, choosing with care the personnel who were to supervise them even if their personal participation was limited.

The rapidity with which Eleanor gave birth shows that she did not nurse her infant children, for it was uncommon for great ladies to nurse their own babies. As queen, her chief responsibility was ensuring continuity of the royal line by bearing children, not rearing them, and it was widely known that breast-feeding inhibited pregnancy. Names of some of the royal children's wet-nurses survive, and they indicate that they were selected from women of free, not servile, status, probably from wives of servants in the royal household. Alexander of Neckham, a scientific writer, Oxford master, and later abbot of Cirencester, proudly claimed that he and Richard Lionheart were "milk-brothers," for his mother had been the prince's wet-nurse.[84] Eleanor felt so fondly toward Agatha, one of her children's wet-nurses, that in 1198, three decades after her child-bearing years, she rewarded her service with a gift of land in Hertfordshire and a year later a more valuable gift, a Devonshire manor. Agatha was a woman whose ambition Eleanor could admire, and such generous gifts would have made her former servant a woman of some means. Some time, probably before becoming John's wet-nurse, Agatha entered into a long-term relationship with Godfrey de Lucy, son of the chief justiciar and himself a royal clerk who would win the bishopric of Winchester in 1189 despite being encumbered with a "wife."[85]

Wet-nurses of Eleanor's children must have resembled nannies in their relations with their charges, providing not only nourishment, but also affection and companionship and remaining with them long after weaning. After John was brought to England during the great rebellion of 1173–74, the pipe roll records a grant of ten marks to "the nurse of the king's son," although he was at least seven years old then.[86] The wet-nurses of Richard Lionheart and John earned their fond feeling, and their affection was returned. When Richard became king, he granted a pension to his nurse, Hodierna.[87] After John's death, his former nurse Agatha, by then a prosperous widow, remembered him and his son when making a gift of land to the nuns of Flamstead "for the soul of King Henry [III] son of King John."[88]

When Henry II's sons were little more than infants, each of them was assigned a "master" or "preceptor" from among members of the royal household. He was assigned responsibility for the young boy, charged with spending on his needs and supervising the servants caring for him. He was not necessarily a cleric, and he did not give lessons; teachers—also called masters—could be recruited from the clerks and chaplains present in any great household. Choosing such a master was Henry's duty, for noble fathers made major decisions about their sons' upbringing, although he was likely to have discussed his selection with Eleanor. A master named Mainard took charge of Young Henry in 1156 when the boy was only a year old, and he remained with him for at least three more years.[89] The division of authority between this official and the child's mother is unknown, but it must have meant that Eleanor was denied full responsibility for her son's care, even in early childhood. Forced to share responsibility for her young sons with a male named by her husband, she nevertheless succeeded at some point in their youths in knitting the affective bonds normally binding sons to their mothers.

In 1159, when Young Henry was only four years old, his father placed him in the household of his chancellor Thomas Becket, where sons of nobles were "educated in gentlemanly upbringing and teaching."[90] There was precedent for Henry's sending his heir away at such an early age: William the Conqueror had placed his second son, William Rufus, the designated heir to the English Crown, in Archbishop Lanfranc's household. Henry II may already have been thinking of naming Becket his archbishop of Canterbury and having his eldest son crowned as king while still a boy. When relations between Henry and Archbishop Becket began to cool, Henry, in October 1163, rebuked his newly installed primate by removing Young Henry from his custody. When the king left for his French territories the next month, he did not send the boy, then about eight years of age, back to Eleanor; instead, he continued to live apart from his mother's household with a new master, William fitz John, a royal administrator.[91]

Young aristocrats were knighted as part of their initiation into manhood, and fathers would find them a mentor to join their household: an older, experienced knight who could prepare them for knighthood with training in the noble occupations of hunting, hawking, and warfare. After Young Henry's coronation in 1170, his father assigned such a mentor to the fifteen-year-old youth, the knight-errant William Marshal, much admired for chivalry, but an illiterate with little interest in administration. According to the *History of William Marshal,* he served as the sort of companion-guide who accompanied heroes of the romances, charged with the Young King's instruction in courtesy and martial arts, preparing him to take up arms as a knight.[92] Hunting sharpened warrior skills, and all of Henry and Eleanor's sons shared their ancestors' love for the chase. Richard during his youth in Poitou would find pleasure in hunting in his mother's ancestral forests in the Vendée. Roger of Howden wrote of Henry II's sons, "They strove to outdo others in handling weapons. They realized that without practice the art of war did not come naturally when it was needed."[93]

Sons of royalty needed to know more than skill in handling horses and weapons, and at twelfth-century princely courts, clerics were advocating a courtly ideal of conduct, challenging old-fashioned knights upholding the traditional warrior ethos of the knightly class. The counts of Anjou had long prized learning in Latin letters, seen in the excellent schooling that Henry II's father provided for him, and Eleanor too knew the value of learning. While less is known about Henry's sons' formal education than his own, it is certain that they acquired a sound grounding in Latin grammar, although no formal office of royal schoolmaster yet existed at the English court. A letter in the archbishop of Rouen's name, addressed to the king when Young Henry was only ten years old, however, expresses a fear that the knightly side of the future king's education was taking precedence over study of the liberal arts.[94] Perhaps the concern stemmed from Henry's removal of his heir from Thomas Becket's custody, and it hints at rivalry between the boy's clerical and knightly tutors over the two groups' diverging values. Richard Lionheart knew Latin well, although he is better known for his French verses. Gerald of Wales's anecdote of the Lionheart's correcting the Latin spoken by his archbishop of Canterbury gives evidence of his competence as a Latinist.[95] John gained an interest in literature during his youth, and as king he built up a considerable library of classics and religious works. He deposited his books at Reading Abbey for safekeeping and sometimes wrote to the abbot requesting that certain volumes be sent to him.[96]

Although great ladies had responsibility for their sons' upbringing only until they reached their sixth or seventh year, aristocratic daughters could remain in their mother's care until adolescence, unless they were betrothed as pre-adolescents and sent away to be brought up by their future in-laws. Like other queens throughout the Middle Ages, Eleanor saw her daughters affianced at early ages to foreign princes chosen for political considerations, and promptly sent far away to grow up at foreign courts. Personal contact by Eleanor with her daughters was difficult once they were sent off to their future husbands' lands in Germany, Spain, and Sicily, and she had little prospect of seeing them again. Yet contacts between royal daughters and their birth-parents were seldom entirely severed, and Eleanor doubtless corresponded with her daughters, although no copies of her letters survive. Royal parents maintained contact with daughters married to foreign princes, for their marriages had been arranged for the purpose of serving the family interest, creating or securing alliances.[97] Matilda, Eleanor, and Joanne, married to princes who were conspicuous as cultural patrons, were almost certainly literate. Late twelfth-century romances depict noble maidens learning their letters, and a renowned preacher, Adam of Perseigne (d. *c.* 1208), sent the countess of Chartres Latin texts that she could give to her daughters to read with the help of her chaplain or a learned nun.[98] Although instruction in letters must have begun before Eleanor's daughters left the English royal household, the major portion of their education would have taken place at the courts of their in-laws.

Eleanor's first years as English queen were fulfilling for her, even though she was very much an alien to her subjects. She created a genuine partnership with Henry II, possessing a post of responsibility as his regent. At the same time that she was deeply involved in royal governance, she was also fulfilling successfully a queen's basic task, bearing children, especially sons, to continue the royal line. Eleanor's degree of involvement in her children's upbringing differs from the ideal of parenting today, but it hardly differs from practises of royalty or the aristocracy in any age, who have always enjoyed the services of nannies, governesses, tutors, or boarding schools in the rearing of their children. A biographer of King George VI (d.1952) writes that for the prince and his brothers and sisters their parents "were 'Olympian figures,' part of a dimly perceived grown-up universe." She adds, "For them the real world was their nursery and the servants and nurses who looked after them."[99] Much the same could be said of Eleanor and Henry II's offspring. It is not so much Eleanor's mothering as her sons' own escapades—persistent revolts against their father, the fecklessness of Young Henry, Geoffrey's repeated treachery, or King John's cruelty and incompetence—that have caused her to be labeled a bad mother centuries later.

CHAPTER 6

A QUEEN'S WORK: REGENT FOR AN ABSENTEE KING, 1155–1168

HENRY Plantagenet, lord of Anjou and Normandy as well as duke in Eleanor's duchy of Aquitaine, would spend even less time in England than had his Anglo-Norman predecessors: not even thirteen years of his thirty-five-year reign. During his first decade as king he visited his island realm only four times, usually staying between a year and a year and a half, and his absences from England lasted up to four years.[1] Obviously the new king needed a trusted and capable representative to govern England while he was away dashing about dealing with the rebellions of nobles and Capetian conspiracies in France. He would turn to his wife Eleanor as his helpmate, reviving the Anglo-Norman practice of naming the queen as regent during the king's absences.

Eleanor's presence in the English kingdom was all the more vital after years of weak rule under Stephen of Blois. A strong and trusted hand controlling England in Henry II's absence was essential in his first decade as king when the administrative machinery of Henry I's reign, weakened during the civil war of the 1140s during the reign of Stephen of Blois, was not yet restored. Henry could turn with confidence to Eleanor to represent legitimate royal authority in England. He saw in her another strong woman similar to his mother, Empress Matilda, who had shown herself able and willing to take the reins of power. Despite Eleanor's responsibilities as regent, she would not remain continuously in England; in most years, she would cross the Channel at least once if only to attend Henry's Christmas court, for it was more often held in his French possessions than in England.

A royal presence in the person of Eleanor as regent was essential to give legitimacy to Henry's deputies carrying out his work of reclaiming royal resources, restoring central authority, and curbing the magnates' power while he was outside his kingdom. Working closely with trusted royal officials, she issued commands that had the same force as the king's commands. Although English chroniclers caught sight of Eleanor "only out of the corner of their eyes," as regent, she had a key role as the personification of monarchy during Henry's many absences from the kingdom.[2] To present to the people their new Angevin king's majesty, riches, and power, it was his queen's task to preside over a magnificent court. Henry II knew that his grandfather's court had been "characterized by its ostentatious display of wealth," and one way of emulating him was to restore the royal court as the center of culture and learning that it had been before its luster had dimmed during the weak Stephen's disputed reign.[3] Henry expected his new queen to take a central role in reflecting his court's splendor, shining like a star. He would provide Eleanor with a generous marriage settlement, dowerlands of manors and towns scattered across England, and in addition, large sums handed over to her periodically that would provide her with a vast income, as much as that of the greatest magnates in the kingdom. After the coronation ceremony in December 1154, Eleanor of Aquitaine found herself "Riche dame de riche rei."[4]

ELEANOR'S ROLE AS QUEEN AND REGENT IN ENGLISH GOVERNMENT

Once Henry Plantagenet and his bride were crowned king and queen of England, the youthful King Henry II was determined to rule as a great king, and he took as his model his grandfather, Henry I. Henry Plantagenet was "determined to be not merely king, but such a king as his grandfather had been," even in the north of the kingdom where royal authority had never been as strong as in southern England.[5] During the long civil war that had preceded Henry's accession, England's earls and barons had consolidated control over their lordships, recruiting armed bands and ignoring the king and his local agents, the sheriffs. Early in 1155 the king headed north, reaching York by the end of January and moving on to take control of Scarborough Castle. Henry remained in his new kingdom for little more than a year, until January 1156, when he left his queen behind as his deputy and returned to France to contend with his brother's rebellion in Anjou.[6] Eleanor acted as her husband's regent until the summer of 1156, when she sailed away to join him in Anjou, taking with her both her children, Young Henry and the infant Matilda. Not long after Christmas, Eleanor would return to England with the two children, and she was again regent early in 1157 until Henry II arrived in the kingdom in April.

No less a person than the learned John of Salisbury, the papal secretary who had encountered Eleanor first in Italy on her return from the Second Crusade, bears witness to her activities as regent. In England in a new post as secretary to Theobald, archbishop of Canterbury, he proved an astute observer of politics, author of the *Policraticus*, or "Statesmen's Book," the most notable political treatise of the twelfth century. John felt first hand the force of the new English king's authoritarian rule, having aroused Henry's hostility while at Rome for impeding royal emissaries' attempts to defend royal control over the English Church and for obstructing papal approval for an English expedition to Ireland.[7] In one of his letters he laments, "The indignation of our most serene lord, our all-powerful king, our most unconquerable prince, has grown hot against me in full force. . . . I alone in all the realm am accused of diminishing the royal dignity." It was Queen Eleanor and the chancellor, Thomas Becket, who would bring John the good news "that the storm which threatened me has abated," when they arrived in England ahead of the king in spring 1157.[8]

A modern biographer of Henry II writes, "To judge from the chroniclers, the most striking fact about Eleanor of Aquitaine is her utter insignificance in Henry's reign." He acknowledges that Eleanor as regent had authority to act in the king's name or in her own, but he finds that her power "seems in practice to have been largely formal."[9] Such an under-estimation of Eleanor's political significance can be challenged, however. Henry had enough confidence in Eleanor's abilities to leave her behind in England in the dangerous early years of his reign, when his control over the kingdom was not yet complete. John of Salisbury was convinced that the royal couple's power was interchangeable, with the queen's power equal to her husband's in ruling the kingdom. In one of his letters, he complained of an unnamed cleric who was teaching the equality of papal and royal power, allegedly instructing the English people that they could appeal "to the Pope and to the king or queen alike." John accused this clerk of seeking to "kindle the indignation of the king or queen to crush the innocent."[10]

Letters by John of Salisbury authored in Archbishop Theobald's name reveal Eleanor acting as authoritatively as any Anglo-Norman or Angevin monarch. One letter shows Eleanor pressuring the bishop of Worcester to secure the post of archdeacon for one of her clerks, Master Solomon. In his letter to the bishop of Worcester, Theobald pointed out that the king and queen desired the post for her clerk and that the bishop should have agreed to appoint such a "learned and honourable man." The letter continued, "But perhaps you will say that Master Solomon does not deserve such a favour, since he has stirred up the queen's mind against your innocence. What else is this than to accuse the queen of lying? For she has excused him in your hearing."[11] Despite Eleanor's pressure on Master Solomon's behalf, she does not appear to have secured the archdeaconry of Worcester for him.[12] Another of the archbishop's letters, addressed to the abbess of Amesbury, complains that the abbess had ejected a cleric from his church "with violence and without any process of law," an act that Theobald condemned as "a wrong done to the holy Roman Church and an affront to the king's majesty." The abbess had made matters worse by refusing to restore the church despite a mandate from "our lady the queen." The archbishop warned her that "if our lady the queen corrects your breach of the king's proclamation by condign punishment, we shall ratify it."[13]

Throughout Eleanor's early years as queen, there must have been much movement from the household of Henry II, following him to war along England's frontiers or in his French territories, to her own entourage. The king took care to leave a small group of trusted companions in charge of the administration to assist her in governing his new kingdom. Based at the exchequer at Westminster, these men could be found from time to time at Eleanor's side in castles where she was residing as far away as Oxford or Salisbury. Chief among them was Robert, earl of Leicester, and Richard de Lucy, joint justiciars, to assist her in governing England. The queen could respect the earl of Leicester, "a powerful, literate, and intelligent magnate," who had an outstanding education for a twelfth-century layman. A cultivated man, he had received his early education at Abingdon Abbey, then as a youth at Henry I's royal court that was something like a palace school. His presence alongside Eleanor advising her reinforced her authority as regent.[14] In contrast to the illustrious earl of Leicester, member of the powerful Beaumont family and Henry's trusted friend since his struggle for the English Crown, Richard de Lucy was of only knightly birth, and he had risen in rank through service to King Stephen. He had readily transferred his allegiance to the new king, however, and soon proved himself a capable administrator, winning Henry's trust.[15]

Another valued adviser for Eleanor as regent was Reginald de Dunstanville, earl of Cornwall. Like Earl Robert of Gloucester, Reginald was one of Henry I's many illegitimate sons; after Robert's death, he had become perhaps the most important advocate among the English baronage for the Angevin cause. He had looked out for Henry's interests after he returned to France to his wife and infant son in March 1154; and he remained influential once Henry and Eleanor arrived in England in December 1154.[16] Eleanor also benefitted from "the faithful care of the archbishop of Canterbury" during the king's absences, as John of Salisbury wrote. While the king was campaigning in Wales in summer 1157, John assisted Archbishop Theobald in the task of ensuring "the safe custody of the illustrious queen of the English and the king's sons."[17] Also counting among the queen's counselors was Thomas Becket when he was not with the king on campaigns across the Channel.

Several lesser-ranking Anglo-Normans who had joined Henry's household before his coronation and who continued to be among his closest associates joined Eleanor's household from time to time, when they were not in France with the king. They include such men as Manasser Bisset, who as steward of the royal household sometimes carried out tasks for the queen, once overseeing the delivery of one of her robes to her, as well as Warin fitz Gerold, charged with seeing to the queen's travel and payments for her supplies. Fitz Gerold, who had been in Henry's service since 1148, was the king's chamberlain. Hugh de Gundeville, who had served earlier in the household of Henry's cousin, the earl of Gloucester, was in charge of works for the queen's chapel, houses, walls, and garden at Winchester.[18]

Keys for assessing Eleanor's power as English queen are her writs—peremptory letters ordering the carrying out of royal commands, most often addressed to sheriffs or other local royal agents. Royal writs dealt with administrative matters or with petitioners' requests to right a wrong, such as unlawful occupation of land or seizure of property. They were crucial instruments for restoring the king's position as the font of all justice after the weakening of royal power during Stephen's reign, and the royal chancery drafted hundreds or even thousands of them each year. Few were preserved, and the number surviving may represent no more than 1 percent of all issued in Henry II's reign.[19] With Henry frequently away from the English kingdom and Eleanor issuing such documents as regent, she had an indispensable part in the restoration of royal authority; but only nine of Eleanor's actual writs survive, although more are known second-hand through references to them in other documents.[20] These are only a tiny fraction of the dozens and dozens undoubtedly issued by her during each of her husband's absences.

Eleanor's writs adopt the same harsh tone of the Anglo-Norman kings' writs; in one addressed to the sheriff of Suffolk, a great earl, the queen took an imperious tone. She warned him that his failure to carry out an earlier command "much displeased my lord the king and me," and she warned him that "if you do not wish [to carry it out], the king's justice will be made to be done."[21] In a writ to the sheriff of London, she concluded, "Until you enforce the king's justice for London, I do not wish to hear more complaints about default of justice. Farewell."[22] Most of Eleanor's writs dealt with routine matters, such as the letters of royal permission to leave the kingdom required of clerics. A letter of John of Salisbury to Thomas Becket, dated early 1164, mentions that he had gone to the queen at Salisbury to secure his "license to depart."[23] He could not take ship without a writ bearing her seal. When petitioners procured writs from the king overseas, it seems that an additional writ from the queen was needed in order to implement them in England. In one petitioner's account, he writes that once he had the king's writ from Normandy in hand, "I proceeded to Salisbury with the same, in order that it might be returned under the queen's seal," noting that her writ cost him two silver marks.[24] Other documents issued by Eleanor are confirmations of covenants that parties to disputes in local courts had settled by compromise and then sought written record of their agreement. While none of Eleanor's confirmations survives from her years as regent, they were occasionally cited in later lawsuits; for example, a litigant in 1204 claimed land under an agreement made between his father and an earlier opponent "according to the confirmation given by the Lady Queen Eleanor."[25]

The two chief justiciars, Earl Robert of Leicester and Richard de Lucy could not act without the approval of either the king or the queen, and when both Henry and Eleanor were far from the kingdom during the 1159 Toulouse expedition, the earl of Leicester would consult a more accessible member of the royal family, the empress Matilda in Normandy.[26] Leicester and Lucy occasionally witnessed the queen's writs, suggesting that they had a hand in drafting them. Yet Eleanor did not hesitate to issue writs overruling the chief justiciars. When the abbot of St Albans could not secure justice against a powerful neighbor due to the earl of Leicester's failure to act in a lawsuit from 1158–59, he approached the queen. The earl had failed to issue a writ protecting the abbot's property from seizure by his opponent while the lawsuit proceeded, and his adversary had cut down a number of trees in his wood; but Eleanor proved willing to intervene in the dispute, issuing her own writ to protect St Albans from further losses.[27] The office of justiciar was not yet the powerful position of "second to the king" that it would become by the end of the twelfth century, and its duties centered on the exchequer and fiscal matters. Later the chief justiciar would oversee all the royal administrative agencies, the exchequer, royal judges, sheriffs, constables, and lesser local officials, leaving the king, traveling with his itinerant household about his Continental possessions, free to concentrate on war and diplomacy.

THE ENGLISH ROYAL COURT

Under Eleanor and Henry II, the English royal court would regain its importance, becoming the largest royal court in Europe and approaching the papal court in numbers. Eleanor would have gloried in her place as a focal point of royal splendor at crown-wearings and other festive occasions, enjoying the contrast with the drabness of the Capetian court that she had left behind. Henry had had less experience of great princely courts while growing up, having spent much of his youth in warfare moving about with only a small retinue. Supposedly he preferred the informality of a military band on the march, yet he well understood the importance of "the theater of power" and his queen's and his own splendid appearance for impressing his subjects with his power. According to one courtier, the king appeared "always robed in precious stuffs, as is right." As a youth Henry had heard stories of grand courts; certainly his mother told him of the glories of her father Henry I's court and her first husband's imperial household in Germany, and later Eleanor could have described to him the grandest court of all, the Byzantine emperor's court at Constantinople.[28]

The new king revived the Anglo-Norman kings' custom of celebrating with much pomp the great festivals of the Church. Christmas, Easter, and Pentecost were occasions for English kings to host impressive assemblies of their nobles combining religious, convivial, and political functions. William the Conqueror and his sons had made them times for ceremonial crown-wearings to remind their subjects of divine sanction for their authority over them. Of all these assemblies coinciding with the liturgical calendar, the Christmas court was the most brilliant. On these ceremonial occasions, the court of Henry II's grandfather afforded him a model, and courtiers from Henry I's reign survived to instruct him in the proper rituals and courtly conduct.[29] At Easter 1158 Henry and Eleanor are said to have worn their crowns ceremonially for the last time, vowing never to take up their diadems again and placing them on the altar of Worcester Cathedral.[30] It seems improbable that they abandoned the Anglo-Norman monarchs' practise of crown-wearings on the three great feast-days, however. A more plausible explanation is that they were donating the crowns that they had worn that Easter to the cathedral, not renouncing all future crown-wearings. Sometimes it is said that this action was due to Henry's disapproval of too much pageantry, or possibly his objection to the bishops' role in crown-wearings that could be seen as emphasizing his subjection to the spiritual power.[31] Both he and the queen knew very well the usefulness of ostentatious court ceremonial, however. They could see great festivals displaying royal power and splendor as political propaganda, and Henry continued to mark significant occasions such as his sons' knighting or solemn assemblies of his magnates with magnificent display and much feasting.

Eleanor occupied a position as a focal point of royal splendor at the crown-wearings and other festive occasions staged by the king. Lavish sums were spent on the queen's clothing, and her garments of rich fabrics decorated with fur and gold or silver embroidery worn at festivals were a means of proclaiming royal wealth and power. The pipe rolls, the exchequer's records of annual audits of royal finances, record a pound paid to her shoemaker, almost seven pounds for cloth, and a robe costing over twenty pounds plus twenty shillings for delivering it to her.[32] At a time when a knight's fee (equivalent to a single manor) produced an annual income of no more than twenty pounds, such a price for a robe was enormous. Numerous miscellaneous entries on the pipe rolls suggest the luxury of Eleanor's life as queen at the English court. Purchases for her kitchen for pepper, cumin, and cinnamon are recorded, and innumerable entries for imported wine and its transport are indications of the high standards for her table. An abundance of elaborately prepared dishes, especially meats, defined a great prince's table; and a king's banquets had a political function, impressing guests with his power, prestige, and wealth. An illustration of Henry II's awareness of the impression that a lavish feast could make is a Christmas dinner given for the native Irish nobles during his 1171 expedition to Ireland; they were amazed by "the sumptuous and plentiful fare of the English table and the most elegant service by the royal domestics." Chestnuts sent to Salisbury to the queen by Henry's writ in 1159 at a cost of three shillings were perhaps a token of his continued affection for her after four years of marriage.[33]

A feature of the English royal court under the new king and queen was its cosmopolitan character, attracting courtiers from across the Channel, many of them men of classical learning, along with numerous English-born clerks who had studied at Paris. As one of them, Peter of Blois, famously observed, in Henry's household "it is school every day."[34] Courtly conduct or courtesy was expected of those gathered there, an ethos that extolled the classical ideal of courtliness: strong moral character, eloquence, refined tastes, and dignified deportment. Also powerful at Henry and Eleanor's court was the knightly ethos of chivalry, the virtues of a courageous and faithful knight, to which literate knights at court added courtesy. Literature, influenced by the clerical ideal of courtliness, presented the knights with heroes who were exemplars of morality and manners as well as prowess. Early in the thirteenth century, a troubadour Raimon Vidal composed a treatise on civility in which he looked back to the days when Eleanor was England's queen, taking Henry II and his sons as his models. He saw them combining the virtues of the courtier and the warrior, and he looked on their time as "the good old days of those who knew how to achieve noble, valorous and sensible acts."[35]

For clerical writers at Henry and Eleanor's court, their histories and romances provided an opportunity to promote their vision of a courtly culture combining knightly virtues of chivalry with moral and ethical values while at the same time providing entertainment. Through poetry and song they sought to persuade great men of their duty to provide support for their young knights without an inheritance or marriage prospects. Although it is impossible to document the part that women at court played in the taming of the unruly males gathered there, they had every reason to encourage the clerics' civilizing efforts. Young knights who were both amorous and ambitious soon learned that courtesy won them favor among ladies who could help them in the quest for patronage by interceding with their husbands on their behalf.[36] Eleanor's upbringing at the sophisticated ducal court at Poitiers ensured that she would have supported writers' attempts to elevate the tone of the English royal court, inculcating higher standards of good manners and civilized conduct among the courtiers. Yet when the queen joined in courtly banter, demonstrating her own wit, as was normal for southern ladies, she would have lowered herself in the eyes of conservative clerical moralists. Doubtless such conduct encouraged them to spread more ugly rumors about her, and Eleanor's enjoyment of gambling may have exposed her to more criticism for frivolity. Some of her household servants held land of her in return for giving her ivory dice yearly. Not only games with dice but board games such as backgammon and chess were played for stakes, and aristocratic ladies favored such games of chance as ways of passing their time.[37]

Under the new Plantagenet monarch, politics in England became court politics, as scions of aristocratic families flocked to court, competing for royal patronage with lesser-ranking newcomers. The ideal of ethical conduct taught to courtiers as an essential part of courtliness was in competition with their ambition for material advancement through a patron's favor. A landless yet loyal household knight who won royal favor could win lucrative offices, custody of manors in the king's hand, marriage to a wealthy heiress or a widow with dowerlands, and remission of debts and tax obligations. A cleric in the king's or queen's service could hope for appointment to lucrative ecclesiastical posts, even to a bishopric. Such appointments to posts in the Church were a common means for English royalty to secure incomes for clerks in their service. In a poem by Peter of Blois depicting a debate between a courtier and a criticizer of the courtier's life, he explained what drew the ambitious to the royal court:

> What binds us to the court
> is more delicate clothing,
> food more exquisite
> and more refined, and there I'm feared, and not afraid,
> and can increase the estate my parents left me, and
> thunder out great words;
> I'm tied there by the counsels
> of the rich, and the chances
> of dignities, which the friendship
> of magnates can bestow.[38]

Anyone who rose through royal favor, however, ran a risk of losing the monarch's goodwill and leaving the court in disgrace.

While enhancing the majesty of royalty was a function of the royal household, duties of the new king's servants ranged from providing physical protection for the royal family to domestic tasks of supplying the royal entourage with food, drink, and other necessities, and assisting the king in the official business of governing the kingdom. The royal household had a public aspect as the royal court, and before the royal administration became professionalized, domestic officials assumed public responsibilities. All this required a huge staff, ranging from titled household officials, bands of knights, chaplains, and clerks, down to huntsmen, horsemen, and menials in the stables and kitchens. One court functionary's title, "water carrier of Queen Eleanor," suggests both a large corps of royal servants' specialized tasks and an elaborate court etiquette prevailing at the English royal court.[39] Richly clothed doorkeepers and ushers stood about to keep order in the hall, escorting the invited into the royal presence and ejecting the unwanted. Perhaps indicative of the moral level of Henry's household was an officer specially charged with "custody of the whores of the royal court."[40] Clearly, Eleanor was now far away from the pious and puritanical atmosphere prevailing at the court of her prudish ex-husband.

Eleanor would find the English royal household's structure similar to her father's and her first husband's households, following a model derived from the Carolingian court. It consisted of three elements: one clerical, the chapel; and two lay ones: a military element of knights or military retainers, and the lay officials of the hall and chamber charged with provisioning the royal household.[41] Prominent in the royal household were clerics performing both priestly and secretarial tasks. The chapel consisted of several priests with liturgical duties, including the queen's personal chaplain who heard her confessions. One of the chaplains or clerks had the title of almoner, charged with distribution of alms; and another might serve his lord's family as physician. Numerous other clerks were attached to the chamber, probably in minor clerical orders, assigned with keeping track of the royal couple's expenditures. Still others served in the royal chancery or writing office, drafting official documents under the direction of the chancellor, formal head of the royal chapel staff. As in other princely households, the head of the secretarial staff was the chancellor. Because the chancellor had custody of the king's seal, it was essential that the king have confidence in him, and early in Henry's reign Thomas Becket left the archbishop of Canterbury's household to take the post.

The king's household consisted of two lay groups. Naturally, one of these was a military element for protection and for maintaining order at court, a band of knights ranging from earls and barons with their own retinues to landless soldiers. This household force could serve in wartime as the nucleus of an army, a general staff for an expanded force of hired foot soldiers, archers, and siege engineers. Eleanor would have had more contact with the second lay element, the staff of the hall. She would have had frequent business with the butler charged with supplying wine, or more generally, the king's table, and with the chamberlains, long ago in charge of the royal bedchamber, but now charged with the household treasury and payment of its expenses. Eleanor and her own steward would have consulted often with the king's stewards, also known as seneschals, who supervised all the domestic officials attached to the hall and to the chamber.[42]

As we have seen, the court, like other twelfth-century royal courts, was itinerant. In the royal entourage's moves about the kingdom, it traveled burdened with goods necessary for impressing the communities through which it passed with the king's wealth and power. One contemporary commented, "It is no wonder that crowds of women and youths or men of the frivolous type rush out to see kings. But even wise and discreet men are driven to go out and watch them . . ."[43] An important household official was the marshal with responsibility for the many horses and carts needed to transport the enormous quantity of baggage required by the king, the queen, and their large retinue. Other servants had duties connected with the royal family's travel, the "bearer of the king's bed" and the "tent-keeper," each with his own servant and pack horse. All officials charged with the hall, chamber, kitchen, and other components of the royal household had carts and carters as well as pack horses for carrying their supplies. In all, well over 100 mounted men, plus a dozen or more pack horses and half a dozen carts or wagons with iron-bound wheels were required for the court's travel.[44]

In Eleanor's first year in England she was often separated from Henry, for he was constantly on the move, cementing his authority over his new kingdom. Henry II was notorious for restless movement about his territories, dashing from one hot spot to another, from the Welsh or Scottish frontiers to the Loire valley and to the unruly southern borders of Poitou. His household often doubled as the headquarters of a general on a military campaign, limited in size because he had to be ready to move at a moment's notice. Eleanor escaped these countless displacements. Both her responsibilities as regent and her frequent pregnancies prevented her traveling with her husband, and she was free to make more leisurely progresses from one English royal castle to another in the south and west of the kingdom. It was her duty as queen to preside over the royal household in all its splendor, maintaining the magnificence worthy of a great king's court, while Henry was on the move with his fighting men throughout his far-flung domains.

Nonetheless, Eleanor's life as Henry II's queen was one of constant movement from castle to castle in England and frequent voyages across the Channel to the Plantagenet possessions in France or to her own duchy. Because roads were little more than tracks that turned to mud during rains, travel of any great distance by land was slow, uncomfortable, and exhausting; and crossing the English Channel in foul weather could be dangerous, with the small vessels violently tossed about in stormy seas. In winter, gales often caused delays in sailing across the Channel, and waiting days for a storm to abate or for favorable winds was common. Channel crossings of queens since the Norman Conquest were so common that some lords held lands of the king in return for servicing the queen's yacht sailing between England and Normandy. Most years

Eleanor would cross the sea at least once if only to attend Henry's Christmas court, for it was more often held in his French possessions than in England. The queen was accompanied on her voyages by a household of three dozen or more servants, requiring several vessels to transport her entourage and her travel goods. As Eleanor in her second marriage was regularly producing children, traveling with toddlers multiplied the difficulties of travel, even with the assistance of numerous servants, and it sometimes proved easier and safer to deposit the children at some secure place in trusted servants' care. Despite the difficulties, however, she would frequently travel with one or two very young children, even taking them with her across the Channel.

ELEANOR'S PERSONAL HOUSEHOLD

As Henry II's queen, Eleanor had a large staff of servants responsible for her needs who formed her own separate household within the larger royal household. Her own household imitated the larger royal one with officials bearing identical titles, her own chancellor, and numerous clerks as well as a steward, butler, and chamberlain.[45] Because of her husband's numerous lengthy absences from the kingdom, her entourage expanded during those periods to include numbers of the king's men. Eleanor's personal household did not number as many as the hundred or more persons in the service of Henry III's queen in the mid-thirteenth century, but she probably had forty or more persons of varying ranks serving her, equivalent in size to the household of any English earl or major baron.[46]

Only a few members of Eleanor's household, her closest associates in her new kingdom, can be identified.[47] Prominent among them is Master Matthew, her chancellor, who seems to have become head of her writing office on her arrival in England until he left the royal household to become dean of Angers Cathedral about 1162. He has been identified as Henry Plantagenet's former tutor, who had earlier taught Count Geoffrey's two sisters.[48] At various times in the 1150s, two other clerks, Master Bernard and Jordan, also held the title of queen's chancellor. Two or more clerks in Eleanor's household bore the name Peter; one can be identified as her chaplain, another was a scribe "Peter of Poitiers," who may be the same "Peter the duchess's notary" who was with her in 1153–54 before her arrival in England.[49] Another of the queen's household clerks was Jocelin de Balliol, of Anglo-Norman ancestry and likely from a Northumberland baronial family. Jocelin, formerly in Empress Matilda's household, witnessed more of the queen's writs than anyone else in her household.[50] The presence of Master Matthew and Jocelin in Eleanor's household suggests that Henry was not allowing her a completely free hand in choosing its members.

Two others also apparently placed in Eleanor's household by her husband were Ralph of Hastings, steward of the queen's household, and William fitz Hamo, a Norman chosen from the king's inner circle. Ralph of Hastings's uncle had served previously as steward to an earlier queen, the second wife and widow of Henry I. Ralph as steward handled payments to Eleanor from the exchequer during her first five years as queen. William fitz Hamo had been serving the counts of Anjou since the mid-1140s. He was one of two trusted members of Henry Plantagenet's household left behind with Eleanor's household in Normandy a few months after their marriage while the young duke was in England fighting for his Crown. The other was Geoffrey de Clères, an Angevin who earlier had served Henry's father along with his two brothers.[51]

At royal courts factionalism sometimes arose as ambitious relatives and courtiers following a foreign princess to her new husband's court competed with native-born courtiers, who feared the newcomers as "an all-powerful alien faction."[52] This had been the case at the court of Louis VII, where members of Eleanor's Poitevin entourage formed a clique that threatened long-standing Capetian courtiers' influence. There was little possibility of a similar situation at the English royal court, however. When Eleanor left Poitiers with Henry for his duchy of Normandy after Easter 1154, she had left behind most of her household assembled during the two years following her flight to Beaugency to Poitou in 1152.[53] When the couple finally set sail for England at the end of the year, she was not accompanied by the large retinue of Poitevins that had followed her to Paris as a young bride, and few Poitevins ever followed her northward to the English court in search of patronage. As a result, the likelihood of her creating a powerful Poitevin faction in England was slim, and her countrymen were not a factor in rivalry for royal patronage. She would be spared the hostility that Henry III's queen, Eleanor of Provence, would arouse in the mid-thirteenth century by attracting hordes of fortune-seeking Provençal and Savoyard relatives to the English court. Apart from general suspicion of the southern French for their frivolity and profligacy, no evidence survives of anti-Poitevin sentiments among native-born courtiers such as that prevalent later in the reigns of King John and Henry III, when the word "Poitevin" became a term of opprobrium.

Despite the paucity of Poitevins in Eleanor's entourage, she could not escape involvement in the scramble for patronage prevalent at royal courts. With an entourage equivalent to a major baronial household in size, the queen had considerable patronage to dispense, and ambitious men in pursuit of patronage from her husband would have sought her to intercede on their behalf. A lucrative queenly perquisite pursued by Eleanor's saintly predecessor, Edith-Matilda, wife of Henry I, was the sale of influence. Petitioners seeking favors from the king or influence at court would not have hesitated to give gifts to the queen, hoping for her intercession with her husband on their behalf. In mid-thirteenth-century England, Henry III's wife, Queen Eleanor of Provence, would take advantage of her access to the king to play an active part in court politics, making a point of cultivating friendships with prominent courtiers, among them powerful royal administrators.[54] Some hint of tensions between Eleanor's household and that of her husband appears in the unhappy lot of the queen's water carrier, however. After Eleanor's fall from favor in 1173, he would meet a bad end, falsely accused of crimes by two of the king's huntsmen and hanged.[55]

No more than four or five members of Eleanor's household at Poitiers after she separated from Louis VII can be pinpointed with certainty in her service later in England, Normandy, or Poitou. Two or possibly three of her clerks bore the name Peter. Most often with the queen was Peter her chaplain accompanying her at Caen at the end of her 1156–57 visit to Poitou and again prominent among her clerks after her return to Poitou in 1168. Peter was still living as late as 1189, when the queen took steps to safeguard his income from a prebend at Rouen Cathedral.[56] Also two Poitevin laymen are found with Eleanor in England: Philip her butler and Bernard de Chauvigny her chamberlain. Bernard's family had supplied hereditary officers for the bishops of Poitiers, managing their lordship of Chauvigny; and he was Eleanor's cousin, descended from the viscounts of Châtellerault through his mother.[57] Bernard ought not be confused with Master Bernard, her chancellor in Poitou following her divorce from Louis VII, for the post of chamberlain was a lay office.

The only Poitevin noble known to have received a land grant in England was Eleanor's uncle Ralph de Faye, although it is uncertain whether he ever visited there. A younger son of the queen's maternal grandfather, the viscount of Châtellerault, Ralph styled himself "de Faye" after his wife's ancestral lordship on the Poitevin–Angevin frontier. Holding posts in Poitou, he was more valuable to Eleanor looking out for her interests in her native county. Eleanor managed to secure for her uncle estates at Bramley, Surrey, in her first year as queen, and his lands enjoyed favors such as pardons from taxes and freedom from visitations of royal justices and foresters. Ralph de Faye succeeded in ingratiating himself with Henry, and he often joined the king's entourage in France until his fall from royal favor in 1173.[58] Eleanor took advantage of her new position to show generosity to other kinsmen belonging to the Châtellerault lineage. For Barthélemy de Vendôme, apparently related to her through Ralph's family, Eleanor found an ecclesiastical living in England. Some time before 1173, she persuaded the abbot of Westminster Abbey to appoint him as priest of one of the abbey's churches in Essex. Barthélemy, dean of Angers Cathedral at the time and elected archbishop of Tours in 1174, would have held the church as an absentee, finding a needy English cleric to carry out his priestly duties.[59]

No doubt others accompanied Eleanor from Aquitaine to England, their names now lost, not important enough to be recorded in documents. She would have brought with her lesser-ranking retainers, such as maidservants, and higher-ranking Poitevins in her household would have brought along their own servants. Other elements of Eleanor's household in England remain largely hidden, although hints survive from accounts of later English queens' households. It was customary for later medieval queens to recruit groups of noblewomen or girls to serve in their households, forerunners of the later "ladies of the bedchamber" or "ladies of honor" of modern queens. No doubt, such aristocratic ladies could be found in Eleanor's household. Twelve shillings were spent in 1165 to purchase a saddle and bridle for a relative of the queen, a lady known as Marchisa, possibly a daughter of the count of La Marche. Perhaps Eleanor had brought her to England as one of the ladies or maidens of her household. Mention of the queen's "girls" or "maidens" survives later, from the time of her captivity after 1173.[60]

A medieval queen's household had a military component—a number of knights functioning as bodyguards and as an armed escort when traveling under the constable's command. Yet evidence for Eleanor's household knights only emerges late, during her sons' reigns. One member of Eleanor's household who seems to have played a military role is "a rather enigmatic personage" known as Saldebreuil. Possibly lord of Sanxay, an estate near Saint-Maixent not far from Poitiers, he had belonged to Eleanor's household in Poitou since shortly before her divorce from Louis VII and was steward of her household at the time of her marriage to Henry. Suggesting that Saldebreuil joined Eleanor's household in England for a time beginning in 1163 and continuing through 1167 are yearly payments to him of sixty shillings and ten pence from the exchequer.[61] The name Saldebreuil became attached to a knightly admirer who won Eleanor's favor with a daring deed in one of the romantic legends that arose centuries after her death. The tale seems to stress her sensuality, centering on the knight's engaging in combat while wearing an intimate article of her clothing. According to the story, Eleanor in jest asked which of her household knights would do battle against a fully armored adversary while clad only in one of the queen's chemises. Saldebreuil volunteered at once, and suffering a wound in the combat, was treated tenderly by Eleanor. That evening, the queen appeared at a banquet wearing the blood-stained chemise, greatly disturbing her husband, the king.[62]

When Eleanor returned to Aquitaine with Henry in autumn and winter 1156–57, some members of her household accompanied her from England, among them Ralph of Hastings and Master Matthew, but she quickly consti-tuted a household of her own composed of Poitevins. Acting as Eleanor's own chancellor and drafting her documents was the Poitevin cleric, Jordan, who was to be once more in the queen's entourage during her residence in Poitou a decade later. Also among the Poitevins holding household offices during this visit was Saldebreuil, now identified as her constable. Another was Hervey Panetarius who had witnessed for her as early as 1140, and whom she named provost of Poitiers during this visit.[63] No first-tier nobles of Aquitaine seem to have joined the duchess's household on her 1156 circuit, and the highest-ranking southern nobles, counts, or viscounts would rarely be in attendance at the courts of Henry or Eleanor.[64] Two prelates, Geoffrey du Loroux, the longtime archbishop of Bordeaux, along with the bishops of Poitiers and Périgueux, were in attendance on Eleanor, however. Also joining the royal entourage was a mid-ranking noble, Ebles de Mauléon, who was becoming an influential figure along the Atlantic coastal area of the county of Poitou.[65]

For Henry II, having his queen live in great state with a large household of her own was part of his program of impressing his new English subjects with his wealth and power. With Eleanor's landed income supplemented by payments from the exchequer, she could maintain a standard of living equal to that of the greatest English barons. Records of royal spending are far from complete, for much money paid in and spent by the king's chamber, his household financial office, never passed through the exchequer and therefore left no trace on the pipe rolls.[66] Yet Eleanor's known English income, without counting other revenues left unrecorded or her receipts as duchess of Aquitaine, would have made her a personage of financial importance in the kingdom. She had sufficient funds to be a powerful source of patronage, able to purchase the loyalty of grateful courtiers, the prayers of monastic institutions, and the praise of writers.

Firstly, some revenues came to the queen from her own duchy of Aquitaine, although no record of transfers of funds to England survives; and her husband controlled her ducal resources to a large extent. Secondly, Eleanor had dower-lands presented to her by Henry, a landed endowment presented by a noble husband to his bride on their wedding day. Once Henry won the English Crown, he bestowed on his queen some—though not all—of the traditional dowerlands of the Anglo-Norman queens, estates given by his grandfather Henry I to his two wives, Edith-Matilda and Adeliza.[67] Eleanor's dower included some twenty-six properties scattered over thirteen English shires, ranging from single manors to income from prosperous towns, as well as some lands in France. For example, she held the barony of Berkhamstead in Hertfordshire that consisted of twenty-two knights' fees stretching across England, as well as other land in Berkshire and Hampshire. Eleanor's lands in Devonshire produced at least £177 each year, including income from tin mines in Devon and from the annual fair at Exeter. In London she controlled a dockland area known as Queenhithe; her privileges there could not be defined precisely as property-holdings or spheres of jurisdiction, but as diverse payments and complex "bundles of rights."[68] Although it is clear that Eleanor was assigned considerable lands as dower, the degree of her control over them is not certain. Many royal estates had passed out of the king's hands during the confusion of Stephen's reign, and it would take time for Henry to restore his domains to their pre-civil war extent. Also a goodly portion of Eleanor's English estates were in the hands of noble tenants who were great lords themselves, producing only intermittent, though occasionally large "feudal" payments.

Supplementing funds coming to the queen from her dowerlands was additional income paid as cash from the exchequer for her living expenses, a pension or "corrody" averaging about £115 annually. In Eleanor's early years as English queen, she issued her own writs authorizing expenditures for her household needs. From time to time she also received cash payments by the king's writ for individual items, sometimes lumped together on the pipe rolls, but often specified. Still another source of income for Eleanor was queen's gold; for every hundred silver marks paid to Henry II by noble heirs when they inherited their lands or as offerings for favors, Eleanor as his consort was entitled to one gold mark; considerably more valuable than the silver mark, equivalent to six pounds of silver.[69] This income was important enough for the queen to have her own clerk at exchequer sessions to see to the collection of her gold.[70]

Eleanor's total revenues amounted to a sum equaling that of the kingdom's richest earls or barons. Payments to her from the exchequer between 1154 and 1159 totaled £1,661, or average annual payments of £415. Although only a rough estimate can be made of baronial incomes early in Henry II's reign, by the beginning of the thirteenth century they ranged from over £800 annually to less than £100 with an average of £202.[71] With such an income, the queen had resources to play a significant role in public life, setting an example of royal power through her standard of living. With that she could offer patronage to recruit friends and to purchase churchmen's goodwill with benefactions to religious houses, but evidence for her distribution of favors is sparse. William Marshal recalled that when he had joined Eleanor's military household in Poitou in 1168, she readily gave him "horses, arms, money, and fine clothes."[72] No doubt she was equally generous with her retainers in England, both clerical and knightly. Yet nothing shows her spending in order to enlist a party or faction among the English nobility to further her interests. No doubt Eleanor did play an active part in court politics, although the evidence does not survive. She would have done well to have cultivated friendships with prominent courtiers and powerful royal administrators, but possibly she was more preoccupied with using her resources as duchess of Aquitaine to purchase a loyal band of men among her Poitevin nobility than with spending her English revenues on recruiting a queen's party at court. Nor is there evidence to suggest that Eleanor of Aquitaine was particularly generous in making gifts to English monastic foundations, although traditionally, English queens had spent large sums founding new religious houses and adding to established foundations' endowments.

ELEANOR AND PATRONAGE OF LITERATURE AT COURT

Entertainment held an important place at the English royal court under Eleanor and Henry II, in contrast to Louis VII's court, known for its sobriety and solemnity. Eleanor's second husband invited *jongleurs* and performers of all sorts to his court, doubtless encouraged by her. English moralists, much like critics of the court of Eleanor's grandfather at Poitiers, condemned the Plantagenet court for immorality, complaining of actors, mimes, and dancers who fostered debauched conduct among the courtiers.[73] Just as with other princes new to power, Henry Plantagenet, after winning the English Crown, attracted to his court singers and writers to compose poems and songs, glorifying him and his lineage.[74] Among the crowd of courtiers were serious writers in Latin and in the Anglo-Norman vernacular, and during Eleanor's years as English queen, troubadour lyric poetry, courtly love, and courtly romances spread to the Anglo-Norman world. A former poet turned monk at Eleanor and Henry's court noted ruefully, "When I frequented the court with the courtiers, I made *sirventes, chansons, rimes* and *saluts* [types of secular lyrics], among the lovers and their mistresses."[75]

Yet a cause and effect relationship between Eleanor's arrival in England and the advent of courtly literature there is dubious. Certainly a uniquely productive literary culture flourished at the royal court under Eleanor and Henry, and learned men flocked there, as evidenced by an extraordinary flowering of literary works in several genres.[76] The queen, of course, had grown up at a court where literature and learning were valued, as had Henry. A contemporary described his father Geoffrey le Bel as "most highly lettered, commanding eloquence which set him far above both clerics and laymen, replete with all good manners."[77] Even before Henry became king, writers were dedicating works to him. It is unlikely that the young duke of Normandy commissioned their works, however; they were dedicated to him in anticipation of his patronage once he took the English throne.

Certainly, the court of Eleanor and Henry II earned a reputation as a beacon for courtly writers. As king of England, Henry was eager to encourage authors writing on varied subjects, no doubt expecting their works to reflect favorably on him as a powerful monarch. He sponsored both Latin language and

Anglo-Norman vernacular works, among them historical works written in England and Normandy and also in Anjou that would give an illustrious past to both his Plantagenet predecessors as counts of Anjou and his Norman ancestors who had captured England's royal Crown. He wished during his quarrel with his archbishop of Canterbury to shore up the English monarchy's sacred character with writings pointing up the sanctity of his predecessors. In his competition with the Capetian kings he needed to claim as forebear some heroic figure equaling their prestigious predecessor Charlemagne, and King Arthur or Edward the Confessor could potentially fulfill that need.

Both of Henry I's wives had been known as patrons of literature, and Henry II, who modeled himself on his grandfather, associated his queen with him in extending patronage to writers, even if no explicit evidence for their commissions of works survives.[78] Yet dedications or eulogies inserted by authors into their works afford indirect evidence that they viewed their monarch or his queen as prospective if not actual sources of patronage. Not all clerics wrote in search of material gain, however; some were impelled to write in the hope of instructing and correcting their prince,[79] and others simply sought to show themselves loyal subjects through passages praising their ruler. There is no evidence that the nun of Barking who translated a Latin life of Edward the Confessor into Anglo-Norman had a commission from Henry II or his queen, although she would have known of the king's support for the Confessor's canonization. Perhaps she hoped to win their favor for her convent through her work. She inserted into her translation a passage calling on God's protection for the king, the queen, and their lineage, and their divine sustenance in sanctity, peace, joy, and plenty.[80] For clerical authors at court who often doubled as royal clerks, it is impossible to separate patronage of their literary activity from payment for their secretarial services. Their reward from Eleanor or Henry often came in indirect forms, as presentations to churches or to cathedral prebends, whether in return for activities as royal scribes or as authors. Best known are clerics writing in Latin at the court of Eleanor and Henry, such as Gerald of Wales, Peter of Blois, or Roger of Howden; but Wace, a writer of histories in Anglo-Norman, was awarded by the king with a prebend at Bayeux Cathedral in the 1160s.[81]

Eleanor had grown up at the Poitevin court that gave birth to troubadour poetry, and she certainly heard, read, and encouraged courtly literature. The royal court of Henry II attracted singers of songs, viol players, pipers, and other musicians; and among these entertainers were poets and composers. No doubt scores of songs were commissioned as propaganda in praise of the monarch and his queen or to commemorate special events such as celebrations of victories or the births and marriages of royal offspring, and once sung were soon forgotten. Occasionally a pipe roll entry records payments to a storyteller (*fabulator*) or a harpist (*citharidus*).[82] Although no documents survive to register Eleanor's own commissions of literary works, handsome sums were regularly handed over to her from the royal treasury that could be used for distributing patronage to writers without leaving any trace in the exchequer accounts. The absence of documents recording Eleanor's payments to writers does not preclude her showing favor to them with cash from her personal treasury or with gifts of precious objects. Royal reward to writers, like favors to other courtiers, could take the form of gifts of robes or other clothing, gold cups, or even horses and mules. A Catalan troubadour writing a decade or more after Henry II's death wrote of hearing how "Sir Henry, a king of England, gave horses and mules as gifts." A week spent entertaining a generous patron could win a singer or poet robes worth more than most peasants earned in a year. Lacking other documentation, however, the poems themselves must bear witness that their authors expected to win the English queen's favor through their writings. At the least, they testify that "while actual evidence of commission of texts by Eleanor . . . may be scarce, the testimony of active literary life at her court is not."[83]

Only one troubadour, Bernart de Ventadorn, a native of the Limousin, "perhaps the tenderest and subtlest of all the Provençal love-poets," can be confirmed as present at the English royal court; apparently, his patron was Henry II, not the queen. Bernart traveled north to Henry's ducal court in Normandy, supposedly after he was forced to leave the viscount of Ventadorn's court because of his love for the viscountess. He entered Duke Henry's service, composing lyrics for him, and crossing the Channel to England after Henry's coronation as king. He declares in one song, "For the king's sake, I am both English and Norman." In this poem, lamenting at being "far from my lady," he indicates that he encountered Eleanor more often on her visits to Normandy than in the English kingdom across the sea. Bernart declares that he wrote it in England, "far from the Norman land, across the wild, deep sea"; and in another of his lyrics, he hints at his devotion to "the queen of the Normans."[84]

Following a troubadour tradition of disguising the identity of one's beloved, Bernart de Ventadorn celebrated his love for an anonymous lady, giving her a code name, *Aziman*, sometimes identified as Henry II's queen. After Eleanor made her residence in England, the poet addressed an Occitan lyric lamenting his sadness at his separation from his anonymous lady and comparing their situation to that of Tristan and Iseult.[85] Within a half century of Eleanor's death, the song had led a biographer of Bernart with a vivid imagination to fabricate a love affair between the poet and the queen. Some modern biographers have followed his lead, while others find in Bernart's declarations of love for the English queen either mere adoration from afar or no more than poetic convention. Although supposedly expressing his deepest feelings in his songs, they cannot be read as history; they were not secret diaries or true confessions, but poems for public presentation following strict conventions of the troubadour genre. No evidence shows Eleanor attracting other poets from Aquitaine to the English court; nor did she inspire natives of Henry's Anglo-Norman domains to compose courtly love lyrics in English, Welsh, or the French spoken by the Anglo-Normans.[86]

During Eleanor's early years as English queen, she seems to have shared her husband's taste for histories, especially those written in the Anglo-Norman vernacular. Henry II commissioned writers experienced at composing romances who could make historical writings available to a courtly audience not well educated in Latin.[87] In about 1155 a royal clerk Wace won a commission to write the *Roman de Brut*, an Anglo-Norman adaptation of Geoffrey of Monmouth's Latin history. Layamon, a priest who translated the *Brut* into English in the first decades of the thirteenth century, claims that Wace had dedicated it to Queen Eleanor and that he wrote of her, "Generous is Eleanor, gracious and wise." Possibly Layamon had seen a now lost presentation copy that contained a dedication to the queen.[88] While his statement is no direct proof for Eleanor's patronage, at least it indicates that she was thought to be a queen interested in literature and capable of offering favors to authors attracting her attention.

Hardly accurate history, the *Roman de Brut* presents the story of the early Britons from the arrival of Brutus, a refugee from the Trojan War, to the Saxon invasions as if a translation of an ancient book in Breton (or Welsh). Although Wace incorporated oral traditions transmitted in minstrels' songs, Geoffrey of Monmouth's *History of the Kings of Britain* was his chief source. His vernacular reworking of legends of the ancient Britons, adding courtly elements, would play a pivotal part in medieval literature as the source for the "matter of Britain," for it proved appealing to composers of later twelfth-century romances centering on King Arthur, Guinevere, and the knights of the Round Table. As a result, the legendary Arthur, his queen, and his knights became as much a part of history for twelfth-century readers as biblical personages or as heroes from the Latin classics, and Wace may have modeled his depiction of Arthur's queen on Eleanor. Perhaps courtiers hearing or reading these romances were tempted to see Henry and Eleanor in the portraits of Arthur and Guinevere. If modern readers can see parallels between fictional characters and historical personalities in twelfth-century romances, then Eleanor and Henry's contemporaries could have seen them even more clearly.[89] Medieval readers expected to uncover more than one level of meaning during their reading, and they were attuned to the allegorical nature of poetry.

Henry II, though materially more powerful than his rival Louis VII, felt himself "ideologically inferior" because of the Capetian king's prestigious ancestry, traced back to Charlemagne.[90] Arthurian material is sometimes said to have provided useful propaganda for Henry in his rivalry with Louis and later with his son Philip II, offering King Arthur as a prestigious royal predecessor from an even earlier time than the Capetians' Frankish predecessors. Yet Henry made only fitful and desultory attempts at constructing an Arthurian ideology to counteract the Capetians' use of Charlemagne. Seeking ideological advantage from Arthurian material was not without risks, for King Arthur and Arthurian legends could serve better the purposes of rebellious English nobles, who found in Arthur and his faithful men gathered at the Round Table an idealized view of earlier kingship. Arthur was closely identified with the inhabitants of the Celtic fringes, people looked on by the English as savages, and Arthurian tales had an especially subversive effect on the Welsh and the Bretons.[91]

Henry II commissioned another book from Wace, the *Roman de Rou*, a history praising his Norman ducal ancestors from Rollo (or Rou), the Viking invader of Normandy, down to his grandfather Henry I; and the clerk prepared himself for the task by reading early Norman chronicles, listening to epic poetry, and even examining charters in Norman churches.[92] After opening with a eulogy in praise of Henry and Eleanor, calling the queen "noble and both kind and wise," Wace gives a brief biography, glossing over the scandalous aspects of her marriage to Louis VII. He writes of their fateful crusade only, "each suffered great hardship and pain there"; and he attributes the couple's separation to "the advice of barons," noting that "this separation did her no harm." Wace also connects Eleanor to Henry's Norman ancestors, writing that Duke William of Poitiers fell in love with the daughter of Rollo, founder of the Norman ducal dynasty, and married her.[93]

Work on the *Roman de Rou*, begun around 1160, stopped sometime after 1170 when Wace lost the king's favor. In his text, Wace wrote that at the king's command Master Benedict (Benoît) of Sainte-Maure was replacing him, and he complained of Henry's failure to give him his promised financial reward. He compared the king's patronage unfavorably with that in the time of Virgil and Horace, writing, "then largess had strength and virtue."[94] Master Benedict, a native of the Touraine, had become a retainer of the counts of Anjou, probably first under Geoffrey le Bel. He was already known for his vernacular account of the Trojan war, *Roman de Troie*, written in the mid- to late 1160s. Eventually Benedict completed a version of the work first assigned to Wace as the *Chroniques des ducs de Normandie*, largely a translation of earlier Latin histories. More pliable than his predecessor, he inserted praises of Henry's Norman ancestors, portraying them in conventional terms as pious and courteous lords, and he hailed his patron as the "flower of the princes of the world."[95]

In Benedict's *Roman de Troie*, he placed immediately after a diatribe against women's follies a passage paying thinly disguised compliments to Eleanor. He hailed her as "one in whom all knowledge abounds," and "the powerful lady of a powerful king, without evil, without anger, without sorrow."[96] Even if Benedict did not "officially" dedicate his *Roman de Troie* to Eleanor, it is evident that he thought of her while writing it, knowing she would read it. The *Roman* tells the familiar story of Helen, carried off from her Greek husband with her agreement by Paris, a Trojan prince who placed her at the center of a court of poets, a life with parallels perhaps too close to Eleanor's. Benedict, aware of this, painted an idealized picture of the love of Helen and Paris, possibly seeking to present them as a romantic analogy with the royal couple. To draw the reader's attention away from Helen's adultery, he criticized another female character, the captive of Achilles, for her unfaithfulness. Another parallel to Eleanor, doubtless pleasing to her, is Benedict's depiction of the worthy Hecuba, queen of Troy, a woman of wisdom, justice, and piety, and like the English queen, mother of eight children—five sons and three daughters.[97]

Benedict's earlier work tracing Henry II's prestigious Trojan origins seems adapted to his political goal of glorifying his lineage. The Trojan past attracted considerable interest among twelfth-century Anglo-Normans, both vernacular and Latin writers, and works in other genres produced genealogies demonstrating Henry's descent from Trojan heroes.[98] An English clerk, Joseph of Exeter composed *Ylias*, a poem on the Trojan War, inserting an evocation of the recently deceased Young Henry into his account of Hector's death. Another work on legendary Troy, an anonymous romance, the *Roman d'Eneas* (*c*.1160), is thought to have been written for the Plantagenet court. Adapted from Vergil's *Aeneid*, it gives less attention to Aeneas's love for Dido than his love for Lavinia, celebrating a successful dynastic marriage and possibly pointing to a parallel with the marriage of Eleanor and Henry. Another romance, the *Roman de Thèbes*, written early in the royal couple's reign, is based on a classical work, Statius's *Thebaid*. In the romance, verses proclaim that kisses of an ancient king's daughters "were worth more than London or Poitiers." Perhaps it is not too speculative to read this linking of two of the Angevin Empire's most important cities as a compliment to Eleanor, queen of England and countess of Poitou. Passages depicting a queen whose husband listened to her counsels with respect would have called to readers' minds the English queen. Also connecting the unknown author to Eleanor is his Poitevin birth, for his native dialect was the French of Poitou.[99]

Seeking Eleanor's favor was another writer in the Anglo-Norman language, Philip of Thaon, author of what can only charitably be called scientific works. One was a treatise written in Latin rhyming couplets before 1120 on computing the dates of moveable feasts, "hardly inspiring subject matter." Another of Philip's books was the first bestiary in the French language, treating beasts and birds, both real and mythical, and concluding with a listing of precious stones and their properties. He had first written his bestiary during Henry I's reign shortly after the king's second marriage, dedicating it to the new queen; but soon after 1154 he presented Eleanor with a copy newly dedicated to her. Obviously angling for patronage, he wrote, "God save lady Alienor, / Queen who art the arbiter / Of honor, wit, and beauty, / Of largess and loyalty." Later lines are addressed to the queen directly, asking her to intercede with the king to obtain his inheritance from his mother.[100]

Eleanor may have had some connection with another scientific work, a medical text in Latin brought from Sicily to England by Robert Cricklade, prior of Saint Fridewide's, Oxford (d. *c.*1171). He was the compiler of a scientific text, an abridgement of Pliny's natural history, that he had dedicated first to King Henry I, then later to Henry II. Like a number of English scholars, Robert traveled in Italy, going to Rome and Sicily in 1156 and returning in 1158. While in Sicily, he was given a copy of the *Gynaecia Cleopatrae*, originating in Constantinople, to take back to England to the queen. Eleanor would have learned of the reputation of Greek medical learning while in Constantinople during the Second Crusade. It is plausible that the English queen, anxious after the early death of her son William, had asked the prior to bring from Sicily medical books on childbirth, care of children, and female disorders. At the time of Robert's departure, Eleanor was left with only one boy, Young Henry. Given her record of bearing only daughters in her first marriage, she may have had dynastic concerns about producing more sons. If so, her fears proved unrealistic, for she quickly produced two more sons in 1157 and 1158.[101]

After Eleanor's first decade as English queen, her public role as her second husband's regent was eroding. After 1163, when Henry's four-year absence from the kingdom ended, the pipe rolls cease to cite her writs as authorization for payments.[102] The disappearance of Eleanor's writs need not point to the couple's estrangement, for other factors can explain her reduced political role. In part, it is explained by Henry's expansion of royal government by 1164; new administrative structures led to a shifting of more and more political activity away from the royal household to the exchequer at Westminster. The joint chief justiciars, Earl Robert of Leicester and Richard de Lucy, presiding over the exchequer, were responsible for royal revenues and the sheriffs' accounts, and as their title indicates, also headed the revived royal judicature. The exchequer was evolving into a nerve center for the everyday work of royal administration, leaving the king's own itinerant household free to concentrate on political, diplomatic, and military decision-making. With a steady stream of messages flowing between these two power centers, the queen's role as an intermediary between the king abroad and an increasingly professional administration in England would decline.

Also contributing to Eleanor's reduced role as regent were her own frequent absences from the English kingdom. She was away for almost a year from May 1165 until Easter 1166, serving as Henry's deputy in Anjou and Maine. Although the queen returned to act as regent in 1166 and 1167, the chief justiciars' sphere steadily expanded during her absences. Early in 1168, Henry, unable to subdue the rebellious Poitevins, would decide to install Eleanor at Poitiers, hoping that ruling indirectly through her would prove more acceptable. Her child-bearing years at an end, she may have found the prospect of an important political role in her native Poitou appealing. Once their eldest son was crowned king in June 1170, he could replace his mother as regent. Henry Senior left the Young King behind in England, conceding to him "all rights and judgements by his new seal," and he authorized writs during his father's absences in France and in Ireland from late June 1170 to November 1172.[103] Eleanor's time in charge of her duchy of Aquitaine would end with the great rebellion of 1173–74, when her conspiracy with her sons against her husband discredited both the queen and Young Henry as regents. With no member of the royal family to represent Henry II during his absences from England, the chief justiciar would take on the role of regent, now second to the king.

1 Church of Notre-Dame-la-Grande, Poitiers, on the market square near the ducal palace, its sculpted façade a splendid example of Poitevin Romanesque art dating from Eleanor's early years.

2 Seal of Eleanor's grandfather William IX, Duke of Aquitaine and Count of Poitou, the 'troubadour duke'.

3 The Eleanor Vase, a rock crystal vase brought from Spain by Duke William IX and presented to Eleanor, who gave it to Louis VII; he later he donated it to Suger of Saint-Denis, who added the jeweled metal base and top.

4 An 1840 painting by Jean-Baptiste Mauzaisse at Versailles depicting Louis VII at Saint-Denis receiving the crusader's banner from Abbot Suger in Eleanor's presence.

5 A nineteenth-century print of the walls of Antioch built by the Byzantines high above the Orontes River valley, they continued to protect the city at the time of Eleanor's visit there on the Second Crusade.

6 Eleanor of Aquitaine's tomb sculpture at Fontevraud Abbey constructed c. 1210, a few years after her death in 1204.

7 Henry II's tomb sculpture at Fontevraud Abbey that Eleanor likely played a role in planning and preparing during her last years at the abbey.

8 Cathedral of Saint-Pierre, Poitiers, east (rear) wall, showing a severity similar to that of Henry II's castles, indicating that his military architects took part in its design.

9 Stained glass Crucifixion window at the cathedral of Saint-Pierre, Poitiers, presented by Henry and Eleanor to the church during her residence at Poitiers, 1168-73.

10 Painting by Margaret Dovaston (1884-1954) depicting Henry II with his lover Rosamund Clifford, commissioned for an illustrated English history c. 1921.

11 Late twelfth or early thirteenth century wall painting in the chapel of Sainte-Radegonde, Chinon discovered in 1964, alleged to depict Eleanor's farewell in 1174 as Henry II led her into captivity, though this is far from certain.

12 Tomb sculpture at Fontevraud Abbey of King Richard I of England, Lionheart, Eleanor's favorite son; she likely oversaw its construction during her retirement at the abbey.

Alienor D. g. Regina Angl Duc. Norman. Aquit
Comit. Andeg. Archiepis. Epis. Comitibus Vicecomitibus Ba-
ronibus. Just. Baillivis et omnibus ad quos pñs Carta pervenerit
salute. ad Universorum Noticiam volumus pervenire qd
cũ mus filius noster Rex Ricardus cuius anima ĩn pace qui-
escat eterna ad petitionem nram nobis dedit & concessit
terram de Hobriteby et de Harfineby cum omnibus
pertinentiis ĩn boscis et ĩn plano ĩn pratis, ĩn pasturis ĩn
aquis ĩn molendinis ĩn stagnis et ĩn omnibus aliis que
ad terram illam dinoscitur pertinere, que terra psolvere
solebat ad scacarium pro sol. annuatim. sciatis igitur quod
nos supradictam terram cum aliis pertinentiis pnotatis
dedimus et concessimus et pñti Carta confirmavimus fideli
servienti nro Ade COCO et Johanne Uxori sue habendam
et tenendam sibi et heredibus suis de nobis et heredibus
nris ĩn perpetuum libere pacifice ĩntegre et quietam de
Cornagio et de omnibus aliis Consuetudinib' que ad rege
Anglorum debent pertinere reddend' per annum ad-
festum scti Michaelis pro omnibus servitiis una libram
cimini Baillivis Regis de Kardolio. Et quia volumus ut
hoc ratu et stabile permaneat ĩn perpetuum pñti Carte
sigilli nri robur apposuimus et munimen'. Testib' Dño
Rad. de Faia et Dño Willelmo fratre suo. Hen-
rico de Bernevall. Conslt de Berkam. Nicholo de
Wiltesir. hunfredo clerico Gausb'. et Willmo de Jaun
Willo de Sto Maxintio clerico nro. Dat. per manũ Rogeri Capellani nri apud fontē Ebr. Anno ĩn carñati Verbi
1200

scellé en cire verte
sur un cordon des
soye brune.

14 The chapel of Fontevraud Abbey, housing the tombs of Eleanor, Henry II, Richard I, and Isabelle of Angoulême, wife of King John and mother of Henry III of England.

15 The great hall of the ducal palace in Poitiers, now the Palais de Justice, renovated during Eleanor's last years in the 'Angevn style' of architecture. The triple fireplace is a fourteenth-century addition.

16 Tomb sculpture at Worcester Cathedral of King John of England, Eleanor's last surviving son, completed twenty years after his death in 1216.

CHAPTER 7

A TASTE OF POWER IN POITOU, 1168–1173

In the first year and a half of Eleanor's second marriage, before her coronation as English queen, she had played the primary role in governing her duchy of Aquitaine, May 1152 to December 1154, and Henry Plantagenet had merely confirmed her acts. Before long, however, the situation would be reversed. December 1154, when Eleanor acquired the new title of Queen of England, marks the beginning of a period of her withdrawal from official activities in her duchy. Eleanor's loss of initiative is partly explained by her almost permanent absence from her native land before her return to Poitiers early in 1168 to take up residence there. On becoming England's queen, she kept busy in her new kingdom acting as Henry's regent and bearing his children. Between her 1156–57 circuit of Aquitaine and her return to Poitou to take charge there in 1168, she found herself relegated more and more to the background in administering her ancestral lands, merely confirming her husband's decisions.

Once Eleanor's new husband became King Henry II of England, he felt capable of taking on what her former husband, Louis VII of France, had fitfully attempted, subjecting the duchy of Aquitaine to his control and integrating it into his Plantagenet collection of family lands. Eventually Eleanor would find herself excluded from power by Henry to a greater degree than by her previous husband. Henry by his right of marriage was count of Poitou and duke of Aquitaine, and he could exercise his wife's hereditary rights by delegation, although he could not lawfully transfer ducal rights without her consent. Eleanor as a married woman could not act alone on her own responsibility without her husband's assent.[1] Henry's quest to centralize his authority over Eleanor's inheritance would end the autonomy enjoyed by her in the brief period between her flight from Paris and her voyage to England to become queen.

As the author of the *History of William Marshal* writes, "the men of Poitou were always in revolt against their lords."[2] Yet crises in Henry II's lands to the north—on the Welsh marches, in Brittany, and along his long frontier with Capetian territory—constantly diverted his attention from Eleanor's lands. By the beginning of 1168, Henry would give up his goal of imposing direct rule on the Poitevins; and he would decide to give them back their duchess, hoping that installing Eleanor at Poitiers and ruling indirectly through her would prove more acceptable to them. She was willing to return to her ancestral duchy, anxious to assume a more important political role and to ensure her second son Richard's succession.[3] The five years following Eleanor's return to Poitou early in 1168 would be the longest period of her direct authority over her ancestral lands.

AQUITAINE IN ELEANOR'S ABSENCE IN THE YEARS PRIOR TO 1168

Soon after Eleanor of Aquitaine married Henry Plantagenet, her new husband showed a tendency to intervene forcefully in the Poitevins' affairs in a manner reminiscent of Louis VII's violent encounters with them. Yet within Eleanor's lands, Henry II would never succeed in asserting his public powers enforced so effectively in his Anglo-Norman realm and to a lesser extent in Anjou. Angevin administration in Aquitaine would always have a rudimentary quality compared to England or Normandy, indicated by the small number of Henry's documents treating Poitevin or Aquitanian matters out of the thousands generated elsewhere.[4] In large expanses of territory—on Poitou's southern edges, the Angoumois, Limousin, Périgord, or Auvergne, and in almost the whole of Gascony—Eleanor and her predecessors held neither castles nor estates, and the lords of those territories acknowledged little more than nominal ducal authority. Henry as duke of Aquitaine had far fewer castles garrisoned by his own men than in Normandy or his family lands of Anjou, Maine, and the Touraine. Eleanor's ducal ancestors had never exercised effective authority over most of Gascony, and they rarely bothered to visit its southern zones beyond the Bordelais.[5]

Just after Henry's marriage to Eleanor, he had shown an eagerness to assert his authority over her subjects with force, tangling with the people of Limoges and destroying the town's newly built walls and a bridge on his first visit there in 1152. Then on the couple's 1156 circuit of Aquitaine, he had angered the ruling family of the Limousin by taking custody of the deceased viscount's minor son despite protests from the boy's uncles. Two years later Henry confronted the powerful viscount of Thouars, besieging his castle, driving him from the town, and placing the viscounty under his own agents. It is possible that Eleanor urged such severity on her new husband, just as she had Louis VII. Whatever his reasons, Henry's determined steps to impress his authority over

Eleanor's subjects only aroused their anger and alarm. They were dismayed to discover that the English king could impose his will "from the furthest parts of England as far as the River Garonne."[6]

Although the Poitevin nobility were willing to acknowledge Henry Plantagenet's pre-eminence as their count-duke, they regarded his attempts to introduce an Anglo-Norman pattern of governing into their duchess's lands as unwarranted meddling. He put them on the defensive in trying to transform vague ties of lordship that had bound to Eleanor's predecessors into the enforceable obligations owed by his Norman and English nobles. The Poitevins only admitted their obligation as landowners to perform for him as count-duke ancient "public" services, and they protested that Henry was infringing on their traditional liberties. As usual, the instigators of resistance were powerful and turbulent regional lords along Poitou's southern frontier in the lower Charente and upper Vienne valleys. These unruly nobles presented barriers blocking the duke's route between their two capitals, Poitiers and Bordeaux. Among the most quarrelsome were the lords of Lusignan, who offer an impressive illustration of lesser lords' expansion into regional powers as they expanded from their eleventh-century castle of Lusignan not far from Poitiers, acquiring castles and lands in southern Poitou. Conspicuous participants in all revolts against the Plantagenets, they habitually joined their neighbors in flouting ducal authority and expanding their power. Other dangerous families along "the soft underbelly of the Angevin Empire" included the Taillefer counts of Angoulême, the counts of Périgord, and the four viscounts of the Limousin: Limoges, Comborn, Ventadour, and Turenne.[7]

Eleanor's own thoughts on Henry's attempts to subject the nobility of Poitou to his rule cannot be known. No doubt she had supported him in the first years of their marriage just as she had her first husband. Over time, however, she seems to have begun to judge Henry's policies as heavy-handed, disrespectful of her own country's traditions, and likely to fail. She would have felt that she knew best how to deal with her people, and the series of noble revolts in defense of their "liberties" resulting from Henry's attempts to subject them to northern "feudal" obligations would not have surprised her. Henry's brutality in crushing resistance, reclaiming and razing many of the rebellious Poitevin nobles' fortifications, accomplished few lasting results. Defeated Poitevin nobles soon rebuilt their demolished fortresses and reinforced town walls. Their power within their own territories was too great for the English king to apply the force that he could muster in his northern territories. He was powerless to halt the consolidation of power by lesser Poitevin lords, who were converting scattered holdings into regional lordships protected by strings of stone fortifications.[8]

Eleanor's own experience at foreign courts, where hostile courtiers made her feel alien, likely led her to sympathize with the anti-foreign sentiments of the nobility of Aquitaine. To them, their duchess's husband was a foreigner, "the king of the North," representing an alien culture. They tended to vent their anger by attacking anyone from Henry's Anglo-Norman realm. Isaac, the English-born abbot of Étoile in Poitou, experienced Poitevin antagonism toward his countrymen. He wrote to a fellow countryman, John of Canterbury, bishop of Poitiers, complaining that a neighboring lord was attacking him and crying from the rooftops that he wished to avenge through him his hatred of all natives of England. Isaac exclaimed, "Would to God that I had never been English or that, exiled in this place, I never had to see another Englishman."[9]

In fact, only a handful of Henry II's subjects from the Anglo-Norman realm or from Anjou held posts of authority in Eleanor's lands. Most prominent was Patrick, earl of Salisbury, who had loyally supported the young Plantagenet prince in his struggle for the English Crown. Henry had named him commander of his military forces in Aquitaine by 1163, giving him priority over the Poitevin constable of Aquitaine, Theobald Chabot, lord of Vouvent in the Vendée.[10] Aside from occasional Anglo-Norman appointees, such as Simon de Tournebu, constable of Thouars Castle, Henry depended on members of the same Poitevin families that had served earlier count-dukes. Henry's agents in his wife's duchy came primarily from the lesser nobility holding castles in the Aunis and Saintonge, the three families of Maingot de Surgères, Mauzé, and Mauléon, whose members had proven their loyalty in posts as ducal provosts and custodians of ducal castles. Both William Maingot I and William de Mauzé had served Eleanor's father and later Louis VII as seneschals of Poitou, acting as deputies during their absences. The Mauléons, with holdings along the Atlantic coast of Poitou and Aunis on the Île de Ré and the Île d'Oléron, were typical in their rapid rise in the twelfth century. They acted as hereditary custodians of the counts' coastal castle and lordship of Talmont, a favored hunting ground of Eleanor's ancestors.[11]

Hardly any Poitevins succeeded in attaching themselves to Henry II's household, even though Poitou and Aquitaine, like other twelfth-century principalities, abounded in ambitious knights and clerks aspiring to become courtiers. Eleanor's uncle Ralph de Faye sometimes found himself in the royal household when the king was in his French territories, although other Poitevin names are rare among the courtiers regularly in his entourage. Ralph enjoyed Eleanor's confidence, and he held the post of seneschal of Saintonge after her departure for England in 1154; indeed, he was in some sense his niece's chief deputy in her duchy.[12] Taking advantage of his powerful position, he gained a reputation as "a notorious oppressor of monastic institutions."[13]

Like Louis VII, Eleanor's second husband made an attempt to place men loyal to him in Aquitaine's bishoprics, seeking to extend to Aquitaine the spiritual privileges that he exercised over the English and Norman churches. As

Eleanor would have known, the dukes of Aquitaine had not controlled effectively the churches of their domains since the eleventh-century reform movement. A ducal role in episcopal elections in the ecclesiastical province of
Bordeaux had been restricted further by Louis vi's action at the time of
Eleanor's marriage to Louis the Younger in 1137. The French king and his son
had renounced any claim to traditional ducal rights over the province of
Bordeaux, ending the dukes' dominance in prelate's elections.[14] Despite this
concession, Louis VII had tried unsuccessfully in 1140 to control the choice of
a new bishop of Poitiers; and Eleanor had supported, perhaps encouraged, her
first husband's high-handed attempts to control episcopal appointments.

The Plantagenet duke would be more successful than Louis, but his power
in selecting bishops was minor compared to his role in his Anglo-Norman
lands. On the death of the longtime primate Geoffrey du Loroux, archbishop
of Bordeaux, in 1158, it was probably at Eleanor's suggestion that Henry tried
to influence the election, seeking to impose the master of the schools at
Poitiers, John d'Asside (or Sie) on the bishops of the Bordeaux region. Since
Henry was not yet well acquainted with his Aquitanian subjects, he would
have solicited Eleanor's opinion; and it was doubtless she who put forward the
schoolmaster's name, hoping to continue the close relationship that she had
enjoyed with Archbishop Geoffrey. When the king-duke's presence intimi-
dated the prelates assembled for the election, only one bold bishop dared
speak out, reminding him, "Lord King, a just election was committed to us; it
is not fitting to deal with the election in your presence." On hearing this,
Henry left in hot anger, having failed to install his candidate, and the assembled prelates elected the bishop of Périgueux as archbishop.[15] They feared
offending their new duke, however; and apparently as a conciliatory signal,
they agreed to John d'Asside's nomination to the bishopric of Périgueux a year
or two later.[16]

A short time after Henry's failure at Bordeaux, the archbishopric unexpectedly fell vacant again, and Hardouin, dean of Le Mans Cathedral, was elected in
1159–60. Henry cherished the cathedral at Le Mans, for it was where he had
been christened and where his father was buried; but he did not have close ties
with Hardouin. It was not long before the archbishopric became vacant yet
again, and a native Gascon, Bernard de Montault (or Montaud), bishop of
Lectour, was elected. He attended several crucial conferences in the course of
Henry's long quarrel with Thomas Becket, where he would take the king's side.
In 1173 toward the end of Eleanor's stay in Aquitaine, an English monk, the
abbot of Reading, William le Templier, was elected archbishop in the king's presence. He was well known to both Eleanor and Henry, who had ties to Reading
Abbey, the burial place of their first son. Yet William can hardly be considered
one of their courtiers, unlike a number of Norman and English bishops.[17]

Soon repercussions of Henry II's bitter quarrel with his archbishop of Canterbury were resounding in the diocese of Poitiers. In 1162 Henry actively supported the candidacy of an English cleric, John of Canterbury (or Jean des Bellesmains) for the bishopric. The king's choice as bishop would prove to be no ally in his conflict with Thomas Becket, for the two were friends, both former members of Archbishop Theobald's household. Bishop John wrote to Becket in a letter dated July 1164, complaining that the king was seeking to introduce into Poitou harsh measures similar to the Constitutions of Clarendon that had triggered the archbishop's struggle against him. John wrote that royal commissioners had brought the king's command that he must not "usurp anything touching the king's dignity." His decree restricted the bishop's jurisdiction within his diocese in disputes involving the clergy or ecclesiastical property, unless the appropriate lay officials had failed to do justice. In addition, the bishop was forbidden to excommunicate any Poitevin baron or anyone else refusing to answer in his episcopal court without first consulting the king's agents. The break between the bishop of Poitiers and Henry II became so bitter that around 1166 rumors reached the bishop's friends of an attempt to poison him; John of Salisbury learned that the bishop was ill and that a monk who had supposedly drunk from the same cup had died. The bishop as a foreigner in Poitou was in a precarious position, however, and knowing that he needed the king-duke's support, he reached a reconciliation with Henry.[18]

The two commissioners who brought Henry's 1164 decrees to Bishop John were Norman Simon de Tournebu, constable of Thouars, and Richard of Ilchester, a courtier–cleric who was a native of Somerset. Henry had enough clout to install Richard in two posts in the Poitevin church—archdeacon of Poitiers and treasurer of the collegiate church of Saint-Hilaire le Grand. Traditionally, the counts of Poitou as lay abbots of Saint-Hilaire had nominated the church's treasurers, who may have carried out some financial tasks for the counts. Richard, very busy in England as one of the king's "evil counselors" during the Becket controversy, was largely an absentee office-holder at Poitiers, and this was one of his rare visits to his post.[19]

In the 1160s, while Bishop John was giving his support to Thomas Becket, Henry II sponsored the early stages of rebuilding the cathedral of Saint-Pierre at Poitiers, no doubt with his queen's approval and participation.[20] Planned as an early gothic hall-church with three aisles of almost the same proportions, its flat and massive rear wall without buttresses is a unique feature not found in any other church, only in fortresses. Since similar walls appear in castle construction under Henry's supervision in England, it appears to be the work of the English king's military architects. The cathedral's choir, completed around 1167, is an appropriate monument to Henry II in its "power, simplicity and grandeur." Another reminder of the Plantagenet dynasty's authority over

Poitiers is the great stained-glass crucifixion window above the high altar, a gift of Eleanor and her husband. Its bottom panel depicts the royal couple holding a model of the window and presenting it to Christ with their four sons joining them, two on each side. The depiction of the four sons places the piece's date after John's birth at the end of 1166, and it certainly predates the rebellion of 1173–74 by Eleanor and three of her sons. One of the few surviving contemporary "portraits" of Eleanor, her image occupies the most prominent place in the bottom panel on the viewer's left, but to the right of God, a place customarily reserved for males. This hints at her initiative in donating the impressive window to the cathedral.[21]

Compounding Henry's difficulties in Eleanor's domains was the ambition of the king of France, who had been duke of Aquitaine during his marriage to Eleanor. In the two centuries before Eleanor's birth, the relationship between the French monarchy and the duchy of Aquitaine had remained ill-defined, and Gascony's status was even more problematic. Even if early dukes had acknowledged the Capetian monarch's superior status as crowned and anointed successor to the Carolingian emperors, they felt that only their lack of a royal title made them in any way inferior. Louis VII as Eleanor's husband had gained a right to intervene in Aquitaine that he did not wish to surrender. After initial antagonism toward Henry as Aquitaine's ruler, he had adopted an accommodating attitude, but his approach would change with the birth of a long-awaited son on 22 August 1165. He wished his heir Philip to rule the French kingdom without any threat from a powerful empire controlling all of its Atlantic coast, and his relations with Henry steadily worsened in the late 1160s. Knowing that French power was inadequate for a head-on challenge, Louis saw his best hope for weakening Henry in encouraging rebellions in the Plantagenet possessions, and the Poitevins' opposition gave him hopes of his adversary's domains splitting into their constituent parts. In addition, Louis found in the English king's embroilment in bitter conflict with Thomas Becket an opportunity for troublemaking, and he offered the archbishop of Canterbury refuge in France after his flight from England. More and more, the Becket conflict became entangled with Angevin–Capetian rivalries, and the exiled archbishop's supporters depicted the English king as not only an oppressor of the Church but also an enemy of the French.[22]

The entire eastern frontier of the duchy of Aquitaine was in dispute with the Capetians throughout Henry and Eleanor's marriage and beyond. The county of Berry, adjoining Poitou, was divided into Plantagenet and Capetian halves, with the northern part, the viscounty of Bourges, part of the French royal domain and Châteauroux, the leading lordship of lower Berry, under Plantagenet influence. The two dynasties continually disputed with each other for domination over Berry lordships lying between Bourges and Châteauroux.[23]

The position of the county of Auvergne, lying to the east of the Limousin, was always puzzling; for the dukes of Aquitaine, the counts of Toulouse, and the Capetians all laid claim to its lordship. In 1163 Louis VII invaded the Auvergne, and Henry resisted assertion of French royal authority there, raising an army to oppose him. Later, the English king claimed ducal jurisdiction through his marriage to Eleanor, intervening in a dispute over succession to the county in 1167. When Henry summoned the Auvergne heir's usurping uncle to his court, the uncle appealed to the court of his lord the French king at Paris. Henry then launched a campaign, ravaging Auvergne, and eventually Louis would acknowledge the duke of Aquitaine's right to lordship over Auvergne.

A greater problem was the county of Toulouse adjoining Gascony, first claimed by Eleanor's grandfather, William IX and his duchess, a claim reasserted by Eleanor and Henry in the inconclusive campaign of 1159. Conflict would continue for forty years, drawing in the kings of Aragon in alternating enmity and alliance with the Plantagenets and the counts of Toulouse. Louis VII took advantage of the Toulousains' hostility to expand his influence, and the city of Toulouse viewed the French monarch as its special protector.[24]

Henry II, forced to spread himself too thinly over domains stretching from the Scottish borders to the Pyrenees, could never give full attention to the duchy of Aquitaine and its independent-minded local and regional leaders. He appeared in person there only once between the 1159 Toulouse campaign and 1166, descending into the Dordogne valley to besiege a castle in the summer of 1161. He never succeeded in creating administrative agencies for Aquitaine, and his failure to assert the supremacy of ducal justice as in his Anglo-Norman possessions is striking. Although Poitou had been experiencing a commercial revolution since the mid-eleventh century, it is impossible to estimate how much Henry and Eleanor profited from its prosperity. Increasing traffic in both coastal and overseas trade at a number of ports undoubtedly benefitted the ducal treasury with port duties and other taxes, yet ducal income lagged behind Henry's English or Norman revenues.

Cultivating the mutual friendship, shared respect, and compromise that Eleanor's ancestors had fostered to secure harmony with their nobles in the Angoumois and Limousin was a policy pursued neither by her husband Henry II nor by her son Richard Lionheart. They made no attempt to co-opt the Poitevin aristocracy or a growing merchant class with ties of patronage, and their royal households remained predominantly Anglo-Norman. Instead, they turned to tactics of ferocity, terror, and retaliation. Annals and chronicles are filled with accounts of punitive campaigns in Poitou and the Limousin fought with brutish foreign mercenaries, the dreaded *Brabançons* or *routiers* that were the Angevin response to numerous revolts in the region. Putting down rebellions rarely involved pitched battles, but instead laid waste and plundered rebels' lands, resulting in the peasantry's impoverishment and sharpened hostility toward foreigners. In dealing with Gascony, Henry could only follow Eleanor's ancestors in limiting his ambition to holding on to its richest portions, Bordeaux and the Garonne valley, and ignoring the more distant parts. Like Eleanor's ducal ancestors, Henry proved unable to bring the lords of the Pyrenean foothills to accept anything more than nominal submission, and some were willing to give their homage to the kings of Aragon or the kings of Navarre. The situation in much of Gascony was comparable to that in northernmost England, where the king could do no more than "show the flag" on infrequent military expeditions to the Scottish border lands.

ELEANOR, RULER IN AQUITAINE, 1168–1174

During the years between Eleanor's 1156 visit to Aquitaine and her installation at Poitiers in 1168, she visited her ancestral lands only once, in advance of the Toulouse campaign of 1159. The responsibilities of her husband in his French territories north of the Loire left him little time for overseeing her duchy. Henry II spent much of 1166 on campaign in Brittany, nominally a vassal state of the dukes of Normandy, bringing it under his control and betrothing his third son Geoffrey to the count's daughter and heir. Even though Henry's attention was constantly diverted from Aquitaine, his periodic attempts at subduing the southern nobles nourished their discontent. Eleanor, acting as her husband's agent at Angers from spring 1165 to summer 1166, was again in close contact with her Poitevin subjects, and she learned first-hand of their dissatisfaction. She heard from her cousin Ralph de Faye and others that the nobles were threatening to withdraw their allegiance from Henry "because of his pruning of their liberties."[25] Dissatisfaction mounted to such a level that the Poitevin bishops sought to end the English king's rule over them by challenging the legitimacy of his marriage to their duchess. When papal legates arrived in Poitou to confer with the Poitevin clergy about the Becket conflict, the prelates drafted a document to present to them detailing the couple's genealogies to demonstrate that the marriage was unlawful because of their relationship within the Church's prohibited degrees of kinship.[26]

The Poitevin nobility's restlessness forced Henry to seek a solution to the strife in his wife's lands south of the Loire valley; and in October 1166 at the end of his Breton campaign, he considered steps for dealing with the obstreperous Poitevins. He decided to summon Eleanor's nobles to a council at Chinon in late November, and there he revealed to them a plan to hold his Christmas court at Poitiers.[27] He appeared in Poitiers in December for the festivities with Young Henry, presenting his heir to the Poitevin magnates, but this gesture was not enough to appease them. This was perhaps because of the absence of their duchess, who was too close to the delivery of her last child to risk traveling from England to Poitou.

In 1167, Henry II not only had to deal with the Poitevin nobles' threatened revolt, but also with the disputed succession to the county of Auvergne and the longstanding dispute with the count of Toulouse. At Grandmont in the Limousin, an austere religious house that Henry much admired, he met with Count Raymond V, but their meeting brought no satisfactory end to the issue.[28] At the beginning of 1168 Henry had to leave Normandy to put down a revolt by major lords on Poitou's southern frontier, led by the counts of Angoulême and La Marche and the lords of Lusignan. In winter weather, the king-duke marched on the castle of Lusignan, former seat of the Lusignan family near Poitiers and an important rebel center. He took Lusignan from them and made the fortress his base for ravaging their lands.[29] Despite Henry's victory, he was forced to conclude that his queen's patrimony could constitute no more than a secondary zone within his Angevin "empire" that could not be ruled by outright occupation, but only through local leaders. He decided to try pacifying the Poitevins by giving them back their own countess—Queen Eleanor.

It is not clear whether Eleanor had accompanied Henry when he left Argentan for Poitou in January. In any case, he had installed her at Poitiers to govern by the end of winter, and she would remain more or less permanently resident there until 1174, preoccupied with governing the unruly Poitevins. By spring 1168, once her husband thought that the rebels were subdued and strategic castles strengthened and garrisoned, he headed north for a meeting with the Capetian king on the Norman frontier, leaving Eleanor behind. Fearful that his wife's presence in Poitou would not be enough to guarantee peace, he continued to take responsibility for all matters related to war, and he left at her side in charge of military matters his trusted lieutenant, Earl Patrick of Salisbury.

Much speculation has arisen over Henry's decision to install Eleanor at Poitiers, since the experiment ended badly for him with her participation in their sons' rebellion of 1173–74. Those unfamiliar with the long separations that had marked the earlier years of Eleanor's marriage to Henry sometimes attribute her return to Poitou to the couple's alienation. Sometimes her absence from his Christmas courts after 1167 is cited as a sign of their troubled marriage.[30] In fact, she joined Henry for the courts of 1170 and 1172, although in December 1171, with Henry far away in Ireland, she remained in Aquitaine, holding a great Christmas court at Limoges with her son Richard.

There has also been speculation that anger at her husband's infidelities, especially jealousy over his infatuation with Rosamund Clifford, triggered her decision to abandon England for Poitou, yet the chronology of this liaison does not support such a view.[31] Nothing points toward Eleanor's fury at Henry's extra-marital affairs either before her return to Poitou or in the years just following. Their marriage had never been a love match, and she was well aware of his affairs with both low-born household servant women and noble ladies. Eleanor had known from childhood that aristocratic husbands were habitually unfaithful and that their wives were expected to ignore their infidelities. There is little doubt, however, that the nature of their marriage was changing, and that the two were drifting apart, no longer the partners that they had been earlier. By 1168 Eleanor's child-bearing years were behind her, and Henry at age thirty-five was still lustful and looking elsewhere for pleasure. It is not unlikely that the decision for Eleanor to return to Poitou was mutual, marking the couple's agreement to an unofficial separation without undue rancor, whether for political or personal reasons.

Little considered as a factor in Eleanor's willingness to take up residence in Aquitaine was her own desire to wield power over her patrimony, a wish to assume her hereditary right as duchess.[32] Medieval moralists hardly considered such a motive, for they had a habit of "personalising the behaviour of women, attributing emotional or irrational motives to their actions," while describing men's actions as "rational," motivated by practical circumstances.[33] Too often, modern writers follow such conventional thinking, assigning medieval women's actions to personal or emotional motives or even to sexual appetites. Eleanor, at her mature age, could aspire to an important political role in her patrimony as she saw her power as regent in England slipping steadily into the chief justiciar's hands. A growing concern for her at a time when Henry II was considering the succession to his domains was the fate of her duchy. Eleanor of Aquitaine saw her own ancestral line as more ancient and more prestigious than Henry's Angevin and Norman forebears, and she had no wish to see her patrimony disappear, absorbed permanently into a Plantagenet empire as simply another province.

Soon after her arrival in Poitou Eleanor found herself almost at once in the thick of a revived rebellion, caught in an ambush that took the life of her protector, Earl Patrick of Salisbury. Following the king's departure, the Lusignans tried to seize the queen's person in late March or early April 1168, probably along the road between Poitiers and Niort.[34] The *History of William Marshal* gives a full account of the incident. At the end of 1167, early in William's career as a knight errant, he had left England to follow his uncle Earl Patrick to Poitou, and he was riding with the queen's party when it was ambushed by a band led by two Lusignan brothers, Geoffrey and Guy. The earl sent the queen to safety in a nearby castle, but before he could mount his horse for combat, "a traitorous assassin struck him right through from behind with his lance," and he died at once.[35] According to the Poitevins' version of the incident, the earl was killed, "though unintentionally," as they defended themselves from an attack while peace talks were under way. By summer, the magnates of Poitou and Angoulême implicated in the earl's death, including the count of La Marche, the viscount of Thouars, Geoffrey de Lusignan, and the abbot of Charroux, were demanding restitution from Henry for damages inflicted on them by him and his men.[36]

William Marshal, enraged by his uncle's killing, fought furiously even after he was unhorsed, but wounded in the mêlée, he was taken captive. His captors held him in hard confinement awaiting a ransom payment, and Eleanor rescued him, handing over hostages as a guarantee for the ransom. To show her gratitude, she supplied all that he needed as a knight of her household, "horses, arms, money, and fine clothes." William's valor in this ambush was a crucial moment for his reputation as an exemplar of chivalry, for it brought him into the queen's service, and he would continue serving her until 1170, when the king chose him to instruct his newly crowned son Henry, not yet dubbed a knight, in courtesy and knightly warfare. The Marshal became chief among his young master's household knights, and after leaving Young Henry's service, he would remain loyal to the Plantagenet line, serving Henry II faithfully, then his two sons Richard and John, and finally his grandson, Henry III.[37]

Between 1168 and 1174, the queen-duchess possessed the greatest degree of autonomy that she would enjoy during Henry II's lifetime, yet her authority was not unlimited. Her husband kept close control over military matters, although it is uncertain whether he named anyone to replace the earl of Salisbury as his commander in Poitou. According to one near-contemporary account, William de Tancarville, hereditary chamberlain of Normandy, held Poitou after Earl Patrick's death, but this is uncorroborated.[38] Although Eleanor had access to Poitevin sources of income, it is likely that Henry kept a share of revenues in his own hands, leaving her without "the two nerves of power that are money and military force." She no longer received the pensions paid to her when in England, but continued to collect some English funds, including almost £100 a year from her Devonshire manors.[39]

Eleanor, now formally in charge of her duchy, issued all major administrative acts—charters, writs, and letters—under her own seal, and an indicator of her public authority is her use of her seal to endorse or guarantee grants or agreements made by others.[40] Such documents show that her effective power extended only over the Poitevin heartland, a limited portion of the vast duchy of Aquitaine. One of Eleanor's first religious benefactions after her return to Poitou was an endowment at the church of Saint-Hilaire, Poitiers, for an anniversary mass to be said annually "for the soul of Earl Patrick who died in our service." The document declares that Eleanor was making the donation to the church where the earl's body lay "by the will and command of my lord the king and my son [Richard]." Henry's interest shows not only his devotion to the memory of a loyal servant and longtime friend, but also his concern for his wife faced with danger that threatened their shared authority over her duchy. No confirmations by Henry of other documents issued by Eleanor survive from the years of her residence in Poitou, nor are there any extant charters in his own name concerning Aquitaine during those years.[41] Only two of Eleanor's letters survive from this period, both requesting papal assistance in restoring one of her kinsmen, Peter-Raymond, as abbot of Saint-Maixent; for unknown reasons, he had been removed from his post at the head of one of Poitou's most prestigious monasteries. Another intervention by Eleanor in a religious house's affairs was her support for the admission of a priest's niece into the aristocratic nunnery of Notre-Dame de Saintes "at the urgent entreaty of the venerable Eleanor."[42] Perhaps this was a compassionate act on Eleanor's part, prodding a house, noted as a refuge for noble ladies, that was reluctant to admit such a girl into its ranks.

By 1170, both Henry II and his queen were intent on ensuring the succession to their patrimonies. Henry was preoccupied with arranging Young Henry's coronation as English king. Because the king's childhood had been dominated by a long struggle for the English Crown between his mother and Stephen of Blois, he feared any uncertainty about the succession on his own death. He had long contemplated following Capetian precedent and having Young Henry crowned king in his own lifetime.[43] Henry's haste in going forward with his son's coronation in 1170 is explained in part by a need to forestall drastic acts by the exiled Thomas Becket. On Palm Sunday 1169, Becket had excommunicated a number of Henry's advisers, including the bishops of London and Salisbury. By autumn, the angry archbishop was threatening to declare the English kingdom under an interdict, prohibiting all public religious services and also threatening Henry with excommunication.[44] For Henry, going ahead with the coronation may have been a scheme for thwarting Becket, reasoning that the archbishop's excommunication would have no effect if a youth innocent of his father's sins against the Church were wearing the crown.

Since the archbishop of Canterbury traditionally crowned and anointed new kings, Henry II drafted the archbishop of York to act in his absence, a step that would, not surprisingly, infuriate Becket. In spite of the complication of Becket's opposition, Eleanor shared Henry's ambition of seeing their eldest son crowned, doubtless delighted that his coronation would elevate her standing as mother of a king. In spring 1170, during the days before Young Henry's coronation, it was clear that Eleanor still had a place among her husband's counselors. According to the *History of William Marshal*, the king's decision to stage the coronation was made "by the counsel of the queen and all her entourage, for such was her duty."[45]

In June 1170, as the coronation was about to take place, Eleanor returned to Normandy at Henry's summons to act as his deputy while he was in England preparing for Young Henry's coronation. Apparently left behind at Caen with Eleanor when Young Henry sailed for England was his wife Margaret, who was to be excluded from the ceremony. It is uncertain whether this was deliberate, designed as an insult to her father Louis VII, but for whatever reason, Margaret would not be crowned queen for more than another two years, when a second ceremony was staged for the Young King's re-crowning in August 1172.[46] One of Eleanor's duties in Normandy was to forestall attempts by Becket or the pope to send letters forbidding the coronation, by stopping any ecclesiastic from taking ship to England until the ceremony had taken place. When Roger, bishop of Worcester, entered Normandy with a papal prohibition and tried to set sail, the queen and the constable of Normandy intervened. After the coronation, Henry II encountered the bishop and upbraided him for not being present at the ceremony, knowing full well that his absence was due to his own order. Roger replied that the queen and the constable had stopped him. Courteously seeking to protect Eleanor from Henry's reproof, the bishop pointed out that "either her respect or fear of you will make her conceal the truth"; and he added, "Or if she states the truth, your indignation will fall upon that noble lady. Better that I should lose a leg than that she should hear one harsh word from you."[47]

At the end of 1170 Eleanor again left Poitou for Normandy. She was present at the hunting lodge of Bur-le-Roi near Bayeux with Henry II and her three younger sons for the fateful Christmas court that preceded Thomas Becket's murder.[48] The festive mood at Bur-le-Roi that December was dispelled by the arrival of bishops from England a few days before Christmas. These prelates, Henry's strong supporters in his bitter conflict with his archbishop of Canterbury, came to complain of their excommunication by Becket, who had recently returned to his archbishopric after a shaky settlement of his long quarrel with the king. This news plunged the royal household into crisis as Henry and his counselors debated measures to counter the archbishop's action. It was from Bur that four of the king's knights set out for Canterbury to murder Becket on 29 December. The queen must have heard the enraged Henry utter his rash remark against his former friend that impelled his knights to plot the archbishop's death and to slip away from court on their deadly mission. The king had moved on to Argentan when, three days later, he learned that they had slain the archbishop in his cathedral. Eleanor probably departed as soon as possible, eager to distance herself from her husband, now denounced as the assassin at least indirectly of an archbishop who would be acclaimed almost at once as a holy martyr and miracle worker.

Nonetheless, the royal couple met again the next year at Chinon for Henry's 1172 Christmas court, along with two of their sons, Richard and Geoffrey. Eleanor wished to see Richard her second son installed safely as her successor in the duchy of Aquitaine, and by seeing his future settled, she hoped to ensure preservation of the duchy of Aquitaine as a distinct political unit. Richard had been designated heir to Eleanor's lands in accordance with widespread custom that second sons should inherit their mothers' landed inheritances, confirmed by Henry at a meeting with Louis VII in January 1169 at Montmirail Castle in Maine. Eleanor traveled throughout her lands, visiting other cities such as Limoges, Niort, Périgueux, and Saint-Jean-d'Angély, to introduce her son to his people. In June 1170 the two traveled to Limoges to lay the cornerstone of the monastery of Saint-Augustin, and while there, they received with great pomp the kings of Aragon and Navarre, who had come on pilgrimage to the tomb of Saint Martial.[49]

In June 1172, Eleanor saw that Richard at age fourteen was solemnly invested as duke in a move paralleling Young Henry's coronation as king of England two years earlier. The boy's ceremonial investiture had two parts, first at Poitiers and then at Limoges, and it was a step that Eleanor was unlikely to have taken without her husband's agreement. Indeed, the Limousin chronicler Geoffrey de Vigeois wrote, "King Henry Senior transferred to Richard by the will of his mother Eleanor the duchy of Aquitaine."[50] Yet Henry II would continue to bear the title "duke of Aquitaine" throughout his reign, and during his father's lifetime Richard was usually addressed by the title "count of Poitou."[51]

Richard's installation began with a splendid ceremony at Poitiers on the Sunday after Pentecost in the church of Saint-Hilaire-le-Grand, where the counts of Poitou had long held the post of lay abbot. With the bishop of Poitiers and the archbishop of Bordeaux presiding, Richard was presented with a lance and a banner, symbols of his authority as count. Following these solemnities at Poitiers was another elaborate ceremony in Saint-Martial Abbey at Limoges housing relics of two of Aquitaine's most revered saints. Saint Martial was allegedly one of Christ's apostles sent to convert the Aquitanians, and Saint Valérie was a holy virgin and martyr, and according to tradition, daughter of a Roman governor of Aquitaine. As the ceremony's key element, the new duke was invested with the sacred ring of Saint Valérie, symbolizing his mystical marriage to the city and to the duchy of Aquitaine. Then the bishop placed a golden circlet on his head and handed to him a rod and a sword.[52] Clerics at Saint-Martial had apparently devised this ceremony inaugurating a new duke during the eleventh century in imitation of royal coronations, and they could cite the coronation of Charles the Bald's son as king of Aquitaine in 855 as precedent. They were eager to enhance their

house's prestige by making its significance for the dukes of Aquitaine equivalent to that of Saint-Denis for the Capetian kings, hoping to attract pilgrimages and patronage.

The people of Limoges must have viewed the ceremony in their city as
public recognition of the new duke's authority, symbolizing the transfer to him
of something of the Carolingian rulers' sacred character.[53] They had no love for
their old duke Henry II, who had twice punished them by leveling their city's
walls. In Eleanor's mind as well, the ceremony must have signaled that young
Richard's authority in Aquitaine had nothing to do with Henry, but symbolized that his right descended from God and from the Carolingian sub-kings of
Aquitaine through her lineage. As Louis VII's queen, she had seen the advantage
to the Capetians of linking their kingship to the cult of Saint Denis, France's
patron saint. She is likely to have seen in the ceremony at Saint-Martial "its
special value in direct opposition to Saint-Denis and the Capetians."[54] No
doubt Eleanor recognized also that Richard's installation as her successor
would bolster the special bond existing between the boy and his mother.

At Christmas 1172 and at the beginning of the new year, Eleanor and her
husband were together for the festivities at Chinon Castle. While at Chinon,
the queen-duchess made a visit to nearby Fontevraud where she witnessed a
gift by a steward of the royal household Manasser Biset and his wife. They gave
the nuns money for annual purchases of herrings during Lent, and Eleanor
confirmed their grant by setting her seal to it. Their charter notes, "This gift
was made in the chapter of Fontevraud, on the Sunday when *Exsurge quare*
was sung in the presence of Eleanor queen of the English . . . and of Richard
her son."[55] Sometime after 1170 Eleanor had begun to associate herself more
and more with the great abbey, making significant gifts to the nuns and to
their dependent priories. She visited Fontevraud at least twice before the
rebellion of 1173, and on one of her visits Abbess Audeburge agreed to act as
witness to one of her charters. The queen-duchess was also present for the
religious profession of a widow, joining the abbess in receiving the gift that
the novice's parents made to the nuns.[56]

Perhaps Eleanor's revived interest in Fontevraud was simply a continuation
of Henry's patronage policy or an expression of gratitude for the nuns' shel-
tering of her young children, John and Joanne, while she was preoccupied
with governing Poitou. A darker explanation, however, is that she was already
contemplating a break with Henry and saw cultivating the great abbey's favor
as a way of winning influence with neighboring nobles, several of whom
would later join the rebellion against her husband.[57] It seems that from about
1170 Eleanor was experiencing an emotional or sentimental distancing from
Henry that paralleled their physical distance. It was becoming clear that her
husband was not allowing her complete freedom to govern her own duchy,

and he did not hesitate to continue intervening personally in Aquitaine. In the spring and summer of 1169, Henry campaigned as far south as Saint-Macaire on the border between the Bordelais and the Bazadais, seizing and razing former rebels' castles.[58] In the spring of 1171, when the townspeople of La Souterraine staged an uprising against their lord, the abbot of Saint-Martial, the abbot did not call on Eleanor for aid. Apparently aware of where final authority lay, he appealed directly to Henry, who rushed to the Limousin and crushed the revolt.[59]

In three documents from that year an alteration in the wording of her charters hints at Eleanor's distancing from Henry II. She modified their form of address to define herself as sole head of her domains, abandoning the previously used phrase "to the king's faithful followers and her own" in favor of the simple words, "to her faithful followers." This omission of any reference to her husband aimed at asserting her authority to act in her own name within Poitou and Aquitaine, not simply as Henry's agent.[60] In implying a rejection of the rights in her patrimony conferred on Henry through their marriage, she seemed to be venturing dangerously close to questioning the marriage itself. Living in Poitou had brought Eleanor face to face with the brutality of her husband's policies there. She learned first-hand of his cruelty to rebels captured in the 1167–68 rebellion from the widow of Robert de Seilhac, a lord of the Limousin, whose imprisonment Henry had ordered. The cruel conditions of captivity commanded by the king had brought about his death. In 1172 or 1173 the queen-duchess affixed her seal as witness to a grant to Fontevraud Abbey by de Seilhac's widow. Eleanor's sympathy for the widow may imply a rebuke to her husband, pointing toward disillusionment with his harsh rule over her people.[61]

ELEANOR'S COURT AT POITIERS

After Eleanor's return to Poitou in 1168, Henry apparently intended to follow his earlier practise of positioning some of his own loyalists in her household, but he did not do so. The paucity of Anglo-Norman or Angevin names in Eleanor's entourage in Poitou testifies that she quickly won freedom to choose her own household officials without her husband's supervision. At Poitiers with Eleanor when she made a grant for Earl Patrick of Salisbury's soul were the Norman Simon de Tournebu, Henry's constable of Thouars Castle in 1164, who later returned to Normandy to serve in the ducal administration there, and an Anglo-Norman, Richard de Camville. After the earl of Salisbury's death, however, northerners soon disappeared from the queen-duchess's household. Only two other Anglo-Norman names appear as witnesses to her charters, both occurring on the occasion of the 1172 Christmas court at Chinon.[62] Henry's failure to plant his own men at his queen's Poitevin court would cost him dearly, for her 1173 conspiracy with her sons against him came as a complete surprise.

Poitevin office holders joining Eleanor's entourage soon after her return indicate that she turned to the families of longtime servants of the counts to constitute a household of her own. Identified as her steward is Porteclie de Mauzé whose father had served both her father and her first husband.[63] Hervey, always identified as *Panetarius*, or butler, had been in Eleanor's service when she was French queen, and she had named him provost of Poitiers on her 1156 visit with Henry; but Philip, her butler earlier in England, was also with her in Poitou, as was Bernard de Chauvigny, her chamberlain in England.[64] While she was in Poitou Eleanor also reconstituted her chancery, and she found scribes capable of adopting a style similar to that of Henry II's official documents without slavish imitation of royal models.[65] Master Bernard, who had acted as chancellor previously in Poitou in 1152, returned to her service, and another Poitevin clerk, Jordan, identified as Eleanor's chancellor on her 1156 visit, is probably the same Jordan appearing with her again in Poitou after 1168 as "clerk" and "notary." Peter, the queen's chaplain earlier in England, seems likely to have doubled as a secretary for her in Poitou. A prominent member of Eleanor's household was her constable Saldebreuil, who had possibly joined her in England for a time.[66] He would have commanded a band of household knights needed for her protection as she moved about turbulent Poitou. As noted above, among her knights was William Marshal, recruited after his uncle Patrick of Salisbury's death.

Once back in her native land, Eleanor renewed contacts with her Poitevin kin, notably the descendants of her maternal grandfather, the viscount of Châtellerault. Among them was her uncle, the current viscount, Hugh II. Occupying a position as the most prominent member of her retinue and as her chief Poitevin counselor, however, was the viscount's younger brother, Ralph de Faye. Even before Eleanor's return, Ralph de Faye had played an important part in Poitou's administration, acting as seneschal of Saintonge and as "procurator" of Aquitaine; and from 1168 he seems to have been seneschal of all Aquitaine.[67] During the queen's residence at Angers in 1165 and 1166, Ralph had frequently attended her court, keeping her informed on conditions in her duchy. Other members of Poitou's noble families rarely appeared at Eleanor's court, other than her own relatives, including her uncle and his brother the viscount of Châtellerault.[68] Except for the count of La Marche, powerful lords on the southern fringes of Poitou such as the count of Angoulême or the viscount of Limoges were absent, and only a few lords below the category of count or viscount appeared at court, for example, Geoffrey, lord of Tonnaye-Charente. Nor were members of the ecclesiastical hierarchy of Aquitaine particularly prominent at Eleanor's court. Among the higher clergy, the bishops of Périgueux and Angoulême occasionally attended their duchess, as did the prior of Sainte-Radegonde, Poitiers; but John of Canterbury, bishop of Poitiers, was more often in her presence than any other prelate. This is not surprising since he was close at hand in Poitiers, but he was hardly a trusted counselor; as a strong partisan of Thomas Becket, he was mistrustful of both the queen and Ralph de Faye. Indeed, in one of the bishop's letters his insinuations can be construed as suggesting scandalous relations between the two similar to the accusations against Eleanor and her uncle Raymond at Antioch years earlier.[69]

More often present at Eleanor's court were lesser-ranking nobles from families with a tradition of service to the counts of Poitou who had continued in Henry II's service. William Maingot II belonged to a family that served as hereditary custodians of the lordship of Surgères, and his father had held posts as seneschal under earlier dukes of Aquitaine, as had Porteclie de Mauzé.[70] Other officials included Fulk de Matha whose father had served Eleanor's father, her first husband, and then Henry Plantagenet as seneschal, and Maingot de Melle, hereditary custodian of the lordship of Melle. Both William Maingot and Fulk de Matha would continue to be prominent in Poitou's administration under Count Richard.

Alongside the queen-duchess at Poitiers was her second son Richard, aged nine at the time of her return to Poitou, and already acknowledged as heir to her duchy.[71] Henry had agreed to her custody of the boy, aware of his need for a special apprenticeship to prepare for ruling his future duchy. Eleanor associated him with her in governing Aquitaine after 1168 with the phrase "I and Richard my son" in two-thirds of her surviving documents.[72] Among the aristocracy second sons, naturally jealous of their first-born brothers, often became particularly devoted to their mothers. During Richard's adolescence, when he was continuously at his mother's court, his attachment to her flowered, a bond that other members of the Plantagenet family seem to have recognized. In his five years spent at her side in Poitou, he came to have in common with Eleanor "an undeniable sense of regional attachment and shared experience" that both bound them to her ancestral homeland and to each other. The trust that Richard would place in her political judgment during his years as English monarch first strengthened during this period. The singular affection formed between mother and son leads some writers, applying outdated psychological theories, to suspect from Richard's emotional dependence on Eleanor in his father's absence that her domineering personality fostered his homosexuality. Yet the Lionheart's adult sexuality is problematic, and no comment from contemporary writers shows them troubled by his close relationship with his mother.[73]

While Richard was with his mother almost continuously in Poitou, it seems that if her other two older sons—the Young King Henry and Geoffrey of Brittany—joined her court, it was only briefly. After Young Henry's coronation at age fifteen in June 1170, his residence was chiefly England where he acted as his father's regent, although he made visits to Normandy where he held his own Christmas court in 1171. It seems that Geoffrey, barely a teenager, was also mainly in England after 1170. Yet Eleanor maintained some contact with these two sons, whether meeting them in Normandy or receiving them in Poitou. She began to concentrate her ambition more and more on these boys after 1167, years that would be critical for her relations with them and with her husband. Although the youths had not yet received their belts of knighthood, they were capable of playing a role in politics as Eleanor's tools at a time when she and her husband were drifting apart. Young Henry would pass through his mother's lands in February 1173 on his way to a great council at Limoges. Made aware of his younger brother's solid position in Poitou, he felt increasing bitterness at his father's refusal to give him domains of his own to govern. Henry II made proposals at Limoges for finding lands to secure his youngest son John's future that would enrage him, and the homage by the count of Toulouse to Henry Senior and to the Young King would incense Eleanor and Richard. The Limoges council would set the stage for the great rebellion by Eleanor and her sons that would soon erupt.

Joining Eleanor's court at Poitiers from 1168 until 1170 was her second daughter, also named Eleanor, although she may have also spent some time at Fontevraud with her younger brother John and her sister Joanne.[74] Earlier Henry II had begun seeking future husbands for his daughters among Spanish princes, hoping for marriage-alliances that would further his ambitions in southwestern France. He wished to isolate Toulouse and also to limit Capetian influence in Spain after Louis VII's marriage to a Castilian princess following his divorce from Eleanor. In 1168 Henry arranged a Spanish marriage for his second daughter, seven years old at the time, betrothing her to young Alfonso VIII, king of Castile. In September 1170 Eleanor made one of her rare visits to Bordeaux, bringing along young Eleanor to hand her over to Castilian envoys. The queen-duchess presided over a great council to settle the terms for her namesake's marriage with Castilian commissioners, a number of Spanish bishops, and nobles headed by the archbishop of Toledo. Also attending the council was a great company of Eleanor's magnates, including the archbishop of Bordeaux and the bishops of Agen, Angoulême, Poitiers, Saintes, and Périgueux, several Gascon viscounts, and faithful Poitevin officials such as Theobald Chabot and William Maingot. At the council's end, young Eleanor was taken in hand by Spanish prelates to cross the Pyrenees to join her future husband in Spain, where their marriage would be solemnized once she reached the age of twelve.[75] After the child left Poitiers for the Castilian court, Eleanor could hardly expect to see her daughter again, but chance would reunite them more than thirty years later in 1202.

The marriage settlement made by Henry II for his second daughter did not provide her with a large sum of money to take to her bridegroom, as was becoming common in noble marriages. Instead, young Eleanor's dowry was to be the duchy of Gascony, although it was not to come into her possession until after her mother's death.[76] No doubt Henry saw his wife's southern duchy as a dispensable outlying zone of Aquitaine in the grip of unruly nobles, where the dukes of Aquitaine had never exercised effective control. Henry had no lawful right to dispose of Eleanor's Gascon patrimony without her agreement, but it is difficult to believe that she would have given her assent freely. Eleanor cannot have been pleased that a prize won by her great-grandfather for the duchy of Aquitaine over a century earlier was to be handed over one day to the Castilian royal line. Years later, in 1204, following Eleanor's death, Alfonso VIII would try to assert his wife's right by invading Gascony.[77] Perhaps Henry's willingness to diminish Eleanor's patrimony by promising Gascony to the Castilian king contributed to her doubts about her husband's commitment to preserving her family's accumulated lands, and it would have caused her to question her own degree of authority over her heritage.

When Eleanor had journeyed from Normandy to Aquitaine in 1168 she was accompanied by the two of her children still in infancy, Joanne and John. These youngsters would not remain with their mother's household at Poitiers, however, but were placed in the nuns' care at Fontevraud Abbey. The abbey's obituary notice for King John's death notes that he "was given to us and to our church as an oblate by his most illustrious father King Henry and for a period of five years was cared for by us."[78] The obituary doubtless is correct in declaring that it was Henry who handed over young John to the Fontevraud nuns, for decisions regarding noble boys' education were the father's preroga-tive. The abbey had enjoyed the Angevin counts' favor since its founding at the beginning of the twelfth century; furthermore, Henry's aunt had been its abbess, and while his two youngest children were there one of his cousins was a nun there. Influencing his decision to house the two children at Fontevraud was Eleanor's preoccupation with other matters, namely the taming of her turbulent duchy, but its location on the Angevin frontier not too far from Poitiers made frequent visits from her possible.

The abbey's obituary is misleading in describing John as an oblate, for the boy was not sent there for education as a cleric, even though it was not uncommon for aristocratic families to place one of their younger sons in the clergy. If Henry II had intended to prepare him for an ecclesiastical career, he would not have sent him to a double abbey ruled by an abbess where males among the religious took a secondary place to the nuns. In this instance, the term "oblate" means simply a boy lodged at the abbey in the nuns' care, for nunneries often took in children of both sexes to nurture and educate. In late twelfth-century England, Saint Hugh of Lincoln sent a five-year-old boy in his custody off to a convent to learn his letters.[79]

John at Fontevraud was unable to enjoy the close maternal ties normally linking sons in affection to their mothers during early childhood. This has led at least one authority on Eleanor, applying psychoanalytic theories, to hold John's lack of contact with her at that crucial time responsible for his "paranoia and unprincipled opportunism."[80] Perhaps John's early separation from his mother inspired negative feelings about his self-worth that impelled him toward despotic rule as king, stimulating his suspicious nature, jealousy, sensitivity to slights, and delight in humbling rivals that he would first display as an adolescent. Yet a Freudian image of Eleanor as a domineering mother distorting her son's psyche can be challenged. His brothers, sisters, and many other aristocratic children also endured early and repeated separations from their parents.[81] Richard, in his mother's company constantly in early adolescence, proved as capable of severe cruelty to enemies and harsh exploitation of his subjects as his much-hated younger brother, despite his reputation as "the standard-bearer of Christianity, the flower of western chivalry." Given the increasingly tense atmosphere of hostility between Henry II and Eleanor and jealousy among their sons, perhaps young John was fortunate in spending his earliest years away from his parents' household in the tranquility of a religious house.[82] In any case, John had cause to feel insecure for reasons other than separation from his mother in early childhood. The youngest of several sons in any medieval noble family had uncertain prospects; and when in January 1169 Henry set forth his scheme for the succession to his collection of principalities at Montmirail, it called for a tripartite partition among his three elder sons with nothing for young John.

ELEANOR AND THE COURTS OF LOVE AT POITIERS

Eleanor's years spent apart from Henry II presiding over her own court at Poitiers have inspired much myth. Romantically inclined writers, imagining the "queen of the troubadours" attracting poets to her court, have found inspiration in a Poitevin chronicler's description. Lamenting the queen-duchess's captivity in England after 1174, he writes, "Once tender and delicate, you enjoyed a royal freedom, you abounded with riches, young girls surrounded you playing the tambourine and the harp, singing pleasant songs. Indeed you enjoyed the sound of the organ, and you leaped to the beating of drums."[83] This brief passage has inspired writers to imagine Eleanor gathering about her swarms of noble maidens and gallants as well as troubadour poets, presiding over courts of love and pronouncing judgments on amorous problems.

Great ladies had a duty to train young knights in their households in courteous conduct to ensure their proper deportment with the women of her entourage. Yet some go so far as to envisage Eleanor establishing a "royal academy" to teach noble youths and maidens not only courtesy or chivalry, but also "courtly love." Supposedly the queen-duchess fostered troubadour doctrines of love at her court at Poitiers, encouraging in these youths a mentality that sanctioned adulterous relationships, giving rise to modern romantic love.[84] "Courtly love" is a term coined by a late nineteenth-century French authority on medieval literature. Troubadours themselves never used the term, employing instead *fin' amors*, even though their songs register the high value they placed on passionate, overpowering love. Among writers today, some limit courtly love to doctrines of love first set forth in troubadours' lyrics, while others apply the term broadly as meaning medieval romantic love in general.

Because Eleanor's name is so often linked with so-called courtly love, its sudden appearance in southern France and the rapid northward spread of its popularity require some explanation. Once the answer was the enthusiastic support given to troubadours and their teachings by aristocratic women such as Eleanor, who supposedly saw their outlook on love as a means of improving their condition.[85] While early twelfth-century troubadour lyric poetry and northern romances composed later in the century did much to promote courtly love among knights in the French and Anglo-Norman realms, it is not certain that their intended audience was female. Although women were among the listeners to courtly lyrics and romances at princely courts, such works do not necessarily reflect a feminine viewpoint. The female characters seem created for a male audience, portrayed as passive objects, victims of violence whose function is to provide the hero an opportunity for making a gallant rescue.[86]

Adulterous love in troubadour lyrics has little relation to reality, and it existed primarily in the poets' imagination, probably little more than a game played by young knights with few prospects for land or marriage. Vying with one another in wooing their lords' wives and displaying their courtesy to win ladies' favor enabled them to reconcile themselves to the deferral or denial of their sexual desires. Possibly troubadour poets in their quest for the love of higher-ranking ladies hoped to enhance their own social standing by presenting themselves as exemplars of perfect courtly conduct.[87] The extramarital nature of this troubadour depiction of love, contradicting ecclesiastical condemnations of lust, adultery, and fornication as serious crimes, presents a barrier to accepting its authenticity, however. Furthermore, poets' employment of the same language of fealty that bound knights to their lords to describe their adoration of a noble lady seems to ignore the realities of a militarized twelfth-century society. Such declarations of vassal-like devotion to a lady may have been paradoxical or ironic, accepted by amused noble audiences as entertaining fictions, even though during Eleanor's childhood some noblewomen still held on to political power in Occitan-speaking lands where troubadour poetry flourished.[88]

Clearly literature influences human emotions; as one writer on the medieval mind states, "In matters of love, life has often sought to imitate art."[89] The extraordinary popularity of courtly love literature, first in Occitan troubadour lyrics and later in northern French romances, suggests that however imaginative or escapist, it reflected to some extent aristocratic society's thoughts. A concept of spontaneous passionate love was rising in the twelfth century despite the Church's ascetic teachings on sexual matters. Learned readers steeped in the classical tradition already knew the power of love from reading Catullus or Ovid, and they could recognize symptoms of lovesickness. They could believe that an "art of love" could be taught. Even theologians and preachers assumed the existence of something akin to romantic love, and they wrote about problems of love and proposed remedies to lovesickness.[90] Twelfth-century vernacular poets were confronting real problems faced by an aristocratic male-dominated society in dealing with matters of love, courtship, and marriage. Their new courtly literature raised relevant issues about free will in love and marriage, and the contrast between the ideal of couples' free choice and actual marriage practices struck a powerful chord, especially among noble ladies. It should not be surprising if Eleanor's two stormy marriages stimulated courtly poets' thoughts on free choice for marriage partners and couples' need for mutual affection.[91]

For readers today, Eleanor's connection with courtly love comes chiefly from persistent legends that during her years in Poitou she gathered around her a group of ladies in "courts of love," handing down judgments on matters of the heart. The source of this legend is Andrew the Chaplain's *On Love*, a handbook for courtly lovers addressed to a friend who was "a new recruit to love."[92] Included in Andrew's book is a collection of twenty-one opinions allegedly pronounced by Eleanor and ladies at her court on disputed questions of love. The ladies giving judgments are, in addition to the English queen: Countess Marie of Champagne, her elder daughter from her first marriage; Ermengarde, viscountess of Narbonne; and the countess of Flanders. Formerly Andrew's work was taken at face value and his accounts of the courts of love accepted as accurate; today, however, its testimony is no longer accepted as proof of ladies actually taking part in such courts at Poitiers. No evidence points to contacts between Marie de Champagne and her mother after Eleanor's 1152 divorce, and if they ever met, it could only have been in the 1190s, when Eleanor passed through Champagne on her way to her captive son Richard in Germany.[93] It is not the presence of these ladies at Poitiers that accounts for Andrew's choosing them to voice unorthodox opinions on love, but their common desire as married women, widows, or divorcees to decide their own destinies and to exercise political power over their lands.[94]

Despite a tradition that Andrew wrote under Countess Marie's patronage, no evidence places him at her court in Champagne; indeed, he identifies himself as a chaplain at the court of Philip II of France, the Plantagenets' bitter enemy. Andrew was a cultivated and courtly cleric writing shortly before 1190 for ambitious and sophisticated young French courtiers who appreciated both classical poets and the satirical poetry of their own day.[95] His *On Love* is so filled with contradictions that some scholars dismiss it as "an elaborate spoof." One contradiction is an ordained priest authoring a learned treatise on sexual love that argues in favor of adultery at a time when the Church was pressing for clerical celibacy. Another incongruity is the contrast between the first two books of *On Love*, devoted to ensuring that Andrew's friend would "lack nothing in the art of love," and a final book condemning the joys of the flesh and exhorting him not to become a lover of women. Andrew disingenuously advised his friend, "Read this book . . . that, invigorated by the theory and trained to excite the minds of women to love, you may, by refraining from so doing, win an eternal recompense and thereby deserve a greater reward from God."[96]

Few today read Andrew's account of the courts of love literally, and it now seems clear that his book, far from praising Eleanor's patronage of courtly love, is either an ironic, humorous account of courtly love or a severe criticism of its doctrines. With premeditated malice and purposeful ambiguity, Andrew attributed to the queen-duchess and the countess of Champagne the most salacious decisions of his imagined courts at Poitiers.[97] In the six rulings ascribed to Eleanor, allusions to her own marital situation appear that would have aroused laughter among French courtiers familiar with gossip that had long circulated about her two marriages. The most shocking judgment in Andrew's treatise—that true love between a husband and his wife is impossible—is set forth in a letter attributed to Marie de Champagne, supposedly written in response to a letter addressed to her posing the question, "whether love can have any place between husband and wife." Eleanor's daughter is depicted as replying, "We declare and hold as firmly established that love cannot exert its powers between two people who are married to each other. For lovers give each other everything freely . . . but married people are in duty bound to give in to each other's desires."[98]

Andrew depicts Eleanor citing with approval Marie's judgment in her own findings. One case concerns a knight in love with a woman who had transferred her love to another man, but who led him to hope that she would return to him, should she lose her current lover's affection. After the lady married the second lover, the knight, thinking that she could not possibly love her husband, demanded that she return to him and give him "the fruit of the hope she had granted him"; she refused, however, "saying that she had not lost the love of the man she had married." Eleanor, referring to Marie's letter as precedent, then ruled that "the lady should grant her [ex-] lover the love she has promised."[99] This opinion depicting Eleanor's disillusionment with marital love would not have surprised Andrew's readers, surely aware of her two unhappy marriages and her imprisonment by Henry II after 1173.

In another of Eleanor's judgments, Andrew depicts her rendering a verdict condemning consanguineous marriages. The problem centers on a man joined in love to a woman without knowing that they are kin, who, once aware of their kinship, seeks to leave her. The woman, wishing to remain with her lover, argues that because they had begun their relationship unaware of their relationship and without sinful intent, their crime must be excused. Eleanor judges harshly, "A woman who under the excuse of a mistake of any kind seeks to preserve an incestuous love is clearly going contrary to what is right and proper. We are always bound to oppose any of those incestuous and damnable actions which we know even human laws punish by very heavy penalties."[100] Andrew's readers at the French court would have guffawed at the irony, knowing that after Eleanor's first marriage was dissolved on account of consanguinity, she promptly entered a second marriage also violating the Church's canons. Some would have found added humor in the queen's taking a harder line on consanguineous marriages than did the pope, who had counseled Eleanor and Louis VII to stay together.[101]

A judgment attributed to Eleanor treating a woman's dilemma in choosing as lover either an upright knight of mature age or a worthless younger man was also selected by Andrew for its satirical effect. Eleanor wins his praise for judging "with wonderful subtlety" in favor of the older man. He has her pronounce judgment that a woman does better to choose her lover "by the man's knowledge and his character and his praiseworthy manners, not by his age." She adds that "young men are usually more eager to gratify [their passion] with older women than with young ones . . . those who are older prefer . . . the embraces and kisses of young women rather than of older ones. But on the other hand a woman whether young or somewhat older likes the embraces and solaces of young men better than those of older ones." Similar is Eleanor's opinion in the case of "a worthless young man and an older knight of excellent character" both seeking the same woman's love. Eleanor's practical opinion was that "a woman does not do very wisely if she chooses to love an unworthy man, especially when a good and eminently worthy one seeks her love."[102] Readers of both judgments would have recalled that Eleanor on her separation from Louis, a husband of her own age, had married Henry, a young man nine years her junior.

Admirers of Eleanor of Aquitaine have nominated a number of prominent twelfth-century writers as members of a literary circle supposedly gathered at

Poitiers enjoying her patronage. As we have seen, troubadours often resorted to code names in their lyrics, disguising the true name of the lady to whom they gave their devotion. Bernart de Ventadorn, one of only two troubadour poets who can definitely be situated in Eleanor's presence, hints at his devotion to "the queen of the Normans"; and in other poems he declares his adoration for a lady identified only by an invented name, inspiring speculation that she was the English queen. To assume that Bernart de Ventadorn's troubadour lyrics express his true feelings for the English queen is to forget that he was a professional composer and singer of songs and that his songs of tormented love conform to a familiar convention. In any case, Bernart's patron was more likely Henry II than Eleanor, he attended the royal court in England and Normandy early in their marriage, and no evidence places him later at her court in Poitiers. The second troubadour to be found at Eleanor's court is Arnaut Guilhem de Marsan, a Gascon noble, documented only at her great court at Bordeaux in 1170. His presence there is explained by his position as lord of Roquefort and Montgaillard in the Landes, not as some wandering poet seeking a patron.[103]

Not only troubadours but northern French writers of romances are reputed to have made their way to Eleanor's court; prominent among them are Marie de France and Chrétien de Troyes, although no evidence places either writer in Eleanor's company at Poitiers. Marie de France, once thought to have been Henry II's half-sister, is best known for her twelve *Lais*, short narrative poems in French probably composed in the 1170s for a sophisticated audience at a prominent princely court. What little is known of her is deduced from her writings, the high level of education exhibited hinting at her aristocratic birth. Her native language was the French of Paris, not English or Anglo-Norman, and in her *Fables*, written after the *Lais*, she identifies herself as coming from France.[104] Yet her *Lais* connect her in a number of ways to the Anglo-Norman realm. They show Celtic sources, demonstrate her knowledge of the English language, and have an English provenance, copied at Reading Abbey. Lending support to her ties with the Plantagenet royal court is their dedication to a *nobles reis* who seems to be Henry II or possibly his eldest son. Marie claims that her *Fables* are her translation of an Old English version of Aesop's fables translated by King Alfred, and she dedicated them to "the count William, the most valiant of this realm," identified as a late twelfth-century English earl, possibly William de Mandeville, earl of Essex (d.1189).[105]

Marie's *Lais* cannot be classified as "courtly love" tales, but these short stories present situations that would have resonated with the aristocracy of Henry's lands, especially noble ladies. Marie through her connections to the English court certainly knew much about Eleanor, whether or not she actually met her; and Eleanor would have found her *Lais* appealing. Unlike courtly romances, they take women's problems as seriously as men's, contrasting the harmful consequences of possessive, selfish love with the healing effect of unselfish love. Marie frequently examines the constraints that a tormented, confining married life imposed on women not unlike the English queen, and her female characters suffer and surrender to their desires, defying their husbands and social convention for the sake of love. Indeed, two of the *Lais* depict women escaping from imprisonment by their husbands, recalling to readers Eleanor's fate after her rebellion against Henry in 1173.[106] Little more connects Marie to Eleanor, however, than the ties to England exhibited in her tales and their appeal for women, with subject matter featuring unhappily married couples.

Because Chrétien de Troyes, the first great composer of romances, acknowledged Marie, countess of Champagne, as his patron, it is sometimes assumed that he frequented her mother's court at Poitiers. The countess's significance as a patron of vernacular literature, commissioning romances by Chrétien de Troyes, does not seem to owe anything to Eleanor's influence, however. Chrétien wrote that Marie de Champagne was the patron who supplied him with Arthurian subject matter for his *Lancelot* or *Le chevalier de la charette*, the first telling of Lancelot and Guinevere's love. He introduced themes of troubadour lyrics into northern French literature in this romance, but he did not find the adulterous subject matter appealing.[107] He abandoned his *Lancelot* before it was finished, and in other romances he tried to counteract the subversive myth of adulterous love and to communicate love and marriage reconciled. Although no evidence places Chrétien at Poitiers, his apparent knowledge of southern England's geography inspires speculation that he had visited the island kingdom, and his *Lancelot* suggests his acquaintance also with Lower Normandy. In two romances, *Erec et Enide* and *Cligès*, he depicts the Britain of King Arthur as if it were Henry II's England, and he may have intended readers to see in Arthur's empire an allusion to Henry's Angevin empire. Some readers of Chrétien's *Erec et Enide* conjecture that his description of King Arthur's splendid court at Nantes derives from his presence at Henry's brilliant Christmas court there in 1169. Yet no direct evidence exists for either Henry's or Eleanor's patronage of Chrétien.[108]

It is only Chrétien de Troyes's subject matter that connects him to Eleanor of Aquitaine. Perhaps Marie de Champagne in selecting the subject of his romance thought of her mother's life that was already becoming legendary. Certainly Chrétien would have heard of Eleanor's two royal marriages as well as rumors of her scandalous conduct that led to the dissolution of her first marriage, and it is not implausible that a romance seeming to sanction adulterous love should have drawn inspiration from the English queen's life. It is likely that readers of Chrétien's romances at princely courts could perceive parallels between Eleanor and Guinevere or Iseult, regarded by twelfth-century readers as historical personalities, even if he had no such parallels in mind. These parallels convince some students of Eleanor that close reading of medieval romances can disclose twelfth-century reality, bringing readers "closer to Eleanor as she actually was, as she was perceived to be in her own age, and even as she may sometimes have perceived herself."[109] Others remain suspicious of extrapolating historical evidence from fiction, and for them, Eleanor in the guise of Guinevere conjures up an unconvincing image.

Eleanor at Poitiers, though busy governing her duchy, may have found time to engage in clever conversation with knights and ladies at her court, possibly including talk centered on love. Her son Richard Lionheart, a composer of songs as an adult, might well have acquired his interest in poetry and music during his youth there. If Eleanor's court at Poitiers functioned as a school for "domesticating" noble youths, polishing them to shine as courteous companions for sensitive and elegant ladies, it was a failure with her son, its most famous pupil. Although renowned as a paragon of chivalry, Richard represented an older chivalry, the prowess of warriors of the *chansons de gestes* rather than the courtesy of knightly lovers in the Arthurian romances.[110] He was hardly noted for extending courtesy toward the ladies, least of all toward his own wife.

Evidence for Eleanor as a pioneer in promoting courtly poetry or courtly practices of love is scanty. While abundant material points to an active literary life at the English royal court, it is far less ample for her court established later at Poitiers. After its revival in 1168, the Poitevin court never became a center for Occitan lyrics as it had been in Duke William IX's days; and during the long years of Eleanor's absence, first at Paris and then in the Anglo-Norman realm, there had been no court at Poitiers to offer patronage. Troubadour poets had to seek patrons at courts to the south at Narbonne, in Aragon, or in Toulouse, and they would not flock back to Poitiers to join Eleanor, although other singers congregating at her court on great ceremonial occasions undoubtedly performed their songs. In fact, far more allusions to two other great ladies as patrons, Ermengarde and Maria de Ventadorn, appear in troubadour poetry of the time than to the duchess of Aquitaine.[111]

Chronology also argues against Eleanor's patronage of romance writers. In the last third of the twelfth century, when romances were first flourishing in northern France, she was no longer in any position to attract patronage seekers, stripped of power after 1173 and banished from the royal court. Nor can the courtly romances afford guidance in reconstructing Eleanor's thinking about matters of love and marriage. Adulterous love stories such as the Iseult and Tristan or Guinevere and Lancelot romances are still studied with the queen's unhappy marital situation in mind, but her legendary life can only be acknowledged as a source for medieval romance writers, giving a "ring of truth" to their invented characters.

It was in the five years after Eleanor's return to Poitou in 1168 that she would find herself wielding genuine power over Poitou and Aquitaine. Once Henry II decided on indirect rule through his wife as a means of dealing with the intractable Poitevins, Eleanor was happy to return to her homeland to take charge. The longer that she resided in her native duchy, the more she identified with her nobility, who resented her husband's infringements on their traditional liberties. She came to see that she held only a shadow of power, while Henry kept for himself the essential elements, military force and money, and his continued interventions made her tenuous position clear. More and more, the couple's political partnership was fraying. In Eleanor's years at Poitiers, she grew more involved with her sons as they approached manhood, and she worked to ensure Richard's succession in Aquitaine. She sympathized with Young Henry's resentment of his father's refusal to share power with him, denying him lands and riches that he felt were his due as a crowned king. Eleanor, like other aristocratic mothers, tended to take her sons' part against their father. Unlike other great ladies, however, she would go so far as to plot outright rebellion with her sons against her husband, and by 1173 she would join them in taking up arms against Henry.

CHAPTER 8

A QUEEN'S DISCONTENT AND HER SONS' THWARTED AMBITIONS, 1173–1174

F EW figures experienced such a dramatic and disastrous turn of the wheel of fortune as did Eleanor of Aquitaine in the autumn of 1173, when she fell from her place as Henry's assistant in ruling his collection of territories to detention as his prisoner in Chinon Castle. Eleanor inspired and participated in her sons' rebellion of 1173–74 that became a widespread revolt against Henry. Spreading throughout his domains, it was the greatest challenge to his authority that he would face until his last days. The record of the royal couple's sons for rebellions against their father and for fighting each other is almost unequaled in medieval history, and the queen's active part in a revolt against her royal husband was near unimaginable to contemporaries. Writers ever since have accused the English queen of fomenting her sons' rebellion, and the family's troubles are still so notorious that they are a subject for films and plays. The chronicler Ralph Diceto writing not many years after the revolt admitted that young Richard, count of Poitou, and Geoffrey of Brittany in fleeing to Paris to join their elder brother in 1173 were "following the advice of their mother Eleanor." He then listed over thirty instances of sons rebelling against their parents, but was unable to specify a single case of an earlier queen rebelling against her royal husband.[1]

The dysfunctional character of the family life of Eleanor of Aquitaine, Henry II, and their sons was no secret to their contemporaries. One late twelfth-century monastic writer likened the English royal family to "the confused house of Oedipus," and another commented that "this father was most unhappy in his most famous sons."[2] Courtiers at the English royal court could only explain the intense hostility by recalling an Angevin legend of the Plantagenet family's diabolical descent, having as ancestor a demon-countess of Anjou. In fact, Henry was largely an absentee father during his sons' early years, and following aristocratic custom, he was content to leave their upbringing in others' hands. Once his sons became adolescents, they resented their father's refusal to share power with them, denying them authority over the lands that he had designated for them in various partition schemes.

The stormy relationship between Henry II and his eldest son is the classic example of relations between medieval aristocratic fathers and their heirs. Among the nobility, an heir could not achieve full adult status or assume governing responsibilities as long as his father held onto the family lands; he was condemned to remain a "youth" for years past adolescence, unable to marry on account of his landless status.[3] Such heirs often joined bands of other landless youths, who were also waiting impatiently to come into their inheritances, and their frustration and boredom often pushed them toward violence. This is especially true of Eleanor and Henry's eldest son, who like other heirs saw his father thwarting his attainment of full manhood, forcing him to seek riches and fame in mock combat at tournaments or in serious warfare. Young Henry was widely admired during his life and much lamented after his death at age twenty-eight, praised for his courtesy and chivalry. A poem described Young Henry as "a worthy, fine, and courtly man, [who] later in his life performed such high exploits that he revived the notion of chivalry, which, at the time, was near to extinction."[4] Eleanor found this thoughtless, whimsical, yet winning boy as appealing as did others, and he was her most favored son after Richard. His father favored him and was ready to forgive his irresponsibility throughout his life.

Not only noteworthy is the hatred of Eleanor and Henry's sons for their father and for each other, but also a growing antagonism between Eleanor and her royal husband that may have fueled their sons' anger. Henry II was a restless man with a violent temper, and his offspring often bore the brunt of his impatience and anger. Hostility between fathers and sons was not unusual in great noble families in the Middle Ages, and in such situations the mother, often trapped in an unhappy marriage, took on the role of her sons' protector and intercessor against their father.[5] Even William the Conqueror's wife had sent money to their eldest son, Robert, while he was in revolt against his father. Eleanor of Aquitaine went much further in supporting her sons, however, and her prodding of them into making war on their father, her own husband, was unprecedented and appalling to contemporaries, highly unusual, if not unique, among medieval aristocratic families. It is hardly surprising that an educated, intelligent woman such as Eleanor, frustrated at the loss of her influence in public life, should have sought power through manipulation of her sons. Clearly she had cemented solid ties of affection, or perhaps in the language of psychology, imposed her domination over them.

As the queen's estrangement from Henry II became apparent during her long sojourn in Poitou after 1168, it had an effect on their children's feelings, and the couple's hostility must account at least partially for the boys' alienation from their father. On reaching adolescence they lacked any loyalty to Henry, and their rebellions would give a tragic quality to his last years. Late twelfth-century chroniclers saw the faithlessness of Eleanor and Henry's sons as God's just punishment for his sins, and moralists compared Young Henry with Absalom, the biblical King David's rebellious son.[6] One of them wrote of Henry's "inordinate love for his sons" and accused him of trampling on others' rights "while he exerted himself unduly for their advancement." In that writer's view, it was God's will that he should be punished by their rebellions and untimely deaths.[7] The disaffected courtier Gerald of Wales also saw Henry's paternal affection, though his love for his sons was not returned:

> On his legitimate children he lavished in their childhood more than a father's affection, but in their more advanced years he looked askance at them after the manner of a step-father; and although his sons were so renowned and illustrious he pursued his successors with a hatred which perhaps they deserved, but which none the less impaired his own happiness. . . . Whether by some breach of the marriage tie or as a punishment for some crime of the parent, it befell that there was never true affection felt by the father towards his sons, nor by the sons towards their father, nor harmony among the brothers themselves.[8]

PLANS FOR THE SUCCESSION TO THE ANGEVIN EMPIRE

Like other twelfth-century aristocratic parents, Henry II and Eleanor were preoccupied with the permanence of their patrimonies and their untroubled transmission to their heirs, but they could not have foreseen how divisive succession plans could prove to be. At the time ruling families made no distinction between succession to personal property or landed estates and succession to public authority, rule over principalities. Yet the bloc of lands comprising Henry's assemblage of family lands, the kingdom of England, the duchy of Normandy, Eleanor's duchy of Aquitaine, and the lands of the counts of Anjou, was far grander than the usual ducal or baronial inheritance. Some at the Plantagenet court probably were aware of the succession schemes of Charlemagne and his successors, who had faced a similar problem of leaving behind both several sons and a large heterogeneous state. Certainly Eleanor and her subjects were conscious of Aquitaine's history as one of the sub-kingdoms within the larger Carolingian empire, assigned to a younger son as ruler, yet subordinate to the heir to the imperial title. The Carolingians'

solution of creating principalities for younger sons within the imperial frame-
work would have proven appealing to the royal couple.

The degree of Eleanor's involvement in her husband's planning for their
sons' succession to his various possessions is doubtful. Since the duchy of
Aquitaine was Eleanor's own patrimony and Henry's rights over it came only
through their marriage, it could not be part of such an arrangement without
her agreement. As it was common in princely families for property brought by
the wife to a marriage to be assigned to the second son, the two followed tradition and allotted Aquitaine to Richard, preserving Eleanor's ancestral duchy as
a distinct domain passing to his descendants. Eleanor would have voiced no
objection to her eldest son's designation as heir to her husband's heritage,
proud that Young Henry would bear his grandmother Empress Matilda's
English crown and the Norman ducal title as well as his paternal ancestors'
title of count of Anjou ruling over family lands in the Loire valley. Henry's
conquest of the county of Brittany, long considered a dependency of the
duchy of Normandy, would supply a heritage for Geoffrey, their third son.

Henry unwisely assumed that advance arrangements would forestall quarrels among his sons over their inheritances, unable to grasp that once he gave
the boys titles they would expect the power that was associated with them.
No doubt he expected his sons to share with him the task of governing his
far-flung domains once he grew old, and to continue working together after
his death, but the boys were unwilling to wait. Henry II's tinkering with his
succession plans fostered in his sons deeper feelings of insecurity and competition with their siblings than were common in princely families, and Eleanor,
like other aristocratic mothers, sympathized with her sons' frustration. Once
it became apparent that Henry expected his wife's duchy to retain some lasting
tie to the Plantagenet line, with Richard owing homage to him and eventually
to his brother Young Henry, Eleanor became suspicious of her husband's
succession scheme. Henry's expectation did not accord with her ambition for
Richard or for her duchy of Aquitaine. Perhaps Henry's desire to provide equi-
tably for all four sons was motivated by genuine affection, but it proved to be
the root cause of his troubles. Once he became preoccupied with securing
lands for his youngest boy John "Lackland," his changing plans at the expense
of his three other sons were bound to rouse them to anger. The Plantagenet
king ignored the biblical injunction, "Let your life run its full course, and then,
at the hour of death, distribute your estate" (Ecclesiastes, 33: 21–23).

Primogeniture, the custom that the eldest son inherits all his father's lands,
was gaining ground in twelfth-century aristocratic families as the preferred
inheritance pattern, but it was not yet fixed as law by the late 1160s when Henry
and Eleanor were pondering the succession to their possessions, and inheritance customs still varied from region to region. Yet great families desired to

preserve their estates as single units and to ensure their safe passage from one generation to the next, while at the same time searching for some means of providing for their younger children.[9] These contradictory feelings explain Henry's periodic proposals for changing the succession. His own desire to leave all his sons a landed legacy was one that few great aristocrats could fulfill, for they rarely had sufficient holdings to provide for several sons. Frequently younger sons in aristocratic families with multiple male children were left landless, unless arrangements were made for them either to marry a girl who was heir to estates or to find them a rich ecclesiastical living. Henry could not bring himself to follow the early Capetians' practice of leaving their younger sons landless; nor could he follow a long tradition among the counts of Anjou of preserving the integrity of their lands by leaving younger sons only insignificant landholdings.[10] Eleanor's own experience as a young girl matched Capetian and Angevin practice. She had seen her uncle, her father's younger brother Raymond, forced to leave the Poitevin court and wander far away to seek his fortune first at the English royal court and later in the Holy Land.

For the vast territories assembled by Henry Plantagenet, strict primogeniture as practiced by lesser lords appeared unworkable, for it would have placed his eldest son in the impossible position of governing far-flung territories with diverse populations while leaving his younger sons landless and disaffected. Although Henry II never called his conglomeration of lands an "empire," he had hopes for its survival as a lasting political entity. Henry expected common family interest to preserve some cohesion for his lands after his demise, despite their partition. His plan unrealistically assumed that his younger sons would accept Young Henry's priority with natural family affection, strengthened by ties of homage.[11] The king was to be sorely disappointed, for his arrangements demanded strong fraternal affection, younger brothers' satisfaction with limited lands, and a willingness to co-operate with their senior brother, all of which were lacking.

Shortly before 1170, both Henry and Eleanor became preoccupied with the issue of succession to their territories. Henry faced the problem of the unity of his dual inheritance—his paternal Plantagenet lands in the Loire valley and his maternal legacy, the Anglo-Norman realm. Eleanor's concern was not the integrity of her husband's possessions, but her own duchy of Aquitaine's preservation as a distinct political unit. She did not share her husband's vision of unity for his possessions, especially as the couple drifted apart. She saw her own ancestral line as more ancient and more prestigious than his lineage, and her chief concern was ensuring Richard's position as the continuator of her lineage. She anticipated that Aquitaine would go its own way after Henry's death, her ancestral line continuing through Richard's offspring and ruling unfettered by links to the Plantagenet dynasty. Eleanor had no wish to see her duchy swallowed up and digested in her husband's empire, reduced to the status of simply another Angevin province.

A complication for the succession to both Henry's Continental lands and Eleanor's duchy was their status as part of the kingdom of France under Louis VII's lordship, and the couple were not to be left alone to dispose of their possessions. Henry as the crowned and anointed king of England was Louis's equal, but within his French domains, the Capetian monarch was his lord. Louis did not desire to see his powerful rival's empire outlive him, and hoped that it would soon break down into its constituent parts even before Henry's death. He quickly grasped that his lordship over Normandy, Anjou, and Aquitaine afforded him a means of promoting this process, once Henry's sons had done homage to him for their assigned portions of their parents' holdings. The French king saw an advantage in fomenting strife between the boys and their father, especially the rancor of his son-in-law Young Henry, by pressing for a premature partition of Henry's lands. Although Louis cultivated the image of a peacemaker, he was willing to stir up discontent among Henry and Eleanor's sons as a means of embarrassing and weakening his powerful rival at little cost.

The question of the Plantagenet succession first arose at conferences between the French and English monarchs in the late 1160s, resulting in a plan adopted at a council in early January 1169 at Montmirail, Maine. Louis VII first proposed that Henry Senior renew his homage for the duchy of Normandy, originally offered on his 1151 visit to the French court with his father, and that his eldest son should do homage for Anjou and Maine. The French monarch's aim was that Young Henry, holding those territories directly of him, should owe nothing to his father or to his brothers, "save what they may deserve, or what natural affection dictates." Louis also proposed that Richard should hold the duchy of Aquitaine directly of him as lord, and to bind the Poitevin heir further, he pledged to betroth to him his daughter, Alix, younger sister of Young Henry's bride Margaret.[12] Louis's proposal shows his grasp of the value of his lordship over Henry's sons as a weapon for eating away at the English king's power.

The two kings reached agreement on a plan at their 1169 meeting at the castle of Montmirail. Henry anticipated that his promise of a future partition would allay the French king's fears by holding out the prospect of a dispersal of Angevin power on his death. According to a contemporary account, the English king came to Louis VII "as a suppliant," acknowledging that because of his earlier homage and fealty to Louis, he owed "all the aid and service due from a duke of Normandy to the king of France."[13] Their agreement specified that the eldest son, Young Henry, was to have all lands that Henry Senior had inherited from his parents: Count Geoffrey's principalities in the Loire region,

Anjou, Maine, and Touraine, together with the Empress Matilda's Anglo-Norman heritage. Young Henry was to do homage to Louis, acknowledging his lordship over his assigned lands that lay within the French kingdom, as Richard was to do for Aquitaine.

Eleanor was absent from the Montmirail conference, doubtless aware that an encounter with her former husband would have been awkward for all parties, but she was doubtless well pleased with the result. For two of her sons—the second-born Richard and Geoffrey, her third—the settlement provided them with lands lying beyond the core Anglo-Norman and Angevin territories. Richard was promised his mother's duchy of Aquitaine in accord with Eleanor and Henry's previous agreement; also his betrothal to King Louis VII's daughter Alix was to go forward. The princess was to be handed over to the English king's custody at once, just as had been her elder sister Margaret at an even younger age.[14] Placing young Alix in Eleanor's care at Poitiers would have been an embarrassment to Louis; indeed, he had insisted in the terms for Margaret's betrothal that she was not to be brought up in Eleanor's household. Instead, Henry decided to place the girl in his own household, a regrettable decision.

With young Richard's formal designation as heir to Aquitaine, Eleanor could be confident of his succession to her ancestral lands, whatever the fate of Henry's other domains. After the queen's return to Aquitaine in 1168, she concentrated her ambition on Richard, cementing his position with installation ceremonies as count of Poitou and duke of Aquitaine. The third son, Geoffrey, had already been positioned to succeed to Brittany, a county that was traditionally under the lordship of the Norman dukes. After Henry enforced his lordship through conquest of Brittany, he betrothed the count's daughter and heir to Geoffrey in 1166, holding great courts where the Breton barons acknowledged Geoffrey as their future count.[15]

The Montmirail settlement effectively left two of Henry II's sons landless: his youngest child, John, and the teenaged Young Henry. John was too young to be given consideration, and Henry refused to give his eldest son lands or responsibilities befitting his status as heir to the Anglo-Norman kings and the Angevin counts. Young Henry was condemned to remain a "youth," without territories of his own to govern or to yield him an income, and his frustration mounted after his coronation in 1170. Henry Senior had no intention of giving the Young King governing responsibilities to match his status as a crowned and anointed monarch, as the boy's new seal as English monarch illustrates. Young Henry's seal did not designate him "King by grace of God," as had all English royal seals since the Norman kings had added it to the royal style; nor did it display his image bearing a sword, as was traditional. Since Henry Senior is known to have supervised the making of his son's seal, the sword's absence seems deliberate, a sign that the Young King was "an heir in waiting," inferior to his father, who was still king "by grace of God."[16] Young Henry knew that he could have none of the substance of royalty until his father's incapacity or death handed him power. Eleanor likely shared her eldest son's disappointment, assuming that he would be assigned lands of his own and some measure of authority over either England or Normandy, diluting her husband's authority.

The Young King's situation grew more vexing when he turned eighteen in 1173 and still had neither lands nor authority, not even estates in the Angevin heartland traditionally handed over to the Plantagenet heir. Young Henry felt his landlessness even more keenly because he had been married to Margaret, daughter of Louis VII of France, since the age of five. Marriage traditionally marked a young noble's transition to full adulthood and settling down with his bride in his own household on some portion of his family's patrimony. Young Henry's powerlessness aroused jealousy of his brother Richard, already installed in his Poitevin inheritance and sharing with his mother political responsibilities far different from his illusory authority as his father's associate ruler. The contrast that Young Henry noted between his lack of power as a crowned and anointed king and Richard's position in his mother's county added to the humiliation he suffered at his father's hands.[17]

CHANGING SCHEMES FOR THE SUCCESSION OF ELEANOR'S SONS

Eleanor and Henry's youngest child, John, born at the end of 1166, had no place in the tripartite partition of Montmirail. Henry did not want his last-born son to remain "John Lackland," however. While custom called for aristocratic fathers to leave their patrimony to their eldest son, they were free to leave their acquisitions to younger children, although the youngest of several sons could expect to inherit nothing more than expendable peripheral lands. Yet John's father was determined to secure him substantial lands, and his attempts at providing for the boy only aroused the ire of his other sons. Young Henry, Richard, and Geoffrey's resentment of their father and jealousy of their youngest brother would ignite into open warfare by 1173. Eleanor did not share her husband's concern for their youngest son's future. This does not mean that she loved him less than her other children, but she simply accepted that prospects for the youngest of four sons were dubious unless a bride with a great inheritance could be found for him, as the experience of her own family showed.

Literature and John's own family's history would have taught him from childhood that younger sons had uncertain prospects. Twelfth-century romances are filled with tales of younger sons forced to leave home to seek their fortunes as knights errant. Insecurity about his future, rivalry with his brothers for lands, and awareness of their resentment over their father's schemes to find a legacy for him likely had a malign influence on John's character. The uncertainty of his prospects would have fostered self-doubts, a sense of inadequacy that the glorious reputations of his brothers Young Henry and Richard only strengthened. In the toxic atmosphere at the Plantagenet court, John could hardly have avoided absorbing some poisons from the suspicion and treachery spreading among Henry's courtiers taking sides with the Young King. This was likely as powerful an influence on young John's character as his early childhood spent separated from his mother at Fontevraud. Eleanor can hardly be blamed for his growing up to be secretive and suspicious, or for his distrustful and autocratic rule after unexpectedly succeeding to the English Crown in 1199.

The Montmirail settlement was reaffirmed in Henry's will when he was stricken with a life-threatening illness in August 1170, though he added to it some provision for his last-born son. He requested that his eldest son take custody of young John "that he might advance him and maintain him," and he expressed a wish that the boy be given the county of Mortain in Normandy, a lordship often held in the past by junior members of the ducal family.[18] It was only Henry's acquisition of lordship over Ireland that would eventually provide a principality for John. In October 1171, a year after his recovery, the king set sail for Ireland where he remained until the next spring asserting his authority over the island. Some time after his expedition, certainly by 1177, he began to think of Ireland as a lordship that would solve the problem of a legacy for his landless last-born son.[19]

In 1173, during Eleanor's residence in Poitou, Henry II saw an exceptional opportunity for young John when a marriage was proposed for the boy that would seal an Angevin alliance with the count of Savoy, Humbert III of Maurienne. John was to be married to Alais, the elder of Humbert's two daughters and heir to his lands. Earlier the count had sent an envoy to Normandy proposing that if the English king should betroth his youngest son to Humbert's elder daughter, their marriage would bring John extensive fiefs in Piedmont and Savoy together with the possibility of succeeding to his county of Savoy. Humbert's county occupied a strategic position high in the Alps, controlling mountain passes that opened a way into Italy from France.[20] Henry's discussions with Humbert were part of a strategy of expanding Plantagenet influence deep into the Mediterranean south, drawn in that direction chiefly by rivalry with the counts of Toulouse, though perhaps also impelled by his more grandiose dreams. Count Raymond V had extended his reach far east of Toulouse to Nîmes, the Rhône and beyond into the southern Alps. Henry could hardly refuse Humbert's offer, with its potential for a vast expansion of Angevin power, possibly extending into Italy, and he "bought" the count's daughter for John, promising the count 5,000 marks.[21] He also agreed to grant John the traditional holding of a younger son of the counts of Anjou: the three castles of Chinon, Loudun, and Mirebeau.

Henry II arranged a meeting with Count Humbert for the beginning of February 1173, and he gathered a brilliant assemblage of nobility at Montferrat (today Clermont-Ferrand) in the Auvergne. Young Henry was summoned from England to join the royal entourage journeying to meet the count of Savoy at Montferrat.[22] They passed through Poitiers en route to be joined by Eleanor. In addition to Henry, Eleanor, and the Young King, the company included the king of Aragon and the count of Toulouse, who sought Henry's arbitration of their longstanding rivalry. Others assembled there included not only magnates from Henry and Eleanor's lands and from Savoy, but also a number of great men from Provence. Standing out among Poitevin nobles present at Montferrat was Eleanor's uncle and adviser Ralph de Faye.[23]

Nothing came of young John's projected marriage since the count's daughter promptly died; nonetheless, it marked the beginning of serious troubles between Henry and his eldest son. Henry Senior's generous provision for his youngest son aroused Young Henry's anger because the three Angevin castles promised to John lay within his assigned territories. He knew they would actually be controlled by his father, not by a child aged five. The Young King, who did not possess a single castle in Anjou or Maine, not even a proper residence for himself and his wife, considered this property transfer without his consent outrageous; and the insult became another grievance contributing to his later rebellion. Relations between Henry and his heir would be complicated by the involvement of a third party, Louis VII, to whom the Young King was bound through marriage and by Louis's lordship over the French lands assigned to him at Montmirail. Young Henry began to look to the French king as a counselor and father-figure, and Louis encouraged his son-in-law to press his grievances against his father. In November 1172 the Young King and his queen made a visit to the French court, where he heard little good about his father and much that was negative. Louis advised Young Henry to go to his father in Normandy and ask him to hand over to him control of either the English kingdom or the duchy of Normandy, and he urged him that if his father refused his demand, then he should return to Paris to his wife.[24]

Archbishop Thomas Becket's murder in December 1170 had already inflamed the Young King's hostility toward his father. Few events in the twelfth century outraged western Christendom more than Becket's brutal death in his own cathedral at the hands of four of Henry II's household knights. The English king's suspected complicity in the crime and his less than whole-hearted repentance at Avranches in 1172 further undermined his son's respect for him. Young Henry had felt fondness for Becket since spending part of his childhood in the chancellor's household. He could see that his coronation had brought the quarrel between the exiled primate and his father to a boiling point, but that it had been no more than a ruse for thwarting Becket's expected excommunication of Henry. He had gained only a royal title, while actual power was retained by his father.[25] As a Flemish chronicler wrote, "Having laid aside the royal crown, [Henry] had his son Henry, a most honorable knight . . . crowned king, retaining for himself all land pertaining to the kingdom with all its fruits and revenues."[26]

The Young King's father-in-law, the pious Louis, "most Christian of princes and the prince of all Christians," to quote one of Becket's friends,[27] had seen the archbishop's assassination as an opportunity to weaken his rival. Soon afterward, Louis had joined his brothers-in-law, the count of Blois and the archbishop of Sens, in writing to the pope to urge retribution for the English king's crime.[28] Whatever the Young King's true feelings about his father's part in the murder, like the French monarch, he sought to exploit the situation. On the eve of his 1173 revolt, he would send letters to potential supporters asserting his bond with his saintly mentor and pointing to his father's lackluster pursuit of Becket's assassins as a justification for taking up arms against him. Some of the boy's allies even argued that the death of the archbishop of Canterbury had deprived Henry II of his right to rule.[29]

Eleanor had been present at the hunting lodge of Bur-le-Roi in Normandy for the 1170 Christmas festivities, and she may have heard Henry II make the fateful remark that inspired his knights to leave the court unnoticed to carry out what they assumed was the king's will. Eleanor would have found an archbishop's brutal murder as shocking as anyone else, and it must have strengthened her in her deepening detachment from her husband. Although the queen is suspected of sharing her uncle Ralph de Faye's hostility toward Thomas Becket, she kept her views to herself. Indeed, she had once joined the empress Matilda in seeking a settlement of Henry's quarrel with his archbishop, and she may have shared her mother-in-law's opinion that Henry's inflexibility in dealing with Becket was a mistake.

After the February 1173 council called by Henry II at Montferrat, the distinguished company of princes moved on with the king and queen to Limoges, where Henry's actions would alarm and anger Eleanor.[30] At Limoges Raymond V, count of Toulouse, alarmed at the prospect of the county of Maurienne falling under Angevin influence, decided to make peace with his longtime enemy. No doubt he hoped that an agreement with Henry would buy him a period of calm needed to consolidate his recent territorial gains in Provence. Raymond consented to do homage for his county of Toulouse to the English king and to his sons Young Henry and Richard. In addition, he promised to perform military service and to make Henry an annual payment of either a hundred silver marks or ten warhorses. Henry's settlement with the count took no account of the duchess of Aquitaine's lordship over Toulouse.[31] Indeed, Raymond's homage to the two kings, father and son, seemed to proclaim the county's permanent subjection to the English monarchy.

Henry II's reconciliation with Count Raymond, coupled with his continued interventions in Poitou after installing Eleanor in power there, caused her to reflect on her husband's unbridled power and to contemplate means of curtailing it. Such thoughts would have strengthened her instinctive sympathy as a mother for the Young King in his powerlessness. She could have seen that her over-mighty husband's succession plans afforded a weapon for cutting him down to size, forcing him to implement the partition proposed at Montmirail devolving power on his sons.[32] By the end of the Limoges council, if not earlier, Eleanor was ready to conspire with her sons against her husband. Count Raymond of Toulouse, before leaving Limoges, took Henry aside to warn him of a plot against him involving his wife and their sons. Apparently this was Henry's first clue that their dissatisfaction had reached the point of actual plotting. He acted on Raymond's warning, taking the precaution of shoring up security at his castles in Poitou. Knowing well the count's bitterness against the duchess of Aquitaine, however, he did nothing to stop her from returning to Poitiers. Richard and another of their sons, Geoffrey of Brittany, either accompanied her from Limoges or else soon joined her at Poitiers. Henry was capable of suspecting his wife of taking her sons' side against him. He is unlikely, however, to have imagined that Eleanor would take the drastic step of making war on him, since that would have required an alliance with her former husband, Louis VII.[33]

ELEANOR'S DISILLUSIONMENT WITH HER SECOND MARRIAGE

What drove Eleanor of Aquitaine to such disillusionment with her marriage to Henry II that she would conspire against him and urge her three eldest sons to rebel against their father in league with her ex-husband? Although mothers in medieval princely families sometimes supported their sons and interceded for them with their father, Eleanor pushed this pattern to a new extreme. The unprecedented example of the English queen participating with her sons in armed revolt against their father in 1173–74 "astonished and scandalized contemporaries," both secular clerks with ties to the royal court and moralistic monastic chroniclers.[34] Swayed by negative views of powerful women that were gaining ground in the twelfth century, these writers would express deep disapproval of Eleanor's part in the rebellion.

Yet late twelfth-century writers provide few clues to the queen's motivations, for they had little interest in speculating on the workings of her mind.

Due to their view of history as exemplary, the chroniclers saw no need to look for a cause other than God at work in the world. They were content with the explanation that the revolt of Henry's sons inspired by his own queen was divine punishment for his sins. If any attempt was made to probe Eleanor's motives, it was merely to attribute her actions to emotion, to a thirst for revenge against Henry, without spelling out reasons for her ire and never taking into account larger political considerations. William of Newburgh, searching to explain Henry II's unfortunate relations with his sons, concluded, "This is believed to have happened deservedly by the just judgment of God for two reasons." The first reason was Henry's marriage to Eleanor, a woman previously the wife of another; and the second was the king's obstinate opposition to the sainted Thomas Becket.[35] Although Newburgh blamed the French monarch for counseling the Young King to rebel, like several English chroniclers he pictured Eleanor as a manipulative mother guilty of encouraging her younger sons Richard and Geoffrey's flight to Paris to join their elder brother. Another monastic chronicler assigned fault chiefly to Louis VII and Count Philip of Flanders. Making only a terse admission of the queen's involvement, he noted that because "she wished to rise up with her sons against [Henry], he imprisoned her for many years."[36]

Eleanor's English subjects were willing to believe the worst of her in 1173 because of scandal attached to her as early as the Second Crusade, scandal that had followed her from France to England. It appeared that for a second time she was breaking one of the basic rules for a married woman, forgetting the submissiveness owed to her husband, just as she had at Antioch during her first marriage.[37] Another factor in the eagerness to implicate her in the conspiracy against Henry II was her semi-separation from him, when she took up residence in Poitou early in 1168. Yet the royal couple's separation was by mutual agreement, for Henry saw indirect rule through his wife as an attractive alternative, little different from her role as regent in England with his trusted agents at her side advising her. Whatever the personal factors in the couple's wish to live apart, Eleanor doubtless welcomed an opportunity to return to her homeland to rule Poitou in her own right.[38] Yet clerics, influenced by conventional teachings on marriage, interpreted the queen's leaving her husband's side as a sign of her refusal to adopt a wife's proper submissiveness.

Unaware of Eleanor's expectation of wielding authority within her inherited lands, her contemporaries failed to credit her with political impulses for turning against her husband. It never occurred to them that a craving for genuine power in her own duchy and disappointment at Henry's continued interventions there could have driven her to take revenge through her sons. Her desire to preserve her own authority in Aquitaine, to protect Richard's right of succession, and to prevent her duchy from becoming merely another of her husband's provinces had as much to do with her revolt as a wronged wife's bitterness. Her wish was to see power pass directly from her as duchess to her second son without passing through the intermediary of Henry or Young Henry. The year 1172, Richard's formal installation as count-duke, may mark the time that Eleanor decided on a break with Henry and on asserting her own authority as ruler over Poitou. By then she was altering the form of address in her charters to exclude any mention of her husband's rights there.[39]

Eleanor had good reasons for harboring doubts about her husband's commitment to the preservation of her ancestral lands. Henry II's promise of Gascony as their daughter Eleanor's dower on her betrothal to the king of Castile cannot have relieved the queen-duchess's worries about his aims for her patrimony. Then the great council at Limoges in February 1173, where the count of Toulouse did homage to Henry and to the Young King, sent a new danger signal. By taking Raymond's homage for Toulouse, Henry was turning his back on Eleanor's longstanding claim to Toulouse as her lawful inheritance and threatening that county's status as a vassal state of Aquitaine. By recognizing Raymond V, a descendant of the usurping Saint Gilles lineage, as rightful successor to Toulouse, Henry was implicitly setting aside her claim to the county through her grandmother's right. His acceptance of the count's homage was all the more disturbing because Eleanor knew that his claim to lordship over Toulouse derived solely from his rights as her husband. Furthermore, she read Count Raymond's homage to the Young King as a claim of English lordship over the duchy of Aquitaine, signaling to her that Richard and succeeding generations of dukes would hold it subject to English monarchs' lordship. Eleanor's hope was for power over Aquitaine to pass directly to Richard without passing through the intermediary of the king of England. Raymond V's homage to Richard seemed no more than an acknowl-edgment of Richard's position as second son standing in reserve as a secondary heir to the English Crown, not a recognition of his lordship as duke of Aquitaine.[40]

Eleanor's incitement of her sons' revolt against Henry II seemed aimed at subverting his intention of turning his diverse domains into a lasting empire under a Plantagenet dynasty. She sought an implementation of the Montmirail settlement of 1169 that would guarantee its prompt partition. This was an aim that she shared with Louis VII, that Henry should be forced to cede authority to his sons in the territories assigned to them, lands for which they already had done homage to the French king. In Eleanor's bitterness, she wished to see her husband stripped of power, leaving him to spend his last years in retirement without resources of his own, or at best merely presiding over his sons as an ineffectual "chairman of the board." To see this happen, she was willing to conspire with her former husband, suggesting that her feelings toward Louis may have mellowed. In comparison to the harsh and fearsome Henry II, the Capetian king's mildness and gentleness possibly appeared as appealing to Eleanor as to other subjects of the Plantagenet king living in fear of his royal "wrath and ill-will."

Strangely, modern writers are almost as reluctant as medieval chroniclers to look for political factors explaining Eleanor's role in her sons' revolt. Most have been content to attribute her urge to wound Henry II to a marriage gone sour, which they ascribe to his adulteries. Others, swayed by Freudian psychology, turn to Eleanor's participation in the 1173–74 rebellion as an indication of her unhealthy relations with her sons, concluding that they "often served as her pawns" in her pursuit of power. Advocates of psychological interpretations of history depict her viewing her sons "as instruments of her will, or obstacles blocking its exercise, rather than as individuals to be nurtured and cherished," and that within her "the domineering rather than nurturant side of mother-hood was strongest."[41] Such denunciation of Eleanor as a domineering mother in a dysfunctional family, grasping for power and responsible for her sons' rejection of their father, reaches beyond the surviving evidence.

Popular historians and novelists find fertile ground for Eleanor's role in the rebellion in Henry II's adulteries, assuming that his infidelity had alienated her perhaps as early as 1166. For them, the fury of a woman scorned is sufficient explanation for the revolt, yet little concrete evidence points to the king's sexual straying as the root cause of the queen's disaffection. Eleanor and Henry's marriage was not a love match, but a political union that each expected to be mutually beneficial. Aristocratic wives were expected simply to ignore their husbands' infidelities, and Eleanor would have learned to look the other way, hiding wounded feelings, although Henry's dalliances with maidens of aristo-cratic rank would have been more hurtful to her than his bedding of peasant girls. Indeed, one of John of Salisbury's letters from 1168 records the count of Brittany's complaint against the English king for the fate of his daughter, handed over to him as a hostage: "She had been a virgin, but that he had made her pregnant, committing treachery, adultery and incest."[42]

Eleanor would have been troubled by Henry's illegitimate son, William Longsword, the product of his liaison with a noble lady. A noble youth fathering a child by some low-born woman was one thing, but a married prince impregnating a noble lady was a disgraceful act, threatening the legiti-macy of her husband's lineage. William, probably born around 1170 during the queen's Poitevin sojourn, was the son of a certain Ida, sometimes identified as a daughter of Roger de Tosny III, an important Norman lord with extensive lands in England. Ida married Roger Bigod II, earl of Norfolk, at the end of 1181, and Longsword's charters refer openly to "Countess Ida my mother." Young William, unlike her husband's other bastard Geoffrey Plantagenet, received little attention from his father, for sons resulting from aristocrats' extra-marital affairs were less well received by their fathers than those resulting from youthful pre-marital affairs. No mention of him occurs in the records until 1188 when he was approaching manhood and his father granted him land in Lincolnshire.[43] Secrets were impossible to keep at a royal court, with courtiers constantly trading information for their advantage, and Eleanor, far away in Poitou, certainly learned of the birth of Henry's bastard by a lady from a prominent Anglo-Norman family. Whatever pain Henry's extra-marital escapades caused Eleanor, it cannot be diagnosed as due to a broken heart, but more likely due to bruised pride. Yet her humiliation by Henry's many adulteries can be counted as one of her grievances against him.

Popular biographers barely acknowledge that Henry II had a son by Ida de Tosney, but they attach much significance to his infatuation with Rosamund Clifford, who has been termed "the great love of his life."[44] Henry's supposed public flaunting of his new mistress is sometimes put forward as the source of the queen's desire for revenge. The fair maiden Rosamund was the daughter of Walter Clifford, a Welsh border lord, and the king may have first met her at a stop at her father's castle during his 1165 campaign in Wales. She was no more than in her early twenties while he was thirty-two, and Eleanor had passed her fortieth year. None of the late twelfth-century chroniclers makes a specific allegation that Rosamund Clifford was the cause of Eleanor's disenchantment with her marriage, however, and the evidence is too thin to suggest that this mistress presented a greater threat to it than had Henry's previous ones.[45]

Most significantly, the chronology of Henry II's affair with Rosamund does not fit the alleged facts. Some biographers have dated the king's affair with her as early as 1166, and they credit the queen's decision to leave the English court for Poitou in 1168 to the humiliation that she suffered. Yet the affair is likely to have begun during Eleanor's Poitevin sojourn, no earlier than 1170 and possibly not until 1173, and it only became a public spectacle after the queen's return to England as a prisoner in 1174, lasting some six years until Rosamund's death in 1176 or 1177.[46] Although Henry's second illegitimate son, William Longsword, was born shortly before or soon after his affair with Rosamund Clifford began, he was definitely not her child. Eleanor's husband was no more faithful to the fair Rosamund than he was to his queen. If Rosamund was indeed the great love of Henry's life, the strongest evidence for his devotion is a house known as Everswell that he ordered to be built near the royal residence at Woodstock, intended for her according to tradition. Constructed around a spring with water running through rectangular pools and surrounded by cloistered courts, it was more like palaces of Norman Sicily than any secular building in northern Europe. In later legend Rosamund's residence would be described as a maze or labyrinth, designed to make certain that Eleanor could never find her rival.[47]

Not even the gossipy Gerald of Wales, always willing to slander the Plantagenets, depicted the queen's incitement of her sons' revolt as resulting from her wrath over Henry's mistress Rosamund Clifford. In one work written only a few years after the great revolt, he implied that Henry had been discreet in his adulteries up to that time: "After the great wrong committed against their father by his sons, under their mother's influence . . . [the king] openly broke his marriage vows." Writing decades later, Gerald declared that the king "was before an adulterer in secret, and was afterwards manifestly such," pointing out that he publicly displayed his liaison with Rosamund only after the queen's imprisonment.[48] Other chroniclers add nothing about Rosamund's role in Eleanor's estrangement from Henry. The sometime royal clerk, Roger of Howden, remained silent about the affair until after the king's death. Rosamund's name only appears in his account of Saint Hugh of Lincoln's visit to the convent of Godstow in 1191, when he ordered her tomb removed from the nuns' chapel and reburied in the churchyard, "for she was a harlot."[49] Eleanor's rage against Henry for his liaison with the fair Rosamund is insufficient to explain her role in her sons' revolt.

The Great Rebellion of 1173–1174

When Young Henry's frustration with his father exploded into a large-scale revolt in 1173, Henry II faced his most serious threat since winning the English Crown.[50] The rebellion of the Young King, his brothers, and their mother triggered both simultaneous uprisings of aggrieved nobles in localities from England to Poitou and also attacks by neighbors who felt threatened by Henry's power. The allies arrayed against Henry included, in addition to his three sons, the Scottish and French kings, four English earls and other disaffected barons, nobles of Angevin-ruled lands in France, and such powerful French princes as the counts of Flanders and Blois. Such a wide-ranging alliance threatened the collapse of Henry II's empire, the most serious threat yet faced by him. Warfare would engulf England, which faced invasion from the Scottish king in the north as well as by sea from Flanders; and fighting would rage throughout Henry's French lands from the Norman frontiers to Poitou's southern fringes.

The source of Young Henry's dissatisfaction was his failure to win lands and income suitable for a crowned king, and his constant disappointment in his expectation of wealth and power. Indeed, as a married man, he saw his landless status thwarting his achievement of full manhood. Due to Young Henry's feckless character, contemporaries faulted others for encouraging his revolt. Walter Map, a courtier who knew Young Henry well, compared him to Absalom, the Israelite King David's rebel son, and described him as "a prodigy of unfaith and prodigal of ill . . . a lovely palace of sin."[51] Strongest suspicion falls on Eleanor of Aquitaine. Not only the queen's contemporaries, but modern scholars have pointed to her as the inciter of her three elder sons, assuming that she sought revenge against her husband through them. A Poitevin chronicler, almost alone in openly supporting the rebellion, admitted her incitement of her sons, writing, "For thou has stirred them up . . . to bring sore affliction on their father." Henry II's treasurer assigned Eleanor a prominent part, declaring, "Since without cause a wife was angry with her husband, sons with their father, menials with their lord, might you not well say that a man was in rebellion against himself?"[52]

According to a chronicler writing two decades after the rebellion, "certain persons" whispered in the Young King's ear that he ought at least to reign jointly with his father, and even that he had a right to rule alone, for having been crowned king, it was as if his father's reign had expired. Certainly Eleanor was not alone in influencing Young Henry to revolt. Among others urging him on were the sons of nobles filling his household who formed factions and bred conspiracies and rumors. Toward the end of Henry II's reign, his longtime treasurer hinted at courtiers, unnamed "little foxes" who had corrupted the king's sons and turned them against him.[53] Young Henry's youthful companions saw his father blocking his access to riches for rewarding them with patronage, the lucrative offices, loans, gifts of cash and lands, and advantageous marriages that they expected. They were so greedy for reward that they were willing to jeopardize the Angevin Empire's stability by inflaming their young lord's hatred of his father. A Welsh chronicler describes the situation succinctly: the Young Henry "had many knights but he had no means to give rewards and gifts to the knights."[54]

Within Young Henry's household, a split developed between companions of his own choosing, contemptuous of Henry II, and officials selected for him by his father who urged restraint. The king, mistrustful of his son's rash young companions, had positioned key clerks in his household loyal to the king, and these were regarded by Young Henry and his friends as informers. This split reflects tensions between clerical and knightly values, between royal clerks' courtly urbanity and the martial values of the Young King's youthful comrades. After a hunting trip with Young Henry and his companions which exposed their irresponsibility, the king undertook a purge of his son's household; and this purge, particularly the dismissal of one of Young Henry's favorite household knights, apparently precipitated his flight to Paris in March 1173.[55]

Such a large-scale conspiracy as the revolt that broke out in April 1173 could not have been entirely the work of such inexperienced youths as Young Henry and his companions. Henry II's Irish expedition, from mid-October 1171 to mid-April 1172, afforded an opportunity for hatching plots. Stormy seas throughout that winter isolated the king in Ireland, limiting his contact with both England and his French lands and creating an opportunity for his enemies to conspire. The Young King was chiefly in England acting as regent after his coronation in June 1170, although he crossed to Normandy in summer 1171, remaining in the duchy until after his Christmas court when he sailed for England. Eleanor's movements in 1171 are largely unknown, although she and Richard were at Limoges for that year's Christmas court. It seems possible that she visited Normandy while Young Henry was there in summer and autumn 1171 and the pipe rolls suggest also the possibility of a visit with him in England some time in 1172.[56] It is certain that the queen and her eldest son met at the beginning of 1173 when he set out for the Auvergne to join his father. Whether or not they had met earlier, they would have kept in contact through messengers.

In England, secular clerks close to the royal court accused the queen and Ralph de Faye of instigating the great rebellion. Roger of Howden implicates the queen along with Ralph de Faye, avoiding responsibility for his accusation by adding, "as is said in some quarters." Ralph Diceto dated Eleanor's plotting from the time of Henry's Irish expedition, writing, "While the king delayed in Ireland, Hugh de Sainte-Maure and Ralph de Faye, uncle of Queen Eleanor, on her advice, so it is said, began to turn away the mind of the young King from his father, suggesting that it seemed incongruous to be a king and not exercise the rule of a kingdom." Echoing these English chroniclers is a major chronicle from Tours that credits the counsel of Ralph de Faye and also Hugh de Sainte-Maure with fueling the strife between Henry and Eleanor and their sons. Hugh, like de Faye, was a noble whose lands along the Poitevin–Angevin frontier lay as much in the Touraine as in Poitou, and the two succeeded in rallying neighboring lords frightened by Henry Senior's dominance.[57] The prominence of Ralph de Faye's name among the conspirators reveals his central role as his niece's counselor. It suggests doubts about a woman's capacity for taking the extreme action of rousing her sons to rebel against their father. Chroniclers' bias required them to search for a man standing at Eleanor's side guiding her, but Eleanor did not need anyone's direction to foment her sons' rebellion.[58]

A letter by Peter of Blois, allegedly written as secretary to Rotrou, archbishop of Rouen, demanded that Eleanor return to Henry's side. Authentic or not, it expresses the thoughts of churchmen about the queen's conduct unsuitable for a wife, quoting the gospel of Matthew (19:6): "Those whom God has joined . . . man must not put asunder." It declares, "That woman who is not subject to her husband violates the condition of nature, the command of the Apostles and the law of the Gospel. For the man is the head of the woman." (Ephesians 5:23). The letter's author found it even worse that Eleanor "enabled the lord king's and your own flesh to rebel against their father, as it is deservedly said by the prophet, 'I reared and brought up sons, but they have rebelled against me.'" (Isaiah 1:2). His condemnation continued, "With your woman's way and childish counsel, you provoke offense against the Lord King, to whom even the strongest kings' necks bow. . . . You should return with your sons to your husband whom you are obliged to obey and to live with." The letter concludes with the archbishop's threat, "Either you return to your husband, or we will constrain you by canon law and will be bound to enforce ecclesiastical censures against you . . . although we shall do it with sorrow and tears."[59]

It was a strange intersection of interests that would align Eleanor with Louis VII. Louis had long recognized the menace that his over-mighty Plantagenet vassal's ambitions presented to the Capetian monarchy, blocking effective exercise of royal power over much of his kingdom. Henry's diplomacy of early 1173, settling the long conflict with Count Raymond of Toulouse and making a marriage alliance with the count of Maurienne, seemed to threaten a vast expansion of Angevin power southward. An extension of Henry's power to the entire region between the Garonne and the Rhône rivers would present a grave danger for Louis's sovereignty over France.[60]

As the Young King's father-in-law and sworn lord, Louis VII was in a position to influence the boy, and he doubtless played a major role in precipitating the revolt. Louis could see the political and legal value of his lordship over Henry II's sons, supplying him with a justification for intervening in the English king's French territories. Contemporary chroniclers point to the French king's collusion, naming him as prominent among those taking part in his son-in-law's treason. In February 1173 at the Limoges council, Young Henry once more demanded effective power over one of the three principalities promised him as his inheritance. His demand that his father hand over to him rule over either Normandy, Anjou, or England was made, according to Roger of Howden, "at the suggestion of the king of France, and of the earls and barons of England and Normandy who disliked his father." He adds that from then on, Young Henry was seeking pretexts for withdrawing from his father, with whom "he could not even converse . . . on any subject in a peaceable manner."[61]

After Henry II refused his eldest son's request for a principality to govern as his own, he resolved to watch him closely, keeping him in the royal retinue at all times. Acting on Count Raymond's warning, he insisted that Young Henry join him as he moved from Limoges northward toward Normandy in mid-March 1173. Stopping on the way at Chinon Castle, the Young King made his escape from his father in what must have been a well-planned operation. In the middle of the night he succeeded in slipping from the bedchamber that he and Henry Senior were sharing, creeping out of the castle undetected, and hastening to his father-in-law at Paris. Henry's action in crowning his son as king in his own lifetime then came back to haunt him. When he sent envoys to Paris to persuade Young Henry to return to his side, Louis VII asked who was seeking his return. When they answered, "The king of the English," Louis replied, "The king of the English is here. . . . Since you seem to address his father, formerly king of the English, as still king, you should know that king is dead. Furthermore, he should correct his habit of conducting himself as king after having resigned his kingdom in favor of his son, as all the world bears witness."[62] This disingenuously simple statement by Eleanor's former husband amounted to a declaration of war against her current spouse.

Once at Paris in spring 1173, the Young King was lavish with promises of lands and cash to French nobles who would fight for him, among them the counts of Blois, Champagne, and Flanders. He also issued a manifesto to churchmen condemning Henry II's persecution of them, and taking up the martyred archbishop Thomas Becket's cause of defending the English Church's liberties, he promised to end his father's habit of exerting royal pressure on episcopal elections.[63] Yet few prelates in Angevin lands were willing to defy the old king, and the pope and the English and Norman bishops rallied around him. Some nobles in all parts of Henry's domains calculated that his sons' revolt was likely to succeed and elected to join them in rebelling, assuming that one day the boys would succeed to the Plantagenet possessions and that those who had stood with them against their father would be remembered and rewarded.[64]

Soon after Young Henry fled to the Capetian court, his brothers, Richard and Geoffrey of Brittany left Eleanor's side to join him at Paris later in the spring of 1173, and the three renewed their homage to King Louis, promising not to make peace with their father without the French monarch's counsel and consent.[65] Their mother was blamed for their flight. One chronicler writes that the two boys followed Young Henry to Paris "by counsel of their mother that they should choose their brother over their father." A Norman chronicler friendly toward Henry II, the abbot of Mont-Saint-Michel, reported of Eleanor's role in her sons' revolt, "At the same time [as Young Henry's flight], Queen Eleanor (*Aliénor*) and her two sons, Richard, Count of Poitou and Geoffrey, count of Brittany were alienated (*alienati*) from [Henry]." The Latin permits a play on the name "Eleanor" and the verb "to alienate."[66] Although Eleanor's sons were precocious youths, their immaturity and inexperience meant that their instigation of the war was impossible, and only she and Louis VII enjoyed sufficient affection and respect to steer them to such action. Without maturity, reputation, or respect, Young Henry at only eighteen, Richard not yet sixteen, and Geoffrey several months short of fifteen could hardly have independently planned the uprising. Not even the eldest of the three had the capacity for organizing such a widespread and co-ordinated effort with almost simultaneous eruptions of warfare along frontiers from the Scottish borders to southern Poitou.

Personal animosities nurtured by Eleanor and other enemies of Henry II cannot alone account fully for the widespread insurrection that broke out in 1173, for its causes are complex, with larger political and societal factors contributing. As the English king's rule grew more abrasive and authoritarian, buttressed by his success in devising new administrative methods, it appeared threatening to magnates in many of his lands, subjecting them to new obligations and imperiling their former control over their own vassals. Eleanor's nobility in Poitou, unaccustomed to strong rule, proved particularly resentful of the English king, viewing him as a foreign lord asserting his authority through military force and violence. Both English barons and Poitevin nobles saw the revolt of Henry's sons as an opportunity to loosen his ever-stronger grip on them. As an English chronicler wrote of those flocking to the Young King's banner, it was "not because they regarded his as the more just cause, but because the father ... was trampling upon the necks of the proud and haughty."[67] The diverse lands and peoples making up Henry's Plantagenet empire reacted with differing degrees of hostility, with a majority at least apathetic about the outcome of the fighting and a significant minority including townspeople and many churchmen active in Henry's support.

Six weeks after the Young King's flight, almost simultaneous warfare broke out all along the frontiers of Henry's French lands and also across the English Channel. Young Henry and his allies, the counts of Boulogne and Flanders, invaded Normandy, where he had a number of partisans among the magnates, while the French king besieged a castle on the duchy's southern frontier. On the Scottish frontier with England the king of the Scots marched south, while numbers of the English baronage, including the earls of Chester, Derby, Leicester, and Norfolk, rose up in revolt. The fighting spurred uprisings by nobles throughout the other Angevin possessions, in Brittany and even in Maine, part of the Angevin heartland, although most nobles in Anjou remained loyal. A chronicler in Poitou rejoiced that Henry's sons were warring against their father, and he saluted the early successes of Poitevin nobility who stood by Eleanor against her husband: "Exult, Aquitaine! Rejoice, Poitou, that the scepter of the king of the North be removed from you!"[68] While a number of powerful Poitevin nobles stood at Eleanor's side, by no means all the aristocracy of Aquitaine played an active part in the revolt. Most lords of the Limousin were too busy fighting each other to join in the rebellion, and almost all the Gascon nobility stood aside from the conflict.[69]

Henry II did not lose his nerve, for he was a capable and confident general; and after a few months of fighting, his victory over his sons and their Capetian ally was not in doubt. Despite the desertions, many of his fighting men in

England, Normandy, and in his Angevin patrimony remained loyal. Equally important, administrative structures held, supplying enormous revenues raised in England and in loyal towns in his French lands, and Henry had treasure piled up in strategically located castles far exceeding Louis VII's funds. Henry's supply of ready cash would ensure his mastery, allowing him to contract for large armies of mercenaries that moved with unexpected speed. In autumn 1173, he made a quick march southward into Poitou from Chinon with his own mercenary force; as he approached Poitiers, Eleanor sought refuge at Faye-la-Vineuse, her uncle Ralph de Faye's lordship. He had preceded his niece in fleeing to Paris, probably setting out to secure from Louis an offer of sanctuary for her.[70]

Fearing capture, Eleanor soon decided that it was time to take flight and find refuge at the court of her former husband at Paris. She must have seen the irony of her flight from her current husband to the court of Louis VII whom she had left twenty years earlier. By late November, however, before she could reach Louis's territory, she was taken prisoner on the road to Chartres, and Henry locked her away in Chinon Castle. Members of her household traveling with her suffered worse fates; according to a Poitevin chronicler, "Some taken from their land are condemned secretly to a foul death, others deprived of sight, others are forced to wander and flee to scattered places."[71]

Gervase of Canterbury, the only chronicler to record specifics of the queen-duchess's foiled flight, adds the detail that she had fled disguised in male dress to join her sons in rebellion. He wrote that "having changed from her woman's clothes, [she] was apprehended and detained in strict custody. For it was said that all these happenings were prepared through her scheming and advice. For she was an extremely astute woman, of noble descent but flighty."[72] Old Testament law declared that for women or men to dress in the other sex's garments was an "abomination" (Deuteronomy 21:5). In the twelfth century, when the Church was attempting to differentiate gender roles more precisely, cross-dressing was considered an offense against the right order of things, and the English chronicler's tale was more likely a metaphor for Eleanor's inappropriate pursuit of masculine power than an accurate account of her costume. It is possible, however, that in her desperation to make a speedy escape she changed into trousers in order to ride astride rather than side-saddle.

By Christmas 1173 Henry II had made the Loire valley safe to serve as his base of operations, and he shifted forces north into Normandy, under attack from Flanders and from the Île de France. Meanwhile in England his faithful chief justiciar Richard de Lucy and loyal earls were confronting the rebels among the English baronage; in the autumn they repulsed an invading force of Flemish mercenaries commanded by the earl of Leicester, son of the late justiciar, one of the king's early supporters. The young earl of Leicester and his wife fell captive to the justiciar's men in autumn 1173, and they were sent across the Channel for imprisonment.[73] When Henry received word of the count of Flanders' plan to come to the aid of the remaining English rebels with a larger invasion, he sailed for his kingdom on 7 July 1174, with his captive queen on board, taking along their two youngest children who had been housed at Fontevraud Abbey, together with the earl of Leicester, his wife, and other high-ranking English prisoners. On landing in his kingdom, Henry consigned Eleanor to captivity in Salisbury Castle. Then he rushed to Canterbury to prostrate himself before the martyred Archbishop Thomas Becket's tomb as a humble pilgrim and to seek absolution as a penitent sinner by submitting to symbolic punishment by the Canterbury monks. Soon the king received a sign of his restoration to God's grace, when news arrived that forces fighting for him in the north of the kingdom had scored a colossal victory, capturing the king of the Scots. With all England again under royal control, Henry sailed back to Normandy in August to deal with his enemies now dispirited by the collapse of their cause across the Channel. By mid-August he had beaten back Louis VII's siege of Rouen, forcing him to retreat and clearing Normandy of invaders. By 8 September the French king agreed to a truce, and the Capetian–Plantagenet rivalry would remain quiescent for the remainder of Louis's reign.

Henry with his "renowned defensive genius and quick-strike ability" survived a great test of the strength of the empire that he had created.[74] Only in Eleanor's native Poitou, where fighting was endemic, did the war continue. Her capture in autumn 1173 had caused the young Count Richard, previously in his elder brother's shadow, to take control of the rebellion in Poitou, and his leadership on campaign marked the beginning of his reputation for bravery. When citizens of the port town of La Rochelle slammed shut their gates in his face, the young prince marched southward to the Charente valley city of Saintes, a commercial rival of La Rochelle, only to be driven out by his father in spring 1174. At the end of the summer, young Richard, contemptuous of his lackluster brothers who had accepted a truce, remained unreconciled, holding out in the near-unassailable fortress of Taillebourg high above the River Charente, while his father proceeded to take control of Poitou.[75]

By the end of September 1174 Richard was forced to join his two brothers in seeking a peace settlement, and they accepted their father's terms in October at Montlouis in Angevin territory between Amboise and Tours. Henry II's success in putting down the great rebellion placed him in an impregnable position, and he offered what he considered generous terms to the rebels. All prisoners were to be released, except for a few prominent ones—the Scottish king, the earls of Chester and Leicester, and Eleanor, who was notably not among those receiving gracious treatment. The rebels would eventually regain their lands, but their castles were demolished, leaving their ruins strewn all over Henry's lands, "visible reminders of the Old King's power and the penalties meted out to rebellious lords."[76] Despite Henry Senior's seeming generosity to his sons, he made certain that they were dependent on him. Soon he would be willing to delegate authority to his second son in Poitou and to his third son in Brittany, but in the Angevin and Anglo-Norman heartlands he refused to share power with Young Henry, then aged nineteen. The Young King was granted two castles in Normandy and a generous annual revenue of £15,000 *angevin* (£3,750 sterling). Although the king occasionally assigned his eldest son military tasks, rarely carried out effectively, he limited him to the margins of high politics and condemned him to economic insecurity. The youth's landless status would force him to follow the tournament circuit across northern France, and he left England in April 1176, "transformed from a king into a knight."[77]

Henry's second son and Eleanor's favorite, Richard, received only two "suitable dwelling-places," unfortified residences in Poitou, and half the revenues of the county. After a short time, however, his father charged him with responsibility for restoring order to Aquitaine, and he took up again his military career begun in 1174 that would win him the sobriquet "Lionheart." The third son Geoffrey was to have half the revenues of Brittany until his marriage to its heir, Constance, at which time her entire inheritance, including the English earldom of Richmond, was to pass to him. Henry also provided for his youngest son John at Montlouis, assigning him revenues from the English royal domain worth £1,000, together with any additional estates his father might choose to grant him, the castle and county of Nottingham, the castle and lordship of Marlborough, and two castles and income of £1,000 *angevin* (£250 sterling) in Normandy, as well as the three castles in Anjou and Maine earlier promised to him, with an additional £1,000 *angevin* in revenues from Angevin territories. Such generosity to an eight-year-old can hardly have pleased Young Henry; indeed, it seemed "almost as if planned purposely to give John a foothold in every part of his eldest brother's future dominions— a strip, so to say, in every one of young Henry's fields."[78]

The great rebellion of 1173–74 had exposed the extent of the hostility permeating the family of Eleanor and Henry II, and the bitter feelings left in its wake could never be expunged. Although Henry extended to his sons what he took to be generous treatment, they continued to nourish resentments against him, and their rebellions would punctuate his last years, weakening in the process the empire that he had assembled. The marriage of Eleanor and Henry was in ruins, and Henry had no intention of reinstating her in her earlier place at his side. The treaty of Montlouis made no mention of the captive queen, and of all the prominent rebels, she paid the heaviest price. After spending several months imprisoned at Chinon Castle, she was brought to England by Henry II in July 1174, along with the earls of Chester and Leicester. The king would release the two earls from their imprisonment and restore their lands to them by 1177, although he razed their castles except for key fortresses that he kept under his control.[79] Henry could never forgive his wife's ferocious act of inciting their sons into taking up arms against him in 1173, however, and Eleanor would not win release as long as he lived. Whatever her reasons for urging her sons to revolt against their father—certainly more than a rejected wife's rage—she had taken a huge chance and she lost her wager, paying the heaviest price of all the rebels. She would be kept under guard throughout the remainder of Henry's reign, denied full freedom until his death in 1189.

CHAPTER 9

A Captive Queen's Lost Years, 1174–1189

After Eleanor was taken captive in November 1173 and imprisoned at Chinon Castle, Henry II took her to England in the summer of 1174 when he set out to deal with the baronial uprising in his kingdom and to stave off an invasion from Flanders by the Young King's allies. The royal entourage made a stormy crossing of the Channel on 7 July along with a number of high-ranking prisoners and hostages, among them the captive queen, her two youngest children, Joanne and John, her daughter-in-law, Margaret, wife of the Young King, and likely two other sons' intended brides, Alix of France and Constance of Brittany.[1] The king sent his queen off to Salisbury Castle, and young Margaret and other hostages were sent to Devizes Castle.[2] Eleanor would remain in England confined in various royal castles for almost sixteen years, with the exception of an extended stay in Normandy in 1185–86, until her husband's death in July 1189.

Terms such as "prisoner" or "captive" calling up images of Tudor queens confined in the Tower of London awaiting execution do not accurately describe the conditions of Eleanor's confinement. Eleanor's detention was not so much comparable to a criminal's treatment as that of a hostage handed over to guarantee his sons' good behavior, and her captivity can be regarded as a means for Henry II to ensure their sons' submission.[3] For the first years after her forced return to England, "house arrest" best describes her situation; she was not housed in a dungeon deep under Salisbury Castle's keep, but in a palatial residence built by the bishop of Salisbury early in the twelfth century within the castle's walls. Whatever conditions Eleanor endured during the first decade of her captivity, she gradually obtained greater freedom as the years passed. From 1184, when her eldest daughter, Duchess Matilda of Saxony, came from Germany to England with her exiled family, her appearances at the royal court increased.

The captive Eleanor won little sympathy from her English subjects, but she still occupied a place in the hearts of the Poitevins, as the chronicle of Richard le Poitevin shows. A sympathizer with the rebel cause in 1173–74, he expressed joy when Henry II's sons ranged themselves against their father. This Poitevin cleric felt strongly the alien character of the English king's rule over Aquitaine, and for him Henry, "the king of the North," was a foreign oppressor. He inserted into his account a lament for the captive queen, declaring that Eleanor had fulfilled the prophecy of Merlin concerning "the Eagle of the Broken Covenant." The prophecies of Merlin had appeared first in Geoffrey of Monmouth's *History of the Kings of Britain*, an early twelfth-century history by "a romance writer masquerading as a historian." Accepted by its readers as authentic history, it popularized the Arthurian legend; and it circulated widely as far away as Aquitaine, influencing Richard le Poitevin.[4] He hailed Eleanor as the "eagle of the two heads," a queen divided in two between England and Aquitaine, between north and south. Having stirred up her eaglets against their father, she was defeated and "removed from thy land and led into a country which thou knewest not is today a captive and humiliated." The passage continues, imagining Eleanor lamenting in captivity the lost pleasures of court life at Poitiers:

> I beseech you, queen divided in two, leave off your continual lamenting. Why does your heart afflict you with daily tears? Return, o captive, return to your cities, if you can; if you cannot, then weep with the king of Jerusalem and say: "Hard is my lot, exiled in Meshech, dwelling by the tents of Kedar!" [Psalm 120:5], for you live among an unknown and coarse people. Weep again and always, and say: "Day and night, tears are my food" [Psalm 42:3], ... Eagle of the broken alliance, how long will you cry out, and not be heard? The king of the North has placed you under siege. With the Prophet, "Shout aloud without restraint; lift up your voice like a trumpet" [Isaiah 58:1], so that your sons will hear your voice. For the day approaches when you will be freed by your sons and you will be returned to your own land.[5]

When the captive queen waited at Barfleur to board ship for the voyage across the Channel, she must have recalled sailing from the same port twenty years earlier, setting out with her new husband filled with hopes for a new life as queen of England. Now, at age fifty, Eleanor feared that she would grow old and die separated from her children, stripped of power, and banished from royal courts where she had always shone as a central character. During the queen's almost sixteen years of captivity, she would lose two of her sons; Young Henry's demise in June 1183 was followed by that of Geoffrey of Brittany three years later. Before their deaths, the two were again challenging their father and jostling with their brother Richard, count of Poitou, to seize as much of the Plantagenet territories for themselves as they could, no doubt with their captive mother's silent applause.

The two sons' deaths forced Henry II to revise his plans for the succession to his territories, and the fate of Eleanor's lands became a cause of contention between the king and Richard, now the eldest son. The survival of Richard and John, more and more his father's favorite, cast doubt on Richard's succession to Aquitaine, formerly assumed to be settled. Continuing to complicate the English king's relations with his sons were his Capetian rivals, Louis VII and, after his death in 1180, his heir, Philip II, later given the appellation "Augustus". With the Plantagenet empire threatened, Henry needed to make certain that his captive queen had no chance of inflaming further their offspring against him.

ELEANOR'S EARLY YEARS OF CAPTIVITY

During the years of Eleanor of Aquitaine's captivity, 1174–89, she disappears almost entirely from sight. According to one account, Henry II ordered her confined in "well guarded strong places"; and she was first housed under close supervision in the royal castle at Sarum, or Old Salisbury, although later she can be located occasionally at other royal castles in southern England.[6] As a woman, Eleanor received more lenient treatment than men captured while taking part in an armed rebellion; and Henry may have chosen Salisbury Castle for her detention as a gesture of leniency, for its residential quarters, a large quadrangle next to the keep, had been one of her favored abodes during her earlier years as queen.[7] According to a chronicler at Limoges, Henry imprisoned his queen at Salisbury Castle, "on guard against her reverting to her machinations."[8] The king's fear was Eleanor's continued involvement in the intrigues of their quarrelsome sons, and he tried to ensure that no communication passed between them. Yet he could not afford to treat her too harshly, for that would only have added to the hatred that Young Henry, Richard, and Geoffrey already felt for him. Earlier, both Anglo-Norman monarchs and counts of Anjou had not hesitated to imprison defeated nobles, including near-relatives, for years, often under such harsh conditions that they lost their health, if not their lives. A queen's long captivity was startling, but imprisonment of great ladies was not unprecedented. In medieval vernacular literature, tales were not uncommon of aristocratic ladies locked away for years, many of them by their own families, and history records many noble maidens whose fathers were forced to turn them over to their lords as hostages.

Henry II could have made other choices for ridding himself of the threat presented by Eleanor to the stability of his rule. She could simply have disappeared during her captivity at Chinon, but young Arthur of Brittany's mysterious disappearance from Rouen Castle later during John's reign shows that such a solution would have created more problems than it solved. Rumors that John had murdered his nephew with his own hands quickly spread, and it sapped his subjects' loyalty to him, crippling him in his contest with his arch-enemy Philip of France. Certainly rumors of Eleanor's death while in Henry's hands following his suspected role in the murder of Becket would have had a similar effect. His wife's murder would have aroused revulsion throughout Europe, and it would have so enraged the Poitevins that Plantagenet rule over them would have been impossible. In any case, Henry's character had little in common with that of the insecure and overly suspicious John, and although severe and vengeful, he lacked his youngest son's depraved cruelty that surfaced once he was king.

An option that great men had often chosen in earlier centuries for dealing with wayward or unwanted wives was immuring them in convents. Henry II considered such a step in 1175–76, when his adulterous affair with Rosamund Clifford was at its most passionate stage. A contemporary writer claimed that Henry, having imprisoned his queen, no longer tried to hide his adultery, and publicly displayed as his mistress, "not a rose of the world (*mundi rosa*) . . . , but more truly might be called the rose of an impure husband (*immundi rosa*)."[9] Apparently Henry was not worried that dissolution of his marriage to Eleanor would threaten his authority over her duchy of Aquitaine. Despite Louis VII's loss of Aquitaine as a result of his divorce, Henry seemed confident that Richard's formal installation as duke of Aquitaine and count of Poitou would keep Eleanor's lands safely in Plantagenet hands.

Henry saw an opportunity to secure a divorce from Eleanor at the time of a mission to England by a papal legate, sent from Rome to settle one of the endless quarrels between the kingdom's two archbishops.[10] On the papal representative's arrival in England in autumn 1175, the king received him with honor, showering him with gifts and flattery. Henry assumed that the cardinal would agree readily to a dissolution of his marriage on grounds of consanguinity, since Louis VII had won a divorce for that reason, and Henry's kinship to Eleanor was even closer than her relationship to her first husband. The English king allegedly offered his queen release from her captivity during his Easter court at Winchester in 1176, if she would agree to enter a religious house, no doubt Fontevraud Abbey, probably with the prospect of becoming abbess there. The abbey had a reputation as a residence for noble ladies seeking refuge from wordly affairs, but Eleanor was unwilling to join them, not even if installed as abbess, and she and her sons resisted Henry's plan. She even appealed to the archbishop of Rouen against being packed off to Fontevraud, and he refused to give his consent to Henry's plan.[11] As the archbishop of Rouen's role shows, the Church's opposition was another obstacle to Henry in ridding himself of Eleanor, and his projected divorce was not to be easily accomplished. After Becket's martyrdom, the English king had little credit with the papacy or with churchmen in England or elsewhere in Europe. He was in no position to pressure a pope firmly opposed to approving a divorce, particularly one who was doubtless aware of rumors that he desired the divorce in order to marry his mistress.

Whatever the possibility of Henry II setting his queen aside and taking Rosamund Clifford as his wife, events intervened to prevent it, for his beloved mistress died late in 1176 or in 1177. His fair Rosamund was buried at Godstow Priory in Oxfordshire only a few miles from their trysting place at Woodstock. Around the time of Rosamund's death the patron of Godstow, an Oxfordshire baron, assigned his patronage rights over the house to Henry in order that it should be held "in chief of the king's crown, as the Abbey of Saint Edmund and other royal abbeys throughout the kingdom of England are constituted." This elevation in Godstow's status reflects Henry's deep feelings for his mistress, a desire to honor the convent that housed her tomb and to place the nuns watching over it under royal protection. In the years following Rosamund's death, Henry showed great generosity to the Godstow nuns, making them cash grants and giving them timber for their building projects.[12]

Soon gossip was circulating that Henry II's desire for an annulment of his marriage was not in order to wed Rosamund Clifford, but so that he could marry instead the sixteen-year-old Alix of France, a maiden whom he had already "unchastely, and with too much want of faith, dishonored."[13] Alix's father Louis VII had betrothed her to Richard at the Montmirail settlement of 1169, and he had handed her over to be raised at her future father-in-law's court. Henry's ravishing of young Alix was far more shameful to contemporaries than his affair with Rosamund Clifford, for he had taken advantage of a girl entrusted to him as his ward when she was only nine to remain in his household until she reached the proper age for marrying Richard. In taking her to his bed, he had not only violated her trust, but also the trust of her father, his lord the French king, as well as that of his own son. This affair had begun during the queen's absences from court, but given the rapid circulation of rumors from the royal court, Eleanor heard of the scandal almost at once, whether still in Poitou or sequestered in England later. The queen would learn that Henry did not limit his adulterous affairs to Alix of France while she was in captivity. He sired another illegitimate son by a Welsh woman, Nest, married to one of his knights from southwestern England. He acknowledged the boy, named Morgan, who became a cleric and eventually was named provost of Beverley, Yorkshire, a lucrative ecclesiastical living that English kings often granted to high-ranking royal servants.[14]

News of the king's liaison with Alix must have left Eleanor appalled, for the king's conduct not only grossly violated aristocratic standards of honorable behavior, but also betrayed and humiliated her favorite son. It gave both Eleanor and Richard yet another grievance against Henry. According to a courtier's hostile account, the king hoped by means of new heirs born to his new favorite that he might "be able effectually to disinherit his former sons by Eleanor, who had troubled him."[15] The story of Henry II's seduction of Alix is not simply another scurrilous tale told by his enemies, for several sources corroborate it.[16] Henry was curiously reluctant to carry out the princess's long-delayed marriage to Richard, despite periodic protests from Louis VII and Philip II and from high-ranking churchmen including the pope complaining on their behalf. Strongest evidence for the accusation's accuracy, however, is Richard Lionheart's own resistance to marrying Alix. Roger of Howden, a chronicler with access to court circles, records Richard's excuse offered to Philip, her half-brother, for refusing to marry his betrothed of many years at the outset of the Third Crusade. He quotes Richard as telling the French king, "I do not reject your sister; but it is impossible for me to marry her, for my father had slept with her and had a son by her." Richard then added that he could present many witnesses capable of testifying to the truth of his statement. At the time, the English king was in the embarrassing position of preparing to take a Spanish princess as his bride, and he needed a potent excuse for breaking off his engagement to Alix. The Lionheart's most respected modern biographer finds it difficult to discount Howden's "explicit statement." Furthermore, the Lionheart need not have lodged such a bitter accusation against his own father in order to justify his rejection of Alix; he could simply have declared that she had borne another man's child without naming the father.[17]

The captive Eleanor was stripped of the revenues that she had enjoyed as queen. Her dowerlands were taken from her, even the paltry sum of twenty-one shillings and a penny a year from wool produced on two Berkshire manors.[18] Henry helped himself to Eleanor's dower when carrying out his bargain for reconciliation with the Church after Becket's murder. For release from a crusading vow sworn as part of his penance, he promised the pope that he would found three new religious houses instead, honoring the newly sainted archbishop. He founded a Carthusian priory at Witham in Wiltshire, and to fulfill his commitment to found two other houses, he transformed existing religious houses into royal foundations, taking portions of Eleanor's dowerlands to endow them. He took a church of secular canons on the queen's estate at Waltham, Essex, and converted it into an abbey of Augustinian canons regular in 1177. Henry also refounded a house of nuns at Amesbury Priory in Wiltshire that had fallen into scandalous condition, as exposed by an episcopal visitation; allegedly the abbess had borne three children since entering the religious life. The king made it a daughter house of Fontevraud, settling at Amesbury twenty-four nuns brought from the mother-house, again taking manors from Eleanor's dowerlands to provide the endowment.[19]

If Eleanor no longer drew income from her dowerlands, periodic payments or pensions that English monarchs made to favored kin, friends, and servants for their maintenance continued to be paid to her at Henry II's command. These were generous payments, considering that the queen's household was now much smaller, ranging from less than £30 to a high of £180; in 1175, her first full year of captivity, payments totaled £161, an income befitting a minor baron. The funds were handed over to trusted men in the king's service, first to Robert Mauduit, constable of Salisbury Castle, where Eleanor was under his guard. It is a strange coincidence that Mauduit belonged to a family that had served previous queens; his ancestors had acted as chamberlains for Henry's mother, the empress Matilda, and for her mother.[20] Later, from 1180 to the end of Henry's reign, another member of an administrative family, Ralph fitz Stephen, a longtime royal servant serving as one of the king's chamberlains, had charge of Eleanor's expenditures. The queen won the respect of her second custodian, and after Henry II's death, Ralph made a gift of land for the king's soul and for Queen Eleanor's salvation, to Stanley Abbey, a Cistercian house in Wiltshire founded by Henry's mother.[21] No doubt others charged with the care of the captive queen came to admire her strength in enduring adversity.

As years passed Eleanor was allowed to make sojourns at other castles, certainly to Winchester and Windsor and perhaps as far west as Devonshire, where she had held substantial lands. Within Winchester Castle was a series of buildings that together formed the equivalent of a royal palace; and during Henry II's reign repairs and additions to the residential quarters were constantly under way. At Winchester, the queen probably encountered her daughter-in-law, Margaret, wife of the Young King, who was a frequent visitor there, for works undertaken in 1174–75 included construction of an addition "where the young queen hears mass."[22] In 1176, Robert Mauduit received a payment of almost three pounds by the king's order, apparently for Eleanor's expenses during Henry's Easter court held that year at Winchester.[23] That court marked the last time that she would see all four of her sons together. Richard and Geoffrey had crossed from France for the feast, and they returned to the Continent with their father. Henry the Young King and his queen also left England after Easter, and he would be away from the kingdom for three years before returning for another Easter court at Winchester.

The dullness of Eleanor's life was brightened by the betrothal of her youngest daughter Joanne in 1176. The captive Eleanor had no voice in negotiations for the eleven-year-old girl's hand, but she would have been filled with pride at Joanne's selection as the bride of William II, king of Sicily. William's kingdom was the creation of eleventh-century Norman adventurers incorporating both Sicily and the southern Italian mainland and heir to traditions of the island's previous occupiers, Greeks, Romans, and Arabs. Years earlier Eleanor had seen first-hand the island's splendors at their height under King Roger II, when her ship from the Holy Land, blown off course, landed her at the cosmopolitan city of Palermo in 1149. By the time William succeeded to the throne, however, Sicily's greatness was fading into a sort of "Indian summer." Henry II had sought a Sicilian marriage for one of his daughters earlier, and the project was revived in May 1176, when ambassadors from the Sicilian royal court came to England. They were entertained at Winchester, where Joanne was residing and where Eleanor had remained for a time after the Easter court. The young princess's beauty impressed the envoys, and Henry agreed to her betrothal to the young Sicilian ruler. English emissaries set off for Sicily to negotiate the marriage settlement, arriving at Palermo in early August.[24] Perhaps the queen helped in readying her daughter's trousseau and prepared her for life at the Sicilian royal court by recalling her own visit there years earlier. After Joanne's departure for her new home, her mother could not have expected to see her ever again, but chance would reunite them on two occasions many years later.

In September 1176 Joanne left Winchester for Palermo, loaded with clothing, gold and silver plate, and other impressive gifts to take to her new island home; the cost of one of her robes, no doubt her wedding dress, was over £114.[25] In February 1177 in the Palatine Chapel at Palermo, she married William, a young man of twenty-two, and her coronation as his queen quickly followed. Joanne's Sicilian marriage aroused greater interest among the English than had her two elder sisters' marriages earlier to foreign princes. English adventurers journeyed south to seek their fortunes, attracted by accounts of the island kingdom's riches. Artistic and literary inspiration flowed northward from Sicily; mosaics in Sicily's Byzantine-style churches influenced English wall-paintings and manuscript miniatures, and the Sicilian kingdom became a setting for English romances.[26]

During the captive queen's imprisonment, expenditures on her behalf indicate that conditions of her detention were far from harsh and that she was housed in comfortable quarters. Circumstances of her confinement were improving by 1177, perhaps not coincidentally the year that Henry II finally released from imprisonment the earls of Chester and Leicester, two prominent participants in the 1173–74 revolt. Considerable and almost continuous repairs and expansions were under way at Salisbury Castle throughout the 1170s, supervised by Robert Mauduit; in 1177 alone over £113 was spent on the castle's residential quarters. Indeed, the evidence suggests that Henry II wished Eleanor to live in a state worthy of a queen, even though she was banished from court. In 1178 two robes of scarlet, a fine woolen cloth often dyed a rich red that was so popular that the cloth's name was given to the color, gray furs, and an embroidered cushion were purchased for Eleanor "and her maid," indicating that the queen had servants assigned to her. The next year more expenses were recorded for clothing made of luxury goods, over eighteen pounds for a great cloak of scarlet cloth; and also for furs and a leather garment for the queen as well as another scarlet cloak, a leather garment and a cape for a maiden in her household. Eleanor was allowed to leave the castle precincts to go horseback riding, for payments are recorded for a gilt saddle covered in scarlet for the queen and a less grand one for her maid.[27] She enjoyed the companionship of high-born maidens, such as Amiria, the sister of Hugh Pantulf, baron of Wem in Shropshire. Years later when Amiria was making a gift of land to the nuns of Amesbury Priory, she described herself as Eleanor's former handmaid and foster-child. The Wiltshire manor that Amiria gave to the nuns had come to her as a gift from the queen, formerly part of her dowerlands.[28]

CONTINUED STRIFE AMONG ELEANOR'S SONS

Although Henry II kept his queen under lock and key to guard against new conspiracies, his stormy relations with their three older sons continued. Their bad relations were worsened by his periodic new proposals for the succession that caused his sons constant uncertainty, deepening resentment of their father, and jealousy of each other that pushed them into continued revolts. This strife had two chief causes. One was Young Henry's continued complaining after the 1173–74 rebellion at his lack of any territory to call his own. His younger brother Richard's possession of the county of Poitou after 1175 galled him, for the contrast with his own powerlessness seemed to announce his royal title's emptiness. Like many aristocratic mothers, Eleanor felt sympathy for her son's chafing at his dependent situation. No doubt she continued to hope to see Henry's domains divided among sons during his lifetime, and it is not unlikely that she managed to contrive some means of communicating with her sons and stirring up their dissatisfaction. She would have been more artful than another imprisoned queen four centuries later, Mary Queen of Scots, in devising means for sending and receiving messages to and from her sons and other sympathizers.

A second factor in Henry Senior's strife with his elder sons was his insistence on finding a landed inheritance for his youngest son John that they suspected would be at their expense. Although John did not appear promising to contemporaries, apparently Henry saw something in him that others missed. He clearly felt closer to his youngest son than to his elder ones, who had been tainted by their taking up arms against him in 1173–74 in association with their mother. Unlike Richard, who was obviously Eleanor's favorite, John had never fallen under the spell of his mother's powerful personality, for he had spent his childhood separated from her and her influence. Furthermore, John's much younger age would have made him seem more compliant. After the boy was brought to England in 1174, his father kept him in his own household, and he would have been in Eleanor's company only on the few great occasions when she was allowed to join the royal court. In 1181 John's father sent him off to the household of the chief justiciar, Ranulf de Glanvill, to prepare him for governing; there the boy found himself in a veritable school for royal administrators. Henry indulged young John while he was with the justiciar's household, supporting three knights who were his companions with generous sums and providing funds for transporting the youth's dogs and their keepers when he crossed the sea to Normandy with Glanvill.[29]

After the peace of Montlouis ending the great rebellion in autumn 1174, Henry II set about finding lands in England for John, violating the kingdom's customary law of inheritance to do so. On two occasions, Henry ignored the precedent of equal partition of lordships among female heirs prevailing since his grandfather's reign, and daughters who wedded before their father's death had to be content with only their marriage portions.[30] In 1175, on the death of Henry's uncle Reginald de Dunstanville, earl of Cornwall, the king took the earldom into his hand for young John, disinheriting the earl's daughters of all but small portions. One of Reginald's daughters was married to the viscount of Limoges, a trouble-making vassal of Eleanor on Poitou's southern frontier, and his wife's disinheritance gave him added excuse for plotting against Plantagenet rule in the queen-duchess's lands.[31] Then in 1176 the king determined to endow John with another great earldom, Gloucester in the west of England. He made a marriage treaty with the earl of Gloucester betrothing John to Isabel, the earl's youngest daughter, effectively disinheriting the girl's two married older sisters.[32] Later Henry would seek a principality for his youngest son to match his brothers' duchies of Brittany and Aquitaine, naming John lord of Ireland at a royal council in May 1177.

Richard, charged with governing his mother's county of Poitou since 1175, had faced repeated revolts by princes of the Angoumois and the Limousin on its southern fringes.[33] In the fighting there, he won fame for his prowess and his boldness to the point of rashness that contributed to the construction of his heroic reputation. The young count's successful siege of the supposedly impregnable fortress of Taillebourg in the Charente valley in May 1179 enhanced his repute as a warrior, impressing his father. After that victory, he visited England, either summoned by Henry, who received him "with the highest honor," or according to one account, on a pilgrimage to the shrine of Saint Thomas Becket at Canterbury. Whatever the purpose of Richard's visit to the kingdom, some time during his stay, the king had Eleanor brought before a council at London and demanded that she formally cede her duchy to her second son. Possibly Eleanor, already wounded by Richard's rapid reconciliation with his father, saw this as another blow to their former strong bond.[34]

In 1182 Count Richard had to confront still another rebellion of nobles in southern Poitou. The rebels leveled grave charges against their count, accusing him of raping their wives and daughters, and then, "after the ardor of his lust had died," handing them over to his knights to use "as common prostitutes." A more likely explanation for the southern aristocrats' outrage is alarm at Richard's iron rule, notably his vigorous attempts to impose on them obligations similar to those traditionally owed by Anglo-Norman barons to their king-duke.[35] The Poitevin rebellion soon became entangled with the dissatisfaction of Richard's brothers. By mid-May 1182 Henry II, fearing that the young count was in danger of losing control over Poitou, rode south to his aid, accompanied by his third son, Geoffrey of Brittany. After arriving in his wife's domains, Henry summoned his eldest son, the Young King, to join in the fighting on Richard's behalf. By midsummer the combined forces of the father and his two eldest sons had convinced the viscounts of Limoges and Périgord to seek peace terms, but the Poitevin conflict would continue.

Young King Henry's chronic discontent transformed the noble rebellion in Eleanor's lands into a contest between her two eldest sons for her duchy. An inauspicious change in the conflict's character occurred once Young Henry arrived, for he listened with sympathy to the Poitevins' long-simmering grievances against Richard and challenged his brother's authority over the county. Since the settlement of Montlouis, the landless Young King's bitterness at his two younger brothers' possession of their own provinces had grown steadily. The Poitevin rebels, captivated with his charm and chivalric conduct and preferring his fecklessness to Richard's tenacity, expressed a desire to have him rule over them, overlooking their lady Eleanor's wishes. Young Henry found an affront that goaded him into rash action in autumn 1182, when his brother Richard constructed his castle of Clairvaux. It lay on the ill-defined Poitevin–Angevin frontier, apparently within the county of Anjou and claimed by the Young King as subject to him as count. During the 1182 Christmas festivities at Caen, he admitted that his frustration with his lack of authority and his anger at Richard over Clairvaux Castle had impelled him to ally with the rebel Poitevins. To settle his sons' quarrel, Henry II took the new castle into his own hands, but this incident forced him to rethink his previous plans for the succession. He had to admit the hollowness of his hope for his sons' co-operation in a shared Plantagenet enterprise and the potential for fighting between them after his death.

Henry II sought once more to draft a stable succession plan, trying to impose another settlement on his sons at Le Mans soon after the 1182 Christmas court, although the arrangement knitted together there unraveled almost at once. While Eleanor was not present at Le Mans, she is not likely to have been unaware of her husband's latest succession scheme. Always fearful that her ancestral lands would be absorbed permanently into an Angevin "empire," she would have understood its ominous implications. The key element of Henry's new plan was the homage of Richard and Geoffrey of Brittany to their elder brother the Young King, Richard for his mother's duchy of Aquitaine and Geoffrey for Brittany, implying that their father hoped for some sort of federation of siblings after his demise, headed by Young Henry. Geoffrey did homage to Young Henry readily, for the Breton counts traditionally had owed homage to the dukes of Normandy. The two had become close companions, for Geoffrey had joined his brother's household shortly after his knighting by his father in August 1178, traveling with him on the tournament circuit across northern France.[36]

Richard, however, refused to do homage, unwilling to accept the subjection of his mother's patrimony to the Young King. He argued that one brother could not be the superior of the other during their parents' lifetime, and he added that if his father's possessions rightly passed to the eldest brother, then his mother's duchy of Aquitaine ought to pass to the second son. Furthermore, the young count of Poitou had already done homage to the French monarch for Eleanor's duchy of Aquitaine, a sign of its special status. He feared that homage to his brother would result in what had long alarmed his mother—reducing her patrimony to another dependent Plantagenet territory, submerging Aquitaine permanently within a larger Plantagenet empire. This perceived threat had led her to raise her sons' revolt against her husband in 1173. Richard withdrew from his father's court in a rage in January 1183, leaving behind in one chronicler's words "nothing but recriminations and threats."[37] Eleanor would have found his outrage a satisfying reaction, even though it led to war among the Plantagenet siblings a month later.

Geoffrey of Brittany and Young Henry entered the fray when sent to the Limousin by their father to negotiate with the Poitevin rebels. Instead, the two joined forces with the insurgents at Limoges early in 1183, mounting raids to loot religious shrines of their rich treasures, not even sparing Grandmont, a monastery revered by their father and designated as his burial place. Soon Henry II, fearing that the two sons were about to defeat Richard, marched to Limoges to his aid, and his army besieged the rebels in the citadel of Saint-Martial but proved unable to take it. While Henry Senior pressed the siege, Richard worked to deliver the Angoumois and Saintonge from rebels and plunderers. Although the warfare was centered in Eleanor's lands, the Old King took precautions against treachery by Young Henry's friends in England, re-imprisoning the earl of Leicester and his wife, whom he had taken prisoner during the 1173–74 revolt.[38] Nothing indicates that the king mandated any significant change in the conditions of Eleanor's confinement in 1183; she was unlikely to have conspired with Young Henry and Geoffrey in their attempt to eject Richard from her ancestral county of Poitou.

The struggle in the south quickly developed into a major crisis with princes from outside the region seeking to take advantage of the family's strife to weaken Henry II. By this time the meek Louis VII was dead, succeeded by his son, Philip II, a much more dangerous opponent for the Plantagenets. Following his father's policy of exploiting any situation that complicated the English king's problems, the new French ruler proved a master at sowing dissension, stimulating Henry's sons' bitterness against their father.

Eleanor would witness the character of the long Plantagenet–Capetian conflict changing during Philip's reign; no longer would Henry II and his sons succeeding him be the aggressors; instead, they were forced to wage defensive campaigns against the Capetian king. Philip sent aid to Young Henry, his brother-in-law, whom he hoped would succeed to the Plantagenet heritage; and Raymond V, count of Toulouse, came in person to fight alongside the Young King.[39] Despite recruiting Raymond's rival, the king of Aragon, as an ally, Richard appeared about to be driven out of Aquitaine, but Young Henry's charm and courtesy were inadequate substitutes for material resources. He quickly ran through his always insufficient funds and was forced to finance his war by plundering the people he supposedly had come to protect from his brother's greed. He sacked the abbey of Saint-Martial at Limoges, not only raiding its treasury, but seizing golden altar frontals, chalices, and crosses.[40] Not long before he died in June 1183, he had looted Rocamadour, one of the most famous shrines in western Christendom with its seven sanctuaries ranging up steep canyon walls.

Richard and Henry II had the Young King on the run, when his sudden death brought a temporary end to the family infighting. In June 1183 at Martel in the Dordogne, Young Henry was struck down with dysentery at age twenty-seven, and he died a good death in the eyes of the faithful, repenting of his sins and reconciled with his enemies before expiring. The Young King dictated a death-bed message to his father, hoping that he would come to him for reconciliation; but Henry Senior, suspecting treachery, refused. Instead, he sent a sapphire ring, expecting that his son would recognize it as a sign of his affection and forgiveness. Young Henry's letter first asked his father to treat Eleanor mercifully in captivity at Salisbury; and then he requested that provision be made for his widow Margaret, peace made with his allies, and restitution paid to churches that he had plundered. He expressed a desire to be buried in Rouen Cathedral, where the bodies of his illustrious ancestors, founders of the Norman duchy, lay.[41] Young Henry asked that he be placed on sackcloth and ashes arranged in the shape of a cross to die in the manner of monks. Knowing that he would not live to fulfill his vow to go on crusade, he bequeathed his crusader's cloak to his former mentor in knighthood, William Marshal, "who loved him with great love," and requested that he take it to Jerusalem in fulfilment of his crusading vow. His companions at his deathbed wept and lamented their loss of a patron who was "the best and handsomest of men who was ever born since the time of Abel." They cried out, "God! What will now become of Generosity, Chivalry and Prowess, once wont to make his heart their home?" Not everyone mourned the Young King so profoundly; one English chronicler wrote that his popularity was only explained by the fact that "the number of fools is infinite."[42]

When Henry II learned of his eldest son's death, he dispatched Thomas of Earley, archdeacon of Wells, to England to bring Eleanor the sad news. Her reaction is recorded as part of a sermon delivered soon afterward by the archdeacon on Young Henry's pious death, which he wished to present as the martyrdom of a saint accompanied by miracles. Among the miracles that the preacher attributes to the recently deceased prince is Eleanor's vision that had already revealed her son's demise before the arrival of the king's messenger. She recounted to the archdeacon her dream in which Young Henry had appeared to her joyous and serene and wearing two crowns, one atop the other. Eleanor's interpretation of the two crowns consoled her, giving her confidence in her son's eternal salvation. She interpreted the lower crown, duller than the shining upper one, as standing for his earthly power and, gleaming above it, the other crown signifying his salvation. She asked, "What significance can be given to that [upper] crown, if it is not eternal bliss that has neither beginning nor end? What is the significance of such an intense radiance, if not happiness on high?" She then answered by quoting Scripture, "Things beyond our seeing, things beyond our hearing, things beyond our imagining, all prepared by God for those who love Him" (First Corinthians 2:9–10).[43] While revealing little of Eleanor's sorrow at her son's death, this account perhaps tells something of her Christian faith, her confidence in his eternal salvation that comforted her in her captivity. Yet Eleanor was a perceptive woman who knew the propaganda value of her pious vision foretelling her eldest son's fate and depicting him almost as if a candidate for canonization. Indeed, she may have inspired Thomas's sermon. Once Eleanor regained control of her dowerlands, she continued to show devotion to the Young King's memory, granting land to one of his servants in gratitude for his services to him.[44]

Young Henry's death caused the collapse of the rebel coalition, but Henry II remained in his wife's duchy to continue his siege of Limoges; and once the city surrendered on 24 June 1183, he destroyed the walls of its citadel, "not leaving one stone upon another." Henry and Richard with their ally the king of Aragon proceeded to take other rebel castles, among them Hautefort, seat of Bertrand de Born, a warmongering troubadour who had sought through his lyrics to inflame the Young King's resentments. Once the Plantagenet monarch had pacified Poitou by seizing and razing castles, he made himself master there, installing his own constables in castles that Richard had formerly controlled as count.[45] Geoffrey too paid for his part in the 1182–83 conflict, stripped of control over his castles in Brittany.

The Last Years of Eleanor's Captivity

Possibly Young Henry's deathbed request for amelioration of Eleanor's conditions of confinement moved his father, but practical concerns raised by the youth's death also brought her greater liberty. Among the repercussions of the Young King's demise was friction between Henry II and Philip II of France over the lands to be assigned to the Young King's widow, Margaret, who was Philip's half-sister. Although contention centered on the Norman Vexin with its fortress at Gisors brought by Margaret as her dowry on her betrothal, a related issue raised by Philip was a demand for dowerlands in England supposedly assigned to her at the time of her marriage. Henry II's reply was that those lands were no longer available for the French king's widowed sister, having been handed over earlier to Queen Eleanor. His determination to avoid seeing his former daughter-in-law Margaret possessed of sizeable English estates likely contributed more to Eleanor's increased liberty than a desire to honor his dying son's plea. The usually well-informed Roger of Howden claims that late in 1183 the king released Eleanor from her long captivity, commanding that the queen, "who had been kept in detention for many years, be freed and that she make a progress about her dowerlands," in proof of her possession of them. Indeed, she did visit her dowerland at Waltham in Essex.[46]

Eventually other issues concerning the rights of the Young King's widow were resolved by negotiations between the French and English monarchs without too much acrimony. Most contentious was the Norman Vexin, for Philip II, like his father, saw Plantagenet possession of it as a threat to their heartland, the Île de France. Yet if it returned to the French king's hands, then

Henry would feel that his Norman duchy's safety was threatened; and surprisingly, he succeeded in keeping custody of that strategically vital territory.
Margaret agreed to accept an annuity in exchange for the Vexin, and Henry
was to keep it as the dowry of another of Philip's half-sisters, Alix, in return
for his promise that Richard's much-delayed marriage to her would finally
take place. Philip hoped that the count of Poitou's marriage to Alix would link
the two princes together as kinsmen and friends as had Young Henry's
marriage to Margaret. Neither Henry nor Richard had any interest in moving
forward with the marriage, however, doubtless for decidedly different reasons.

Another important element in improving Eleanor's situation was the
arrival of her eldest daughter Matilda, duchess of Saxony, in Plantagenet territory in summer 1182; and once Matilda crossed from Normandy to England,
the queen made a number of public appearances at the royal court. Matilda
and her husband Henry the Lion, duke of Saxony, took refuge in her father's
lands after the duke's rivalry with the Holy Roman Emperor Frederick I
(Barbarossa) had forced him to leave Germany. Henry and his duchess
went into exile, and seeking a haven in her father's lands, they traveled to
Normandy, accompanied by their eldest son, also named Henry, a second
son, Otto, their daughter Richenza, and a large company of knights and other
attendants, while a third son was left behind in Germany, held there as a
hostage. Henry II left off his campaigning in Poitou to hasten northward to
meet them.[47] Not long after the exiles' arrival in Normandy, Matilda gave
birth to a fourth son at Argentan, but he apparently lived only a short time.

Once Matilda arrived in England in June 1184, her mother's seclusion
ended for a time as she traveled to Winchester for a reunion, and Eleanor
enjoyed her eldest daughter's company for almost a year—more time than
she was ever to spend with her other adult daughters. After the birth of
Matilda's fifth son at Winchester in summer 1184, she and her mother
were together at Berkhamstead and Windsor. In late November Henry held a
great council at London that became a family reunion, attended by Eleanor,
the duchess of Saxony and her husband, and all three of the royal couple's
surviving sons, whom the queen had not seen for almost a decade. A
month later, Eleanor was again with her extended family at Windsor for
the Christmas court. Then early in 1185, she and Matilda were summoned
from Windsor to Winchester by the king to share in the good news of Henry
the Lion's pardon by the German emperor. After Easter, the king commanded
his queen, his daughter, and her husband, the duke of Saxony, to join him
in Normandy for another council, and Eleanor traveled with her daughter
and son-in-law to Portsmouth, where they set sail.[48]

With the success of the English king's efforts to reconcile Henry the Lion
and the emperor, the duke and duchess continued their journey, setting out

from Normandy for their ducal palace at Brunswick in Saxony. After Matilda's return to Saxony, Eleanor would never see her eldest daughter again, for she would die in Germany in June 1189. The family alliance sealed by Matilda's marriage to the duke of Saxony held strong after her death, however. Eleanor's granddaughter Richenza, or Matilda as she was called by the English, and her Saxon grandsons were left behind in England after their parents' return to Germany, one of them still there after Henry II's death.[49] Both Richard and John as English kings would prove dependable supporters of one of Matilda's sons, Otto of Brunswick, in his contest with the Hohenstaufens for the imperial Crown.

In the years of Matilda's English exile, an improvement in Eleanor's material circumstances is clear. Even before her daughter's arrival in England, she was moved from Salisbury to Windsor Castle; and a Canterbury chronicle notes that in 1184–85, "Queen Eleanor was for a little time, at the petition of Archbishop Baldwin of Canterbury, freed from prison where she had been held confined for almost twelve years."[50] Whatever the truth of this unconfirmed report, payments for the queen's expenses increased at this time. Over £55 was spent for cloth to make hoods and capes of samite, a rich fabric of heavy silk, for the queen and for "Bellebelle," apparently her maid; later expenses recorded for the journey of Eleanor and her daughter Matilda from Windsor to London show the sum of £104 allocated for their maintenance. Eleanor was once again receiving some income from her dowerlands in Devon as well as revenues from Queenhithe, a part of her dower lying along the Thames in London.[51]

Young Henry's death called for new arrangements for the succession, and Henry II met with his three surviving sons at Angers after the Young King's burial at Rouen. It was only natural for Richard to replace his deceased elder brother as heir to the English Crown and to Normandy as well as to the Angevin patrimony of Anjou, Maine, and the Touraine.[52] Yet the Capetian ruler Philip II, as his father had, took a great interest in Henry's plans for the succession to the principalities comprising his empire lying within the French kingdom. Earlier Philip could have counted on the bulk of Henry's possessions passing to his brother-in-law, Young Henry, whom he regarded as an ally and whom he also reckoned lacked his father's keen political judgment.[53] Now he was forced to rethink his policy toward the Plantagenets, and conflict between the two kings threatened. Richard, too much his mother's son, had never enjoyed the strong paternal affection that Henry had felt for the deceased Young Henry, and his father had no intention of having him crowned king. It soon became clear that John Lackland was taking the favored place in Henry's heart that the Young King had previously occupied. Richard was aware of Henry's wish to provide much more for John than the youngest son in an aristocratic family could normally expect, and he feared that the king's inordinate love for his youngest son would result in cheating him—the eldest surviving son—of Poitou, the province that he saw as "his own especial possession."[54] The young Capetian monarch would work to promote this increasing hostility, as earlier his father Louis had encouraged Young Henry's hatred for his father.

The fate of Eleanor's patrimony, the duchy of Aquitaine, became the focus of contention over Henry II's new succession scheme. He tried throughout the winter of 1183–84 to pressure Richard into handing over the duchy to John. Possibly one of his reasons for bringing Eleanor to Windsor in 1183 was to coerce her into agreeing to his new plan for her patrimony, but she would have strongly opposed it. Richard, unwilling to renounce power in Poitou in exchange for Henry's implied promise of his Anglo-Norman realm and his Angevin patrimony, rode off from his father's court without giving an answer and later sent word from Poitiers of his refusal. Allegedly, the king then angrily told John, aged seventeen, to lead an army into Poitou and take his brother's lands by force. John had fallen under the influence of his brother Geoffrey of Brittany, nine years older, and the two brothers shared personality traits. A contemporary at court described the young count of Brittany as "able to corrupt two kingdoms with his tongue . . . a hypocrite in everything, changeable and a dissembler."[55] Geoffrey and John raised a force to invade their brother's county of Poitou in August 1184, after Henry's return to England, but their attack backfired when Richard in retaliation invaded Brittany. Henry summoned his three sons to England for a meeting at Westminster in late autumn, where their mother was present, doubtless a participant in the discussions; and afterward, the royal family moved on to Windsor to celebrate Christmas. Eleanor, aged sixty, could have recalled that her coronation had taken place thirty years earlier, in December 1154, and that she had passed a third of her time as queen as a prisoner. By 1184, the contrast in her age with her much younger husband's was no longer noticeable, for Henry's years of hard riding and rough living bolting from one end of his far-flung lands to the other had aged him beyond his fifty years.

By the Christmas court's end, Henry II had pressured his sons into making peace, but he was unsuccessful in imposing his scheme of replacing Richard with John in Aquitaine. Henry turned to Eleanor, seeing her title as duchess of Aquitaine as a tool for bringing Richard to heel, and she was brought to Normandy for another family council convened in May 1185. The king planned to exploit his wife's hereditary right to strip Richard of the power that he had held over Aquitaine since 1175 by restoring her nominal authority as duchess that she had been forced to surrender in 1179. At Alençon, Henry warned Richard that if he did not hand over Poitou to his mother, then she "would come in person at the head of a great army to devastate his land." A loving son, Richard obeyed, "and he returned all Poitou with its castles and fortifications to his mother."[56] For the young count of Poitou, his surrender was a price worth paying for quashing Henry's scheme for replacing him with John, and also he grasped that Eleanor's restoration to nominal rights as duchess of Aquitaine would strengthen her position. He returned to Poitou, confident that the special place of his mother's duchy within the Plantagenet dominions remained intact, although his father in fact held a tight rein on the Poitevin administration.[57] The young count's insecurity about his position as Henry's primary heir made him seek clear acknowledgment of his status, but he would never win a precise pledge from his father. Henry Senior resolved not to repeat the mistake that his premature installation of Young Henry as heir had been, and after 1185 he aimed at keeping his surviving sons uncertain about their futures, a policy that only pushed Richard into rebellion.

While at Alençon, Eleanor made two grants to Fontevraud Abbey, a house that had enjoyed the generosity of her own ancestors as well as Henry II's Angevin forefathers. Henry himself had always been a generous patron of the abbey, but Eleanor had not proven particularly bounteous before the 1170s. Her 1185 charters recording the two grants are the only ones known to survive from all the years of her captivity. Although Eleanor may have made some other grants between this interlude at Alençon and Henry's death in July 1189, the survival of only two official documents between 1174 and 1189 seems to stand as evidence for her political impotence during the years.

The first of the two documents assigned Fontevraud £100 annually from Eleanor's Poitevin revenues. Its text survives in full, and the words seem to suggest the queen-duchess's lack of complete freedom of action. Eleanor declared that she was acting "with the assent and at the will of her lord Henry, King of England, and of Richard, Geoffrey and John, her sons." Stating such an authorization by her husband and her sons as well is unusual in her Poitevin charters. The grant continues with language customary for gifts to religious foundations, declaring its purpose "for the salvation of the soul of my lord the king and for the salvation of my own soul and of my son Richard and my other sons and my daughters and my predecessors." Witnesses' names show that several of her devoted Poitevin nobles, among them Geoffrey, lord of Tonnay-Charente, his kinsman Raoul, John, lord of Rexe, and the seneschal of Poitou and the count's chief deputy, Robert de Montmirail, had traveled to Normandy to pay their respects to her. Another Poitevin witness was Chalon de Rochefort, conspicuous as a member of Eleanor's military household during her years as a widow.[58]

Eleanor's second grant in favor of Fontevraud awarded another £50 for founding a priory, Sainte-Catherine at La Rochelle affiliated with the abbey.

This grant is apparently Eleanor's only foundation of a new religious house in Poitou, and she is not known to have founded any others in her two husbands' kingdoms. Like the previous document, this one probably depicts Eleanor carrying out her husband Henry's wishes.[59] Henry's political calculations may well lie behind the two grants, for cultivating the favor of both La Rochelle and Fontevraud Abbey was worthwhile to him. One was a town with a growing economy, a source of vital revenues for Plantagenet Poitou; the other was a great religious foundation with a strategic location only a few miles from Chinon Castle, the site of his Angevin treasury, and influential among the local nobles.

Eleanor remained in Normandy almost a year, no doubt taking advantage of her time there to visit her eldest son's tomb in the cathedral at Rouen. She and Henry sailed for England at the end of April 1186,[60] and little is known of her life from then until Henry's death in the summer of 1189 which would bring a full restoration of her freedom. The improved conditions that she had enjoyed during Matilda's visit continued, however. While not entirely free, she was no longer confined to Salisbury Castle, but spent time also at the royal palace at Winchester. In the annals of one English monastery an entry recorded under the year 1187 reads, "King Henry and Queen Eleanor were reconciled," suggesting wide awareness that she was no longer being held in close confinement. Added evidence is the renewal of payments of queen's gold to her soon after her return from Normandy.[61] In spring 1187 Eleanor was receiving a pension that amounted to about thirteen shillings daily or about twenty pounds a month, a sum equivalent to the annual income of many knights; and that same year she received generous clothing allowances for herself and the maidens of her household.[62]

While Ralph fitz Stephen still had responsibility for monies assigned to the queen, in one instance Eleanor's own clerk Jordan received twenty-four pounds "for her expenses." A clerk of the same name had witnessed one of her charters during her 1156–57 visit to Poitou, then identified as her chancellor; and again in Poitou in 1168–73, a certain Jordan had witnessed as her "clerk and notary."[63] Although it seems improbable that the Jordan serving her in 1187 was the same clerk who had belonged to her household thirty years earlier in Poitou, the name suggests the intriguing possibility that a faithful Poitevin was again in her service in England at the end of Henry II's reign. If so, Jordan's position as Eleanor's secretary in 1187 may indicate that her husband was no longer attempting to control her correspondence.

The future of Eleanor and Henry's youngest son, John Lackland, still preoccupied the king after the council at Alençon. Henry, temporarily abandoning his proposal to turn over the queen's patrimony to John, revived his earlier plan for making Ireland a separate lordship for him. In spring 1185 he knighted the eighteen-year-old lad at Windsor Castle and sent him off to Ireland at the head of a large-scale expedition that required many ships, horses, and supplies for a massive force of fighters and administrators. Probably Henry's hope was that John could impose some order on the island, as his brothers Richard and Geoffrey were doing in other lands on the Plantagenet periphery. John's Irish expedition was hardly a success, however; he clearly failed his first test in exercising authority, and he had to withdraw in frustration without imposing order on the island. John was in England waiting for a favorable wind to return to Ireland when news of the death of Geoffrey of Brittany, Eleanor and Henry's third son, in August 1186 caused the king to postpone any Irish plans. He needed John to play a part in new plans for disposition of his Continental possessions. Until then he had been planning the boy's coronation as king of Ireland, and in January 1187 papal legates arrived from Rome with a crown of peacock feathers that was never to be used. John would remain merely "lord of Ireland," even after he became a king in England.[64]

Geoffrey of Brittany had fled to Paris to Philip II's court, and he died there, allegedly trampled to death under horses' hooves while fighting in a tournament. The second of Eleanor's adult sons to predecease her, he left two daughters and a widow, Constance of Brittany, pregnant with a third child. Geoffrey's posthumous son Arthur, named after the legendary king of the Britons, would inherit his father's place in the Plantagenet line of succession. Eventually this would cause his grandmother's estrangement from him, for her hatred of the boy's mother, Constance of Brittany, and the Breton nobles' discontent with Plantagenet rule impelled them to turn to the French king for protection. With Arthur a protégé of Philip, Eleanor would consider her young grandson a threat to her son John's right to succeed to the Plantagenet territories in France on Richard's death in 1199. Geoffrey's death in 1186 advanced John one step closer to the succession, and his inheritance to all Henry II's lands appeared a possibility. His father was in his fifties and suffering from poor health, his brother Richard was unmarried and preparing to embark on a perilous crusading venture to the Holy Land, and his nephew Arthur was not yet born. Clearly Henry was seeking to place John in a stronger position than any younger son had a right to expect, and Richard felt so threatened that he imagined that his father was about to alter the succession in John's favor.[65]

By 1187–88, Henry II was again proposing to shift John to Eleanor's patrimony. Rumors circulated that the Old King planned that Richard should succeed only to his English kingdom and that the duchy of Normandy with all his other French possessions, including Aquitaine, should pass to John. Whatever Henry's actual succession plans, Richard had no intention of surrendering Poitou, where he had held power for a dozen years, for the uncertain possibility of some day receiving a royal crown. No doubt, Eleanor shared Richard's rancor at this scheme for transferring her patrimony to John, and if she had the opportunity, she would have urged him to resist the proposal. Although Henry's ambition for John was probably less threatening than Richard imagined, he failed to win from his father the clear recognition that he sought as heir to the English Crown. The young count of Poitou's fears of being supplanted in the line of succession soon climbed to new heights, fed by rumors spreading from Philip II's court at Paris.

Eleanor could appreciate that Philip of France, following his accession in 1180, was proving more persistent and effective in exploiting the tensions between Henry II and his sons than his father had. Having first cultivated the friendship of Geoffrey of Brittany who died at the Capetian court, Philip II then turned to Richard who joined him at Paris as his guest in the summer of 1187. As Roger of Howden reports, "Between the two of them there grew up so great an affection that King Henry was much alarmed."[66] With Richard at Philip's court as his constant companion, the French king could plant additional doubts in his mind about Henry's supposed plan to replace him as heir, and Richard demanded that his father publicly designate him as his successor, refusing Henry's requests that he leave Paris and join him. Eventually Richard left Paris and returned to his mother's domains in the south to deal with the long-running conflict between the dukes of Aquitaine and the counts of Toulouse that had begun with Eleanor's grandmother.

Richard again made war on Toulouse in the spring of 1188, throwing his mercenaries into a massive assault on Count Raymond V's territory, long claimed by Eleanor, occupying a number of castles, ravaging the countryside, and approaching the city of Toulouse. Philip II came to Raymond's aid, trying to divert Richard's attention from Toulouse with an attack on the county of Berry on Poitou's eastern frontier; and in mid-June 1188 the fall of Châteauroux, long under Poitevin influence, had the desired effect. Henry was so alarmed at the potential threat of Capetian control of Berry to his own Angevin heartland that he left England in July, leading a large army to force the Capetian ruler's withdrawal. Henry, making what proved to be his final departure from England, paused at Salisbury, where Eleanor often resided, before moving on to the Channel coast. Perhaps the royal couple met there and spoke together at a final meeting.[67]

Despite Philip II's earlier support for the count of Toulouse, he and Richard had come to a secret agreement by autumn 1188, combining against Henry II, who was being worn down by incessant combat and recurrent illness. One can only guess what Eleanor knew of this new conspiracy against her hated husband. In Henry's last year of life, as his grip on power was loosening, it is likely that she had no trouble finding informants to tell her news of his perilous situation. At a mid-November confrontation between Henry and the two new allies at Bonmoulins on the Norman frontier, the English king knew that he was betrayed when he saw his son arriving in the company of Philip. Seeking to sharpen the enmity between father and son, the French king made demands of Henry in support of Richard. He insisted that the marriage of his half-sister Alix to Richard finally must go forward, that Richard take possession not only of his mother's duchy of Aquitaine, but of all his father's French provinces, and that the English barons do homage to Richard in acknowledgment that he was heir to the kingdom of England. The count of Poitou, driven by fears that the Old King was going to deprive him of his inheritance, then defied his father by kneeling before Henry's arch-enemy the French monarch and doing homage to him, asking his aid as lord in winning his rightful heritage. Henry left the meeting "full of fury and rage," saying "My children will never do anything that is good, all they will do is destroy me and themselves; they have always done me harm and injury."[68] The rivalry between the Plantagenet and Capetian monarchs turned into a war of succession before Henry's death with his heir allied with Philip II. Eleanor was about to have her wish for her husband's downfall fulfilled.

Negotiations in spring 1189 failed to defuse the crisis, and Richard's homage to the French monarch brought on more warfare that would wear Henry II down to his death. After Christmas 1188, his health was failing, and he was too ill to attend peace talks early in the new year. When he was well enough to take part in talks after Easter 1189, he found Philip II's conditions unacceptable. Soon after the talks broke down, Richard and Philip invaded Anjou and Maine to harry the ailing Henry, forcing him to flee. In this final struggle, Philip and his new ally drove a wedge into the Angevin heartland, prying Normandy apart from Aquitaine. As they overran the cities of the Loire valley, Henry, broken in body and in spirit, took refuge at Chinon Castle, ancestral stronghold of the counts of Anjou. Following the fall of Tours, the exhausted and defeated Henry set off to meet with his adversaries in such pain that he could neither sit nor stand. Only two days before his death, he meekly submitted to Philip's demands, recognizing Richard as lawful heir to all his lands, promising to do homage to the Capetian monarch for all his possessions in France, and admitting Capetian supremacy over disputed territories in the Auvergne and Berry. In addition, he promised to pay Philip a large cash indemnity, and he agreed to French occupation of three castles in either the Norman Vexin or in Anjou to guarantee fulfillment of his promises.

Henry II's hope of permanence for the domains that he had accumulated were doomed by the extraordinary hostility of his sons against him and against one another, and conflicts with his progeny had given a tragic quality to his last years. Doubtless his unfortunate marital situation—his wife held prisoner while he openly consorted with a series of mistresses—had reinforced his sons' hatred, extinguishing any filial feeling for him. Contemporaries saw the faithlessness of Henry's sons as God's just punishment for his sins, and many believed that prominent among his sins was his bigamous and incestuous marriage to Eleanor, lawfully wedded to Louis VII. News of the Old King's betrayal by John Lackland, his most beloved son, is thought to have hastened his death. Henry, on learning that John had gone over to Philip's side, asked, "Is it true that John, dear to me as my own heart, whom I have loved above all my sons, and for the sake of whose advancement I have endured all these evils, is it true that he has deserted me?"[69] At this news, weakened from his final illness and heart-broken at hearing John's name read out heading a list of traitors, Henry headed back to Chinon Castle. The Old King lost the will to continue his struggle for life. He lingered, unconscious, for three days, then died on 6 July 1189 at age fifty-six.

Henry II's faithful barons paid him the honor and respect due him in death. Preparing his body for public view, "They clothed him in his royal garments, since he was a king crowned and anointed, according to law and holy decree." Then they carried his bier from Chinon Castle for burial at Fontevraud Abbey, only a short distance away, where "with plain chant and a fine service [the nuns] received him as their master, as a mighty king ought to be received." It was left to two of the king's steadfast subjects, William Marshal and Geoffrey Plantagenet his bastard son, to make the burial arrangements. On Henry's death, an extraordinary midsummer heat wave forced the king's faithful followers to make a quick decision about his burial. They could spare no time transporting the king's body over the sea to Reading Abbey in England, intended by Henry's grandfather as a royal mausoleum, or by a long land journey to Grandmont Abbey in the Limousin, where Henry had expressed a wish to be buried. Nor could they take Henry's body to Le Mans for burial in the cathedral next to his father's tomb, for the city was in Philip II's hands.[70] Nor was there time to send to England for Eleanor to come to his entombment, even if she had felt a desire to be present. The spiteful writer Gerald of Wales pointed out the irony that Henry II's final resting place should have been Fontevraud, "a place so obscure and unsuitable for so great majesty," and "where he had striven eagerly with such great desire and such earnest endeavors to confine Queen Eleanor in a nun's habit."[71] Yet the austere beauty and peace of the chapel at Fontevraud with its four great domes over the nave supported by massive piers seems an appropriate setting for the tomb of Henry Plantagenet, a man careless of the outer trappings of power, but whose whole life was a ceaseless search for it.

Following Henry II's burial, his heir Richard Lionheart hastened to take control over his father's English kingdom and its rich resources. One of Richard's first acts was to order his mother Queen Eleanor liberated, even though her custodians had set her free as soon as rumors of the Old King's death reached England. Richard sent William Marshal, a knight known for his loyalty first to Young Henry and later to the Old King, to England with messages to important personages there. Among the recipients was Eleanor, now aged sixty-five, whom William Marshal found at Winchester, "now a free woman and in a more comfortable situation than she was wont to be." In the passage recording their meeting, the poet of the *History of William Marshal* points out that the name Aliénor was "an amalgam of 'pure' (*ali*) and 'gold' (*or*)," a compliment intended to signal that she lived up to her name.[72] The comment is uncharacteristic of an author who otherwise had little to say about women in his biography. Eleanor, however, had played a major role in launching Marshal's career, taking him into her service as a reward for his capture while defending her during the infamous foiled attempt to kidnap her two decades earlier in Poitou.

Eleanor had prevailed over Henry II by enduring a decade and a half of forced withdrawal from the royal court. The grim word "imprisonment" does not define accurately those years, as conditions improved for her over time, most markedly in the time between Matilda's arrival in England and Henry's death in July 1189. Yet in addition to Eleanor's isolation, those years brought to her the added sadness of the deaths of two of her sons, Young Henry in 1183 and Geoffrey of Brittany in 1186, and the loss of her eldest daughter Matilda in 1189. Worse for the queen was her frustration at her own political powerlessness, her inability to assist Young Henry in his quest for power to match his royal title or to aid Richard in opposing his father's changing succession schemes.

Simply by enduring and surviving her loss of freedom during Henry II's last years, Eleanor demonstrated the forbearance and fortitude that brought her victory over him. During the reigns of her surviving sons, Richard I and John, Eleanor would finally win the political influence that she had always craved, and her years as a widow would prove to be the most fulfilling of her life. In the last fifteen years of Eleanor's life, she would play an important role in England's politics, showing to all that she had preserved "not merely vitality and ability, but mental resources also of no ordinary character."[73] It is ironic that she should have profited from her contemplation during long hours of solitude imposed on her by her hated husband to draw lessons that she would apply later, working for the preservation of his Angevin empire.

CHAPTER 10

THE QUEEN-MOTHER: RICHARD'S REIGN, 1189–1199

It was in Eleanor of Aquitaine's widowhood that she came to exercise true political power, at last earning the reluctant respect of her contemporaries. During the reigns of her two surviving sons, Richard Lionheart, 1189–99, and John Lackland, 1199–1216, Eleanor manifested her strongest maternal feeling as she struggled to assist them in securing their inheritances and preserving their possessions. Widowhood was the time when aristocratic ladies gained greatest freedom of action, controlling their dowerlands, and Eleanor took advantage of her new-found freedom. She did not imitate some noble widows and quietly withdraw to her dowerlands, even though the purpose of a dower was to rid the heir's house of his mother's presence, leaving him with only his wife beside him.[1] Eleanor, long deprived of the political influence that she craved, had vast reserves of energy saved up during her 1174–89 captivity that she would willingly expend during her two sons' reigns, years that would be the most burdensome, yet active and rewarding, of her long life.[2]

Eleanor would live fifteen years as a widow, from age sixty-five to her death at age eighty, an extraordinary old age even though women in her epoch were living longer than men.[3] Her widowhood would consist of periods of semi-withdrawal from activity punctuated by two phases of furious activity, when she turned her energies to seeing her sons firmly in control of their scattered domains. During the first half of the Lionheart's reign, his mother's efforts at assisting him in securing the kingdom of England and protecting his hold on it during his absence on crusade and in captivity, 1190–94, were phenomenal for a woman of her advanced age. Following the Lionheart's death in April 1199, she flew into action after five years of repose to promote John's succession to Henry II's heritage. Although her primary consideration was always her own duchy of Aquitaine, she never doubted that her ancestral lands now belonged within the larger Angevin "empire" assembled by her hated husband. With her two sons succeeding him, she viewed those far-flung territories as a Poitevin empire as much as a Plantagenet one, and her weightiest cares would revolve around preserving their unity and dynastic continuity.

One consequence of Eleanor's activity as a widow was the English people's greater appreciation of her, indicated by a less negative tone adopted toward her by chroniclers, who added lighter shadings to their dark descriptions written during her two marriages. Only as a widow wielding power in defense of her son, Richard Lionheart, would Eleanor win her former critics' acceptance and forgiveness. So long as she was acting on behalf of the heroic crusader king, her straying into masculine spheres, exercising royal authority, even riding into battle, could be overlooked, and writers were willing to express their admiration for her. Richard of Devizes, the only chronicler to have left a character sketch of the queen, demonstrates a new desire to flatter Eleanor and her son. He describes her as "an incomparable woman, beautiful yet virtuous, powerful yet gentle, humble yet keen-witted, qualities which are most rarely found in a woman, who . . . had two kings as husbands and two kings as sons, still tireless in all labours, at whose ability her age might marvel."[4]

Eleanor's two royal sons shared strong feelings for her, and during their reigns she took precedence over their wives, enjoying the perquisites of a queen-consort.[5] During dangerous periods of transition from one reign to another, she symbolized as queen-mother the continuity of the Plantagenet line. Visible testimony to her high standing is her third seal used after her release from captivity. The new seal is similar to her earlier ones, except for some significant differences. It is the first of her seals to describe her as queen "by grace of God," a phrase adopted by Henry II in 1172. The portrait on the seal's obverse presents her in a more regal manner than on earlier ones, bearing the attributes of royalty. She wears a wimple topped by a three-pointed crown, and she holds in her right hand a scepter, a branch-like object with a fleur-de-lis atop it; in her left hand she no longer holds a bird, as on her previous seals, but an orb topped with a cross with a bird sitting on it. This unimpressive bird is sometimes identified as a falcon, common on aristocratic seals, or even as an eagle, perhaps a reminder of Merlin's prophecy that "the eagle of the broken covenant shall rejoice in her third nesting." Ralph Diceto in his account of the queen's release from captivity quoted this passage from the prophecies of Merlin found in Geoffrey of Monmouth's pseudo-history. He assumed that his readers could identify the eagle as Eleanor and the "third nesting" as a reference to her third son Richard. The bird on Eleanor's seal probably is not an eagle, however, but a dove, for a dove-topped orb is part of the English coronation regalia, and Henry II on his great seal was depicted holding such an orb.[6]

ELEANOR AND RICHARD'S ACCESSION TO ENGLAND'S CROWN

It is unlikely that any king ever received more valuable assistance from his mother than did Richard from Eleanor.[7] The new English monarch empowered her to hold England until he could arrive to take charge himself, and as a crowned queen she symbolized lawful royal authority in the kingdom until his arrival for his coronation. With her strong personality, she could dominate royal officials and assure administrative continuity. Although official records fail to reflect Eleanor's efforts on Richard's behalf, contemporary writers vividly depict her exertions. One chronicler wrote, "Queen Eleanor, who for many years had been under close guard, was entrusted with the power of acting as regent by her son. Indeed, he issued instructions to the princes of the realm, almost in the style of a general edict, that the queen's word should be law in all matters." He concluded, "To make up for his many excesses, [Richard] took care to show his mother all the honor that he could, that by obedience to his mother he should atone for the offenses committed against his father."[8]

Although Eleanor's position in England's government was not comparable to that of Philip II's mother in France, who was proclaimed official regent while her son was away on crusade,[9] she swiftly exerted herself on Richard's behalf, securing the kingdom for him and remedying the late king's abuses. Representing royal power, she gave legitimacy to the authority of the experienced and capable chief justiciar Ranulf de Glanvill, and his writs sometimes stated their authorization "by the queen's precept." The respect given Eleanor as queen-mother would give her a prominent part in English politics during the turbulent years of 1190–94, when the kingdom was threatened by her younger son John, count of Mortain, and by the Capetian king. She was a prominent force in England, enforcing royal directives, prohibiting a papal legate from entering the kingdom, attesting royal charters, and attending gatherings of the king's great council.[10]

Eleanor once more presided over an elaborate household after her release from imprisonment. It is not surprising that no Poitevin names appear among them after so many years of absence from her native land, not even Jordan, who had been her clerk in the days before Henry II's death. Prominent among her household officials was her butler, Ingelram. Pay for three men employed in her household was provided by annual grants from the exchequer: a clerk of her chapel, her cook, and a third described simply as "the queen's man." The duties of Adam her cook must have extended beyond the kitchen, for in April 1194, Richard I granted Adam land in Cumberland "for his service which he performed for our mother and our dear nephew Otto, son of the duke of Saxony," and Eleanor was recorded as the first witness to the charter.[11] She showed her gratitude to faithful servants with gifts, and before her retirement to Fontevraud late in Richard's reign, she made grants to her children's former wet-nurse, to a former servant of her eldest son, Young Henry, and after she settled at the abbey, to her butler Ingelram.[12]

The queen-mother's prominence in England's governance after her release from captivity required her to issue many letters and charters, and in her household were a half dozen or more clerks. Those employed as scribes were likely royal clerks temporarily transferred to her service.[13] Although none bore the official title of chancellor, a likely candidate for head of her writing office is Herbert le Poer, archdeacon of Canterbury before he became bishop of Salisbury in 1194. Herbert was a longtime royal clerk, probably transferred to the queen-mother's household soon after she was freed. He belonged to an administrative family and was possibly an illegitimate son of Richard of Ilchester, whose service to Henry II as one of his "evil counselors" during the Becket quarrel had won him the wealthy bishopric of Winchester in 1173. Other household clerks were attached to the queen's chapel, for example Adam of Wilton, "clerk of the queen's chapel," serving her spiritual needs as chaplains or as her almoner distributing alms on her behalf.[14]

A chronicler described Eleanor after her release from captivity: "Circulating with a queenly court, she set out from city to city and castle to castle just as it pleased her." The chronicler must have chosen the uncommon term "queenly court" instead of "royal court" purposely to draw attention to the extraordinary sight of a female exercising royal authority. The queen sent representatives to all the counties of England to take free men's oaths of fidelity to their new king. These royal agents were ordered to release captives imprisoned by the king's will alone, not by the law of the realm, and also those held for offences against the arbitrary forest law, while those lawfully imprisoned were to be released once they found sureties for their appearance at trial. The chronicler continued, commenting, "In her own person she demonstrated how grievous unjust imprisonment was for men, and how release aroused in them joyful revival of spirits." He added that Eleanor freed prisoners because her own experience had taught her that "confinement is distasteful to mankind, and that it is a most delightful refreshment to the spirits to be liberated therefrom."[15] Certainly Eleanor could feel for those arbitrarily imprisoned by her late husband, but her proclamation was not a general amnesty emptying the jails, for conditions for prisoners' release were specific and consistent with legal principles and practices. The monastic writer William of Newburgh, nonetheless, was disgusted that freeing them had unleashed "these pests" back onto society only to terrorize decent subjects more confidently in the future.[16] Another chronicler commented more favorably, recognizing her action as redressing Henry II's despotic deeds. She curbed "the depredations of those . . . charged with the care of the forests, intimidating them with the threat of severe penalties"; he also hails her ending of Henry's habit of housing his horses in the stables of abbeys, remarking that she "distributed them with pious liberality."[17]

Although Eleanor's first concern in the weeks after Henry's death was assisting Richard's smooth accession to England's throne, she did not forget a widow's duty to provide prayers for her departed husband's soul. She assigned income of the vacant bishopric of Winchester as alms on Henry's behalf and also made grants to the nuns of Amesbury and to the Carthusian brothers for his soul.[18] In old age, Eleanor was finally fulfilling the role that her English subjects considered proper for their queens, tempering the king's harsh rule with mercy and busying herself with spiritual matters.

Eleanor met Richard at Winchester soon after his landing at Portsmouth on 13 August 1189 to join his entourage. When he learned that English castles on the southern frontier of Wales were being attacked by the Welsh, his first impulse was to march immediately to their relief, but heeding his mother's counsel, he continued on his way to Westminster for his coronation.[19] In preparation for the queen-mother's participation in the coronation festivities, over £100 was spent on clothing, furs, horses and their harness, and other items to ensure that she and her entourage made an appropriately splendid impression. Her household now included a number of noble maidens in her care, among them Alix of France, Richard's long-suffering fiancée and victim of Henry II's lust; Count John's betrothed, Isabelle, daughter of the deceased earl of Gloucester; and Denise of Déols, heir to the lordship of Berry and soon to be the bride of Andrew of Chauvigny, one of Richard's Poitevin stalwarts.[20] Andrew had ties of kinship with Eleanor through her Châtellerault ancestors, and his kinsmen had supplied officials for the counts of Poitou. Bernard de Chauvigny had served as the queen's chamberlain during her first years in England, and Richard as count of Poitou had made Geoffrey de Chauvigny his chamberlain.[21] Eleanor acknowledged her ties to both Andrew and Denise by attending their wedding at Salisbury.[22]

Richard took care to ensure that his mother had adequate wealth for maintaining a standard of living appropriate for a great queen, although as duchess of Aquitaine she was already rich and powerful in her own right. The division of the duchy's resources between Richard and his mother is unclear, but Eleanor evidently felt no constraint on making grants from Poitou's revenues. As duke of Normandy, Richard granted his mother income from some Norman administrative agencies.[23] As English king, he confirmed to her as queen-mother the dowerlands granted her by Henry II, adding a proviso that she should have all that Henry I and Stephen had bestowed on their queens, providing her with a substantial income independent of annual exchequer grants.[24] Eleanor's dower included twenty-six properties in England, among them such rich towns as Chichester, Northampton, and Exeter, and three baronial honors, Arundel, Berkhamstead, and Berkeley. Among her dower-lands on the Continent were three Norman towns that brought her the equivalent of more than £200 sterling a year, three other towns in the Touraine, and one in Maine as well as Poitevin lands and castles.[25]

Supplementing Eleanor's dower income were other sources of cash, expense monies paid from the exchequer for such items as clothing for herself and for the maidens in her household. As Henry II's consort, Eleanor had received queen's gold, a portion of sums paid to the king by petitioners as offerings for favors; and she continued to collect queen's gold throughout her life, even after Richard Lionheart's marriage to Berengaria of Navarre and John's marriage to Isabelle of Angoulême.[26] Its value is shown by an 1190 incident in the midst of Richard's fund-raising for his crusade, when Eleanor received as queen's gold a great golden chalice valued at 100 marks (about £67), offered by the monks of Bury Saint Edmunds instead of cash. The queen returned the vessel to the monks for the sake of the soul of her late husband Henry II.[27]

In spring 1190, after Richard had crossed to Normandy, he summoned his mother, his brother John, his illegitimate brother Geoffrey Plantagenet, and several bishops to a great council at Nonancourt. This council's purpose was to lay out plans for governing the new king's lands during his expedition to the Holy Land, and he provided funds for his mother's travel. Richard had taken the cross in 1187, and it is his leadership of the Third Crusade, 1190–92, that makes him the best known of all medieval English monarchs. During Eleanor's voyage across the Channel her mind must have turned to her own hardships endured on the Second Crusade more than forty years earlier, and her memories would have aroused fears for her son's safety. Making the crossing with Eleanor were noble maidens in her entourage, among them her granddaughter Eleanor of Brittany, the unfortunate Alix of France, and the daughter of the countess of Eu. Also traveling with her was a great lady, Hawise, countess of Aumale, Normandy, lady of Skipton and Holderness in northern England, and the widow of the earl of Essex.[28] A strong-willed lady similar to the queen-mother, a contemporary described her as "a woman who was almost a man, lacking nothing virile except the virile organs." Richard aimed to give her in marriage to William de Forz, one of his faithful knights in Poitou and a descendant of functionaries in the service of Eleanor and her predecessors.[29]

At the Nonancourt council, the new king made provision for his sole surviving brother during his absence on crusade. He handed over to John control of six shires in England and the county of Mortain in Normandy, and he confirmed his title of lord of Ireland, making him a dangerously over-mighty subject in the British isles. Richard's generosity to John in his strongly governed kingdom and his wealthiest French province gave his brother scope for causing trouble, although the king apparently felt confident that his weak character left him incapable of causing serious mischief. Establishing the new count of Mortain in so powerful a position led some of Richard's subjects to surmise that he did not expect to return from his crusade, and they feared that if he did, "His brother, already no less powerful than he and eager to rule, would defeat him and drive him out of the kingdom."[30] Richard's lavish grants to John seemed an implicit declaration of his intent that John should be his heir in case of his death overseas. He saw that an explicit statement, however, would have encouraged the count's bad behavior, as Henry II's unhappy experience with Young King Henry had shown.

The Lionheart perhaps expected that two checks would discourage his brother from doing harm. One was their mother Eleanor's influence, and the other was John's oath to remain outside England during his brother's absence from the kingdom, but neither worked as expected. First, Eleanor was away from England for several months in 1190–91, accompanying Richard as far as Chinon in Anjou, then crossing Aquitaine to Spain and across the Midi to conduct Richard's bride to his camp at Messina in Sicily, where he was wintering before sailing to the Holy Land. The second precaution, Count John's promise at Nonancourt not to return to England for three years, was soon undone apparently through Eleanor's pressing Richard to free him from his oath.[31] She hardly knew her youngest son, who had grown up during her long captivity, and like Richard, she underestimated his capacity for trouble-making, or perhaps she expected that John's awareness of his advantage as Richard's presumed heir would induce him to behave himself. In fact, John surfaced "in active mischief" once his mother was far from England on her long journey to Spain and Sicily, although open moves against the regency government would begin only after he heard of his brother's formal declaration of young Arthur of Brittany as heir late in 1190.[32] Once the queen-mother returned to the Anglo-Norman realm in 1191 she exerted her maternal pressure on her last-born son, succeeding in preventing him from rushing off to join Philip II following the French king's premature return from the crusade in anger and frustration at Richard.

At Nonancourt, the Lionheart named two chief justiciars to govern England jointly in his absence, but this scheme promptly collapsed on the death of one of them, William de Mandeville, earl of Essex. The king then began tinkering with his plan that ultimately would leave one of the co-justiciars, William Longchamp, bishop of Ely, solely in charge of the kingdom. Longchamp's power rested on his control over the royal seal as royal chancellor, a sign of Richard's confidence that in effect handed over to him the administration of the realm. By limiting authority of the other co-justiciar, the bishop of

Durham, to the north of England, Richard had given Longchamp an excuse to exclude him from Westminster, the center for royal administration. Finally in June 1190, Richard acknowledged Longchamp's supremacy, declaring him chief justiciar of all England. On the same day that the king's letter arrived, news came that the pope had conferred on Longchamp spiritual authority over the Church in the island kingdom as papal legate. One chronicler's claims that Longchamp had "three titles and three heads" and that he had become "Caesar and more than Caesar" ring true.[33] Apparently Richard's trust either created or encouraged an arrogance and ambition within his chancellor that would ultimately bring him to ruin.

The issue of Richard's marriage was doubtless a topic for discussion during the Nonancourt conference. It may have been at that time that he revealed to his mother his plan to marry Berengaria of Navarre, and he requested her to travel to Spain and bring his bride to him in Sicily.[34] Among Eleanor's weightiest concerns was the Lionheart's marriage and the birth of a son and heir that would ensure dynastic continuity and preserve the unity of the Plantagenet holdings. She knew well the many dangers that lay ahead for a crusader king. Years earlier, Richard had been betrothed to Alix, daughter of Louis VII and half-sister of Philip II, but he had always balked at wedding the Capetian princess, probably because of his belief that his own father had seduced her.[35]

Despite Eleanor's anxieties, Richard himself showed few worries about the succession, confident that he would survive the dangers of an expedition to the Levant and live long enough to sire heirs.[36] His mother was wary of the potential heirs to Richard—his sole surviving brother, John, count of Mortain in Normandy; her grandson Arthur of Brittany; and Richard's half-brother Geoffrey Plantagenet, a cleric in minor orders. At Messina in Sicily, before sailing for the Holy Land, the Lionheart would name his nephew, Arthur of Brittany as his heir. Eleanor considered the child Arthur unacceptable because of the ferocious hostility of his Breton mother toward her Plantagenet in-laws. Eleanor can hardly have had much sympathy for Geoffrey, her late husband's beloved bastard son, and she opposed Richard's honoring his father's wishes by naming him archbishop of York.[37] Before Geoffrey could be consecrated, he had to take priestly vows, making him less credible as a potential king, and like John, he was barred from entering the kingdom for three years. Notwithstanding any doubts that Eleanor harbored about her youngest son's character, she apparently viewed him as the sole suitable successor to the English throne should Richard die without direct heir, and possibly her insistence that Richard release John from his obligation of remaining outside the kingdom reflects her concern for his succession.

A chronicle from the crusader kingdom maintains that Eleanor was the instigator of Richard's marriage to Berengaria because her hatred and resentment of the king of France and his offspring led her to prevent at any price her son's marriage to a daughter of Louis VII.[38] This work is a continuation of William of Tyre's chronicle that had recorded the Antioch affair that had brought public attention to Eleanor's troubles with her first husband. It is unlikely, however, that Richard Lionheart was "bullied into marriage by his formidable mother" or that she can be credited with negotiating his marriage to Berengaria of Navarre.[39] Despite Eleanor's feelings about Richard's choice of a bride or her fears for the succession, her son's marriage to a princess from the Pyrenean kingdom must be seen as his own plan. Allying himself with Berengaria's father, King Sancho VI (d.1194), and her brother, the future Sancho VII, formed part of a program for stabilizing Gascony. Richard saw the match as "an ingenious diplomatic device . . . in order to cut his way through a thicket of political problems," probably proposed by him as early as February 1190 at a great council of the Gascon nobility at La Réole. It was appropriate to discuss the proposal with his Gascon lords, for the duchy of Gascony featured in discussions of the marriage alliance. He proposed granting his income from Gascony to his bride as her dower to enjoy until Eleanor's death when she would gain possession of all the queen-mother's dowerlands in England and Normandy. Because Navarre and other Christian kingdoms in northern Spain played important roles in the politics and diplomacy of southwestern France, Richard's alliance gained him aid in protecting his southern flank from aggression by Count Raymond V of Toulouse. The count, the only important neighboring prince who had not taken the cross, was a potential trouble-maker during Richard's long absence on crusade.[40]

ELEANOR AND ENGLAND DURING RICHARD'S ABSENCE, 1190–1194

At Chinon on 24 June 1190, Eleanor said farewell to Richard, and he rode off to meet Philip II at Vézelay to set out on the Third Crusade. Before leaving the Loire valley, she took time to sit on a tribunal at Saumur alongside the seneschal of Anjou to settle a dispute between the abbess of Fontevraud and the town's mayor.[41] Soon afterward, Eleanor, then in her mid-sixties, set off for Spain to fetch her son's bride Berengaria and bring her to him in Sicily, where he would be wintering in 1190–91. Although it is unlikely that the queen-mother had taken part in Richard's marriage negotiations, there is no doubt that her mission to Sancho VI was a delicate one requiring shrewd diplomacy, for she had to reassure him about the seriousness of her son's intention to set aside his French fiancée in favor of the Navarese princess.[42] Sancho would have demanded assurances that the English king had extricated himself from his previous betrothal, a difficult task since Richard dared not confront Philip II about his wish to break off the betrothal. He feared that such an affront to the honor of the French king's sister would so infuriate Philip that he would refuse to continue their joint crusading mission. By late January 1191, Eleanor had crossed the Alps with Richard's bride, and once they reached Italy, they continued southward for sixty-eight days, meeting the Lionheart at Reggio on 30 March.[43] Richard could not postpone approaching Philip II, by then in Sicily, about release from his betrothal to Alix, and only the news that his sister had borne Henry II a child caused the French king to comprehend that Richard would never consent to a marriage with her.[44] This scandalous revelation embittered all the more relations between the two crusader kings.

During the queen's travels from Spain to Sicily, it was becoming clear to the English that Richard's plan for governing the kingdom in his absence faced two dangerous threats. One was widespread animosity against his Norman-born viceroy, William Longchamp, and the other was reckless plotting by Count John. Due to the grave situation in England, Eleanor could not tarry after delivering Richard's bride, and she remained in Messina only three days before beginning the long journey back to Angevin territory. She could enjoy only a hurried reunion with her youngest daughter, Joanne, widowed queen of Sicily, whom she had not seen since 1176.[45] Yet Eleanor took advantage of her brief visit with Joanne to insist that she accompany her brother and his bride on the voyage to Palestine to see that Richard's wedding would actually take place, since it could not be held until the end of Lent. Joanne and Berengaria would sail away with Richard's crusading fleet only to be shipwrecked off the coast of Cyprus, but on the island on 12 May 1191 Eleanor's desire that Richard should finally be married was fulfilled, and now she could hope for a grandchild.

Eleanor's daughter Joanne, a young and childless widow, found herself in a pitiable position in Sicily, stripped of funds, until her brother came to her rescue after his landing there at the end of summer 1190. Her marriage to King William II was childless, and his death left the succession to the Sicilian Crown uncertain. Taking advantage of the disputed succession to seize control of the kingdom was the late king's bastard nephew, Tancred of Lecce; but his claim was contested by a powerful rival, the German ruler and claimant to the imperial title, Henry VI. He claimed the Sicilian Crown through the right of his wife, the late king's aunt, and he was planning an expedition to Sicily to confront Tancred. Because Tancred had sequestered Joanne's dowerlands, one of Richard's reasons for his long stopover on the island was to recover her dower right, as well as to claim treasure left by her late husband to finance the crusade that he did not live to join. The Lionheart pressured Tancred into promptly releasing Joanne and restoring her extensive properties.[46] Because of the complicated Sicilian situation, Eleanor had taken on the task of meeting with Henry VI once she reached northern Italy in January 1191 on her journey southward with Richard's bride.[47] She needed to assure him that her son would do nothing during his stopover in Sicily to jeopardize his claim to the southern kingdom.

Once the queen returned to the north from Italy, she seems to have passed the winter of 1191–92 at one of her dower manors, Bonneville-sur-Touques in Normandy.[48] Soon, however, she had to cross to England once more to deal with the collapse of Richard's flawed scheme for governing England in his absence. Longchamp, bishop of Ely and royal chancellor, was concentrating all authority in his own hands. Eleanor's role and her effectiveness during the resulting crises can refute any notion that she was "merely a royal figurehead" for the competent professional clerks and household knights who staffed the Angevin royal administration. Possibly an indicator of her assurance of her own authority is that she began to attest documents with the phrase, *teste me ipsa*, meaning "as my own witness," as she had done occasionally in Poitou earlier. She used this phrase chiefly in orders sent to regional officials to redress grievances that had come to her attention, and it reveals her "personal interest and intervention" as well as her "direct responsibility."[49]

William Longchamp was seizing complete control of England's governance, and he used his position as chancellor in custody of the king's seal to confirm his standing as Richard's chief deputy.[50] He aimed to take full advantage of the free hand that the king had given him. Longchamp's pride and his certainty of royal support made him careless, however, and he engaged in activity that snowballed into political disaster. Despite Longchamp's administrative abilities and the king's confidence, as a foreigner of obscure origin he lacked the respect of the English baronage; and his financial extortions, imperious manner, contempt for the English, and ignorance of their customs soon aroused the barons' incipient xenophobia. Furthermore, his "foreign" origin inspired mockery of his physical appearance and innuendo about his sexual proclivities with claims that he stocked the Ely cathedral chapter with handsome young canons to satisfy his lust.[51]

Longchamp's chief problem in governing the kingdom was the power of the king's brother, Count John, whose position not only as an over-powerful magnate but as the likely successor to the English throne presented insurmountable difficulties for the low-born chancellor.[52] The count of Mortain seized the opportunity presented by Longchamp's unpopularity to enhance his position by heading baronial opposition to the chancellor's authoritarian rule. Before setting sail from Sicily for Palestine, the Lionheart had refused to listen to complaints from England about his deputy's high-handed conduct. Even if Eleanor tried to convince Richard of Longchamp's misconduct, she could not have confirmed the charges against him or convinced the king to take action, for she had been absent from the kingdom for too long to have been aware of recent outrages. By the time she met her son at Messina at the end of March 1191, he had already sent letters to England responding to the alarming reports of his viceroy's misgovernment.[53]

Royal representatives were sent off to England to act as counter-weights to Longchamp's authority. Most important was Walter of Coutances, archbishop of Rouen and a longtime royal servant, who accompanied Eleanor on the return to Angevin territory from Sicily. Walter arrived in England in the spring of 1191 in time to try to mediate the quarrel between the chancellor and Count John. The archbishop carried with him letters from the Lionheart, whose contents had the effect of forcing Longchamp to share authority with him as one who knew the king's will, thereby undermining the chancellor's authority. Once Walter landed in England, he found that the situation was indeed critical. A council was called for the end of July at Winchester to relieve tensions between Count John and the chancellor, but both arrived accompanied by large armed bands. In the historic city a truce was patched together that pulled the opponents back from the brink of warfare. Although the Winchester agreement clearly worked to Longchamp's disadvantage, neither John nor Walter of Coutances left with any greater role in the government than before. Longchamp continued to disregard the king's command that he include the archbishop in his inner circle of advisers, claiming that his innate knowledge of the king's will trumped royal letters brought by Walter, which he dismissed as fraudulent.

The other counter-weight to Longchamp sent to England by the king was Geoffrey Plantagenet, Richard's bastard half-brother, whom he had nominated as archbishop of York. Once installed as archbishop, Geoffrey could be expected to restrain Longchamp's power over the English Church as papal legate. Eleanor had stopped in Rome on her way from Sicily in order to lobby a newly installed pope for Longchamp's confirmation in his post of papal legate. At the same time, setting aside her hostility toward Geoffrey, she sought his swift consecration as archbishop of York, and she spent heavily to purchase support at the papal *curia*, changing 800 marks with Roman money-changers.[54] When Geoffrey Plantagenet landed at Dover in September 1191 on his way to his new archiepiscopal see, Longchamp overplayed his hand and had him seized by force and jailed. Geoffrey's mistreatment called to mind another authoritarian ruler's attack on another English archbishop two decades earlier.

The outrage against Archbishop Geoffrey of York on his landing at Dover energized Longchamp's opponents and neutralized his supporters. Rising to the occasion, John summoned a great council at Marlborough, where he lodged complaints before the bishops and barons, charging that the truce negotiated at Winchester had been broken and his half-brother unlawfully arrested. Longchamp was summoned to answer these indictments at a later session of the council, where John and his followers raised charges of Geoffrey's arrest, and Archbishop Walter of Rouen added an accusation of obstructing the implementation of royal commands. After several days the chancellor surrendered to the council, and he was stripped of his authority as chief justiciar, compelled to hand over the king's seal, and forced to flee the country. He headed for Dover, and according to his adversaries' accounts, he suffered additional indignities before his escape across the Channel to Normandy at the end of October, caught fleeing in a woman's disguise. The assembly now had to determine his successor, and Count John gained recognition as heir to the Crown and the title of supreme governor of England, but won no meaningful role in government, while Walter of Coutances was to head the administration, taking on the chief justiciar's duties.

The *History of William Marshal* states that Walter of Coutances "acted well and wisely, by the advice of the Marshal and of the barons, and also by the advice of the queen." Eleanor was a central figure in Walter's counsels from his arrival in England in spring 1191 until the end of 1193, and her endorsement was essential for giving credibility to his governance in the king's absence. Gerald of Wales, no fan of Eleanor, states that his appointment as an envoy to the Welsh came from the authority of the queen, Walter as justiciar, and the chancellor Longchamp.[55] Philip II's return to western Europe in the summer of 1191 after withdrawing from the crusade added to the difficulties in holding England for the absent King Richard. It tempted Count John, already thwarted in securing a larger role in the regency, to betray his brother. In January 1192, Eleanor had to deal with Philip's demand that his sister Alix, the rejected fiancée of Richard, be returned to the French court.

The queen-mother, while on her estates in Normandy, learned of the Capetian king's courtship of John with the tempting offer of all Richard's French lands and marriage to Alix. She sailed for England on 11 February 1192 to alert Walter of Coutances and to intercept "the light-minded youth" before he could cross the Channel to join Philip II's court. John's flirtation with Philip was only circumvented by Eleanor's insistence that he remain in England. At a series of councils, "through her own tears and the prayers of the nobles," John was persuaded to promise that he would not go to Philip.[56] Count John remained quiet for the time being, and a precarious peace prevailed until word reached England that the Lionheart had been taken captive in Germany. Despite Eleanor's efforts at corralling the wayward John, she found time to turn to lesser matters of state. She joined the citizens of London in appealing for easy terms for a citizen saddled with a heavy fine of over £500 for counterfeiting. She also sought, unsuccessfully, to reconcile two quarrelling northern prelates, Geoffrey, archbishop of York, and Hugh de Puiset, bishop of Durham, by summoning them to a council at London.[57]

Eleanor also tried to relieve the ill-effects of the bitter quarrel between the exiled William Longchamp and Walter of Coutances. When Longchamp placed his diocese of Ely under an interdict and excommunicated his former colleagues in the English government, the archbishop of Rouen excommunicated him in retaliation and seized his episcopal estates.[58] The queen-mother, making a circuit of Cambridgeshire in 1192, saw the misery that Longchamp's sanctions were causing the devout of his diocese. She witnessed "a people weeping and pitiful with bare feet, unwashed clothes, and unkempt hair," lamenting that their deceased relatives were denied burial in consecrated ground. "They spoke by their tears," and Eleanor understood at once their distress without an interpreter, despite her ignorance of the English language after almost forty years as queen of England. Moved by their suffering, she became a prime mover in forcing the chancellor and the archbishop to patch up their quarrel causing such woe to innocent people, persuading them to withdraw their mutual excommunications of each other and their supporters. Richard of Devizes asked, "And who could be so savage or cruel that this woman could not bend him to her wishes?"[59] As a perceptive writer notes, in this episode, Eleanor's determination in dealing with these two powerful prelates was "entirely typical of Angevin methods of government: it might have been employed by Henry or Richard."[60]

On Eleanor's return to London in March 1192, new difficulties awaited her, for Longchamp had landed at Dover seeking to reclaim some measure of authority—at least his post as papal legate. She had some sympathy for the deposed justiciar, a faithful official of her son Richard, and she suspected that the king would not have sanctioned his removal, had he been fully informed of the situation. The new justiciar, Walter of Coutances, and other great men had no interest in rehabilitating Longchamp, although they were unwilling to act against him without the approval of either the queen-mother or Count John. Contentious talks at a great council convinced Eleanor that she could never overcome their opposition, and she gave up any attempt at reconciling the chancellor and the magnates. She warned Longchamp to leave England at once to avoid arrest, and he departed in haste.[61]

The greatest crisis of the Lionheart's reign was his imprisonment in Germany, and the queen-mother assumed a position of direct authority in England early in 1193, once news arrived. Count John had menaced the kingdom's peace since Philip II's return from the crusade, and now he saw his elder brother's captivity as an opportunity to carry out his claim to be the successor to the Plantagenet domains; indeed, he acted as if Richard's return from Germany alive was unlikely.[62] As soon as John learned of his brother's imprisonment, he rushed to France in early January 1193, making straight for the Capetian court to do homage to Philip for his brother's French domains. When John later returned to England with a mercenary force, declaring his brother dead and demanding recognition as king, the regency government, rallied by Eleanor, refused to believe him and remained loyal to the captive king. Following the council's flat refusal to support John, hostilities broke out as he occupied castles and the government sent forces to besiege them, and low-level conflict would continue almost until Richard's return to his kingdom. The possibility of a French invasion in aid of John loomed, and Eleanor took action in February 1193 to defend England from a hostile fleet, ordering that the coasts facing Flanders be strongly fortified. In a Canterbury chronicler's words, these orders were issued "by command of Queen Eleanor, who at that time ruled England."[63] The expense of fighting Count John could no longer be borne once a huge ransom was demanded for the king's release, making a truce essential for the regency government in order to conserve funds required for freeing Richard. When the truce was arranged, John surrendered the royal castles of Windsor, Wallingford, and the Peak "into the hand of Queen Eleanor," although two, Nottingham and Tickhill, remained in his hands.[64]

The queen-mother played an active part in ecclesiastical affairs during Richard's absence, involving herself as early as November 1189 in the long-simmering dispute between the archbishop of Canterbury and his monks of Christchurch Cathedral. When a papal legate landed in England to settle the controversy, Eleanor stopped him at Canterbury because of his arrival without royal permission, and she prevented his proceeding farther.[65] Also illustrating Eleanor's influence is her role in the Canterbury election of 1193 during Richard's captivity. The archbishopric of Canterbury fell vacant twice while the king was beyond the sea. During the first election at the end of 1191, the queen-mother also was absent from the kingdom; nonetheless, the Canterbury monks wrote to her, entreating her to support their right of free election.[66] Exercising their right of election without waiting for royal approval, they provoked the regency council's protests, but the conflict soon ended when their choice as archbishop died only a month after his consecration.

Eleanor played an active part in the second Canterbury election, made necessary by the new archbishop's sudden death. Only in early 1193, while Richard was a prisoner in Germany, did his wishes in this election become known. The king nominated as new primate his trusted adviser in the Holy Land, Hubert Walter, bishop of Salisbury, and he sent three letters from Germany on 30 March authorizing an election by the monks of Canterbury Cathedral and supporting Hubert Walter's candidacy. The first letter, addressed to Eleanor, recounted Hubert Walter's efforts at the papal court and before the German emperor seeking his release and asked her to work for his election. In Richard's letter to Eleanor, he used more affectionate language than normal in royal letters, calling her "dearest mother" and "sweetest mother." The second letter was addressed to government officials, urging them to support Hubert Walter; and the third, addressed to the Canterbury monks, commanded them to seek the advice of Queen Eleanor and William de Sainte-Mère-Eglise, a trusted royal clerk, when choosing their new archbishop. The Canterbury monks elected Richard's candidate in May 1193, with Eleanor quieting the spat that perennially arose between the prelates and the Christchurch monks over their rival claims to the right of election. Richard, unaware that the election had taken place in accordance with his wishes, wrote from Germany again in early June urging his mother to settle the matter by going to Canterbury herself.[67]

Richard Lionheart's imprisonment must have raised his mother's dismal memories of her own years spent in confinement, and three letters in Eleanor's name seeking papal support for Richard's liberation survive. These letters display a mother's pain and distress, as well as her contempt and anger at the pope's passivity. The pope was the newly elected Celestine III, chosen by the cardinals after a stalled election because he was the oldest among them at age eighty-five. As pontiff, he was preoccupied with maintaining good relations with the German emperor Henry VI, and he was not prepared to challenge the emperor for Richard's sake, even if the captive king was, as a crusader, under papal protection.

The queen-mother in her fury at her son's unjust imprisonment styles herself in one letter "Eleanor, by the wrath of God Queen of England," but in another more anguished one, she is "Eleanor, pitiable and hoping in vain to be pitied." In the letters she expresses an almost religious devotion for Richard, describing him as "the soldier of Christ, the anointed of the Lord, the pilgrim of the cross." She stresses Richard's sacral character derived from his coronation, constantly referring to him as "the Lord's anointed." She blames herself for his misfortune. "Mother of mercy look upon a mother so wretched, or else if your Son, an unexhausted source of mercy, requires from the son the sins of the mother, then let him exact complete vengeance on me, for I am the only one to offend, and let him punish me, for I am the irreverent one." The unhappy queen's angry words reveal both her combative spirit and her disquiet over her inability to secure his release. She reproaches the two monarchs, Philip II and Henry VI, who were standing in the way of his release: "the cruelty of the tyrant who does not stop making an unjust war against the king because of his greed; that tyrant who keeps him bound in prison-chains (after the king had been caught during a Holy Crusade, under the protection of God above and under the safeguard of the Roman Church)." Eleanor denounces Celestine III for tolerating their shameful crimes of imprisoning her crusader son and ravaging his lands, pointing out that he sees all these wrongs, "yet keeps the sword of Peter sheathed, and thus gives the sinner added boldness, his silence being presumed to indicate consent." She acidly reminds the pope of his failure to give Richard the protection owed him as a crusader, declaring that "you have not sent those princes even one messenger from those around you ... you still do not send even one sub-deacon, not even one acolyte ..." She suggests that the Holy See would not be harmed "if you had gone to Germany in person for the release of such a great prince."[68]

These three letters are often labeled inauthentic, dismissed as simply rhetorical exercises neither written by Eleanor nor for her. Even if royal letters were routinely composed by clerks, the possibility of their reflecting something of their nominal author's own feelings can be conceded. One of Eleanor's biographers writes, "I like to think that [in certain phrases] we have either Eleanor's own words or the words of someone who captured her feelings exactly." It seems clear that the letters were written on Eleanor's behalf by Peter of Blois, one of the greatest twelfth-century letter writers. Peter had accompanied the queen-mother on her return to the north from Sicily in 1191, and afterward was a sometime member of her household. Peter wrote two other letters seeking Richard's release, one to the pope in the name of the archbishop of Rouen and another in his own name to the archbishop of Mainz, a friend from student days in Paris years earlier.[69] Genuine or not, the three letters are an accurate reflection of the aged Eleanor's anguish and anger, showing her awareness that her own efforts to free her captive son were crucial, since she could not count on the pope's help.

Eleanor's immediate concern was the prompt raising of the staggering sum of 150,000 marks demanded by the German emperor as ransom for her son's release. In a letter addressed to his mother and the regency council in April 1193, Richard urged them to begin raising quickly an initial 70,000 marks to expedite his release in exchange for hostages. Eleanor, sharing responsibility for raising the ransom with Walter of Coutances, risked the popularity that she had won since Henry II's death in approving the burdensome levies required. They demanded a quarter of the value of all moveable goods and one pound on each knight's fee along with all English churches' gold and silver, although the austere Cistercian and Gilbertine houses, lacking treasure, contributed their wool crop instead. Levies for Richard's ransom fell not only on the English, but also on his subjects across the Channel; all monastic houses in Aquitaine were compelled to pay an aid.[70]

The monks of Bury Saint Edmunds offered as part of their contribution the golden chalice previously presented to Eleanor as queen's gold and returned to them by her. Indicating her authority and her charity is her action in redeeming the costly cup and restoring it to them once more. In appreciation, the monks responded with a charter promising never again to let the chalice out of their house's possession.[71] In early June the queen-mother attended a council at St Albans where trustees were named to hold the treasure raised for the king's ransom; they were to deposit it in chests at Saint Paul's Cathedral sealed with her seal and that of the archbishop of Rouen. The campaign for raising the ransom was complete by December when Henry VI announced that Richard would be released in mid-January 1194.

Richard's mother and his new archbishop of Canterbury, Hubert Walter, set out for Germany with the first ransom money, and it is remotely possible that her journey took her through the county of Champagne. If so, Eleanor may have had a reunion there with the countess Marie, her daughter by Louis VII. It is unlikely that they had seen each other since Eleanor's departure from the Capetian court in 1152, when Marie was a girl of seven; and it was their last opportunity to meet, for Marie would die in March 1198 at the age of fifty-three.[72] Eleanor's second daughter by her first marriage, Adelicia, widow of the count of Blois, also died about this time, although the exact date of her death is unknown.

The queen-mother arrived at Cologne for the feast of the Epiphany, and by mid-January 1194 she had reached Speyer, where her son was being held. She attended an assembly of bishops and magnates meeting at Mainz on 2 February to consider final terms for Richard's release. One detail to settle was the selection of hostages to be left behind to guarantee full payment of the 150,000-mark ransom; among the hostages were two of Eleanor's German grandsons—sons of her daughter, Matilda, duchess of Saxony. When Henry VI at the last minute pressured Richard to surrender England to him as an imperial fief, paying an annual tribute of £5,000, Eleanor counseled her son to accede to the demand in order to speed his release.[73] Two days later, on 4 February, the English king was finally freed, landing safely in England on 13 March. Eleanor accompanied him on his progress about the kingdom and was present at the end of March and in early April at a great council in Nottingham, when the king reordered his kingdom. He dealt harshly with Count John's supporters and ordered his brother to come to England in May to stand trial as a traitor. Later Eleanor witnessed Richard's solemn crown-wearing on 17 April at Winchester Cathedral, a symbolic reassertion of his sacral status as England's king. At the ceremony, she sat facing the king in the chancel of the cathedral in the place of honor as queen-mother. She did not have to share her honored position with the queen-consort, for Berengaria never visited England during her husband's reign. Afterward Eleanor traveled with her son until he reached Portsmouth on 24 April, where he waited more than two weeks for a favorable wind to take him to Normandy.[74]

With the Lionheart once more free and in his own lands, the queen-mother's uncertainty about the Plantagenet succession revived. Eleanor, dissatisfied with both her last-born son and her grandson as heirs, had hoped that Richard and Berengaria's marriage would produce an heir. Because of the king's crusade and captivity, the couple had spent very little time together, and their separation would continue after his return from Palestine. Richard's crown-wearing at Winchester Cathedral would have presented an appropriate setting for Berengaria's coronation as queen, yet she was not brought to England for the ceremony. The Lionheart was almost constantly fighting the French after his return from Germany, and circumstances separated him from his wife, although at other times he apparently preferred being apart from her. In 1195 a holy hermit appeared before the king and rebuked him for his sins, urging Richard to reform his life and admonishing him, "Remember the destruction of Sodom and abstain from illicit acts." After this reproof from the hermit, the king was briefly reconciled with his wife, but no pregnancy followed.[75] The hermit's reprimand and Richard's failure to father a child by Berengaria are "the two main planks" for constructing a case for his homo-sexuality. Whatever the truth about Richard's sexuality, warning flags were raised to alarm Eleanor about her son's marriage. By 1197 or 1198 it was clear that Richard's marriage was unsuccessful on two counts: first, it had failed to produce an heir for the Plantagenet possessions; and second, after his peace treaty with Raymond VI of Toulouse, the alliance with the king of Navarre was no longer useful.[76]

Eleanor found her grandson, Arthur of Brittany, poisoned by the anti-Plantagenet sentiments of his Breton mother Constance and his protector Philip II, unacceptable as Richard's heir. His very name was "a badge of Breton independence and hostility toward the Plantagenets." Because Constance, since her husband Geoffrey's death in 1186, and the Breton aristocracy both harbored powerful hostility against their suzerain, the duke of Normandy, Eleanor wanted to block little Arthur from becoming head of the Plantagenet house. Constance's fury against the Angevin line had blinded her to the advantage that an upbringing at Richard's court would have given her son— an opportunity to strengthen ties with his uncle that might have won him formal nomination as the childless English king's heir. In 1196, when the Lionheart demanded custody of the boy, the Bretons hid him away until he could be smuggled to Philip II's court. With Arthur a pawn of the French monarch, neither Eleanor nor Richard could bear to contemplate his succes-sion. As hope of a son as heir to Richard dimmed, Count John was left as his brother's likely successor.[77]

It is possible that the aged duchess's eyes fixed on another grandson as a potential heir after Arthur's flight to Paris: the German prince Otto of

Brunswick, son of Henry and Eleanor's daughter Matilda, wife of the duke of Saxony. Eleanor's influence may have inspired the Lionheart's nomination of Otto as count of Poitou in the spring of 1196. If she had become reconciled to the fact that her son would not produce an heir, she may have sought to see someone solidly established in her patrimony to prevent any succession struggle there on her death.[78] Otherwise, Richard's grant of Poitou to his nephew is difficult to explain, for it seems to contradict his earlier tenacity in holding on to his southern inheritance. In any case, the youth was never invested formally as ruler of Poitou; and it does not appear that he exercised independent authority, for Richard's seneschals in Aquitaine and Gascony continued to administer the county. By 1197 the grander possibility of Otto's succession to the German imperial title arose on Emperor Henry VI's death, and he returned to Germany to pursue his candidacy. With Otto's withdrawal and Arthur of Brittany in his enemy's household, Richard tacitly acknowledged his brother John as his heir to the Angevin empire. Yet Arthur would continue to cause his grandmother worry, since he provided "a trump card" for his Capetian protector Philip II to play in his political game against John after Richard's death in 1199.[79]

ELEANOR'S FIRST RETIREMENT, 1194

Once Richard was released from captivity and restored to power in England by spring 1194, he and Eleanor returned to France, knowing that his kingdom was secure. In mid-May, soon after the two had reached Normandy, John joined them at Lisieux, having ignored his summons for trial in England, and the queen-mother fostered her two surviving sons' reconciliation. Documents that had come into the Lionheart's hands gave evidence of his brother's conspiring with the French monarch against him at the time of his release from captivity, and Richard had previously summoned John to come before a great council at Northampton to answer for his treason. Although Richard did not trust his brother enough to allow him custody of any castles or estates, he received the tearful and repentant John in May 1194 "with good-humoured contempt." This was achieved "through the mediation of Queen Eleanor their mother," and soothing the king's wrath, she saved John from the disgrace of a trial by battle, the traditional means of trying great men accused of treachery against their lord.[80]

When the queen-mother decided that it was safe for her to withdraw from public affairs, she settled not at Poitiers, but at Fontevraud, the prestigious abbey lying on the Angevin–Poitevin frontier. Eleanor's generosity to the abbey had steadily increased over the years. Although Fontevraud's chapel housed Henry's tomb, it is unlikely that this would have figured heavily in her choice of residence. No doubt the abbey, a mixed house where the resident monks were subject to a powerful abbess, appealed to Eleanor, long frustrated in her own desire to exercise power, and it was a house that traditionally had attracted aristocratic ladies, including women of her late husband's family.

Eleanor made Fontevraud her chief residence for the rest of her life. After she settled there she devoted herself increasingly to her own spiritual needs and to personal matters involving her household and other intimates sharing her life at the abbey. Death was ever present to people in the Middle Ages, especially to one who had reached Eleanor's age and had outlived most of her kin; and like other medieval Christians, she hoped to die a good death. Yet neither her withdrawal to a religious house nor her advanced age meant that she had retired entirely from the secular world and from public concerns. Political considerations would have dictated her choice of residence as much as family allegiance or religious devotion. Fontevraud's strategic location linking the Plantagenet possessions lying on both banks of the Loire provided her "a convenient base of operations" from which she could work to tighten dynastic links with nobles of the region that were constantly threatening to unravel in the face of her sons' struggle against their nemesis, Philip II.[81] From Fontevraud, she could easily make periodic visits to nearby Poitiers; however, she never returned to England.

During Eleanor's semi-retirement after 1194, she maintained a large household at Fontevraud including, in addition to domestic servants, lesser knights, serjeants, and several clerks. By this time she had replaced her longtime chaplain, Peter, who had traveled with her from Poitou to England in 1154 and returned with her to Poitiers in 1168. Eleanor showed her appreciation for her aged chaplain's service, taking steps to provide for him soon after her liberation from captivity in 1189. When Archbishop Walter of Rouen was adding prebends for more canons for his cathedral church with rents from a chapel in Nottinghamshire, the queen-mother requested that one of the new posts be reserved for Peter in his old age. A later tradition connects Eleanor with that Nottinghamshire chapel, located within the walls of Tickhill Castle, alleging that she had been its founder.[82]

After Eleanor's return to the Continent, she had a large staff of clerics who served as her scribes, although none bore the title of chancellor. The names of four scribes at Fontevraud, sometimes identified as her chaplains, indicate that she continued to maintain an active correspondence. Other clerics in the queen-mother's household held the post of almoner, one of whom continued to serve her after her retirement to Fontevraud, probably drafting charters for her.[83] Knights charged with overseeing her English dowerlands came occasionally to Fontevraud to present their accounts, indicating that English revenues continued to flow to her in her retirement. Among them was Henry de Berneval, steward for her English lands, whom Eleanor rewarded with rents from her lands in Wiltshire, as well as Geoffrey de Wancy, identified as constable of her estate of Berkhamstead, and Wandrill de Courcelles, her seneschal, a Norman knight likely administering her dowerlands in the duchy.[84]

Eleanor found among the nuns at Fontevraud great ladies who had taken the veil there, and others who, like her, had retired there without taking vows. During her residence at the abbey, her granddaughter, the child of the countess of Blois, her second daughter from her marriage to Louis VII, was one of the nuns. A visitor to Eleanor at the abbey some time between May 1194 and the following spring was her daughter Joanne. The unfortunate Sicilian queen had been in the entourage of her brother's bride Berengaria of Navarre since their return from the Third Crusade. In the autumn of 1196, Richard would marry her off to Raymond VI of Toulouse to seal the settlement of the long quarrel between the dukes of Aquitaine and the counts of Toulouse. Eleanor could hardly have been confident of a happy marriage for her daughter, for it was the count's fourth marriage, and he had two former wives still living.[85]

Widows were expected to make pious gifts to favored religious foundations on behalf of their families, and Eleanor's benefactions to Fontevraud increased during the last decade of her life. The great abbey became the chief institutional beneficiary of her gifts, and she issued over a dozen documents during this period either recording her own grants, confirming those made by members of her household, or registering her own gifts to retainers. During Richard's captivity she had won for Fontevraud a dispensation from the contributions to his ransom demanded from other religious houses. Among gifts made during her retirement were revenues granted from her Poitevin lands, for example, annual rents amounting to £130 *poitevin* to maintain the abbey's kitchen, as well as a £10 *poitevin* yearly rent for a chaplain to celebrate masses in the chapel of Saint Laurence that she had founded there. Eleanor also acted in favor of her chosen refuge in other ways, mediating disputes that resulted in judgments favorable to Fontevraud, inspiring her petitioners to make gifts and then witnessing the documents recording their donations.[86]

During the Lionheart's last five years, while he was busy resisting his Capetian rival, little evidence of Eleanor's activities survives. Perhaps she joined Richard at his Christmas court in Poitiers in 1195, but no proof of her presence remains; Richard's remaining Christmases, observed in Normandy in the midst of dangerous warfare, were unlikely to have been festive events. Occasionally documents surface to show Eleanor's continued involvement in matters of state. In 1196 settlement of a dispute between the nearby abbey of Bourgueil and her men of Jaunay in Poitou took place in her presence at

Fontevraud. The next year she joined Archbishop Walter of Coutances in asking the king to remit a debt owed by a longtime royal servant, and Richard responded by cancelling half the debt. In 1198 the monks of Canterbury Cathedral wrote to the queen seeking her intervention in their still-simmering dispute with their archbishop.[87]

Richard Lionheart, fatally wounded by a crossbowman's arrow at the siege of Chalus, near Limoges, at the end of March 1199, survived for ten days, and Eleanor had time to rush to his deathbed, attended by the abbot of Turpenay in the Touraine. Following the king's death on 6 April, she accompanied his body to Fontevraud Abbey for burial in the chapel next to his father's tomb, as he had requested. In accord with his wishes, his heart was sent to Rouen Cathedral to be buried before the high altar opposite his brother Henry's tomb. Bishop Hugh of Lincoln, who was in Anjou making his way to Richard to resolve a quarrel with the king, hastened to Fontevraud to preside over the funeral mass on Palm Sunday, 11 April; also participating in the service were the bishops of Angers and Poitiers, the abbot of Turpenay and the abbot of Le Pin, the king's former almoner.[88]

Two weeks after Richard's interment, Eleanor issued a charter along with her last surviving son, John, granting property to the abbey of Saint-Marie de Turpenay. In this document, she expresses her awareness of the special attachment that Richard had felt for her; she stated that he "had complete confidence in us (after the Saviour) that we would provide for his salvation . . . in accord with our maternal solicitude." She declared that she was making the gift "because our beloved Luke abbot of Turpenay was present with us at the illness and funeral of our dearest son the king and labored above all others at his obsequies." Present at Fontevraud to witness this grant was a distinguished company, including several who had attended Richard's funeral. Clerical witnesses included Cardinal Peter of Capua, the bishop of Poitiers, and the bishop of Agen, who earlier had given the last rites to another of Eleanor's sons, Young Henry. Also present were Count John, Richard's heir; the late king's widow Queen Berengaria, the seneschal of Anjou, and two noble ladies residing at Fontevraud, Eleanor's granddaughter, and Matilda, countess of Perche.[89] Several weeks later the queen granted £100 *poitevin* to Fontevraud for the souls of her husband Henry II, her son Henry the Young King, her other sons and daughters, and for "that mighty man King Richard."[90]

During Richard I's reign Eleanor of Aquitaine had moved from isolation and confinement following Henry II's death in 1189 to a premier position in England's government, a place that she had long assumed to be her right. The respect that the English accorded her as queen-mother and as regent in all but name during Richard's absence on the Third Crusade and his captivity in Germany marks a high point in her political influence and power. It is more remarkable for having occurred in an age when women's exercise of power was declining, due to both the growth of bureaucratic structures and the Church's more restrictive gender definitions that condemned women's activity in the public sphere. Eleanor took her political responsibilities seriously, and she carried them out with great energy, not allowing her advanced age to stop her from rushing to Spain, to Sicily, and to Germany on missions on her son's behalf.

After the Lionheart's release from his imprisonment in 1194, Eleanor withdrew from England to Fontevraud Abbey, expecting to pass her last years among the nuns there in calm and contemplation. Events would soon disturb her quiet, however, and Richard's unexpected death without a direct heir in spring 1199 would force her to re-enter worldly affairs. In her mid-seventies she would rouse herself to action again, becoming busier than ever in a battle for the right of her last remaining son, John, to succeed to the Plantagenet heritage and to her own patrimony.

CHAPTER 11

SECURING THE PLANTAGENET LEGACY: JOHN'S REIGN, 1199–1204

FOLLOWING the Lionheart's death, Eleanor had no time for the indulgence of grieving in quiet contemplation over her son's tomb at Fontevraud. At an age that few medieval women attained, the queen-mother again was forced to rouse herself to activity. Hardly any secular ruler in the eleventh or twelfth centuries—male or female—remained so active at the advanced age of seventy-five. Yet one of the busiest periods in her entire life came in the months following Richard's death, when uncertainty about the succession cast a shadow over the Plantagenet domains. The succession to Richard was unclear, contested by his younger brother John and his adolescent nephew Arthur, son of Geoffrey of Brittany. Eleanor had no illusions about her last surviving son; writing to the pope during Richard's captivity, she had acknowledged that his brother John was "killing the people of the prisoner's kingdom with the sword . . . ravaging the land with fires."[1] Setting aside her memories of John's treachery, however, she would give him unstinting support against her grandson, Arthur.

Eleanor had no wish to see the assemblage of Angevin lands partitioned between her son and her grandson because of her deep distrust of her Breton daughter-in-law, Constance, whose chief concern was bringing an end to Plantagenet influence over Brittany. Indeed, the struggle following the Lionheart's death can be seen as a conflict between two mothers, each one fighting for her son's right.[2] Eleanor had never been close to John, her youngest son; preoccupied with administering Aquitaine during his first years and imprisoned during his adolescence, she had had little opportunity to "bond" with him. Yet she would not have had any intimation that his early childhood separation from her could have contributed to shaping his adult personality, his secretive, suspicious, and scheming nature that would determine the unfortunate character of his rule. While well aware of her last surviving son's character faults, she may have seen in his willfulness enough of herself in her earlier life to arouse her maternal instincts. Now she unhesitatingly threw herself into the struggle to secure his succession to the entire Plantagenet and Poitevin legacy. She raced around France to pacify Poitou and to shore up support in Anjou and Aquitaine while John solidified his hold on the Anglo-Norman realm.

By the time of Eleanor's death in 1204, it would have become clear that John was losing his struggle to defend the Plantagenet empire from Philip II of France, a cunning prince who more than matched his opponent in craftiness and cruelty. Perhaps no English king could have withstood the advancing Capetian monarchy, for its resources would equal if not surpass the Angevins' wealth during John's reign. Yet some continued to blame Eleanor's marriage to Henry Plantagenet for the troubles facing his empire. Following John's accession, the saintly bishop of Lincoln, Hugh of Avalon, predicted that Philip would take revenge against the sons of "the adulteress who forsook her lawful husband shamelessly for his rival, the king of the English." He foresaw the fulfillment of words in the Bible in the destruction of Henry and Eleanor's line. "Bastard shoots will not have deep roots," and "The offspring of an adulterous union will be destroyed."[3]

A SUCCESSION DISPUTED BY ELEANOR'S SON AND GRANDSON

Richard Lionheart, dying of his wound at Chalus, knew that he would leave behind a disputed succession with the possibility of fighting between John and Arthur. In such a situation, the priority of one relative over another as heir was not yet fixed, although some authorities argued that the nephew as "representative" of a deceased elder brother should be favored over a surviving younger brother. The king's companions around his deathbed urged him to name a successor. The English barons did not support Arthur's right to the English Crown because of his tender age, aware that a minor as monarch would subject the Plantagenet empire to weak rule at a critical time, facing the menace of the increasingly powerful Philip II. Also they could recall that John had served his brother capably enough as a soldier during Richard's final five years, gaining military experience.[4]

Eleanor did not hesitate to add her voice to those supporting her last surviving son against her grandson. She would never have wanted to see her despised daughter-in-law become regent of the English kingdom. While it is uncertain whether Richard declared his wishes, it seems likely that, pressed by his mother and his magnates, he acknowledged his brother Count John as his heir before he expired. John was visiting his nephew in Brittany when Richard received his fatal wound. Most likely a secret message from Eleanor informed him of his brother's serious condition, and he slipped away from the Breton court and headed for Anjou to join his mother at Fontevraud in mourning Richard's death. Richard's seneschal of Anjou, a loyal English knight, turned over to him the castles of Loches and Chinon with their treasuries, perhaps at Eleanor's urging.[5]

With the English and Norman magnates opting for Richard's brother and the nobles of Anjou, Maine, and Touraine proclaiming Arthur of Brittany as their lord, the disputed succession allowed Philip II to revive the Capetian policy of pitting one member of the Plantagenet family against another. Although well into her seventies, Eleanor strode into action in order to win John's recognition as heir to Henry II's entire legacy. While John worked to secure Normandy and England, she would assert control over lands to the south. An invading force led by Arthur and Constance marched into Anjou and Maine, and once they occupied Le Mans, Philip II went there to take the boy's homage. The Breton prince then moved on to Tours. As John hurried to Rouen to be invested as duke of Normandy on 25 April, Eleanor joined with Mercadier, Richard's steadfast mercenary captain, in ravaging the countryside around Angers because the Angevins had gone over to Arthur's side, and Poitevin nobles loyal to her marched northward to Tours to confront Arthur's army.

Eleanor's exertions on her son John's behalf received little notice from the English people, unlike her energetic efforts for Richard Lionheart. One reason is that activity assisting John took place in the Loire valley and in her native Aquitaine, leaving most people in England uninformed to any but the most spectacular incidents. Another factor is the deaths soon after the beginning of a new century of two of the major English chroniclers writing at the end of the twelfth century, Roger of Howden (d. *c*.1203) and Ralph Diceto (d. 1201). Although Howden duly recorded without comment Eleanor's 1199 punitive military expedition in Anjou alongside Mercadier, he doubtless deemed her participation in it "unwomanly."[6] Another chronicler writing two or three decades after the queen-mother's death was less discreet, adding to his account that Eleanor and Mercadier had devastated Angers, "and basely carried off the captured citizens."[7] Yet poets found inspiration in the image of an aged lady riding off to war; the epic *Aliscans* written at the end of the twelfth century features a fictional lady boasting, "Though my hair is grey and white, my heart is bold and thirsts for war."[8]

John, unlike his brother, was not in possession of Aquitaine at the time of his accession to the English throne, and the possibility of troublesome activity there by Philip of France in favor of young Arthur required Eleanor's assertion of authority over her duchy. The queen-mother hastened from Fontevraud to Aquitaine by the end of April to take her subjects' homage, while John sailed to England for his coronation as king on 25 May. As one of her charters states, "Henry, as well as our son Richard, who succeeded him, having both since died, and God having left us still in the world, we have been obliged, in order to provide for the needs of our people and the welfare of our lands, to visit Gascony."[9] Also to secure her duchy from the Capetian king's interference, she swallowed her pride and sought out Philip II in mid-July to do homage to him for her county of Poitou, an action that implied her homage for all Aquitaine as well. Her duchy's relationship to the French monarch remained ill-defined, and the status of Gascony was even less clear, although Capetian kings had long asserted a right to intervene in cases claiming default of ducal justice. Eleanor's action, likely her own idea, was unprecedented, for at that time women did not normally do personal homage to their lord, but had a relative do homage on their behalf.[10]

From late April to early July 1199 Eleanor was traversing her duchy from Loudun near the Angevin frontier to Bordeaux, issuing charters confirming properties and privileges in an attempt to win her subjects over to John's side. It was vital for her to placate her Poitevin subjects who had endured the ruthlessness of Richard's rule over them. On her spring and summer circuit she sought to shore up the loyalty of townspeople and ecclesiastics, generously issuing confirmations of the privileges of religious houses and towns. The queen-duchess confirmed the privileges and possessions of the ancient religious foundations traditionally favored by the count-dukes, among them Montierneuf; Saint-Eutrope; Sauve-Majeure; and also Richard's own foundation, the Cistercian abbey of Notre-Dame de Charon.[11]

Eleanor continued Henry II's and Richard's policies of purchasing the support of towns by recognizing their communes, associations for municipal self-government. She granted charters for Poitou's chief cities, including La Rochelle, Oléron, Niort, Poitiers, Saintes, and Bordeaux, confirming their liberties. In exchange, these towns acknowledged certain obligations to their lady, swearing fidelity and promising to supply the men of their militias for the duchy's defense.[12] The people of Bordeaux petitioned her to abolish "certain evil impositions, unheard of and unjust," imposed by Richard, and she obliged, noting that she was "expecting of the afore-mentioned people the fidelity and devotion that we and our predecessors and our dearest son John king of England have always had." In July, John confirmed to the citizens of Bordeaux "all liberties and customs" that his mother had conceded and confirmed.[13] Eleanor recognized that townspeople's support, especially the service of their militias, could offset the fickle fidelity of the Poitevin nobility who were taking advantage of the Plantagenet–Capetian rivalry to wring concessions from her and her son. Although her action in granting away ducal financial resources ultimately would reduce dangerously the power of ducal government, it proved successful in purchasing the commercial centers' loyalty to John. The cities of Poitou would reject the Capetian king's blandishments as long as their queen-duchess lived.

Winning the shifting loyalties of the Aquitanian aristocracy was a more difficult task, but Eleanor tried to win them over to John's cause, restoring properties to them that Richard had confiscated and remedying his unjust actions. The grieving queen in a charter dated "on the day of her dearest son Richard's burial" restored to William de Mauzé land that the late king had seized from him; then, at Eleanor's "will and petition", Mauzé made a gift of £100 angevin annually for the nuns of Fontevraud.[14] More difficult to placate were the troublesome Lusignan nobles, Hugh IX, and Ralph, count of Eu, who were regular members of her entourage on her 1199 circuit. When Eleanor was passing through their lands, according to some accounts, Hugh IX took her hostage and released her only after she agreed to recognize his right to the county of La Marche, which his family had long claimed. Equally likely is Eleanor's acceptance of his claim to the county as an inducement to win his support for John's succession. Whatever the circumstances, King John recognized Hugh as count and took his homage for La Marche by the end of January 1200.[15]

Eleanor sought to rally to John's side Poitevin families with a tradition of ducal service, notably two families rising from middling ranks of the nobility—the Mauléons and the Maingots de Surgères—who had proven loyal servants to the Plantagenets as provosts and seneschals. The Mauléons, descendants of castellans who had expanded their lands along the coast of Poitou and the Aunis, were traditionally custodians of the ducal lordship of Talmont. Ralph de Mauléon sought to gain from the uncertain succession in spring 1199 by offering himself to whatever candidate promised more. In a "piece of political blackmail," he went to Eleanor to declare his claim to hereditary rights of lordship over Talmont and La Rochelle, offering to prove his right by his own oath and that of a hundred knights. Eleanor had little choice other than to compromise with him. She was willing to grant him Talmont, but refused to surrender complete control over the profitable port of La Rochelle, offering him instead £500 annually from her profits from the town plus the castle of Benon in return for his liege homage and his renunciation of any hereditary right to La Rochelle. She made clear that this concession to Ralph was due to necessity, declaring that it was made "because we wish to have his service which is necessary for us and our son John."[16] Another family, the Maingots, had a history of service to the counts of Poitou since the eleventh century as custodians of the counts' castle of Surgères, and in 1199 Eleanor cemented William III Maingot's continued loyalty by recognizing him as its hereditary lord. Eleanor also sought to buy the support of Andrew de Chauvigny, one of Richard's faithful Poitevin knights, with a grant of Saint-Sevère-sur-l'Adour, but she failed, for he eventually rallied to young Arthur's cause.[17]

In turbulent Poitou, a military element was an essential part of Eleanor's household, and several knights and serjeants accompanied her as she moved across her domains. They included her beloved uncle's son, Ralph de Faye II, and occasionally his younger brother William. Other knights in her entourage were Chalon de Rochefort and Laon Ogier, and Pierre, a local military official at Chauvigny. Also one of her knights was Geoffrey de Chauvigny, Richard Lionheart's chamberlain in Poitou in the 1180s, whose family was related to Eleanor through her Châtellerault connections. Her serjeants included Hugh de Jaunay, to whom Eleanor granted land in Poitou. Also traveling with the queen-duchess from time to time were a number of her administrators. Most prominent among them were Pierre Bertin, seneschal of Poitou since 1190, and Raymond Bernard, seneschal of Gascony. Less often present was the English-born Robert of Thornham, who had served as seneschal of Anjou in Richard's last years, then as seneschal of Poitou after 1200. Other office-holders in Eleanor's entourage include her provosts of La Rochelle and Montreuil-Bonnin, and Savaric the Younger, named by her to be master of the mint at Poitiers in 1199.[18]

The number of official documents that Eleanor issued during the months following Richard's death leaves no doubt about the significance of her activity on John's behalf. Between April 1199 and her death in the spring of 1204 she issued over sixty charters, two-thirds of them dating to within a year of John's accession; their number amounts to more charters than the total granted in the fifteen years following her captivity.[19] During Eleanor's circuit of Aquitaine, two prelates were her most valued counselors; Henry, bishop of Saintes, and Maurice, bishop of Poitiers. At Bordeaux on 1 July 1199, the queen-duchess presided over a great gathering of Gascon magnates, including the archbishop of Bordeaux, the bishops of Saintes and Lectoure, but also Gascon lords rarely seen at her court, such as Gaston VI, count of Bigorre and viscount of Béarn, the count of Foix and the viscount of Tartas.[20]

During the course of Eleanor's 1199 circuit of Aquitaine, her youngest daughter, Joanne, widow of King William II of Sicily and wife of Raymond VI, count of Toulouse, had joined her at Niort. Joanne's marriage to the count had resulted in a son, the future Count Raymond VII, but it brought her no happiness. When she was left to contend with a rebellion in her husband's domains alone, abandoned by him, she earned the praise of an English annalist as "a woman whose masculine spirit overcame the weakness of her sex."[21] Nonetheless, she was forced to flee from the county of Toulouse in the spring of 1199 to seek refuge at her brother's court in Normandy. Joanne reached her mother Eleanor in Poitou only to learn of Richard's death, making their reunion a sorrowful occasion. Although pregnant and exhausted from her flight, she rushed to her brother's grave at Fontevraud Abbey.

Joanne accompanied her mother to Rouen to join John's court. Traveling with them were prominent Poitevins in her service, including Ralph de Faye II, Eleanor's cousin.[22] By the time that Joanne and her mother reached Rouen, the unfortunate countess was seriously ill and in a desperate condition. Sensing that she would not survive the strain of giving birth, she made her will, witnessed by Eleanor, bequeathing her body and goods, valued at more than 1,000 marks, to Fontevraud.[23] Joanne begged to be allowed to die wearing the habit of a Fontevraudist nun, despite the obstacle of having a husband who opposed her request, and the archbishop of Canterbury agreed to a special dispensation. Soon after receiving the veil, in September 1199, Joanne died following a caesarian section, delivering a son who survived only long enough to be baptized. At the end of August John had made a grant of money for his sister, "by the counsel of our dearest lady and mother"; and after her death he issued a charter witnessed by Eleanor assigning to two of Joanne's maids pensions from the town of Saumur's revenues.[24] Eleanor seems to have acted as executor of Joanne's will, and she probably oversaw the removal of her daughter's body from its first burial place in Rouen Cathedral for re-interment in the nuns' cemetery at Fontevraud. While crossing Gascony to her last surviving daughter Eleanor's court in Castile, early in 1200, she took time to seek out Joanne's former husband, Raymond VI of Toulouse, to see that he implemented his late wife's bequests.[25] Death spared the unhappy Joanne the pain of knowing that her husband would be denounced by the pope as a protector of the heretical Cathars and a crusade proclaimed against his lands in 1208.

During Eleanor's summer visit to King John's court at Rouen, she exchanged charters with him, establishing a sort of condominium over Aquitaine by mother and son. In Eleanor's charter, she acknowledged her son as her rightful heir, ceded Poitou (all Aquitaine is implied) to him and accepted his homage; and she transferred the homage, fealty and service of the bishops and lay nobility of the county to him. John in turn issued a charter returning the province to her for her lifetime or for as long as she wished, to rule as his lady (*domina*). This exchange of charters acknowledged their "co-ordinate and co-extensive" authority, holding jointly the sort of property rights commonly shared by husband and wife, for neither could alienate possessions without the other's consent. King John appointed the seneschals who headed the administration in Poitou and Gascony, yet his mother's authority there was genuine. The arrangement created by Eleanor's homage to Philip II and these two charters must be considered "a diplomatic masterstroke." By positioning her as the French king's direct vassal for Aquitaine, and not John, it appeared to preclude for the remainder of Eleanor's life any meddling in the duchy by the Capetian monarch during his clashes with the English king. In acknowledging John as lawful heir to the duchy and associating him with her authority as duchess, Eleanor cemented his position in southwestern France and forestalled Philip's intervention on behalf of Arthur at her death.[26]

After this spurt of activity, Eleanor returned to Fontevraud, expecting to spend her last years in prayer, meditation, and good works. Her lifelong concern for the souls of her relatives—providing funds for marking the anniversaries of their deaths with prayers—continued. A dozen or so clerics' names appear on documents issued by Eleanor identified as her clerks or chaplains, indicating that her household included an impressive ecclesiastical element. Indeed, it has been said that the numbers of clerics in her entourage "rivalled those of many a bishop,"[27] indicating that she maintained an elaborate schedule of liturgical services in her chapel for the souls of her deceased kin. Other evidence points to her interest in the daily round of worship services, for example her gifts of liturgical objects to Fontevraud Abbey during her retirement there and expenditures on incense and other items for her household chapel in England recorded on the pipe rolls. Perhaps her son Richard's enthusiasm for the music of the royal chapel, encouraging the choir to sing out at full volume, sprang from her own interest in the liturgy.[28] In her old age at Fontevraud Eleanor doubtless derived comfort from attending daily masses, contemplating Christ's sacrifice, and as a mother who had only two children left alive at her death, sharing Mary's pain at her son's suffering. Her lavish expenditures in support of her chapel may explain her less than generous record as a donor of lands to religious houses.[29] Eleanor did not seem to see patronage of religious foundations as a sphere in which she could purchase influence as did other noble ladies, who found their benefactions to monks and nuns a means of rising above the limitations that society imposed on women.

Among the clerics in Eleanor's entourage at Fontevraud were a number who served as her scribes, indicating that she maintained an active writing office even while supposedly living in retirement. Documents bearing the note, "given by the hand of Roger our chaplain," show that he was acting as her secretary during the spring and summer of 1199. Roger had accompanied Eleanor to Fontevraud, and as a brother of the abbey he received an annual rent of £10 from Oléron, and he had also the revenue from an oven and a house at Poitiers previously constructed by her. Eleanor provided this income to cover the costs of masses that he celebrated in the chapel of Saint-Laurence established by her at Fontevraud.[30]

Although Roger's origin is unknown, another clerk drafting Eleanor's charters in the years after 1199, William of Saint-Maixent, described as "our clerk" or "our notary," was Poitevin. His name links him with one of Poitou's most important abbeys, controlled by Eleanor's ducal ancestors for centuries. He served the queen-mother until 1203, when he joined King John's household as a clerk of his chamber. Another of Eleanor's clerks early in John's reign was English, although active mainly at Poitiers, Master Richard of Gnosall, identified as "clerk of our chamber." In 1203 the queen-mother had two other chaplains in her service, although no more is known of them than their names—Ralph and Jocelin. Several laymen appear among the circle of retainers continuing to serve Eleanor in her new residence at Fontevraud, among them Henry de Berneval, steward of her English dowerlands since Henry II's death, who continued to appear to present his accounts.[31]

Eleanor enjoyed the company of the Fontevraud nuns and noble widows who, like her, had retired to the great abbey. Among the nuns during Eleanor's residence there was her granddaughter, daughter of her own daughter Adelicia, countess of Blois, who was prioress and, after her grandmother's death, abbess. In the queen-mother's last years at Fontevraud, nuns or noble widows who had retired to the great abbey sometimes acted as her witnesses, although this was unusual for women. Some cannot be identified precisely; they include a "Countess Matilda," identified variously as countess of Eu, Perche, or viscountess of Aunay, "A. duchess of Borbonie," and "M. countess of Tornodori (Tonnère?)." All these ladies accompanied her at Poitiers in 1199 shortly after Richard's death. Also among those traveling to Poitiers with her was the abbess of Fontevraud.[32]

By early autumn 1199 Arthur of Brittany's attempt to win recognition as his uncle Richard's heir in the Plantagenet's French lands was languishing. The boy's leading supporter among the Angevin nobility, William des Roches, had come to believe that Philip II was manipulating him for his own advantage, and he came to terms with King John. Des Roches managed to remove Arthur from the French king's custody and in October at Le Mans a formal treaty of reconciliation ended the struggle between John and his nephew, though only for a time. This forced the two monarchs to agree to a truce that would prepare the way for the treaty of Le Goulet in May 1200, a formal accord that appeared to solidify John's position with permanent peace. By its terms, Philip recognized the English king's right to Anjou, and he ratified Brittany's status as a fief held of John as duke of Normandy; however, John failed to gain custody of young Arthur, and his nephew returned to Paris.

To symbolize the peace between the Capetians and Plantagenets negotiated at Le Goulet, a marriage was arranged for Philip II's heir, Prince Louis (the future Louis VIII), grandson of Eleanor's first husband and heir to the French

Crown, to one of King John's nieces. Young Louis's bride was to be a daughter of John's sister Eleanor and her husband King Alfonso VIII of Castile. Early in 1200 the queen-mother, now in her late seventies, once again would set off on the long journey to Spain to fetch a royal bride. Her willingness to undertake overland travel for such a long duration under medieval road conditions is evidence of her extraordinary good health for a woman of her years at a time when medicine could offer no relief from the aches and pains of old age. Eleanor's namesake, known in Spain as Leanor of Castile, was the only one of her children left alive in addition to John. Perhaps desire for a reunion with her daughter whom she had not seen since she surrendered her to Spanish envoys at Bordeaux in 1170, over thirty years earlier, impelled her to accept this perilous mission.

Leanor had given birth to ten children, six of whom survived to adulthood; five were daughters, and four of them would become queens. According to a late Spanish chronicler, it was left to Eleanor once she arrived in Castile to choose between her two granddaughters who were of marriageable age, and she selected the younger, Blanca, because she feared that her elder sister's Spanish name, Urraca, would be impossible for the Parisians to pronounce. Once married to Louis, Blanca would become known as Blanche of Castile, mother of France's saint-king, Louis IX. The trip to Castile was Eleanor's last long journey, and she remained two months at the royal court to become reacquainted with her daughter and to acquaint herself with her grandchildren, and no doubt to recover strength for the return journey.[33]

On the queen-mother's return journey, she reached Bordeaux in time to celebrate Easter. There, after enduring the physically exhausting journey from Spain, she experienced a shocking episode—the murder of Mercadier, the loyal mercenary captain of both her sons, killed by one of the seneschal of Gascony's soldiers. Mercadier most likely had come to provide protection for her as she made her way north across hostile Lusignan territory to deliver young Blanca to her betrothed. Eleanor lacked the strength to escort her granddaughter any further, and she charged the archbishop of Bordeaux with accompanying the girl to Normandy, where John would hand her over to her future husband, and Eleanor headed for Fontevraud.

ELEANOR'S SECOND RETIREMENT

The chronicler Roger of Howden last mentions Eleanor in respectful terms recording her retirement on her return from Spain in 1200: "Aged and wearied by the labors of her long journey, Queen Eleanor withdrew to the abbey of Fontevrault and remained there."[34] No doubt she expected to spend her last years behind the walls of Fontevraud in quiet devotions in her chapel there, yet great matters continued to intrude on her retirement as John's failings as ruler were exploited by Philip of France. From time to time Eleanor had to leave her retreat to visit Poitiers; indeed, one Angevin chronicler who surely would have been aware of her retirement to Fontevraud recorded Poitiers as the place of her death.[35]

At Poitiers, Eleanor inspired a large-scale construction project, one that perhaps she actively supervised during her visits to the city—an elegant renovation of the great hall of the ducal palace in the "Angevin style." This undertaking had begun some time during Richard's last years and continued until Eleanor's death. The palace, dating to the Merovingian era, had undergone major reconstruction following a fire early in the eleventh century under her great-grandfather, Duke William VIII; and her grandfather, William IX, had added the tower called Maubergeon that gave its name to the dissolute duke's mistress. Today Eleanor's hall still stands, forming the lobby of the present-day Palais de Justice; three of the hall's walls appear as they did following her remodeling, but elaborate fireplaces added in the fourteenth century replace the southern wall. The great hall's architecture and sculptural decor seem linked to other construction projects at Poitiers associated with Eleanor and Henry, notably the exterior east wall of the cathedral of Saint-Pierre. The stark surface of the hall's stone walls is broken on two sides by two sets of rounded blind arches resting on slender pilasters, one above the other, while the western wall has only the upper arches with the lower portion left plain, possibly to accommodate tapestries. The upper series of arches rests on sculpted corbels representing human and mythical creatures' heads.[36] This spacious and imposing hall stands as testimony to Eleanor's desire to display the power and prestige of her ancestral ducal line at a time when its continuity was being threatened by the Capetian king.

Soon poor judgment by Eleanor's last remaining son generated crises that called her back into political activity. King John created another opportunity for Philip II and Arthur of Brittany in August 1200 with an ill-considered marriage. Having set aside his marriage to Isabelle of Gloucester, he took as his wife another Isabelle, heir to the county of Angoulême, without regard for his bride's prior betrothal to Hugh IX, lord of the county of La Marche and head of the troublesome Lusignan clan in lower Poitou. This marriage, often depicted as due to John's passion for a beautiful maiden, appeared at the time an astute diplomatic move, bringing to him the rebellious county of Angoulême. The Angoumois was a strategic territory, lying on the route between Poitiers and Bordeaux, and the English king's possession of it would have kept castles threatening the Plantagenets' passage from Poitou to Gascony from falling under Hugh IX's direct control. Eleanor had no love for the Lusignan clan, and her son's rash marriage that blocked a major expansion of their power must have pleased her. Whatever her doubts about the sudden marriage, she accepted it, and she gave her approval to John's designation of two important towns of her domains, Niort and Saintes, as part of her new daughter-in-law's dowerlands.[37]

While John may have viewed his action in tearing young Isabelle away from her fiancé as a clever move, it would have disastrous consequences. He had committed "an unprovoked act of dishonor" that angered and humiliated the Lusignan family;[38] and he outraged other powerful nobles along Poitou's southern fringes. John unwisely made no effort to placate the Lusignan clan's wounded pride by offering compensation; instead, his contemptuous treatment spurred Hugh's family to revolt. By autumn 1201, Hugh de Lusignan had taken his complaint to the court of King Philip II, superior lord over the counts of Poitou, and the French royal court on 28 April 1202 condemned John for failure to appear in Paris to answer his vassal's charges.[39] This led to another round of the long Capetian–Plantagenet conflict, with Philip taking advantage of the crisis to revive Arthur of Brittany's claim to a share of the Plantagenet heritage. The young duke rejected his vassalage to John for Brittany, and the French king recognized him as his vassal for Anjou and Poitou as well as for Brittany. The revived conflict would result eventually in Arthur's murder and John's loss of Normandy to his Capetian rival.

During this new crisis facing King John, Eleanor's sound political instincts impelled her to attempt to shore up his position in Aquitaine. Between 1200 and 1203 she issued at least ten charters concerning Aquitanian matters, seeking to preserve alliances with lay and ecclesiastical lords necessary for the duchy's cohesion.[40] Most important was Eleanor's effort to protect John's position in Poitou by winning over Aimery, viscount of Thouars, perhaps the most powerful Poitevin noble with a dozen castles dominating the north and west of the county. The viscount's loyalty to the English king was problematic; he had supported John's succession in spring 1199, but had turned toward Arthur and Constance in the autumn. John revoked his custody of Chinon Castle to grant it to William des Roches, his seneschal of Anjou, as a reward for delivering Arthur of Brittany from Philip II's clutches. Also about this time, Aimery's brother, Guy of Thouars, became the third husband of Arthur's mother, Constance of Brittany, tying him more closely to Arthur's faction.

In February or March 1201, the queen-mother, although ill, summoned Aimery of Thouars to Fontevraud to entreat him to remain faithful to John despite his friendly relations with the Bretons and with Hugh de Lusignan. In a letter to her son describing the visit, Eleanor reported that she and her faithful agent, Guy de Dives, a former marshal in Richard's household and constable of Dinan, had met with Aimery. The visit had gone well, and as a result she could assure John that she was convalescing better than usual. She had pointed out to the viscount that he alone of all those in the king's service had done no injury to her son, unlike other Poitevin barons. She had then warned Aimery that he "ought to feel great shame and sinfulness because he had stood by while other barons unjustly disinherited you," and that he "heard and understood our words." Eleanor assured John that Aimery had "promised to do everything he can to bring back to your obedience the lands and castles that some of his friends have seized without your leave or will," if he could keep all his own possessions. The viscount had renewed his fealty, promising "that he will be in your service well and faithfully against all men," and Eleanor and Guy de Dives had agreed to act as pledges that he would do whatever was commanded. Aimery wrote to John, giving his account of the meeting and assuring the king of his loyalty.[41] It was the queen-mother's quick action that prevented the viscount of Thouars from becoming the Lusignan's most dangerous ally. Her work would not last, however, and by 1202 Aimery of Thouars had joined William des Roches in deserting the English king and aligning himself with young Arthur of Brittany's forces.

The fifteen-year-old Arthur of Brittany, once more in Philip II's care, again furnished the Capetian monarch with a weapon against John, and he acknowledged the boy as duke of Aquitaine, sending him off at the head of an invasion force bound for Poitou in the summer of 1202.[42] Arthur's grandmother, although approaching eighty, left Fontevraud for Poitiers in July 1202 on a mission to keep her homeland from falling into his hands. When Eleanor stopped at Mirebeau Castle north of Poitiers near the end of the month, she found herself under attack by Arthur's forces and his Lusignan allies. Besieged in the castle, she somehow got a letter out to John, and his strong feelings for his mother moved him to his most robust action in his largely listless defense of his Continental domains, 1202–04. The English king acted with unaccustomed speed on a daring mission to rescue Eleanor and, making a forced march of eighty miles from Le Mans in less than two days with a mobile force of mercenaries, he surprised the besiegers and freed his mother. John's exultant letter describing his mother's rescue survives, telling how his force caught the enemy force off guard eating breakfast, and he took prisoner a number of important rebels, including his nephew Arthur, the Lusignan brothers, and Andrew de Chauvigny.[43]

John's good fortune did not continue, however; as so often happened, his lack of judgment and instinct for cruelty caused him to over-reach. Eleanor would have learned of the deaths of a number of his captives—her own Poitevin subjects—from harsh conditions of their imprisonment in England. Soon word of her son's murder of her grandson, Arthur of Brittany, would reverberate across John's territories, even into the cloister at Fontevraud. In mid-April John sent a messenger bearing a letter addressed to Eleanor and several Aquitanian magnates. The letter does not tell the news; that would have been conveyed orally by the messenger, but it contains a phrase, "the grace of God is even more with us than [the messenger] can tell you," a veiled reference to Arthur's demise.[44] Hearsay about John's part in his nephew's death soon led to his loss of much of the Loire valley, and defections by major magnates of Anjou and Poitou followed. By the end of 1203 Eleanor would have known that her son's defense of Normandy had failed and that he had fled the duchy, sailing to England. This was followed by the capture in early March 1204 of the supposedly invulnerable fortress of Château-Gaillard, built by Richard Lionheart to dominate the Seine valley, leaving Rouen vulnerable to French conquest. The Norman capital would fall to Philip's forces a month later.

In Eleanor's last years she had to confront the likelihood that the great empire that she had presided over alongside Henry II was unlikely to survive for long after her death. Although this saddened her final days, her greatest concern was her knowledge that death was approaching, and she turned her attention to contemplating her immortal soul's fate. In earlier life Eleanor had not been a notably generous contributor to monastic houses, never earning a reputation for pious gifts or for interceding with her two husbands on behalf of the Church in the manner that had won churchmen's affection for earlier queens. Throughout her life Eleanor followed the custom of great ladies when making gifts to religious houses, designating them for prayers for the souls of relatives, especially her spouse and her children, showing a strong sense of family. In her last years she made generous grants for commemorations of the anniversaries of her loved ones' deaths, directed toward the salvation of the souls of her ancestors, her spouse Henry II of England and her sons young Henry and Richard Lionheart. In six grants made after her estranged husband's death in 1189, she included his name among those for whom she was making gifts to procure spiritual benefits. Only in a gift to the monks of the major Poitevin abbey of Saint-Maixent in 1200 did she request prayers for the remission of her own sins. In recompense for the damages done to the monks by her "dearest son Richard," she granted them services formerly rendered to her by her foresters, and she asked in return that the abbot and monks feed three paupers each day in their refectory and celebrate two masses on her behalf.[45]

During Eleanor's final days at Fontevraud she found comfort in commemorating Henry II and Richard I through overseeing the construction and placement of their tomb-sculptures, and also in planning her own tomb, completed sometime before 1210.[46] In constructing a Plantagenet family mausoleum, Eleanor was fulfilling one of the duties often undertaken by noble ladies, but she also desired to reunite in death her family that had been estranged in life.

The effigies in the chapel at Fontevraud are among the earliest life-size recumbent figures of royal personages sculpted in medieval Europe, and they rank as "pivotal innovations in the evolution of tomb sculpture." Eleanor may have found inspiration for Henry and Richard's funerary monuments in the tombs of her first husband, Louis VII, and her former mother-in-law, Adelaide of Maurienne (d.1154). The tomb slab of Adelaide at the convent of Saint-Pierre de Montmartre, where she had retired, is a flat sculptural representation, the first life-size image to be carved for one of Eleanor's royal contemporaries. The site of Louis's tomb was at the Cistercian house he had founded at Barbeau, not at Saint-Denis, and it marks the first fully sculpted representation of a deceased Capetian monarch. Eleanor would have known of these burial monuments, and she doubtless intended that the tombs of her second husband and her favorite son should surpass in splendor those of their Capetian rivals.[47]

The figures of Henry and his son, the work of a single sculptor following precise instructions, are indeed splendid. They represent recreations of their ceremonial lying in state, when their coronation regalia were displayed alongside their bodies to recall the authority and legitimacy of their kingship.[48] Although Fontevraud had longstanding ties to the counts of Anjou, and Henry II proved to be a prominent patron and protector of the abbey, it became the necropolis of Plantagenet monarchs almost by accident. Henry had earlier made known his desire to be buried at Grandmont Abbey in the Limousin, an austere house that he favored, and he had begun rebuilding the abbey church in grand style by 1166.[49] Henry's interment at Fontevraud Abbey in July 1189, due to the necessity for a quick burial in the midst of a summer heat wave, led to his son Richard and his daughter Joanne's entombment there in 1199, followed by his widow Eleanor in 1204.

Eleanor had played no part in the decision to inter her husband at Fontevraud, yet she was probably a major figure in negotiations with the nuns on the siting of his tomb within the abbey's chapel. She could feel a strong sense of family solidarity with Henry and his Plantagenet empire that he had assembled despite bitterness surviving from their troubled marriage, for through her sons it was as much an Aquitanian empire, heir to the ambitions of her own ducal ancestors. It seems clear that she was thinking dynastically when planning an arrangement of the tombs in the Fontevraud chapel as a family group, reuniting in death a house that had been alienated in life. Eleanor must have gone to great lengths to secure the location that she desired for Henry's tomb, since it was highly irregular for a male to be entombed in the chapel of a religious house of women and all the more unusual for one to be buried within the nuns' choir.[50]

It is not improbable that Eleanor anticipated that the chapel of Fontevraud, located on the borders of the territories of husband and wife, would become a royal mausoleum, proclaiming the glories of a dynasty that united the Angevin and Poitevin ruling houses. Despite the collapse of the "empire" that she had presided over as Henry II's queen, and the extension of Capetian control over Fontevraud, her aim was partially accomplished. Her grandson, Henry III of England, showed affection for the great abbey that was the burial place of his grandparents and his famous uncle, and years after it had fallen under Capetian control he continued to acknowledge the abbey's significance for his family. His mother, Isabelle of Angoulême, had died a nun at Fontevraud, and he later had her body moved from the sisters' burial ground into the choir to lie with the other royal tombs. Henry also had his father John's heart sent to the abbey, and eventually his own heart would be enshrined there.[51] The imposing tombs in the Fontevraud chapel, now impressively positioned at the crossing of the nave and transepts, stand as silent testimony to Eleanor's dedication to the idea of a not purely Plantagenet but also Poitevin empire that she struggled to preserve after Henry II's death, short-lived though that empire proved to be.

An Adventure-filled Life Ends, a Legend Begins

Less than a month after Rouen fell to the French, placing Normandy under Capetian control, Eleanor of Aquitaine died at Fontevraud Abbey on 31 March or 1 April at the extraordinary age of eighty. Her last recorded visit to Poitiers was on 8 February 1202, and it is unlikely that she traveled far after that date.[52] As late as 1203 Eleanor kept busy trying to shore up support for John. She granted land to Aimery de Rochefort, who had remained faithful to her son, and she reissued a charter granting the townspeople of Niort a commune.[53] Sensing death approaching, she expressed her wish to take the veil of a Fontevraud nun and to be buried in the nuns' chapel. An Angevin chronicle describes King John's reaction to his mother's death: "By her death the king, most violently saddened, feared greatly for himself and was disquieted more than enough to withdraw from Normandy."[54] While the chronology is incorrect, for John had abandoned Normandy in December 1203, the writer doubtless captured the depth of the king's feeling for his mother. Obviously Eleanor's own knowledge of her son's failure to defend his Plantagenet heritage and her awareness of the potential impact on Poitou of his loss of Normandy, threatening its conquest by the Capetian king, would have saddened her last days. The death of the duchess of Aquitaine meant that Poitevin nobles such as Viscount Aimery of Thouars, loyal to her Plantagenet sons only out of respect for her, would quickly abandon John and rush to do homage to Philip of France.

   Although Eleanor apparently had made a will in 1202, it does not survive.[55] No doubt, it expressed her wish to be interred in the chapel at Fontevraud

Abbey alongside Henry II's tomb. Her own effigy there is similar to her husband's and her son Richard's, but it is plainly the work of a different artist skilled in the "1200s style," rendering her body even more three-dimensional than the earlier ones through skillful treatment of the folds of the clothing. It may follow her own instructions, portraying her as she wished to be remembered, not as an octogenarian but as a woman in the perfection of her mature years. Like her husband and her son, she is crowned, though without any other symbol of royal power sometimes depicted on the tombs of queens, such as a scepter. Unlike Henry and Richard Lionheart, she is depicted as living, holding a book, not reading, but lost in contemplation with eyes closed. Eleanor's effigy is a pioneering work, the earliest medieval sculptural representation of a lay woman holding an open book. No similar effigies appeared on women's tombs in England before the mid-thirteenth century. Given Eleanor's alleged role as a patron of courtly love literature, some like to believe the book to be one of romances, but it is certainly a devotional book, a psalter or a prayer book. A reminder of the queen-duchess's last years spent in a community of devout women preparing herself for eternal salvation, it recalls a romance's description of a grieving widow: "Reading psalms from a prayerbook / Illuminated in letters of gold."[56]

At Fontevraud the nuns left an obituary of Eleanor that records her generosity to their house in extravagant language, listing the deceased queen's costly gifts to them and exaggerating by declaring that "she was from her earliest life a patron of the church of Fontevraud." She had paid for a wall built around their cloister, and presented them with a processional cross of gold ornamented with precious stones, a gold cup, and several other gold and silver vessels and some silk vestments. The nuns' obituary expresses pride that Eleanor had rejected other religious houses to take the veil of their order, and it is silent on the controversies that had circulated around her while living. Instead it describes her as a queen who had "brightened the world with the splendor of her royal progeny," and who "by the merit of her incomparable rectitude, surpassed almost all the queens of the world."[57] In Normandy, at Rouen Cathedral, the anniversary of her death was commemorated annually, as it was across the Channel in England by the monks of Canterbury Cathedral. At Reading Abbey, the monks remembered the recently deceased queen with prayers usually reserved for monks of the house, as they had promised her not long after she had become their queen. Her son John was moved to mercy by his loss, and two weeks after his mother's death he ordered that all prisoners be set free, regardless of the seriousness of their crime, "for the love of God and for the salvation of the soul of our dearest mother." Such an act was uncharacteristic of John, who rarely showed compassion, but a suitable commemoration of his mother Eleanor who had suffered a long loss of her liberty.[58]

Among the English people, the reaction to Eleanor's death was muted; those chroniclers who recorded her passing noted it without comment.[59] One obscure Londoner, however, writing in the year of Eleanor's death, paused in his work of compiling the English laws to call to mind his late queen. Ignoring the "black legend" of her misdeeds that was already taking shape, he recalled her simply as "a noble queen indeed and a spirited and wealthy lady." In 1216 Gerald of Wales, a thwarted patronage seeker turned satirist, was writing at a time when he had no fear of King John who was busy fighting off a baronial rebellion. Gerald let loose a barrage of bitter anti-Plantagenet propaganda that slandered Eleanor. Condemning her marriage to Henry II as adulterous, he declared that she was cursed with the inherited licentiousness of her Poitevin lineage. A generation after Eleanor's passing, the still influential chronicler Matthew Paris recorded her death in one of his histories. In his obituary, he was kind to Eleanor, describing her as "an admirable lady of beauty and cleverness."[60] Elsewhere he was scathing in his comments on Henry II's queen, however, contributing to her "black legend" by embellishing rumors of her misconduct on the Second Crusade.

On Henry II's death in 1189, Eleanor of Aquitaine, at an age when most great ladies would have withdrawn from activity, had thrown herself energetically into the cause of securing her son Richard's succession to the English throne, protecting his inheritance, the so-called Angevin empire, during his absence on crusade and in captivity. Then on the Lionheart's death in 1199, when Eleanor was seventy-five, she still had reserves of strength to fight to preserve for John, her last surviving son, the integrity of the block of lands amassed by Henry II. Despite her failed marriage to Henry and her earlier efforts to further the partition of his "family assemblage" of lands, she no longer desired to see its dismemberment once her sons were its rulers. As her offspring and heirs to her ancient duchy of Aquitaine, their territories on both sides of the English Channel constituted as much a Poitevin as a Plantagenet empire. Yet she would be linked throughout history with the fate of the empire assembled by Henry II, as a French historian writing in 2004 notes: "It is fascinating to consider how much the death of Eleanor of Aquitaine accelerated the dissolution of the Angevin Empire, as if one could not survive without the other. . . . Eleanor of Aquitaine personifies, in sum, the rise and the fall of the Angevin dynasty."[61]

Eleanor of Aquitaine had lived her life on her own terms, refusing to accept the increasingly restricted role allowed to women by religion and custom. She paid a high price for her insistence on choosing her own destiny, witnessing the ruin of her reputation, estrangement from two husbands, and even enduring years of imprisonment. In her widowhood Eleanor at last achieved the political power that she had always assumed was her right. In exercising authority, Eleanor showed herself deeply devoted to her sons, applying her political skills in their service. Her role in safeguarding England for Richard Lionheart while he was away on Crusade and then confined in captivity was essential for the kingdom's internal order and external security. On Richard's death, Eleanor's activity in Anjou and Aquitaine forestalled attempts to secure the succession of her grandson, Arthur, under the thumb of King Philip of France.

Eleanor's positive political actions on behalf of her two sons in her last years rebut unflattering views of her by twelfth-century authors of histories. Applying to her a standard for judging English queens set in the Anglo-Norman age and prejudiced by gossip that had become attached to her since the incident at Antioch years earlier, most contemporary writers found Eleanor, granddaughter of a dissolute southern duke, falling short of their image of a proper queen. Even before her death, gossip and rumor were being magnified into myths. Unfortunately for Eleanor's reputation, many historians in succeeding centuries have followed her contemporaries in their negative judgment.

CHAPTER 12

OVERWHELMED BY A BLACK LEGEND

Eleanor of Aquitaine was the object of more scurrilous gossip in her lifetime than any queen except possibly Marie Antoinette, and resulting depictions of Eleanor as a loose and frivolous woman would define her for centuries. Ugly gossip about Eleanor's alleged sexual impropriety first arose during the Second Crusade at her uncle's court at Antioch, first revealing the crisis in her marriage to Louis VII, and an open break with him ensued. Resulting from the incident at Antioch was a "black legend," fastening onto her a reputation for sexual promiscuity that still undermines her reputation today, despite a lack of actual proof. Rumors followed the royal couple back to France where they soon took on a life of their own, and gossip of Eleanor's serial adulteries was circulating in her own lifetime.

Insinuation and innuendo in contemporary chronicles expanded into outright fiction in the years following her death, as stories circulating during her lifetime coalesced with older legends, and a legendary Eleanor was created bearing little resemblance to the actual queen-duchess. Such myths chiefly interest the historian of mentalities and of folklore, although the historian of Eleanor must grapple with the reasons for the hatred that they express.

No doubt the pervasive misogyny of medieval churchmen and intellectuals encouraged Eleanor's excoriation by her contemporaries. Medieval texts studied by candidates for the clergy were filled with anti-female views, teaching that women were more aggressive sexually than men, with ravenous sexual appetites; and even medieval medical teaching reinforced the belief that women were exploding volcanos of sexual desire, less capable than men of taming their passions. Almost all writings about Eleanor since the early thirteenth century have been tainted by the hostility perpetuated in these legends, not only repeating rumors about her misbehavior on crusade but readily adding new tales of her serial adulteries. Even in the modern era, popular writers have continued to recycle these fictions.

Historians throughout the later Middle Ages and in much of the modern era adopted a moralistic approach to historical personalities similar to the monastic writers' standard that was "essentially a moral judgment upon an individual sinner." Nineteenth-century Victorian writers, even those influenced by an emerging professional approach to the study of history, still followed chroniclers' estimates of members of medieval princely families. Both assumed that a queen's immoral behavior could have evil effects on her royal husband's governance and on his kingdom's equilibrium. Eleanor would have aroused the same fear, revulsion, and hatred in nineteenth-century writers that contemporary chroniclers had felt when confronted with her desire for liberty and power. Popular writers even today cannot resist the temptation to continue propagating the myth of Eleanor's prodigious sexual appetites.[1]

A ballad first published in England in the seventeenth century, though doubtless recycling earlier stories, recites the crimes credited to Eleanor. In the ballad the queen confesses her sins to two friars, actually Henry II and William Marshal in disguise, admitting to a number of sins: not only adultery, but also murder. Accusations that Eleanor had murdered her husband's beloved Rosamund Clifford had arisen by the fourteenth century, and they continued even into the nineteenth century. Soon after the queen's death another legend arose and spread widely—an accusation of her demonic descent, apparently transferring to her folk tales of lords' marriages to ladies with demonic features who vanished when their secret became known. Among these tales was one of an early count of Anjou with a demon-wife, who had the mysterious habit of always leaving church before the elevation of the host. Once restrained from departing, she had suddenly flown through a window never to be seen again.[2] Somehow these later legends coalesced into the story of the demon lady Melusine, and Eleanor, or a fictional character standing in her place, became its central figure. Only near the end of the nineteenth century did a rehabilitation of Eleanor's reputation begin, and the result was a new myth of her as "the troubadour queen."

ELEANOR AS MULTIPLE ADULTERER

Like many great women in history, Eleanor of Aquitaine's reputation is stained with tales of sexual impropriety. Accusations of multiple adulteries began with gossip about alleged indiscretions with her uncle, Raymond, prince of Antioch, while on the Second Crusade. The rumors spawned a black legend that took on a life of its own, until she became eventually "a sort of quasi-mythic figure, the very symbol of feminine infidelity."[3] In Eleanor's own lifetime, contemporaries hinted that she was the sexual partner not only of Raymond of Antioch, but also of Geoffrey de Rancon, a powerful Poitevin lord, while on the road to the Holy Land, and after her return to France, of Geoffrey, count of Anjou, who was about to become her father-in-law. After her marriage to Henry II, she was accused of improper relations with another uncle, Ralph de Faye.

Following Eleanor's death new names were added to the list of her lovers, among them the troubadour Bernart de Ventadorn. An imaginative mid-thirteenth-century biography of Bernart claimed that she had been his mistress, although the author's sketchy knowledge of Eleanor's life discredits his account. He shows Bernart going to Normandy where Eleanor was duchess to seek her favor, but their love affair ended when she married Henry, king of England. In fact, Bernart de Ventadorn had been present at the Plantagenet court in Normandy and England for a time early in Henry and Eleanor's marriage, but his affair with the queen-duchess is imaginary.[4] About the same time, a famous Paris preacher told an anecdote of Eleanor in a sermon, accusing her of having attempted to seduce Gilbert de la Porrée, bishop of Poitiers (1147–54), her senior by more than forty years. Referring to Eleanor only as "a certain queen of France," the preacher claimed that she desired Master Gilbert, and called him to her presence. Noticing his fair hands, she took his hand in hers, and said, "Oh, how fitting if these fingers should touch my sides!" Quickly withdrawing his hand, he replied, "Lady, let this not be done for if my fingers thus touched you, with what could I ever eat again?"[5]

In the course of the thirteenth century, Eleanor's reputation had sunk to such a point that common opinion pointed to her adulteries as Louis VII's reason for divorcing her. Early in the century, a French chronicler Hélinand de Froidmont (d. *c.*1230) included a brief account of Eleanor's two marriages in his work. Hélinand, a former *trouvère* in Philip Augustus's entourage, had become a Cistercian monk, but continued writing in the cloister, composing a universal chronicle in Latin. In his passage on Eleanor's divorce, he writes, "It was on account of her lasciviousness that Louis gave up his wife, who behaved not like a queen but more like a harlot."[6] Like Gerald of Wales, Hélinand was writing near the end of the long Capetian–Plantagenet conflicts, and as a onetime courtier of Philip Augustus, he took care to accent the moral failings of the king's enemies. A generation later the chronicle of another French Cistercian, Aubri des Trois Fontaines, recorded only one event for the year 1152: Eleanor's divorce and remarriage. His entry parallels that in Hélinand's chronicle: "Henry of England took as wife the woman whom the king of France had just got rid of ... Louis had let her go on account of the lasciviousness of this woman, who behaved not like a queen, but more like a public woman."[7] In the early fourteenth century, Hélinand's account was

copied by a Dominican inquisitor and author, Bernard Gui, in one of his
historical works.[8]

Not long after Eleanor's death, writers were expanding on her sexual
adventures during the Second Crusade, and earlier guarded allusions to her
indiscretion with Raymond of Antioch were transformed into allegations that
her paramour at Antioch was not her uncle, but a Muslim prince, eventually
identified as Saladin. The chronicles of Matthew Paris (d. *c.*1259), a monk
of St Albans Abbey, afford a prime example of this shift.[9] In his account of
Louis vii's crusade, he merely mentioned that the queen had accompanied
him without alluding to the Antioch affair. When discussing Eleanor's divorce,
however, he could not contain his predilection for "unscrupulous falsifica-
tion,"[10] and he transmuted Eleanor's supposed dalliance with her uncle in
the east into affairs with Saracens. The St Albans chronicler charged her not
only with multiple adulteries, but "especially infidelity with a certain infidel
prince in the East, perpetrated while her husband devoted himself to the
business of war."[11]

A collection of historical anecdotes composed in French by an anonymous
minstrel of Reims about 1260 likely had greater influence than Matthew Paris
on later accounts of the incident at Antioch. He too spins a tale of Eleanor's
involvement with a Muslim prince, falling in love with the sultan Saladin,
her son Richard's adversary during the Third Crusade. In fact, Saladin would
not have been even a teenager at the time of Eleanor's visit to the Holy
Land. Nonetheless, the minstrel's account—more that of a *jongleur* than a
historian—has her falling madly in love before meeting him. Having heard of
his many qualities that contrasted with Louis vii's pious and passive character,
she promised to renounce Christianity if the Muslim leader should succeed
in abducting her. Her husband stopped her as she was preparing to flee
to Saladin, and when he asked her why she was deserting him, she replied,
"On account of your *mauvestié* [translated variously as cowardice, worthless-
ness, or fecklessness], in God's name; for you are not worth a rotten apple!
And I've heard such good reports of Saladin that I love him better than
you." On returning to France, the king followed his barons' advice and separated from Eleanor. The minstrel's account stresses Eleanor's wealth, "the
noblest and richest lady in Christendom," holding "fully three times as
much land as the king." He commented that Louis had "acted like a fool," for
in sending his queen away, he lost her land, "which was vast and rich," to
Henry Plantagenet.[12]

Other late medieval French chronicles follow the Reims minstrel's version
of Eleanor's adventures on crusade. An unpublished fourteenth-century
manuscript includes a shorter version of the minstrel's account, and it too
condemns Louis vii for losing her lands. In this chronicle, the French king

again asked his men's advice about what to do with his wayward wife once he had intercepted her flight with Saladin, and he followed it, sending her back to her own country. The author comments that this "was a foolish thing to do," and when Louis's former wife married the king of England, "He knew that he had acted foolishly by not walling up Countess Eleanor, but it was too late."[13] Another history, a fifteenth-century *Chronique de Flandre*, follows the Reims minstrel less closely, yet it clearly shares some elements that reveal it as its source. In this account, Eleanor was at Tripoli, and she planned to run away with "the Sultan Rehaudin." When she and her husband Louis returned to the west, he went to Rome to ask the pope for a divorce.[14]

By the sixteenth century, printed books were appearing that reported Eleanor and her supposed liaison with Saladin. Widely read was Jean Bouchet's *Annales d'Acquitaine*, first published in 1524. Bouchet, a Poitevin native, had sought a career at court as a poet, but returned to Poitiers to practice law and to write. His *Annales*, a prose chronicle of his native province, proved popular, printed in numerous editions down to 1644, five of them revised and reissued by the author.[15] In his book, he sought to re-establish a more honorable memory for the great duchess, and he reworked her portrait along the lines of depictions of ideal queens. Bouchet gave voice to the accusation of Eleanor's sexual misconduct on crusade through the words of one of the bishops at the council at Beaugency in 1152 considering Louis VII's demand for a divorce. According to Bouchet, the bishop in advocating the divorce raised the issue of Eleanor's adultery, accusing her of having given herself "to Sultan Saladin, whose image and portrait she had seen."[16]

Jean Bouchet, wishing to depict Eleanor in a favorable light, portrayed her not as a criminal, but as the victim of her jealous husband, Louis VII. In his discussion of the incident at Antioch, he presented her taking Count Raymond's side against her husband because she held her ties of blood to Raymond to be more powerful than her marital bond. According to Bouchet, the queen knew nothing of the council at Beaugency until the archbishop of Bordeaux informed her of its approval of Louis's demand for a dissolution of their marriage. At the news, she fainted and remained speechless for two hours, and when she revived, she asked how she had displeased the king. Told that their marriage was consanguineous, she accepted the need to separate, but asked for the return of her ancestral lands to her. Wounded in her pride, she soon accepted the proposal of Henry Plantagenet. Bouchet's rehabilitation of Eleanor found some favor with other late sixteenth-century writers, but his influence had little long-term impact.[17]

At the end of the seventeenth century, the first biography of Eleanor of Aquitaine appeared, authored by the French historian Isaac de Larrey (d.1719), an exiled Protestant. Rejecting the story of the queen's attachment to Saladin, Larrey conjectured that she had written to the Muslim leader seeking the release of a captive relative, Sambreuil (rightly Saldebreuil), a Poitevin lord. Saladin, touched by the letter's tone, released his prisoner without demanding any ranson, and Eleanor responded with a courteous letter of thanks. According to Larrey, when Louis VII learned of his wife's negotiations with the Christians' enemy without consulting him, he became jealous and accused her of "a criminal commerce" with Saladin, becoming his lover with her uncle Raymond's connivance. Eleanor dismissed this accusation contemptuously and afterward could no longer love Louis, causing her to propose that they separate. Larrey noted that after the couple's return to France, the rejected queen met Henry Plantagenet, whom she found more cultivated than Louis.[18]

Larrey's attempted rehabilitation had little effect, as did the critical spirit of the eighteenth-century age of reason; and for most eighteenth-century French historians Eleanor remained a shameless harlot. One wrote of Eleanor's conduct at Antioch, "Accustomed to the time and the place, she so abandoned herself to the voluptuousness of the Levant that the foul odor of her incontinence spread everywhere before the king became aware of it."[19] A Poitevin who later became an ardent revolutionary published a history of Poitou just before the 1789 Revolution with a sympathetic treatment of Eleanor, though it had little effect on her reputation among the French as a bad wife and a bad queen.[20] The Revolution perhaps harmed Eleanor's reputation, for stories of Marie Antoinette's indiscretions brought to mind parallels with her twelfth-century predecessor. Neither the restoration of the monarchy nor the re-establishment of a republic would bring an improvement in Eleanor's reputation in France.[21]

Across the Channel in Britain, the Scottish rationalist philosopher David Hume did not hesitate to repeat in his popular *History of England* the rumor of Eleanor's dalliance with a Muslim prince, although he took care to categorize it as mere suspicion. In his account of Henry II's marriage to the duchess of Aquitaine, he noted her earlier crusading adventure with Louis VII, writing that "there having lost the affection of her husband, and even fallen under some suspicion of gallantry with a handsome Saracen," Louis's divorce from her followed.[22] Elsewhere he wrote that "Queen Eleanor, who had disgusted her first husband by her gallantries, was no less offensive to her second . . . and . . . carried to extremity, in different periods of her life, every circumstance of female weakness."[23]

Two movements, romanticism and nationalism, dominating early nineteenth-century culture, had a major impact on the writing of history, encouraging an interest in the Middle Ages as the formative period in the evolution of the modern nations. All the qualities of romantic and nationalistic history writing are illustrated in the major work of the French historian Jules Michelet (1798–1874), his monumental *Histoire de France*. He continued the vilification of Eleanor of Aquitaine; his characterization of her as "passionate and vindictive as a woman of the Midi" is repeated by innumerable writers. He saw Eleanor as a prototype of the women liberated by the twelfth-century revival of classical learning and by courtly culture who felt entitled to their freedom. Yet he condemned her as "a veritable Melusine, mixed with contradictory natures, mother and daughter of a diabolical generation." He went so far as to claim that on account of her affair with Geoffrey le Bel, "the sons that she had of Henry risked greatly being the brothers of their father."[24] In the 1930s a distinguished French medievalist echoed Michelet's description, writing that Eleanor was a "southern adventuress," and continuing, "Coquette, capricious and sensual, Eleanor is a real pagan."[25]

In Victorian England old canards about the twelfth-century queen continued to be copied and embellished even though serious study of history was passing from learned amateurs to university-trained professionals striving for an objective scientific method. Yet non-professionals continued turning out histories that attracted large numbers of readers, including a new reading public of middle-class women. A work popular with them was the six-volume *Lives of the Queens of England* by Agnes Strickland (1806–74), first published 1840–49 and often reissued. Surprisingly, Strickland, reporting the Antioch episode in her chapter on Eleanor, does not accuse the French queen directly of adultery with her uncle, Prince Raymond, writing, "It seems strange that the man who first awakened the jealousy of king Louis should stand in such very near relationship to his wife; yet . . . she commenced such a series of coquetries with her handsome uncle, that king Louis, greatly scandalized and incensed, hurried her out of Antioch one night . . ." She points out, however, "It is true, many authorities say that Raymond's intrigues with his niece were wholly political."[26]

Strickland repeats stories of Eleanor's affair with Saladin, reporting that after leaving her uncle's court, Eleanor engaged in "a criminal attachment . . . to a young Saracen emir of great beauty, named Sal-Addin." She mentions that letters of Suger of Saint-Denis supply the evidence, doubtless meaning the abbot's letter actually referring only to the king's suspicions aroused at Antioch. According to Strickland, the queen's misconduct led Louis to express his intention of separating from her as soon as he returned to his kingdom, but he was dissuaded by Suger. The king's trusted counselor pointed out that such an action would lead to the loss of Eleanor's rich inheritance, and that their daughter, Marie, would not inherit her mother's duchy should the queen remarry. Suger's warning persuaded the French king to permit the unhappy Eleanor to return with him to Paris, and it was his dread of losing Aquitaine that "allowed her to retain the dignity of queen of France."[27]

While writers of the twentieth and twenty-first centuries no longer hypothesize an affair between Eleanor and the Muslim Saladin, some are nonetheless still willing to posit a sexual dimension to her relationship with her uncle Raymond of Antioch. One popular biographer recently wrote, "In the face of all the reliable contemporary evidence, it is puzzling to find that most of Eleanor's modern biographers do not accept that she had an adulterous affair with Raymond."[28] Even respectable scholars can indicate their own suspicions with innuendo worthy of a judgmental monastic chronicler. One writes, "Raymond welcomed her with open arms—all too open, some were to hint."[29]

ELEANOR AS MURDERER

A body of legend about Henry II's love affair with Rosamund Clifford captured popular imagination. As the story of their love became the subject of poetry, dramas, even operas, Eleanor's alleged quest for revenge, even plotting her rival's murder, became a central aspect of the legend. At first, Eleanor's role was simply that of the wronged wife, and it was Henry and Rosamund's conduct that was condemned. This was the view presented by a mid-fourteenth-century monastic chronicler Ralph of Higden in his *Polychronicon*, a universal history and encyclopedia. In his book, he tells of Henry's love for Rosamund and the hideaway that he constructed for her, a labyrinthine palace or "maze" at Woodstock. His explanation that the purpose of the maze was to prevent Henry's queen from finding Rosamund may have provided an opening for speculation by later writers that Eleanor desired to do her harm.[30] *Polychronicon* became one of the most popular chronicles in late medieval England, and it passed into English-language literature when it was translated into the vernacular in the 1380s by John of Trevisa.[31]

Taking up Higden's hint, the mid-fourteenth-century *Chroniques de London* appears to be the first work that depicts a vindictive and jealous Eleanor causing Rosamund's death. Its anonymous author describes in gory detail the unhappy fate of the Fair Rosamund at the queen's hands, "a noble young lady, the most beautiful known to man, put to death, accusing her of being the king's concubine."[32] Throughout his account, he confuses the king and queen with Henry III and Eleanor of Provence, dating Rosamund's death to 1262. His gruesome telling of Rosamund's death begins with the queen's placing the naked Rosamund in a closed room between two fires and threatening to burn her; then she has her put into a bath, and an old woman is summoned to cut her veins in both arms. While she is bleeding to death, another aged woman brings two toads to place on her breasts, which they begin to suckle. Two more hags enter to hold the bleeding Rosamund by her arms until she expires, while the queen stands by laughing and mocking her. Eleanor has her body buried in a dirty ditch, but later the grief-stricken king has a tomb constructed for her at Godstow Abbey.[33]

New versions of Eleanor's pursuit of Fair Rosamund continued to appear in the early modern era. The Woodstock maze appears in an early sixteenth-century chronicle by Robert Fabyan of London, obviously borrowing from the Greek legend of Theseus and the minotaur. In Fabyn's version, Eleanor adopts Theseus's navigation of the labyrinth by using a ball of string to find Rosamund; then the vengeful queen "dealt with her in such manner that she lived not long after."[34] After this, a staple of Rosamund tales became Eleanor's use of string to reach Rosamund in the maze-like bower built for her by Henry II at Woodstock. It appears in Samuel Daniel's poem, *The Complaint of Rosamond*, printed in 1592, and again in a ballad *Fair Rosamonde*, dating from the end of the sixteenth century, although only published two centuries later.[35] The ballad again has Eleanor finding Rosamund in her bower at Woodstock, "so cunningly contriv'd, / with turnings round about, / That none but with a clue of thread / Could enter in or out." Despite Rosamund's pleas for mercy, Eleanor forces her to drink a cup of poison. A ballad from Scotland, *Queen Eleanor's Confession*, charges Eleanor not only with the poisoning of Rosamund, but also the attempted poisoning of her own husband. This ballad, first printed in the late seventeenth century, probably originated much earlier; for the theme of an unsuspecting wife confessing her infidelities to her husband disguised as a confessor was popular in later medieval vernacular literature.[36]

The rivalry between Eleanor and Rosamund lent itself to dramatization. The essayist and poet Joseph Addison early in the eighteenth century composed an opera, *Rosamond*, in which Eleanor confronts her rival and gives her the choice of death by a poisoned cup or a dagger. Addison wanted a happy ending, however; and in his operatic version of the legend, the cup is found to contain only a sleeping potion, not poison. The opera ends with Eleanor and Henry reconciled, and Rosamund left to live out her life at Godstow Abbey.[37] In the Victorian age, the poet Alfred Lord Tennyson composed a verse drama *Becket* in 1884 that intertwined the political theme of the quarrel between Thomas Becket and Henry II with the legend of Queen Eleanor's hounding of her husband's mistress. When the Fair Rosamund is cornered by Eleanor armed with a dagger, she cries out, naming the queen's own paramours:

And I will fly . . . to heaven,
and shriek to all the saints . . .
"Eleanor of Aquitaine, Eleanor of England!

Murder'd by that adultress Eleanor,
whose doings are a horror to the east,
A hissing in the west!" Have we not heard
Raymond of Poitou, thine own uncle—nay,
Geoffrey Plantagenet, thine own husband's father—
Nay, ev'n the accursed heathen Saladdeen—Strike!
I challenge thee to meet me before God.[38]

No doubt Tennyson's source for the Rosamund story was Alice Strickland's *Lives of the Queens of England*, which became a standard work. Strickland admitted that it was no easy task to sort through the many tales concerning Eleanor and her rival, but she placed too much faith in unreliable sources and her own imagination. In her chapter on Eleanor, she even asserts that Henry had met Rosamund in his youth before his coronation as king, and that he had privately contracted a marriage with her. After bringing Eleanor to England, he had kept Rosamund hidden away at Woodstock, ignorant of his marriage. The queen eventually discovers his secret, however, finds her way through the maze, and confronts her husband's mistress. Strickland writes that "it is certain that the queen did not destroy her rival either by sword or poison, though in her rage it is possible that she might threaten both." Nonetheless, Henry had to separate from Rosamund, and Strickland calculates that she lived for another twenty years "in great penitence" after taking religious vows at Godstow.[39]

ELEANOR AS A DEMON LADY

An archetypal narrative of folklore centers on the "man-with-fairy-mistress" theme. A mysterious lady encounters a young noble whose passion she arouses and, wishing to hide a dark secret, will not agree to become his lover until she extracts a promise of secrecy from him. Then when her beloved breaks his promise, she suddenly disappears without a trace. Eventually this fairy mistress would receive the name Melusine, and she would be transformed from a fairy into a demonic creature. Such tales became attached to Eleanor by the early thirteenth century, allegedly deriving from accusations voiced at the time of her divorce from Louis VII. No doubt the image of womanhood that Eleanor presented seemed so contrary to the subordinate role that society assigned to medieval women that the conclusion was that she could only be of diabolical descent.[40] The first written accounts of such a demon mistress appear in books by Walter Map and Gervase of Tilbury, two writers who were among Henry II's courtiers.

Walter Map in his book on courtiers' follies includes an account of such a mysterious lady, "that beautiful pestilence," the bride of an eleventh-century

Norman baron "who always shunned the sprinkling of holy water." Her curious mother-in-law spied on her after she left the church and watched her go into her bath, where she turned into a dragon. When her husband and a priest arrived to sprinkle her with holy water, she vanished through the roof.[41] A few years later, Gervase of Tilbury, who had moved on to the court of the German emperor, completed a book of anecdotes that he had begun for Henry the Young King in which he included a similar tale. Gervase set his version in Provence, where the lord of a castle near Aix, out riding one day, came upon a beautiful lady whom he desired greatly, but she would not give in to his desire unless he agreed to marry her. She warned him that "he would enjoy the utmost earthly prosperity in his wedded life [only] as long as he did not see her naked." The lord agreed never to attempt to see her unclothed, but finally his curiosity overcame him, and he spied on her in her bath. When his lady became aware that he had seen her, she turned herself into a serpent, plunged beneath the bath-water, and was never seen again.[42]

About the same time that Gervase of Tilbury was writing in the Holy Roman Empire, Gerald of Wales in England was spinning another version of the demon bride tale, this one featuring an early countess of Anjou. Gerald wrote of an ancestor of Henry Plantagenet who very seldom came to church and showed little or no devotion during the service, always leaving immediately after the reading of the gospel and never remaining for the consecration of the host. Eventually the count, concerned at her strange conduct, had her forcibly restrained by his men when she attempted to leave the church. She took under her arm two of her young sons, and flew out of an upper window of the church in the sight of all the congregation, leaving behind two other sons. Gerald concluded, "And so this woman, more fair in face than in faith, having carried off her two children with her, was never afterwards seen there." According to him, Richard Lionheart often told this Plantagenet family legend as an explanation for his and his brothers' quarrelsome natures. Richard allegedly joked that "all had come of the devil, and to the devil they would go." Gerald's tale had the subversive purpose of "placing a she-devil at the very heart of the Plantagenet dynasty."[43]

In the decades following Eleanor's death, if not earlier, these older legends of women of demonic ancestry came to merge with tales told of her as her reputation steadily worsened. Matthew Paris listed among the reasons for Louis VII's divorce of Eleanor that she "was descended from the devil."[44] Two little-known Norman vernacular histories dating from the early thirteenth century also take up the demon legend, applying it to Eleanor. Both include an account of her after leaving Louis VII's court disrobing before her Poitevin subjects to prove that she was no devil. They offer, however, a version favorable to the newly divorced queen, demonstrating that she was indeed no demon and refuting tales circulating of her devilish descent. The shorter of these two histories appears to have been written no later than a generation after Eleanor's death, or even earlier. A manuscript of it seems to have belonged to the Abbaye aux Dames at Caen. Perhaps the nuns there, some of them noble ladies from distinguished families, cherished a more sympathetic memory of their last duchess of Normandy than other tales of her circulating at the time. This history tells of how, after men of Poitou had come to take her away after her separation from Louis, she disrobed and said to them, "Lords, what sort of beast am I?" And they told her, "By God! There is no more beautiful woman living in this age." She then replied to them, "I am not the devil that the king of France called me just now." The second vernacular history from Normandy, dating from early in the second half of the thirteenth century, is much longer, but its story is essentially the same.[45] Clearly the Norman historians who included these two stories intended to salvage Eleanor's reputation, not to sully it. They seem unlikely to have meant that Eleanor exposed herself naked to her nobles, but that she only removed her outer garments to demonstrate the beauty of her entirely human body, lacking any demonic characteristics.[46]

A few years later, Philippe Mouskès in his *Chronique rimé* also shows Eleanor, stung by her repudiation by Louis, gathering her Poitevin nobles together and disrobing before them. She asks them, "Is not my body delightful? And yet the king says that I am a devil." Her barons reassure her of her beauty and that she will soon find another husband. Mouskès, nonetheless, connected Eleanor to the demonic legend through her mother. After reciting the story of the rejected queen's undressing before her barons, he adds an account of her parentage. He tells how the "count" of Aquitaine while out hunting met a beautiful lady; married her, and had several children with her, including Eleanor. Then after a time the countess suddenly disappeared as usual in such tales, flying off through the church roof.[47]

In the mid-thirteenth century, the anonymous minstrel of Reims gave an account of Louis after his return from crusade, seeking his barons' advice about what to do with his queen, to which the French nobles replied, "Truly, the best advice we could give you is to let her go; for she's a devil, and if you keep her much longer we're afraid she'll have you murdered." The king took their advice, although the minstrel commented, "He would have done better to have her walled up, so that he would have had her great land all his life."[48] A direct borrowing from the Reims minstrel appears in the fifteenth-century *Chronique normande* by Pierre Cochon. His account also depicts the French king seeking his barons' counsel about Eleanor's fate after the couple had returned from the crusade. This late chronicler also records the barons' advice "to let her go to the devil . . . where she had come from." Cochon copies the minstrel's suggestion: "That was bad advice because it would have been better if he had walled her up. And besides, he had no child from her."[49]

The Middle English romance *Richard Coeur de Lion*, composed in or near London around 1300, continues the conflation of Eleanor with earlier tales of a demon bride. This romance does not give the name of the hero's mother as Eleanor, but names her Cassodorien. Like the demon-countess of Anjou, Cassodorien had the mysterious habit of always leaving mass before the elevation of the host; and when forced to remain for that high point of the mass, she had suddenly flown out the window of a chapel never to be seen again.[50] In the romance, likely based on an earlier Anglo-Norman poem, Henry II married Cassodorien, the beautiful daughter of the king of Antioch, after she and her father had sailed to England, inspired by a vision. After fourteen years of marriage never daring to let her eyes fix on the consecrated host, one Sunday the king forced Cassodorien to remain in church while the priest elevated the host. At that moment, "She took her daughter by the hand, nor would she be without her son. She made her way out through the roof in full view of them all." Young John fell, however, and broke his thigh; but she and her daughter flew away, and were never seen again. Strangely, Eleanor appears in the romance under her own name at one point, depicted accurately as bringing Richard's bride Berengaria of Navarre to him in Sicily.[51]

The definitive version of the demon lady legend, a romance giving her the name Mélusine, is a late fourteenth-century work by Jean d'Arras. His *Mélusine* omits direct references to Eleanor, but the action is set in Poitou, telling the story of the Lusignan family's origins, an example of so-called "ancestral romances." In Jean's account, Mélusine, the bride of the lord of Lusignan, had exacted from her husband a promise never to see her on Saturdays, for on those days she took the form of a serpent. Her husband could not resist spying on her while she was in her bath on a Saturday, however, and he was appalled to see that she had a serpent's body from the waist down. Mélusine then turned into a fifteen-foot-long serpent and flew away.[52] A similar version of the Mélusine story linking her with the Lusignan family, *Le Roman de Mélusine ou Histoire de Lusignan*, was written about the same time by Coudrette, possibly a native of Poitou.[53]

A NEW MYTH OF ELEANOR AS "QUEEN OF THE TROUBADOURS"

In the early nineteenth century, two movements, romanticism and nationalism, combined to foster a new interest in medieval vernacular languages, and in France this led to a recovery of the troubadour poets' songs in Occitan. Late in the century, scholars' study of the troubadour songs resulted in the discovery of "courtly love," a term coined by Gaston Paris (1839–1903), the greatest French philologist of his day and a professor at the Collège de France. This widely used term has no single accepted meaning today, but it introduced the novel notion of an unrequited, but ennobling and almost idolatrous love of a knight for a lady of higher rank, propagated by the troubadour poets. Some scholars saw noble ladies' patronage of the literature of "courtly love" as evidence for their growing influence in medieval society.

In the course of the nineteenth century, history was becoming a profession dominated by academics and demanding advanced studies; since then, Eleanor of Aquitaine's fate has suffered at the hands of professional historians who were largely a male-dominated group. These scholars, relying primarily on Latin chronicles, tended to leave Eleanor in the shadows, or when they did take notice of her, followed moralizing medieval clerics' conventional character assessments. Most academic historians throughout much of the twentieth century were willing to leave such "softer topics" as studies of medieval women's lives to students of literature, an academic sphere where women were once more likely to find careers.[54] Women are prominent among Eleanor's modern biographers, and they often give Eleanor their "unreflecting empathy."[55] With their background in medieval literature they have tended to emphasize her emotional life and her literary activity. A result is that studies of Eleanor's life written by specialists in medieval vernacular literature have focused on her role as a patron of poets or her life as inspiration for episodes in the romances. To the dismay of political historians working primarily with Latin sources, some "literary" historians look to the portraits of Arthur's queen Guinevere in romances for a disclosure of the real-life Eleanor. A respected scholar of French literature concluded in his 1993 biography of Eleanor that the best means of delineating her is through "a composite picture ... from the more sympathetic of the portrayals of Guenevere in courtly romance." Such writers have inspired a new, more positive myth of Eleanor as "queen of the troubadours." Missing Andrew the Chaplain's irony in uncritical readings of his book *On Love*, they picture the queen-duchess as sponsor of the new doctrine of courtly love at her court at Poitiers, 1168–74, sitting in judgment in "courts of love."[56]

Amy Kelly in her widely read 1956 book, *Eleanor of Aquitaine and the Four Kings*, describes Eleanor's court as an academy for civilizing "truculent youths, boisterous young from the baronial strongholds of the south." According to her, the queen-duchess saw it as her duty to "subdue to civility a generation that had lacked the disciplines of a somewhat fixed and authentic court." Kelly even proposed that Eleanor summoned her elder daughter by Louis VII, Marie, countess of Champagne, to head the "royal academy at Poitiers," even though there is no evidence whatsoever that Marie ever visited her mother at Poitiers.[57] Marion Meade in her 1977 book, *Eleanor of Aquitaine*, takes

Eleanor's "academy" as a starting point for creating an image of her as feminist revolutionary. Meade depicts her carving for women an elevated position in medieval society by taming belligerent young knights, teaching them a new courtly code through her courts of love. She writes of the ladies at Eleanor's court, "They saw themselves as innovators of a rational new world, a prototype for the future perhaps, in which women might reign as goddesses or at the least mistresses of their own destinies."[58] Thus the myth-making continues in a new age, although it is now more favorable to Eleanor.

No other medieval queen's reputation was so tarnished as Eleanor's by an accumulation of gossip, rumor, and outright fabrication. Soon after her death, stories circulated incorporating legends that had nothing to do with her, and any trace of the real Eleanor, the queen and mother, was overcome by a black legend that only grew over the centuries. Why Eleanor aroused such hostility is difficult to explain, although shifting attitudes toward women offer clues. By her first years, the unique situation that had prevailed in the chaotic tenth and eleventh centuries, when lack of governmental structures enabled strong women to seize roles as leaders, had ended. In the twelfth century, a woman confident of her own abilities and eager to exercise power appeared threatening to good order, violating standards for feminine behavior laid down by both the Church and aristocracy. Blackening Eleanor's reputation with charges of personal immorality was the opinion shapers' response to her shocking refusal to conform to medieval society's norms. In succeeding centuries the myth totally triumphed over reality. Today stripping away such legends is essential if a "truthful image" of Eleanor is to be recovered.

Abbreviations

AHP	*Archives historiques du Poitou*
ANS	*Anglo-Norman Studies*
Aurell, ed., *Aliénor*	Martin Aurell, ed., *Aliénor d'Aquitaine, 303: art, recherches et création*, extra series (Nantes, 2004)
BEC	*Bibliothèque de l'école des chartes*
Becket Correspondence	*The Correspondence of Thomas Becket, Archbishop of Canterbury, 1162–1170*, ed. and trans. Ann J. Duggan, 2 vols (Oxford, 2001)
BSAO	*Bulletin de la société des antiquaires de l'ouest*
Cal. Chtr. Rolls	*Calendar of Charter Rolls*, Public Record Office, 6 vols (London, 1903–27)
Cal. Docs. France	*Calendar of Documents Preserved in France*, I, *918–1206*, ed. J. H. Round (London, 1899)
CCM	*Cahiers de civilisation médiévale*
Chron. Turon. mag	*Chronicon Turonense magnum*, in A. Salmon, ed., *Recueil des chroniques de Touraine* (Tours, 1854)
CMH	*Cambridge Medieval History*, eds H.M. Gwatkin, J.P. Whitney, J.R. Tanner, C.W. Previté-Orton, and Z.N. Brooke, 8 vols (Cambridge, 1911–36) (see also *New CMH*)
La Cour Plantagenêt	Martin Aurell, ed., *La Cour Plantagenêt (1154–1204), Actes du colloque tenu à Thouars du 30 avril au 2 mai 1999* (Poitiers, 2000)
Delisle-Berger, *Actes*	Léopold Delisle and Elie Berger, eds, *Recueil des actes de Henri II*, 3 vols (Paris, 1916–27)

Delisle-Berger, *Intro.*	Léopold Delisle and Elie Berger, eds, *Recueil des actes de Henri II, Introduction* (Paris, 1909)
Dict. M.A.	*Dictionary of the Middle Ages*, ed. J.R. Strayer, 13 vols (New York, *c.* 1982–89)
DNB	*Oxford Dictionary of National Biography*, ed. Leslie Stephen (1885–1901) (see also *Oxford DNB*)
EHR	*English Historical Review*
Eleanor: Lord and Lady	John Carmi Parsons and Bonnie Wheeler, eds, *Eleanor of Aquitaine: Lord and Lady* (New York, 2003)
Eyton, *Itin. H. II*	R.W. Eyton, *Court, Household, and Itinerary of King Henry II* (London, 1878)
Fasti	John le Neve, *Fasti Ecclesiae Anglicanae 1066–1300*, ed. Diana E. Greenway, 9 vols (London, 1968–)
Geoffrey de Vigeois	*Geoffroi de Vigeois, Chronica*, ed. Père Labbé, in *Novae bibliotheca manuscriptorum*, vol. 11 (Paris, 1657); also *RHGF*, vol. 12
Gerald of Wales	*De principis instructione*, ed. G.F. Warner, in *Giraldi Cambrensis opera*, 8 vols, Rolls Series (London, 1861–91)
Gervase of Canterbury	*Gervase of Canterbury: Historical Works*, ed. William Stubbs, 2 vols Rolls Series (London, 1879–80)
Gesta Regis	*Gesta Regis Henrici Secundi Benedicti Abbatis*, ed. William Stubbs, 2 vols (London, 1867)
Howden, *Chronica*	*Chronica Rogeri de Houedene*, ed. William Stubbs, 4 vols Rolls Series (London, 1868–71)
HSJ	*Haskins Society Journal*
JMH	*Journal of Medieval History*
John of Salisbury, *Letters*	W.J. Miller and C.N.L. Brooke, eds, *The Letters of John of Salisbury*, 2, *Oxford Medieval Texts* (Oxford, 1979, 1986)
Kibler, ed., *Eleanor*	W.W. Kibler, ed., *Eleanor of Aquitaine, Patron and Politician* (Austin, 1976)
Labande, "Pour une image"	E.-R. Labande, "Pour une image véridique d'Aliénor d'Aquitaine," *BSAO*, 4th ser., 2 (1952); reprinted in Labande, *Histoire de l'Europe Occidentale XIe-XIVe siècles* (London, 1973)
Landon, *Itinerary*	Lionel Landon, *The Itinerary of King Richard I*, Pipe Roll Society, new series, 13 (London, 1935)
Medieval Queenship	John Carmi Parsons, ed., *Medieval Queenship* (New York, 1993)

Migne, *PL*	J.P. Migne, ed., *Parologiae cursus completus . . . series Latina*, 221 vols (Paris, 1844–1903)
MSAO	*Mémoires de la Société des antiquaires de l'Ouest*
New *CMH*	*The New Cambridge Medieval History*, eds Paul Fouracre, Rosamond McKittrick, Timothy Reuter, David Luscombe, Jonathan Riley-Smith, David Abulafia, Michael Jones, and Christopher Allmand, 9 vols (Cambridge, 1995–)
Norgate, *Angevin Kings*	Kate Norgate, *England under the Angevin Kings*, 2 vols (London, 1887; reprint New York, 1969)
Oxford DNB	*Oxford Dictionary of National Biography*, ed. H.C.G. Matthews, Brian Harrison, and Lawrence Goldman, 20 vols (Oxford, 2004), at www.oxforddnb.com
Plantagenêts et Capétiens	*Plantagenêts et Capétiens: Confrontations et héritage*, eds Martin Aurell and Noël-Yves Tonnerre (Turnhout, 2006)
PR	*The Great Roll of the Pipe . . . King Henry II*, Publications of the Pipe Roll Society (London 1884–1925); *Great Roll of the Pipe*, Pipe Roll Society, new ser., ed. Doris M. Stenton (London, 1925–)
PR H. II, Second-Fourth Years, ed. Hunter	*The Great Rolls of the Pipe for the Second, Third, and Fourth Years of the Reign of King Henry the Second, A.D. 1155, 1156, 1157, 1158*, ed. Joseph Hunter, Record Commission (London, 1844)
Ralph of Coggeshall	*Radulphi de Coggeshall Chronicon Anglicanum*, ed. J. Stevenson, Rolls Series (London, 1875)
Ralph Diceto	*Radulphi de Diceto, Opera Historica: The Historical Works of Master Ralph de Diceto, Dean of London*, ed. William Stubbs, 2 vols Rolls Series (London, 1876)
RHGF	Martin Bouquet et al., eds, *Recueil des historiens des Gaules et de la France*, 24 vols (Paris 1734–1904)
Richard Coeur de Lion	John Gillingham, *Richard Coeur de Lion: Kingship, Chivalry and War in the Twelfth Century* (London, 1994)
Richard, *Comtes*	Alfred Richard, *Histoire des comtes de Poitou*, 2 vols (Paris, 1903)
Richard of Devizes	*The Chronicle of Richard of Devizes*, ed. and trans. J.T. Appleby, Medieval Texts (London, 1963)

Robert of Torigni	*Chronicles of the Reigns of Stephen, Henry II, and Richard I*, ed. R. Howlett, 4 vols, Rolls Series (London, 1885–90), 4: *The Chronicle of Robert of Torigni*
Rot. Chart.	*Rotuli Chartarum, 1199–1216*, ed. T. Duffus Hardy, Record Commission (London, 1837)
Rot. Lit. Claus.	*Rotuli Litterarum Clausarum*, ed. T. Duffus Hardy, 2 vols, Record Commission (London, 1833–4)
Status, Authority, Power	Jane Martindale, *Status, Authority, and Regional Power: Aquitaine and France, Ninth to Twelfth Centuries* (Aldershot, 1997)
Walter Map	Walter Map, *De nugis curialium*, eds C.N.L. Brooke and M. R. James, Oxford Medieval Texts (Oxford, 1983), revised edn
William of Malmesbury	*Willelmi Malmesbiriensis de Gestis regum*, ed. William Stubbs, 2 vols, Rolls Series (London, 1887–89)
William of Newburgh	*Chronicles of the Reigns of Stephen, Henry II and Richard I*, ed. R. Howlett, 4 vols, Rolls Series (London, 1885–90), 1–2: *Historia Rerum Anglicarum*
World of Eleanor	Catherine Léglu and Marcus Bull, eds, *The World of Eleanor of Aquitaine: Literature and Society in Southern France between the Eleventh and Thirteenth Centuries* (Woodbridge, 2005)

NOTES

INTRODUCTION: SEARCHING FOR A "TRUTHFUL IMAGE" OF ELEANOR OF AQUITAINE

1. Martin Aurell, *L'Empire des Plantagenêts 1154–1224* (Paris, 2003), p. 45.
2. Jane Martindale, "Eleanor of Aquitaine" in *Status, Authority, Power*, art. 11, p. 24.
3. Phrase of Aurell, "Aux origines de la légende noire d'Aliénor d'Aquitaine," pp. 89–102.
4. John Barrie, Columbia Pictures, 1968.
5. Gillingham's phrase, *Richard I* (New Haven, 1999), p. 44, n. 14.
6. Martindale, "Eleanor of Aquitaine," pp. 37–39.
7. John Carmi Parsons, *Eleanor of Castile: Queen and Society in Thirteenth-century England* (New York, 1996), p. 6.
8. Elizabeth A.R. Brown, "Eleanor of Aquitaine: Parent, Queen, Duchess" in Kibler, ed., *Eleanor of Aquitaine*, is the most influential example of psycho-history, along with Georges Duby in his article "Les 'jeunes' dans la société aristocratique dans la France du Nord-Ouest."
9. Richard Barber, "Eleanor of Aquitaine and the Media" in Léglu and Bull, eds, *The World of Eleanor of Aquitaine*, p. 26. Also Caroline Bynum, "Did the Twelfth Century Discover the Individual?" in *Jesus as Mother* (Berkeley, 1993), pp. 82–109.
10. Elizabeth Fox-Genovese, "Culture and Consciousness in the Intellectual History of European Women," *Signs*, 12 (1987), p. 536.
11. V.H. Galbraith, "Good Kings and Bad Kings in English History," in *Kings and Chroniclers*, art. 2, pp. 119–32.
12. D.D.R. Owen, *Eleanor of Aquitaine: Queen and Legend* (Oxford, 1993), p. 108.
13. A chronicle of Louis VII's crusade written by his confessor was edited after her marriage to the French king had ended to delete references to her. Virginia G. Berry, ed. and trans., Odo of Deuil, *De profectione Ludovici VII* (New York, 1948), p. xxiii, n. 67.
14. *Historia Anglorum: The History of the English People* by Henry of Huntingdon (d.1156) only mentions her divorce and remarriage, ed. Diana Greenway, pp. 756–59. For the "golden age" of medieval English historiography, see Antonia Gransden, *Historical Writing in England c. 550–1307* (Ithaca, NY, 1974); and Beryl Smalley, *Historians in the Middle Ages* (New York, 1974).
15. On this group, see Ralph V. Turner, "Eleanor of Aquitaine, Twelfth-century English Chroniclers and her 'Black Legend,'" *Nottingham Medieval Studies*, 52 (2008), pp. 17–42.

16. Sharon Farmer, "Persuasive Voices: Clerical Images of Medieval Wives," *Speculum*, 61 (1986), p. 519.

17. Geoffrey Koziol, "Political Culture," in Marcus Bull, ed., *France in the Central Middle Ages 900–1200* (Oxford, 2002), p. 63.

18. Lois L. Huneycutt, "Female Succession and the Language of Power in the Writings of Twelfth-century Churchmen" in Parsons, *Medieval Queenship*, pp. 189–91; also Betty Bandel, "English Chroniclers' Attitude toward Women," pp. 113–18; and Pauline Stafford, "The Portrayal of Royal Women in England, mid-tenth to mid-twelfth Centuries" in *Medieval Queenship*, pp. 143–67.

19. Eleanor's own documents, which remained uncollected and unedited until the end of the twentieth century. They will be available soon in a single collection as part of the Plantagenet *Acta* Project, chair, Sir James Holt, *The Acta of Eleanor of Aquitaine and Richard Duke of Aquitaine and Count of Poitou* (Oxford, forthcoming).

20. First quotation, *Richard of Devizes*, p. 25; second quotation, the title of Labande's article, "Pour une image véridique d'Aliénor d'Aquitaine," reprinted in Labande, *Histoire de l'Europe Occidentale XIe–XIVe siècles* (London, 1973), pp. 175–235; and recently reprinted as a book (Poitiers, 2005), introduction by Martin Aurell.

Chapter 1: Growing Up in the Ducal Court of Aquitaine, 1124–1137

1. Notably a wall painting discovered in 1964 in a chapel in the rocks below Chinon Castle. See Kenaan-Kedar, "Aliénor d'Aquitaine conduite en captivité," *CCM*, 41 (1998). Opposing views: Cloulas, "Les peintures murales de Saint-Radegonde de Chinon," and Kleinmann and Garcia, "Les peintures murales commémoratives de Saint-Radegonde de Chinon," *CCM*, 42 (1999); Nilgen, "Les Plantagenêt à Chinon. A propos d'une peinture murale dans la chapelle Saint-Radegonde."

2. John W. Baldwin, *Aristocratic Life in Medieval France: The Romances of Jean Renart and Gerbert de Montreuil, 1190–1230* (Baltimore, 2000), p. 128. See Labande, "Pour une image," p. 198, n. 108, for chroniclers on Eleanor's beauty.

3. Jane Martindale, "Peace and War in Early Eleventh-century Aquitaine," in *Status, Authority, Power*, art. 6, pp. 163, 170, citing Adémar de Chabannes, *Chronique*, ed. Yves Chauvin and Georges Pon (Turnhout, 2003). Members of the ducal family changed their names to William on taking power as dukes of Aquitaine.

4. Paul Courteault, *Histoire de la Gascogne et de Béarn* (Paris, 1938), pp. 55–56; Zimmermann, "West Francia, the southern principalities," in *New CMH*, 3, ch. 16, p. 440.

5. Yves Renouard, "Les Institutions du duché d'Aquitaine," in Lot and Fawtier, *Histoire des institutions françaises au moyen âge*, 1, *Institutions seigneuriales* (Paris, 1957), pp. 162–63.

6. Patrick Geary, "Vivre en conflit dans une France sans état," pp. 1107–33, trans. and reprint in Geary, *Living with the Dead in the Middle Ages* (Ithaca, NY, 1994).

7. The "standard model" of social and political history in tenth- and eleventh-century western Europe is set forth in Georges Duby, *La société aux XIe et XIIe siècles dans la région mâconnaise* (Paris, 1953), depicting a "feudal revolution" or "feudal transformation" expanding from northern France c. 1000, a picture now rejected by many historians. For recent views on a "stateless" society and the rise of "feudalism", see Frederic L. Cheyette, "Some Reflections on Violence, Reconciliation, and the 'Feudal Revolution,'" in Warren. C. Brown and Piotr Górecki, eds, *Conflict in Medieval Europe* (Aldershot, 2003), pp. 243–64.

8. Frederic L. Cheyette, *Ermengard of Narbonne and the World of the Troubadours* (Ithaca, NY, 2002), pp. 233–34, 237.

9. E.g. Alfred Richard, ed., *Chartes et documents de Saint-Maixent*, 2, no. 401, mentions the forest of La Sèvre; *Rot. Chart.*, p. 35, forest of Bordeaux; 147b, forest of Branchin

outside Bordeaux; Louis de la Boutière, ed., *Cartulaire d'Orbestier*, pp. 6–10, no. 4, forest of Orbestier or Talmont. Forest revenues were still important in the mid-thirteenth century, Francis X. Hartigan, ed., *Accounts of Alphonse of Poitiers 1243–1248* (Lanham, MD, 1984), p. 11.

10. Charles Higounet, *Histoire de l'Aquitaine, Documents* (Toulouse, 1973), p. 109; citing J. Viellard, ed., *Le Guide du pélerin de Saint-Jacques de Compostelle* (Mâcon, 1938).

11. Olivier Jeanne-Rose, "Ports, marchands et marchandises: aspects économiques du littoral poitevin," *MSAO*, 5th ser., 4 (1996), pp. 115–42.

12. Helmets: Gaston Dez, "Histoire de Poitiers," *MSAO*, 4th ser., 10 (Gaston, 1969), p. 42. Wines: Olivier Guyotjeannin, *Atlas de l'histoire de France* (Paris, 2005), p. 36. Salt: *Rot. Chart.*, p. 62, King John's renewal of Richard's grant to the Grandmont monks of salt from his *salinum* at Bordeaux; *Rot. Chart.*, p. 110, John's confirmation of Richard's charter concerning a saltwork at Oléron.

13. Cheyette, *Ermengard of Narbonne*, pp. 25–35. See also Linda Paterson, *The World of the Troubadours* (Cambridge, 1993), pp. 224–25.

14. Cheyette, *Ermengard of Narbonne*, p. 25.

15. For Philippa, see Cheyette, *Ermengard of Narbonne*, pp. 25–35. For other examples, Stafford, "Powerful Women in the early Middle Ages, Queens and Abbesses" in Peter Lineham and Janet L. Nelson, eds, *The Medieval World* (London, 2002), p. 401.

16. On her career, Isabelle Soulard-Berger, "Agnès de Bourgogne," *BSAO*, 5th ser., 6 (1992), pp. 45–55.

17. Charles Higounet, *Bordeaux pendant le haut moyen âge* (Bordeaux, 1963), pp. 156–57.

18. Léglu and Bull, *World of Eleanor*, Introduction, pp. 2–3.

19. First quotation, Cheyette, *Ermengard of Narbonne*, p. 125; see also Paterson, *World of Troubadours*, pp. 85, 153. Second quotation, Higounet, *Histoire de l'Aquitaine, Documents*, p. 109; citing Viellard, ed., *Guide du pélerin de Saint-Jacques*. The German abbot, Siegfried of Gorze, cited by Jaeger, *The Origins of Courtliness* (Philadelphia, 1985), pp. 178–79.

20. John of Salisbury, *Letters*, 2: 179, no. 176. See Gillingham, "Events and Opinions: Norman and English Views of Aquitaine" in *World of Eleanor*, pp. 57–81.

21. For pre-Plantagenet Aquitaine's endemic warfare, Jane Martindale, "Aimeri of Thouars and the Poitevin Connection" in *Status, Authority, Power*, art. 9, pp. 224–45; and "Cavalaria et orgueil," *ibid.*, art. 10, pp. 87–116.

22. Ruth E. Harvey, "The Two Wives of the 'first troubadour', Duke William IX of Aquitaine," *JMH*, 19 (1993), pp. 307–25, maintains that William had only one wife, Philippa of Toulouse, and denies that Philippa had been married previously.

23. Jean Flori, *Aliénor d'Aquitaine: La reine insoumise* (Paris, 2004), pp. 33–34.

24. Philippe Wolff, ed., *Histoire du Languedoc*, ch. 5 (Toulouse, 1967), Philippe Wolff, "Epanouissement du Languedoc," pp. 176–77.

25. Villard, "Guillaume IX d'Aquitaine et le concile de Reims," *CCM*, 16 (1973), pp. 296, 300, 301, 302. Cheyette, *Ermengard of Narbonne*, p. 371, n. 48; Jean-Marie Bienvenu, "Aliénor d'Aquitaine et Fontevraud," *CCM*, 29 (1986), p. 16. Villard finds Philippa retiring temporarily to a religious house after 1119, but living after William's death on her dowerland. Harvey, "The Two Wives of the 'first troubadour," argues that neither William nor Philippa sought to repudiate one another during their long marriage and that their mutual interest in taking Toulouse held them together.

26. Villard, "Guillaume X," regards the two poems as authentic, p. 299; Harvey, "Wives of the 'first troubadour," pp. 319–20, rejects Hildebert's authorship of the two poems.

27. *Geoffrey de Vigeois, RHGF*, 12, p. 430.

28. George T. Beech, "The Eleanor of Aquitaine Vase, William IX of Aquitaine, and Muslim Spain," *Gesta*, 32 (1993), pp. 3–10: also Beech, "The Eleanor of Aquitaine Vase," in Parsons and Wheeler, *Eleanor: Lord and Lady*, pp. 369–76.

29. Orderic Vitalis: Marjorie Chibnall, ed., *The Ecclesiastical History of Orderic Vitalis*, 5, pp. 324, 328, 330, 336, 338, 340, 342; cited by George T. Beech, "Contemporary Views of William the Troubadour" in *Medieval Lives and the Historian*, pp. 79–80. None of these poems survived, Beech, 'The Ventures of the Dukes of Aquitaine into Spain and the Crusader East," *HSJ*, 5 (1993), p. 65. *William of Malmesbury*, 2, pp. 379, 447–48, 510–12; cited by Beech, p. 80; and Martindale, "Cavalaria et Orgueil," p. 89.

30. Quotation, Beech, "Contemporary Views of William," pp. 74 and 81. See also Beech, "L'attribution des poèmes du comte de Poitiers à Guillaume ix d'Aquitaine," *CCM*, 31 (1998), pp. 3–16. On William's learning, Martindale, "Cavalaria et Orgueil," pp. 91, 114; René Crozet, *Histoire du Poitou* (Paris, 1949), pp. 46–47. See Peter Dronke, "Profane Elements in Literature," in Robert L. Benson and Giles Constable, eds, *Renaissance and Renewal* (Cambridge, MA, 1982), pp. 580–81, on William as writing within a tradition.

31. *Chronique de Saint-Maixent*, ed. Jean Verdon (Paris, 1979), pp. 194–95. See Alfred Richard, *Histoire des Comtes de Poitou*, 2, p. 2. For La Rochelle, Beech, *A Rural Society in Medieval France, The Gâtine of Poitou* (Baltimore, 1964); Robert Favreau, "Les débuts de la ville de La Rochelle," *CCM*, 30 (1987), pp. 3–6.

32. Flori, *Aliénor*, pp. 40–41.

33. David Crouch, *The Image of Aristocracy in Britain, 1000–1300* (London, 1992), pp. 281–84.

34. Jacques Boussard, *Le gouvernement d'Henri II Plantagenêt* (Paris, 1956), p. 353; Renouard, "Les institutions du duché d'Aquitaine," pp. 161–62.

35. Martindale, "Cavalaria et Orgueil," pp. 96, 97, 98; Higounet, *Bordeaux pendant le haut moyen âge*, pp. 58, 64.

36. Higounet, *Bordeaux pendant le haut moyen âge*, pp. 157–59.

37. *Rodulfus Glaber, The Five Books of the Histories*, eds John France, N. Bulst, and P. Reynolds (Oxford, 1989), p. 117.

38. On students at Poitiers, see Gillingham, "Events and Opinions," p. 69. Quotation, David Bates, *William the Conqueror* (Stroud, Gloucs., 2001); also see Gransden, *Historical Writing*, pp. 99–100, on William of Poitiers.

39. Paterson, *World of Troubadours*, p. 100.

40. Laura Kendrick, "Jongleur as Propagandist: The Ecclesiastical Politics of Marcabru's Poetry" in Bisson, *Cultures of Power*, pp. 259–86.

41. Marcabru: Flori, *Aliénor*, p. 40; Beech, "L'attribution des poèmes," pp. 4–5; Simon Gaunt and Sarah Kay, eds, *Troubadours: An Introduction* (Cambridge, 1999), pp. 281–82, 287. Jaufre Rudel: Elizabeth Salter, "Courts and Courtly Love," in David Daiches and Anthony Thorlby, eds, *Literature and Western Civilization: The Medieval World* (London, 1973), p. 419.

42. Sarah Kay, "Contradictions of Courtly Love and the Origins of Courtly Poetry: The Evidence of *Lauzengiers*," *Jl. Medieval and Early Modern Studies*, 26 (1996), p. 212.

43. Kay, "Contradictions of Courtly Love," p. 215.

44. Cheyette, *Ermengard of Narbonne*, p. 237, citing "Non es meravelha s'eu chan."

45. Paterson, *World of Troubadours*, pp. 88, 258–59, 262.

46. Géraldine Damon, "La place et le pouvoir des dames dans la société au témps d'Aliénor," in *Plantagenêts et Capétiens: Confrontations et héritage*, eds Martin Aurell and Noël-Yves Tonnerre (Turnhout, 2006), pp. 125–41.

47. Thesis of Jaeger, *Origins of Courtliness*.

48. Georges Duby, "La situation de la noblesse en France au début du xiiie siècle" in *Hommes et structures du moyen âge* (Paris, 1973), pp. 43–48; Eric Koehler, "Observations historiques et sociologiques sur la poésie des troubadours," *CCM*, 7 (1964), pp. 27–51.

49. Paterson, *World of Troubadours*, p. 88; Koziol, "Political Culture," in Bull, ed. *France in the Central Middle Ages*, p. 63.

322   *Notes to pp. 28-36*

50. Richard, *Comtes*, 2, pp. 10–11, 18.
51. Andrew W. Lewis, "The Birth and Childhood of King John: Some Revisions" in Parsons and Wheeler, *Eleanor: Lord and Lady*, p. 161.
52. For Raymond's career, Steven Runciman, *A History of the Crusades*, 2, pp. 199–200; and Jonathan Phillips, "A Note on the Origins of Raymond of Poitiers," *EHR*, 106 (1991), pp. 66–67.
53. Richard, *Comtes*, 2, pp. 6, 34; Jean-Philippe Collet, "Le combat politique des Plantagenêts en Aquitaine: l'exemple des vicomtes de Thouars (1158–1199)" in Martin Aurell, ed., *Noblesses de l'espace Plantagenêt (1154–1224)* (Poitiers, 2001), p. 141, n. 10.
54. Julien Boureau, Richard Levesque, and Isabelle Sachot, "Sur les pas d'Aliénor, l'abbaye de Nieul-sur-l'Autise," in Aurell, ed., *Aliénor*, pp. 129–35.
55. Richard, *Comtes*, 2, pp. 44–45, 51.
56. Charlotte A. Newman-Goldy, *The Anglo-Norman Nobility in the Reign of Henry I: The Second Generation* (Philadelphia, 1988), p. 35; David Herlihy, *Medieval Households* (Cambridge, MA, 1985), p. 83; Nicholas Vincent, "King Henry II and the Poitevins," in *La Cour Plantagenêt*, pp. 122–23.
57. Philippe Ariès, *L'Enfant et la vie familiale sous l'Ancien Régime* (Paris, 1960; reprint 1973), p. 313; trans. Baldic, *Centuries of Childhood*, pp. 396–97.
58. Quotation, Herlihy, *Medieval Households*, p. 158. For a survey of recent historical writings, see Barbara Hanawalt, "Medievalists and the Study of Childhood," *Speculum*, 97 (2002), pp. 440–60.
59. Sarah Bradford, *The Reluctant King: The Life and Reign of George VI 1895–1952* (New York, 1989), p. 20.
60. Higounet, *Bordeaux pendant le haut moyen âge*, p. 65.
61. Kimberley LoPrete, "Adela of Blois as Mother and Countess" in Parsons and Wheeler, *Medieval Mothering*, pp. 315–16; Guibert de Nogent, *De vita sua*, trans. C.C. Swinton Bland; *Self and Society in Medieval France*, ed. John F. Benton (New York, 1970), p. 45.
62. Charles Victor Langlois, *La vie en France au moyen âge* (Paris, 1926–28), 2, p. 12.
63. *Conscholaris* and *sodalis*, given by a certain Richard Animal. Elisabeth Van Houts, "Les femmes dans le royaume Plantagenêt: gendre, politique et nature" in *Plantagenêts et Capétiens*, p. 104 and n. 44.
64. Paterson, *World of Troubadours*, pp. 259–60.
65. One from the Auvergne before 1156 and another by a Catalan active in the late thirteenth century, Paterson, *World of Troubadours*, pp. 253–55.
66. Baldwin, *Aristocratic Life in Medieval France*, ch. 7, "Aristocratic Religion," pp. 194–247.
67. Langlois, *La vie en France au moyen âge*, 1, p. 210.
68. Michael T. Clanchy, "Images of Ladies with Prayer Books," *Studies in Church History*, 38 (2004), pp. 107–11.
69. John W. Baldwin, *The Language of Sex: Five Voices from Northern France* (Chicago, 1994), pp. xx–xxi. See also Robert Bartlett, *England under the Norman and Angevin Kings* (Oxford, 2000), pp. 562–66; Jacques Dalarun, "The Clerical Gaze," in Klapisch-Zuber, *Silences of the Middle Ages*, ch. 2, pp. 15–42; and Farmer, "Persuasive Voices," p. 519.
70. René Metz, *La femme et l'enfant dans le droit canonique médiéval* (London, 1985), "Le statut de la femme en droit canonique médiéval," art. 4, pp. 74, 103, 105. Also Huneycutt, "Female Succession and the Language of Power," pp. 189–91; and Stafford, "Portrayal of Royal Women in England," pp. 143–67.
71. Quotation, Paterson, *World of Troubadours*, p. 271. See Claude Thomasset, "The Nature of Women," in Klapisch-Zuber, *Silences of the Middle Ages*, pp. 43–69.
72. Coss, *The Lady in Medieval England 1000–1500* (Stroud, Gloucs., 1998), pp. 21, 29–31; Koziol, "Political Culture," p. 63.
73. Christopher Harper-Bill, "The Piety of the Anglo-Norman Nobility," *ANS*, 2 (1978), p. 69.

74. Jean Verdon, "La femme en Poitou aux xe et xie siècles," *BSAO*, 4th ser., 15 (1977), p. 95; Géraldine Damon, "Dames du Poitou au temps d'Aliénor," in Aurell, ed., *Aliénor*, p. 50. On the scarcity of women's houses, Paterson, *World of Troubadours*, pp. 241–43.

75. Quotation, *Chronique de Saint-Maixent*, pp. 126–27. Richard, *Comtes*, 2, pp. 71–72, 78, conflates her with another abbess, Agnès de Barbezieux, 1162–74.

76. Bienvenu, "Aliénor d'Aquitaine et Fontevraud," p. 16; Paterson, *World of Troubadours*, pp. 243–44.

77. *Chronique de Saint-Maixent*, p. 194.

78. Cited by Rebecca A. Baltzer, "Music in the Life and Times of Eleanor of Aquitaine," in Kibler, ed., *Eleanor of Aquitaine*, p. 65.

CHAPTER 2: BRIDE TO A KING, QUEEN OF THE FRENCH, 1137–1145

1. Higounet, *Bordeaux pendant le haut moyen âge*, pp. 97–99. Roger Aubent et al., eds, *Dictionnaire d'histoire et de géographie écclésiastique* (Paris, 1912–), "Geoffroi Babion," 20, p. 531.

2. Suger, *The Deeds of Louis the Fat*, ed. and trans. Richard Cusimano and John Moorhead (Washington DC, 1992), p. 156. For the will, *Chronicon Comitum Pictaviae*, *RHGF*, 12, pp. 409–10. See Achille Luchaire, *Louis VI Gros, Annales de sa vie et de son règne* (Paris, 1890), p. 264, who doubts the will, as does Richard, *Comtes*, 2, pp. 51–52.

3. Quotation, *Walter Map*, p. 441. See Fawtier, *The Capetian Kings of France* (London, 1960), p. 19.

4. Ives Sassier, *Louis VII* (Paris, 1991), p. 76; Eric Bournazel, "Suger and the Capetians," ed. Paula Lieber Gerson, in *Suger and Saint-Denis: A Symposium* (New York, 1986), p. 66.

5. Higounet, *Bordeaux pendant le haut moyen âge*, p. 66.

6. Suger, *Deeds of Louis the Fat*, p. 156; Mirot, ed., *Chronique de Morigny*, p. 67; also the Norman chronicler *Orderic Vitalis*, Chibnall, ed., 6: p. 491.

7. Richard, *Comtes*, 2, p. 56.

8. Ruth Harvey, "Eleanor of Aquitaine and the Troubadours," in Léglu and Bull, *World of Eleanor*, pp. 103–04.

9. Quotation, Cusimano and Moorhead, *Deeds of Louis the Fat*, p. 156. See also Jane Martindale, "Succession and Politics in the Romance-Speaking World" in *Status, Authority, Power*, art. 5, pp. 39–40.

10. Ferdinand Lot and Robert Fawtier, eds, *Histoire des institutions françaises au moyen âge*, 3 vols (Paris, 1957–62), 2: *Institutions royales*, p. 109.

11. Cusimano and Moorhead, *Deeds of Louis the Fat*, pp. 156–57.

12. Aubert et al., *Dictionnaire d'histoire et de géographie*, "Geoffroy de Lèves," 20, pp. 456–47; Richard, *Comtes*, 2, p. 57.

13. David Herlihy, "The Family and Religious Ideologies in Medieval Europe," in his *Women, Family, and Society*, p. 160.

14. Quotation, Herlihy, "Family and Religious Ideologies," p. 160.

15. The date of Louis's birth is no more certain than that of Eleanor; various chronicles give 1120, 1121, 1122, or 1123 as birth dates. Gasparri, ed. and trans., *Suger, Oeuvres*, 1, p. 244, n. 17.

16. His first royal seal shows his long hair, Jim Bradbury, *Philip Augustus King of France 1180–1223* (Harlow, 1998), p. 18; Cusimano and Moorhead, *Deeds of Louis the Fat*, p. 150, "a very handsome youth." On his youth, Pacaut, *Louis VII*, p. 31.

17. For Philip's death, Cusimano and Moorhead, *Deeds of Louis the Fat*, p. 149; Louis's coronation, Chibnall, ed., *Orderic Vitalis*, 6: pp. 422–23, 446–47.

18. Hallam and Everard, *Capetian France*, p. 155, citing Stephen of Paris, *Fragmentum Historicum de Ludovico VII*, *RHGF*, 12: p. 89.

19. Marceal Pacaut, *Louis VII et son royaume* (Paris, 1964), ch. 2, "La politique de grandeur et d'illusion, 1137–1154."

20. Pacaut, *Louis VII*, pp. 33, 36, 59.

21. Richard, *Comtes*, 2, p. 90.

22. *William of Newburgh*, 1, p. 93, bk 1, ch. 31, writing in the last decade of the twelfth century; translation in P.G. Walsh and M.J. Kennedy, *History of English Affairs Book I*, (Warminster, 1988).

23. Marjorie Chibnall, ed., *Historia Pontificalis of John of Salisbury* (Edinburgh, 1956), pp. 60–61 and pp. 52–53. *William of Newburgh*, 1, pp. 92–93, described Louis's love for Eleanor as "vehement passion."

24. Pacaut, *Louis VII*, p. 59.

25. Robert Bartlett, *England under the Norman and Angevin Kings*, p. 563; Flori, *Aliénor*, pp. 47, 343, citing Baldwin, *Language of Sex*, French edn.

26. Suggestion of Aurell, "Aux origines de la légende noire," p. 93. See also Flori, *Aliénor*, pp. 322–24, 333–35.

27. Higounet, *Bordeaux pendant le haut moyen âge*, pp. 188–89.

28. Cusimano and Moorhead, *Deeds of Louis the Fat*, p. 157.

29. Régine Pernoud, *Aliénor d'Aquitaine* (Paris, new edn 1965), p. 18, quoting L. Mirot, ed., *Chronique de Morigny*.

30. Verdon, "La femme en Poitou," p. 94; for another French region, Duby, *Société mâconnaise*, pp. 53–54.

31. Beech, "The Eleanor of Aquitaine Vase," *Gesta*, pp. 3–10. Pernoud, *Aliénor*, p. 38, maintains that Eleanor presented the vase to Louis after his return from his unsuccessful Toulouse expedition.

32. Pacaut, *Louis VII et les élections épiscopales*, p. 78; Jörge Peltzer, "Les évêques de l'empire plantagenêt et les rois angevins" in *Plantagenêts et Capétiens*, p. 470.

33. Charles Higounet and Arlette Higounet-Nadal, eds, *Grand Cartulaire de la Sauve Majeure* (Bordeaux, 1996), 2, pp. 729–30, no. 1278; Louis VII's confirmation, 2, pp. 730–31, no. 1279.

34. Richard, *Comtes*, 2, p. 57.

35. Achille Luchaire, *Études sur les actes de Louis VII* (Paris, 1885), no. 165, dated 1146.

36. Painter, "Castellans of the Plain of Poitou in the Eleventh and Twelfth Centuries," in Cazel, *Feudalism and Liberty*, p. 37; Hivergneaux, "Autour d'Aliénor d'Aquitaine" in *Plantagenêts et Capétiens*, p. 63.

37. 8 August, Richard, *Comtes*, 2, p. 61; Chibnall, ed., *Orderic Vitalis*, 6, pp. 490–91.

38. Higounet, *Bordeaux pendant le haut moyen âge*, p. 65; Sassier, *Louis VII*, p. 61.

39. Cusimano and Moorhead, *Deeds of Louis the Fat*, p. 158.

40. Mirot, *Chronique de Morigny*, p. 70.

41. Urban T. Holmes, Jr, *Daily Living in the Twelfth Century* (Madison, 1964), pp. 57–77.

42. Amy Kelly, *Eleanor of Aquitaine and the Four Kings* (Cambridge, MA, 1956), citing a letter of Pierre de la Celle to John of Salisbury, Migne, ed., *PL*, 202, col. 519.

43. Flori, *Aliénor*, p. 55.

44. *Carmina Burana*, 108a, cited by Helen Wadell, *The Wandering Scholars* (Garden City, NY, 1995), p. 234.

45. Crouch, *Image of Aristocracy*, pp. 293–94.

46. A comparison made by John Carmi Parsons, "Damned If She Didn't and Damned When She Did," in Parsons and Wheeler, *Eleanor: Lord and Lady*, pp. 265–99.

47. Pacaut, *Louis VII*, p. 36; Margaret E. Howell, *Eleanor of Provence: Queenship in Thirteenth-century England* (Oxford, 1998), pp. 56–57, 186–87.

48. Marion Facinger, "A Study of Medieval Queenship: Captain France 987–1237," *Studies in Medieval and Renaissance History*, 5 (1968), p. 36; Howell, *Eleanor of Provence*, pp. 186–87.

49. John W. Baldwin, "Image of the Jongleur in Northern France around 1200," *Speculum*, 72 (1997), pp. 639–40.
50. Sassier, *Louis VII*, pp. 75–83.
51. A poem of Bernart de Ventadorn, Harvey, "Eleanor of Aquitaine and the Troubadours," p. 101; see also pp. 103–04. Pierre Bec, "Troubadours, trouvères et espace Plantagenêt," *CCM*, 29 (1986) pp. 9–14, finds that of the 22 most famous *trouvères*, a majority came from Picardy (14), the second largest group from Champagne, and only a third from the Île de France.
52. For examples from Anglo-Saxon England, Stafford, "Portrayal of Royal Women in England," pp. 143–67. Cheyette, *Ermengard of Narbonne*, p. 25, for a prime example from the Midi.
53. Parsons in John Carmi Parsons and Bonnie Wheeler, eds, *Eleanor of Aquitaine: Lord and Lady* (New York, 2003), p. 275.
54. Chibnall, ed., *Orderic Vitalis*, 6, pp. 508–09; Orderic makes no mention of Eleanor.
55. Sassier, *Louis VII*, pp. 86–87.
56. Lois L. Huneycutt, "The Creation of a Crone: The Historical Reputation of Adelaide of Maurienne," in Nolan, *Capetian Women*, p. 28; Facinger, "Study of Medieval Queenship," pp. 27, 28.
57. Facinger, "Study of Medieval Queenship," p. 27.
58. Facinger, "Study of Medieval Queenship, pp. 34–35, documented in 92 acts over 22 years."
59. Facinger, "Study of Medieval Queenship," pp. 33–34; Hivergneaux in *Eleanor: Lord and Lady*, p. 56, citing Luchaire, *Études sur les actes de Louis VII*, nos 18, 119, 177.
60. Koziol, "Political Culture," pp. 62–63; Facinger, "Study of Medieval Queenship," pp. 24, 27.
61. Facinger, "Study of Medieval Queenship," p. 35.
62. R. Thomas MacDonald, "Ralph de Vermandois (d.1152)," in *Medieval France: An Encyclopedia*, p. 781.
63. *Histoire de Louis VII* in Gasparri, *Suger, Oeuvres*, 1, pp. 162–65; Pacaut, *Louis VII*, p. 40; Sassier, *Louis VII*, p. 86.
64. Facinger, "Study of Medieval Queenship," p. 35.
65. Sassier, *Louis VII*, p. 90.
66. Barber, "Eleanor of Aquitaine and the Media," p. 27.
67. Pacaut, *Louis VII*, p. 41, and Sassier, *Louis VII*, suggest Eleanor's increasing influence; Richard, *Comtes*, 2, p. 215.
68. Pernoud, *Aliénor*, p. 37.
69. Pacaut, *Louis VII*, pp. 36, 37; quotation, Pacaut, p. 38.
70. Facinger, "Study of Medieval Queenship," p. 35; Hivergneaux in *Eleanor: Lord and Lady*, p. 57.
71. Guillaume le Breton spoke of Poitou as "terre belliqueuse, et de foi instable," cited by Labande, "La civilisation d'Aquitaine à la fin de la période ducale," p. 19; and William Marshal shared a similar view, *History of William Marshal*, eds, Holden, Gregory, Crouch, lines 1577–80. For modern scholars' views on the Aquitanian nobility's "love of strife for its own sake," see Debord, *Société laïque dans la Charente*, p. 397; and earlier Norgate, *Angevin Kings*, 2: 203. Jane Martindale in "Eleanor of Aquitaine," in *Status, Authority, Power*, art. 11, pp. 24–33, expresses doubts about Aquitaine's supposed "anarchy".
72. Pacaut, *Louis VII*, p. 41; Sassier, *Louis VII*, p. 154; Hivergneaux in *Eleanor: Lord and Lady*, p. 58.
73. Hivergneaux in *Eleanor: Lord and Lady*, p. 59.
74. Mauzé: Debord, *La société laïque dans la Charente Xe–XIIe siècles* (Paris, 1984), p. 372. The archbishop: Hivergneaux in *Plantagenêts et Capétiens*, p. 63.
75. Hivergneaux in *Plantagenêts et Capétiens*, p. 62; also Hivergneaux in *Eleanor: Lord and Lady*, p. 58.

76. Hivergneaux in *Eleanor: Lord and Lady*, pp. 58, 60–62. T. Grasilier, *Cartulaires inédits de la Saintonge* (Niort, 1871) 2, p. 36, no. 29; p. 51 no. 48, Eleanor's confirmation of Louis vII's charter of liberties granted for Notre-Dame, Saintes.

77. Quotation, Debord, *Société laïque*, p. 370. For another view, see Jean Dunbabin, *France in the Making 842–1180* (Oxford, 1985; 2nd edn 2000), p. 342.

78. Most prominent was the lord of Lezay, who controlled Talmont Castle, Sassier, *Louis VII*, pp. 89–90; Pacaut, *Louis VII*, p. 41.

79. Sassier, *Louis VII*, p. 90. Gasparri, ed. and trans., *Histoire de Louis VII* (Paris, 1996), pp. 166–73, dates the Poitevin revolt April 1138; others date it in September. Pernoud, *Aliénor*, p. 36, attributes Louis's anger and violent reaction to Eleanor. Flori, *Aliénor*, p. 58, notes that no text depicts Eleanor playing any role at all, but "No text, it is true, prohibits it either."

80. Glyn S. Burgess, "Social Status in the *Lais* of Marie de France," p. 69.

81. Sassier, *Louis VII*, pp. 99–101; Pacaut, *Louis VII*, p. 68.

82. Flori, *Aliénor*, p. 58; Pernoud, *Aliénor*, pp. 37–38; Sassier, *Louis VII*, p. 102.

83. Cheyette, *Ermengarde of Narbonne*, p. 25; Jane Martindale, "An Unfinished Business: Angevin Politics and the Siege of Toulouse," *ANS*, 23 (2000), pp. 117–19, for the basis for Eleanor's claim.

84. Boureau, Levesque, Sachot, "Sur les pas d'Aliénor," p. 129, citing BNF, ms, coll. DeBaluze, t. 47, f. 304; also D. Sainte-Marthe, ed., *Gallia Christiana in provinciis ecclesiasticas distribua*, 2: *instrumenta*, pp. 385–86.

85. Pernoud, *Aliénor*, p. 40, attributes Louis's efforts at controlling episcopal elections to Eleanor's views, influenced by her family background of quarrels with ecclesiastical authorities.

86. K.-F. Werner, "Kingdom and Principality in Twelfth-century France," in Timothy Reuter, ed., *The Medieval Nobility* (Amsterdam, 1979), pp. 266, 269.

87. Flori, *Aliénor*, p. 59; Sassier, *Louis VII*, pp. 91, 101–02, 107–09.

88. Pernoud, *Aliénor*, p. 39. For accounts of this affair, Flori, *Aliénor*, pp. 59–60; Pacaut, *Louis VII*, pp. 43–44; Sassier, *Louis VII*, pp. 109–13.

89. Flori, *Aliénor*, pp. 38–39, 59; Sassier, *Louis VII*, p. 110.

90. Flori, *Aliénor*, pp. 59–60; Pacaut, *Louis VII*, p. 44; Sassier, *Louis VII*, pp. 112–13.

91. Flori, *Aliénor*, p. 60; Pernoud, *Aliénor*, p. 34; Sassier, *Louis VII*, pp. 113–14.

92. Quotation, Bruno Scott James, trans., *The Letters of St. Bernard of Clairvaux* (London, 1953), no. 297, pp. 364–65; Pacaut, *Louis VII*, p. 44; Sassier, *Louis VII*, pp. 113–17.

93. Sassier, *Louis VII*, pp. 124–25, and Scott James, *Letters of St. Bernard*, no. 300, p. 371.

94. Pacaut, *Louis VII*, p. 44; Sassier, *Louis VII*, p. 126. Others give the dedication of the new abbey of Saint-Denis, 11 June 1144, as the date of the peace agreement.

95. Scott James, *Letters of St. Bernard*, no. 302, p. 3 73; Sassier, *Louis VII*, pp. 128–29.

96. Flori, *Aliénor*, pp. 62–63; quoting *S. Bernardi vita prima auctore Gaufrido*, ch. 3, Migne, *PL*, 194: col. 332; Sassier, *Louis VII*, pp. 129–30.

97. Herlihy, *Medieval Households*, p. 118; Herlihy, "Family and Religious Ideologies," pp. 156–58.

98. Baldwin, *Language of Sex*, pp. 213–14.

99. Chibnall, ed., *Historia Pontificalis*, p. 12.

100. MacDonald, "Raoul de Vermandois," p. 781. They had a son who succeeded to the county of Vermandois and two daughters.

101. Quotations, Beech, "Eleanor of Aquitaine Vase," *Gesta*, pp. 3–10. See Brown, "Eleanor of Aquitaine Reconsidered: The Woman and her Seasons" in *Eleanor: Lord and Lady*, p. 20; also Pernoud, *Aliénor*, p. 48; Sassier, *Louis VII*, pp. 135–36.

102. Pacaut's title for ch. 2 of *Louis VII*, p. 39.

CHAPTER 3: ADVENTURES AND MISADVENTURES ON THE SECOND CRUSADE, 1145–1149

1. Accounts in standard crusade histories, Kenneth M. Setton gen. ed., *A History of the Crusades*, 1, *The First Hundred Years* (Madison, 1969), ch. 15, Virginia G. Berry, "The Second Crusade," p. 465. Steven Runciman, *History of the Crusades* (Cambridge 1952) 2, p. 248; Jonathan Riley-Smith, *The Crusades: A History*, 2nd edn (New Haven, 2005), pp. 104–05; Jonathan Phillips, *The Second Crusade: Expanding the Frontiers of Christendom* (New Haven, 2007), pp. xxvii–xxviii.
2. Sassier, *Louis VII*, pp. 142, 145; Giles Constable, "The Second Crusade as seen by Contemporaries," *Traditio*, 9 (1953), p. 247.
3. Berry, ed. and trans., Odo of Deuil, *De profectione Ludovici VII*, pp. 6–7, n. 3. Also Pacaut, *Louis VII*, p. 47.
4. Berry in Setton, *History of the Crusades*, pp. 467–68.
5. Riley-Smith, *Crusades*, p. 121; Sassier, *Louis VII*, pp. 142–44.
6. Riley-Smith, *Crusades*, p. 121. Quotation, Migne, *PL*, p. 185, Bernard epist. no 247: col. 947, trans. Runciman, *History of the Crusades*, 2, p. 254.
7. Constable, "Second Crusade Seen by Contemporaries," pp. 244, 247.
8. Flori, *Aliénor*, pp. 64–65. The only account mentioning Eleanor taking the cross at Vézelay is an anonymous continuation of Suger, *Histoire du roi Louis VII*, written some thirty years later, *RHGF*, 12, p. 126.
9. Flori, *Aliénor*, p. 69.
10. Explanation written a half-century after the Second Crusade by *William of Newburgh*, 1, pp. 92–93; translation, *History of English Affairs Book I*, pp. 128–29. See also Labande's speculation, "Pour une image," p. 181.
11. Cheyette, *Ermengard of Narbonne*, p. 257; Flori, *Aliénor*, pp. 69–70; Pernoud, *Aliénor*, p. 60.
12. Runciman, *History of the Crusades*, 2, p. 262; Flori, *Aliénor*, p. 67.
13. *William of Newburgh*, 1, pp. 92–93; trans., *History of English Affairs*, pp. 128–29. On his elevation of chastity, see Nancy Partner, *Serious Entertainments: The Writing of History in Twelfth-Century England* (Chicago, 1997), pp. 70–73, citing *Newburgh*, 1, p. 66.
14. Sassier, *Louis VII*, p. 154.
15. Sassier, *Louis VII*, p. 157; Riley-Smith, *Crusades*, p. 123.
16. Sassier, *Louis VII*, pp. 155–58; Riley-Smith, *Crusades*, p. 126; Pernoud, *Aliénor*, pp. 62–63.
17. Pernoud, *Aliénor*, p. 64.
18. Sassier, *Louis VII*, pp. 158–60; Riley-Smith, *Crusades*, p. 125.
19. Runciman, *History of the Crusades*, 2, pp. 253, 257.
20. Runciman, *History of the Crusades*, 2, p. 257; Riley-Smith, *Crusades*, p. 124; Constable, "Second Crusade Seen by Contemporaries," pp. 263–64. John of Salisbury accuses the two French bishops of "boasting" that they were papal legates, though they actually had no such commission, Chibnall, ed., *Historia Pontificalis*, p. 54.
21. Berry, ed. and trans., Odo of Deuil, *De profectione*, pp. 21–22. The archbishop was Samson of Mauvoisin.
22. Sassier, *Louis VII*, pp. 160, 201; Pacaut, *Louis VII*, pp. 57, 58.
23. Berry, ed. and trans., Odo of Deuil, pp. 16–17; Sassier, *Louis VII*, p. 162.
24. Berry, ed. and trans., Odo of Deuil, pp. 18–19; Phillips, *The Second Crusade*, pp. 126–27.
25. Baltzer, "Music in the Life and Times of Eleanor of Aquitaine," p. 65.
26. William B. Stevenson, "The First Crusade," *CMH*, 5, ch. 7, pp. 278, 298, estimates the number on the First Crusade including non-combatants as some 25,000 or 30,000, of whom 12,000 to 15,000 were actual fighting men. Sassier, *Louis VII*, p. 163, notes that

very large medieval armies consisted of 5,000 knights and 40,000 light cavalry and infantry, a very high estimate of the non-knightly element.

27. Flori, *Aliénor*, p. 65, citing Nicetas Choniatae, *Historia*, ed., I. A. Van Dieten, *Corpus fontium Historiae Byzantinae*, vol. 11, 1 (Berlin, 1975), p. 60. See Agnes Strickland, *Lives of the Queens of England from the Norman Conquest*, 6 vols, reprint (London 1893–99), "Eleanora of Aquitaine," 1, pp. 164–201, at p. 169; Kelly, *Eleanor and Four Kings*, pp. 35, 38–39; for discussion of this legend, see Flori, *Aliénor*, pp. 65–67; Owen, *Eleanor*, pp. 148–52.

28. Sassier, *Louis VII*, pp. 163, 165.

29. Quotation, Berry, ed. and trans., Odo of Deuil, pp. 24–25. On medieval travel conditions, Danny Danziger and John Gillingham, *1215 the Year of Magna Carta* (London, 2003; reprint New York, 2005), p. 35. Holmes, *Daily Living in the Twelfth Century*, p. 55; Margaret W. Labarge, *Medieval Travellers, The Rich and Restless* (London, 1982), p. 37.

30. Runciman, *History of the Crusades*, 2, p. 262.

31. Berry, ed. and trans., Odo of Deuil, p. 27; Sassier, *Louis VII*, p. 156.

32. Berry, ed. and trans., Odo of Deuil, pp. 32–33.

33. Sassier, *Louis VII*, p. 163; Pacaut, pp. 55–56; Berry in Setton, *History of the Crusades*, 1, p. 501.

34. Berry, ed. and trans., Odo of Deuil, pp. 30–33, 44–45; Runciman, *History of the Crusades*, 2, p. 263; Sassier, *Louis VII*, pp. 167, 168.

35. Riley-Smith, *Crusades*, p. 128; Sassier, *Louis VII*, p. 169; Paul Magdalino, "The Byzantine Empire, 1118–1204," *New CMH*, 4, pt 2, pp. 620–21.

36. Berry in Setton, *History of the Crusades*, 1, pp. 486, 489.

37. Berry, ed. and trans., Odo of Deuil, pp. 58–59, ed. citing Louis's letter to Suger, *RGHF*, 15, p. 488, no. 13.

38. *Dict. M.A.*, 3, Gilbert Dagron, "Constantinople," pp. 552–53.

39. Berry, ed. and trans., Odo of Deuil, pp. 64–65.

40. Berry, ed. and trans., Odo of Deuil, pp. 58–59 and n. 34. Odo's work mentions Eleanor only four times, pp. 17, 57, 77, 79, referring to her only as "the queen," never by name. Berry, ed., p. xxiii, n. 67, suggests that his omission of Eleanor points to a later redaction of his text after her first marriage ended, deleting all references to her to avoid blemishing the king's reputation.

41. Quotation, Berry, ed. and trans., Odo of Deuil, pp. 66–67; also pp. 72–73, n. 29; and Pernoud, *Aliénor*, p. 70.

42. Berry, ed. and trans., Odo of Deuil, pp. 56–57, and n. 47. Odo wrote in one of his few mentions of Eleanor, "Occasionally the empress wrote to the queen," then quickly changed the subject. His sudden transition from their correspondence to the Byzantines' effeminate character most likely results from his suppression of Eleanor from his text, Flori, *Aliénor*, p. 73; also Pernoud, *Aliénor*, p. 71.

43. Lynda Garland, "Imperial Women and Entertainment at the Middle Byzantine Court," in Garland, ed., *Byzantine Women: Varieties of Experience, 800–1200* (Aldershot, 2006) pp. 177–78, 182.

44. Pernoud, *Aliénor*, p. 75.

45. Kelly, *Eleanor and Four Kings*, p. 42. Also Pernoud, *Aliénor*, p. 74; and Jean Markale, *Aliénor d'Aquitaine* (Paris, 1979; 2nd edn 2000), pp. 34–35; like Pernoud, he finds symptoms of a lack of sympathy between Louis and Eleanor at Constantinople.

46. Runciman, *History of the Crusades*, 2, p. 269; Berry, in Setton, *History of the Crusades*, 1, p. 492.

47. Sassier, *Louis VII*, p. 170.

48. Berry, ed. and trans., Odo of Deuil, p. 57.

49. Quotation, James Bruce Ross and Mary Martin McLaughlin, eds, *The Portable Medieval Reader* (New York, 1950), p. 445. See also Runciman, *History of the Crusades*, 2, p. 275.

50. Berry, in Setton, *History of the Crusades*, 1, p. 491; Riley-Smith, *Crusades*, p. 128.
51. Emily Atwater Babcock and A.C. Krey, eds, *William of Tyre, A History of Deeds Done Beyond the Sea* (New York, 1943), 2, pp. 170–71.
52. Berry, in Setton, *History of the Crusades*, 1, pp. 495–96; Sassier, *Louis VII*, pp. 171, 174.
53. Berry, ed. and trans., Odo of Deuil, pp. 104–05.
54. Runciman, *History of the Crusades*, 2, p. 270; Sassier, *Louis VII*, p. 177.
55. Runciman, *History of the Crusades*, 2, p. 272; Sassier, *Louis VII*, pp. 177–78.
56. Berry, ed. and trans., Odo of Deuil, p. 109.
57. For the Cadmos Mountain crossing, see Curtis Howe Walker, "Eleanor of Aquitaine and the Disaster at Cadmos Mountain on the Second Crusade," *American Historical Review*, 55 (1949–50), pp. 857–61; also Berry in Setton, *History of the Crusades*, 1, p. 499; Flori, *Aliénor*, p. 75; Sassier, *Louis VII*, pp. 18–79; Phillips, *The Second Crusade*, pp. 199–201.
58. Berry, ed. and trans., Odo of Deuil, pp. 118–19.
59. Quotation, Berry, ed. and trans., Odo of Deuil, pp. 114–15, 122–25. See also Babcock and Krey, *William of Tyre*, 2, p. 177; Pacaut, *Louis VII*, p. 51.
60. Pernoud, *Aliénor*, p. 78; Flori, *Aliénor*, pp. 76–77. Those blaming Eleanor include Kelly, *Eleanor and Four Kings*, p. 49; Marion Meade, *Eleanor of Aquitaine* (New York, 1977; reprint 1991), pp. 99–100; Alison Weir, *Eleanor of Aquitaine: By the Wrath of God, Queen of England* (London, 2000), p. 63. They follow Richard, *Comtes*, 2, p. 92, who claims that "Eleanor, seeing a green valley . . . wished to descend there. Geoffrey, indeed, attempted to resist, but was weak enough to yield to the wishes of the queen." *William of Tyre*, 2, p. 175, blames Geoffrey's guides.
61. Pernoud, *Aliénor*, pp. 89–90.
62. Berry, in Setton, *History of the Crusades*, 1, p. 499.
63. Berry, ed. and trans., Odo of Deuil, pp. 128–29; Sassier, *Louis VII*, p. 180.
64. Berry, ed. and trans., Odo of Deuil, pp. 128–37.
65. Berry, ed. and trans., Odo of Deuil, pp. 138–43; Runciman, *History of the Crusades*, 2, pp. 273–74; Sassier, *Louis VII*, pp. 181, 182; also Berry in Setton, *History of the Crusades*, 1, pp. 502, 503.
66. *William of Tyre*, 2, p. 179. Among the knights were Charles de Mauzé and Payen de Faye; Pernoud, *Aliénor*, p. 83.
67. Quotation, Pernoud, *Aliénor*, p. 90; also Kelly, *Eleanor and Four Kings*, pp. 57–59; Owen, *Eleanor*, p. 214; R.C. Smail, *Crusading Warfare (1097–1193)* (Cambridge, 1956; reprint New York, 1995), p. 43.
68. Sassier, *Louis VII*, p. 184; Pacaut, *Louis VII*, p. 52.
69. *William of Tyre*, 2, p. 179.
70. Berry in Setton, *History of the Crusades*, 1, p. 504; Pacaut, *Louis VII*, p. 52; Runciman, *History of the Crusades*, 2, p. 279; Sassier, *Louis VII*, p. 185.
71. *William of Tyre*, 2, pp. 180–81.
72. Meade, *Eleanor*, p. 110; Sassier, *Louis VII*, p. 186; Martindale, "Eleanor of Aquitaine," in *Status, Authority, Power*, art. 11, p. 40. Pernoud, *Aliénor*, p. 83.
73. Flori, *Aliénor*, pp. 297–98.
74. Labande, "Pour une image," p. 185.
75. Chibnall, ed., *Historia Pontificalis*, pp. 52–53.
76. Duby, *Women of the Twelfth Century: Eleanor of Aquitaine and Six Others*, trans. Jean Birrell (Chicago, 1997) 1, p. 16; Flori, *Aliénor*, pp. 326–30; Sassier, *Louis VII*, p. 188.
77. Chibnall, ed., *Historia Pontificalis*, p. 53, quotation, Ovid, *Heroides*, iv, 138. Confirmation of Louis's distress is a letter of Abbot Suger, hinting that Louis had disclosed his unhappiness with Eleanor to him, Suger's letter in *RHGF*, 15, pp. 509–10, no. 69.
78. Chibnall, ed., *Historia Pontificalis*, p. 53. See also Aurell, "Aux origines de la légende noire d'Aliénor," pp. 91–92; and Flori, *Aliénor*, pp. 521–23.

79. Peter W. Edbury and John Gordon Rowe, *William of Tyre: Historian of the Latin East* (Cambridge, 1988). William only completed his history in 1184, but he would have heard of the Antioch incident from aging eye-witnesses, p. 26. *erat . . . mulier imprudens et contra dignitatem regis, legem negligens maritalem, tori conjugalis oblita,* Migne, *PL,* p. 207, col. 670; my modification of Babcock and Krey's translation, *William of Tyre,* 2, pp. 180–81.
80. Flori, *Aliénor,* pp. 333, 334.
81. Chibnall, ed., *Historia Pontificalis,* pp. 60–61; and pp. 52–53. See also Aurell, "Aux origines de la légende noire," p. 93; and Flori, *Aliénor,* pp. 322–24, 333–35.
82. Quotation, Berry in Setton, *History of the Crusades,* 1, p. 504.
83. Translation, Owen, *Eleanor,* p. 105. Ruth E. Harvey, *The Poet Marcabru and Love* (London, 1989), p. 195, identifies this poem of Cercamon's as "Ab lo pascor."
84. Barber, "Eleanor and the Media," p. 26.
85. *Richard of Devizes,* pp. 25–26. Writing in the same era, *Gervase of Canterbury* ed. William Stubbs, 2 vols (London, 1879), merely mentioned "a certain discord between [Louis] and his queen Eleanor" on their return from the Holy Land and about which, "according to certain persons it was perhaps better to keep silent," 1, p. 149. *Gerald of Wales,* 1: 299, bk 3, ch. 27; trans. Joseph Stevenson (London 1858; reprint Felinfach, Dyfed, 1994), p. 97.
86. Pacaut, *Louis VII,* p. 53; Flori, *Aliénor,* p. 79; quotation, Chibnall, ed., *Historia Pontificalis,* pp. 52–53.
87. Kelly, *Eleanor and Four Kings,* p. 62, quotes Suger's letter, *RHGF,* 15, p. 510, no. 69. French translation, Suger, *Oeuvres,* ed. and trans. F. Gasparri, 2, pp. 32–37, letter 6.
88. *William of Tyre,* 2, pp. 182, 183; Kelly, *Eleanor and Four Kings,* pp. 65, 66.
89. *William of Tyre,* 2, pp. 184–85; Sassier, *Louis VII,* pp. 189–90; Runciman, *History of the Crusades,* 2, p. 280.
90. Runciman, *History of the Crusades,* 2, pp. 280–81; Riley-Smith, *Crusades,* p. 129; Sassier, *Louis VII,* pp. 191–92; Phillips, *The Second Crusade,* pp. 215–18.
91. Quotation, Runciman, *History of the Crusades,* 2, p. 284; *William of Tyre,* 2, pp. 187–93; Sassier, *Louis VII,* pp. 193–95.
92. Constable, "Second Crusade seen by Contemporaries," pp. 266, 271, 273.
93. Ibid., p. 275, citing a letter of Pope Adrian IV, Migne, *PL* 188: col. 1615.
94. Quotation, *Historia Pontificalis,* p. 59; *William of Tyre,* 2, p. 195; Sassier, *Louis VII,* p. 196.
95. Pacaut, *Louis VII,* p. 54.
96. Pernoud, *Aliénor,* p. 94.
97. Kelly, *Eleanor and Four Kings,* pp. 68–69, citing Suger, *RHGF,* 15, pp. 509–10, no. 69.
98. *William of Tyre,* p. 196; Pacaut, *Louis VII,* p. 58; Runciman, *History of the Crusades,* 2, p. 285.
99. Labarge, *Medieval Travellers,* p. 30; Barbara M. Kreutz, "Ships and Shipbuilding, Mediterranean," *Dict. M.A.,* 11: 233; Flori, *Aliénor,* p. 79.
100. *Historia Pontificalis,* p. 60, is jumbled; see also Runciman, *History of the Crusades,* 2, p. 286; Sassier, *Louis VII,* p. 198.
101. In Louis's letter to Suger about their rescue, he "expresses himself . . . with great dryness on the subject of his companion." Labande, "Pour une image," p. 189, citing Suger's letter, *RHGF,* 15, pp. 513–14, no. 81. See also Kelly, *Eleanor and Four Kings,* pp. 69–71; Sassier, *Louis VII,* p. 198.
102. *William of Tyre,* 2, p. 198.
103. Sassier, *Louis VII,* pp. 199–200; Berry in Setton, *History of the Crusades,* 1, p. 511.
104. Pernoud, *Aliénor,* pp. 95–96; Sassier, *Louis VII,* p. 199.
105. *Historia Pontificalis,* pp. 61–62.
106. Labarge, *Medieval Travellers,* p. 28; Pacaut, *Louis VII,* p. 55, Sassier, *Louis VII,* p. 200.
107. Richard, *Comtes,* 2, p. 95.
108. Pacaut, *Louis VII,* pp. 55–56, 58; Dunbabin, *France in the Making,* p. 293.

CHAPTER 4: A HUSBAND LOST, A HUSBAND GAINED, 1149–1154

1. Dunbabin, *France in the Making*, p. 293.
2. Facinger, "Medieval Queenship," pp. 35, 36. All but one of her charters as French queen date from before the Second Crusade. Hivergneaux, in *Eleanor: Lord and Lady*, p. 56.
3. Pacaut, *Louis VII*, pp. 60–61.
4. Kelly, *Eleanor and Four Kings*, p. 74.
5. Sassier, *Louis VII*, pp. 224–25.
6. Pacaut, *Louis VII*, p. 63; Pernoud, *Aliénor*, pp. 102, 103.
7. Duby, *Women of the Twelfth Century*, 1, 13; Aurell, "Aux origines de la légende noire," pp. 99–100.
8. *Walter Map*, pp. 474–77.
9. *Gerald of Wales*, pp. 300–01, bk 3, ch. 27, *abusus fuerat*; Pacaut, *Louis VII*, p. 61.
10. Markale, *Aliénor*, p. 161.
11. Thomas K. Keefe, "England and the Angevin Dominions, 1137–1204," ch. 18, *New CMH*, 4, pt 2, p. 559.
12. Bernard Bachrach, "The Idea of the Angevin Empire," *Albion*, 10 (1978), pp. 298–99. Kate Norgate, *England under the Angevin Kings*, 2 vols (London, 1887; reprint New York, 1969), 1, pp. 374–76; on the Angevin court and courtliness, see Jaeger, *Origins of Courtliness*, pp. 201–04. Quotation, *Gervase of Canterbury*, 1, p. 125.
13. Peter of Blois, *Epistolae*, Migne, *PL*, 207, letter 66.
14. Owen, *Eleanor*, p. 30.
15. Labande, "Pour une image," p. 193; Pacaut, *Louis VII*, p. 61.
16. Pacaut, p. 60; Flori, *Aliénor*, pp. 85, 87.
17. Bradbury, *Philip Augustus*, p. 26.
18. Labande, "Pour une image," p. 198.
19. Flori, *Aliénor*, p. 89; Sassier, *Louis VII*, pp. 225–26.
20. *Zelotypiae spiritu inflammatus*, in A. Salmon, ed., *Chronicon Turonensis magnum* (Tours, 1854), p. 135, cited by Flori, *Aliénor*, p. 92; see Sassier, *Louis VII*, p. 227.
21. Marie-Bernadette Bruguière, "A propos des idées reçues en histoire: le divorce de Louis VII," *Mémoires de l'Académie des sciences, inscriptions et belles-lettres de Toulouse*, 140, 15th ser., 9 (1978), p. 200; Sassier, *Louis VII*, p. 232.
22. Quotation, Labande, "Pour une image," p. 193. Flori, *Aliénor*, p. 80.
23. Louis was descended from Robert II's eldest son, King Henry I, and Eleanor from another son, Duke Robert of Burgundy; Constance Brittain Bouchard, "Eleanor's Divorce from Louis VII: The Uses of Consanguinity" in *Eleanor: Lord and Lady*, p. 226, figure 10.1.
24. For the shared ancestry of Louis and his second and third wives, Bruguière, "Le divorce de Louis VII," pp. 197–99; and Bouchard, "Eleanor's Divorce," pp. 230–31.
25. *Gervase of Canterbury*, 1, p. 149; and a chronicle of Saint-Germain-des-Prés cited by Bruguière, "Le divorce de Louis VII," p. 193.
26. Sassier, *Louis VII*, p. 233.
27. John Carmi Parsons, "Damned If She Didn't and Damned When She Did" in *Eleanor: Lord and Lady*, p. 267.
28. Gillingham, "Love, Marriage and Politics in the Twelfth Century" in Gillingham, *Richard Coeur de Lion*, pp. 251–52.
29. Bruguière, "Le divorce de Louis VII," pp. 192–93, 197, followed by Sassier, *Louis VII*, p. 232.
30. Kelly, *Eleanor and Four Kings*, p. 79; Parsons, "Damned," p. 269.
31. Flori, *Aliénor*, p. 80, citing *Robert of Torigni*, p. 164.
32. James A. Brundage, "The Canon Law of Divorce in the Mid-twelfth Century: Louis VII v. Eleanor of Aquitaine," in *Eleanor: Lord and Lady*, pp. 217–19.

33. Flori, *Aliénor*, p. 82.
34. Theodore Evergates, "Aristocratic Women in the County of Champagne," in Evergates, ed., *Aristocratic Women in Medieval France* (Philadelphia, 1999), pp. 77–79; Flori, *Aliénor*, p. 82.
35. Pacaut, *Louis VII*, p. 108; Pernoud, *Aliénor*, p. 104.
36. Quotation, Flori, *Aliénor*, p. 83, citing *Chron. Turon. magn.*, p. 135. Martindale, "Eleanor of Aquitaine," pp. 41–42.
37. Quotation, W.L. Warren, *Henry II* (Berkeley, 1977), p. 45; see also Margaret Aziza Pappano, "Marie de France, Aliénor d'Aquitaine, and the Alien Queen," in *Eleanor: Lord and Lady*, p. 347.
38. Flori, *Aliénor*, pp. 80, 87–88, 92, 93; Pacaut, *Louis VII*, p. 60.
39. *William of Newburgh*, 1, p. 281, bk 3, ch. 26.
40. *Gervase of Canterbury*, 1, p. 149.
41. Flori, *Aliénor*, p. 84, citing *William of Newburgh*, bk 1, ch. 31, para 3; Pernoud, *Aliénor*, p. 109.
42. Quotation, Richard Benjamin, "The Angevin Empire," *History Today* (February 1986), p. 21; also Warren, *Henry II*, p. 44.
43. Quotation, Greenway, ed., *Henry of Huntingdon, Historia Anglorum*, pp. 756–59. For Louis's view, Dunbabin, "Henry II and Louis VII," in Harper-Bill and Vincent, *Henry II: New Interpretations*, p. 49.
44. View of Fawtier, *Capetian Kings*, p. 24, echoed by Pacaut, *Louis VII*, p. 67.
45. Flori, *Aliénor*, p. 95.
46. *Roger of Wendover*, trans. J.A. Giles, 2 vols (London, 1849), 1, p. 505.
47. Opinion is divided on a formal condemnation by the French royal court, see Bradbury, *Philip Augustus*, p. 27; Fawtier, *Capetian Kings*, p. 140 and n.1; Norgate, *Angevin Kings*, 1, pp. 393–94 and n.1, p. 394. Sassier, *Louis VII*, pp. 238, 241, is skeptical, as is Martindale in *Status, Authority, Power*, art. 11, p. 32, n. 31, who writes: "there is no evidence for such a formality in the 1150s."
48. For the little-noticed son who died in infancy between 1159 and 1164, see Lewis, "The Birth and Childhood of King John," pp. 161, 165 and n. 10, p. 170, citing *Ralph Diceto*, ed. William Stubbs, 2 vols (London, 1876), 2, pp. 16–17, 269–70.
49. Chris Given-Wilson and Alice Curteis, *The Royal Bastards of Medieval England* (London, 1984), pp. 103–04; Marie Lovatt, "Geoffrey (1151?–1212), archbishop of York." *Oxford DNB*.
50. *Calendar of Charter Rolls 1341–1417* (London, 1916), p. 282, no. 18; p. 286, no. 16; David Knowles, C.N.L. Brooke, and Vera C.M. London, eds, *The Heads of Religious Houses in England and Wales 940–1216* (Cambridge, 1972), p. 208. Since Matilda died around 1202, her birth probably occurred around the 1150s, shortly before Henry and Eleanor's marriage.
51. First quotation, Harvey, *The Poet Marcabru*, p. 195; second, pp. 135–38. Marcabru's poem xv, lines 27–30, Harvey, p. 126: "But the lady who takes two or three lovers and who does not want to pledge herself to one alone indeed damages her reputation and decreases her worth each time."
52. *Gautier Map, Contes pour les gens de cour*, trans. Alan Keith Bate (Turnhout, 1993), Introduction, pp. 31–32. Also Richard Barber, "Eleanor and the Media," p. 26.
53. Aurell, *L'Empire des Plantagenêt*, pp. 51–52, citing Walter Map and Gerald of Wales. Churchmen who condemned the marriage as bigamous or incestuous include two chroniclers, William of Newburgh and Gervais of Canterbury, a canonist, Robert de Courson, and Saint Hugh of Avalon, bishop of Lincoln.
54. *William of Newburgh*, 1, pp. 92–93; trans., Walsh and Kennedy, pp. 128–29. See Flori's comments, *Aliénor*, p. 88.
55. *Gervase of Canterbury*, RS, 1, p. 149.
56. Pappano in *Eleanor: Lord and Lady*, pp. 349–50.

57. Hivergneaux discusses the two charters in *Eleanor: Lord and Lady*, pp. 63–65. Edouard Audouin, ed., *La commune et la ville de Poitiers (1063–1327)*, AHP, 44 (1923), pp. 35–36, no. 20; Richard, ed., *Chartes et documents de Saint-Maixent*, pp. 352–53, no. 335.

58. By April 1153, Z.N. Brooke and C.N.L. Brooke, "Henry II, Duke of Normandy and Aquitaine," *EHR*, 61 (1946), pp. 83, 88; *Regesta Regum A.-N.*, nos. 193, 306, 339, 363a–b, 364, 575, 710, 840, 901.

59. H.G. Richardson, "The Letters and Charters of Eleanor of Aquitaine," *EHR*, 74 (1959), p. 193. For the grant to Viscount Hugh, Hivergneaux in *Eleanor: Lord and Lady*, p. 64, citing A. Bardonnet, *Les comptes et enquêtes d'Alphonse, comte de Poitou (1253–1269)*, *AHP*, 8 (1879), dated 1153–54.

60. *Recueil des Actes de Henri II*, ed. Léopold Delisle and Élie Berger, 3 vols (Paris, 1916–27), 1, pp. 31–32, no. 24. Trans. Régine Pernoud, *Women in the Days of the Cathedrals* (San Francisco, 1998), p. 136.

61. Brown, "Eleanor Reconsidered," in *Eleanor: Lord and Lady*, p. 21.

62. Bienvenu, "Aliénor d'Aquitaine et Fontevraud," pp. 18–19.

63. On her seal, Hivergneaux in *Eleanor: Lord and Lady*, pp. 64, 65; and Brown in ibid., pp. 20, 23. On her titles, Hivergneaux in ibid., p. 65, citing a charter for the abbey of La Trinité-de-Vendôme; Charles Métais, ed, *Cartulaires saintongeais de la Trinité-de-Vendôme*, pp. 103–04, no. 62. As late as October 1153, the archbishop of Bordeaux recognized only the duchess's authority in one of his documents, making no mention of either Henry or Louis, Hivergneaux in *La Cour Plantagenêt*, p. 65.

64. Sassier, *Louis VII*, pp. 239–40; *Regesta Regum A-N*, "Itinerary of Henry fitz Empress, Duke of Normandy."

65. It is unclear whether ceremonies marking Henry's formal installation as duke took place at this time; *Geoffrey de Vigeois* merely states that he was received with jubilation (*cum tripudio*), *RHGF*, 12, p. 438.

66. Debord, *Société laïque*, p. 380.

67. Robert Hajdu, "Castles, Castellans and the Structure of Politics in Poitou, 1152–1271," *JMH*, 4 (1978), pp. 25–53; Debord, "La politique de fortification des Plantagenêts dans la seconde moitié du XIIe siècle," in Marie-Pierre Baudny, ed., *Les fortifications dans les domaines Plantagenêts* (Poitiers, 2000), pp. 10–11.

68. Frédéric Boutoulle, "La Gascogne sous les premiers Plantagenêts" in *Plantagenêts et Capétiens*, pp. 286–88.

69. *Regesta Regum A-N*, "Itinerary of Henry," p. xlvii.

70. *Gesta Stephani*, ed. and trans. K.R. Potter and R.H.C. Davis (Oxford, 1976), p. 83 on Empress Matilda, "an extremely arrogant demeanour, instead of the modest gait and bearing proper to a gentle woman"; also "arbitrary or rather headstrong" and displaying "extreme haughtiness and insolence," p. 79. See Huneycutt, "Female Succession and Language of Power," pp. 189–201.

71. Richard, *Comtes*, 2, p. 115.

72. *Robert of Torigni*, p. 235.

73. Métais, ed., "Cartulaire saintongeais de la Trinité-de-Vendôme," pp. 103–04, no. 62; also Richard, *Comtes*, 2, p. 115. For fitz Hamo, see Delisle-Berger, *Introduction*, p. 479; Graeme J. White, *Restoration and Reform 1153–1165: Recovery and Civil War in England* (Cambridge, 2001), p. 83. For Geoffrey de Clères, who had served Henry's father along with his two brothers, see Delisle-Berger, *Introduction*, "Hugo de Claiers," pp. 387–88. Peter, the duchess's notary who drafted the Vendôme charter, would serve Eleanor again during her Poitevin residency, 1168–73.

74. Labande, "Pour une image," p. 199; Marjorie Chibnall, *The Empress Matilda; Queen Consort, Queen Mother, and Lady of the English* (Oxford, 1991), p. 156.

75. For the civil war, see Edmund King, *The Anarchy of King Stephen's Reign* (Oxford, 1994); and Warren, *Henry II*, ch. 2, "The Pursuit of an Inheritance (1135–54)," pp. 12–53.

76. Chibnall, *Empress Matilda*, pp. 151, 159, 161, 166; also Chibnall, "The Empress Matilda and her Sons," in Parsons and Wheeler, eds, *Medieval Mothering*, pp. 285, 288, and n. 69.
77. Norgate, *Angevin Kings*, 1, pp. 404, 405; Boussard, *Gouvernement*, p. 400.
78. *Regesta Regum A-N*, 3, pp. 287–88, no. 783; the Norman bishops were Philip of Bayeux, Arnulf of Lisieux. For Èbles, see Martine Cav Carmichael de Baiglie, "Savary de Mauléon," pp. 270–72; Debord, *Société laïque*, p. 385; Marcel Garaud, *Les Chatelains de Poitou et l'avenement du régime féodale xie et xiie siècles* (Poitiers, 1967), pp. 56–57, 69. Agnès was abbess of Saintes *c.* 1137–62.
79. *Robert of Torigni*, ed. R. Howlett, RS, 4 (London, 1867), p. 176; Labande, "Pour une image," p. 199. Geoffrey witnessed, Two of Henry's charters for Fontevraud, *Regesa Regum A-N*, nos. 331, 332.
80. Emilie M. Amt, *Accession of Henry II in England: Royal Government Restored 1149–1159* (Woodbridge, Suffolk, 1993), p. 21, citing *The Anglo-Saxon Chronicle: A Revised Translation*, eds Dorothy Whitelock, David C. Douglas, Susie I. Tucker (London, 1961), pp. 202–03.
81. Amt, *Accession of Henry II*, pp. 15–16.
82. Flori, *Aliénor*, p. 99.

CHAPTER 5: ONCE MORE A QUEEN AND MOTHER: ENGLAND, 1154–1168

1. Norgate, *Angevin Kings*, 1, p. 405.
2. Percy Ernst Schramm, *A History of the English Coronation* (Oxford, 1937), p. 57; Lois L. Huneycutt, *Matilda of Scotland: A Study in Medieval Queenship* (Woodbridge, Suffolk, 2003), pp. 50–51. Labande, "Pour une image," p. 200, accepts *Gervase of Canterbury*, 1, p. 160, over *Robert of Torigny*'s earlier account that makes no mention of Eleanor's coronation.
3. Her children by Henry II: William, 1153–56; Henry, 1155–83; Matilda, 1156–89; Richard, 1157–99; Geoffrey, 1158–86; Eleanor, 1161–1214; Joanne, 1165–99; John 1166–1216, and possibly an unnamed son who died in early infancy.
4. Notably, Brown, in *Eleanor: Lord and Lady*, p. 18, writes, "In her pursuit of power and advantage her children often served as her pawns"; and "To the end of her life, Eleanor's penchant for intrigue and her political impulses were more pronounced than her maternal inclination."
5. H. M. Colvin, *Essays in English Architectural History* (New Haven, 1999), pp. 1–2.
6. Kelly, *Eleanor and Four Kings*, p. 93, citing *Gervase of Canterbury*, 1, p. 160.
7. *Brute y Tywysogyon*, ed. and trans. Thomas Jones (Cardiff, 1955), p. 41, cited by Bartlett, *England under the Norman and Angevin Kings*, p. 342. On London generally, see Caroline M. Barron, "London", in *Dict. M.A.*, 7, pp. 660–63.
8. William fitz Stephen, "Description of London" in F.M. Stenton, *Norman London* (New York, 1990), p. 48 and pp. 26–28, 55.
9. First quotation, *Richard of Devizes*, ed. Appleby, p. 65; second, Stenton, *Norman London*, p. 51.
10. Stenton, *Norman London*, pp. 48, 49. *PR 13 Henry II* (1166–67), 1, records expenses of £64; see R. Allen Brown, H.M. Colvin, and A.J. Taylor, eds., *History of the King's Works* (London, 1963), 1, pp. 45, 86; Judith A. Green, "Henry I and the Origins of the Court Culture of the Plantagenets," *Plantagenêts et Capétiens*, p. 488.
11. Thomas K. Keefe, "Place-Date Distribution of Royal Charters and Historical Geography of Patronage Strategies at the Court of King Henry II Plantagenet," *HSJ*, 2 (1990), pp. 182–83. Eleanor issued five documents at Salisbury, three at Winchester, two at Oxford, two at Bermondsey, just outside London, and only one each at London, Westminster, Hungerford, and Waltham in the years 1155–67.

12. Green, *Plantagenêts et Capétiens*, p. 488.
13. Brown, Colvin, and Taylor, *History of the King's Works*, 2, pp. 910, 1010, 1014; 1, pp. 65, 79–80; *PR 6 Henry II*, p. 49. Henry's wall painting at Winchester Palace described by Gerald of Wales, *On the Instruction of Princes*, p. 95, bk 3, ch. 26.
14. Bartlett, *England under the Norman and Angevin Kings*, pp. 486–87, quoting Walter Map, p. 476, bk 5, ch. 6. On language, Ian Short, "On Patrons and Polyglots: French Literature in Twelfth-century England," in *ANS*, 14 (1992), pp. 242–43, 244; see also J. Dor, "Langues françaises et anglaises, et multilinguisme à l'époque d'Henri II Plantagenêt," *CCM*, 29, p. 71. In 1192 during Richard's reign, she still needed an interpreter when speaking with monolingual English commoners, *Richard of Devizes*, pp. 59–60.
15. Stafford, "Portrayal of Royal Women in England" in *Medieval Queenship*, pp. 156–57.
16. Quotation, Marjorie Chibnall, "Women in *Orderic Vitalis*," *HSJ*, 2, p. 112. See also Huneycutt, "Creation of a Crone," p. 36, citing Laura Gathagan, "Embodying Power: Gender and Authority in the Queenship of Mathilda of Flanders," unpublished doctoral dissertation (City University of New York, 2001).
17. Francis J. West, *The Justiciarship in England 1066–1232* (Cambridge, 1966), pp. 14–15.
18. Lois L. Huneycutt, "Intercession and the High-Medieval Queen: The Esther Topos" in Jennifer Carpenter and Sally-Beth Maclean, eds, *Power of the Weak: Studies on Medieval Women* (Champagne-Urbana, 1995), pp. 126–46, citing Walter Frölich, trans., *The Letters of St. Anselm of Canterbury*, 3 vols (Kalamazoo, MI, 1990), 3, p. 29, no. 320.
19. Flori, *Aliénor*, p. 394.
20. Supposedly Tickhill was part of Eleanor's dowerland, R.T. Timson, ed., *The Blyth Priory Cartulary* (London, 1973), pp. cxxiv, ccxxviii. Henry II granted the chapel to Walter in 1174. For Eleanor's role in securing revenues for her chaplain Peter, *Calendar of Documents Preserved in France*, ed. J.H. Round (London, 1899), p. 12, no. 46; p. 13, no. 52.
21. *PR 5 Henry II*, p. 55; Huneycutt, *Matilda of Scotland*, pp. 105–06.
22. *PR Henry II, Second–Fourth Years*, ed. Hunter, p. 17, danegeld pardoned by the king in queen's demesne and her canons, £9 3s. Amt, *Accession of Henry II*, p. 70, notes that Waltham Abbey had been claimed both by Stephen for his wife, Queen Matilda, and by Adeliza, widow of Henry I.
23. Richardson, "Letters and Charters," pp. 209–11; citing BL Harl. MS 391, f 51b–52, dated 1193, Eleanor's acknowledgment that the abbot of Waltham supplied her with a clerk for collecting queen's gold at the exchequer. A chaplain of Matilda, Henry I's queen, was a canon of Waltham, Huneycutt, *Matilda of Scotland*, p. 100.
24. Nicholas Vincent, "Patronage, Politics, and Piety in the Charters of Eleanor," in *Plantagenêts et Capétiens*, pp. 22–24. Only one charter records her founding a new religious house, a Fontevraudist priory, Sainte-Catherine at La Rochelle in 1185. *Grand Cartulaire de Fontevraud*, eds Jean-Marc Bienvenu, Robert Favreau, and Georges Pon, *AHP* 63 (Poitiers, 2000), 1, pp. 588–89; citing a lost charter known only from a 17th-century inventory; also cited by Hivergneaux, "Queen Eleanor and Aquitaine," p. 71.
25. Jean-Marie Bienvenu, "Henri II Plantagenêt et Fontevraud," *CCM*, 37 (1994), p. 31.
26. On Reading, C. Warren Hollister, *Henry I* (Berkeley, 2001), pp. 282–87.
27. Vincent, "Patronage, Politics, and Piety," p. 22, n. 50.
28. Christopher R. Cheney, "A Monastic Letter of Fraternity to Eleanor of Aquitaine," *EHR* 51 (1936), pp. 488–93.
29. John of Salisbury, *Letters*, 2, p. 224, no. 185, cited by Laurence Moulinier-Brogi, "Aliénor et les femmes savantes du XIIe siècle," Aurell, ed., *Aliénor*, p. 148.
30. Moulinier-Brogi, "Aliénor et les femmes savantes," p. 148, also Joan M. Ferrante, "Correspondent: 'Blessed is the Speech of Your Mouth'" in Barbara Newman, ed., *Voice of the Living Light: Hildegard of Bingen and Her World* (Berkeley, 1998), p. 94.

31. William the Conqueror's queen was Matilda, daughter of the count of Flanders; Henry I married first Edith-Matilda, daughter of the Scottish king and an Anglo-Saxon princess, and second Adeliza, daughter of the count of Louvain; King Stephen's queen was a daughter of the count of Boulogne.
32. Orderic Vitalis and William of Malmesbury. See Beech, "Contemporary Views of William the Troubadour," pp. 73–89.
33. John of Salisbury, *Letters*, 1, p. 199, no. 121.
34. White, *Restoration and Reform*, p. 5.
35. Norgate, *Angevin Kings*, 1, pp. 428, 429–30.
36. *Cartulary of Holy Trinity, Aldgate*, ed. Gerald A.J. Hodgett, London Record Society (1971), app. 14, p. 232; Hollister, *Henry I*, p. 397. *Ralph Diceto*, 1, p. 301, states that Henry was christened by the bishop of London.
37. The Norman administrators were Geoffrey de Neubourg, brother of Rotrou III, count of Perche, and an Anglo-Norman baron, William Pantulf, *Geoffrey de Vigeois*, *RHGF*, 12, p. 439.
38. Hivergneaux in *Eleanor: Lord and Lady*, p. 66: Eleanor's charter confirming the privileges of the abbey of Sauve-Majeure near Bordeaux followed one issued by Henry a few days earlier; another confirming Henry's grants to the monks of Notre-Dame de Luçon; and a third ratifying their settlement of a property dispute between the chapter of Saint-Hilaire, Poitiers, and the collegiate church's treasurer. Orders to her agents concerning Fontaine-le-Comte and Sablonceaux.
39. Hivergneaux, *Eleanor: Lord and Lady*, pp. 63, 66; and Hivergneaux, *La Cour Plantagenêt*, p. 66.
40. Richard le Poitevin, *RHGF*, 12, p. 417 and Louis Halphen, ed., *Annales Angevines et Vendômoises, Saint-Aubin* (Paris, 1903), pp. 14–15.
41. R.W. Eyton, *Court, Household, and Itinerary of King Henry II* (London, 1878); also Owen, *Eleanor*, Chronology, pp. 219–20.
42. Cheyette, *Ermengard of Narbonne*, p. 25; Martindale, "An Unfinished Business," pp. 117–19, for a critique of modern historians' depiction of the expedition; pp. 143–51, on Eleanor's claim.
43. Quotation, Warren, *Henry II*, p. 84; see p. 83, map v. Also Martindale, "Eleanor of Aquitaine," in *Status, Authority, Power*, art. 11, pp. 26–27; Gillingham, "Angevin Empire," in Gillingham, *Richard Coeur de Lion*, 2nd edn (Oxford, 2001), p. 26.
44. For Becket and Toulouse, J.D. Hosler, "The Brief Military Career of Thomas Becket," *HSJ*, pp. 88–100; also Frank Barlow, *Thomas Becket* (Berkeley, 1986), p. 57.
45. Cheyette, *Ermengard of Narbonne*, p. 259.
46. Elizabeth Hallam and Judith Everard, *Capetian France, 987–1328*, 2nd edn (Harlow, Essex, 2001), p. 160.
47. Lindsay Dippelmann, "Marriage as Tactical Response: Henry II and the Royal Wedding of 1160," *EHR*, 119 (2004), pp. 559–60.
48. Robert de Neubourg, Flori, *Aliénor*, p. 109.
49. Bisson, "Aragon, Crown of," *Dict. M.A.*, 1, pp. 408–11.
50. *RHGF*, 12, p. 417, cited by Martindale, "An Unfinished Business," p. 120; see also p. 133.
51. Quotation, Amt, *Accession of Henry II*, pp. 182–83; Warren, *Henry II*, p. 86.
52. E.g. John of Salisbury, *Letters*, 2, pp. 104–05, no. 168, to Bartholomew, bishop of Exeter, June 1166.
53. Martindale, "An Unfinished Business," pp. 134–41; Warren, *Henry II*, pp. 86–87; Barlow, *Becket*, pp. 57–58.
54. Two of her English documents appear to be dated during Henry's Toulouse campaign, *Gesta Abbum S. Albani*, ed. H.T. Riley, RS (London, 1867), 1, p. 161, text also in R.C. Van Caenegem, ed., *English Lawsuits, from William I to Richard I*, 2 vols,

Selden Soc., 106, 107 (London, 1990–91), 2, pp. 354–58, no. 396; and *Cartae Antiquae Rolls 11–20*, ed. Conway Davies, Pipe Roll Society, new ser., 33 (1960), pp. 71–72, no. 410. See Martindale, "An Unfinished Business," p. 154.

55. Dippelmann, "Marriage as Tactical Response," pp. 954–64.
56. *Robert of Torigni*, p. 211.
57. Edina Bozoky, "Le culte des saints et des reliques dans la politique des premiers rois Plantagenêt," *La Cour Plantagenêt*, p. 281; Martin Aurell, "Les Plantagenêts, la propagande et la relecture du passé" in Aurell, ed., *Culture politique des Plantagenêts*, pp. 16–17.
58. *PR 8 Henry II*, p. 43.
59. For the first view, Kelly, *Eleanor and Four Kings*, p. 97; and for the second, Owen, *Eleanor*, p. 43.
60. Barlow, *Becket*, p. 68.
61. Meade, *Eleanor*, pp. 177–78, citing Becket's letter to Idonea, May 1170, *The Correspondence of Thomas Becket, Archbishop of Canterbury 1162–1170*, ed. and trans. Ann J. Duggan, 2 vols (Oxford, 2001), 2, pp. 1233–34, no. 289.
62. Eyton, *Itin. H. II*, p. 58.
63. Frank Barlow, *Edward the Confessor* (Berkeley, 1970), pp. 281–84; Barlow, *Becket*, p. 95.
64. Barlow, *Becket*, pp. 52–54, 98; I.J. Sanders, *English Baronies* (Oxford, 1960), p. 14.
65. *PR 12 Henry II*, pp. 101, 109.
66. *In curia domine regine*, Daniel Power, "The Stripping of a Queen: Eleanor in Thirteenth-Century Norman Tradition" in *World of Eleanor*, p. 116, n. 8, cites three cases from Anjou showing Eleanor taking part in judgments. Also Delisle-Berger, *Introduction*, p. 174, dated *c.* 1160; and Delisle-Berger, *Actes*, 1, pp. 408–09, no. 263, probably dated 1166 recording settlement of a dispute "judged at Angers in the court of the most excellent king of the English Henry and the venerable queen Eleanor."
67. Flori, *Aliénor*, pp. 116–18; Warren, *Henry II*, p. 101.
68. Whether he had the title seneschal of Aquitaine or simply seneschal of one region, Saintonge, is disputed. Boussard, *Gouvernement*, p. 354, doubts that he was ever seneschal of Aquitaine, while Debord, *Société laïque*, p. 400, and Hivergneaux, *La Cour Plantagenêt*, p. 70, disagree.
69. For Sainte-Radegonde, *Becket Correspondence*, 2, p. 216, n. 9. Oléron: Flori, *Aliénor* p. 117; Vendôme: Richard, *Comtes*, 2, p. 136.
70. First quotation, *Becket Correspondence*, 2, pp. 214–18, no. 51. Doubtless, the disreputable deeds (*infamies*) were Faye's anti-clerical actions, but some writers have suggested that the tendencies (*presumptiones*) coming to light alluded to rumored scandalous relations between Ralph and his niece, Flori, *Aliénor*, p. 117; Meade, *Eleanor*, p. 230; and Owen, *Eleanor*, p. 54. Second quotation, John of Salisbury, *Letters*, 2, pp. 343–47, no. 212, dated January 1167.
71. John of Salisbury, *Letters*, 2, pp. 62–63, no. 162. For Matilda's disagreement with Henry over the Becket business, see Chibnall, "Empress Matilda and her Sons," pp. 188–89.
72. Meade, *Eleanor*, pp. 234–38; Flori, *Aliénor*, p. 119; Owen, *Eleanor*, pp. 55–56.
73. Richardson, "Letters and Charters," p. 197.
74. F.M. Powicke and E.B. Fryde, eds, *Handbook of British Chronology*, 2nd edn (London, 1961), pp. 32–33; supplemented by Lewis, "Birth and Childhood of King John," pp. 161–65.
75. Owen, *Eleanor*, Chronology, pp. 220–21; Flori, *Aliénor*, p. 121.
76. Labande, "Les filles d'Aliénor d'Aquitaine," p. 106.
77. Damon, "Dames du Poitou au temps d'Aliénor," p. 50.
78. Gillingham, "Love, Marriage, and Politics in the Twelfth Century," p. 253.
79. Georges Duby, *William Marshal: The Flower of Chivalry*, trans. Richard Howard (New York, 1985), pp. 135–36.

80. Eyton, *Itin. H. II*; Owen, *Eleanor*, Chronology, pp. 219–20; Flori, *Aliénor*, pp. 108–22.
81. Much of this section derives from two articles, Ralph V. Turner, "Eleanor of Aquitaine and her Children: An Inquiry into Medieval Family Attachment," *JMH*, 14 (1988), and "The Children of Anglo-Norman Royalty and their Upbringing," *Medieval Prosopography* (1990).
82. Lois L. Huneycutt, "Public Lives, Private Ties: Royal Mothers in England and Scotland, 1070–1204" in Parsons and Wheeler, *Medieval Mothering*, pp. 306–07.
83. Ibid., pp. 298–303.
84. Orme, *From Childhood to Chivalry: The Education of the English Kings and Aristocracy, 1066–1530* (London, 1984), pp. 11–12.
85. Eleanor's gifts to Agatha, land at Hamelhamstead, Berkhamstead, and Lufton manor, Devon, *Rot. Chart.*, p. 18. On Agatha, see Mary G. Cheney, "Master Geoffrey de Lucy, an Early Chancellor of the University of Oxford," *EHR*, 82 (1967), pp. 759–60.
86. *PR 22 Henry II* (1175–76), p. 141. On medieval wet-nurses, see Goodich, "Bartholomeus Anglicus on Childrearing," *History of Childhood Quarterly / Journal of Psychohistory*, 3 (1975), p. 81. A mark was two-thirds of a pound, 13 shillings and 6 pence.
87. *PR 2 Richard I*, p. 118; *PR 3 and 4 Richard I*, pp. 118, 281.
88. Cheney, "Master Geoffrey de Lucy," p. 760.
89. *PR Henry II, Second–Fourth Years*, ed. Hunter, pp. 66, 101, 180; *PR 5 Henry II*, p. 58.
90. J.C. Robertson, ed., *Materials for the History of Thomas Becket*, 7 vols, RS (London, 1875–85), 3, p. 22.
91. Eyton, *Itin. H. II*, p. 86; *PR 11 Henry II*, p. 73; *PR 12 Henry II*, pp. 96, 100; *PR 13 Henry II*, pp. 169, 171; Warren, *Henry II*, p. 185.
92. *History of William Marshal*, eds A.J. Holden, S. Gregory, and D. Crouch (London, 2002), lines 2427–2432; Sidney Painter, *William Marshal* (Baltimore, 1933), pp. 31–49.
93. Roger of Howden, *Chronica*, ed. William Stubbs, 4 vols, RS (London, 1868–71), 2, p. 106.
94. Authored by Peter of Blois, Migne, *PL*, 207, cols 210–12.
95. Gillingham, *Richard I* (New Haven, 1999), p. 256, citing Gerald of Wales, *De Invectionibus*.
96. *Rot. Lit. Claus.*, p. 108.
97. John Carmi Parsons, "Mothers, Daughters, Marriage, Power: Some Plantagenet Evidence, 1150–1500," in *Medieval Queenship*, p. 69.
98. Georges Duby, "Women and Power" in Bisson, *Cultures of Power*, pp. 80, 81; citing Migne, *PL*, 211, col. 685.
99. Sarah Bradford, *The Reluctant King*, p. 16.

CHAPTER 6: A QUEEN'S WORK: REGENT FOR AN ABSENTEE KING, 1155–1168

1. *Handbook of British Chronology*, eds Powicke and Fryde, p. 32, Henry's absences from England: 10 January 1156 to April 1157; 14 August 1158 to 25 January 1163; *c.* February to *c.* May 1165; *c.* March 1166 to 3 March 1170.
2. Owen, *Eleanor*, p. 108.
3. Judith Green, "Henry I and the Origins of the Court Culture of the Plantagenets" in *Plantagenêts et Capétiens*, pp. 485–95, at p. 492.
4. Benedict of Saint-Maure, *Roman de Troie*, lines 13, 457–13, 470.
5. Warren, *Henry II*, p. 59.
6. Norgate, *Angevin Kings*, 1, p. 431.
7. Giles Constable, "The Alleged Disgrace of John of Salisbury," *EHR*, 69 (1954), pp. 67–76.
8. John of Salisbury, *Letters*, 1, pp. 31–32, no. 19 to Peter, abbot of Celle; and 1, pp. 50–51, no. 31.

9. Warren, *Henry II*, pp. 120, 260.
10. John of Salisbury, *Letters*, 1, p. 89, no. 51, to Pope Adrian IV.
11. John of Salisbury, *Letters*, 1, pp. 151–52, no. 98, dated *c.* 1158–60. *PR Henry II, Second–Fourth Years*, ed. Hunter, p. 13, records a payment of 66s 8d to "Solomon the queen's clerk."
12. *Fasti*, 2, *Monasti Cathedrals*, pp. 30, 105.
13. John of Salisbury, *Letters*, 1, p. 189, no. 115, dated 1160. The cleric was Jordan, treasurer of Salisbury, *c.* 1154–55 to 1159–60, *Fasti*, 4, *Salisbury*, p. 30.
14. David Crouch, *The Beaumont Twins: The Roots and Branches of Power in the Twelfth Century* (Cambridge, 1986), pp. 7, 86–88, 207, 210; David Bates, "The Origins of the Justiciarship," *ANS*, 4 (1987), p. 11.
15. Emilie M. Amt, "Richard de Lucy, Henry II's Justiciar," *Medieval Prosopography*, 9 (1988), pp. 61–87.
16. Amt, *Accession of Henry II*, p. 20.
17. John of Salisbury, *Letters*, 1, p. 52, no. 32, to Peter de Celle, dated July–August 1157.
18. *PR Henry II, Second–Fourth Years*, ed. Hunter, p. 171, Bisset responsible for carrying the queen's robe from Winchester to Oxford. On Bisset, see Amt, *Accession of Henry II*, pp. 22, 163; White, *Restoration and Reform*, pp. 46–47, 83. Fitz Gerold, *PR Henry II, Second–Fourth Years*, pp. 107, 171. On Fitz Gerold, see Amt, *Accession of Henry II*, p. 76; Chibnall, *Empress Matilda*, p. 126; *Regesta regum A-N*, 2, p. xxxv. Gundeville, *PR 6 Henry II*, 1159–60, p. 49; see Amt, *Accession of Henry II*, p. 41.
19. Michael T. Clanchy, *From Memory to Written Record: England 1066–1307*, 2nd edn (Oxford, 1993), p. 58.
20. Twenty-nine are authorizations of payments recorded on the exchequer's pipe rolls, *PR Henry II, Second–Fourth Years*, ed. Hunter, 5 for 1155–56; 7 for 1157–58, *PR 5 Henry II* (1158–59), 5 writs, 13 for 1159–60, *PR 6 Henry II*; none for 1160–63, *PR 7 Henry II*; and one in 1162–63, *PR 8 Henry II*.
21. Dated before 1162, *Calendar of Charter Rolls*, 5, *15 Edward III–5 Henry V*, p. 61; the same phrase occurs in a writ to the knights of Abingdon Abbey, *c.* 1159–60, *Chronicon Monasterii de Abingdon*, ed. J. Stevenson, 2 vols, RS, 2, p. 225; English translation, *English Historical Documents*, 2, *1042–1189*, 936, no. 266.
22. Dated 1156 or 1157, H.G. Richardson, ed., *Memoranda Roll 1 John*, p. lxviii, citing BL Harl. ms 1708, f 113b.
23. John of Salisbury, *Letters*, 2, p. 7, no. 136.
24. Richard of Anstey's account of his lengthy lawsuit, bouncing back and forth between royal and ecclesiastical courts, *c.* 1158–63; Van Caenegem, ed., *English Lawsuits*, nos. 397–404, no. 386E; discussed in Richardson, *Memoranda Roll 1 John*, p. lxxx.
25. Cyril T. Flower, *Introduction to Curia Regis Rolls, 1199–1230 A.D.*, Selden Society, 62 (London, 1944), p. 304.
26. Crouch, *Beaumont Twins*, p. 89; White, *Restoration and Reform*, pp. 182, 183.
27. Abbot of St Albans versus Robert of Valognes, Van Caenegem, ed., *English Lawsuits*, 2, pp. 354–58, no. 396; Warren, *Henry II*, pp. 327–29.
28. Quotation, Gillingham, "The Cultivation of History, Legend, and Courtesy at the Court of Henry II," Kennedy and Meecham-Jones, *Writers of the Reign of Henry II*, p. 41, citing *Walter Map*, p. 116. Green, "Henry I and the Origins of the Court Culture of the Plantagenets," p. 485.
29. Green, *Plantagenêts et Capétiens* pp. 485–95.
30. *Ralph Diceto*, 1, p. 302; Howden, *Chronica*, 1, p. 216.
31. Schramm, *History of the English Coronation*, p. 58; H. G. Richardson, "The Coronation in Medieval England," *Traditio*, 16 (1960), p. 127; Bartlett, *England under the Norman and Angevin Kings*, pp. 127–28. Also Matthew Strickland, "The

Upbringing of Henry, the Young King," in Harper-Bill and Vincent, *Henry II: New Interpretations*, p. 197.

32. *PR Henry II, Second–Fourth Years*, ed. Hunter, p. 5; *PR 5 Henry II*, p. 1; *16 Henry II* (1169–70), p. 15. See also James H. Ramsay, *A History of Revenues of the Kings of England, 1066–1399*, 2 vols (Oxford, 1925), 1, p. 189.

33. *PR Henry II, Second–Fourth Years*, ed. Hunter, p. 175; and numerous entries for wine, *PR 6 Henry II* (1159–60), pp. 13, 16, 23, 49. See R.R. Davies, *Domination and Conquest: The Experience of Ireland, Scotland and Wales 1100–1300* (Cambridge, 1990), p. 49, citing Gerald of Wales, *Expugnatio hibernica*, ed. and trans. A.B. Scott and F.X. Martin (Dublin, 1978), pp. 96–97, bk 1, ch. 33; Howden, *Chronica*, 2, p. 32. Chestnuts, *PR 5 Henry II*, p. 25.

34. Letter 66 in Migne, *PL*, 207.

35. Georges Duby, *The Three Orders: Feudal Society Imagined*, trans. Arthur Goldhammer (Chicago, 1980), p. 272; Jaeger, *Origins of Courtliness*, pp. 206–07, 209. For Vidal, Aurell, "Les Plantagenêts, la propagande et la relecture du passé," p. 12.

36. Jaeger, *Origins of Courtliness*, p. 268.

37. Robert B. Patterson, ed., *Earldom of Gloucester Charters: The Charters and Scribes of the Earls and Countesses of Gloucester to A.D. 1217* (Oxford, 1973), Introduction, p. 12; p. 71, no. 65. For another example of land held by the service of supplying three dice, see *Rot. Chart.*, pp. 18, 128, a Devon manor, part of Eleanor's dower that she had granted to her former wet-nurse, is to be held of King John's bride Isabelle by the service of three dice. See also Achille Luchaire, *Social France at the Time of Philip Augustus*, trans. Edward Benjamin Krehbiel (New York, 1912; reprint 1967), p. 552; Danziger and Gillingham, *1215*, p. 61.

38. Translation, Peter Dronke, "Peter of Blois and Poetry at the Court of Henry II," *Mediaeval Studies*, 38 (1976) p. 207.

39. Richardson, "Letters and Charters," p. 208, n. 3, her ewer, Philip fitz Vital. See also Crouch, *Image of Aristocracy*, pp. 294, 296, 297.

40. Ranulf de Broc, Harper-Bill, and Vincent, *Henry II: New Interpretations*, p. 332, n. 2.

41. J.E.A. Jolliffe, *Angevin Kingship*, 2nd edn (London, 1963), pp. 192–206.

42. For Manasser Biset, steward of the king's household, and Hastings, the queen's steward, *PR Henry II, Second–Fourth Years*, ed. Hunter, p. 176.

43. Bartlett, *England under the Norman and Angevin Kings*, pp. 134–35, citing Henry of Huntingdon, *De contemptu mundi*, p. 604.

44. Labarge, *Medieval Travellers*, pp. 35, 39. Bartlett, *England under the Norman and Angevin Kings*, pp. 133–34.

45. E.g. Herman, Eleanor's chaplain, and John, "the queen's clerk," *Cart. S. Iohannis Baptiste in Colecestria*, 1, p. 38; and Elias, former clerk of the earl of Gloucester, identified in one of the earl's charters as "clerk of the Lady Eleanor queen of England," Patterson, ed., *Earldom of Gloucester Charters*, p. 12; p. 71, no. 65. For John de Waurai, her butler, *PR 9 Henry II*, p. 45; *10 Henry II*, p. 19; *14 Henry II*, p. 174; Adam, her chamberlain, *PR 18 Henry II*, p. 15.

46. Howell, *Eleanor of Provence*, p. 267; Crouch, *Image of Aristocracy*, pp. 293–94.

47. A charter issued at Bermondsey, c. 1154–1162, BL ms Harl. 4757 fo.2v, abstract only, s.xvii, names several with their titles. I am grateful to the Plantagenet *Acta* Project for supplying me with this reference.

48. On Master Matthew, see Richardson, ed., *Memoranda Roll 1 John*, Introduction, p. lxviii. Witnessing charters for Henry before his coronation, *Regesta Regum A–N*, no. 666, 13 April 1149 at Devizes; no. 776, 9 November 1151 at Angers.

49. Peter of Poitiers: *Gallia Christiana*, 11, *Instrumenta*, col. 82, no. 16; *Petrus notaruns*, Métais, ed., "Cartulaire saintongeais de Vendôme," pp. 103–04, no. 62; also Vincent, "Patronage, Politics and Piety," in Aurell and Tonnerre, p. 36. Métais, ed., "Cartulaire saintongeais de la Trinité-de-Vendôme," pp. 103–04, no. 62.

50. Richardson, "Letters and Charters," p. 197; Hivergneaux, *Plantagenêts et Capétiens*, p. 70. The Balliols came from Bailleul-en-Vimeu (Somme). Sanders, *Baronies*, p. 25; and Lewis C. Loyd, *The Origins of Some Anglo-Norman Families*, Herleian Soc., 103 (Leeds, 1951; reprint Baltimore, 1985), p. 11.

51. For Geoffrey, Delisle-Berger, *Introduction*, "Hugo de Claiers," pp. 387–88.

52. Howell, *Eleanor of Provence*, pp. 186–87.

53. Labande, "Pour une image," p. 199, citing *Robert of Torigni*, p. 176.

54. Huneycutt, *Matilda of Scotland*, p. 59; Howell, *Eleanor of Provence*, pp. 186–87.

55. Philip fitz Vital, Richardson, "Letters and Charters," p. 208, n. 3.

56. Lewis, "Six Charters of Henry II and his Family for Dalon," pp. 659–61; Marchegay, *Cartulaires du Bas-Poitou*, p. 109; Clouzot, "Cartulaire, de l'abbaye de Notre-Dame de la Merci-Dieu," pp. 78–79; Redet, "Documents pour l'histoire de Saint-Hilaire," pp. 180–81, no. 153. For his Rouen prebend, *Cal. Docs. France*, p. 12, no. 46; p. 13, no. 52.

57. *PR Henry II, Second–Fourth Years*, ed. Hunter, p. 176, £6 corrody by Ralph of Hastings and Bernard de Chauvigny. For the Chauvigny family, see G. Devailly, *Berry du Xe au milieu du XIIIe siècle* (Paris, 1973), p. 423, n. 8; Theodore Evergates, "Nobles and Knights in Twelfth-century France," in Bisson, *Cultures of Power*, p. 31. Later Geoffrey de Chauvigny was Count Richard's chamberlain, *Cal. Docs. France*, p. 467, no. 1286.

58. Vincent, *La Cour Plantagenêt*, pp. 122–23. *PR Henry II, Second–Fourth Years*, ed. Hunter, p. 11, payment to Ralph de Faia 32s for his danegeld; p. 12, Ralph pardoned by king's writ of 104s and also of 45s; p. 162, Ralph pardoned of 34s. *PR 13 Henry II*, p. 205, 71s 11d pardoned for Ralph de Faye by the king's writ. Gerald of Wales tells an anecdote that suggests Ralph's presence with the king at Woodstock, *Gemma Ecclesiastica*, in Gerald of Wales, *Opera*, 1, p. 54, 2, p. 162, cited in Vincent, "Court of Henry II" in *Henry II: New Interpretations*, p. 323.

59. Barthélemy's letter testifying to Eleanor's role, Emma Mason, ed., *Westminster Abbey Charters*, London Record Society, 25 (1988), pp. 298–99, no. 463. For his kinship to Eleanor, Peltzer, *Plantagenêts et Capétiens*, p. 473 and n. 31.

60. Marchisa identified as her *cognata*, *PR 11 Henry II*, p. 40. For identification, see Vincent, in *Plantagenêts et Capétiens*, p. 46. Pipe roll entries during Eleanor's captivity after 1173 refer to her "girls" or her "maidens [*puellae*]," *PR 24 Henry II* (1177–78), p. 128; *PR 30 Henry II* (1183–84), p. 217, and *PR 33 Henry II* (1186–87), p. 181. See also Howell, *Eleanor of Provence*, pp. 104–05.

61. Hivergneaux in *Plantagenêts et Capétiens*, p. 68; Painter, "The Lords of Lusignan in the Eleventh and Twelfth Centuries," in Cazel, ed., *Feudalism and Liberty*, pp. 68–69: Sanxay was in the hands of the Lusignans in the thirteenth century, probably acquired by them sometime in the twelfth century. An act of Eleanor for Fontevraud from 1152, Delisle-Berger, 1, p. 32, no. 24, gives him the title *dapifer meus*; elsewhere he is called *constabularius*. Saldebreuil in pipe rolls, *PR 9 Henry II*, p. 71; *11 Henry II*, p. 30, *12 Henry II*, p. 130; payment of 60s 10d, *PR 13 Henry II*, p. 2; *PR 14 Henry II*, p. 2; Saldebreuil's payment transferred to others, *PR 16 Henry II*, p. 14. A son or other relative may be the Saut de Bruil who fought with Richard Lionheart on crusade forty years later, and who served as Richard's messenger, sent to the Holy Land following his release from captivity in February 1194 to announce his plan to return there. Lionel Landon, *The Itinerary of King Richard I*, Pipe Roll Society, new ser. 13(1935), pp. 59, 83, citing Howden, *Chronica*, 3, p. 233.

62. Markale, *Aliénor*, pp. 163–64, no source cited. The knight Saldebreuil appears in François de Belle-Forest, *Grandes annales et histoire générale de France*, 2 vols (Paris, 1579), 1, p. 510; then amplified by Augustin Thierry, *Histoire de la conquête de l'Angleterre par les Normands*, 4 vols (Paris, 1846), 3, p. 60. I owe these references to the kindness of Dr Ursula Vones-Liebenstein.

Notes to pp. 165-169

63. Jordan "my chancellor," *Recueil des documents de l'abbaye de Fontaine-le-Comte*, ed. Georges Pon, *AHP*, 62 (1982), pp. 36–38, no. 24. For Saldebreuil and Hervey, Hivergneaux, *Capétiens et Plantagenêts*, pp. 63, 68. For the Mauzé family, see Hivergneaux, *Capétiens et Plantagenêts*, p. 63.

64. Debord, *Société laïque*, pp. 382–85.

65. He witnessed Henry's charter confirming Eleanor's grant to the monks of Luçon, Delisle-Berger, Actes, 1, pp. 132–33, no. 32, at Chizé.

66. Amt, *Accession of Henry II*, pp. 97–98.

67. Bartlett, *England under the Norman and Angevin Kings*, pp. 43–44.

68. Based on Richard I's charter granting traditional dowerlands to his bride Berengaria, in Dom Edmond Martene and Dom Ursin Durand, *Veterum scriptorum et Monumentorum historicorum, dogmaticorum, moralium, amplissima collectio* (Paris, 1724), vol. 1: col. 995–97; summarized by Cloulas, "Le Douaire de Bérengère de Navarre, veuve de Richard Coeur de Lion," *La Cour Plantagenêt*, pp. 90–91. In addition, pipe rolls record exemptions from danegeld for Eleanor's lands, Amt, *Accession of Henry II*, p. 76. On Lufton Hundred, Devon, White, *Restoration and Reform*, p. 119; for Queenshithe, Brooke, *London: The Shaping of a City*, p. 156.

69. A silver mark's value was two-thirds of a pound. Charles Johnson, ed., *The Course of the Exchequer* (London, 1950), p. 122.

70. Richardson, "Letters and Charters," pp. 210–11, notes Eleanor's receipt of queen's gold in 1167; *PR 10 John*, p. 25, charter of 1194 acknowledging that Jurnet the Jew of Norwich paid 40 marks of queen's gold, owed since Henry II's time.

71. Sidney Painter, *Studies in the History of the English Feudal Barony* (Baltimore, 1943), p. 170. After the queen's return in 1157 from a long visit to Aquitaine, her expenses for that year alone totaled more than £500. *PR Henry II, Second–Fourth Years*, ed. Hunter, pp. 111–86.

72. *History of William Marshal*, lines 1876–82.

73. Peter of Blois, Migne, *PL*, 207, col. 49A, p. 14.

74. Howden, *Chronica*, 3, p. 143, describing William Longchamp's patronage of singers and *jongleurs*, cited by Aurell, *L'Empire des Plantagenêts*, p. 98.

75. Bartlett, *England under the Norman and Angevin Kings*, pp. 497–98, citing Denis Piramus, *La Vie seint Edmund le rey*, lines 16–19, in *Memorials of St. Edmund's Abbey*, ed. T. Arnold, 3 vols, (London, 1890–96), 92, p. 137.

76. Ian Short, "Literary Culture at the Court of Henry II" in Harper-Bill and Vincent, *Henry II: New Interpretations*, pp. 341–50; also Charles H. Haskins, "Henry II as a Patron of Literature" in A.G. Little and F.M. Powiche, eds, *Essays in Medieval History Presented to Thomas Frederick Tout* (Manchester, 1925), pp. 71–77.

77. Breton d'Amboise, cited by Jaeger, *Origins of Courtliness*, p. 203, from Halphen and Poupardin, eds, *Chroniques des comtes d'Anjou et des seigneurs d'Amboise*, p. 71.

78. Eleanor's literary patronage is a much debated issue. Writers of a previous generation depicted her as a great patron of the troubadours, who flocked to her "courts of love" at Poitiers, e.g. Amy Kelly, Rita Lejeune, Régine Pernoud. In a reaction against this romantic depiction, some scholars deny her significance as a patron, notably Karen Broadhurst, "Henry II of England and Eleanor of Aquitaine: Patrons of Literature in French?", *Viator*, 27 (1996), pp. 53–84.

79. Jaeger, *Origins of Courtliness*, e.g. pp. 233–35; he sees this as the primary motivation for clerical writers of vernacular romances.

80. Broadhurst, "Henry II and Eleanor," pp. 62–63. *Vie d'Edouard Confesseur*, ed. Ö. Södergård (Uppsala, 1948), written between 1163 and 1179, based on Ailred of Rievaulx's Latin life of Edward.

81. Flori, *Aliénor*, p. 403.

82. Aurell, *La Cour Plantagenêt*, pp. 34–35. Haskins, "Henry II as a Patron," p. 73, citing *PR 18 Henry II*, p. 4; *PR 21 Henry II*, p. 204, and post-1176 pipe rolls.

83. Quotation, Derek Pearsall and Nicolette Zeeman, eds, *Elizabeth Salter: English and International Studies in the Literature, Art, and Patronage of Medieval England* (Cambridge, 1988), p. 37, citing H.J. Chaytor, *Troubadours and England* (Cambridge, 1923). See also Baldwin, "Image of the Jongleur in Northern France," p. 640. Second quotation, Pappano, "Marie de France, Aliénor, and the Alien Queen," *Eleanor: Lord and Lady*, p. 361, n. 15.

84. Poems 26 and 33, Ruth Harvey, "Eleanor and the Troubadours," pp. 101, 104–06; from S.G. Nichols et al. eds and trans., *The Songs of Bernart de Ventadorn* (Chapel Hill, NC, 1962).

85. Flori, *Aliénor*, p. 410; Owen, *Eleanor*, pp. 40–41; Salter, "Courts and Courtly Love," pp. 420–21: More pain of love I feel / Than Tristan, that lover / Who suffer much agony / For the fair-haired Iseult. Text from F.R. Hamlin, P.T. Ricketts, and J. Hathaway, *Introduction à l'étude de l'ancien provençal* (Geneva, 1967), no. 24.

86. Kelly, *Eleanor and Four Kings*, pp. 85–87; Pernoud, *Aliénor*, pp. 143–47; Meade, *Eleanor*, pp. 159–60. Also Bec, "Troubadours, trouvères et espace Plantagenêt," pp. 9–14. The only example is Richard Lionheart, who wrote a song in both French and Occitan versions during his captivity in Germany.

87. Jaeger, *Origins of Courtliness*, p. 206.

88. *Franche est Alienor et de bonaire et sage*, Lejeune, *CCM*, pp. 25–26. Flori, *Aliénor*, pp. 403, 406–08; Broadhurst, "Henry II and Eleanor," pp. 70–72.

89. Fiona Tollhurst, "What Ever Happened to Eleanor? Reflections of Eleanor of Aquitaine in Wace's *Roman de Brut* and Lawman's *Brut*," in *Eleanor: Lord and Lady*, pp. 326, 329, 331; Owen, *Eleanor*, p. 166.

90. Werner, "Kingdom and Principality," p. 275.

91. John W. Baldwin, "The Capetian Court at Work under Philip II," in Edward Haymes, ed., *The Medieval Court in Europe* (Munich 1986), pp. 80–81; Gillingham, "Cultivation of History, Legend, and Courtesy," pp. 28, 36–37. Also Aurell, "Henry II and Arthurian Legend" in Harper-Bill and Vincent, *Henry II, New Interpretations*, pp. 362–94.

92. Aurell, "Les Plantagenêts, la propagande et la relecture du passé," p. 17.

93. Glyn S. Burgess and Elisabeth van Houts, eds, *Wace's Roman de Rou* (Woodbridge, Suffolk, 2004), p. 3, pt. 1, lines 24–36, pp. 39–40; pt. 2, lines 1565–87.

94. Flori, *Aliénor*, pp. 403–04. Quotation, *Roman de Rou*, trans. Burgess, p. 3, pt. 1, lines 1–16.

95. Broadhurst, "Henry II and Eleanor," pp. 56–58; Flori, *Aliénor*, pp. 403–04, 407; Peter Damian-Grint, "Benoît de Saint-Maure et l'idéologie des Plantagenêts," in *Plantagenêts et Capétiens*, pp. 412–27.

96. Lines 13, 457–70, *en cui tote scïence abonde, a la ci n'est nule seconde . . . . Riche dame de riche rei, senz mal, senz ire, senz tristece*; trans. Tamara O'Callahan, "Tempering Scandal: Eleanor of Aquitaine and Benoît de Saint-Maure's *Roman de Troie*," in *Eleanor: Lord and Lady*, pp. 302–03.

97. O'Callaghan, "Tempering Scandal," pp. 301–17, on Helen and Briseida; Flori, *Aliénor*, pp. 408–10, on Hecuba, Joan M. Ferrante, *To the Glory of her Sex: Women's Role in the Composition of Medieval Texts* (Bloomington, 1997), p. 120. Eleanor had eight known children, possibly a ninth.

98. Aurell, *L'Empire des Plantagenêts*, pp. 174–75.

99. Renate Blumenfeld-Kosinski, "Antiquity, Romances of" in Kibler and Zinn, *Medieval France: an Encyclopedia*, p. 49. On the *Roman de Thèbes*: Lejeune, "La femme dans la littérature française," pp. 201–16; Owen, *Eleanor*, p. 167; also Martindale, "Eleanor: The Last Years" in S.D. Church, ed., *King John: New Interpretations* (Woodbridge, Suffolk 1999), pp. 137–38, 164.

100. First quotation, Short, "Patrons and Polyglots," pp. 241–42; Broadhurst, "Henry II and Eleanor," pp. 72–73. Bestiary translation, Kelly, *Eleanor and Four Kings*, p. 101.

101. Van Houts, "Les femmes dans le royaume Plantagenêt," pp. 95–112.

102. West, *Justiciarship in England*, pp. 33–35; Richardson, "Letters and Charters," p. 195.
103. *Gesta regis*, 1; p. 6; see R.J. Smith, "Henry II's Heir, the *Acta* and Seal of Henry the Young King, 1170–83," *EHR*, 116: Appendix, nos 3–8.

CHAPTER 7: A TASTE OF POWER IN POITOU, 1168–1173

1. Richardson, "Letters and Charters," pp. 197, 199.
2. *History of William Marshal*, ed. Holden, Gregory, and Crouch, lines 1566–1580.
3. Hivergneaux in *La Cour Plantagenêt*, p. 70, writes that it is impossible to prove whether Eleanor's return to Poitou was due to jealousy or lovers' spite. Equally significant were her political ambitions. On Henry's failure to establish his personal rule over Aquitaine, see Nicholas Vincent, *La Cour Plantagenêt*, pp. 118–19.
4. J.C. Holt, "The Writs of Henry II," John Hudson, ed., *The History of English Law: Centenary Essays on "Pollock and Martland,"* Proceedings of the British Academy, 89 (London, 1996), p. 54.
5. Debord, "La politique de fortification," pp. 10–11; Boutoulle, "La Gascogne sous les premiers Plantagenêts," *Plantagenêts et Capétiens*, pp. 286–88.
6. Richard le Poitevin, cited by Vincent, *La Cour Plantagenêt*, p. 128.
7. Gillingham, "The Unromantic Death of Richard I," p. 41, in *Richard Coeur de Lion: Kingship, Chivalry, and War in the Twelfth Century* (London, 1994).
8. Hajdu, "Castles, Castellans, and the Structure of Politics in Poitou," pp. 27–54.
9. Pierre Boissonade, "Administrateurs laïques et ecclésiastiques anglo-normands en Poitou à l'époque d'Henri II Plantagenêt (1152–1189)," *BSAO*, 3rd ser., 5 (1919), p. 189, citing Migne, *PL*, 194, col. 1896.
10. See Boissonade, "Administrateurs laïques et ecclésiastiques anglo-normands en Poitou," pp. 156–90. *Ralph Diceto*, 1, p. 331, *Comes Patricius in Aquitania princeps militiae regis Anglorum*. For Theobald Chabot, Boussard, *Gouvernement*, p. 117.
11. Boussard, *Gouvernement*, pp. 117, 125, 353; Debord, *Société laïque*, p. 375. Painter, "Castellans of Poitou," p. 34. Renouard, "Les institutions du duché d'Aquitaine," pp. 161–62.
12. Warren, *Henry II*, pp. 103, 129.
13. Quotation, Duggan, *Becket Correspondence*, 2, p. 216, n. 9; Delisle-Berger, *Introduction*, p. 416; Richard, *Comtes*, 2: 136. For Faye's career, see Vincent, in *La Cour Plantagenêt*, pp. 122–23.
14. Jean Gaudemet, "Structure de l'Église de France," in Lot and Fawtier, *Histoire des institutions françaises au moyen âge*, 3, *Institutions écclesiastiques* (Paris, 1962), p. 173.
15. Jacques Boussard, ed., *Historia Pontificum et comitum Engolismensium* (Paris, 1957), pp. 44–45.
16. Peltzer, "Les évêques de l'empire Plantagenêt," p. 471.
17. André Musset, "L'espace et le temps Plantagenêt: les problèmes d'une architecture," *CCM*, 29 (1986), p. 126; Peltzer, "Évêques de l'empire Plantagenêt," pp. 471–72; Cheney, "A monastic letter of fraternity to Eleanor," pp. 488–93.
18. Quotation, Duggan, *Becket Correspondence*, 1, pp. 128–33, no. 34. See also Philippe Pouzet, *L'Anglais Jean dit Bellesmains* (Lyon, 1927), pp. 9–15; Peltzer, "Évêques," pp. 472–73.
19. Duggan, *Becket Correspondence*, 1, pp. 128–33, no. 34. Charles Duggan, "Richard of Ilchester, Royal Servant and Bishop," *Trans. Royal Hist. Soc.*, 5th ser., 16 (1966), pp. 1–21. Ilchester witnessed one of Henry II's charters at Surgères, 1167–68, Delisle-Berger, *Actes*, 1, p. 417, no. 269.
20. Lindy Grant, "Le patronage architectural d'Henri II et de son entourage," *CCM*, 37 (1994), pp. 75–79. For the completion date, Françoise Perrot, "Le portrait d'Aliénor dans le vitrail de la *crucifixion* à la cathédrale de Poitiers" in Aurell, ed. *Aliénor*, p. 182.

21. Jean Louise Lozinski, "Henri II, Aliénor d'Aquitaine et la cathédrale de Poitiers," *CCM*, 37 (1994), pp. 91–100.

22. Barlow, *Becket*, p. 178.

23. Devailly, *Berry*, pp. 351–426, 438.

24. Warren, *Henry II*, pp. 105–06; Duggan, *Becket Correspondence*, 1, pp. 99–109, letter 31, John, bishop of Poitiers to Becket, dated 24 June 1164, pp. 106–07, and n. 14; also n. 5, pp. 127–28. Richard Benjamin, "A Forty-Year War: Toulouse and the Plantagenets, 1156–90," *Historical Research*, 61 (1988), p. 274.

25. *Gervase of Canterbury*, 1, p. 267.

26. Norgate, *Angevin Kings*, 2, p. 61; Warren, *Henry II*, p. 103.

27. Meade, *Eleanor*, p. 233.

28. Benjamin, "A Forty-Year War," pp. 273–74.

29. John of Salisbury, *Letters*, 2, pp. 564–65, no. 272, dated April–May 1168; also *Geoffrey de Vigeois*, *RHGF*, 12, p. 442. According to the *History of William Marshal*, lines 1566–1580, 1590–92, pp. 80–82, the king was in England when news of the revolt reached him, and he crossed the Channel accompanied by Eleanor, Earl Patrick, and other English barons.

30. Hivergneaux, *Eleanor: Lord and Lady*, p. 68.

31. E.g. Kelly, *Eleanor and Four Kings*, pp. 134–35.

32. Hivergneaux in *La Cour Plantagenêt*, p. 70.

33. Ann Trindade, *Berengaria: In Search of Richard the Lionheart's Queen* (Dublin, 1999), p. 63; also Pappano, "Marie de France, Aliénor, and the Alien Queen," p. 350.

34. Boissonade, "Administrateurs," p. 161; Painter, *William Marshal*, p. 26, n. 29, locates it near Luisgnan Castle.

35. *History of William Marshal*, lines 1590–1651, pp. 82–85.

36. John of Salisbury, *Letters*, 2, pp. 566–67, no. 272; pp. 602–03, no. 279; Delisle-Berger, *Actes*, 2, pp. 145–46, no. 566. Henry, who had taken the abbey of Charroux under his protection as "advocate, patron and defender," declared that since the abbey belonged to him, he offered the abbot nothing.

37. *History of William Marshal*, lines 1879–1883, 1939–1948; Painter, *William Marshal*, pp. 31–49; David Crouch, *William Marshal: Court, Career, and Chivalry in the Angevin Empire 1142–1219* (Harlow, 1990), p. 37.

38. *Walter Map*, pp. 492–93.

39. Hivergneaux, *La Cour Plantagenêt*, p. 73. *PR 15 Henry II* (1168–69), pp. 47, 48; *PR 16 Henry II* (1169–70), p. 97; *PR 17 Henry II* (1170–71), p. 24; *PR 18 Henry II* (1171–71), p. 98. Also *PR 18 Henry II*, p. 15, Eleanor still had an official in her service in England, Adam the queen's chamberlain.

40. E.g. confirmation of a settlement that her kinsman Ralph de Faye and his son made ending their dispute with a citizen of La Rochelle; Alexandre Teulet, Henri-François Delaborde, and Élie Berger, *Layettes du Trésor des Chartes*, 5 vols (Paris, 1863–1909), 1, p. 149, no. 352. Other times she warranted grants benefitting Fontevraud Abbey. Early in 1173 at Chinon, Eleanor was a witness to her husband's charter confirming the abbey's rights at Angers and Saumur; also Eleanor witnessed a gift by a certain Ginosa: Bienvenu, "Aliénor et Fontevraud," p. 20.

41. Delisle-Berger, *Introduction*, pp. 411–12; *Actes*, 1, p. 425, no. 278; and L. Redet, "Documents pour l'histoire de Saint-Hilaire," pp. 180–81, no. 153; comments by Hivergneaux in *La Cour Plantagenêt*, p. 71. Twenty of Eleanor's documents survive from this period; fifteen are charters recording grants or confirmations of earlier grants with religious houses as the chief beneficiaries, although two are for townsmen, Pierre de Ruffec of La Rochelle and Geoffrey Berland, a rich merchant of Poitiers, Hivergneaux, *Eleanor: Lord and Lady*, pp. 66–71.

42. One to Pope Alexander III and another to the cardinal-deacon Hyacinthus, Luc d'Achery, *Veterum scriptorum spicilegium*, 3 vols (Paris, 1723), 2, pp. 528–59. Richard,

Comtes, 2, p. 104, identifies the abbot as Pierre-Raimond, apparently a member of the family of the counts of l'Isle-Jourdain. For Petronilla, daughter of a priest of Saint-Macou, T. Grasilier, ed., *Cartulaires inédits de la Saintonge*, 2, p. 78, no. 86.

43. As early as 1162, he had purchased gold for the boy's crown and for his regalia. *PR 8 Henry II*, p. 43.

44. Barlow, *Becket*, pp. 195–96.

45. *History of William Marshal*, lines 1908–22, especially lines 1910–15: *Si li prist talent e corage / De faire son filz coroner. / Si fu a cest conseil doner / La reïne e tot son poeir, / Quer ce fu bien sen deveir.*

46. Warren, *Henry II*, p. 111; Barlow, *Becket*, p. 206. For Eleanor at Caen, *Becket Correspondence*, 1, pp. 1248–53, no. 296.

47. *Becket Correspondence*, 2, pp. 1219–25, no. 286, Becket to Bishop Roger, dated May 1170. For the encounter between king and bishop, William fitz Stephen, in *Materials for Thomas Becket*, RS 3, p. 103, translation, Kelly, *Eleanor and Four Kings*, p. 144.

48. *Robert of Torigni*, p. 249; Howden, *Chronica*, 2, p. 14.

49. *Geoffrey de Vigeois*, RHGF, 12, p. 442, dates their Limoges visit 1170; Gillingham, "Richard I and Berengaria of Navarre" in *Richard Coeur de Lion*, p. 40, gives 1171, also Flori, *Aliénor*, p. 133; Richard, *Comtes*, 2, p. 161; Labande, "Pour une image," p. 206.

50. Quotation, *Geoffrey de Vigeois*, RHGF, 12, pp. 442–43 and note. Vigeois's date is 1170, accepted by Richard, *Comtes*, 2, pp. 150–51; and following him, Barlow, *Becket*, p. 204: they date the ceremonies 31 May 1170. Kate Norgate, *Richard the Lion Heart* (London, 1924; reprint New York, 1966), p. 11, and Gillingham, *Richard I*, p. 40, support 1172. This is more likely, since Henry recalled Eleanor to Normandy in spring 1170, while he was in England.

51. Delisle-Berger, *Actes*, 2, pp. 82–83, no. 519, dated 1172–78, confirmation of La Rochelle's liberties conceded, *Richardo filio meo presente, herede meo Pictavie*; also Ralph V. Turner, "The Problem of Survival for the Angevin 'Empire,'" *American Historical Review*, 100 (1995), p. 85.

52. *Geoffrey de Vigeois*, RHGF, 12, pp. 442–43; also an order for the blessing of the duke of Aquitaine, RHGF, 12, pp. 451–53.

53. Pernoud, *Aliénor*, pp. 193–94. On the ceremony's significance, see Daniel F. Callahan, "Eleanor of Aquitaine, the Coronation Rite of the Duke of Aquitaine and the Cult of St. Martial," in *World of Eleanor*, p. 29.

54. Callahan, "Eleanor, the Coronation Rite and the Cult of St. Martial" in *World of Eleanor*, pp. 31–37.

55. Delisle/Berger, *Actes*, 1, p. 404; *Cal. Docs. France*, p. 378, no. 1067. She also witnessed Henry II's charter for Fontevraud, Delisle-Berger, *Actes*, 2, p. 541, no. 413.

56. Bienvenu, "Aliénor et Fontevraud," pp. 19–21; Hivergneaux in *Eleanor: Lord and Lady*, pp. 68–69. For Abbess Audeburge as witness, A. Buhot de Kersers, *Histoire et statistique monumentale du département de Cher*, 8 vols (Paris and Bourges, 1875–98), 6, p. 81, no. 1, reference supplied with thanks from the Plantagenet *Acta* Project.

57. Bienvenu, "Aliénor et Fontevraud," pp. 15–27.

58. Boutoulle, "La Gascogne sous les premiers Plantagenêts," pp. 70, 200–01.

59. Hivergneaux, "Eleanor and Aquitaine," p. 70; Richard, *Comtes*, 2, p. 158.

60. Hivergneaux in Parsons and Wheeler, *Eleanor: Lord and Lady*, p. 68.

61. A gift for a dependent priory at Montazais in Poitou; Hivergneaux in *La Cour Plantagenêt*, p. 72. Geoffroi de Vigeois, RHGF, 12, p. 442: *crudeliter ferro indutum, pane arcto atque aquâ breve cibavit donec defecit.* Norgate, *Richard the Lion Heart*, p. 8, n. 1, replacing the name usually given as Robert de Silly or Sillé with Robert de Seilhac, a lord of the Limousin, correcting what she had written in her *Angevin Kings*, 2, p. 137.

62. Hivergneaux in *Capétiens et Plantagenêts*, pp. 70, 71; Delisle-Berger, *Introduction*, p. 458. The two Anglo-Normans at Chinon were Manasser Biset and Jocelin de Bailleul.

63. For the Mauzé family, see Hivergneaux in *Capétiens et Plantagenêts*, p. 63.

64. For Hervey, Hivergneaux, *Capétiens et Plantagenêts*, p. 68; he had witnessed Eleanor's attestation and confirmation of a charter granted by Louis VII, *c.* 1140 at Orléans, Grasilier, *Cartulaires inédits de la Saintonge*, 2, p. 51, no. 48. For Philip *pincerna*, Paul Marchegay, ed., "Chartes de Fontevraud concernant l'Aunis et La Rochelle," *BEC*, 19 (1958), p. 321. For Bernard, J.-L. Lacurie, *Histoire de l'abbaye de Maillezais* (Fontenay-le-Comte, 1852), pp. 271–72, *preuve* 51.

65. Vincent in *Plantagenêts et Capétiens*, p. 40; disagreeing with Richardson, "Letters and Charters," p. 204.

66. Master Bernard and Peter, chaplain, Eleanor's charter for Earl Patrick's soul, Delisle-Berger, *Introduction*, pp. 411–12; *Actes*, 1, p. 425, no. 278. Marchegay, "Chartes de Fontevraud," p. 329, at St-Jean-d'Angély, lists Peter, chaplain, and Jordan, clerk and notary; Métais, *Cartulaire saintongeais*, pp. 114–16, no. 70, Peter, chaplain, and Jordan, clerk. Other listing of Peter the chaplain with Eleanor after 1167: Lewis, "Six Charters of Henry II and his Family," pp. 659–60, at Périgueux; Peter, the queen's chaplain, Marchegay, *Cartulaires du Bas-Poitou*, p. 109, no. 24 at Poitiers; Clouzot, *Cartulaire de l'abbaye de la Merci-Dieu*, pp. 78–79, no. 87; also *Cal. Docs. France*, p. 453 at Poitiers. Saldebreuil witnessed at least 13 of Eleanor's Poitevin charters: Hivergneaux, *Capétiens et Plantagenêts*, p. 68.

67. Hivergneaux, *La Cour Plantagenêt*, pp. 70, 71; Debord, *Société laïque*, p. 400; Boussard, *Gouvernement*, p. 354, doubts that he was actually seneschal of Aquitaine.

68. Hugh witnessed three of her charters, all at Poitiers; Ralph witnessed thirteen of his niece's charters, Hivergneaux, *Capétiens et Plantagenêts*, pp. 66, 67.

69. Duggan, *Becket Correspondence*, no. 51, pp. 214–18.

70. On Maingot, Painter, "Castellans of Poitou," pp. 35, 37; and "The Houses of Lusignan and Chatellerault 1150–1250" in Cazel, *Feudalism and Liberty*, p. 88; on Mauzé, Boussard, *Gouvernement*, pp. 353, 484.

71. John of Salisbury, *Letters*, 2, pp. 553–71, no. 272, *destinato duci Aquitaniae.*

72. Hivergneaux in *Eleanor: Lord and Lady*, p. 67.

73. Quotation, Martindale, in *Status, Authority, Power*, art. 11, p. 22; on aristocratic mothers and their sons, Duby, "Women and Power," pp. 81–82. For a survey of views on Richard's sexuality, see Flori, *Richard Coeur de Lion* (Paris, 1999), pp. 448–64; also Gillingham, *Richard I*, pp. 263–66, for a stout defense of his heterosexuality.

74. Kelly, *Eleanor and Four Kings*, pp. 159, 328, situates her both at Fontevraud and at Poitiers. E.-R. Labande, "Les filles d'Aliénor d'Aquitaine: étude comparative," *CCM*, 29 (1986), p. 107, places her at Fontevraud, following Kelly.

75. Labande, "Les filles d'Aliénor," p. 107. A document dated September 1170 assigning dower to the princess records those present at Bordeaux, Julio Gonzalez, *El reino de Castilla en la epoca de Alfonso VIII*, 3 vols (Madrid, 1960), 1, pp. 190–93; also pp. 188–89, n. 172, a chronicle account that adds names, notably Ralph de Faye, "seneschal of Aquitaine," and Élie, count of Périgord.

76. Gillingham, "The Angevin Empire," pp. 31, 34, 70.

77. Gillingham, "Richard I and Berengaria," pp. 124–25.

78. Bienvenu, "Aliénor et Fontevraud," p. 20, citing B. Pavillon, *La Vie du Bienheureux Robert d'Arbrissel* (Paris and Saumur, 1666), p. 535, preuve 90. Bienvenu notes that, to his knowledge, this is the only source giving this information.

79. Decima L. Douie and Hugh Farmer, ed. and trans., *Life of St. Hugh of Lincoln*, 2 vols (Edinburgh, 1961–62), 1, pp. 132–33, the boy was sent to Elstow Abbey.

80. Brown, in Kibler, ed., *Eleanor*, p. 24.

81. Lewis, "The Birth and Childhood of King John," p. 168.

82. Quotation, Flori, *Richard Coeur de Lion*, p. 484; Flori's suggestion, *Aliénor*, p. 126. See also H.G. Richardson and G.O. Sayles, *The Governance of Medieval England from the Conquest to Magna Carta* (Edinburgh, 1963), p. 326.

83. Richard le Poitevin, *RHGF*, 12, p. 420; Labande, "Pour une image," pp. 213–14, n. 202.
84. See pp. 311–13 below.
85. The view of Gaston Paris (1839–1903), who originated the term *amour courtois* or courtly love, popularized by Sidney Painter, *French Chivalry* (Baltimore, 1940).
86. Baldwin, *Aristocratic Life in Medieval France*, p. 123; Duby, *Love and Marriage in the Middle Ages*, trans. J. Dunnet (Chicago, 1994), pp. 56–63.
87. Views of Erich Köhler adopted by Duby, *Medieval Marriage: Two Models from Twelfth-century France* (Baltimore, 1978), esp. pp. 12–14; also Duby, "Women and Power," pp. 69–85.
88. Cheyette, *Ermengard of Narbonne*, p. 237.
89. Quotation, Baldwin, *Aristocratic Life in Medieval France*, p. 265; see also p. 153.
90. For example, Baldwin, *Language of Sex*, on Peter the Chanter, pp. 24–25, 251; and on Thomas of Chobham, pp. 133–34; and Baldwin, *Aristocratic Life in Medieval France*, p. 153.
91. Flori, *Aliénor*, pp. 365–68.
92. Andreas Capellanus, *The Art of Courtly Love*, ed. and trans. John Jay Parry (New York, 1990), Preface, p. 27.
93. John F. Benton, "The Court of Champagne as a Literary Center" in Benton, *Culture, Power and Personality* (London, 1991), pp. 580, 589; Joan Martin McCash, "Marie de Champagne and Eleanor of Aquitaine: A relationship re-examined," *Speculum*, 54 (1979), p. 710.
94. Flori, *Aliénor*, p. 383.
95. Pascal Bourgain, "Aliénor d'Aquitaine et Marie de Champagne mises en cause par André le Chapelain," *CCM*, 29 (1986), pp. 29–36; also Flori, *Aliénor*, pp. 368–74.
96. Andreas Capellanus, *Art of Courtly Love*, p. 187, bk 3.
97. Baldwin, *Language of Sex*, pp. 18–19; Brown in Kibler, ed., *Eleanor*, pp. 18, 19, and n. 77; Flori, *Aliénor*, pp. 375–76.
98. Andreas Capellanus, *Art of Courtly Love*, pp. 167–77, bk 2, ch. 7; quotations, pp. 106–07.
99. Andreas Capellanus, *Art of Courtly Love*, p. 175, no. 17.
100. Andreas Capellanus, *Art of Courtly Love*, pp. 170–71, no. 7.
101. Flori, *Aliénor*, pp. 379–80.
102. Andreas Capellanus, *Art of Courtly Love*, p. 176, no. 20; and p. 170, no. 6.
103. On Bernart, see p. 169 above. Also Frederic L. Cheyette, "Women, Poets, and Politics in Occitania," in Theodore Evergates, ed., *Aristocratic Women in Medieval France*, pp. 140–44, 171. For Arnaut, see Harvey in *World of Eleanor*, p. 109.
104. Epilogue, lines 3–4, *Marie ai num, si sui de France*. On Marie, see Joan M. Ferrante, "The French Courtly Poet: Marie de France" in Katharina M. Wilson, ed., *Medieval Women Writers* (Athens, GA, 1984), pp. 64–69; also Short, "Patrons and Polyglots," p. 240; and Pappano, *Eleanor: Lord and Lady*, pp. 339, 340.
105. Painter, "To Whom were Dedicated the *Fables* of Marie de France?" reprinted in Cazel, *Feudalism and Liberty*, pp. 107–10.
106. Ferrante, "The French Courtly Poet: Marie de France," p. 66; Pappano in *Eleanor: Lord and Lady*, p. 340.
107. Broadhurst, "Henry II and Eleanor: Patrons of Literature in French?" p. 80; Evergates, "Aristocratic Women in the County of Champagne," p. 79; Flori, *Aliénor*, pp. 362–63, 365.
108. Beate Schmolke-Hasselmann, "Henry II Plantagenêt, roi d'Angleterre, et la genèse d'*Erec et Enide*," *CCM*, 24 (1981), pp. 241–46; Carlton W. Carroll, "Quelques observations sur les reflets de la cour d'Henri II dans l'oeuvre de Chrétien de Troyes, *CCM*, 37 (1994), pp. 33–39. See also Aurell, "Henry II and Arthurian Legend," pp. 378–79, 380. For a more sceptical attitude, see Gillingham, "Cultivation of History," p. 37.

109. Quotation, Owen, *Eleanor*, pp. 163–64, 213. He concludes his 1993 biography of Eleanor by noting that the best means of delineating her is with "a composite picture . . . from the more sympathetic of the portrayals of Guenevere in courtly romance." See also Flori, *Aliénor*, pp. 350–51, 432–35.
110. Flori, *Richard Coeur de Lion*, pp. 442–43.
111. Harvey, "Eleanor and the Troubadours," pp. 109–13.

Chapter 8: A Queen's Discontent and her Sons' Thwarted Ambitions, 1173–1174

1. *Ralph Diceto*, 1, p. 350; also 1, p. 355, Gillingham, *Richard I*, p. 43, citing *Diceto*, 1, pp. 355–66.
2. *Richard of Devizes*, p. 3; *William of Newburgh*, 1: 280–82.
3. Described by Duby, "Les 'jeunes' dans la société aristocratique."
4. *History of William Marshal*, lines 2637–41, *Pu[i]s vos di que li giemble rei[s], / Qui fu bons e beals e corteis, / Le fist puis si bien en sa vie / Qu'il raviva chevalereie / Qui a cel tens ert près de morte.*
5. Herlihy, *Medieval Households*, pp. 121–22.
6. E.g. *Walter Map*, pp. 280–93; *William of Newburgh*, 1, p. 233.
7. *William of Newburgh*, 1, p. 281; trans, *English Historical Documents*, 2, *1042–1189*, p. 372.
8. Gerald of Wales, *Expugnatio hibernica*, trans, *ibid.*, 2, *1042–1189*, pp. 387–88.
9. Waugh, *The Lordship of England: Royal Wardships and Marriages in English Society and Politics, 1217–1327* (Princeton, 1988), p. 8.
10. For the Capetians, Andrew W. Lewis, *Royal Succession in Capetian France: Studies on Familia Order and the State* (Cambridge, MA, 1981), p. 59. For Angevin tradition, see Bachrach, "The Idea of the Angevin Empire," pp. 293–99.
11. See Turner, "The Problem of Survival for the Angevin 'Empire'," pp. 78–96.
12. Alix brought Richard no dowry, but he was promised a gift of land, perhaps Bourges, once they were married, John of Salisbury, *Letters*, 2, pp. 564–65, no. 272.
13. John of Salisbury, *Letters*, 2, pp. 636–38, no. 288.
14. Flori, *Aliénor*, p. 104; John of Salisbury, *Letters*, 2, no. 272.
15. *Robert of Torigni*, p. 242.
16. Smith, "Henry II's Heir," pp. 304–06.
17. Smith, "Henry II's Heir," pp. 310–13.
18. Norgate, *John Lackland*, pp. 3–4, citing *Gesta regis*, 1, p. 7; Howden, *Chronica*, 2, p. 6.
19. Warren, *Henry II*, p. 204 and n. 1.
20. Cheyette, *Ermengard of Narbonne*, pp. 266–67; *Robert of Torigni*, p. 250.
21. *Gesta regis*, 1, p. 36.
22. Howden, *Chronica*, 2, p. 41.
23. Delisle-Berger, *Actes*, 1, p. 520, no. 389. For witnesses to the treaty between Alfonso of Aragon and Raymond of Toulouse, see Vincent, *Plantagenêts et Capétiens*, p. 34.
24. Howden, *Chronica*, 2, pp. 40–41.
25. Thesis of Ursula Vones Liebenstein, "Aliénor d'Aquitaine, Henri le Jeune et la révolte de 1173: un prélude à la confrontation entre Plantagenêts et Capétiens?" in *Plantagenêts et Capétiens*, pp. 75–93.
26. Vones-Liebenstein, *Plantagenêts et Capétiens*, p. 81, citing L. Vanderkindere, ed., *La chronique de Gislebert de Mons* (Brussels, 1904), p. 110; also, citing William fitz Stephen, companion and biographer of Becket, who saw the aim of Henry's action as preventing the archbishop from imposing punishment on the English kingdom for his misdeeds, "because he was no longer king." *Vita Sancti Thomae*, Robertson, ed., *Materials for Thomas Becket*, 3, p. 107.

27. *Materials for Thomas Becket*, 6, p. 43.
28. Warren, *Henry II*, pp. 112–13.
29. Vones-Liebenstein, *Plantagenêts et Capétiens*, pp. 87–88.
30. Delisle-Berger, *Actes*, 2, p. 3, no. 455.
31. *Geoffrey de Vigeois, RHGF*, 2, p. 443, states: "In the following yr. [1171 or 1172?], Raymond count of Toulouse coming to Limoges, and before the king of England and his wife and his son Richard did homage for the city of Toulouse and received said city from them as a benefice." *Ralph Diceto*, 1, pp. 353–54, states that the count did homage to Henry on 12 February 1173; but that Richard was not present, and he dates his homage to Richard at Pentecost, late May. Also *Gesta regis*, 1, p. 36, and Howden, *Chronicon*, 2, p. 45, state that at the peace settlement with the count in February 1173, the count became the man of Henry, Henry the Young King, and Richard.
32. Pernoud, *Aliénor*, pp. 191–94.
33. Flori, *Aliénor*, pp. 141, 142, citing Geoffroi de Vigeois, *RHGF*, 12, p. 443; Gillingham, *Richard I*, pp. 42–43.
34. Flori, *Richard Coeur de Lion*, pp. 42–43.
35. William J. Brandt, *The Shape of Medieval History: Studies in Modes of Perception* (New Haven, 1996), pp. 151–52, quoting *Newburgh*, 1, pp. 280–82.
36. *Ralph of Coggeshall*, ed. J. Stevenson, (London, 1875), pp. 17–18; *Gervase of Canterbury*, 1, p. 80, also depicts Eleanor inciting Richard and Geoffrey to flee.
37. Duby, *Women of the Twelfth Century*, 1, p. 14; Flori, *Richard Coeur de Lion*, pp. 42–43.
38. Pernoud, *Aliénor*, p. 186.
39. Duby, *Women of the Twelfth Century*, 1, p. 14; Martindale, *Status, Authority, Power*, art. 11, p. 44; Warren, *Henry II*, p. 121; Hivergneaux, *La Cour Plantagenêt*, pp. 72, 73; Hivergneaux in *Eleanor: Lord and Lady*, p. 69.
40. Gillingham, *Richard I*, pp. 46–47; also Martindale, "Eleanor, suo jure duchess of Aquitaine c. 1122–1204," *Oxford DNB. Geoffrey de Vigeois, RHGF*, 12, p. 443, makes no mention of Young Henry.
41. Brown in Kibler, *Eleanor*, p. 10; and Brown in *Eleanor: Lord and Lady*, p. 18.
42. John of Salisbury, *Letters*, 2, p. 603, no. 279; dated July 1168. Henry's crime was also incest because the count's wife was the daughter of an illegitimate daughter of Henry I, thus half-sister to Henry's mother, the empress Matilda.
43. Land at Appleby, in Lincolnshire, Given-Wilson and Curteis, *Royal Bastards*, p. 100; Matthew Strickland, "Longespée [Lungespée], William (I)," *Oxford DNB*.
44. Warren, *Henry II*, p. 601.
45. E.g. Kelly, *Eleanor and Four Kings*, pp. 134–35; Pernoud, *Aliénor*, pp. 178–80; Warren, *Henry II*, p. 601. Labande, "Pour une image," p. 209, writes, "Eleanor did not avenge herself by assassinating Rosamund. She did better. She raised rebellion in Poitou."
46. Gerald of Wales, *Expugnatio hibernica*, pp. 128–29. Flori, *Aliénor*, p. 119, rejects any suggestion that the liaison became known to Eleanor c. 1166. Warren, *Henry II*, p. 601, follows Gerald.
47. Brown, Colvin, and Taylor, *History of the King's Works*, 1, *The Middle Ages*, p. 86. For the labyrinth legend, see ch. 12, pp. 306–08.
48. First quotation, Gerald of Wales, *Expugnatio hibernica*, pp. 128–29; for its date, Gransden, *Historical Writing*, p. 244; second, *Gerald of Wales*, trans. Stevenson, p. 17, bk 2, ch. 4.
49. Howden, *Chronica*, RS, 3, pp. 167–68. *William of Newburgh*, 1, pp. 280–82, writing after Henry's death, got the king's adulteries totally wrong, asserting that he "begot illegitimate offspring in pursuing pleasure" only once the queen had passed child-bearing age. See Given-Wilson and Curteis, *Royal Bastards*, ch. 7, pp. 97–102.

50. For accounts of the rebellion, see Norgate, *Angevin Empire*, 2, pp. 134–68; Warren, *Henry II*, pp. 117–41.

51. *Walter Map*, p. 283, dist. 4, ch. 1.

52. *RHGF*, 12, p. 420, trans, Barber, "Eleanor of Aquitaine and the Media," pp. 22–23; and Richard Fitz Neal, *Course of the Exchequer*, p. 76.

53. Flori, *Aliénor*, p. 140; citing *William of Newburgh*, p. 170, bk 2, ch. 27; *Course of the Exchequer*, p. 76.

54. Bartlett, *England under the Norman and Angevin Kings*, p. 5, citing *Brut y Twysogyion*, ed. and trans. Thomas Jones (Cardiff, 1955), p. 161.

55. Hasculf/Asculf de Saint-Hilaire, *Robert of Torigni*, pp. 255–56; Howden, *Chronica*, 2, p. 51; also *Ralph Diceto*, 1, p. 371.

56. Smith, "Henry II's Heir," pp. 298, 307; Eyton, *Itin H. II*, pp. 163, 168–70; also Norgate, *Angevin Kings*, 2, p. 129. Richardson, "Letters and Charters," p. 198, n. 2, citing *PR 19 Henry II*, p. 184, a payment by the king's writ for robes of "the king son of the king [Young Henry] and the queen his mother and the queen his wife [Margaret]." Also *PR 18 Henry II*, p. 79, "40 shillings for a palfrey for the queen's work."

57. *Ralph Diceto*, RS, 1, p. 350; also *Gesta regis*, 1, pp. 34, 42, 43, and Howden, *Chronica*, 1, p. 32; and *Chron. Turon. Mag.*, p. 138. On Hugh de Saint-Maure, see Aurell, *L'Empire des Plantagenêts*, p. 217; Boussard, *Gouvernement*, p. 478, n. 4.

58. Flori, *Richard Coeur de Lion*, pp. 43–44.

59. *RHGF*, 16, pp. 629–30; Migne, *PL*, 207, cols 448–49. For Peter of Blois at Rouen, David S. Spear, "Les chanoines de la cathédrale de Rouen pendant la période ducale," *Annales de Normandie*, 41 (1991), p. 147.

60. Sassier, *Louis VII*, pp. 448, 449.

61. Howden, *Chronica*, 1, pp. 366–67.

62. *William of Newburgh*, 1, p. 170, bk 2, ch. 27.

63. Vones-Liebenstein *Plantagenêts et Capétiens*, pp. 87–89, citing his letter to Pope Alexander III, *RHGF*, 16, pp. 643–48, no. 66.

64. Cheyette, *Ermengard of Narbonne*, p. 332.

65. *Gesta Regis*, 1, p. 44.

66. *Ralph Diceto*, 1; p. 355; *Robert of Torigni*, p. 256. *William of Newburgh*, 1, pp. 170–71, bk 2, ch. 27, adds an unlikely detail that the Young King, told by the French that his brothers could bring the Aquitanians and the Bretons to his cause, secretly went to Aquitaine to bring the two boys back to Paris.

67. Warren, *Henry II*, p. 124; citing *Ralph Diceto*, 2, p. 371.

68. *Richard le Poitevin*, *RHGF*, 12, p. 416; cited by Flori, *Aliénor*, pp. 157–58.

69. Gillingham, *Richard I*, p. 47.

70. Pernoud, *Aliénor*, p. 219.

71. Labande, "Pour une image," pp. 210, 214, and n. 202, citing *Richard le Poitevin*, *RHGF*, 12, p. 420.

72. *Erat enim prudens femina valde nobilibus orta natalibus, set instabilis*, Gervase of Canterbury, 1, pp. 142–43.

73. *Gesta regis*, 2, p. 61; David Crouch, "Breteuil, Robert de," *Oxford DNB*.

74. Keefe, "England and the Angevin Dominions," *New CMH*, p. 570.

75. Gillingham, *Richard I*, pp. 49–50.

76. Gillingham, *Richard I*, p. 50.

77. Delisle-Berger, *Actes*, 2, p. 19, no. 468, October 1174. Quotation, *Ralph Diceto*, 1, p. 428

78. Norgate, *John Lackland*, pp. 5–6.

79. Warren, *Henry II*, pp. 138–39, 366–67.

CHAPTER 9: A CAPTIVE QUEEN'S LOST YEARS, 1174–1189

1. *Gesta regis*, 2, p. 61.
2. Norgate, *Angevin Kings*, 2, p. 159.
3. Martindale, *Status, Authority, Power*, art. 11, pp. 33–34, n. 35.
4. Gransden, *Historical Writing*, pp. 202–03.
5. *Richard le Poitevin, RHGF*, 12, p. 420, trans. Barber, "Eleanor and the Media," pp. 22–23.
6. *Gervase of Canterbury*, 1, p. 256. Only Roger of Howden in *Gesta Regis* tracked her movements, 1, pp. 305, 313, 333, 334, 337, 345. *Geoffrey de Vigeois, RHGF*, 12, p. 442, states that she was held chiefly at Salisbury.
7. Vincent, "Patronage, Politics and Piety," p. 20.
8. *Geoffroi de Vigeois, RHGF*, 12, p. 443.
9. *Gerald of Wales*, pp. 165–66; trans. Stevenson, p. 17.
10. *Gervase of Canterbury*, 1, pp. 256–57.
11. Kelly, *Eleanor and Four Kings*, p. 240 and p. 190.
12. Quotation from The National Archives, PRO E164/20, fl4v; Clark, ed., *English Register*, no. 5. I owe this reference to the kindness of Prof. Emilie Amt, who is preparing an edition of the Godstow Charters. R. Allen Brown, H.M. Colvin; see also Brown, Colvin, and Taylor, *History of the King's Works*, 1, *Middle Ages*, p. 90.
13. *Gerald of Wales*, trans. Stevenson, p. 57.
14. The wife of Ralph Bloet, Crouch, *William Marshal*, p. 139; Given-Wilson and Curteis, *Royal Bastards*, p. 99.
15. *Gervase of Canterbury*, 1, pp. 256–57; *Gerald of Wales*, trans. Stevenson, p. 58, bk 3, ch. 2.
16. See Gillingham, *Richard I*, p. 82, n. 24, citing Andreas of Marchiennes, *Historia regum Francorum, Mon. Ger. Hist., SS* 26, p. 211, writing in the mid-1190s that "Henry had kept her always with him and never handed her over to his son Richard. On this subject many things are said, but I think it improper to include uncertain gossip in a true history." The chronicle of Meaux in Yorkshire reports that Alix bore Henry a child who "did not survive," E.A. Bond, ed., *Chronica monasterii de Melsa*, 3 vols, RS (1866–68), 1, p. 256. Although the chronicle dates from the end of the fourteenth century, it is knowledgeable about events over two centuries earlier.
17. *Gesta regis*, 1, p. 159; Gillingham, *Richard I*, p. 142 and n. 5.
18. *PR 19 Henry II* (1172–73), p. 64; *PR 20 Henry II* (1173–74), p. 112.
19. Elizabeth Hallam, "Henry II as a Founder of Monasteries," *JI of Ecclesiastical History*, 28 (1977), pp. 118, 124–25. For the rebuilding of Waltham, see Brown, Colvin, and Taylor, *History of the King's Works*, 1, p. 88.
20. Huneycutt, *Matilda of Scotland*, pp. 96–97 and n. 116; barons of Hanslope, Bucks, Sanders, *Baronies*, pp. 50–51.
21. Robert Mauduit: *PR 20 Henry II* (1173–74), p. 29; *PR 21 Henry II* (1174–75), pp. 100, 106. Ralph fitz Stephen: *PR 27 Henry II* (1180–81), pp. 5, 129; *PR 28 Henry II* (1181–82), pp. 109, 159; *PR 33 Henry II* (1186–87), p. 181, joined by Eustace fitz Stephen; *PR 1 Richard I*, Hunter, ed., p. 5. For Stanley Abbey, *Victoria County History, Wiltshire* 3, p. 269, citing Dugdale, *Monasticon*, 5, p. 565; also BL, Lord Frederick Campbell's Charters, xxiii. 20.
22. Brown, Colvin, and Taylor, *History of the King's Works*, 1, *Middle Ages*, 2, p. 857.
23. Winchester, *PR 22 Henry II* (1175–76), pp. 171, 198; *PR 26 Henry II* (1179–80), p. 195, payments from Devon and Wiltshire accounts; *PR 29 Henry II* (1182–83), likely at Windsor, since this was paid out of Berkshire revenues.
24. Eyton, *Itin. H. II*, pp. 202, 204, 205, 206.
25. *PR 22 Henry II*, pp. 12–15, 47, 152, 198–99.
26. *Gesta regis*, 1, pp. 115–17, 119–20, 157–58, 169–72; Howden, *Chronica*, 2, pp. 95–98; *Ralph Diceto*, 1, pp. 416–17; *Robert of Torigni*, p. 278. Also Labande, "Les filles

d'Aliénor," *CCM*, pp. 105–07. For artistic influences, see Ralph V. Turner, "Les Contacts entre l'Angleterre normano-angevine et la Sicile normande," *Études Normandes*, 35 (1886), pp. 39–60.

27. Brown, Colvin, and Taylor, *History of the King's Works*, 1, *Middle Ages*, 2, p. 826; *Victoria County History: Wiltshire*, 6: 57. Eleanor's expenses: *PR 23 Henry II* (1176–77), p. 166, £5 17s. 9d; *PR 24 Henry II* (1177–78), p. 128; *PR 25 Henry II* (1178–79), p. 125.

28. Amiria is called the queen's *domicella et nutrita*. She gave the manor of Winterslow, *Cal. Doc. France*, 387, no. 1091; and Eleanor's confirmation, p. 387, no. 1090 and note. Amiria and Hugh Pantulf's father died in 1175, Sanders, *Baronies*, p. 94.

29. *Gesta Regis*, 1, pp. 303, 305, 308; *PR 27 Henry II* (1180–81), p. 15; *PR 28 Henry II* (1182–83), p. 160; *PR 29 Henry II* (1183–84), p. 74.

30. Norgate, *John Lackland*, pp. 6–7; Sanders, *Baronies*, p. 6.

31. Sanders, *Baronies*, pp. 14, 21, 60.

32. *Earldom of Gloucester Charters*, p. 5

33. See Gillingham, *Richard I*, ch. 5, "Duke of Aquitaine, 1175–83," pp. 52–75; and Ralph V. Turner and Richard R. Heiser, *The Reign of Richard Lionheart: Ruler of the Angevin Empire, 1189–1199* (London, 2000), ch. 4, "Richard's Apprenticeship," pp. 57–71.

34. *Ralph Diceto*, 1, p. 432; *Robert of Torigni*, p. 282; *Geoffrey de Vigeois*, RHGF, 12, p. 442. Howden, *Chronica*, 2, p. 93, dates Richard's visit to England at Easter 1179, before his taking of Taillebourg. *PR 25 Henry II* (1178–79), pp. 101, 107, reveals expenses for Richard's crossing to England. For Eleanor's feelings toward Richard, Labande, "Pour une image," p. 213.

35. Quotation, *Gesta Regis*, 1, p. 292. Richard provoked a contest over custody of the county of Angoulême with the deceased count's two brothers, Debord, *Société laïque*, p. 381; Gillingham, *Richard I*, p. 64.

36. *Ralph Diceto*, 1, p. 426; *Gesta Regis*, 1, p. 207; Howden, *Chronica*, 2, p. 166.

37. *Gesta Regis*, 1, pp. 291–92, quotation, p. 292; *Ralph Diceto*, 2, pp. 18–19.

38. Crouch, "Breteuil, Robert de," *Oxford DNB*.

39. See Turner and Heiser, *Reign of Richard Lionheart*, ch. 3, "The Problem of Philip Augustus and Growing French Royal Power," pp. 41–56. Richard, *Comtes*, 2, p. 211; Gillingham, "Unromantic Death," p. 39; Benjamin, "A Forty Year War," p. 276.

40. Bernard Itier, *Chroniques de Saint-Martial de Limoges*, ed. H. Duplès-Agier (Paris, 1876), p. 27.

41. *Geoffrey de Vigeois*, reprinted in Smith, "Henry II's Heir," *EHR*, no. 21; *Robert of Torigni*, p. 306.

42. *History of William Marshal*, lines 6880–6915, 6935–43, and line 5048, *Qui molt l'amout de grant amor*. Jaundiced view of *William of Newburgh*, RS 1, p. 234, bk 3, ch. 7.

43. *Sermo de morte et sepultura Henrici regis juniori*, included in *Ralph of Coggeshall*, pp. 272–73.

44. Vincent, *Plantagenêts et Capétiens*, p. 43; also Hanna Vollrath, "Aliénor d'Aquitaine et ses enfants: une relation affective?" pp. 119–21. Her land grant to Nicholas fitz Richard of Wiltshire, King John's confirmation, *Rot. Chart.*, p. 71.

45. Howden, *Gesta Regis*, 1, pp. 293, 302–03; Richard, *Comtes*, 2, p. 222; Norgate, *Richard the Lion Heart*, pp. 55–56.

46. *Gesta Regis*, 1, p. 305; *PR 30 Henry II* (1183–84), p. 217, 3s for carrying the saddles of the queen and her maidens to Waltham.

47. *Ralph Diceto*, 2, p. 13; *Gesta regis*, 1, p. 288; Howden, *Chronicon*, 2, p. 269. See Kate Norgate, revised by Timothy Reuter, "Matilda, duchess of Saxony (1156–1189)," *Oxford DNB*.

48. *Gesta Regis*, 1, pp. 313, 333, 337; Howden, *Chronicon*, 2, pp. 288, 304.

49. *Gesta Regis*, 1, p. 345; *PR 33 Henry II* (1186–87), p. xxii; *PR 1 Richard I*, ed. Hunt, Record Commission, p. 6; William was still in England in 1191, *PR 2 Richard I*, p. 137. Labande, "Les filles d'Aliénor," pp. 105–06.
50. *PR 29 Henry II* (1182–83), p. 134; *Gervase of Canterbury*, 1, p. 326.
51. *PR 26 Henry II* (1179–80), p. 95; *PR 30 Henry II* (1183–84), pp. 58, 70, 134, 138.
52. For struggles between Richard and his father after Young Henry's death, see Gillingham, *Richard I*, ch. 6, "The Uncertain Inheritance, 1184–89," pp. 101–22.
53. Warren, *Henry II*, pp. 610–11.
54. Quotation, Norgate, *Richard the Lion Heart*, p. 59.
55. *Gerald of Wales*, trans. Stevenson, p. 26, bk 2, ch. 11.
56. *Gesta Regis*, 1, pp. 337–38.
57. *Ralph Diceto*, 2, p. 40; Richard, *Comtes*, 2, p. 232.
58. Marchegay, ed., "Chartes de Fontevraud," pp. 330–31. Hivergneaux, *Eleanor: Lord and Lady*, p. 71, n. 68; Hivergneaux, *La Cour Plantagenêt*, p. 74, Eleanor was "only a plaything in Henry II's hands."
59. Hivergneaux, *Eleanor: Lord and Lady*, p. 71, n. 68, citing a lost charter known only from a seventeenth-century Fontevraud inventory. See also Bienvenu, "Aliénor et Fontevraud," pp. 19, 21, and Bienvenu, Favreau, Pon, eds, *Grand Cartulaire de Fontevraud*, 1, pp. 588–89.
60. *Ralph Diceto*, 2, p. 40.
61. *PR 33 Henry II* (1186–87), p. 194; *Annales monastici*, 2, *Waverley*, p. 241. For queen's gold, Richardson, "Letters and Charters," pp. 209–10.
62. £12 5s 10d as her Easter allowance, and over £26 as the Michaelmas clothing allowance, *PR 33 Henry II* (1186–87), p. 40.
63. *PR 33 Henry II*, p. 39. On Jordan, see above, p. 192.
64. Ralph V. Turner, *King John* (London, 1994), reissued as *King John: England's Evil King?* (Stroud, Gloucs. 2005), p. 33.
65. Turner, *King John*, pp. 33–34.
66. *Gesta regis*, 2, p. 7.
67. Kelly, *Eleanor and Four Kings*, p. 235.
68. *History of William Marshal*, lines 8196–8201.
69. *Gerald of Wales*, trans. Stevenson, p. 95, bk 3, ch. 25.
70. *History of William Marshal*, lines 9215–20, 9229–37; Bienvenu, "Henri II et Fontevraud," p. 31.
71. *Gerald of Wales*, trans. Stevenson, p. 101, bk 3, ch. 28.
72. *History of William Marshal*, lines 9503–11.
73. William Stubbs, *Seventeen Lectures on the Study of Medieval and Modern History* (Oxford, 1900; reprint New York, 1967), p. 139.

CHAPTER 10: THE QUEEN-MOTHER: RICHARD'S REIGN, 1189–1199

1. Duby, "Women and Power," pp. 71–72.
2. Pernoud, *Aliénor*, p. 257.
3. Herlihy, "Natural History of Medieval Women," p. 58.
4. *Richard of Devizes*, p. 25; Gillingham, "Royal Newsletters, Forgeries and English Historians: Some Links between Court and History in the Reign of Richard I," *La Cour Plantagenêt*, p. 175.
5. Richardson and Sayles, *Governance of Mediaeval England*, p. 153.
6. *Ralph Diceto*, 2, p. 67. See Flori, *Aliénor*, pp. 164–65; and Brown, "Eleanor Reconsidered," pp. 24–25.
7. John Gillingham, "Telle mère, tel fils: Aliénor et Richard," in Aurell, ed., *Aliénor*, p. 27.
8. *Ralph Diceto*, 2, p. 67.

9.   John W. Baldwin, *The Government of Philip Augustus: Foundations of French Royal Power in the Middle Ages* (Berkeley and Los Angeles, 1986), p. 102.

10. West, *Justiciarship in England*, p. 65; Landon, *Itinerary*, pp. 2, 13, 16, 18, 26. For her writs, *PR 1 Richard I*, ed. Hunter, pp. 163, 180.

11. She granted land to Ingelram, *Cal. Docs. France*, no. 1093; Eleanor's confirmation of Ingelram's gift to Dunstable Priory, *Cal. Docs. France*, no. 1094. Adam of Wilton, *PR 6 Richard I*, pp. 76, 231, 240; *PR 7 Richard I*, pp. 119, 173; *PR 8 Richard I*, pp. 101, 275; *PR 9 Richard I*, p. 120; *PR 1 John*, p. 21; *PR 4 John*, pp. 131, 172; *PR 6 John*, pp. 113, 145. Osbert, the queen's man, *PR 5 Richard I*, p. 154; *PR 7 Richard I*, p. 251; *PR 4 John*, pp. 12, 273; *PR 5 John*, pp. 5, 224; *PR 6 John*, pp. 17, 102. Adam the cook, *PR 5 Richard I*, p. 75; *PR 7 Richard I*, p. 27; *PR 8 Richard I*, p. 21; *PR 1 John*, pp. 210, 212; *PR 4 John*, p. 254; *PR 6 John*, pp. 141, 142; Landon, ed., *Cartae Antiquae rolls 1–10*, no. 195.

12. Charters issued by John after his succession confirming Eleanor's earlier grants to Agatha, a wet-nurse, *Rot. Chart.*, pp. 7b–8, 10b; p. 71b, to her cook Adam; pp. 25, 71b, to Roger, another cook; and p. 71, to Nicholas fitz Richard, who had served both "the Lady Eleanor our mother and King Henry our brother."

13. E.g. Master Henry of London, Richardson, "Letters and Charters," pp. 204–05; printed in Dugdale, *Monasticon*, 3, p. 154; possibly to be identified with the Master Henry *de Civitate*, who witnessed at Westminster before November 1193; *Cal. Docs. France*, no. 1093.

14. Also known as Herbert of Ilchester, his father found a place for him at the exchequer, and he occasionally served as a royal justice *c.* 1190–97, *Fasti, Monastic Cathedrals*, p. 14; *Fasti, Salisbury*, p. 3; *Fasti, Lincoln*, p. 127. He attested her charters before her retirement to France in 1194, *HMC Various Collections, 1* (1901), p. 183; Richardson, "Letters and Charters," p. 211; and Davies, ed., *Cartae Antiquae rolls 11–20*, no. 369. Adam of Wilton, *PR 6 Richard I*, p. 231.

15. Quotations, *Gesta Regis*, RS, 2, pp. 74–75; Howden, *Chronica*, 3, pp. 4–5, trans. Riley, 2, p. 112. *Curia reginalis*, not *curia regalis* or *curia regis*, Martindale, "Eleanor of Aquitaine and a 'Queenly Court'?" in *Eleanor: Lord and Lady*, p. 429.

16. *William of Newburgh*, 1, p. 293.

17. *Ralph Diceto*, 2, p. 68.

18. *PR 1 Richard I*, ed. Hunter, pp. 6, 197.

19. *Gervase of Canterbury*, 1: 457.

20. *PR 1 Richard 1*, ed. Hunter, pp. 223–24.

21. Geoffrey as Richard's chamberlain, Landon, *Itinerary*, pp. 8, 10–12, 14, 19, 27; for Andrew, Devailly, *Berry*, pp. 423, 438, 441; for the Chauvignys' kinship with Eleanor, Evergates, "Nobles and Knights in Twelfth-century France," p. 31.

22. Vincent, *Plantagenêts et Capétiens*, p. 46, citing Howden, *Chronica*, 3, p. 7.

23. E.g. money grants to Fontevraud from the revenues of the prévôté of Oléron, Marchegay, "Chartes de Fontevraud," pp. 337–41. For Normandy, *Richard of Devizes*, p. 14; Howden, *Chronica*, 3, p. 2.

24. Howden, *Chronica*, 3, p. 27.

25. From a charter listing Berngaria's dower arrangements, summarized by Ivan Cloulas, "Le Douaire de Bérengère de Navarre, veuve de Richard Coeur de Lion," *La Cour Plantagenêt*, pp. 90–91. For the figures on income from the Norman towns of Falaise, Bonneville-sur-Touques, and Domfront, see Power, "The Stripping of a Queen," *World of Eleanor*, p. 118.

26. Funds for Eleanor, *PR 2 Richard I*, pp. 2, 155. On queen's gold, Richardson, "Letters and Charters," pp. 209–11; Eleanor's 1193 acknowledgment that the abbot of Waltham supplied her with a clerk for queen's gold, *PR 10 John*, p. 25; writ of 1194 acknowledging that Jurnet the Jew of Norwich paid 40 marks of queen's gold owed since Henry II's time, *PR 10 John*, p. 15.

27. Jocelin of Brakelond, *Chronicle of the Abbey of Bury St. Edmunds*, trans. Diana Greenway and Jane Sayers (Oxford, 1989), p. 42.
28. *Gesta Regis*, 2, p. 101; Howden, *Chronica*, 3, p. 28; Landon, *Itinerary*, p. 26; *PR 2 Richard I*, pp. 2, 131.
29. Quotation, *Richard of Devizes*, p. 10. On Hawise, see Ralph V. Turner, "William de Forz, Count of Aumale, an early Thirteenth-century English Baron," *Proc. American Philosophical Soc.*, 115 (1971), pp. 223–24.
30. *Richard of Devizes*, p. 6.
31. Howden, *Chronica*, 3, pp. 32, 217, does not credit Eleanor with securing John's release from his oath; Landon, *Itinerary*, p. 198.
32. William Stubbs, *Historical Introductions to the Rolls Series*, ed. Arthur Hassall (London, 1902), p. 224.
33. *Richard of Devizes*, 13; *William of Newburgh*, 1, p. 331.
34. Gillingham, "Richard I and Berengaria," pp. 160–62.
35. Gillingham, "Richard I and Berengaria," pp. 129–30.
36. E.g. the March 1191 treaty with Philip of France made provision for anticipated sons, Landon, *Itinerary*, p. 230.
37. Landon, *Itinerary*, p. 3.
38. Flori, *Aliénor*, p. 451, citing M.R. Morgan, ed., *La Continuation de Guillaume de Tyr* (Paris, 1982), p. 110.
39. Gillingham, "Some Legends of Richard the Lion Heart." For the historiography, see Gillingham, "Richard I and Berengaria," pp. 121–22, both in his *Richard Coeur de Lion*.
40. On the day of his marriage to Berengaria of Navarre on Cyprus, May 1191, a charter listed all dowerlands that were to pass to Berengaria. Gillingham, "Richard I and Berengaria," pp. 120, 124–25, 130–32.
41. *Cal. Docs. France*, no. 1087; cited by T.S.R. Boase, "Fontevraud and the Plantagenets," *Jl British Archaeology Association*, 3rd ser., 34 (1971), p. 6.
42. Gillingham, "Richard I and Berengaria," pp. 120–27, 130–31.
43. Landon, *Itinerary*, pp. 45, 193–94.
44. Gillingham, "Richard I and Berengaria, pp. 127–30.
45. Labande, "Les filles d'Aliénor," pp. 108–09.
46. For Joan, Richard, and Sicily, see Gillingham, *Richard I*, pp. 130–39.
47. Landon, *Itinerary*, p. 45.
48. Richardson, "Letters and Charters," p. 201.
49. Martindale, "Eleanor: The Last Years," pp. 146, 148–52, quoting Holt, "Ricardus rex Anglorum et dux Normannorum," pp. 79, 80.
50. For Longchamp as chief justiciar, see Turner and Heiser, *Reign of Richard Lionheart*, pp. 115–29.
51. The chief gossips were Gerald of Wales and Hugh of Nonant, bishop of Coventry. On anti-foreign feelings against Longchamp, see Turner and Heiser, *Reign of Richard Lionheart*, pp. 120–21; on his alleged homosexuality, see John Boswell, *Christianity, Social Tolerance, and Homosexuality* (Chicago, 1980), p. 229, n. 69.
52. West, *Justiciarship in England*, p. 73.
53. Landon, *Itinerary*, p. 46, letters of 20 and 23 February to his associate justiciars.
54. Howden, *Chronica*, 3, p. 100; *PR 3 Richard I*, p. 29.
55. *Par le conseil del Mar[eschal] e par les baons ensemble ouvra [il] bien & sagement, et par conseil de la reïne*, lines 9876–82, trans. Mullally, "Loyalty of Eleanor and William Marshal" in *Eleanor: Lord and Lady*, p. 244. Robert Bartlett, *Gerald of Wales 1146–1223* (Oxford, 1982), p. 15.
56. Quotations, *Richard of Devizes*, pp. 58, 60–64; *Gesta Regis*, 2, pp. 236–37.
57. *PR 4 Richard I*, p. 303; and *Gesta Regis*, 2, pp. 237–38.
58. *Richard of Devizes*, pp. 53–54.

59. *Richard of Devizes*, pp. 59–60.

60. *Richard of Devizes*, pp. 59–60; Martindale, *Status, Authority, Power*, art. 11, p. 49.

61. *Richard of Devizes*, pp. 58, 61–63; *Gesta Regis*, 2, pp. 237–40; Norgate, *Richard*, pp. 42–43. Longchamp resumed his duties as chancellor following Richard's release from captivity, returning to England briefly in spring 1194, Landon, *Itinerary*, pp. 86, 90.

62. Brown in Kibler, ed. *Eleanor*, p. 21; Richardson, "Letters and Charters," pp. 201–02. On Richard's captivity and John's rebellion, see Turner and Heiser, *Reign of Richard Lionheart*, pp. 130–40.

63. *Gervase of Canterbury*, 1, p. 515; see also Landon, *Itinerary*, app. E, pp. 204, 205; the queen-mother assured the prior and monks of Canterbury that fortifications erected there by her prayer would not diminish their liberties.

64. Howden, *Chronicon*, 3, p. 208; also *Gesta Regis*, 2, pp. 232–34.

65. *Gesta Regis*, 2, p. 97; *Ralph Diceto*, 2, p. 72; Landon, *Itinerary*, pp. 16, 18.

66. William Stubbs, ed., *Epistolae Cantuarensis* in *Chronicles and Memorials, Richard I*, 2 vols, RS (London, 1864–65), 2, p. 332, no. 352, p. 358, no. 403, the prior to the queen.

67. *Epistolae Cantuarensis*, no. 362, 363, 364; Landon, *Itinerary*, pp. 74, 76. For the election, see *Ralph Diceto*, 2, p. 108; *Gervase of Canterbury*, 1, p. 517; and Turner, "Richard Lionheart and English Episcopal Elections," *Albion*, pp. 7–8.

68. Quotations, Migne, *PL*, 207, cols 1262–71; Letters of Peter of Blois, nos 2–4; also, Brown, citing the first letter, in Kibler, ed., Eleanor, p. 21; also found in Anne Crawford, ed. and trans., *Letters of the Queens of England* (Stroud, Gloucs., 1994), pp. 36–43 from *Rymer's Foedera*, 1066–1383. I have chosen the traditional translation over Crawford's "Eleanor, in God's anger, Queen."

69. Quotation, Barber, *World of Eleanor*, p. 27. Doubting the letters' authenticity are Beatrice Lees, "The Letters of Queen Eleanor of Aquitaine to Pope Clement III," *EHR*, 21 (1906), pp. 73–93, and Owen, *Eleanor*, pp. 87–88. Supporting their authenticity are Richardson, "Letters and Charters," p. 202; and Southern, "Blois, Peter of (1125/30–1212)," *Oxford DNB*; also Brown, in Kibler, pp. 21, 32, n. 108; and Flori, *Aliénor*, pp. 230–35. For a charter witnessed by Peter: 1193 at Berkamstead, Richardson, "Letters and Charters," p. 211.

70. Howden, *Chronica*, 3, pp. 208–10; Landon, *Itinerary*, p. 75; Duplès-Agier, ed., *Chroniques de Saint-Martial*, p. 192. Saint-Martial's contribution was 100 silver marks.

71. Howden, *Chronica*, 3, pp. 208–11; *Richard of Devizes*, pp. 42–43; Jocelin of Brakelond, *Chronicle*, p. 42. Eleanor's charter, Dugdale, *Monasticon*, 3, p. 154; Martindale, "Eleanor: The Last Years," pp. 148, 149.

72. McCash, "Marie de Champagne and Eleanor," p. 710; Evergates, "Aristocratic Women in the County of Champagne," p. 79.

73. Howden, *Chronica*, 3, pp. 202–03; for the hostages, Gillingham, *Richard I*, p. 248, n. 94.

74. Landon, *Itinerary*, pp. 86–93. Martindale, "Eleanor: The Last Years," pp. 142, 146–47.

75. Howden, *Chronica*, 3, pp. 288–90. Their reconciliation took place at Le Mans, 4 April 1195, Landon, *Itinerary*, p. 101.

76. Gillingham, *Richard* I, pp. 263–64; and Gillingham, "Richard I and Berengaria," pp. 133–38.

77. Quotation, Meade, *Eleanor*, p. 332. See Labande, "Pour une image," pp. 225–26; Gillingham, "Richard I and Berengaria," p. 138.

78. Richard, *Comtes*, 2, p. 300.

79. Quotation, Duby, *France in the Middle Ages*, p. 218. On Constance, Arthur, and the succession, see Yannick Hillion, "La Bretagne et la rivalité Capétiens-Plantagenêts. Un exemple: La duchesse Constance," *Annales de Bretagne*, 92 (1985), pp. 118–19; Landon, *Itinerary*, app. E, pp. 207–08; J.C. Holt, "Aliénor, Jean sans terre et la succession de 1199," *CCM*, 29 (1986), pp. 97–99.

80. First quotation, Barlow, *Feudal Kingdom of England*, p. 362. Second, Howden, *Chronica*, 3, pp. 134, 252, *mediante Alienor regina matre eorum*; also *William of Newburgh*, 2, p. 424; and *Annales monastici*, 1, Burton, p. 192.
81. Bienvenu, "Aliénor d'Aquitaine et Fontevraud," pp. 23–24.
82. Peter and the chapel of Blyth, Notts., *Cal. Docs. France*, p. 12, no. 46, no. 52. For Eleanor and the chapel of Blyth, Timson, ed., *Blyth Priory Cartulary*, p. cxxiv.
83. John Piner or John "our chaplain" may have drafted some; he witnessed her 1190 charter at Périgueux in Lewis, "Six Charters of Henry II and his Family," pp. 663–64; Roger "our chaplain" drafted charters, 1194–99, *Cal. Patent Rolls 1232–47*, p. 393. Also after her withdrawal to Fontevraud another chaplain, Ranulph, served her along with Peter Morinus and Master William, her clerks, *Cal. Docs. France*, no. 1092. She provided William with four pounds *angevin* annually from her dowerland at Bonneville-sur-Toque in Normandy, Vincent, "Patronage, Politics and Piety," *Plantagenêts et Capétiens*, p. 33. Richard, the queen-mother's almoner, with her at Westminster in June 1193, Dugdale, *Monasticon*, 2, p. 154.
84. Hivergneaux, *La Cour Plantagenêt*, p. 78. For Eleanor's gift to Henry, *Rot. Chart.*, p. 8a. D.M. Stenton, ed., *Pleas before the King or his Justices*, Selden Society, 83 (1966), 3, pp. 160–61, no. 993, identifies Geoffrey de Wancy as the queen's "seneschal" in a plea concerning Eleanor's lands in Somerset.
85. Hivergneaux, *La Cour Plantagenêt*, p. 78; Labande, "Pour une image," p. 225.
86. Hivergneaux, *La Cour Plantagenêt*, pp. 77–78; Bienvenu, "Aliénor d'Aquitaine et Fontevraud," pp. 23, 25–26. Rents from the *prévoté* of the Île d'Oléron, Marchegay, "Chartes de Fontevraud," pp. 337–38. A grant of the vill of Jaunay for the kitchen, *Cal. Docs. France*, no. 1098. Chapel of Saint Laurence, Marchegay, "Chartes de Fontevraud," pp. 339–40. When a petitioner regained confiscated land after Richard's death, Eleanor required that he donate £100 to purchase garments for the Fontevraud nuns, Marchegay, "Chartes de Fontevraud," pp. 334–35.
87. *Cal. Docs. France*, no. 1092; *PR 9 Richard I*, p. 98, remission of Hugh Bardolf's debt concerning his suit against the powerful earl of Chester; and Stubbs, ed., *Epistolae Cantuarensis*, pp. 437–38.
88. Landon, *Itinerary*, pp. 144–45.
89. *Cal. Docs. France*, p. 472, no. 1301; also printed in Teulet, ed., *Layettes du Trésor des Chartes*, 1, p. 200, no. 489. For the bishop of Agen, Kelly, *Eleanor and Four Kings*, pp. 218–20.
90. Round's translation of *potentis viri regis Ricardi* in *Cal. Docs. France*, no. 1101, p. 390.

CHAPTER 11: SECURING THE PLANTAGENET LEGACY: JOHN'S REIGN, 1199–1204

1. Crawford, *Letters of the Queens of England*, p. 40.
2. F.M. Powicke, *The Loss of Normandy*, 2nd edn (Manchester, 1960), p. 133.
3. Douie and Farmer, *Life of St. Hugh of Lincoln*, 2, pp. 184–85.
4. Sidney Painter, *The Reign of King John* (Baltimore, 1949), pp. 1–8; Richard, *Comtes*, 2, pp. 333–35.
5. Painter, *Reign of King John*, pp. 7–9; Richard, *Comtes*, 2, p. 334.
6. Howden, *Chronicon*, 4, p. 88; see comments of Martindale, "Eleanor: The Last Years," pp. 152–53.
7. Roger of Wendover, *Flores Historiarum*, 1, p. 286.
8. Cheyette, "Women, Poets, and Politics in Occitania," p. 156; citing *Aliscans*, ed. Claude Regnier (Paris, 1990), 1, lines 3105–09.
9. Cirot de la Ville, *Histoire de Sauve-Majeure*, 2, pp. 141–42, trans. Kelly, *Eleanor and Four Kings*, p. 353.

10. Eleanor's homage to Philip is known only from the Capetian historian *Rigord*. See Pierre Chaplais, "Le Traité de Paris de 1259 et l'inféodation de la Gascogne allodiale" in Chaplais, *Essays in Medieval Diplomacy and Administration* (London, 1981); Martindale, "Eleanor: The Last Years," pp. 154–56; Labande, "Pour une image," p. 228.

11. Hivergneaux, *La Cour Plantagenêt*, p. 81.

12. Hivergneaux, *La Cour Plantagenêt*, p. 81.

13. H. Barckhausen, ed., *Archives Muncipales de Bordeaux, Livre des Coutumes* (Bordeaux, 1890), pp. 437–38, no. 45; for King John's confirmation, *Rot. Chart.*, p. 4b.

14. Marchegay, "Chartes de Fontevraud," pp. 334–35; also *Cal. Docs. France*, no. 1097. It was probably during this period that the lord of Parthenay, Hugh l'Archévêque, recovered from Eleanor his castle of Secondigny that had been taken from him by Richard. He had recovered his castle by 1202, *Rot. Lit. Pat.*, p. 11.

15. Painter, "Lords of Lusignan," p. 66. The chronology is confused; Labande, "Pour une image," p. 227, n. 268, dates the incident at the end of 1199, when Eleanor was en route to Castile; a journey that actually took place after the 1200 treaty of Le Goulet. See also W.L. Warren, *King John* (Berkeley, 1977), p. 68.

16. Martindale in *King John: New Interpretations*, pp. 161–62; Hivergneaux, *La Cour Plantagenêt*, p. 83, citing BNF Paris, ms 5914, collection Gaignères, vol 1, p. 469; John's confirmation, *Rot. Chart.*, p. 24b.

17. Maingot, *Rot. Chart.*, p. 25. Chauvigny, Hivergneaux, *La Cour Plantagenêt*, p. 85, citing Teulet, ed., *Layettes du Trésor des Chartes*, 1, no. 508. See also Devailly, *Berry*, pp. 438–41.

18. Hivergneaux, *La Cour Plantagenêt*, p. 82. Geoffrey as Richard's chamberlain, Landon, *Itinerary*, pp. 8, 10–12, 14, 19, 27; he witnessed ten of Eleanor's charters after 1199, Vincent, in *Plantagenêts et Capétiens*, p. 49. For Hugh de Jaunay, *Rot. Chart.*, p. 13; for Savaric, *Rot. Chart.*, p. 11.

19. Hivergneaux, *La Cour Plantagenêt*, pp. 80–81; Richardson, "Letters and Charters," p. 207; Irène Baldet, *Essai d'itinéraire et regestes d'Aliénor reine d'Angleterre 1189–1204*, mémoire de maîtrise (University of Poitiers, 1963) p. 22.

20. Grant of £10 *poitevin* to her granddaughter witnessed by the bishops of Poitiers and of Saintes, "by whose counsel and authority this gift was made and confirmed," Marchegay, "Chartes de Fontevraud," pp. 340–41. See also Hivergneaux, *La Cour Plantagenêt*, p. 78; Martindale, *Status, Authority, Power*, art. 11, p. 19. Magnates at Bordeaux, Cirot de la Ville, *Histoire de Sauve-Majeure*, 2, pp. 141–42.

21. *Annales monastici*, 2, *Winchester*, p. 64.

22. One of her charters issued there lists "our dear daughter Queen Joanne" as one of the witnesses, *Cal. Docs. France*, no. 1090 n.

23. *Cal. Docs. France*, no. 1105; Bienvenu, "Aliénor et Fontevraud," p. 24 and n. 78.

24. 25 *livres angevin*, *Rot. Chart.*, pp. 13, 25b.

25. On Joanne's two burials, *Histoire des ducs de Normandie et des rois d'Angleterre*, ed. Francisque Michel (Paris, 1840; reprint New York, 1965), pp. 83–84. Eleanor's journey to Gascony, *Cal. Docs. France*, no. 1105, no. 142.

26. *Rot. Chart.*, pp. 30–31. See Holt, "Aliénor, Jean et la succession de 1199," pp. 92, 96–98; Richardson, "Letters and Charters," pp. 205–07; Martindale, "Eleanor: The Last Years," pp. 156–58.

27. Vincent, "Patronage, Politics and Piety," *Plantagenêts et Capétiens*, p. 42.

28. For Richard and church music, Gillingham, *Richard I*, p. 255.

29. Vincent, "Patronage, Politics and Piety," pp. 42–44.

30. *Cal. Docs. France*, no. 1107; no. 1090 n; no. 1248; no. 1307; and Marchegay, "Chartes de Fontevraud," pp. 340–41; also Richardson, "Charters and Letters," pp. 206–07. For Roger and Eleanor's chapel, Marchegay, "Chartes de Fontevraud," pp. 339–40; *Cal. Docs. France*, no. 1100.

31. Vincent, *Plantagenêts et Capétiens*, p. 37. For William, Martindale, *Power, Status, Authority*, art. 11, p. 19 and n. 6; Richardson, "Letters and Charters," pp. 206–07. He served John in Poitevin financial administration, Hardy, ed., *Rot. Norm.*, p. 108, and was named dean of Saint Martin's, Angers, 1214, *Rot. Chart.*, p. 199b. For Master Richard *de Gnowesale* or simply Master Richard, Audouin, ed., *Documents concernant Poitiers*, no. 32; Marchegay, "Chartes de Fontevraud," pp. 338–39, 340–41, 390; Pon, ed., *Recueil de Documents de Fontaine-le-Comte*, no. 27; and Richardson, "Letters and Charters," p. 208. Ralph and Jocelin, Richardson, "Letters and Charters," pp. 207–08; Berneval, *Rot. Chart.*, p. 8a.

32. Teulet, ed., *Layettes du Trésor des Chartes*, 2, no. 703. For Adelicia, see Marchegay, "Chartes de Fontevraud," pp. 340–41; and Boase, "Fontevraud and the Plantagenets," p. 6. In a charter, Eleanor referred to her as her "dearest ward [*dilecte alumpne*]," Marchegay, "Chartes de Fontevraud," pp. 338–39.

33. Labande, "Les filles d'Aliénor," pp. 106–08.

34. Howden, *Chronica*, 4, pp. 114–15.

35. Paul Marchegay and E. Mabille, eds, *Chronique de Saint-Aubin d'Angers* (Paris, 1869), p. 53.

36. Nurith Kenaan-Kedar, "The Impact of Eleanor on the Visual Arts in France" in Aurell, ed., *Culture politique des Plantagenêts*, pp. 47–51; Claude Andrault-Schmitt, "L'Architecture 'Angevine' à l'époque d'Aliénor" in Aurell, ed., *Aliénor*, p. 102.

37. Labande, "Pour une image," p. 231; Nicholas Vincent, "Isabelle of Angoulême" in Church, *King John: New Interpretations*, pp. 185, 187, citing *Rot. Chart.*, pp. 74b–75.

38. William Chester Jordan, "Isabelle d'Angoulême, by the Grace of God, Queen," *Revue belge de philologie et d'histoire*, 69 (1991), p. 824.

39. *Ralph Diceto*, 2, p. 174; Baldwin, *Government of Philip Augustus*, p. 98.

40. E.g. grant to Andrew de Chauvigny, a great lord of Berry, of the fief of Sainte-Sevère, August 1199, *Cal. Docs. France*, no. 1307; her request to John to grant to the abbey of Saint-Maixent rights of immunity from tallage and other customs, and from the services of the foresters of Sèvre, September 1200, Richard, *Chartes et documents de Saint-Maixent*, 2, pp. 14–15, no. 401; she granted land to Aimery de Rochefort in 1203, Teulet, ed., *Layettes du Trésor des Chartes*, 2, no. 703.

41. Eleanor's letter, *Rot. Chart.*, pp. 102b–103. See Hivergneaux, *La Cour Plantagenêt*, p. 85. For Guy de Dive, Landon, *Itinerary*, pp. 8, 10, 11, 12, 22, 26–27, 87, 90.

42. Martindale, "Eleanor: The Last Years," p. 160; Powicke, *Loss of Normandy*, p. 138.

43. *Ralph of Coggeshall*, pp. 137–38, records John's letter announcing his victory. The letter must have circulated widely, for usually terse monastic annals also give accounts of his victory at Mirebeau, *Annales monastici, Margam*, 1, p. 26; *Waverley*, 2, p. 254; *Winchester*, 2, pp. 78–9.

44. *Rot. Lit. Pat.*, p. 28b; trans. Kelly, *Eleanor and Four Kings*, p. 380.

45. Vincent, *Plantagenêts et Capétiens*, pp. 27–28, 43. Eleanor's charter for Saint-Maixent, Richard, ed., *Chartes et documents de Saint-Maixent*, 2, no. 402, 6 October 1200 at Fontevraud.

46. Bienvenu, "Aliénor et Fontevraud," pp. 24–25, 27.

47. On the Capetian tombs, see Kathleen D. Nolan, "The Queen's Choice: Eleanor of Aquitaine and the Tombs at Fontevraud" in *Eleanor: Lord and Lady*, pp. 389–91.

48. Nolan, "The Queen's Choice," pp. 377–405; Alain Erlande-Brandenburg, "Le gisant d'Aliénor d'Aquitaine" in Aurell, ed., *Aliénor*, p. 176.

49. Charles T. Wood, "La mort et les funérailles d'Henri II," *CCM*, 38 (1994), pp. 120–21; Bienvenu, "Aliénor et Fontevraud," p. 19.

50. Erlande-Brandenburg, "Le gisant d'Aliénor," p. 176; Charles T. Wood, "Fontevraud, Dynasticism, and Eleanor of Aquitaine," in *Eleanor: Lord and Lady*, pp. 414–16.

51. Boase, "Fontevraud and the Plantagenets," p. 7; Wood, "Fontevraud, Dynasticism and Eleanor," p. 417.

52. Only the Waverley Annals records the exact date of Eleanor's death; other chronicles supply only the year, *Annales monastici*, 2, p. 256. For her visit to Poitiers, Pon, ed., *Documents de Fontaine-le-Comte*, no. 27.
53. Hivergneaux, *La Cour Plantagenêt*, p. 86.
54. Bienvenu, "Aliénor et Fontevraud," p. 26, n. 98, prints the nuns' obituary from B. Pavillon, *La Vie du Bieneureux Robert d'Arbrissel* (Paris and Saumur, 1666), p. 589, *preuve* no. 97. *Annales de Saint-Aubin*, Halphen, ed., *Recueil d'annales angevines et vendômoises*, p. 21.
55. *Rot. Lit. Pat.*, p. 14b–15, John's consent that she make "a reasonable testament", 22 July.
56. Quotation, Chrétien de Troyes, *Yvain, The Knight of the Lion*, trans. Burton Raffel (New Haven, 1987), p. 44, lines 1414–15; see Clanchy, "Ladies with Prayer Books," pp. 115–16. On the tomb-sculpture, Nolan, "The Queen's Choice," pp. 392–95; also Brown, "Eleanor Reconsidered," pp. 27–29; Erlande-Brandenburg, "Le gisant d'Aliénor," pp. 176–77; and Peter Coss, *The Lady in Medieval England*, pp. 76 and 194, n. 7.
57. Latin text in Bienvenu, "Aliénor et Fontevraud," p. 26, n. 98.
58. Cheney, "A Monastic Letter of Fraternity to Eleanor," pp. 488–93; Nicholas Vincent, "Aliénor, Reine d'Angleterre," in Aurell, ed., *Aliénor*, pp. 61–66. John's command, *Rot. Lit. Pat.*, p. 54.
59. E.g. William Stubbs, ed., *Walter of Coventry*, 2 vols, RS (London, 1872–73), 2, p. 196; *Ralph of Coggeshall*, p. 144; Waverley Annals, *Annales monastici*, RS, 2, p. 256.
60. *Regina vero sua vocabatur Alienor, regina scilicet generosa et domina animosa et locuplex*, Manchester, Rylands lat. 155, f. 125, reference provided by John Gillingham in a talk, "A Contemporary London View of the Loss of Normandy," Haskins Society Conference, London, 11 September 2004. *Gerald of Wales*, pp. 300–01, bk 3, ch. 27. Matthew Paris was mistaken about her burial place, however, giving it as Beaulieu Abbey in England, founded by her son John. *Historia Anglorum*, ed. F. Madden, 3 vols, (1866–69), 2, pp. 102–03.
61. Martin Aurell, "Aliénor d'Aquitaine en son temps," in Aurell, ed., *Aliénor*, p. 16.

CHAPTER 12: OVERWHELMED BY A BLACK LEGEND

1. Brundage, "Canon Law of Divorce in the Mid-Twelfth Century", *Eleanor: Lord and Lady*, p. 213. Allison Weir's best-selling biography, *Eleanor of Aquitaine: By the Wrath of God, Queen*, pp. 67–70, is an example of a popular writer elaborating as factual the reports of the Antioch incident by later English chroniclers or moralists.
2. Robert L. Chapman, "Note on the Demon Queen Eleanor," *Modern Language Association Notes* (June, 1995), p. 393.
3. Flori, *Aliénor*, p. 311.
4. Frank McMinn Chambers, "Some Legends Concerning Eleanor of Aquitaine," *Speculum*, 16 (1941), pp. 462–63.
5. Peggy McCracken, "Scandalizing Desire: Eleanor of Aquitaine and the Chroniclers" in *Eleanor: Lord and Lady*, p. 358, translating. Etienne de Bourbon, *Anecdotes historiques, légendes et apologues*, ed. A. Lecoy de la Marche (1877), p. 212.
6. Owen, *Eleanor*, p. 111, translating. Hélinand de Froidmont, *Chronicon* (excerpted by Vincent of Beauvais), Migne, *PL*, 212, cols 1057–58; For Hélinand's career, Baldwin, *Government of Philip Augustus*, pp. 570–71, n. 28.
7. Public woman, *communem* in Latin, Duby, *Women of the Twelfth Century*, 1, p. 8; Flori, *Aliénor*, p. 305.
8. *RHGF*, 12, p. 231, cited by Daniel Power, "The Stripping of a Queen," p. 128, n. 73.

9. Richard Vaughn, *Matthew Paris* (Cambridge, 1958), pp. 32–33, 143, 152; Galbraith, "Roger Wendover and Matthew Paris," *Kings and Chroniclers*, essay 10.

10. Quotation, Vaughn, *Matthew Paris*, p. 134.

11. Matthew Paris, *Historia Anglorum*, 1, p. 288; and a shorter account in *Chronica Majori*, ed. H.R. Laud, 7 vols, RS (1872–83), 2, p. 186.

12. Flori, *Aliénor*, p. 312; Owen, *Eleanor*, pp. 105–07 translating Natalis de Wailly, ed., *Récits d'un ménestrel de Reims au XIIIe siècle*, Société de l'histoire de France (Paris, 1876), pp. 3–7; another translation, McCracken, "Scandalizing Desire," in *Eleanor: Lord and Lady*, pp. 251–52.

13. McCracken, p. 253; citing *Chronique Abrégée*, Paris BnF, fr. 9222, fols 16v–17r.

14. McCracken in *Eleanor: Lord and Lady*, pp. 253–54; citing *Istoire et chronique de Flandre d'après de divers manuscrits*, ed. Kervyn de Lettenhove (Brussels, 1879), pp. 44–55.

15. On Bouchet, Jennifer Britnell, *Jean Bouchet* (Edinburgh, 1986), pp. 1–4, 258.

16. Labande, "Pour une image," p. 187, n. 54, citing Bouchet, *Annales d'Aquitaine* (1644 edn), p. 140. This appears in the first and succeeding editions, 1524 edition, 1557 edition, and 1664 edition, cited by Martin Aurell, Catalina Girbea, and Marie-Aline de Mascureau, "A propos d'un livre récent sur Aliénor d'Aquitaine: portée et limites du genre biographique," *CCM* (2005), 48, p. 235.

17. For a summary of Bouchet's account, see Didier Le Fur, "Le souvenir d'Aliénor à l'époque moderne" in Aurell, ed., *Aliénor*, p. 206.

18. Le Fur, "Le souvenir d'Aliénor," p. 207, citing Isaac de Larrey, *L'Histoire de Guyenne ou histoire d'Aléonor* (Paris, 1692), p. 124.

19. Jean de Serres, *Inventaire général de l'histoire de France*, cited by Philippe Delorme, *Aliénor d'Aquitaine, épouse de Louis VII, mère de Richard Coeur de Lion* (Paris, 2001), p. 77.

20. Le Fur, "Le souvenir d'Aliénor," p. 207, citing Antoine Thibaudeau, *Abrégé de l'histoire du Poitou* (Paris, 1788).

21. Le Fur, "Le souvenir d'Aliénor," pp. 207–08.

22. David Hume, *The History of England from the Invasion of Julius Caesar to the Abdication of James the Second, 1688*, new edn, 6 vols (New York, 1850), 1, p. 284.

23. Barbara Hanawalt, "Golden Ages for the History of Medieval Women" in Susan Mosher Stuard ed., *Women in Medieval History and Historiography* (Philadelphia, 1987), p. 3, citing Hume's *History of England*.

24. Jules Michelet, *Histoire de France*, vol. 1, *Depuis les origines jusqu'à l'avènement de Charles V* (Paris, 1869), pp. 311, 312, cited by Flori, *Aliénor*, p. 19.

25. Flori, *Aliénor*, pp. 19–20, citing Joseph Calmette, *Le monde féodale* (Paris, 1934; new edn 1951), p. 307.

26. Strickland, *Lives of the Queens of England*, "Eleanora of Aquitaine," 1, pp. 164–201, quoting pp. 170–71.

27. Strickland, *Lives of the Queens of England*, 1, pp. 171–72.

28. Weir, *Eleanor*, p. 68.

29. See Owen, *Eleanor*, pp. 24–25; also Flori, *Aliénor*, pp. 321, 323, 328, 332–33.

30. Owen, *Eleanor*, pp. 115, 116.

31. On Higden, see Gransden, *Historical Writing*, 2, pp. 43–57; and Frank Taylor, *The Universal Chronicle of Ranulf Higden* (Oxford, 1966).

32. Owen, *Eleanor*, p. 116, citing *Chroniques*, ed. G.J. Aungier (London, 1844), pp. 3–5.

33. Owen, *Eleanor*, pp. 116–18; Chapman, "Legends Concerning Eleanor," p. 464.

34. Owen, *Eleanor*, pp. 118–19.

35. *Complaint of Rosamond*, Owen, *Eleanor*, pp. 125–28, citing Samuel Daniel, *The Complete Works*, ed., A.B. Grosart (n p, 1185), 1, pp. 79–113. *Fair Rosamonde*, Owen, pp. 122–24, citing Thomas Percy, *Reliques of Ancient English Poetry*, ed., R.A. Willmott (London, n.d.), pp. 251–52.

36. Owen, *Eleanor*, pp. 156–60, citing Percy, *Reliques*, pp. 257–59.

37. Chambers, "Legends Concerning Eleanor," p. 464; Owen, *Eleanor*, pp. 128–33, citing Joseph Addison, *The Miscellaneous Works*, ed. A.C. Guthkelch (London, 1914), 1, pp. 293–332.

38. Owen, *Eleanor*, pp. 145–46, citing Alfred Lord Tennyson, *The Life and Works*, 9 (*The Works*, 8 [London, 1899]), *Becket.*

39. Owen, *Eleanor*, pp. 141–42, citing Strickland, *Lives of the Queens of England*, 1, pp. 237–93.

40. Meade, *Eleanor*, Preface, p. x; and Short, "Literary Culture at the Court of Henry II," pp. 341–47.

41. *Walter Map*, pp. 155–59, dist. 2, ch. 12.

42. Gervase of Tilbury, *Otia Imperialia*, ed. and trans. S.E. Banks and J.W. Binns (Oxford, 2002) pp. 88–91.

43. *Gerald of Wales*, pp. 300–01; Stevenson trans., *Instruction of Princes*, pp. 96–98; and Short, "Literary Culture at the Court of Henry II," p. 346; see also Short, p. 348.

44. *Chronica Majora*, RS, 2, p. 186.

45. Daniel Power, "Stripping of a Queen," pp. 128–33, discussing Cambridge UL, Ii.vi.24, f. 19r–49v, 95r–100v; and Paris, Bibliothèque de l'Arsenal, 3516, ff. 304v–315r.

46. Power, "Stripping of a Queen," p. 126. The Norman French verb *se defubler* translated "to disrobe" is ambiguous. The same verb appears in Chrétien de Troyes's *Cligès*, when the hero removes only his cloak to reveal to the court his physical attractiveness.

47. Philippe Mouskès, *Chronique rimé*, ed. Baron de Rieffenberg, 2 vols (Brussels, 1836–38), 2, pp. 244–45, lines 18, 704–711; cited by Chapman, "Note on the Demon Queen Eleanor," p. 395.

48. Owen, *Eleanor*, pp. 105–07, translation of Natalis de Wailly, *Récits d'un ménestrel de Reims au XIIIe siècle*, pp. 3–7.

49. McCracken, "Scandalizing Desire," pp. 252–53; quoting Pierre Cochon, *Chronique normande*, ed. Charles de Robillard de Beaurepaire (Rouen, 1870), pp. 2–3.

50. Chapman, "Note on the Demon Queen Eleanor," pp. 393–96.

51. Owen, *Eleanor*, pp. 178–80; citing Karl Brunner, ed. and trans., *Der Mittelenglische Versroman über Richard Löwenherz*, Weiner Beiträge zur Englischen Philologie 42 (Vienna and Leipzig, 1913).

52. *Jean d'Arras, Mélusine*, ed. A.K. Donald, Early English Text Society (London, 1895), extra ser., 68.

53. Owen, *Eleanor*, p. 177, citing *Le Roman de Mélusine ou Histoire de Lusignan par Coudrette*, ed. Roach.

54. Margaret Labarge, *A Medieval Miscellany* (Ottawa, Canada, 1997), p. 20.

55. Martindale in *Status, Authority, Power*, art. 11, pp. 36, 38.

56. See ch. 7 above, pp. 198–200.

57. Kelly, *Eleanor and Four Kings*, pp. 159–60.

58. Meade, *Eleanor*, pp. 250, 251.

BIBLIOGRAPHY

PRIMARY SOURCES

Adémar de Chabannes, *Chronique*, ed. Yves Chauvin and Georges Pon (Turnhout, 2003)

Andreas Capellanus, *The Art of Courtly Love*, ed. and trans. John Jay Parry (New York, 1990)

Annales monastici, ed. H. R. Luard, 5 vols, RS (1864–69)

Bernard of Clairvaux, *The Letters of St. Bernard of Clairvaux*, trans. Bruno Scott James (London, 1953)

Bernard Itier, *Chroniques de Saint-Martial de Limoges*, ed. H. Duplès-Agier (Paris, 1876); also Jean-Loup Lemaître, ed. and trans., *Bernard Itier Chronique* (Paris, 1998)

Bernart de Ventadorn, *The Songs of Bernart de Ventadorn*, ed. and trans. Stephen G. Nichols, Jr, John A. Galm, and A. Bartlett Giamatti (Chapel Hill, NC, 1965)

Bertran de Born, *The Poems of the Troubadour Bertran de Born*, ed. W. D. Paden, Jr, T. Senkovitch, and P. H. Stäblen (Berkeley, CA, 1986)

Blyth Priory Cartulary, ed. R. T. Timson (London, 1973)

Calendar of Charter Rolls, 5, *15 Edward III–5 Henry V*, Public Record Office (London, 1916)

Calendar of Documents Preserved in France, 1, *918–1206*, ed. J. H. Round (London, 1899)

Calendar of Patent Rolls Henry III, 3, *1232–47*, Public Record Office (London, 1906)

Cartae Antiquae rolls 1–10, ed. Lionel Landon, Pipe Roll Society, new ser., 17 (1939)

Cartae Antiquae rolls 11–20, ed. J. Conway Davies, Pipe Roll Society, new ser., 33 (1960)

Cartulaire de l'abbaye de la Grace notre-dame ou de Charon, ed. L. de Richemond, *Archives historiques de la Saintonge et de l'Aunis*, 11 (1893)

Cartulaire de l'abbaye de Notre-Dame de la Merci-Dieu, ed. Etienne Clouzot, *AHP*, 34 (1905)

Cartulaire de l'abbaye d'Orbestier, ed. Louis de la Boutière, *AHP*, 6 (1877)

Cartulaire de l'église collégiale de Saint-Seurin de Bordeaux, ed. Jean-Auguste Brutails (Bordeaux, 1897)

Cartulaires du Bas-Poitou, ed. Paul Marchegay (Les Roches-Baritaud, 1877)

Cartulaires inédits de la Saintonge, ed. T. Grasilier, 2 vols (Niort, 1871)

Cartulaire saintongeais de la Trinité-de-Vendôme, ed. Charles Métais, *Archives historiques de la Saintonge et de l'Aunis*, 22 (1893)

Cartulary of Holy Trinity, Aldgate, ed. Gerald A. J. Hodgett, London Record Society (1971)

Chartes de la commanderie magistrale du temple de La Rochelle, ed. Meschinet de Richemond, *Archives historiques de la Saintonge et l'Aunis*, 1 (1874)

"Chartes de Fontevraud concernant l'Aunis et La Rochelle," ed. Paul Marchegay, *BEC*, 19 (1858)

"Chartes du XIIIe siècle relatives à Saint-Martial de Limoges," ed. Henri Omont, *BEC*, 90 (1929)

Chartes et documents pour servir à l'histoire de l'abbeye de Saint-Maixent, ed. Alfred Richard, 2 vols, *AHP*, 16 (1886)

Chrétien de Troyes, *Arthurian Romances*, trans. William Kibler and Carleton W. Carroll (London, 1991; revised 2004)

———, *Yvain, The Knight of the Lion*, trans. Burton Raffel (New Haven, 1987)

Chronicon Monasterii de Abingdon, ed. J. Stevenson, 2 vols, RS (London, 1858)

Chronicon Turonensis magnum in A. Salmon, ed., *Recueil des chroniques de Touraine* (Tours, 1854)

Chronique de Morigny (1095–1152), ed. L. Mirot (Paris, 1909)

Chronique de Saint-Aubin d'Angers, ed. Paul Marchegay and E. Mabille in *Chroniques des églises d'Anjou* (Paris, 1869)

Chronique de Saint-Maixent, ed. Jean Verdon (Paris, 1979)

Chroniques des comtes d'Anjou et des seigneurs d'Amboise, ed. Louis Halphen and R. Poupardin (Paris, 1913)

Cirot de la Ville, abbé, *L'Histoire de l'abbaye et de la congregation de Notre-Dame de Grand-Sauve en Guienne*, 2 vols (Bordeaux, 1844–45)

Crawford, Anne, ed., *Letters of the Queens of England 1100–1547* (Stroud, Gloucs., 1994)

"Documents pour l'histoire de l'église de Saint-Hilaire," ed. L. Redet, *MSAO*, 14 (1847)

Dugdale, William, *Monasticon Anglicanum*, ed. John Calley, Henry Ellis, Ulkeley Bandinel, new edn, 6 vols in 8 (London, 1817–30; reprint 1846)

Earldom of Gloucester Charters: The Charters and Scribes of the Earls and Countesses of Gloucester to A.D. 1217, ed. Robert B. Patterson (Oxford, 1973)

English Historical Documents, gen. ed. David Douglas, 12 vols, 2, *1042–1189*, ed. David Douglas and George W. Greenaway (London, 1968)

English Lawsuits from William I to Richard I, ed. R. C. Van Caenegem, 2 vols, Selden Society, 106, 107 (London, 1990–91)

Epistolae Cantuarensis, 1187–1199 in William Stubbs, ed., *Chronicles and Memorials, Richard I*, 2 vols, RS (London, 1864–65)

Foedera, Conventiones, Literae, etc.; or Rymer's Foedera, 1066–1383, ed. Adam Clarke, J. Caley, J. Bayley, F. Holbrook, and J. W. Clarke, new edn (London, 1816–69)

Gallia Christiana in provincias ecclesiasticas distributa, ed. D. Sainte-Marthe, 16 vols (Paris, 1739–1877)

Geoffroi de Vigeois, Chronica in *RHGF*, 12; also in Père Labbé, ed., *Novae Bibliotheca Manuscriptorum*, vol. 2 (Paris, 1657)

Gerald of Wales, *De principis instructione*, ed. G. F. Warner in *Giraldi Cambrensis Opera*, 8 vols, RS (London, 1861–91), 8; trans. Joseph Stevenson, *Concerning the instruction of princes* (London, 1858; reprint Felinfach, Dyfed, 1994)

———, *Expugnatio hibernica*, ed. and trans. A. B. Scott and F. X. Martin (Dublin, 1978)

Gervase of Canterbury: Historical Works, ed. William Stubbs, 2 vols, RS (London, 1879–80)

Gervase of Tilbury, *Otia Imperialia*, ed. and trans. S. E. Banks and J. W. Binns (Oxford, 2002)

Gesta Stephani, ed. and trans. K. R. Potter and R. H. C. Davis (Oxford, 1976)

Grand Cartulaire de Fontevraud, 1, ed. Jean-Marc Bienvenu with Robert Favreau and Georges Pon, *AHP* (Poitiers, 2000)

Grand Cartulaire de la Sauve Majeure, ed. Charles Higounet and Arlette Higounet-Nadal, 2 vols, *Études et documents d'Aquitaine*, 3 (Bordeaux, 1996)

Great Rolls of the Pipe for the First Year of Richard the First, ed. Joseph Hunter (London, 1844)

Great Rolls of the Pipe for the Second, Third, and Fourth Years of the Reign of King Henry the Second, A.D. 1155, 1156, 1157, 1158, ed. Joseph Hunter (London, 1844)

Guibert de Nogent, *De vita sua*, trans. C. C. Swinton Bland; *Self and Society in Medieval France*, ed. John F. Benton (New York, 1970)

Henry of Huntingdon, *Historia Anglorum: The History of the English People*, ed. Diana Greenway (Oxford, 1996)

Histoire des ducs de Normandie et des rois d'Angleterre, ed. Francisque Michel (Paris, 1840; reprint New York, 1965)

Historia Pontificum et comitum Engolismensium, ed. Jacques Boussard (Paris, 1957)

Historical Manuscripts Commission, *Report on Manuscripts in Various Collections*, 1 (London, 1901)

History of William Marshal, ed. A. J. Holden, S. Gregory, and D. Crouch (London, 2002)

Jocelin of Brakelond, *Chronicle of the Abbey of Bury St. Edmunds*, trans. Diana Greenway and Jane Sayers (Oxford, 1989)

John of Salisbury, *Historia Pontificalis of John of Salisbury*, ed. Marjorie Chibnall (Edinburgh, 1956)

———, *The Letters of John of Salisbury*, ed. W. J. Miller and C. N. L. Brooke, 1. *The Early Letters (1153–1166)*; 2. *The Later Letters (1163–1180)* (Oxford, 1979; 1986)

Jordan Fantosme's Chronicle, ed. P. Johnston (Oxford, 1981)

Layettes du trésor des chartes, ed. Alexandre Teulet, Henri-François Delaborde, and Élie Berger, 5 vols (Paris, 1863–1909)

Lewis, Andrew W., "Six Charters of Henry II and his Family for the Monastery of Dalon," *EHR*, 110 (1995)

The Life of St. Hugh of Lincoln, ed. and trans. Decima L. Douie and Hugh Farmer, 2 vols (Edinburgh, 1961–62)

Livre des coutumes, ed. H. Barckhousen, *Archives Municipales de Bordeaux*, 5 (Bordeaux, 1890)

Materials for the History of Thomas Becket, ed. J. C. Robertson, 7 vols, RS (London, 1875–85)

Matthew Paris, *Historia Anglorum* in *Historia Minor*, ed. F. Madden, 3 vols, RS (1866–69)

———, *Chronica Majori*, ed. H. R. Luard, 7 vols, RS (1872–83)

Memoranda Roll 1 John, ed. H. G. Richardson, Pipe Roll Society, new ser. 21 (1943)

Odo of Deuil, *De profectione Ludovici VII*, ed. and trans. Virginia Gingerick Berry (New York, 1948)

Orderic Vitalis, *The Ecclesiastical History of Orderic Vitalis*, ed. and trans. Marjorie Chibnall, 6 vols (Oxford, 1969–80)

Peter of Blois, *Epistolae*, in Migne, *PL*, 207, cols 1–560

Pleas before the King or his Justices 1198–1212, ed. Doris M. Stenton, 3, Selden Society, 83 (1966)

Publications of the Pipe Roll Society, *The Great Roll of the Pipe for Five King Henry II . . . Thirty-four Henry II*, original ser., 38 vols (1884–1925); new ser., *Two Richard I . . .* (1925–)

Ralph of Coggeshall, *Radulphi de Coggeshall Chronicon Anglicanum*, ed. J. Stevenson, RS (London, 1875)

Ralph Diceto, *Radulphi de Diceto, Opera Historica*, ed. William Stubbs, 2 vols, RS (London, 1876)

Ralph Glaber, *Rodulfus Glaber, The Five Books of the Histories*, ed. and trans. John France, N. Bulst, and P. Reynolds (Oxford, 1989)

Ralph Niger, *The Chronicle of Ralph Niger*, ed. R. Anstruther (London, 1851)

Recueil d'actes relatifs à l'administration des rois d'Angleterre en Gascogne au XIIIe siècle, ed. Charles Bémont (Paris, 1914)

Recueil d'annales Angevines et Vendômoises, Annales de Saint-Aubin, ed. Louis Halphen (Paris, 1903)

Recueil des actes de Henri II, ed. Léopold Delisle and Élie Berger: *Introduction* (Paris, 1909); *Actes*, 3 vols (Paris, 1916–27)

Recueil des documents concernant la commune et la ville de Poitiers, ed. E. Audouin, AHP, 44 (1923)

Recueil des documents de l'abbaye de Fontaine-le-Comte, ed. Georges Pon, AHP, 62 (1982)

Recueil des documents relatifs à l'abbaye de Montierneuf de Poitiers (1076–1319), ed. Fr. Villard, AHP, 59 (1973)

Rédet, L., "Mémoire sur les Halles et les Foires de Poitiers," *MSAO,* 12 (1847 for 1845)

Regesta Regum Anglo-Normannorum 1066–1154. eds H. W. C. Davis, C. Johnson, H. A. Cronne, and R. H. C. Davis, 4 vols (Oxford, 1913–69)

Richard fitz Neal, *The Course of the Exchequer by Richard, Son of Nigel,* ed. Charles Johnson (London, 1950)

Richard le Poitevin, *Ex Chronico Richardi Pictaviensis, RHGF,* 12 (new edn, 1877)

Richard of Devizes, *The Chronicle of Richard of Devizes,* ed. and trans J. T. Appleby (London, 1963)

Roger of Howden, *Gesta Regis Henrici secundi Benedicti Abbatis,* ed. William Stubbs, 2 vols, RS (London, 1867)

———, *Chronica Rogeri de Hovedene,* ed. William Stubbs, 4 vols, RS (London, 1868–71)

Robert of Torigni, *Chronicles, Stephen, Henry II and Richard I,* ed. R. Howlett, RS, 4, *The Chronicle of Robert of Torigni* (London, 1890)

Roger of Wendover, *Flores Historiarum,* ed. H. G. Hewlett, 3 vols, RS (1886–89); trans. J. A. Giles, 2 vols (London, 1849)

Ross, James Bruce and Mary Martin McLaughlin, eds, *The Portable Medieval Reader* (New York, 1950)

Rotuli Chartarum, 1199–1216, ed. T. Duffus Hardy (London, 1837)

Rotuli Litterarum Clausarum, ed. T. Duffus Hardy, 2 vols (London, 1833–34)

Rotuli Litterarum Patentium, ed. T. Duffus Hardy (London, 1835)

Rotuli Normanniae in Turri Londinensi asservati, ed. T. Duffus Hardy (London, 1835)

Royal Writs in England from the Conquest to Glanvill, ed. R. C. Van Caenegem, Selden Society, 77 (London, 1958–59)

Saint-Eutrope et son prieuré, ed. Louis Audiat, *Archives historiques de la Saintonge et de l'Aunis,* 2 (1875)

Song of Aliscans, trans. Michael A. Newth (New York 1992)

Suger, *Lettres de Suger, Chartes de Suger, Vie de Suger par le moine Guillaume,* ed. and trans. F. Gasparri, *Suger, Oeuvres,* 2 (Paris, 2001)

———, *The Deeds of Louis the Fat,* eds and trans. Richard Cusimano and John Moorhead (Washington, DC, 1992)

———, *Histoire de Louis VII,* ed. and trans. Françoise Gasparri, *Suger, Oeuvres,* 1 (Paris, 1996)

Thomas Becket, *The Correspondence of Thomas Becket Archbishop of Canterbury, 1162–1170,* ed. and trans. Ann J. Duggan, 2 vols (Oxford, 2001)

Thomas of Walsingham, *Gesta Abbatum Monasterii S. Albani,* ed. H. T. Riley, 3 vols, RS (London, 1867)

Wace, *The History of the Norman People: Wace's Roman de Rou,* trans. Glyn S. Burgess and ed. Elisabeth van Houts (Woodbridge, Suffolk, 2004)

———, *Wace's Roman de Brut, A History of the British,* ed. J. Weiss (1999; 2nd edn, Exeter, 2000)

Walter Map, *De nugis curialium,* ed. C. N. L. Brooke and M. R. James, revised edn (Oxford, 1983)

———, *Gautier Map, Contes pour les gens de cour,* trans. Alan Keith Bate (Turnhout, 1993)

Walter of Coventry or Barnwell Chronicle, *Memoriale Walteri de Coventria,* ed. William Stubbs, 2 vols, RS (London, 1872–73)

Westminster Abbey Charters, ed. Emma Mason, London Record Society, 25 (1988)

William fitz Stephen, "A Description of London," in F. M. Stenton, *Norman London* (New York, 1990); reprint of Historical Association leaflets 93 and 94 (London, 1934)

William IX of Aquitaine, *The Poetry of William VII, Count of Poitiers, IX Duke of Aquitaine,* ed. and trans. Gerald A. Bond (New York, 1982)

William of Malmesbury, *Willelmi Malmesbiriensis de Gestis regum,* ed. William Stubbs, 2 vols, RS (London, 1887–89)

William of Newburgh, *Historia Rerum Anglicarum of William of Newburgh*, in *Chronicles, Stephen, Henry II and Richard I*, ed. R. Howlett, 4 vols, RS (London 1885–90); trans. as *History of English Affairs Book I*, ed. and trans. P. G. Walsh and M. J. Kennedy (Warminster, 1988)

William of Tyre, *A History of Deeds Done Beyond the Sea*, ed. and trans. Emily Atwater Babcock and A. C. Krey, 2 vols (New York, 1943)

Secondary Sources

Amt, Emilie M., "Richard de Lucy, Henry II's Justiciar," *Medieval Prosopography*, 9 (1988)

———, *The Accession of Henry II in England: Royal Government Restored 1149–1159* (Woodbridge, Suffolk, 1993)

Andrault-Schmitt, Claude, "L'Architecture 'Angevine' à l'époque d'Aliénor," in Aurell, *Aliénor, 303*

Ariès, Philippe, *L'Enfant et la vie familiale sous l'Ancien Régime* (Paris, 1960; reprint 1973)

Aubert, Roger et al., eds, *Dictionnaire d'histoire et de géographie écclésiastique*, 30 vols (Paris, 1912–)

Aurell, Martin, ed., *La Cour Plantagenêt (1154–1204), Actes du Colloque tenu à Thouars du 30 avril au 2 mai 1999* (Poitiers, 2000)

———, "Aliénor d'Aquitaine (1124–1204) et ses historiens: la destruction d'un mythe?" in J. Paviot and J. Verger, eds, *Guerre, pouvoir et noblesse au Moyen Age: Mélanges en l'honneur de Philippe Contamine* (Paris, 2000)

———, ed., *Culture politique des Plantagenêts: Actes du Colloque tenu à Poitiers du 2 au 5 mai 2002* (Poitiers, 2003)

———, "Les Plantagenêts, la propagande et la relecture du passé" in Aurell, ed., *Culture politique des Plantagenêts*

———, *L'Empire des Plantagenêts 1154–1224* (Paris, 2003)

———, ed., *Aliénor d'Aquitaine, 303: Arts, recherches et création*, extra series (Nantes 2004)

———, "Aliénor d'Aquitaine en son temps," in Aurell, ed., *Aliénor*

———, "Aux Origines de la légende noire d'Aliénor d'Aquitaine," *Royautés imaginaires (XIIe–XVIe siècles), Colloque de l'Université de Paris X-Nanterre du 26 au 27 septembre 2003*, ed. Anne-Hélène Allirot, Gilles Lecuppre, and Lydwine Scordia (Turnhout, 2005)

———, "Henry II and Arthurian Legend" in Harper-Bill and Vincent, *Henry II: New Interpretations*

Aurell, Martin and Noël-Yves Tonnerre, eds, *Plantagenêts et Capétiens: Confrontations et héritage* (Turnhout, 2006)

Aurell, Martin, Catalina Girbea, and Marie-Aline de Mascureau, "A Propos d'un livre récent sur Aliénor d'Aquitaine: portée et limites du genre biographique," *CCM* (2005)

Bachrach, Bernard, "The Idea of the Angevin Empire," *Albion*, 10 (1978)

———, "Toward a Reappraisal of William the Great, Duke of Aquitaine (995–1030)," *JMH*, 4 (1979)

Baldet, Irène, *Essai d'itinéraire et regestes d'Aliénor reine d'Angleterre 1189–1204*, mémoire de maîtrise (University of Poitiers, 1963)

Baldwin, John W., *The Government of Philip Augustus: Foundations of French Royal Power in the Middle Ages* (Berkeley and Los Angeles, 1986)

———, "The Capetian Court at Work under Philip II" in Edward Haymes, ed., *The Medieval Court in Europe* (Munich, 1986)

———, *The Language of Sex: Five Voices from Northern France around 1200* (Chicago, 1994)

———, "The Image of the Jongleur in Northern France around 1200," *Speculum*, 72 (1997)

———, *Aristocratic Life in Medieval France: The Romances of Jean Renart and Gerbert de Montreuil, 1190–1230* (Baltimore, 2000)

———, "The Kingdom of the Franks (a) Crown and Government," *New CMH*, 4, pt 2

Baltzer, Rebecca A., "Music in the Life and Times of Eleanor of Aquitaine" in Kibler, ed., *Eleanor of Aquitaine, Patron and Politician*

Bandel, Betty, "English Chroniclers' Attitude toward Women," *Jl. History of Ideas*, 16 (1957)

Barber, Richard, "Eleanor of Aquitaine and the Media," in Léglu and Bull, *World of Eleanor*

Barlow, Frank, *Edward the Confessor* (Berkeley, 1970)

——, *Thomas Becket* (Berkeley, 1986)

——, *The Feudal Kingdom of England 1042–1216*, 4th edn (London, 1988)

Bartlett, Robert, *Gerald of Wales 1146–1223* (Oxford, 1982)

——, *England under the Norman and Angevin Kings 1075–1225* (Oxford, 2000)

Bates, David, "The Origins of the Justiciarship," *ANS*, 4 (1987)

——, "The Prosopographical Study of Anglo-Norman Royal Charters," in Katherine S. B. Keats-Rohan, *Family Trees and the Roots of Family Politics: The Prosopography of Britain and France from the Tenth to the Twelfth Century* (Woodbridge, Suffolk, 1997)

——, *William the Conqueror* (Stroud, Gloucs., 2001)

Baudry, Marie-Pierre, "La Politique de fortification des Plantagenêts en Poitou, 1154–1242," *ANS*, 24 (2001)

Bec, Pierre, "Troubadours, trouvères et espace Plantagenêt," *CCM*, 29 (1986)

Beech, George T., *A Rural Society in Medieval France: The Gâtine of Poitou in the Eleventh and Twelfth Centuries* (Baltimore, 1964)

——, "Contemporary Views of William the Troubadour, ixth Duke of Aquitaine, 1086–1126," in Neithard Bulst and Jean-Philippe Genet, eds, *Medieval Lives and the Historian: Studies in Medieval Prosopography* (Kalamazoo, MI, 1986)

——, "L'Attribution des poèmes du comte de Poitiers à Guillaume IX d'Aquitaine," *CCM*, 31 (1988)

——, "The Ventures of the Dukes of Aquitaine into Spain and the Crusader East in the Early Twelfth Century," *HSJ*, 5 (1993)

——, "The Eleanor of Aquitaine Vase, William IX of Aquitaine, and Muslim Spain," *Gesta*, 32 (1993)

——, "The Eleanor of Aquitaine Vase," in Parsons and Wheeler, *Eleanor: Lord and Lady*, ch. 17

Benjamin, Richard, "A Forty-Year War: Toulouse and the Plantagenets, 1156–90," *Historical Research*, 61 (1988)

——, "The Angevin Empire," *History Today* (February 1986)

Benton, John F., "The Court of Champagne as a Literary Center" in Benton, *Culture, Power and Personality* (London, 1991)

——, "Clio and Venus: An Historical View of Medieval Love," in *Culture, Power and Personality*

Berman, Constance H., "Women as Donors and Patrons to Southern French Monasteries in the Twelfth and Thirteenth Centuries," in Berman, Charles W. Connell, and Judith R. Rothschild, eds, *The Worlds of Medieval Women: Creativity, Influence, Imagination* (Morgantown, WV, 1985)

Berry, Virginia G., "The Second Crusade," in Kenneth M. Setton, general ed., *A History of the Crusades*, 1, *The First Hundred Years* (Madison, 1969), ch. 15

Bienvenu, Jean-Marie, "Aliénor d'Aquitaine et Fontevraud," *CCM*, 29 (1986)

——, "Henri II Plantagenêt et Fontevraud," *CCM*, 37 (1994)

Bisson, Thomas N., "Aragon, Crown of (1137–1479)," *Dict. M.A.*, 1

——, "Unheroed Pasts: History and Commemoration in South Frankland before the Albigensian Crusade," *Speculum*, 65 (1990)

——, ed., *Cultures of Power: Lordship, Status and Process in Twelfth-century Europe* (Philadelphia, 1995)

Blamires, Alcuin, *The Case for Women in Medieval Culture* (Oxford, 1997)

Blumenfeld-Kosinski, Renate, "Antiquity, Romances of" in Kibler and Zinn, *Medieval France: An Encyclopedia*

Boase, T. S. R., "Fontevraud and the Plantagenets," *Jl. British Archaeology Association*, 3rd ser., 34 (1971)

Boissonade, Pierre, "Administrateurs laïques et ecclésiastiques anglo-normands en Poitou à l'époque d'Henri II Plantagenêt (1152–1189)," *BSAO*, 3rd ser., 5 (1919)

Boswell, John, *Christianity, Social Tolerance, and Homosexuality* (Chicago, 1980)

Bouchard, Constance Brittain, "Eleanor's Divorce from Louis VII: The Uses of Consanguinity," in Parsons and Wheeler, *Eleanor: Lord and Lady*, ch. 9

———, "*Those of My Blood*": *Constructing Noble Families in Medieval France* (Philadelphia, 2004)

Boureau, Julien, Richard Levesque, and Isabelle Sachot, "Sur les Pas d'Aliénor, l'abbaye de Nieul-sur-l'Autise," in Aurell, ed., *Aliénor*

Bourgain, Pascal, "Aliénor d'Aquitaine et Marie de Champagne mises en cause par André le Chapelain," *CCM*, 29 (1986)

Bournazel, Eric, "Suger and the Capetians," ed. Paula Lieber Gerson, in *Suger and Saint-Denis: A Symposium* (New York, 1986)

Boussard, Jacques, *Le Gouvernement d'Henri II Plantagenêt* (Paris, 1956)

Boutoulle, Frédéric, "La Gascogne sous les premiers Plantagenêts (1154–1199)" in Aurell and Tonnerre, *Plantagenêts et Capétiens*

Bozoky, Edina, "Le culte des saints et des reliques dans la politique des premiers rois Plantagenêts" in Aurell, *La Cour Plantagenêt*

Bradbury, Jim, *Philip Augustus King of France (1180–1223)* (Harlow, Essex, 1998)

Bradford, Sarah, *The Reluctant King: The Life and Reign of George VI 1895–1952* (New York, 1989)

Brandt, William J., *The Shape of Medieval History: Studies in Modes of Perception* (New Haven, 1996)

Broadhurst, Karen M., "Henry II of England and Eleanor of Aquitaine: Patrons of Literature in French?" *Viator*, 27 (1996)

Brooke, C. N. L., *London 300–1216: The Shaping of a City* (Berkeley, 1975)

Brooke, Z. N. and C. N. L. Brooke, "Henry II, Duke of Normandy and Aquitaine," *EHR*, 61 (1946)

Brown, Elizabeth A. R., "Eleanor of Aquitaine: Parent, Queen, Duchess," in Kibler, ed., *Eleanor of Aquitaine*

———, "The Prince is Father of the King: The Character and Childhood of Philip IV" in Brown, *The Monarchy of Capetian France and Royal Ceremonial* (Aldershot, 1991)

———, "Eleanor of Aquitaine Reconsidered: The Woman and her Seasons," in Parsons and Wheeler, *Eleanor: Lord and Lady*

Brown, R. Allen, H. M. Colvin, and A. J. Taylor, eds, *The History of the King's Works*, 1, *The Middle Ages* (London, 1963)

Bruguière, Marie-Bernadette, "A Propos des idées reçues en histoire: le divorce de Louis VII," *Mémoires de l'Académie des sciences, inscriptions et belles-lettres de Toulouse*, 140, 15th ser., 9 (1978)

Brundage, James A., "The Canon Law of Divorce in the Mid-twelfth Century: Louis VII c. Eleanor of Aquitaine" in Parsons and Wheeler, *Eleanor: Lord and Lady*

Burgess, Glyn S., "Social Status in the *Lais* of Marie de France" in Glyn S. Burgess and Robert A. Taylor, eds, *The Spirit of the Court: Selected Proceedings of the Fourth Congress of the International Courtly Literature Society* (Woodbridge, Suffolk, 1983)

Bynum, Caroline, "Did the Twelfth Century Discover the Individual?" in *Jesus as Mother: Studies in the Spirituality of the High Middle Ages* (Berkeley, 1993)

Callahan, Daniel F., "Eleanor of Aquitaine, the Coronation Rite of the Duke of Aquitaine and the Cult of St. Martial of Limoges," in Léglu and Bull, *World of Eleanor*

Cambridge Medieval History, ed. H. M. Gwatkin, J. P. Whittney, J. R. Tanner, C. W. Previté-Orton, and Z. N. Brooke, 3 vols (Cambridge, 1911–36)

Camus, Marie-Thérèse and Robert Favreau, *Églises de Poitiers: Parcours et visites* (Poitiers, 2006)

Carmichael de Baiglie, Martine Cav, "Savary de Mauléon (*ca* 1180–1233), chevalier-troubadour poitevin: traîtrise et société aristocratique," *Le Moyen Âge*, 105 (1999)

Carpenter, David, "Abbot Ralph of Coggeshall's Account of the Last Years of King Richard and the First Years of King John," *EHR*, 113 (1998)

Carroll, Carlton W., "Quelques Observations sur les reflets de la cour d'Henri II dans l'oeuvre de Chrétien de Troyes," *CCM*, 37 (1994)

Cazel, Fred A., Jr, ed., *Feudalism and Liberty* (Baltimore, 1961)

Chambers, Frank McMinn, "Some Legends concerning Eleanor of Aquitaine," *Speculum*, 16 (1941)

Chaplais, Pierre, "Le Traité de Paris de 1259 et l'inféodation de la Gascogne allodiale," *Essays in Medieval Diplomacy and Administration* (London, 1981)

Chapman, R. L., "Note on the Demon Queen Eleanor," *Modern Language Association Notes* (June, 1955)

Cheney, Christopher R., "A Monastic Letter of Fraternity to Eleanor of Aquitaine," *EHR*, 51 (1936)

———, *Hubert Walter* (Walton-on-Thames, 1967)

Cheney, Mary G., "Master Geoffrey de Lucy, an Early Chancellor of the University of Oxford," *EHR*, 82 (1967)

Cheyette, Frederic L., "Women, Poets, and Politics in Occitania," in Theodore Evergates, ed., *Aristocratic Women in Medieval France*

———, *Ermengard of Narbonne and the World of the Troubadours* (Ithaca, NY, 2002)

———, "Some Reflections on Violence, Reconciliation, and the 'Feudal Revolution'," in Warren C. Brown and Piotr Górecki, eds, *Conflict in Medieval Europe: Changing Perspectives on Society and Culture* (Aldershot, 2003), pp. 243–64

Chibnall, Marjorie, "Women in Orderic Vitalis," *HSJ*, 2 (1990), pp. 105–21

———, *The Empress Matilda: Queen Consort, Queen Mother, and Lady of the English* (Oxford, 1991)

———, "The Empress Matilda and her Sons" in Parsons and Wheeler, *Medieval Mothering*

Church, Stephen D., ed., *King John: New Interpretations* (Woodbridge, Suffolk, 1999)

Clanchy, Michael T., *From Memory to Written Record: England 1066–1307*, 2nd edn (Oxford, 1993)

———, "Images of Ladies with Prayer Books," *Studies in Church History*, 38 (2004)

Cloulas, Ivan, "Le Douaire de Bérengère de Navarre, veuve de Richard Coeur de Lion, et sa retraite au Mans," Aurell, ed., *La Cour Plantagenêt*

———, "Les Peintures murales de Saint-Radegonde de Chinon: à propos d'un article récent," *CCM*, 42 (1999)

Collet, Jean-Philippe, "Le Combat politique des Plantagenêts en Aquitaine: l'exemple des vicomtes de Thouars (1158–1199)" in Martin Aurell, ed., *Noblesses de l'espace Plantagenêt (1154–1224)* (Poitiers, 2001)

Colvin, H. M., *Essays in English Architectural History* (New Haven, 1999)

Constable, Giles, "The Second Crusade as Seen by Contemporaries," *Traditio*, 9 (1953)

———, "The Alleged Disgrace of John of Salisbury," *EHR*, 69 (1954)

Coss, Peter, *The Lady in Medieval England 1000–1500* (Stroud, Gloucs., 1998)

Courteault, Paul, *Histoire de la Gascogne et de Béarn* (Paris, 1938)

Cox, J. C., "Mary, Abbess of Shaftesbury," *EHR*, 25 (1910); 26 (1911)

Crouch, David, *The Beaumont Twins: The Roots and Branches of Power in the Twelfth Century* (Cambridge, 1986)

———, *William Marshal: Court, Career and Chivalry in the Angevin Empire 1142–1219* (Harlow, Essex, 1990)

———, *The Image of Aristocracy in Britain, 1000–1300* (London, 1992)

———, "Breteuil, Robert de," *Oxford DNB*

Crozet, René, *Histoire du Poitou* (Paris, 1949)

Cunningham, Hugh, "Histories of Childhood," review essay, *AHR*, 103 (1998)

Dalarun, Jacques, "The Clerical Gaze" in Klapisch-Zuber, ed., *Silences of the Middle Ages*

D'Alverny, Marie-Thérèse, "Comment les Théologiens et les philosophes ont vu les femmes," *CCM*, 20 (1970)

Damian-Grint, Peter, "Benoît de Saint-Maure et l'idéologie des Plantagenêts" in Aurell and Tonnerre, *Plantagenêts et Capétiens*

Damon, Géraldine, "Dames du Poitou au temps d'Aliénor," in Aurell, ed., *Aliénor*

———, "La Place et le pouvoir des dames dans la société au temps d'Aliénor d'Aquitaine" in Aurell and Tonnerre, *Plantagenêts et Capétiens*

Danziger, Danny and John Gillingham, *1215 the Year of Magna Carta* (London, 2003; reprint New York, 2005)

Davies, R. R., *Domination and Conquest: The Experience of Ireland, Scotland and Wales 1100–1300* (Cambridge, 1990)

Debord, André, *La Société laïque dans les pays de Charente Xe–XIIe siècles* (Paris, 1984)

———, "The Castellan Revolution and the Peace of God in Aquitaine," in R. Landes, ed., *The Peace of God: Social Violence and Religious Response in France around the Year 1000* (Ithaca, NY, 1992)

———, "La Politique de fortification des Plantagenêts dans la seconde moitié du XIIe siècle" in Marie-Pierre Baudry, ed., *Les Fortifications dans les domaines Plantagenêt XIIe–XIVe siècles, Actes du Colloque international tenu à Poitiers du 11 au 13 novembre 1994* (Poitiers, 2000)

Delorme, M., "'Facts not Opinions': Agnes Strickland," *History Today*, 38 (1988)

Descroix, J., "Poitiers et les lettres latines dans l'Ouest au début du XIIe siècle," *BSAO*, 3rd ser., 13 (Poitiers, 1942–45)

Devailly, G., *Le Berry du Xe au milieu du XIIIe siècle* (Paris, 1973)

Dez, Gaston, "Histoire de Poitiers," *MSAO*, 4th ser. 10 for 1966 (Poitiers, 1969)

Dillange, Michel, *Les Comtes de Poitou: ducs d'Aquitaine (770–1204)* (Mougon, France, 1995)

Dippelmann, Lindsay, "Marriage as a Tactical Response: Henry II and the Royal Wedding of 1160," *EHR*, 119 (2004)

Dor, J., "Langues françaises et anglaises, et multilinguisme à l'époque d'Henri II Plantagenêt," *CCM*, 29 (1986)

Dronke, Peter, "Peter of Blois and Poetry at the Court of Henry II," *Mediaeval Studies* 38 (1976)

———, "Profane Elements in Literature" in Robert L. Benson and Giles Constable, eds, *Renaissance and Renewal in the Twelfth Century* (Cambridge, MA, 1982)

Duby, Georges, *La Société aux XIe et XIIe siècles dans la région mâconnaise* (Paris, 1953; 2nd edn Paris, 1982)

———, "Les 'Jeunes' dans la société aristocratique dans la France du Nord-Ouest au XIIe siècle," *Annales*, 27 (1964), reprinted in Duby, *Hommes et structures du moyen âge* (Paris, 1984), trans. C. Postan, as "Youth in Aristocratic Society: Northwestern France in the Twelfth Century," in Duby, *The Chivalrous Society* (Baltimore, 1976)

———, "La Situation de la noblesse en France au début du XIIIe siècle" in Duby, *Hommes et structures du moyen âge*

———, *Medieval Marriage: Two Models from Twelfth-Century France* (Baltimore, 1978)

———, *The Three Orders: Feudal Society Imagined*, trans. Arthur Goldhammer (Chicago 1980)

———, *Le Chevalier, la femme, et le prêtre* (Paris, 1981)

———, *William Marshal: The Flower of Chivalry*, trans. Richard Howard (New York, 1985)

———, *Love and Marriage in the Middle Ages*, trans. J. Dunnet (Chicago, 1994)

———, *Dames du XIIe siècle: Héloïse, Aliénor, Yseult et quelques autres* (Paris, 1995); trans. Jean Birrell, *Women of the Twelfth Century: Eleanor of Aquitaine and Six Others* (Chicago, 1997)

———, *France in the Middle Ages 987–1460*, trans. Juliet Vale (Oxford, 1991)

———, "Women and Power" in Bisson, ed., *Cultures of Power*

Duggan, Anne, *Thomas Becket* (London, 2004)

Duggan, Charles, "Richard of Ilchester, Royal Servant and Bishop," trans. Royal Historical Society, 5th ser., 16 (1966)

——, "Bishop John and Archdeacon Richard of Poitiers" in Duggan, *Canon Law in Medieval England* (London, 1982)

Dunbabin, Jean, *France in the Making 842–1180* (Oxford, 1985; 2nd edn 2000)

——, "Henry II and Louis VII" in Harper-Bill and Vincent, *Henry II: New Interpretations*

Edbury, Peter W. and John Gordon Rowe, *William of Tyre: Historian of the Latin East* (Cambridge, 1988)

Erlande-Brandenburg, Alain, "Le Gisant d'Aliénor d'Aquitaine" in Aurell, ed., *Aliénor*

Erler, M. and E. Kowaleski, eds, *Women and Power in the Middle Ages* (Athens, GA, 1988)

Evergates, Theodore, "Aristocratic Women in the County of Champagne" in Evergates, ed., *Aristocratic Women in Medieval France* (Philadelphia, 1999), pp. 74–110

——, "Nobles and Knights in Twelfth-Century France" in Bisson, *Cultures of Power*

Eyton, R. W., *Court, Household, and Itinerary of King Henry II* (London, 1878)

Facinger, Marion, "A Study of Medieval Queenship: Capetian France 987–1237," *Studies in Medieval and Renaissance History*, 5 (1968)

Farmer, Sharon, "Persuasive Voices: Clerical Images of Medieval Wives," *Speculum*, 61 (1986)

Favreau, Robert, "Les Écoles et la culture à Saint-Hilaire-le-Grand de Poitiers des origines au début du xiie siècle," *CCM*, 3 (1960), pp. 473–78

——, "Le Palais de Poitiers au moyen âge," *BSAO*, 4th ser., 11 (1971)

——, *Histoire de Poitiers* (Toulouse, 1981)

——, "Les Débuts de la ville de La Rochelle," *CCM*, 30 (1987)

Fawtier, Robert, *The Capetian Kings of France*, trans. L. Butler and R. J. Adam (London, 1960)

Ferrante, Joan M., "Correspondent: 'Blessed is the Speech of Your Mouth'" in Barbara Newman, ed., *Voice of the Living Light: Hildegard of Bingen and Her World* (Berkeley, 1998)

——, *To the Glory of her Sex: Women's Role in the Composition of Medieval Texts* (Bloomington, 1997)

——, "The French Courtly Poet: Marie de France" in Katharina M. Wilson, ed., *Medieval Women Writers* (Athens, GA, 1984)

Fildes, Valerie, *Wetnursing: A History from Antiquity to the Present* (Oxford, 1988)

Flori, Jean, *La Chevalerie en France au Moyen Âge* (Paris, 1995)

——, *Richard Coeur de Lion* (Paris, 1999)

——, *Aliénor d'Aquitaine: La reine insoumise* (Paris, 2004)

Flower, Cyril T., *Introduction to the Curia Regis Rolls, 1199–1230 A.D*, Selden Society, 62 for 1943 (London, 1944)

Fox-Genovese, Elizabeth, "Culture and Consciousness in the Intellectual History of European Women," *Signs*, 12 (1987)

Galbraith, V. H., "Good Kings and Bad Kings in English History," *History*, 30 (1945) reprinted in *Kings and Chroniclers: Essays in English Medieval History* (London, 1982), art. 2

——, "Roger Wendover and Matthew Paris" in *Kings and Chroniclers*, art. 10

Garaud, Marcel, *Les Châtelains de Poitou et l'avènement du régime féodale, xie et xiie siècles* (Poitiers, 1967)

Garland, Lynda, "Imperial Women and Entertainment at the Middle Byzantine Court" in Lynda Garland, ed., *Byzantine Women: Varieties of Experience, 800–1200* (Aldershot, 2006)

Gaudemet, Jean, "Structure de l'Église de France" in Lot and Fawtier, *Histoire des institutions françaises au moyen âge*, 3, *Institutions écclesiastiques* (Paris, 1962)

Gaunt, Simon and Sarah Kay, eds, *The Troubadours: An Introduction* (Cambridge, 1999)

Geary, Patrick, "Living with Conflicts in Stateless France: A Typology of Conflict Management Mechanisms, 1050–1200" in Geary, *Living with the Dead in the Middle Ages* (Ithaca, NY, 1994)

Gillingham, John, "Royal Newsletters, Forgeries and English Historians: Some Links between Court and History in the Reign of Richard I," in Aurell, *La Cour Plantagenêt*
———, "Events and Opinions: Norman and English Views of Aquitaine, *c.* 1152–*c.* 1204" in Léglu and Bull, *World of Eleanor*
———, *Richard Coeur de Lion: Kingship, Chivalry and War in the Twelfth Century* (London, 1994)
———, "The Angevin Empire" in Gillingham, *Richard Coeur de Lion*, 2nd edn (Oxford, 2001)
———, "Richard I and Berengaria of Navarre" in Gillingham, *Richard Coeur de Lion*
———, "Love, Marriage and Politics in the Twelfth Century," in Gillingham, *Richard Coeur de Lion*
———, *Richard I* (New Haven, 1999)
———, "Two Yorkshire Historians Compared: Roger of Howden and William of Newburgh," *HSJ*, 12 (2002)
———, "Telle Mère, tel fils: Aliénor et Richard," in Aurell, ed., *Aliénor*
———, "The Cultivation of History, Legend, and Courtesy at the Court of Henry II" in Kennedy and Meecham-Jones, *Writers of the Reign of Henry II*, ch. 2
Given-Wilson, Chris and Alice Curteis, *The Royal Bastards of Medieval England* (London, 1984)
Gold, Penny S., *The Lady and the Virgin: Image, Attitude, and Experience in Twelfth-Century France* (Chicago, 1985)
Goodich, Michael, "Bartholomeus Anglicus on Childrearing," *History of Childhood Quarterly/Journal of Psychohistory*, 3 (1975)
Gransden, Antonia, *Historical Writing in England c. 550–1307* (Ithaca, NY, 1974)
Grant, Lindy, "Le Patronage architectural d'Henri II et de son entourage," *CCM*, 37 (1994)
———, "Aspects of the Architectural Patronage of the Family of the Counts of Anjou in the Twelfth Century" in John McNeill and Daniel Prigent, eds, *Anjou: Medieval Art, Architecture and Archeology*, British Archaeological Association Conference Trans 26 (Leeds, 2003)
Green, Judith A., "Henry I and the Origins of the Court Culture of the Plantagenets," in Aurell and Tonnerre, *Plantagenêts et Capétiens*
Guyotjeannin, Olivier, *Atlas de l'histoire de France IXe–XIVe siècle* (Paris, 2005)
Hajdu, Robert, "A History of the Nobility of Poitou," unpublished Ph.D. dissertation (Princeton University, 1973)
———, "Castles, Castellans and the Structure of Politics in Poitou, 1152–1271," *JMH*, 4 (1978)
———, "The Position of Noblewomen in the *pays de coutumes*, 1000–1300," *Jl. of Family History*, 9 (1980)
Hallam, Elizabeth, "Henry II as a Founder of Monasteries," *Jl. of Ecclesiastical History*, 28 (1977)
Hallam, Elizabeth and Judith Everard, *Capetian France, 987–1328*, 2nd edn (Harlow, Essex, 2001)
Hanawalt, Barbara, "Golden Ages for the History of Medieval Women" in Susan Mosher Stuard, ed., *Women in Medieval History and Historiography* (Philadelphia, 1987)
———, "Medievalists and the Study of Childhood," *Speculum*, 97 (2002), pp. 440–60
Harper-Bill, Christopher, "The Piety of the Anglo-Norman Nobility," *ANS*, 2 (1978)
Harper-Bill, Christopher and Nicholas Vincent, eds, *Henry II: New Interpretations* (Woodbridge, Suffolk, 2007)
Hartigan, Francis X., ed., *Accounts of Alphonse of Poitiers 1243–1248* (Lanham, MD, 1984)
Harvey, Ruth E., *The Poet Marcabru and Love* (London, 1989)
———, "The Two Wives of the 'First Troubadour' Duke William IX of Aquitaine," *JMH*, 19 (1993)
———, "Courtly Culture in Medieval Occitania" in Simon Gaunt and Sarah Kay, eds, *The Troubadours: An Introduction* (Cambridge, 1999)

————, "Eleanor of Aquitaine and the Troubadours" in Léglu and Bull, *World of Eleanor*

Haskins, Charles H., "Henry II as a Patron of Literature" in A. G. Little and F. M. Powicke, eds, *Essays In Medieval History Presented to Thomas Frederick Tout* (Manchester, 1925)

Herlihy, David, *Medieval Households* (Cambridge, MA, 1985)

————, "Medieval Children" in Herlihy, *Women, Family and Society in Medieval Europe: Historical Essays, 1978–1991* (Providence, RI, 1995)

————, "The Natural History of Medieval Women" in Herlihy, *Women, Family and Society*

————, "The Family and Religious Ideologies in Medieval Europe," in Herlihy, *Women, Family and Society*

Higounet, Charles, *Histoire de Bordeaux, 2, Bordeaux pendant le haut moyen âge* (Bordeaux, 1963)

————, *Histoire de l'Aquitaine, Documents* (Toulouse, 1973)

Hill, John Hugh and Laurita Lyttleton Hill, *Raymond IV, Count of Toulouse* (Syracuse, NY, 1962)

Hillion, Yannick, "La Bretagne et la rivalité Capétiens-Plantagenêts. Un exemple: la duchesse Constance," *Annales de Bretagne*, 92 (1985)

Hivergneaux, Marie, *Recherches sur la reine Aliénor. Rôle et pouvoir d'une femme au XIIe siècle, mémoire de maîtrise* (University of Paris XII, Val de Marne, 1995)

————, "Aliénor d'Aquitaine: le pouvoir d'une femme à la lumière de ses chartes (1152–1204)" in Aurell, *La Cour Plantagenêt*

————, "Queen Eleanor and Aquitaine, 1137–1189" in Parsons and Wheeler, *Eleanor: Lord and Lady*, ch. 2

————, "Aliénor et l'Aquitaine: le pouvoir à l'épreuve des chartes (1137–1204)," in Aurell, ed., *Aliénor*

————, "Autour d'Aliénor d'Aquitaine: entourage et pouvoir au prisme des chartes (1137–1189)" in Aurell and Tonnerre, *Plantagenêts et Capétiens*

Hollister, C. Warren, *Henry I* (Berkeley, 2001)

Holmes, Urban T., Jr, *Daily Living in the Twelfth Century* (Madison, 1964)

Hosler, J. D., "The Brief Military Career of Thomas Becket," *H S J*, 15 (2004)

Holt, J. C., "Aliénor d'Aquitaine, Jean sans terre et la succession de 1199," *CCM*, 29 (1986)

————, "The Writs of Henry II," John Hudson, ed., *The History of English Law: Centenary Essays on "Pollock and Maitland," Proceedings of the British Academy*, 89 (London, 1996)

Howell, Margaret E., *Eleanor of Provence: Queenship in Thirteenth-Century England* (Oxford, 1998)

Huneycutt, Lois L., "Images of Queenship in the High Middle Ages," *HSJ*, 1 (1989), pp. 65–79

————, "Female Succession and the Language of Power in the Writings of Twelfth-Century Churchmen" in Parsons, *Medieval Queenship*, 189–201

————, "Intercession and the High-Medieval Queen: The Esther Topos" in Jennifer Carpenter and Sally-Beth Maclean, eds, *Power of the Weak: Studies on Medieval Women* (Champagne-Urbana, 1995), pp. 126–46

————, "Public Lives, Private Ties: Royal Mothers in England and Scotland, 1070–1204" in Parsons and Wheeler, *Medieval Mothering*

————, "The Creation of a Crone: The Historical Reputation of Adelaide of Maurienne" in Nolan, *Capetian Women*

————, "*Alianora Regina Anglorum*" in Parsons and Wheeler, *Eleanor: Lord and Lady*

————, *Matilda of Scotland: A Study in Medieval Queenship* (Woodbridge, Suffolk, 2003)

Jaeger, C. Stephen, *The Origins of Courtliness* (Philadelphia, 1985)

Jeanne-Rose, Olivier, "Ports, marchands et marchandises: aspects économiques du littoral poitevin (IXe–XIIe siècles)," *MSAO*, 5th ser., 4 (1996)

Johns, Susan, *Noblewomen, Aristocracy and Power in the Twelfth-Century Anglo-Norman Realm* (New York, 2003)

Jolliffe, J. E. A., *Angevin Kingship* (2nd edn, London 1963)

Jordan, William Chester, "Isabelle d'Angoulême, by the Grace of God, Queen," *Revue belge de philologie et d'histoire*, 69 (1991)

Kay, Sarah, "The Contradictions of Courtly Love and the Origins of Courtly Poetry: The Evidence of the *Lauzengiers*," *Jl. Medieval and Early Modern Studies*, 26 (1996)

Keefe, Thomas K., "Place-Date Distribution of Royal Charters and the Historical Geography of Patronage Strategies at the Court of King Henry II Plantagenet," *HSJ*, 2 (1990)

———, "England and the Angevin Dominions, 1137–1204," ch. 18, *New CMH*, 4, pt 2.

Kelly, Amy, *Eleanor of Aquitaine and the Four Kings* (Cambridge, MA, 1956)

Kenaan-Kedar, Nurith, "Aliénor d'Aquitaine conduite en captivité: les peintures murales commémoratives de Sainte-Radegonde de Chinon," *CCM*, 41 (1998)

———, "The Impact of Eleanor of Aquitaine on the Visual Arts in France," in Aurell, *Culture politique des Plantagenêts*

———, "The Wall Painting in the Chapel of Sainte-Radegonde at Chinon in the Historical Context," in *Cinquante années d'études médiévales. À la confluence de nos disciplines. Actes du Colloque organisé à l'occasion du cinquantenaire du CESCM*, ed. Claude Arrignon, Marie-Hélène Debiès, Claudio Galderisi, and Eric Palazzo (Turnhout, 2005)

Kendrick, Laura, "Jongleur as Propagandist: The Ecclesiastical Politics of Marcabru's Poetry" in Bisson, *Cultures of Power*

Kennedy, Ruth and Simon Meecham-Jones, eds, *Writers of the Reign of Henry II: Twelve Essays* (Basingstoke, 2006)

Kibler, William W., ed., *Eleanor of Aquitaine, Patron and Politician* (Austin, TX, 1976)

Kibler, William W. and Grover A. Zinn, *Medieval France: An Encyclopedia* (New York, 1995)

Klapisch-Zuber, Christiane, ed., *Silences of the Middle Ages* (Cambridge, MA, 1992), vol. 2 of Georges Duby and Michelle Perrot, general eds, *A History of Women in the West*

Kleinmann, Dorothée and Michel Garcia, "Les Peintures murales commémoratives de Sainte-Radegonde de Chinon: à propos d'un article récent," *CCM*, 42 (1999)

Knowles, David, C. N. L. Brooke, Vera C. M. London, eds, *The Heads of Religious Houses, England and Wales 940–1216* (Cambridge, 1972)

Koehler, Eric, "Observations historiques et sociologiques sur la poésie des troubadours," *CCM*, 7 (1964)

Koziol, Geoffrey, "Political Culture," in Marcus Bull, ed., *France in the Central Middle Ages 900–1200* (Oxford, 2002)

Kreutz, Barbara M., "Ships and Shipbuilding, Mediterranean," *Dict. M.A.*, 11, p. 233

Labande, E.-R., "Pour une Image véridique d'Aliénor d'Aquitaine," *BSAO*, 4th ser., 2 (1952); reprint, Labande, *Histoire de l'Europe Occidentale XIe–XIVe siècles* (London, 1973); new edn, ed. Martin Aurell (Poitiers, 2005)

———, "La Civilisation d'Aquitaine à la fin de la période ducale," *Bulletin du Centre international d'études romanes*, 1–2 (1964)

———, "Dans l'Empire Plantagenêt" in Labande, ed., *Histoire du Poitou, du Limousin et des Pays Charentais* (Toulouse, 1976)

———, "Les Filles d'Aliénor d'Aquitaine: étude comparative," *CCM*, 29 (1986)

Labarge, Margaret W., *Medieval Travellers, the Rich and Restless* (London, 1982)

Landon, Lionel, *The Itinerary of King Richard I*, Pipe Roll Society, new ser. 13 (1935)

Langlois, Charles-Victor, *La Vie en France au moyen âge de la fin du XIIe siècle au milieu du XIVe siècle d'après des romans mondains du temps*, 4 vols (Paris, 1926–28)

Lees, Beatrice, "The Letters of Queen Eleanor of Aquitaine to Pope Clement III," *EHR*, 21 (1906)

Le Fur, Didier, "Le Souvenir d'Aliénor à l'époque moderne" in Aurell, ed., *Aliénor*

Legge, M. Dominica, "La Littérature anglo-normande au temps d'Aliénor d'Aquitaine," *CCM*, 29 (1986)

Léglu, Catherine and Marcus Bull, eds, *The World of Eleanor of Aquitaine: Literature and Society in Southern France between the Eleventh and Thirteenth Centuries* (Woodbridge, Suffolk, 2005)

Lejeune, Rita, "Le Rôle littéraire d'Aliénor d'Aquitaine et de sa famille," *Cultura Neo-Latin*, 14 (1954)

———, "Le Rôle littéraire de la famille d'Aliénor d'Aquitaine," *CCM*, 1 (1958)

———, "La Femme dans les littératures françaises et occitanes du XIe au XIIIe siècles," *CCM*, 20 (1977)

Le Saux, Françoise H. M., *A Companion to Wace* (Woodbridge, Suffolk, 2005)

Lewis, Andrew W., *Royal Succession in Capetian France: Studies on Familial Order and the State* (Cambridge, MA, 1981)

———, "The Birth and Childhood of King John: Some Revisions" in Parsons and Wheeler, *Eleanor: Lord and Lady*

Lindsay, Jack, "Guilhem of Poitou" in Lindsay, *The Troubadours and their World* (London, 1976)

LoPrete, Kimberley, "Adela of Blois as Mother and Countess" in Parsons and Wheeler, *Medieval Mothering*

Lot, Ferdinand and Robert Fawtier, eds, *Histoire des institutions françaises au moyen âge*, 3 vols (Paris, 1957–62)

Lovatt, Marie, "Geoffrey (1151?–1212), archbishop of York," *Oxford DNB*

Loyd, Lewis C., *The Origins of Some Anglo-Norman Families*, Harleian Society 103 (Leeds, 1951; reprint Baltimore, 1985)

Lozinski, Jean Louise, "Henri II, Aliénor d'Aquitaine et la cathédrale de Poitiers," *CCM*, 37 (1994)

Luchaire, Achille, *Études sur les actes de Louis VII* (Paris, 1885)

———, *Louis VI le Gros. Annales de sa vie et de son règne* (Paris, 1890)

———, *Social France at the Time of Philip Augustus*, trans. Edward Benjamin Krehbiel (New York, 1912; reprint 1967)

Luscombe, David and Jonathan Riley-Smith, eds, *New CMH*, 4, c. *1024–c. 1198*, pt 2

Lutan, Sara, "Le Porche septentrional de la Collégiale Saint-Martin de Candes (v. 1180) et l'image dynastique des Plantagenêts," *CCM*, 45 (2002)

MacDonald, R. Thomas, "Ralph de Vermandois (d.1152)," in *Medieval France: An Encyclopedia*

Maddox, Donald and Sara Sturm-Maddox, *Melusine of Lusignan: Foundling Fiction in Late Medieval France. Essays on the Roman de Mélusine (1393) of Jean d'Arras* (Athens, GA, 1996)

Magdalino, Paul, "The Byzantine Empire, 1118–1204" in *New CMH*, 4, pt 2

Markale, Jean, *Aliénor d'Aquitaine* (Paris, 1979; 2nd edn 2000)

Martindale, Jane, "Eleanor of Aquitaine" in *Status, Authority, Power*, art. 11

———, "Eleanor of Aquitaine: The Last Years" in S. D. Church, ed., *King John: New Interpretations* (Woodbridge, Suffolk, 1999)

———, "Succession and Politics in the Romance-Speaking World, c. 1000–1140" in *Status, Authority, Power*, art. 5

———, "Peace and War in Early Eleventh-century Aquitaine" in *Status, Authority, Power*, art. 6

———, "Aimeri of Thouars and the Poitevin Connection" in *Status, Authority, Power*, art. 9

———, "Cavalaria et Orgueil: Duke William IX of Aquitaine and the Historian" in *Status, Authority, Power*, art. 10

———, "An Unfinished Business: Angevin Politics and the Siege of Toulouse," *ANS*, 23 (2000)

———, "Between Law and Politics: The Judicial Duel under the Angevin Kings (Mid-Twelfth Century to 1204)" in Pauline Stafford, Janet L. Nelson, and Jane Martindale, eds, *Law, Laity and Solidarities: Essays in Honour of Susan Reynolds* (Manchester, 2001)

———, "Eleanor of Aquitaine and a 'Queenly Court'?" in Parsons and Wheeler, *Eleanor: Lord and Lady*

———, "Eleanor, suo jure duchess of Aquitaine c. 1122–1204," *Oxford DNB*

Matthews, H. C. G. and B. Harrison, eds, *Oxford Dictionary of National Biography*, 20 vols (Oxford, 2004) www.oxforddnb.com

McCash, Joan Martin, "Marie de Champagne and Eleanor of Aquitaine: A Relationship Re-examined," *Speculum*, 54 (1979)

McCracken, Peggy, "Scandalizing Desire: Eleanor of Aquitaine and the Chroniclers," in Parsons and Wheeler, *Eleanor: Lord and Lady*

Meade, Marion, *Eleanor of Aquitaine* (New York, 1977; reprint 1991)

Metz, René, "Le Statut de la femme en droit canonique médiéval" in Metz, *La femme et l'enfant dans le droit canonique médiéval* (London, 1985), art. 4

Mitchell, Rosemary, *Picturing the Past: English History in Text and Image 1830–1870* (Oxford, 2000)

Moulinier-Brogi, Laurence, "Aliénor et les femmes savantes du XIIe siècle," in Aurell, ed., *Aliénor*

Musset, André, "L'Espace Et le temps Plantagenêt: les problèmes d'une architecture," *CCM*, 29 (1986)

Newman-Goldy, Charlotte A., *The Anglo-Norman Nobility in the Reign of Henry I: The Second Generation* (Philadelphia, 1988)

Nilgen, Ursula, "Les Plantagenêts à Chinon. A propos d'une peinture murale dans la chapelle Sainte-Radegonde," *Iconographia: Mélanges Piotr Skubiszewski* (Poitiers, 1999)

Nolan, Kathleen D., *Capetian Women* (New York, 2004)

———, "The Queen's Choice: Eleanor of Aquitaine and the Tombs at Fontevraud" in Parsons and Wheeler," *Eleanor: Lord and Lady*

Norgate, Kate, *England under the Angevin Kings*, 2 vols (London, 1887; reprint New York, 1969)

———, *Richard the Lion Heart* (London, 1924; reprint New York, 1966)

———, revised by Timothy Reuter, "Matilda, Duchess of Saxony (1156–1189)," *Oxford DNB*

O'Callahan, Tamara, "Tempering Scandal: Eleanor of Aquitaine and Benoît de Sainte-Maure's *Roman de Troie*," in Parsons and Wheeler, *Eleanor: Lord and Lady*

Orme, Nicholas, *From Childhood to Chivalry: The Education of the English Kings and Aristocracy 1066–1530* (London, 1984)

———, *Medieval Children* (New Haven, 2001)

Owen, D. D. R., *Eleanor of Aquitaine: Queen and Legend* (Oxford, 1993)

Pacaut, Marcel, *Louis VII et les élections épiscopales dans le royaume de France* (Paris, 1957)

———, *Louis VII et son royaume* (Paris, 1964)

Painter, Sidney, *William Marshal* (Baltimore, 1933)

———, *Studies in the History of the English Feudal Barony* (Baltimore, 1943)

———, *The Reign of King John* (Baltimore, 1949)

———, "Castellans of the Plain of Poitou in the Eleventh and Twelfth Centuries" in Cazel, *Feudalism and Liberty*

———, "The Houses of Lusignan and Châtellerault, 1150–1250" in Cazel, *Feudalism and Liberty*

———, "The Lords of Lusignan in the Eleventh and Twelfth Centuries" in Cazel, *Feudalism and Liberty*

———, "To Whom were Dedicated the *Fables* of Marie de France?" in Cazel, *Feudalism and Liberty*

Pappano, Margaret Aziza, "Marie de France, Aliénor d'Aquitaine, and the Alien Queen" in Parsons and Wheeler, *Eleanor: Lord and Lady*

———, "*La Regina Bisperta*: Aliénor d'Aquitaine et ses relations littéraires au XIe siècle" in Aurell, ed., *Aliénor*

Parsons, John Carmi, ed., *Medieval Queenship* (New York, 1993)

———, "Mothers, Daughters, Marriage, Power: Some Plantagenet Evidence, 1150–1500" in Parsons, *Medieval Queenship*

———, *Eleanor of Castile: Queen and Society in Thirteenth-Century England* (New York, 1995)

———, "Damned If She Didn't and Damned When She Did: Bodies, Babies, and Bastards in the Lives of Two Queens of France," in Parsons and Wheeler, *Eleanor: Lord and Lady*

Parsons, John Carmi and Bonnie Wheeler, eds, *Medieval Mothering* (New York, 1996)
———, *Eleanor of Aquitaine: Lord and Lady* (New York, 2003)
Partner, Nancy, *Serious Entertainments: The Writing of History in Twelfth-Century England* (Chicago, 1977)
Paterson, Linda, *The World of the Troubadours* (Cambridge, 1993)
Pearsall, Derek and Nicolette Zeeman, eds, *Elizabeth Salter: English and International Studies in the Literature, Art and Patronage of Medieval England* (Cambridge, 1988)
Perrot, Françoise, "Le Portrait d'Aliénor dans le vitrail de la *crucifixion* à la cathédrale de Poitiers" in Aurell, ed., *Aliénor*
Peltzer, Jörge, "Les Évêques de l'empire Plantagenêt et les rois angevins" in Aurell and Tonnerre, *Plantagenêts et Capétiens*
Pernoud, Régine, *Aliénor d'Aquitaine* (Paris, new edn, 1965)
———, *Women in the Days of the Cathedrals*, trans. Anne Côté-Harriss (San Francisco, 1998)
Phillips, Jonathan, "A Note on the Origins of Raymond of Poitiers," *EHR*, 106 (1991)
———, *The Second Crusade: Expanding the Frontiers of Christendom* (New Haven, 2007)
Pon, Georges, *Histoire du diocèse de Poitiers* (Paris, 1988)
Pontfarcy, Yves de, "Si Marie de France était Marie de Meulan," *CCM*, 38 (1995)
Pouzet, Philippe, *L'Anglais Jean dit Bellesmains* (Lyon, 1927)
Power, Daniel, "The Stripping of a Queen: Eleanor in Thirteenth-Century Norman Tradition," in Léglu and Bull, *World of Eleanor*
Powicke, F. M., *The Loss of Normandy*, 2nd edn (Manchester, 1960)
Powicke, F. M. and E. B. Fryde, eds, *Handbook of British Chronology*, 2nd edn (London, 1961)
Prescott, Hilda, "The Early Use of 'Teste Me Ipso'," *EHR*, 35 (1920)
Ramsay, James H., *A History of Revenues of the Kings of England, 1066–1399*, 2 vols (Oxford, 1925)
Renouard, Yves, "Les Institutions du duché d'Aquitaine (des origines à 1453)," in Lot and Fawtier, *Histoire des institutions françaises au moyen âge*, 1, *Institutions seigneuriales* (Paris, 1957)
Reuter, Timothy, ed., *New CMH*, 3, *c.900–c.1204* (Cambridge, 2000)
Richard, Alfred, *Histoire des comtes de Poitou*, 2 vols (Paris, 1903)
Richardson, H. G., "The Letters and Charters of Eleanor of Aquitaine," *EHR*, 74 (1959)
———, "The Coronation in Medieval England," *Traditio*, 16 (1960)
——— and Sayles, G. O., *The Governance of Mediaeval England from the Conquest to Magna Carta* (Edinburgh, 1963)
Riley-Smith, Jonathan, *The Crusades: A History*, 2nd edn (New Haven, 2005)
Rosenthal, Joel T., ed., *Medieval Women and the Sources of Medieval History* (Athens, GA, 1990)
Runciman, Steven, *A History of the Crusades*, 3 vols (Cambridge, 1952; reprint Harmondsworth, 1978), 2, *The Kingdom of Jerusalem and the Frankish East 1100–1187*
Salter, Elizabeth, "Courts and Courtly Love" in David Daiches and Anthony Thorlby, eds, *Literature and Western Civilization: The Medieval World* (London, 1973)
Salzman, L. F., *Building in England down to 1540* (Oxford, 1952)
Sanders, I. J., *English Baronies* (Oxford, 1960)
Sassier, Ives, *Louis VII* (Paris, 1991)
Schmolke-Hasselmann, Beate, "Henry II Plantagenêt, roi d'Angleterre, et la genèse d'*Erec et Enide*," *CCM*, 24 (1981)
Schramm, Percy Ernst, *A History of the English Coronation* (Oxford, 1937)
Seward, Desmond, *Eleanor of Aquitaine* (New York, 1979)
Short, Ian, "Patrons and Polyglots: French Literature in Twelfth-Century England" in *ANS*, 14 (1992)
———, "Literary Culture at the Court of Henry II," in Harper-Bill and Vincent, *Henry II: New Interpretations*

Smail, R. C., *Crusading Warfare (1097–1193)* (Cambridge, 1956; reprint New York, 1995)

Smalley, Beryl, *Historians in the Middle Ages* (New York, 1974)

Smith, R. J., "Henry II's Heir: The *Acta* and Seal of Henry the Young King, 1170–83," *EHR*, 116 (2001)

Soulard-Berger, Isabelle, "Agnès de Bourgogne, duchesse d'Aquitaine puis comtesse d'Anjou. Oeuvre politique et action religieuse (1019–v. 1068)," *BSAO*, 5th ser., 6 (1992)

Southern, R. W., "Blois, Peter of (1125–1212)," *Oxford DNB*

Spear, David S., "Les Chanoines de la cathédrale de Rouen pendant la période ducale," *Annales de Normandie*, 41 (1991)

Stafford, Pauline, *Queens, Concubines and Dowagers: The King's Wife in the Early Middle Ages* (Athens, GA, 1983)

———, "The Portrayal of Royal Women in England, Mid-Tenth to Mid-Twelfth Centuries" in Parsons, *Medieval Queenship*

———, "Powerful Women in the Early Middle Ages, Queens and Abbesses" in Peter Lineham and Janet L. Nelson, eds, *The Medieval World* (London, 2002)

———, "Writing the Biography of Eleventh-Century Queens" in David Bates, Julia Crick, and Sarah Hamilton, eds, *Writing Medieval Biography, 750–1250: Essays in Honour of Frank Barlow* (Woodbridge, Suffolk, 2006)

Stafford, Pauline and Anneke Mulder-Bakker, eds, *Gendering the Middle Ages* (Oxford, 2000)

Stevenson, William B., "The First Crusade," *CMH*, 5, ch. 7

Strickland, Agnes, *Lives of the Queens of England from the Norman Conquest*, 6 vols, reprint (London, 1893–99), "Eleanora of Aquitaine"

Strickland, Matthew, "The Upbringing of Henry, the Young King" in Harper-Bill and Vincent, *Henry II: New Interpretations*

———, "Longespée [Lungespée], William I," *Oxford DNB*

Stuard, Susan Mosher, "Fashion's Captives: Medieval Women in French Historiography" in Stuard, ed., *Women in Medieval History and Historiography* (Philadelphia, 1987)

Stubbs, William, *Seventeen Lectures on the Study of Medieval and Modern History* (Oxford, 1900; reprint New York, 1967)

———, *Historical Introductions to the Rolls Series*, ed. Arthur Hassall (London, 1902)

Taylor, Frank, *The Universal Chronicle of Ranulf Higden* (Oxford, 1966)

Thomasset, Claude, "The Nature of Women" in Klapisch-Zuber, *Silences of the Middle Ages*

Tollhurst, Fiona, "What Ever Happened to Eleanor? Reflections of Eleanor of Aquitaine in Wace's *Roman de Brut* and Lawman's *Brut*," in Parsons and Wheeler, *Eleanor: Lord and Lady*

Trindade, Ann, *Berengaria: In Search of Richard the Lionheart's Queen* (Dublin, 1999)

Turner, Ralph V., "William de Forz, Count of Aumale: An Early Thirteenth-Century English Baron," *Proceeds of the American Philosophical Society*, 115 (1971)

———, "Les Contacts entre l'Angleterre normano-angevine et la Sicile normande," *Études Normandes*, 35 (1986)

———, "Eleanor of Aquitaine and her Children: An Inquiry into Medieval Family Attachment," *JMH*, 14 (1988), pp. 21–35

———, "Changing Perceptions of the New Administrative Class in Anglo-Norman and Angevin England: The Curiales and their Conservative Critics," *Jl. British Studies*, 29 (1990)

———, "The Children of Anglo-Norman Royalty and their Upbringing," *Medieval Prosopography*, 11 (1990)

———, *King John* (London, 1994) reissued as *King John: England's Evil King?* (Stroud, Gloucs., 2005)

———, "The Problem of Survival for the Angevin 'Empire'," *AHR*, 100 (1995)

———, "Richard Lionheart and English Episcopal Elections," *Albion*, 29 (1997)

———, "Richard Lionheart and the Church in his Continental Domains," *French Historical Studies*, 21 (1998)

————, "Eleanor of Aquitaine in the Governments of her Sons Richard and John" in Parsons and Wheeler, *Eleanor: Lord and Lady*

————, "Eleanor of Aquitaine, Twelfth-Century English Chroniclers and her 'Black Legend,'" *Nottingham Medieval Studies*, 52 (2008)

Turner, Ralph V. and Richard R. Heiser, *The Reign of Richard Lionheart: Ruler of the Angevin Empire, 1189–1199* (London, 2000)

Van Eickels, Klaus, "Gendered Violence: Castration and Blinding as Punishment for Treason in Normandy and Anglo-Norman England," *Gender and History*, 16 (2004)

Van Houts, Elisabeth, "Le Roi et son historien: Henri II Plantagenêt et Robert de Torigni, Abbé de Mont-Saint-Michel," *CCM*, 37 (1994)

————, *History and Family Traditions in England and on the Continent, 1000–1200* (Aldershot, 1999)

————, "Les Femmes dans le royaume Plantagenêt: gendre, politique et nature" in Aurell and Tonnerre, *Plantagenêts et Capétiens*

Vauchez, André, ed., *Dictionnaire encyclopédique du Moyen Âge chrétien* (Paris, 1997)

Vaughn, Richard, *Matthew Paris* (Cambridge, 1958)

Verdon, Jean, "La Femme en Poitou aux xe et xie siècles," *BSAO*, 4th ser., 15 (1977)

Vessey, D. W. T. C., "William of Tyre and the Art of Historiography," *Mediaeval Studies*, 35 (1973)

Villard, François, "Guillaume ix d'Aquitaine et le concile de Reims de 1119," *CCM*, 16 (1973)

Vincent, Nicholas, *Peter des Roches: An Alien in English Politics, 1205–1238* (Cambridge, 1996)

————, "Henry II and the Poitevins," in *La cour Plantagenêt*

————, "Isabelle of Angoulême: John's Jezebel" in Church, *King John: New Interpretations*

————, "Aliénor, Reine d'Angleterre," in Aurell, ed., *Aliénor*

————, "Patronage, Politics and Piety in the Charters of Eleanor," Aurell and Tonnerre, *Plantagenêts et Capétiens*

————, "Introduction: Henry II and the Historians" and "The Court of Henry II" in Harper-Bill and Vincent, *Henry II: New Interpretations*

Vollrath, Hanna, "Aliénor d'Aquitaine et ses enfants: une relation affective?" Aurell and Tonnerre, *Plantagenêts et Capétiens*

Vones-Liebenstein, Ursula, "Aliénor d'Aquitaine, Henri le Jeune et la révolte de 1173: un prélude à la confrontation entre Plantagenêts et Capétiens?" in Aurell and Tonnerre, *Plantagenêts et Capétiens*

Waddell, Helen, *The Wandering Scholars*, reprint (Garden City, NY, 1955)

Walker, Curtis Howe, "Eleanor of Aquitaine and the Disaster at Cadmos Mountain on the Second Crusade," *AHR*, 55 (1949–50)

————, *Eleanor of Aquitaine* (Chapel Hill, NC, 1950)

Warren, W. L., *King John* (Berkeley, 1962)

————, *Henry II* (Berkeley, 1977)

Waugh, Scott L., *The Lordship of England: Royal Wardships and Marriages in English Society and Politics, 1217–1327* (Princeton, 1988)

Weir, Allison, *Eleanor of Aquitaine: By the Wrath of God, Queen of England* (London, 2000)

Werner, K.-F., "Kingdom and Principality in Twelfth-Century France" in Timothy Reuter, ed. and trans., *The Medieval Nobility* (Amsterdam, 1979)

Wertheimer, Laura, "Adeliza of Louvain and Anglo-Norman Queenship," *HSJ*, 7 (1995)

West, Francis J., *The Justiciarship in England 1066–1232* (Cambridge, 1966)

White, Graeme J., *Restoration and Reform 1153–1165: Recovery and Civil War in England* (Cambridge, 2001)

Wolff, Philippe, "L'Epanouissement du Languedoc" in Wolff, ed., *Histoire du Languedoc* (Toulouse, 1967), ch. 5

Wood, Charles T., "Fontevraud, Dynasticism, and Eleanor of Aquitaine" in Wheeler and Parsons, *Eleanor: Lord and Lady*

———, "La Mort et les funérailles d'Henri II," *CCM*, 38 (1994)

——— "The Doctor's Dilemma: Sin, Salvation, and the Menstrual Cycle in Medieval Thought," *Speculum*, 56 (1981), pp. 710–27

Zimmermann, Michel, "Western Francia: The Southern Principalities," *New CMH*, 3, ch. 16

INDEX